this bridge
we call home

radical visions for transformation

EDITED BY

gloria e. anzaldúa AND
analouise keating

ROUTLEDGE
NEW YORK AND LONDON

Published in 2002 by
Routledge
29 West 35th Street
New York, NY 10001
www.routledge-ny.com

Published in Great Britain by
Routledge
11 New Fetter Lane
London EC4P 4EE
www.routledge.co.uk

Routledge is an imprint of the Taylor & Francis Group.

Printed in the United States of America on acid-free paper.

10 9 8 7 6 5 4 3 2 1

Library of Congress Cataloging-in-Publication Data

This bridge we call home : radical visions for transformation / edited by Gloria E. Anzaldúa
and AnaLouise Keating.
        p. cm.
    ISBN 0-415-93681-0 (HB : alk. paper) — ISBN 0-415-93682-9 (PB : alk. paper)
    1. Lesbians' writings, American. 2. Lesbians—Literary collections. 3. Lesbians—United
States—Biography. 4. Minority women—Literary collections. 5. Minority women—United
States—Biography. 6. Women—United States—Literary collections. 7. American literature—
Women authors. 8. American literature—20th century. 9. Radicalism—Literary collections. I.
Anzaldúa, Gloria. II. Keating, AnaLouise, 1961–

PS509.L47 T48 2002
810.8'09206643—dc21   2002012821

contents

ii. *"still struggling with the boxes people try to put me in" . . . resisting the labels*

iii. *"locking arms in the master's house"* . . . omissions, revisions, new issues

iv.   *"a place at the table"* . . . surviving the battles,
shaping our worlds

v. *"shouldering more identity than we can bear"* . . . seeking allies in academe

vi.   *"yo soy tu otro yo—i am your other i"* . . . forging common ground

vii. *"i am the pivot for transformation"* . . . enacting the vision

giving thanks

So many people poured energy into *this bridge we call home,* providing contact information, advice, and other forms of support: Awiatka, Jacqui Alexander, Joanne Barker, Gloria Bird, Ginny Carney, Valerie Chase, Janet Francendese, Cynthia Franklin, Jancie Gould, Lynda Hall, Joy Harjo, Inés Hernández-Ávila, Mary Lee Hope, Theresa May, Deborah Miranda, Chela Sandoval, Caridad Souza, Kim Springer, and many others. We thank you for your assistance.

Contributors: this book is the product of your prayers, good wishes, and affirmative thoughts. Mil gracias for your faith in our vision, your confidence in this project, your willingness to write from your bodies, from your hearts. You are a fiercely creative folk. Thanks to you who participated in the listserv discussions and debates for your enthusiasm, challenges, and suggested titles, especially Deborah Miranda whose title we chose, and Renae Bredin for a similar title. We thank those contributors who loaned their words for the section titles: Iobel Andemicael (i); Leticia Hernández-Linares (ii); mary loving blanchard (iii); Marisela Gomez (iv); tatiana de la tierra (v); Irene Lara (vi); y Susan Guerra (vii). To the people at Routledge, particularly Bill Germano, Damian Treffs, and Julie Ho, thanks for being flexible and supportive of our process. Special thanks to our familias, compañeras/os for putting up with our workaholic tendencies.

AnaLouise: For emotional sustenance, friendship, and much more, I thank Renae Bredin, Jesse Swan, Eddy Lynton (baby: tú eres todo el hombre y mujer que necesito), mi querida hijita Jamitrice KreChelle (ojalá que esté libro te inspire when you're older), y Yemanja. For assistance with the pre-production process thanks to Carol Lang, Debra Zoppa, Emily Rivendell, and Amy Calvert. For assistance with references thanks to Glenda Lehrman, and for ongoing encouragement thanks to Claire Sahlin and my sistahs at TWU. Thanks to Nadine Barrett and Doreen Watson for making the index. Thanks also to Eastern New Mexico University, Aquinas College, and Texas Woman's University. Thank you, Gloria, for agreeing to take on this project which has grown so much larger than we anticipated. You have taught me—you *teach* me—so much . . . about writing, editing, risk-taking, and friendship.

Gloria: AnaLouise, gracias por todo comadre: you won our months-long debate about whose name goes first. Though you initiated the project and devoted the most time and energy, though I wanted your name to go first, the publishers wanted mine. We made a deal—mine would be first in the initial print run, yours in the second. I commend you for being an exemplary co-editor and a terrific writing comadre—a joy to work with. Gracias, mi comadres in writing, Randy Conner, Liliana Wilson Grez, Carmen Morones, Kit Quan, and Irene Reti. Agradesco también a mis muertos—mi papa, mis mamagrandes, y mis antepasados. Thanks to nature—trees, sea, sky—for inspiring me.

Orishas y espiritus, thanks for guiding us, whispering words of encouragement that nourished our hearts, energized our bodies, and inspired our vision.

Si se puede, pa' adelante, contigo en la lucha.

(Un)natural bridges, (Un)safe spaces

At sunset I walk along the bluffs gazing at the shifting sea, a hammered sheet of silver. A full moon rises over the cliffs of Natural Bridges like an opalescent ball. Under my feet pressure and heat are continuously changing the layers of sedimentary rock formed 100,000 years ago. It took the waves thousands of years to cut out a remnant headlands and thousands more to wear holes or arches through its flanks and shape three stone bridges. Year after year these same waves expanded the arches until the weight of the overlying rock collapsed the outermost bridge twenty-one years ago. In a few seconds the 1989 Loma Prieta earthquake brought down the innermost bridge. Today only the middle one remains, a lone castlelike seastack with an arched hole for an eye.

Whenever I glimpse the arch of this bridge my breath catches. Bridges are thresholds to other realities, archetypal, primal symbols of shifting consciousness. They are passageways, conduits, and connectors that connote transitioning, crossing borders, and changing perspectives. Bridges span liminal (threshold) spaces between worlds, spaces I call nepantla,° a Nahuatl word meaning tierra entre medio. Transformations occur in this in-between space, an unstable, unpredictable, precarious, always-in-transition space lacking clear boundaries. Nepantla es tierra desconocida, and living in this liminal zone means being in a constant state of displacement—an uncomfortable, even alarming feeling. Most of us dwell in nepantla so much of the time it's become a sort of "home." Though this state links us to other ideas, people, and worlds, we feel threatened by these new connections and the change they engender. I think of how feminist ideas and movements are attacked, called unnatural by the ruling powers, when in fact they are ideas whose time has come, ideas as relentless as the waves carving and later eroding stone arches. Change is inevitable; no bridge lasts forever.

I used to cross a trestle bridge near the Boardwalk until a winter storm demolished it. Recently I watched the workers rebuild this historic land-

---

° I use the word *nepantla* to theorize liminality and to talk about those who facilitate passages between worlds, whom I've named nepantleras. I associate nepantla with states of mind that question old ideas and beliefs, acquire new perspectives, change worldviews, and shift from one world to another.

mark, leaving intact some of the original foundation but supporting it with heavy buttresses and integrating it with other new materials. In *this bridge we call home: radical visions for transformation* we've taken the model provided by *This Bridge Called My Back* and given it a new shape—hopefully without compromising the inherent character and structure of the original. Every generation that reads *This Bridge Called My Back* rewrites it. Like the trestle bridge, and other things that have reached their zenith, it will decline unless we attach it to new growth or append new growth to it. *this bridge we call home* is our attempt to continue the dialogue, rethink the old ideas, and germinate new theories. In these pages we move from focusing on what has been done to us (victimhood) to a more extensive level of agency, one that questions what we're doing to each other, to those in distant countries, and to the earth's environment. The knowledge that we are in symbiotic relationship to all that exists and co-creators of ideologies—attitudes, beliefs, and cultural values—motivates us to act collaboratively.

As swells break against the Santa Cruz mudstone promontories I feel that we who struggle for social change are the waves cutting holes in the rock and erecting new bridges. We're loosening the grip of outmoded methods and ideas in order to allow new ways of being and acting to emerge, but we're not totally abandoning the old—we're building on it. We're reinforcing the foundations and support beams of the old puentes, not just giving them new paint jobs. While trying to hold fast to the rights feminists, progressives, and activists have carved out for us with their fingernails, we also battle those who are trying to topple both old and new bridges.

Twenty-one years ago we struggled with the recognition of difference within the context of commonality. Today we grapple with the recognition of commonality within the context of difference. While *This Bridge Called My Back* displaced whiteness, *this bridge we call home* carries this displacement further. It questions the terms *white* and *women of color* by showing that whiteness may not be applied to all whites, as some possess women-of-color consciousness, just as some women of color bear white consciousness. This book intends to change notions of identity, viewing it as part of a more complex system covering a larger terrain, and demonstrating that the politics of exclusion based on traditional categories diminishes our humanness.

Today categories of race and gender are more permeable and flexible than they were for those of us growing up prior to the 1980s. *this bridge we call home* invites us to move beyond separate and easy identifications, creating bridges that cross race and other classifications among different groups via intergenerational dialogue. Rather than legislating and restricting racial identities, it tries to make them more pliant. The personal and cultural narratives are not disinterested, objective questionings of identity politics, but impassioned and conflicted engagements in resistance. They show the ruptures y los desconocimientos (ignored knowledge) around identity issues, revealing how much has shifted in the last twenty years, but also how little has changed. In our efforts to rethink the borders of race, gender, and identity, we must guard against creating new binaries.

Expanding on *This Bridge Called My Back* we incorporate additional underrepresented voices such as those of transgendered people, and Arab and South Asian/Indian Americans. We attempt to break the impasse between women of color and other groups. By including women and men of different "races," nationalities, classes, sexualities, genders, and ages we complicate the debates within feminist theory both inside and outside the academy and inside and outside the United States. Gathering people from many geographies in a multicultural approach is a mark of inclusivity, increased consciousness, and dialogue. This inclusivity reflects the hybrid quality of our lives and identities—todas somos nos/otras. Living in multi-cultural communities and the complexities of our age demand that we develop a perspective that takes into account the whole planet.

Our goal is not to use differences to separate us from others, but nei-ther is it to gloss over those differences. Many of us identify with groups and social positions not limited to our ethnic, racial, religious, class, gender, or national classifications. Though most people self-define by what they exclude, we define who we are by what we include—what I call the new tribalism. Though most of us live entremundos, between and among worlds, we are frustrated by those who step over the line, by hybridities and ambiguities, and by what does not fit our expectations of "race" and sex.

I fear that many mujeres de color will not want whites or males to be contributors in our book. We risk their displeasure. It would have been easier for AnaLouise and me to limit the dialogue to women of color. Many women of color are possessive of *This Bridge Called My Back* and view it as a safe space, as "home." But there are no safe spaces. "Home" can be unsafe and dangerous because it bears the likelihood of intimacy and thus thinner boundaries. Staying "home" and not venturing out from our own group comes from woundedness, and stagnates our growth. To bridge means loosening our borders, not closing off to others. Bridging is the work of opening the gate to the stranger, within and without. To step across the threshold is to be stripped of the illusion of safety because it moves us into unfamiliar territory and does not grant safe passage. To bridge is to attempt community, and for that we must risk being open to personal, political, and spiritual intimacy, to risk being wounded. Effective bridging comes from knowing when to close ranks to those outside our home, group, community, nation—and when to keep the gates open.

Sometimes we feel most unsafe with people of our own group. On September 11 as I listened to the rhetoric of retaliation and war, I realized it masked feelings of bewilderment, sorrow, and fear—the U.S. borders of "safety" had been violated and many people could no longer see our country the same way. Rather than reflect on this arrebato (breach), some of us screamed for revenge. I recalled the internal strife that flared up months earlier in the postings of the listserv we set up for our contributors. I think the listserv conflict also masked feelings of fear—this supposedly safe space was no longer safe. The contentious debates among Palestinian women and Jews of Latina, Native, and European ancestry churned a liquid fire in our guts.

Conflict, with its fiery nature, can trigger transformation depending on how we respond to it. Often, delving deeply into conflict instead of fleeing from it can bring an understanding (conocimiento) that will turn things around. In some of the responses to the heated discussions, I saw genuine attempts to listen and respect all sides. With generous conciliatory responses a few contributors tried to heal las rajaduras split open by mistrust, suspicions, and dualisms. Where others saw borders, these nepantleras saw links; where others saw abysses, they saw bridges spanning those abysses. For nepantleras, to bridge is an act of will, an act of love, an attempt toward compassion and reconciliation, and a promise to be present with the pain of others without losing themselves to it.

A bridge, such as this book, is not just about one set of people crossing to the other side; it's also about those on the other side crossing to this side. And ultimately, it's about doing away with demarcations like "ours" and "theirs." It's about honoring people's otherness in ways that allow us to be changed by embracing that otherness rather than punishing others for having a different view, belief system, skin color, or spiritual practice. Diversity of perspectives expands and alters the dialogue, not in an add-on fashion but through a multiplicity that's transformational, such as in mestiza consciousness. To include whites is not an attempt to restore the privilege of white writers, scholars, and activists; it is a refusal to continue walking the color line. To include men (in this case, feminist-oriented ones) is to collapse the gender line. These inclusions challenge conventional identities and promote more expansive configurations of identities—some of which will soon become cages and have to be dismantled.

The anthology we originally conceived was even more inclusionary than the book you hold. The challenge AnaLouise and I faced was to be as inclusive as possible within the page and word limitations set by our publisher. Due to the current economics in the book industry and the subsequent conviction that teachers would not include a big and pricey book in their syllabi, we had to reduce our original 1,300-page manuscript to 850 pages, the original 108 pieces to 80, and the 113 contributors to 87. In order to keep our commitment to all our contributors we moved an entire section into a second book, one on telling stories and bearing witness. Making these changes took more time and energy than we expected. We agonized over the cuts. Lengthier pieces had to be trimmed and every piece tightened, a task we took on with repugnance but also with dedication. What kept our shoulders to the task was our vision of empowering others, encouraging conocimiento (deep awareness), and striving for social justice.

For positive social change to occur we must imagine a reality that differs from what already exists. The wish to repair, to heal our wounds—what I call the Coyolxauhqui imperative—animates the creation of this book, our teaching, and activism. To treat the wounds and mend the rifts we must sometimes reject the injunctions of culture, group, family, and ego. Activism is the courage to act consciously on our ideas, to exert power in resistance to ideological pressure—to risk leaving home. Empowerment comes from ideas—our revolution is fought with concepts, not with guns, and it is fueled by vision. By focusing on what we want to happen, we change the present. The healing images and narratives we imagine will eventually materialize.

Este libro celebra y encarna el espiritu y linaje of *This Bridge Called My Back*. With it we honor las luchadoras que nos dejaron un legado de protesta y activismo por medio de la pluma. Ours is the responsibility of marking the journey and passing on the torches and rituals left by those who have already crossed many types of bridges. The eighty-seven voices in this collection transmit knowledge and wisdom, plant ideas in our minds, and initiate us into awareness, igniting the passion that in turn sparks activism. We honor those whose backs are the bedrock we stand on, even as our shoulders become the ground for the generations that follow, and their bodies then will become the next layer. Though we're aware of the danger of losing our individuality to the collective fires and the risking of our safe spaces, this undertaking empowers us to become sentinels, bearers of witness, makers of historias.

I descend down the steep bluffs to the tide pool terraces between sea and cliffs. Squatting, I stare at a sea anemone in a pocket of water on the pitted rock. Biologically, we are a single gene pool with minor variations and superficial cultural and genetic differences; we are interconnected with all life. I prod the anemone; it shudders and shakes, contracting into a protective ball. We all respond to pain and pleasure in similar ways. Imagination, a function of the soul, has the capacity to extend us beyond the confines of our skin, situation, and condition so we can choose our responses. It enables us to reimagine our lives, rewrite the self, and create guiding myths for our times. As I walk back home along the cliffs, a westerly wind buffeting my back, the crashing breakers scour the shoulders of the bluffs, slowly hewing out keyholes, fledgling bridges in the making.

Gloria E. Anzaldúa
November 2001

Charting Pathways, Marking Thresholds . . .
A Warning, An Introduction

AnaLouise Keating

*How do we house a combination of ideas, connections, cultures, and discon-
nections which, taken in pieces or whole, are the stuff of revolution?*
                                                              —Amira Jarmakani

Genesis

Summer 1998

Sitting at the computer, swamp cooler blowing moist air on my back, I
read the latest exchange on my favorite listserv. (The Internet is my lifeline, my intellectual sustenance, my connection out of this small dusty
town in eastern New Mexico.) Someone has written, with startled surprise, that she can't use *This Bridge Called My Back: Writings by Radical
Women of Color* in her course next semester because Kitchen Table Press
is no longer in business and the book is OUT OF PRINT!!! Her query
generates other comments about the book's importance. Such a coincidence: I'd just finished reading Cynthia Franklin's *Writing Women's
Communities* and was especially struck by her analysis of *Bridge's* impact.

I start thinking . . . *This Bridge* is almost twenty years old, but look
at the strong feelings expressed about it today. *Bridge* represented an
urgent call for new kinds of feminist communities and practices, a call
that simultaneously invited women of color to develop a transformative,
coalitional consciousness leading to new alliances and challenged "white"
middle-class feminists to recognize and rectify their racism, their classism, and other biases. Have these invitations to transformation been
met? What's changed? What remains the same? Given the enormous
vision expressed in *This Bridge*, coupled with readers' appreciation for
this anthology, you'd think it would have been inevitable that we'd have
made significant progress by now, almost twenty years later. Yet I feel
there's still a lot of work to be done. The term "woman of color" is bandied
about and, yes, employed in empowering ways, but when used does it
indicate a radically altered consciousness? Or have the promises of this
potentially radical term become enmeshed in restrictive forms of identity
politics? It appears that, with some vital exceptions, many still cling
fiercely to the old categories and labels. And what about these self-identified "white" feminists who cite *Bridge* as a turning point in the feminist

movement and claim that reading it transformed them? My own experiences during this past year make me wonder. I've heard similar reports from others—instances of racism, of "white" women feminists ignoring insights, tokenizing, or imposing their own imperial standards on colleagues of color. I'm skeptical. Am I alone in this skepticism?

I have no answers, it's too hot to think, and I'm sweating. The temperature outdoors and in the house has been climbing, the swamp cooler tries to keep up but can't do it. To cool off, I go for my daily swim.

As I walk to the university pool, bracing myself against the hot wind, squinting to keep the blowing dust out of my eyes, my thoughts return to *This Bridge*. Why are these women still talking about it with such passion? Did it change their lives, like it changed my own? Has *Bridge* transformed feminism? Are "we" multicultural—truly, radically-mixed multicultural? Or, as Norma Alarcón suggested back in 1991, is the reverential respect toward *This Bridge* on the part of "Anglo-American" feminists still mainly "cosmetic," just a nod toward diversity?

Arriving at the pool, I rush into the locker room, change into my swimsuit, oil my hair, pull on my swim cap, and quickly walk to the pool. Jump in. Ahhhh. The shock of cold water, after hours of dry heat and parched wind. It feels so good that, for a while, I let my thoughts go and just enjoy my swim—arms slicing through cool water—lap after lap, flip turn after flip turn.

Mesmerized by this rhythm I think back to my own first encounter with *Bridge*, in (of all places) an occult bookshop in Chicago one humid summer day ten years ago during grad school. I was cruising the used book section and the cover caught my attention. I bought it on a whim. What I read changed my life. Despite my African ancestry, despite my woman lover, I was passing as "white," passing as "straight," desperate to fit. But not succeeding. In *Bridge* I met other women who didn't fit, some of whom had tried fitting, some of whom perhaps had not. Unlike me, though, they defiantly spoke out and rejected the restrictive norms. They challenged the categories, demonstrated the labels' limitations. It feels corny to think it (and even cornier to write it), but when I first read *This Bridge* I felt—finally—like I was coming home. Like maybe, just maybe, there were others who thought and felt somewhat like me. And if this was the case—that there are "almas afines," kindred souls, in this world—then I'm not alone.

Bridge contributors combined calls for visibility with an insistence on our radical interconnectedness. It's this paradoxical, crucial linking of commonalities and differences that still thrills me, almost ten years later. Andrea Canaan's rejection of the paralyzing labels that confine us; Audre Lorde's call for "interdependency" among women; Gloria's sense of difference and alienation, coupled with her solution—El Mundo Zurdo, a place where those of us who don't fit in come together, doing our work to bring about revolutionary transformation. These writings moved me, they challenged me to change.

My pace picks up as I relive this life-altering event. For me, *This Bridge* was a call to action, a shout for recognition, and a quest for new forms of community, alternate ways of perceiving each other and ourselves. Such urgency. I was struck by the faith that radical change—material, spiritual, personal, political—is possible. I marveled at the editors' boldness and their confidence that writing can transform us. The authors live out the words on the pages, and they invite others to join them, to enact the transformations they envision. When I read *This Bridge* I crossed a threshold into uncharted territory, and I've never looked back. It was my conversion experience, the first step on my journey into radical woman-of-color feminism. I had never taken a course in women's studies nor even any classes taught by feminists (of whatever color). After *This Bridge* I wanted more. I began reading Audre Lorde, Cherríe Moraga, Chrystos, Luisah Teish, Anzaldúa, and others with similar visions, visions driven by the desire for social justice, visions fueled by the faith that change can occur. And again I wonder: Is *this* what others feel when they read *This Bridge*? Did reading this book radically alter their lives too?

Immersed in my reflections, I lose track of time; the guard's whistle blows and I hear, "Dr. Keating, we're closing now . . . Dr. Keating . . . " Dazed, I wrench myself back to the present and reluctantly climb out of the pool, apologizing as I grab my towel.

Later that day, back at the computer, I continue with my current project: editing a collection of interviews with Gloria. I'm working on Linda Smuckler's transcript and encounter another question about *Bridge*'s creation. It's a recurring theme: Gloria's original vision for compiling *This Bridge*, her feelings of exclusion from "white" feminist groups, her desire to challenge these feminists and to create new alliances among women of color. The vision is so strong, her desire so articulate.

And again I wonder: Where are we now, almost twenty years later? If (as I fear) we haven't progressed as much as some seem to believe, how can we re-energize the dialogue and make change occur? Perhaps we need another *Bridge*-like book, not a sequel but an anthology measuring the progress and—more important—stimulating new conversation: "Where are we now? Where should we go?" I wonder . . . Would Gloria would be willing to co-edit such a collection? But she's so busy, so many writing projects. And the diabetes. It slows her down. I don't want to add to her workload.

Pushing these thoughts aside, I go back to the task at hand. Yet still, the idea nags at me. Like the relentless New Mexico summer days, like the persistent wind whipping the dust skyward, my questions don't go away. They just intensify. And then I read Gloria's statement in the interview with Andrea Lunsford where she associates her work as an anthologist with activism: "Making these anthologies is also activism. In the process of creating the composition, the work of art, the painting, the film, you're creating the culture. You're rewriting the culture, which is very much an activist kind of thing. Writers have something in common with people doing grassroots organizing and acting in the community: It's all about rewriting culture."

Of course! It's so obvious. Why didn't I realized it before? *Bridge* is infused with an activist vision, a concrete belief that we can and must assert ourselves and redefine our world; working together, we *create* the world we want to inhabit. (Perhaps it's this desire and belief that partially account for the book's continued relevance.) They're rewriting culture. That's it! I want to rewrite culture. I see a need for further change, so why not engage in some anthology-making activism?

The wind has picked up even more. I hear it pushing the patio furniture into the wall. But no break in the temperature. The wind just circulates hot air and more hot air. I wipe the sweat from between my breasts, pick up the phone, and dial Gloria's number. After chatting for a short while, I ask if she'd be interested in editing a follow-up book, an anthology that marks *Bridge*'s importance, celebrates its loud shout but goes further—measures its impact and assesses our next steps. We talk awhile. She sounds interested but tentative, not willing to commit to the project without giving it some hard thought. "Making anthologies is a lot of work, AnaLouise. Let me think about it and talk to Randy and Irene and some of my other friends."

A week later, we talk. Gloria agrees to take on this project. She warns me, again, that compiling an anthology is a lot of work. I accept the challenge and we brainstorm: Who should be included: just women of color? women and men of color? people of all colors and genders? If we really want to get an idea of where things are and where they can go, we must be as open as possible. We must also invite men, "white" women, and Jewish people to contribute, and we must break out of our U.S. borders. Together, we hammer out a call for papers, focusing on four areas: *Bridge*'s influence, the current status of issues raised in *This Bridge*, new issues confronting us today, and envisioning change.

I send out our call for papers—to various listservs, to journals, to websites like chicana.com and feminista.com. (The Internet makes a tremendous difference, compared to the difficulties Gloria and Cherríe experienced. Gloria has told me about the time-consuming effort involved in spreading the call for papers; they relied on word of mouth, women's journals, and the mail.[1]) We track down original contributors; Gloria gives me names of friends and colleagues; I write letters and e-mails, inviting them to participate.

Initial Response

Winter 1999

The response surprises me yet also confirms my belief in *Bridge*'s importance. I receive e-mails, letters, phone calls from women who tell us how important this book has been, how excited they are about this project. "It changed my life," I read and hear—again and again. "Reading *This Bridge* changed my life." I'm especially struck by the abstract from Nova Gutierrez. She reminds me of my own first encounter with *Bridge* and reflects the feelings of many others:

> I remember how angry I felt when I first read *This Bridge Called My Back*— angry that I survived for 18 years without it, angry that I didn't have enough money to buy a copy for everyone I knew who would devour its pages the way I did. I remember I called up my family in South Texas and other women of color with whom I had been surviving in our mid-west campus hell and read paragraph after paragraph screaming, "Can you believe this exists? This is about us! These women know what we're going through. Everything we've been talking about is all here. You've got to read this." And so I passed it on. Like a chain letter, I photocopied pages and mailed them with insistent urgings that its readers pass them on as well.

Some people ask me if our call for papers means that we're republishing *This Bridge*. I hope Gloria and Cherríe will republish the book, I tell them, but our anthology is composed of new pieces. *This Bridge* is the mother text, and our book will pick up on and (we hope) extend *Bridge* issues. I explain our vision: "We see this new anthology both as a chance to take a good hard look at where we're at (define the 'we' how you will!); and as an opportunity to generate dialogues that will lead to change—transformation on multiple levels."

Over the next few months, abstracts keep coming in, way past our deadline. Over three hundred submissions. There's that much interest in this new book. It looks like we'll have lots of material that simultaneously draws on and extends *Bridge* issues—especially concerning invisibility and representation. We have abstracts from self-identified Arab-American women, South Asian Indian women, mixed-"race" women, much more variety of Asian-American women than found in *This Bridge*. We've also received some very promising critiques of "whiteness," a few abstracts from women located outside the States . . . Canada, Australia, Europe. No submissions thus far from men. (Why is this? We made it clear in our call for papers that we were interested in receiving work from men.) I'm looking forward to reading the complete pieces. Where will these authors take their ideas and concerns? Will they repeat different (more nuanced) versions of the identity politics we've already seen? Will they open new spaces? Will they do both? Will they do something else entirely?

I'm worried, and kind of sad, because the abstracts we've received thus far seem to confirm my belief that we haven't made much progress. The battles remain the same, although the battlefields have altered slightly: Still, the calls for visibility. Still, the need to break silence. Still, the critique of stereotypes and the desire to invent new identities. But I fear that contributors won't take these critiques far enough: What happens, once you're visible, once you have your new label(s)? Do you isolate yourself, splinter off into your own comforting home until internal conflicts arise and you begin recognizing differences between yourself and others who seem to share your specific label? (This recognition, I believe, is inevitable.) What happens, once you've made others aware of your presence, once you've shattered the stereotypes? What's the next step? What do you envision for the future . . . for your children's, your grandchildren's future?

I understand these issues and their importance: I've been there! But I also see labels (even when self-chosen) as potentially imprisoning and in other ways dangerous. So often, so very often, labels become frozen and turn into walls dividing "us" from each other, preventing us from recognizing common cause and creating new alliances. Part of *Bridge*'s power stems from the authors' ability to transform walls into bridges, into spiraling paths from self to other, from other to self. Our anthology must do even more.

The Work Continues, The Fears Grow

August 1999

Here I am now. It's summer again and, once again, I'm at the computer screen. But my computer and I are in Michigan now, where I begin a new job in less than three weeks. The weather is much cooler, the landscape much greener. Trees everywhere! The branches hang down heavy with leaves. So much life. For years, I've felt a special intimacy with trees, and I smile as I look out the window, at the thick blanket of green, so thick that I can't even see the apartments behind this one. But I miss the heat, the sun, and—yes, even the wind. Not the manure smell, not the dust. I'm not used to all this rain. I still haven't finished unpacking; there are boxes everywhere . . . too many books. Although I should probably continue unpacking, I return to the stack of manuscripts and look through them. As I do so, I'm filled with doubts—doubts only partially triggered by my recent move to this northern state. There's so much material! How will we ever decide what to include, and how will we divide it into sections?

Fall 1999

The book begins taking shape, my excitement and my fears are growing. How can we possibly follow *This Bridge*? What audacity! How can we avoid disappointing those readers who will turn to this "sister volume"[2] and expect almost the same shock of recognition, the thrill of surprise, the sense of "coming home" they experienced upon reading *This Bridge*— whether they read it in the early 1980s, the late '80s, the '90s, or maybe even last week? We can't replicate the voices, the perspectives, the visions, and the positions found in that groundbreaking text. Nor should we try to do so. *This Bridge* was the product of a specific point in time. We can't repeat the past, not even those moments that gave us great satisfaction.

Our deadline was several months ago, August 31 to be exact, and although a number of people have written to us requesting extensions, we have a big stack of submissions to read. I'm excited by the wealth of material. Like the contributors to *This Bridge*, our contributors draw on their personal experiences to examine classism, homophobia, racism, identity politics, community building, and activism. Yet they explore additional topics as well, including third wave feminism, lesbian childbirth, transgendered issues, and the roles reading plays in transformation. And there's more: Shirley Geok-lin Lim explores the absence of maternal voices and subjectivities in *Bridge* and proposes a "maternal imagination in diaspora"; Max Valerio (Anita Valerio in *This Bridge*) describes his transition from female to male; and Cheryl Clarke revisits the current status of issues she raised in her *Bridge* essay, "Lesbianism as an Act of Resistance," to mention only a few.

But I'm worried. Many submissions are quite theoretical, and in this sense indicate a remarkable change from *This Bridge*, which has been used as a model for how women of color don't theorize in "white" academic ways. Piled in stacks all over my dining room floor as I type these words are theoretical pieces by self-identified women of color. Even more remarkable: they don't apologize for or justify their use of high theory. They simply use it and, by so doing, attempt to analyze and take apart the master's houses. My first reaction was a jumbled mixture of astonishment, bewilderment, dismay, and concern. "I don't get it," I said to Gloria last month. "*Bridge* has been repeatedly praised for its oppositional stance to the academy, for its use of nontheoretical language, for its challenge to high theory. How could so many people respond to our call for papers, which so clearly links our new book with *This Bridge Called My Back*, with such theoretical pieces? Yes, I realize that many of our contributors, unlike most *Bridge* contributors, locate themselves—with great discomfort and ambivalence—*inside* the academy. And yes, I know that many first encountered *Bridge* within academic settings. But does this use of theory indicate that they've been seduced by the academy, that they're 'white' academic clones/drones? Or is there something else going on here? More to the point: Is this use of theoretical language something we should encourage contributors to revise or delete?"

I have no answers to these new concerns, but then I go to a feminist conference on rhetoric. In some ways, it's fantastic: there are wonderful, thought-provoking papers by highly intelligent women. The keynoters are remarkable: the famous gender theorist, the well-known working-class butch author, the in-your-face literary theorist, and so on. But these women and, in fact, almost everyone at this conference looks "white." There's only one keynote with women of color, and the organizers seem to have defined women of color exclusively as "black." To make matters worse, this panel is in the afternoon, rather than one of the big evening events. Worse still, the conference organizers eat up part of the presentation time with announcements. To top it all off, they've imported an African-American woman from elsewhere on campus to introduce this panel of African-American women. How typical! Talk about tokens. I'm incensed. There are four women on this panel; there's no way they can deliver their entire papers. Several presenters make a point of saying so: "I will run out of time; I must cut." It's clear that they worked very hard on these papers. The only other invited women-of-color speakers are here to perform: a well-known lesbian mixed-blood poet, a Puerto Rican woman author, a famous Native poet and her excellent band. When I mention this color divide to a friend, she reminds me of Barbara Christian's often-cited essay, "The Race for Theory," which would imply that maybe it's not an oversight, maybe it's because most women of color don't do high theory.

Sure—a few months ago, I might have accepted this explanation with only slight reservations. But after reading dozens of theoretically astute submissions, I reject this possibility. I have concrete proof that "the race for theory" is multicolored, de todos colores. (As if I needed more proof, after reading Chela Sandoval, Jacqui Alexander, Chandra Mohanty, and so many other self-identified women of color. But still, it's good to see the proof stacked in piles around me as I type these words. It's so tangible.) For a while, now, I've been rather troubled by how scholars use Christian's essay to assert that people of color theorize, but in nonacademic ways. After all, I used a lot of theory in my first book, and I've read highly astute theoretical pieces by other self-identified women of color. They know the lingo, they use the terms and theories with grace . . . but they don't theorize simply to put themselves forward, to achieve status within the academic system. Yes, perhaps that's the difference: not necessarily the words used or avoided but rather the contexts, the intentions, and the visions with which theoretical language is infused. Theorizing not just for survival but for transformation . . . transformation of ourselves and the world. That's what I'm doing, and it's what many contributors do as well.

Attending this conference has taught me a valuable lesson: you can't make simplistic assumptions about who does and does not use theory. Maybe academic theory is not necessarily/automatically "white." Maybe Audre Lorde was wrong, maybe in academic guerilla battles we can use the "master's tools" without being assimilated or in other ways destroyed. At this point, I still don't know for sure which pieces will end up in the book, I don't know whether Gloria and I will request that contributors either make the theory more accessible or delete it. And I certainly don't know what readers will make of the more theoretical pieces, should we decide to include them. But I do know that I must actively resist the belief that women of color don't "do theory." It's another false division.

Spring 2000

My worries increase during one of our weekly phone chats, when I learn from Gloria that some of her friends are concerned with our desire to link this new book with *Bridge*. *This Bridge*, it seems, is an icon of sorts. Opening it up to men of all colors, to "white" women, to Jewish women, is viewed as irreverent. Gloria isn't surprised (she's warned me we'd get flak), but she takes these objections very seriously.

For a few days, I'm stunned. I don't know how to respond. I talk to Renae, who tells me that she understands the objections and believes that our working title, *"This Bridge Called My Back, Twenty Years Later,"* can be misinterpreted to indicate that we're simply reprinting *This Bridge*. As my fears grow I return to *This Bridge*, reread the forewords and introductions. Clearly, both Cherríe and Gloria want to open a conversation with all sorts of people: "We see the book as a revolutionary tool falling into the hands of people of all colors" (xxvi).

Although my fears diminish, they don't disappear. The last thing I want is for this book to incite new divisions among women of color. For the next week, I live with these concerns. As I care for my daughter, interact with my partner, teach my classes, swim (especially while swimming!),

I let the fears live inside me. Thoughts race through my mind, jumbled at first but gaining clarity as I circle through the issues . . .

This Bridge is not the Bible, and even the Bible is open to change. No book is—nor can be—frozen in time, not even a book as significant as *This Bridge*. Should we remove the words "This Bridge" from the title? To do so would contradict the potential openness in which *Bridge* was written, the invitation to create new alliances. And what about the contributors? For over a year now they've believed their voices will be specifically joined to the dialogue initiated in *Bridge*. In fact, many responded *because* of our title, because *This Bridge* was so important to them personally; they want to attach themselves, visibly, to it. They view their contributions as gifts. Moreover, *This Bridge* grew out of Gloria's experiences, out of her vision and desire for change. She's the one who, with encouragement from Merlin Stone, first decided to put together *This Bridge*. If she believes that expanding the vision is appropriate, then no one should object.

But really . . . who owns *This Bridge*? Not Gloria, not Cherríe, not the other contributors, not the people who will read this new book. Unless, in different ways, we *all* own it. Once it traveled "out there"—into the world—*Bridge* left the hands of its original creators. It's been picked up, embraced, and "owned" by the many readers who encountered it. It has spoken—it continues speaking—to each person who reads it whether that reader identifies as "of color" or "white," as "female"or "male" or "transgendered," as "lesbian" or "straight" or "bisexual" or "queer." But *ownership* is perhaps the wrong term here. Maybe we don't possess it but rather it possesses us? After all, *This Bridge* speaks to each of us in different ways; different pieces grab hold of different readers. So who has the final word? No one. There is no final word. This openness to unknown readers is part of the risk involved in writing and publishing. Sure, you could try to control who has a say in *This Bridge*—manage the voices, allow only those conforming to your beliefs, your identity politics, your vision. To some extent, inevitably, Gloria and I do this too. But we've decided to cast the net widely, to include voices by people who identify as "male," as "white," as "Jewish," as "TG," as non-U.S. residents. Not all readers will be pleased with this inclusivity, and surely some will object that we violate the spirit of the original volume, the mother text. Do we violate this spirit, or do we invite it to grow? Obviously, I believe the latter.

We must refer to *"This Bridge"* in the title or use other words clearly linking our two books. For the writers included in this new anthology, it's not just the "faith of activists" Cherríe Moraga describes in her preface to the first edition of *Bridge* that moves us; it's also the faith of *Bridge's* readers, faith in the visions outlined within this small but potent book.

During the next few months, Gloria and I return to the question of titles again and again. She, too, has similar feelings; she respects her friends' objections yet feels it's important to maintain continuity in titles. As she states in an e-mail to a colleague:

> I do think it's necessary that some part of the original title be used. It gives a particular lens through which to look both backwards and forwards from the point of _This Bridge_. People are interested in continuing the dialogue presented in _This Bridge_. The contributors in this new anthology were and are inspired by _This Bridge_ and many talk about the impact it has had on their lives and scholarship. Today, as evidenced by the contributions AnaLouise and I have received, that legacy is very much alive and continues. Cherríe and I have always seen _This Bridge_ as an alliance making tool between different groups of people, we've seen it as a bridge. This new book extends that bridge.

Amen, comadre. Amen!

Coming Together

Summer 2000

I'm back from Santa Cruz, where I spent time with Gloria going over the poetry and artwork. Our excitement about this anthology is growing as we begin seeing more clearly the interconnections among the various pieces. And now, although Michigan still doesn't feel like "home," I'm fairly relaxed as I sit outdoors in the shade, surrounded by my sister trees. It's windy today, but unlike the winds of New Mexico—which move fiercely over the dry land, spreading and intensifying the heat—these Michigan winds carry water. The moving green branches sound like waves hitting the shore, or like a rushing brook, like a waterfall. I'm tired and feeling overwhelmed as I sit listening to these winds, feeling a hint of moisture hit my bare skin. There's still so much to do: keeping in contact with contributors, requesting additional changes, collecting biographical statements.

Gloria has suggested that we're ready to finalize the book's organization, and I arrange to make another trip to Santa Cruz in August. We've already grouped the pieces into a tentative table of contents with seven sections (seven is an important number for us both). Now we need to read through the entire manuscript, rethink each section's internal organization, rearrange where necessary, decide on section titles, and insert poetry and artwork. We have sections on *Bridge*'s impact; breaking categories; omissions, revisions, and new issues; survival tactics; academia; alliance making; and envisioning change. Since many pieces enact several themes, placing them is difficult; we rely on other criteria as well . . . genre, length, transitions, shared metaphors. I'd be lost without Gloria's guidance; I've read anthologies for years, but I had absolutely no idea about the amount of work—the meticulous planning—that goes into anthology-making.

Our task would be easier if we had all the submissions, but we're still missing key pieces. And we continue working with some contributors, encouraging them to make additional revisions. "What this essay still needs is a sense of your passion, a sense of what really matters to you. Give the specifics of your emotional and intellectual experience, include concrete details. Put yourself into your words," we tell them, "write from your body, write from your heart." Even as I type these words, I wonder . . . Are we imposing our visions and standards as readers and writers? (In this regard it's perhaps both a help and a hindrance that Gloria and I are so much in agreement about what constitutes "good writing"—pieces with the potential to shift and transform people.)

But the "end" is now in sight. Although we probably won't have a complete manuscript by the end of the summer, it won't be much longer.

Invitation and Caveat to Readers

I chart the pathways to this book. I give you a map, guidelines, should you decide to compile an anthology of this nature. I tell you this story to draw you into our process. I want you to understand the desire for transformation motivating this collection, and I want this desire to touch you, to stimulate your own desires for transformation. Just as our book's cover image invites you to stand on the bridge, we invite you to share our perspectives, our views from *this bridge we call home*. Woven into this story is also a warning: If you've opened this book expecting to find a carbon copy of *This Bridge Called My Back*, don't bother. Stop now. Although it picks up on issues and concerns expressed in *Bridge*, there are many differences, including an expanded diversity of voices, the particular issues we explore, and this volume's relationship to the academy and to "white" feminism. And yet, simultaneously, the two books have much in common. We, too, are rewriting culture. We seize what Toni King and her co-authors describe as "the generative power of the spoken word," and we translate that spoken word into print: "Through our words, first spoken and now written, we deepen and expand the connections between us." Our contributors believe that words can initiate change and evoke new forms of alliance, "[f]orming coalitions . . . that cut across boundaries" (in this volume).

Our goal is not simply to commemorate *This Bridge* but to examine the current status of multicultural feminist theorizing and to reinvigorate *Bridge*'s call for new forms of community, identity, and activism. Much has changed in the past twenty-plus years, and these changes alter how we read *Bridge*, as well as the cultural work it can do in the twenty-first century. We have not (yet?) arrived. Nor have we fully envisioned what this arrival entails. While the overwhelming response we've received confirms *Bridge*'s continuing importance, contributors note that the anthology cannot—entirely—speak to the complexity of our identities, needs, and concerns in the coming years. We must be "endlessly open to revision within and without, while owning the history and density of the multiple descriptions that have made us what we are" (Lorenz, in this volume).

"Spiritual Activism," Nepantla . . . Moving Toward Transformation

At the National Women's Studies Association Conference in Boston I organized a roundtable on *Bridge*. NWSA, though not my favorite conference, offered a good opportunity to discover what others think about the issues raised in *This Bridge*. And indeed it was. Our roundtable was well-received, and the conversation among ourselves and with audience members was remarkable. It confirmed (yet again) my sense that *Bridge* is still extremely relevant to today's issues, as well as my belief that we have a long journey ahead of us before we'll achieve the visions put forth in *Bridge*. I was especially struck by a tension between two apparently contradictory trends that arose during our time together: On the one hand, continued reliance on identity politics, on the importance of self-naming, claiming a specific location—marked by some precise mixture of class, color, culture, gender, and/or sexuality—from which to speak. On the other hand and almost simultaneously, a spontaneous shift toward spirituality, or what Ramona Ortega and Jacqui Alexander described as "spiritual activism." I'm thrilled by this second trend. Although Gloria has been using the term "spiritual activism" for over ten years,[3] I didn't realize that the concept had moved out into the world. Unlike "New Age" versions of spirituality, which focus almost exclusively on the personal (so that the goals become acquiring increased wealth, a "good life," or other solipsistic materialistic items), spiritual activism begins with the personal yet moves outward, acknowledging our radical interconnectedness. This is spirituality for social change, spirituality that recognizes the many differences among us yet insists on our commonalities and uses these commonalities as catalysts for transformation. What a contrast: while identity politics requires holding onto specific categories of identity, spiritual activism demands that we let them go.

So how do we reconcile this apparent contradiction? What roles do categories—of gender, class, color, sexuality, and so forth—play in this vision of radical interconnectedness? How do we synthesize the two? Maybe the point is to live with this contradiction. I don't know. But I do believe that holding tightly to the labels, even when self-chosen, can be destructive—erecting walls that separate us from each other. *Bridge* contributors explored this divisive labeling process in great detail, and demonstrated how very restrictive it can be. And yet, at times, the labels are still necessary. Okay, I can accept this necessity, but I wonder . . . What happens to these names and labels when we embrace spiritual activism? My experiences have taught me that the recognition of our radical interconnectedness offers a vital key to long-term individual/collective change, a crucial point of departure in our work for social justice: if we're all radically interconnected, then the events and belief systems impacting my sisters and brothers in South America or Central Park or Jerusalem have a concrete effect on me. Spiritual activism insists that we all rise or sink together. Gloria made a similar point in her 1983 preface to *Bridge*: "many of us are learning to sit perfectly still, to sense the presence of the Soul and commune with Her. . . . We have come to realize that we are not alone in our struggles nor separate nor autonomous but that we—white black straight queer female male—are connected and interdependent. We are accountable for what is happening down the street, south of the border or across the sea" (n.p.). Viewed from within the Soul's presence, there's no "me" or "you." There's just "us." And yet, this "us" has been shattered and fragmented—split into a multiplicity of pieces marked by the many forms our identities take. I believe, with all my heart, that spiritual activism can assist us in creating new ways to move through these boundaries.

When I described this roundtable to Gloria, focusing especially on the concerns raised above, she reminded me of her belief that we're living in a place/time of nepantla, a point where we're exiting from the old worldview but have not yet entered or created a new one to replace it. Yes, I thought, that's it. This dialogue illustrates where "we" are as a movement: we're slowly breaking down barriers between separate groups (hell, some of the writers in *Bridge* were doing this boundary-breaking work two decades ago). And still, even as we acknowledge their limitations we cling to the labels and claim the power of self-naming in the face of erasure. For me, nepantla represents a threshold, a place of potential transformation: Do we choose to enter into and cross over this threshold, or do we continue clinging desperately to the place we're now at?

I believe that to move forward, we need to cross over, although I don't know what's on the other side. Nor do I know, precisely, *how* to cross over. In the face of uncertainty, we must believe there are ways to accomplish this task. It's this belief that compelled Gloria and me to open up this anthology to people who don't identify as "women of color," despite the risks involved (and these risks are real).

I began working on this anthology because I was extremely dissatisfied with the state of feminist movement. In my dissatisfaction, I returned to *This Bridge*, a book challenging simplistic notions of sisterhood—the belief that, as women, we automatically have things in common. Sisterhood and, more generally, unity, are neither automatic nor guaranteed. They must be imagined and enacted, and to do so is hard work. Our new book confirms and extends this vital insight, inviting readers—inviting *you*—to rethink the existing categories and invent new individual and collective identities, transformational alliances. This anthology demonstrates that the work proposed in *This Bridge* is not yet complete, the vision articulated within its pages is not yet fulfilled. There is more work to be done. New communities we must build. New thresholds to enter into and cross over.

May this book be a threshold, a marker of change, a place of and invitation to transformation. May this book make a difference, jar us out of complacency, revitalize the dialogue, bring readers face-to-face with these thresholds, challenge you to choose, challenge *us* to cross over.

Notes

Mil gracias y abrazos to Gloria E. Anzaldúa and Caridad Souza for encouragement and *extremely* helpful comments on earlier drafts.

1. For more on *Bridge*'s production history see Kayann Short.

2. This phrase is Shirley Geok-lin Lim's. See her essay in this volume.

3. See my introduction to *Interviews/Entrevistas*, especially 8–12, and see Gloria's comments on 38 and 178.

AfterBridge: Technologies of Crossing

Chela Sandoval

Toni Cade Bambara's twentieth-century foreword to *This Bridge Called My Back: Writings by Radical Women of Color* was meant to provoke action. "This Bridge needs no Foreword," she claims. "It's the Afterword that will count" (viii). Now is that post time of Bambara's imagination; we inhabit her imagined afterword. In what ways does this new book, and my own foreword, measure this twenty-first century afterwor(l)d? How do we go about evaluating, weighing, and enumerating the achievements that "U.S. radical women of color" have secured and cherish?[1]

Many U.S. progressives, leftists, feminists, and race, sex, queer, and Marxist activists either dismissed or were outraged by the 1981 *Bridge*; they considered the book a breach of faith, another act of left-wing failure, even blasphemy. Audre Lorde's *Bridge* essay "The Master's Tools Will Never Dismantle the Master's House" (first delivered at a 1979 conference) demonstrates how, in revolutionary times, the book could be viewed as betrayal. Lorde's 1979 challenge to leftists was that it is "arrogance to assume" any discourse of social progression or liberation "without examining our many differences." The "absence," she continued, of "significant input from poor women, black and third-world women, and lesbians," the dismissal of outsider forms of "consciousness," sanctions "a serious gap" in progressive democratic principles. This is what Lorde referred to in her well-circulated but misunderstood warning: "the master's tools will never dismantle the master's house."

Lorde and the other *Bridge* authors knew what was at stake for progressives. Those readers who did cross the *Bridge* were asked to enter what Bambara called "a contract," a narrative contract (viii). This agreement demanded a truce, a sworn intention, a pledge between contending readers, writers, text, and worlds. The pledge encouraged us to self-consciously become; to act and write upon the world; to call up constituencies of radical women of color, countrypeople, feminists, anti-racists, queer lovers, the disabled, the working classes, third world allies, the original, and the unoriginal, and to "shock yourselves into new ways of perceiving the world, shock your readers into the same. Stop the chatter inside their heads. . . . Write of what most links us with life, the sensations of the body, the images seen by the eye, the expansion of the psyche in tranquility: moments of high intensity, its movement, sounds, thoughts.

Even though we go hungry we are not impoverished of experiences" (Anzaldúa, "Speaking," 172).

This Bridge was constructed as a mechanism meant to call up and recognize experiences—and to make them matter differently. In 1981, this mechanism changed the authors themselves, who became the very warriors they swore to become through the publication of their words. *Bridge* effected this affirmative transformation in writers and readers alike in much the same way that a contract assures, confirms, promises. The writing or reading of *Bridge* incurred a debt of honor: its narrative worked in perception in much the same way as a vow, an action that requires a heightened moral consciousness by persons performing it. Through this vow—which was performed as litany, promise, covenant, or guarantee—"radical feminists of color" became women of words, speaking, writing, commanding, directing, giving meaning to silence, and, as Anzaldúa writes in this volume, transcending the word through code: a password: "I act with my heart in my hand," she explains. We disputed the Logos even as we were after the word. The *post* word.

This Bridge was ceremoniously crossed in June 1981 at the National Women's Studies Association Conference, when many of the books' radical feminist-of-color contributors read portions of their writings aloud on stage. Their combined achievement became a ritual of speech, spoken word performance at its finest, "theory in the flesh" (Moraga, *Bridge,* 23), the real appearing in their Acts. Earlier, essays from the book had been depreciated as "insignificant" by institutionally literate feminist activists. But now these same activists became listeners, shocked into stunned silence by what they finally heard, changing them. This hearing, this unavoidable taking-in, developed unanticipated revelations in all those recipients and vessels of the voice, and in all those rendering and giving voice.

What I commemorate in this volume is not so much the publication of that 1981 book, but the unavoidable emergence of the 1970s U.S. third world feminist social movement it marked and celebrated, a social movement that even today remains unlike any other. Its activists were self-consciously aware of themselves as makers and inhabitants of previously unknown modes of being. They knew they were devising a distinct social movement and peoples who might build and occupy an altered world. They envisioned a fresh evolution of human society, being, cultures, genders, sexualities. To these ends many radical feminists of color dedicated the length of their lives: Audre Lorde, Pat Parker, Rosa Villafañe-Sisolak, Barbara Christian, Sharon Lew, Toni Cade Bambara—all of us.

Twenty years later, where is this political movement that calls itself a "women-of-color" movement? Who mobilizes within it? And on what terms? Post U.S. third world feminist politics continue to operate as apparition politics—they inhabit the aftertime of the twentieth century; they are a social movement that haunts the afterspace and -word of twenty-first-century emancipation politics. This 1970s–1980s movement devised by so-called "U.S. third world feminists" was concocted so that it could never belong to any one people. But their anomalous politics left behind a roadmap—readable, available for anyone to follow. The 1981 *This Bridge Called My Back* identified the warriors, their passions, their tactics. What remains are the aftereffects: distinct languages, tastes, thoughts, peoples, procedures, sexualities, worlds, methods.

In December 1999 Vandana Shiva, East Indian feminist, third world activist, member of the Foundation of Science, Technology and Ecology, addressed the International Forum on Globalization.[2] Her overriding message was that in order to liberate planetary citizen-subjects who are categorized as "third world" ethnic peoples, economically, socially, or culturally, citizen-warriors must understand and learn to shape the relations that ardently link technology, morality, and globalization. UNESCO has responded to this call by supporting a "Women on the World Wide Web" network that passionately spans and transits the globe, touching the amulets of blackgrrrls.com with those of the Zapatistas in Chiapas. Gayatri Spivak recommends that activist citizen-warriors shift our thinking away from the notion that the fight is against globalization. The alternative, she says, is to think in terms of a politics capable of comprehending "the planet itself" as a species of alterity *that must be defended.*[3] But how do we go about waging such "planetary politics," how do we defend a planet circulated by cash/capital exchanges? Exchanges regulated through and by corporation city-states? The defended nuclear family held in place? The encompassing interworld digital network? The demands of everyday life? How do we free our individual desires from the grids of domination and subordination evolved by our histories? How do we liberate love, power, race, gender, sex, class, physiognomy, geographies from the very hierarchies that shape them?

The method that elevated the experiences of radical women of color into a connecting "bridge" during the 1970s is summarized in brief by the Mayan code of honor: In Lake´ch: I am another yourself (Argüelles, 196). This verbal address, like Anzaldúa's salutation "I meet you with my heart in my hand," refers to a political system of recognition, the terms of which built Lorde's "house of difference" (*Zami,* 226). The authors you read in this anthology identify and describe emotional, psychic, and social technologies that embody and circumscribe identities necessary for recognizing power, and changing its conditions on behalf of equalizing power between socially and psychically differing subjects. These technologies give practitioners an opening that leads to another distinct mode of consciousness. This differential consciousness is what many writers in this book also describe as connection to "spirit," to the "divine," or as a practice of "love"—la conciencia de la mestiza (Anzaldúa, *Borderlands/La Frontera* 77–91).

This political/spiritual consciousness must be pursued. Its profusions are accessed by and through social movement action organized around what Cornel West calls "prophetic democracy"—Anzaldúa's "open-hand/heartedness." Entry to its endowments requires using an apparatus comprised of five different applications, or technologies. These technologies connect and transit through one another until they are recognizable as a singular method. This method provides cognitive and emotional maps necessary for guiding internal and collective external action. Briefly put, the five technologies of this method are: (1) reading power, as in radical semiotics, la facultad, or "signifyin"; (2) deconstruction, or coatlicue; (3) meta-ideologizing; (4) differential perception, or nepantla; and (5) democratics, the ethical or moral technology that permits the previous four to be driven, mobilized, and organized into a singular methodology for emancipation. This method asks practitioners to collectively and strategically distinguish, evaluate, and select tactics, among which may include integrationism, revolutionary action, supremacism, separatism, anarchism, political defense or redefinition of the human, or complete defiance of that category. However different, each tactic is strategically accomplished in order to intervene in and democratically refocus social and psychic powers through identifying "situated knowledges" (Haraway) that can understand and match globalizing psychic, cultural, and national sites (Spivak, "In a Word"). This methodology of emancipation functions as a place-based ecological activism—it works through self-consciously identifying and producing invigorating political and cultural planetary geographies.

This methodology provides passage to that unfastened, differential juncture of being—la conciencia de la mestiza. What *Bridge*, this book, and others like them call for is a method that permits an evolutionary seeing, interpreting, and changing of the planet. This method vitalizes a twenty-first-century hermeneutics: "Love" understood as a mode of individual and collective social movement (hooks). This social movement spans and conveys transnational citizenry into a dissident force. The aim of this dissident force and of its methodology of love is creative renewal of the planet.

In the *Bridge* of 1981, lesbians of color put their bodies on the front line for the sake of a united, global Third World Liberation, for an inter- and trans-national women's movement, for sex, gay, lesbian, and queer liberation, for the sake of the planet. They named their political theory "radical Third World feminism," describing its politics as follows: "The vision of radical Third World Feminism necessitates our willingness to work with the colored, the queer, the poor, the female, the physically challenged. From our blood and spirit connections with these groups, we women on the bottom throughout the world can form an international feminism. . . . [U]ltimately, we must struggle together. *Together* we form a vision which spans from the self-love of our colored skins, to the respect of our foremothers who kept the embers of revolution burning, to our reverence for the trees—the final reminder of our rightful place on this planet" (Anzaldúa, 196). U.S. third world feminist politics rose out of this liberation movement organized by progressive activists of every color, sex, class, race, gender, physiology, culture. These activists envisioned the five entwined technologies I listed above, to eventually identify these as a method for bringing about utopian social and psychic structures. Theirs was an interdisciplinary discourse that rose out of U.S. third world feminist engagement with European, U.S., Latin American, hegemonic feminist, African, Asian, indigenous, third, and fourth world oppositional discourses. The internationalist principles forwarded by U.S. feminists of color and described in this current book as "the next social evolution of human society," the "multi-matrix," a "metaphysics of interconnectedness," or as a "physics of love" are symptoms of a political consciousness that is tied to the spirit, as well as a methodology of love that is tied to human politics.

This method, its technologies and their interactions, and its effects on identity and social reality work to emancipate citizen-subjects from institutionalized hatred, domination, subordination: it is a methodology of love. To deploy its psychic and social technologies requires a concomitant evolutionary step for human consciousness, and the rise of a new mode of citizen-subject, citizen-warrior, spiritual-activist. The authors of this book call for a science that can bring together the best wisdom of past indigenous spiritual traditions with current techno-digital knowledges, with the purpose of exploring and affirming the multi-dimensional places where body, mind, and spirit assemble, where spiritual work is seen as political work, where political work is seen as spiritual work, and where the erotics of love invest both. Becoming one such spiritual activist rewires one's brain, body, and erotics, in a process that opens the apertures between worlds. Peoples meet there, and transit to new perceptions.

Bridge was performative. It summoned up the very politics for which it called. This same "live action" occurs as one reads this new book, offered twenty years later. It too enacts the "collective I" for which *Bridge* called, reminding us that even across tremendous human differences, In

Lake´ch: I am another yourself. The countrypeople who contributed to this 2001 volume are authors who together have formulated a catalyzing driving force in their writings designed to move through bodies. Their aim? To summon up that afterworld of spirit, this planetary alterity, the utopian post-history for which innumerable peoples have given their lives. This new generation are activators of post U.S. third world feminism, the politics of radical women of color, the methodology of the oppressed, the hermeneutics of love.[4] In the year 2001 "feminist of color" alliances are meeting across the territories to conference on the "marginalization of Womyn and Grrrls of Color in 'Liberation.'" Gender and race remain contested issues here, but sex is perhaps the most charged of all. For only in freeing our erotics as readers, writers, activists, thinkers, spiritualists, lovers, thinkers, bodies can we fully engage this methodology of emancipation.

This new book comprises a ritual of restoration. Here, radical spiritual warriors carry these commitments across time, traversing spaces of lack, fear, toil, hope, love, and the unknown, with courage, faith, and ardor, for the sake of prophetic democracies they will fight for, and acquire. We can think of this book as a basic text in emancipation and slavery studies, the ways in which we enslave ourselves and others, the forms of emancipation we can imagine and deploy. But this book is not about moral redemption, nor is it about moral punishment. It is about survival, evolution, and emancipation; about the moral dimensions of freedom under global capitalism; and about the progression of political, social, and spiritual movements for justice, peace, and love.

Notes

1. For recent books on varying forms of U.S. third world feminism see Naomi Zack, AnaLouise Keating, and T. Denean Sharpley-Whiting and Renee T. White.

2. CNN, November 20, 1999.

3. Gayatri Spivak said this during her talk at the Women and Globalization conference at The University of California, Berkeley, 1998.

4. See my *Methodology of the Oppressed.*

i.

"looking for my own bridge to get over" . . . exploring the impact

one

Open the Door

Nora Gutierrez

two

Chameleon

Iobel Andemicael

Someone was screaming in the hallway. You could hear the screech of sneakers on the polished floor followed by a slamming of doors that shook An's reflection in the mirror of the medicine cabinet. With her open palm she steadied the glass and started again on the red outline of her mouth. Lips pursed and face leaning close to her reflection in the stark bathroom light, she tried—as she had since she could remember—to see herself as others did. Very dark eyebrows, lashes and eyes, skin somewhere between yellow ochre and olive brown, and pigment discoloration—splotches of white like dry salt lakes on an amber plain—at the temples and jaw. She knew the details minutely, each birthmark and imperfection, but still failed—as she had since she could remember—to perceive the whole face as a stranger might and ascertain the identity, ethnicity, culture, and race of the woman before her. Was she beautiful? Was her complexion sallow or seductive? Was she black? Was she so pale and soft-featured as to be mistaken for white? Was she dark enough to be *Latina*? Discernibly Colombian? Or did she simply look mixed—too indefinable to be seen as anything authentic at all?

Doing her childhood dance with her reflection she turned away then swung back suddenly to catch herself unaware. Nothing. She turned off the lights and tried to clear her mind, then flicked them on again and stood blinking; nothing. Who did people see?

Frustrated yet resigned, she shrugged at her reflection. She should be feeling better: her grades were strong enough to keep her pre-med, and she was learning how to step carefully between friends like a hiker crossing over water on stones; yet she was more apprehensive than ever, and acutely felt she still did not fit in. She wasn't invisible, just unseen; familiarity, rather than helping people understand her better, allowed them to impose their expectations more. She still cringed when asked what she was, "ethnically," by people gauging her allegiances. Like the last student left in a classroom at the end of a math exam, she sat paralyzed: even with all the variables she needed listed on the blackboard before her, she was stymied and unable to compute the solution.

With a last quick glance at her flushed reflection, An opened the bathroom door. Kate was pulling her fair hair back into a ballerina-style bun and surveying herself in the full-length mirror on the back of their door. "You promised me you'd go to the movies with us," she said quietly.

"I just found out there was a meeting before the party." An sat awkwardly on Kate's desk chair.

"What'll you miss? Come on," Kate cajoled, "come with us. Everyone's coming over for tequila after the movie and you can go to the party late." Her voice was gentle, with less of the edge that had set in when An had announced she was joining the Black Students' Center a month before. Still anxious to mollify her, An gave in.

"Good choice." Kate moved to stand behind An and examined An's black curls, arranging and rearranging the hair in different positions. "It's so curly and long," she said warmly, snagging her fingers as she tried to straighten the thick strands.

There was a clamor outside the door and after a perfunctory knock, Kate's girlfriends—their friends—pushed into the room in a wave of herbal shampoo and flowery perfume.

"I knew they wouldn't be ready," Emily said over her shoulder to Christie as they crowded into the room, sitting where they could and picking up random objects within their reach. As An was painfully self-contained—as much as she could, she kept everything crammed into her trunk, dresser, desk, and bookshelf—most of the things were Kate's. But Christie was opening a red notebook that An recognized with a sickening jolt.

"Whose poems are these? Or notes anyway."

As nonchalantly as she could, An reached a hand out for her notebook. "It's for an English class."

"Oh, have you finally caught up?" Emily asked.

"No, she's still blocked," Kate said with a melodramatic flourish, her hands deep in An's hair. "She has a semester's worth of poems to turn in to pass the class," she told Christie, "and we have one-on-one tutorials with the professor tomorrow. But An's pre-med—she's too pragmatic to write poetry."

"I think she'd just rather fail the class and wreck her precious GPA than open up about herself." Emily avoided An's eyes.

"What's the assignment?"

"Poems based on Sartre's 'words are actions' or 'acts' or something. And identity. We have to turn in a portfolio with one poem per week for the entire semester. That's our whole grade for the class." Emily turned to An. "At least you're interesting. You should have a lot to say." With a smile she approved each hairdo that Kate tangled together on An's head.

"I'm blank," An said. "I don't know what to say."

"Just speak your mind," Kate said. "Or else you could just cook some of your plantains and do a show-and-tell," she added, laughing knowingly with Emily.

"I like plantains." Christie smiled at An.

"These aren't normal plantains, they're plátanos maduros. They look like pieces of shit on a plate." The room reverberated with barely repressed laughter. "The place smells for weeks."

"And she plays her music when she cooks," Emily added, mimicking a little salsa step. Then seeing An's taut expression, she went over and put her arms around her. "You know we love you. That's why we tease you."

"Where're you from?" Christie asked politely.

"Colombia."

"Her mother's Colombian. Her father's white," Kate corrected in a proprietary tone.

"Afro-Colombian," An added.

"I'd love to meet your family." Christie was animated. "I'd love to see what produced you."

"They're very eccentric," An said, awkwardly clasping her hands together. "Colombian with big doses of immigrant suspicion and single motherhood thrown in."

"Movie's starting in five. We've got to go," Emily jumped up and the group mobilized.

Passing the mirror, An was shocked to see her hair, straightened to an electric frizz, tangled and matted around her head like unspun wool.

"Kate, wait," she gasped, "I can't go out like this! Why didn't you tell me?"

Turning back Kate guffawed and grabbed for Emily. "Look what I did—oh An, I'm so sorry." She laughed again and tried unsuccessfully to press the frizzy mass down with her hands. "It's not so bad."

"Wait. I'll put something in it." An hurried to the bathroom.

"Not that smelly shit, please. You look fine."

"Go ahead," An said, rubbing gel in her hands.

"Isn't that for black hair?" Emily asked, peering over An's shoulder and grimacing.

"Look, just go ahead."

"Hurry up," Kate sighed.

With An's hair finally twisted into a knot and stuffed under a crocheted tam, they ran to the auditorium, which was overflowing for the Saturday-night showing of *Scarface*. As Tony Montana burst into the Colombians' hotel room and was greeted by a whorish, vicious-looking, heavily made-up woman with mannish features reclining on the bed, An watched her friends' expressions carefully. Their faces were absorbed—not indignant or surprised but not amused or disgusted either. Uneasy, An gripped the arms of her chair as the eruptions of cocaine grew into mountains and Michelle Pfeiffer suffered the excesses of her Latin man in white-hot silence. Confused and disembodied, she puzzled out her discomfort. On the one hand she felt dirty, vulgar and un-American, like a creeping, insidious, sinister, enemy "other"; on the other she felt violated, like someone had spit or urinated on her from an apartment above as she walked alone, minding her own business. She felt violated as a Colombian and guilty for the violation as an American.

As the women gathered together in the bathroom after the film, chatting about weekend events and scrutinizing themselves and each other, An relaxed a little. The frown softened on her reflection, but her face looked distorted, crooked somehow. Her complexion—not pink or translucent, freckled or rouged like her neighbors'—seemed muddy, blemished, discolored. Like turgid water churned up at the edge of a pond, or slush shoveled unceremoniously on freshly fallen snow.

"You should wear red," Emily was saying to her, drawing her in from the margin. You have the coloring for it. Like a *Carmen*." All the women in a row paused to examine An and nod, almost in unison.

"Guys like that exotic thing."

The women laughed. An smiled tentatively, trying to gauge the feelings percolating around her in the bathroom.

"Don't mess with her," Kate said, grinning at An. "Colombians'll *fock jou op*."

Back at the dorm, people crowded into their room as Kate pulled tequila and limes from her mini-fridge. Listening to the laughter from the bathroom, An meticulously kohl-lined her eyes and fought her hair with gel until it lay still and gleamed. She smoothed gloss over her lips instead of lipstick and pinched her sallow cheeks until they glowed and she was satisfied with the boldness of her reflection. Then she joined the others in pounding tequila shots, licking salt from their hands, and pushing limes into their mouths, laughing as the juice ran down their chins. But afterwards, she and Kate were silent as they weaved across the campus, An heading to the BSC party and Kate on an off-campus food run with the others. As they reached the heaving basement party room, she and Kate squeezed hands and went their separate ways.

An pushed inside and made her way immediately to the BSC contingent knotted in the center of the room. Shyly sliding into a rhythm, An sidled up to the group, willing the ranks to part a little for her yet trying to look unconcerned if they didn't. An arm stretched out and pulled her into orbit at the periphery like a comet or moon held by a planet's gravitational pull. James, his hand still on her wrist, seamlessly moved out of the center of the group and joined her.

"Are you okay?" he asked, leaning into her ear and squeezing her shoulder. "You look messed up."

She nodded, leaning her weight into him. "Been a long night."

"Well come home and relax, baby." He opened his arms and she was absorbed into his rhythm until the end of the song.

"We missed you at the meeting tonight," he said when they stepped outside to cool off.

"I know. I promised Kate I'd go to the movies with her."

"You went to the movies with 90210 instead of coming to a meeting? You have to get your priorities straight. No wonder you've been having a rough time."

They sat companionably together, enjoying the cool air.

"There's no rule that says you have to pledge to your roommate's friends when you come to college. You need to be where you're most comfortable. In fact, you're welcome to move over to the BSC house if you want. There's a room free since Alice moved off campus."

"I don't know. I don't want to hurt my roommate. She'd take it personally."

"And that's your problem—how, exactly?"

"We're friends, in our own way."

James shrugged. "It's your call. Just be sure the decision's for you and not for other people."

An closed her eyes and tried to ease the spins by breathing slowly and deeply. "I'll think about it." She stood up. "I think I'm going to head out."

"I'll walk you."

The air from the underbrush was cloying and sweet as they walked along the campus's nature trail, each one synchronizing their footsteps to the other's.

"You finish your poem portfolio?" An asked as they stopped under a streetlamp in front of her dorm.

"Are you kidding? Weeks ago. But poetry's what I do. I've got a lot to say about—well, most things." Seeing her doleful expression he pulled her into a hug. "Try not to worry. Just speak your mind. Worrying just chokes you up."

Upstairs in her room, Kate stirred as An settled into her bed in the darkness.

"How'd it go? Did you pay your BSC dues?" she asked dryly.

"Please don't take my joining so personally."

"Whatever. Isn't your Mom coming tomorrow?"

"My mother and grandparents."

"That's nice." After a long pause she added: "You shouldn't be so preoccupied with race. You should just be yourself."

Lying in the darkness and listening to Kate's breathing deepen in sleep, An wondered who that might be.

Watching her mother's car drive through the college gates the next morning, An felt a queasy mix of excitement and apprehension. Her mother,

her black hair relaxed and newly styled to curl attractively below her ears, waved from the driver's seat. Beside her, Abuela was examining the campus around her with narrowed eyes, her red lips pursed in mid-judgement. In the back seat, Abuelito, looking grayer and more wan, was craning his neck to see his granddaughter and squinting his eyes.

As they toured the campus with Abuela walking impatiently ahead in a cloud of perfume, her skirts swishing and jewelry glimmering in the sun, An kept her arm securely linked to her grandfather's, clinging to him as her mother grilled her.

"It's bad enough you've wasted your time in the first place with a poetry class," she was saying, "but now you're telling me you might do badly and destroy your GPA?! How could you risk your future over some stupid class and then not even know what the professor expects?"

"I think she dislikes me."

They sat down at a circle of benches under a spreading oak with a marble table in the middle. Abuela smoothed her pleated skirt and smiled her smile—still coquettish after all these years—at a young man passing with a bookbag. Her gray hair was pulled back into a bun and she sat with the posture and bearing of a great beauty who refused to let the passing years erode her confidence.

"Who dislikes you?" she asked pertly.

"My English professor," An said, bracing herself.

"So what? Why is being liked so important to you? It just gets in your way. It's good if somebody gives you a hard time for a change," she said, not unkindly. "Things are too easy for you jóvenes here. You've no appreciation. Or motivation. And with all the sacrifices that have been made for you." She turned accusingly to her daughter. "She's too American. She thinks everything should come easily." She leaned over and pinched An's forearm. "Have a thicker skin, m'hijita. You won't get very far without it."

"What people think of you is moot if you're successful," her mother said. She sat easily in gray slacks and a white silk shirt, as understated as her own mother was flamboyant. She exuded a cool, detached confidence that An knew was studied; she had weathered the threats of her mother's disappointment enough times to know.

"Whatever you do, don't let your grades slide," her mother went on, then sighed heavily. "I'm still uncomfortable with your not being a science major. I don't see how you have the time." She sat back, palms flat on the table, shaking her head and tightening her lips in disapproval the way she did when An swam out too far in the sea—farther than she herself could go—and she could not physically bring her back.

"I like poetry," Abuelito said suddenly. He had been sitting with his eyes closed, hands crossed on the head of his cane and chin resting on his knuckles. "Maybe she gets it from me. Besides," he insisted as his wife and daughter both started to break in, "no matter what she does we will have our doctor in the family. She can do it all." He rested his head, white hair curled tightly and gleaming against his dark skin, on his knuckles again and closed his eyes.

"I joined the Black Student Center," An blurted out.

Her mother sighed but looked aloof and unperturbed. She had no issue there, as long as grades came first. But Abuela's eyes widened incredulously. "This again?" she exclaimed. "What for? You're not black." She grabbed An's braid and tugged it. "You have good hair. Your skin is trigueña. The one good thing about your mother's fiasco with that man was improving the race. And now you want to go backwards?"

Abuelito stirred, tilting his head back and inhaling loudly. "With your eyes closed the day smells almost like home. Like sun drying wet earth."

"Don't be so naive Mamá," An's mother said wearily. "We're all black here."

Abuela smacked her mouth impatiently. "But look at your child. Back home she'd never be called black. People here are crazy. Why voluntarily stigmatize yourself?"

"Where have you been living Mamá? For an old woman," she paused to let the insult take effect; then, gratified by the indignation on the older woman's face, she continued, "you're not very wise. As for you, An, it's great you joined the BSC, but I wish you'd spend less energy on always trying to fit in and more on your studies."

"A beautiful woman," Abuela said, raising her voice, "should never fit in. She should stand out, be original. Unforgettable."

"It's not about fitting in," An said. "It's about being aware and having support. Giving support. It's about not being indifferent."

"It's about not being different?" Abuela asked smugly.

"Instead of thinking of yourself as not fitting, can't you think of yourself as a bridge between groups?" Abuelito asked as though thinking aloud.

The familiar argument exasperated An. "You romanticize bridges. It's exhausting to constantly try to explain people to each other. Bridges may join two places but they themselves are nowhere—over precipices or cold water or highways. They're defined by the things they connect and by the people who cross them—people who are going somewhere. A bridge is what people trample to get where they're going."

Abuela brightened. "People appreciate a beautiful bridge. Maybe that's what immortalizes a bridge, grace and ingenuity."

"Think of all that a bridge makes possible," Abuelito said quietly, as though he were speaking privately to An. "They unite people who might otherwise never meet."

"They make it easier for armies to cross and invade," An said.

"Yes," Abuelito tapped his cane on the ground for emphasis, "but they can bring progress, trade, communication, and enlightenment."

"And sometimes," Abuela said, her painted nails catching the sunlight as she illustrated her point, "people blow them up."

An looked away, across the green, at the students sitting in groups in the sunshine. "Well mostly I feel like a fugitive at a cliff looking for my own bridge to get over."

"To where?" Her mother's eyes and voice were cool and collected.

An was silent.

"Or maybe I should say from what?" Suddenly impatient, An's mother stood up and straightened her shirt. "Let's get some lunch."

"And I need a toilet," Abuela said.

As the three women washed their hands in the bathroom, An glanced surreptitiously at their reflections: beside the cocky, flamboyant posture of her brown grandmother and the sophisticated, driven countenance of her brown mother, she saw a flaccid young girl, disheveled, sodden and disoriented, messy and inconvenient as caramel oozing at the edges of perfect dark chocolate shells. A pink-brown worm squirming in fertile, freshly turned brown soil.

"I'll go check on mi abuelito," An said, and left without waiting for a reply.

"You know that nobody fits in everywhere," Abuelito said as An sat down beside him and put her head against his shoulder.

"But people want to know your loyalties. I'm tired of feeling out-of-place all the time and I don't want to worsen it. I'm afraid to articulate how I feel. Besides, no one I know would relate to it. At least if I'm quiet I can't be exposed as a traitor or fraud—or, worse, a phony."

"If you're quiet you're at the mercy of others. If you speak frankly you can't be accused of being a fraud. People always test limits, especially if they can't tell where someone stands, and it's dangerous if you don't have any. It makes you weak and malleable, and all insults and compliments go right to your head." He turned to look at his granddaughter and touched his forehead to hers.

"Take strength from who you are, corazón, not weakness from who you're not. Figure out the relationships between things and see where you fit. And even if it's in the spaces between things, then that's your place. Who are you to question it?"

After settling them in their car and waving them out the gate, An walked slowly along the main tree-lined avenue of the college to her professor's house for the tutorials. A little early, she paused near the stoop of the rambling house and watched a row of sunflowers swaying like a muted chorus in the breeze.

"I hope you have a good excuse," Kate said, coming up behind her with Emily. "She wants her poems."

"I'll get them done by deadline."

"How, by getting yourself locked in the library all night again?" Kate's tone was both mocking and concerned.

"What're you talking about?" Emily linked her arms through Kate's and An's and leaned in.

"She does it all the time. To study for English, poli-sci—all the non-pre-med stuff that she leaves to the last minute."

"To do reserve reading you can't take out," An said, trying to hide her irritation at having her secret exposed. "But the night gets really long—and you can't get out until they open the doors in the morning because you'd set off the emergency alarms. You basically have to be desperate. The last time I had the entire semester of reserve reading to do for Dorman's U.S.–Latin American relations class, so I got locked in and read as much as I could and then went straight to the exam in the morning."

"It'd be fun to do in a group—take food and stuff." Emily was intrigued.

Kate pursed her lips with distaste. "All night? In the dark?"

"How do you do it?" Emily asked An.

"They keep the lights on behind the main desk where the reserve reading is."

"Doesn't it freak you out?"

"Sometimes. You have to be desperate."

"And you're desperate in this class, that's for sure." Kate squeezed An's arm supportively.

"Funny thing," Emily said, "is that you were supposed to be her pet. She loved you in the beginning, always wanted to know what you thought. But then you barely said anything."

Coming up the path, James was talking earnestly to several friends but waved when he saw her. "Hey," he called, "I want to catch you up on the other night's meeting. We're sitting by the maple tree around front." After a moment he added: "Hey Kate, Emily."

"So where're you going to sit?" Kate asked when he had passed.

"What?"

"With them or us?" When An hesitated, Kate turned to Emily. "She's such a chameleon." Her face was inscrutable, her voice deadpan.

"Is that good or bad?"

Kate considered. "I don't know. Both. Or maybe a chameleon's just a chameleon."

"Meaning that she eats worms?"

They both laughed. "She changes color based on her environment." They had begun walking toward the house, leaving An standing, her head burning, on the path. Like a child facing strangers on her first day of school, An stared at the ground, struggling to staunch her rising apprehension. When she looked up again the professor was leaning on the doorjamb with her arms folded and a phone cradled between her shoulder and chin.

"Don't be afraid of me," she said. "Come in. My son has me on hold."

The house was lined with overstuffed bookshelves and crammed like an art or curio dealer's back room with masks, ebony goddesses, elaborately woven carpets and textiles. Hanging across one wall above leaning bookshelves were embroidered pullovers stretched and mounted, their arm- and neck-holes taut, onto polished wooden frames with sharp and tiny tacks.

"Huipíles," the professor said behind her. "Women's shirts from Guatemala. That blue and turquoise one is from Panajachel on Lake Atitlán. It's one of my favorites. Each one uses distinct colors and patterns. It's how you can tell where a woman is from. I bought those when I was there in eighty-nine. Very sad. Women were selling them for money to feed their families. It was a bad time." She shook her head, hands on her hips. "Very sad. And not our finest hour."

At An's silence she added: "Ours, America's. Humanity's. Terrible violations of human rights. Hello?" She gestured that An should sit and walked briskly into the other room with the phone.

An walked instead close to the huipíles stretched lifelessly against the wall and traced the patterns with her finger. Peripherally she could see the professor sitting on the edge of her desk, and though her voice was lowered it was urgent enough to be overheard.

"Look," she was saying through clenched jaws, "I don't care what you do with her. Just take precautions. I don't want or need any third world babies. And you don't know what her agenda is. She could ruin your life." She paused, listening. "You know I don't mean it that way," she snapped. "And I don't like the implication. You know perfectly well what I meant."

Hastily, An retreated into the corner of a sunken couch and opened her notebook. She heard the receiver clack into its cradle and then the shuffle of papers. The professor reappeared and dropped into a wide-armed chair with lion-pawed feet.

"What interested you in Latin America?" An asked, gesturing around the room.

The professor steepled her fingers beneath her chin and sat back as though in the spotlight of a public television interview. "Very compelling, colorful, historical importance." Suddenly she grinned and leaned forward conspiratorially. "Loved the food, adored the people. And I could handle Spanish." Then the worried scowl descended again. She was like a mime, shifting features from one extreme to another almost quicker than the eye could follow. "Such a sad and beautiful place. Passionate. Caught my imagination."

After a moment's awkward silence in which both women smiled immediately and broadly at each other, the professor clapped her hands together. "So, where're my poems?"

She settled into her blood-red cushion and put her hands to the enormous carved wooden beads around her neck. On her fingers, large silver-and-turquoise, amber-and-gold, and amethyst rings made her hands seem heavy; on her feet, the fringed copper-colored moccasins seemed to belong on a different body. Laden and bedecked with symbolism, she looked like a composite head-body-feet puzzle where the pieces had been shuffled to comical effect.

"To date you've handed in a few half-finished poems when I should have one for every week." She passed An the small sheaf of papers; they were disordered and crumpled and the top page had rings of coffee across the center. But even more jarring was the fact that she could hardly see the poems for the red lines and comments running through them, like angry graffiti across a freshly painted wall.

"I know you're not a poet, but your words are just so—inauthentic." She paused to let the word take effect, her eyes unwaveringly on An's.

"Inauthentic?" Anger began to pulse in An's head but she was confused and keenly aware of the professor sitting like a cat waiting for a mouse to run from its hole.

Sensing her resistance and impatient for the chase, the professor's eyes flashed dangerously. "Yes, inauthentic."

Taking a deep breath, An said tremulously, "That's why I'm afraid to write."

"Let me read to you —" The professor reached out to recover the pages, and An suddenly noticed the windows open around them and the hum of conversation from students waiting their turn out in the grass.

"You ask what I am?" the professor read in a loud, slightly mocking tone. "Am I black or am I white? I am both so I am neither. I am no one. But what are you? Who are you to need to know?"

"That's inauthentic?"

"Uninteresting. I've heard it all before, I've read the literature. Don't you have anything original to say?" Her face was flushed and her eyes wide and engaged.

An gripped her hands together to keep them from trembling and felt an unfamiliar sense of outrage stirring inside her. "It's what I feel. What do you want me to write about?"

"I want you to make a choice and write about it."

"But the point is not choosing. Not being able to choose."

"Bo-ring," the professor intoned childishly. "Wishy-washy middle ground. Come down on one side."

An swallowed hard. "Choosing sides is authentic? Because it's easier for you?"

"Ah! Such drama!" She laughed but when she leaned forward her eyes were intent. "So what are you then? I'll call you whatever you want."

The students' silence outside the windows triggered An's adrenaline as she imagined the faces—embarrassed, curious, entertained—as they looked when she was singled out in class. "But what will you call me behind my back?"

The professor's jaw set. "Bottom line, An, you are failing my class."

Words, accusations, and pain rushed through her like blood gushing from a severed artery, but she could not speak. "You'll fail me for not being who you think I should be?" she managed at last. "But it's my transcript, my future."

"Then I would focus if I were you."

"I can't write—I don't know what to say."

But words were in turmoil inside her head; after a lifetime of being silent and compliant they were charged in her like colliding atoms by the professor's smug arbitrariness. Yet she felt desperation, too—a dragging, drowning, helpless feeling of going under in a strong current because she didn't know how to fight it.

"I'm sure you'll think of something," the professor said and picked up her student appointment sheet.

Trembling, An got up without another word and left the house. She walked quickly, averting her eyes from the students assembled in the grass and aware that nobody called after her. Stunned and frightened by her sudden isolation, An hurried to seek the sanctuary of the library. Safe in its womb she lay her head down on a desk and listened to the social sounds outside—the clunk of a frisbee against the stone building, a voice calling out an assignment across the green. Overhead, sunlight filtered through simple stained-glass windows. Thoughts were so loud in her head that the words were distorted, unintelligible. Finding your voice was one thing; knowing how to express it another. Restlessly, An got up and wandered through the library carrels, examining books absently as she passed. A word caught her eyes—bridge . . . *This Bridge Called My Back*—and a brown book cover with a woman on her hands and knees—and she was so overwhelmed with homesick pain and powerlessness that she sank down in a chair, her eyes burning with tears and anxiety, loneliness and rage.

> Many of us are learning to sit perfectly still, to sense the presence of the Soul and commune with her. We are beginning to realize that we are not wholly at the mercy of circumstance, nor are our lives completely out of our hands.
> (Gloria Anzaldúa)

> The bridge I must be
> Is the Bridge to my own power,
> I must translate
> My own fears
> Mediate
> My own weaknesses
>
> I must be the bridge to nowhere
> But my true self
> And then
> I will be useful
> (Donna Kate Rushin)

> We are the queer groups, the people that don't belong anywhere, not in the dominant world nor completely within our own respective cultures . . .
> (Gloria Anzaldúa)

Hypnotic and comforting, the women's voices encircled An where she sat, immobilized in a stranger's carrel, tears soothing her face. Women in another, parallel dimension had suddenly become visible to her and she was surrounded, kneaded, drawn in, understood, reassured by the anguished knowing in their voices, enfolded in their pain, and purged—in a slowly seeping motion—of little portions of her own. She read as the light died around her and, to her amazement, for the first time she began to see herself. Like a hologram, she appeared and disappeared according to the angle and the light; after years of loneliness and invisibility, the women's words in her consciousness, like a pencil revealing invisible drawings on a magic pad, brought her form to life. Curled into the dark library carrel, An began to reappear.

> *I am amorphous, transparent. I am a test tube in a racial centrifuge.*
> *I am a mote of dust in a stream of light. I am not the dust.*
> *I am a ray of light refracted by the stained-glass pane. I am not the light.*
> *I am a leaf slapping against its will against others in the wind. I am not the leaf.*

I am a genie or a hologram, the lighted stream of dust that carries an image from the projector to the screen; molecular, metaphysical, I am nothing and I am all.

I am my pounding heart, heavy, insistent, stubborn, and young. I am not my heart.

I am not invisible, nor should I be.

When the fifteen-minute warning that the library was closing crackled over the PA system, An took the book and her backpack and made her way against the crowd, eyes lowered, to a section of deserted carrels among the stacks. She slipped into a bathroom and crouched with her feet up inside the last stall, clasping her belongings to her chest. After several minutes there was a rap on the bathroom door and then the squeak of hinges.

"Security. Library's closed." After a perfunctory once-over the guard flicked off the lights and the door thudded shut behind him. Keenly An listened as the distant clamor and laughter receded, leaving her suspended in the darkness with her pounding heart.

When she couldn't crouch any longer, she stepped down lightly and felt her way to the door, opening it as quietly as she could and listening. Except for the red glow of exit signs and intermittent fluorescent lighting in the hallways between the stacks, the library was dark. An walked the windowless passageways, reveling in the feeling—anxious yet exhilarated—of her solitude opening around her. Other nights, before settling down to study, she had run through the library, or lain on the broad oak tables with her feet up to read, or wandered among the seniors' carrels examining the photographs and quotations they had taped to the walls.

Now, searching restlessly for a place to write where she could safely turn on the lights, she explored the rooms near the library offices. Discovering a sofa in the windowless librarians' bathroom, she settled in with her notebook and *This Bridge Called My Back* and waited for something more to come, watching the hands on a white wall clock flick through an hour.

Halfway into the second hour, An was struck suddenly. She locked the door as a precaution, and then in the stark white light she stripped off her clothes, averting her eyes from the mirror as she did so and tossing the clothes onto the sofa. Her pulse racing, she shed layer after layer, sloughing everything from her body like outgrown skin. When she was naked, her toes curling on the cold tiled floor and her pores tingling, she took a deep breath and turned to face her reflection. Inch by inch she examined her body, first in the mirror and then close at hand, trying to claim every inch of her skin. Turning slowly in front of the mirror, she watched her reflection morph from brown to white to red to yellow to black—and was still the same intact person: a woman of color, flushed and olive-skinned with tones of gold and brown; a woman impolitic and yet sincere; a woman not authentically One yet empathetically Many, her changing colors reflecting the world around her as much as her ability to change. In her posture and bearing, and in the center of her eyes, she could discern—when the light and the angle were right—those who had come before and those who were yet to come.

After a lifetime—passive, timid, and apologetic—of seeing, worrying about, and compensating for what she was not, she suddenly longed to see who she was.

Still naked, An retrieved her notebook, and with intermittent glances at her reflection began to write.

> to record what others erase when I speak, to rewrite the stories others have miswritten about me, about you. To become more intimate with myself and you. To discover myself, to preserve myself, to make myself, to achieve self-autonomy. (Gloria Anzaldúa)

three

Del puente al arco iris: transformando de guerrera a mujer de la paz—From Bridge to Rainbow: Transforming from Warrior to Woman of Peace

Renée M. Martínez

Holding *This Bridge Called My Back* in my hands, I sense a familiar comfort. I flip through it; the pages flutter by, each one bringing forth strong echoes of the nearly two decades since I first picked up the book. *Bridge* has the power and impact of a mother, a sister, a compañera—walking beside me, her gentle hand upon my back. It has not pushed or prodded me forward, but simply and gently reassured, "It's okay, mija, go ahead. You can do it, don't be afraid. You are not alone, no matter how lonely you may sometimes feel."

In my transformation from warrior to peacemaker *This Bridge* illuminates possible future paths, still teaching me new lessons. My understanding and appreciation evolve as I change. It helped me become the woman I am today—writer, artist, educator, peace activist—and yes, a bridge of sorts, a bridge among cultures, generations, worldviews. Now I go willingly, like a shapeshifter, and try to facilitate peace. I no longer feel like the bridge, my back an oft-neglected, unappreciated, and perhaps exploited pathway for others; instead I am now Acro Iris–Rainbow. I am learning how to help people honor and also transcend fundamental differences, in the name of peace and reconciliation.

Arco Iris–Rainbow: One foot in the white world, the other in the Brown; one foot in the world of bureaucrats, the other in that of activists; one foot in the world of administrators and academicians, the other in that of students; one foot in middle class, the other in poverty; one foot in a heterosexual world, the other in Lesbian/Gay—and it goes on and on. We all know the many forces used to dominate and separate, the many identities we embrace, assert, or are burdened by. I no longer feel so torn or pulled apart. Instead I am honored to travel within and between worlds, like dancing light—asking others to follow, to lay down their swords and allow the transcendental qualities of humanity help them find both peace *and* justice.

I am the fifth of six children born to a Mexican-American father and a white mother. Since my dad and his culture were dominant in our household, it never occurred to me that my mom's race or my mixed ancestry made me any "less" Mexican American—nor did my fair skin, since my dad's family fills a spectrum from peach to deep brown. My father raised us to be proud of our Mexican heritage. Unlike most of my Chicana contemporaries, I am a second-generation college graduate. In the 1930s my grandfather said that Mexicans in the United States were treated like dogs; the only way to have a better life was to return home to Mexico or stay and get an education. My father is one of very few Mexican Americans of his era to attend college and receive a graduate degree. He grew up in Claremont, a southern California community segregated between whites and Mexicans, attended the Mexican schools, and was prevented access to many other supposed public facilities. However, in the logic of racism, authorities required his more fair-skinned siblings to attend white schools.

In the early 1940s when my grandfather died, my grandmother Guadalupe was widowed with ten children. The family began working as migrant farm laborers. This difficult life disrupted the children's school year. Still, my father maintained his dream of becoming educated, but it was a battle. When the schools were eventually forced to desegregate, like other non-English speakers he was tested in English and subsequently identified as mentally retarded. He and others were punished and ridiculed for speaking Spanish. Later, a high school counselor tried to dissuade him from taking algebra, encouraging him to enroll instead in auto shop because "Mexicans are good with their hands." After fighting his way into college prep classes, he was accused of cheating because he performed better than the white students. Yet he persevered and succeeded.

I, too, learned to be a fighter—sometimes literally, but usually by dominating in sports or in the classroom. I had a reputation for my quick, violent temper. I grew up in a virtually all-white mountain community and felt under siege, especially for my ethnicity. As a teen, my barely veiled lesbian relationship made me even more vulnerable. Emboldened by love, I ignored the homophobia that constantly licked at my heels like flames from hell.

Leaving for college, I thought I discovered how to start anew, almost reinventing my self. I began showing my gentler side and adopting a calmer demeanor. Yet despite the campus's tolerant attitudes and progressive teachings, by my second year at the University of California, Santa Cruz, I fled for the closet. My lesbianism seemed to disappear, while my racial politics grew and flourished. I lived at a residential college that housed most of the campus's Students of Color and advanced a theme of multicultural pluralism. There were ongoing battles and concerns around racial issues; I supported causes like the hunger strikers' fight for Native American and Third World studies, but the tactics often felt too radical for me and I silently committed to fight "within the system."

College was the first step on my way to getting a Ph.D. and becoming a university professor. With my biology major I rode the wave of academic scientific objectivist privilege. In science courses students were required only to learn the right answers and apply scientific theories correctly. We were rarely asked to think critically or ponder substantive social concerns. However, my double major in environmental studies allowed me to read radical social, political, and economic theory, and question natural resource degradation. I constantly raised issues of environmental policies' racial and social equity, although few of my professors did likewise. Though committed to environmentalism, I sometimes worried that for most environmentalists, "saving the whales" was more important than the lives of people—especially the poor, People of Color, and Third World.

In 1983, during my senior year, I met *This Bridge Called My Back*— the required text for an Intro to Feminism course that I audited (foolishly believing this class ranked far below my "real" courses). Deep down I was actually scared of being too closely associated with anything feminist, fearful it might be considered "queer." Even though the women's studies instructor and class were the most popular on campus, I was certain that when I walked through the door people would somehow "know" my true nature. Fresh from a break-up with a boyfriend, I was terrified of my own soul's truth—that I could never feel more loved than in the embrace of a woman.

Only nine months earlier, I had admitted to myself that I was a Lesbian. But I couldn't accept this reality; it had no place in my life. Instead I stood poised to walk toward self-destruction, certain that suicide might be the only way to reconcile seemingly irreconcilable contradictions—being a Chicana and a Lesbian, my parents' daughter and a Lesbian, alive and a Lesbian. This saga of a young adult's struggle for sexual and cultural identity may seem almost a cliché. Yet even as I write these words, it seems as though I walked through fire—through the deeply ingrained homophobia of my world, outside and within. *This Bridge* helped me see new pathways, options, realities. I am forever indebted to its words, for I still remember my life before having *Bridge's* truths to support my existence.

This Bridge was like a cool refreshing awakening. For the first time I heard the voices of Women of Color, especially Chicanas, proudly proclaim their lesbianism; other daughters of mixed-race ancestry spoke of passing; and all writers unabashedly and unapologetically named racism and societal privilege. I had never been so moved by nor felt so included in any text, or any description of reality. I knew all kinds of radical theory, which I used to write, speak, shout, and protest—but nowhere had I ever been able to sit quietly and simply feel as though I belonged. Among those pages, it was like coming home—a contrast to my literal home, where I'd never have the huge Mexican church wedding, where I worried that my parents feared the shame possibly brought by their fifth child's sexuality.

This Bridge was beside me as I fell back into the arms of another woman—a classmate in my women's studies course. This act itself felt like a celebration of what we'd learned about loving ourselves as women. But here I also bore both the external and internalized condemnation of church, family, friends, and culture. Long-buried pain of homophobia surfaced. I'd carried a lifetime of deflected accusations and bitter hatred, but *Bridge* helped me see and believe in my own integrity. It helped me cut through the myths infused in my culture, the unspoken but ingrained warnings against being Queer: being a Lesbian would sever me from everything that counted in my life; homosexuality, the ultimate betrayal of my Mexican heritage, was only for white people, I'd be disowned for the shame my lesbianism brought upon my family and my people. *This Bridge* reminded me otherwise.

Autumn 1983, *This Bridge Called My Back* packed away in my boxes, we headed together to Los Angeles for graduate school. At UCLA I enthusiastically searched for social equity in the field of public policy development, but was bitterly disappointed. The academy did not want my questions. The university environment, a place that once fed my intellectual growth, now tried to silence me. I felt betrayed, abandoned, and heartbroken. Into the ivory tower, I brought *This Bridge* as a selected text for a graduate student–directed seminar. It felt almost dangerous to discuss issues of racism in this mostly white class, yet we all learned from the experience. I remember a white friend honestly admitting how painful and difficult it was to read *Bridge's* words. We all—men and women, white and of Color, heterosexual and Queer—let *This Bridge* catch our tears and reflect our anger. Like my co-facilitators, I felt such relief and pride to have it as a resource for initiating and guiding a discussion too painful to embark upon alone.

This Bridge was with me as I walked away from the academic life I'd envisioned. The absence of voices like those in *This Bridge* was too disturbing. While serving on tenure and hiring committees I saw the institution's ugly underbelly, academia's sordid politics and values. *This Bridge* gave me strength and conviction to follow my principles and ultimately make one of the most important and best decisions of my life. My own legitimacy, intellectual or otherwise, does not depend upon institutions of so-called higher learning. *Bridge* enabled me to deflect a graduate professor's commentary about my decision to be an educator in the community when she offered, as an intended compliment, "Such a waste!" Onward I went with *This Bridge* both in my heart and on my mind. Together we have traveled, in and out of meetings with white feminists and Men-of-Color activists, onto the streets with Lesbians and Gays of Color. Building coalitions, attending meetings, parades, conferences, rallies, and demonstrations—at times dodging police in riot gear.

The anger and outrage captured on the pages of *This Bridge Called My Back* especially provided voice and solace while I walked in worlds that could not understand or relate to the profound experiences it describes. *Bridge* gave me license to feel and cry, and reminded me not to ignore my emotions for the sake of analysis. I built upon both the indignation of injustices and the celebrations of resistance and survival. *This Bridge* gave me strength to develop theory authentic to my world, when Women-of-Color lives were ignored by narrowly defined male or eurocentric worldviews. We could be at the center, not on the periphery or an afterthought.

This Bridge strengthened me as a warrior. I've fought many battles in various venues. Even when I was isolated and exhausted, *Bridge* helped me maintain commitment and remain open. I've participated at many women's spaces, meetings, conferences, and festivals where painful discussions of race and privilege occurred. In the streets, but more so in meetings with university administrators or politicians, I've confronted racism, sexism, homophobia. But I was never alone; *Bridge* was always there beside me. I stayed when I was convinced that I didn't belong. I kept my voice in the room, even when I thought I could no longer bear another denial, excuse, apology, or token gesture. By virtue of my class, education, and fair skin, I've had access to many worlds. It often felt as though I was the lead flank or advance reconnaissance into the enemy camp. As "una güera" (a light-skinned) Chicana, of mixed heritage no less, and as one who can pass as white, I understand the dynamics of white privilege. I allow those comfortable with my appearance, or who think I'm the "right kind" of Mexican—half-white, educated, middle class—to take me into their confidence, allow me through their gates. I'm often their token. But then they discover that my silence was not part of the bargain.

As a child, I learned always to anticipate some kind of battle. My father, born in the 1920s, perhaps embodies the cruel and ironic contradictions of surviving in a racist society. For many people, he fits the bill as someone who "pulled himself up by the bootstraps." However, his resistance had a quiet rage that surfaced in the privacy of our family. While expecting nothing less than "the best" from his children, he likewise taught us that we would need to be twice as good to be considered equal. He consistently, though almost covertly, instructed us to demand our rights while expecting that they would otherwise be denied. I came of age as a Chicana through the tutelage of my older sisters, where "the struggle" was further shaped in openly confrontational terms. These were the parameters that defined my expectations, my analysis, and my very existence—I cultivated the instincts of a warrior.

Then something in my core began changing. It was not an entirely conscious choice, but peace became a necessity. I don't know exactly when or where the shift occurred. Maybe it was knowing one too many youths involved in gang violence or my horror at watching the Pentagon's sanitized war images of "smart bombs" launched like the latest version of a new video game. Perhaps it was the days of fire and rage in Los Angeles. Whatever happened, peace became a priority.

During this quiet inner revolution, I still felt *Bridge*'s presence, its wise tones guiding me. *Bridge* was beside me in the aftermath of the first Rodney King trial; it brought me wisdom to stay indoors that first night, knowing I had no peaceful voice to raise in response. It was there the following day, as I watched the smoke and ashes dissipate among the cries of "No justice, no peace!" What future could we offer our children? A day later, I gathered peacefully downtown with other activists. Hundreds came together, not knowing what to expect. We watched military convoys fill the streets, and were then harassed and cornered by police. My bitter frustration mounted. I couldn't bear the 1992 presidential politicians' and the media's "Can't We All Get Along" spin on events, or the images of multicultural crews of residents sweeping the streets. Where were real answers for the youths who had violently questioned the verdict?

As an educator in several multiracial high schools, I was overwhelmed by the extreme racial tensions among African Americans, Latinos, Asians, whites, and others. These young folks seemed united only in their mutual distrust. I worried when a colleague asserted that an educator must have hope in the future. I felt only despair—mine and others'. Our children deserved better than what we were giving them. While students sincerely claimed a dedication to peace, one school's Peace Committee meetings sometimes erupted into racial insults and fights, particularly between Latinos and Blacks. At such times my role as peacemaker became clearer. In the midst of teaching nonviolent conflict resolution, I slowly abandoned the sensibility of a warrior.

My commitment to peace also grew as I broadened my activism to include more diverse groups. I returned to the table with white feminists and heterosexuals, engaging them as allies, not adversaries. I tried to find commonalties, build stronger and more authentic coalitions. I tried not to define myself, the world, and my vision according to the dominant society. I stopped focusing so much on the injustice, and began looking at future possibilities.

We have so often been depicted from a deficit model, seen for who we weren't rather than for ourselves—called "Non-white" or "minority," defined in reference to the dominant culture. And also, as a friend once said, "made to pay twice for their sins," dealing with racism and then somehow held responsible for taking care of our perpetrators' guilt. *This Bridge* implored us to move beyond such chains. Something in peacemaking shifts the focus. It pushes beyond the violence and hurt, even the unfocused anger, past the tired, worn-out "master's tools"; it replaces domination and power over, vengeance and retribution, with another sense of justice. It looks for reconciliation that holds people accountable, but not at the cost of their dignity.

My commitment to peace developed as I realized how my narrow definitions prevented me from living honestly or wholly. My worldview of "us" versus "them," "friend" versus "foe" left me under siege, constantly embattled and completely exhausted. I had drawn far too many battle lines that I feared crossing. But what happens when the people you love, your family, your friends begin to appear as the "other"? What happens when you see shadow images of bashings, or hear their faint echoes of racism? How do I respond to my dear heterosexual friend's homophobia? What could I do when my life's kindred spirit sounds so much like the administrators from the "community" organizations I fought with for equal access? How do I handle the knowledge that family members, no matter how hard they try, would probably never be proud of my lesbianism? Did that make them my enemies? And what of my fair-skinned reflection in the mirror, the face of a white woman looking back at me? If all these people were my foes, who were my allies? When could I stop fighting?

Our society rarely teaches us about the strength or power of peace and nonviolence. I adopted a less warlike approach, searching for the courage and faith to walk the same path as those who once looked like enemies. Taking such a risk requires faith in the possibility of a world of peace and harmony. The process has meant trusting in the integrity of my principles and not relying on rigid categories of oppositional thinking. It has been about discovering the difference between having a critical analysis and simply being judgmental or condemning. I've learned not to focus exclusively on the gaps or conflicts, but on areas of intersection that will become pathways toward reconciliation. Slowly, I have become a Woman of Peace—Mujer de la Paz.

Peace exists in many forms. Only as I approached forty did I find the honesty and dignity to begin integrating my mother's Anglo-American ancestry into my life, learning to reconcile my fair skin's protective buffer with the painful legacy of racism that has always defined my understanding of the world and my place in it as a Chicana. Whether embraced or not, passing is always a palpable privilege, but, ironically, passing is not a painless privilege in a racist society. How do I describe my commitment to peace? The shifts, though internally revolutionary and profound, can't be documented by my work as an activist. How do you explain the quiet impact of a pebble breaking the water's surface, the significance of the ripples flowing outward? But I somehow believe that my commitment to peace might be the most important contribution I have yet to make in this world.

My peace activism lies in the radical internal changes that are slowly moving outward. First and foremost, my pacifism manifests itself spiritually. It lives and grows in my art and writing. It touches every area of my life, asserting itself as a priority in all conflict, both personal and political. It's present as I commit to transcending all forms of violence—emotional, spiritual, and physical. I'm inspired by peace efforts in my city and around the world—in Ireland, South Africa, the Middle East—or in Los Angeles with groups like Homies Unidos. What once appeared impossible now seems essential. Former enemies change in ways before unimaginable. The goals of peace and reconciliation have become a shared priority— more important than killing and fighting, even over lost family lives, or previously non-compromising positions of principle and integrity. Compromise and concession facilitate the path of this new way of being in the world.

Unfocused anger has self-destructive properties. Destruction may purge and even on some levels purify, but I'm no longer convinced it facilitates healing—perhaps even the opposite. Our answers somehow lie in building and creating, moving forward and beyond, allowing wounds to heal and scars to fade gracefully. Not to forget or deny pain, but to embrace it and move on. We must believe that atrocities and injustices will not prevent us from flying, or even from soaring. I don't know if I understand forgiveness, or even advocate it in the abstract. But I'm tired of seeing energy drained into a dark pit of despair, rather than amplified by hope. When I teach young people—those whose lives are touched by and at times engulfed in violence and destruction—I reach out with avenues for creativity, self-expression, and nonviolence. My activism is in making spaces for their hopes to flourish and grow, despite the injustices and harm in their lives. My activism is in providing places for young people to learn peaceful solutions to conflict, to make art and find creative expression so that their energies and self-definition can become part of a constructive process. I'm walking down this path in my own life, and trying to open up such avenues for others.

For nearly twenty years, in *all* ways, and always, *This Bridge* plays like the lyrics of a beloved song in my head and heart. Quotations, adages, emotions, and images weave themselves around the life I've lived and into the future I'm creating. I see *Bridge*'s long-standing wisdom and vision, but in new ways. As I now read its final section, I smile. Although at times it seems I am talking about something "new," so many thoughts in *This Bridge* reflect much of where I stand and where I'm heading. Once again *Bridge* is a jumping-off point for my forward movement.

This Bridge has helped me assert that my life experience—as a Chicana, as a Lesbian, as a woman, as a person—should be honored with the dignity and passion it deserves. So, too, it taught me the value of honoring others' lives, and, in their absence, hearing their silence. Gandhi once said, "We must live the change that we wish to see." I would add that we must live the life we dream. *This Bridge Called My Back* has inspired me to dare to dream, to struggle audaciously for a world that does the same.

four

Nacido en un Puente/Born on a Bridge

Hector Carbajal

extiende
los brazos
extiéndelos
que toquen

tus manos
mi orilla

yo recorreré
tu cuerpo
como quien
cruza
un Puente
y se salva

—Francisco X. Alarcón, "Puente"¹

This Bridge Called My Back: Radical Writings by Women of Color is the locale of self-identification, self-discovery, and the inspiration for a new consciousness. I believe that this book speaks to anyone seeking liberation, affirmation, and political action. As a Latino queer, I side with the women of this book in voicing anger, frustration, and activism. I side with anyone else seeking the same.

I first read *This Bridge* two years ago while writing a research project on Gloria Anzaldúa's *Borderlands/La Frontera*. I remember identifying with Anzaldúa's "La Prieta" and its subject of alienation. The essay made me think of my childhood, my family in Texas, and the feelings of pain and loss from being hurt by them. I remember being called "El Prieto" by my family and always feeling "different" from my light-skinned siblings. I remember being regarded as "strange" for preferring to stay in my room to read and write. I remember my mother telling me, "I'll kill myself if I find out you're a joto." In high school, I considered myself a complete "Other" when classmates stigmatized my skin color as "Arabic" or "Indian." They laughed at me and called me a "terrorist." This was not typical teenage angst. This was about race and sexuality, which I quickly put away in the back of my mind. It was painful to repress my pain and anger over fearing and denying my race and sexuality. However, *This Bridge*, especially "La Prieta," made me realize that I was not alone. I have learned to purge my anger and pain through words, just like the testimonies in *This Bridge*. I affirm my identity and hear my voice through words. The words form images in which I am visible. I am alive without shame and confusion. Collected words on a page are my experience, and I hope they appear similar to others who read them.

This Bridge has also taught me that "bridges" are not built on anyone's backs. They are built, as Francisco Alarcón's poem suggests, when we extend our arms to each other. They are built through alianzas. Bridges and alliances form a special foundation for experience, knowledge, understanding and revolution. The power of written words and "bridges" create the strength we need to fight, purge, appeal, revise, subvert, affirm, and revolutionize.

When I first heard of this anniversary anthology, I was told that not many men had expressed interest in collaborating on this project. I see it as a shame that men, whether heterosexual or homosexual, have not been more influenced by *This Bridge*; the book speaks to women and men of all classes, races, genders, and sexual orientations. The book taught me to think about my ties to patriarchy, to culture, to family, and to religion. It also made me examine how each has enslaved me with its repressive ideology. *This Bridge* inspired me to seek liberation and control as a new man, queer and Latino. Now, my written words and my faith in them have created the path toward breaking free into self-identification, self-discovery, and a new consciousness.

I would love to live in El Mundo Zurdo, where all inhabitants make alliances. We all examine one another as we do ourselves. We all learn— as Anzaldúa said in *Borderlands*—how to shift identities and contradictions. We create a new consciousness and share our space with others. We teach others and we are taught. We are part of a cycle of love—sharing and rejoicing. However, much work is still to be done to further the transformation of this world.

We need to start the process by examining gender, race, sex, class, and sexuality (in no particular order or hierarchy) in terms of identity. *This Bridge* explores how these categories constitute identity. These "categories" are not mutually exclusive but a whole that define a person's politics. I believe different identities, histories, and peoples can come together and agree on similar oppressions. We can voice our anger and frustration, and we can believe in our powerful words to create a new consciousness. I'm speaking especially to the men out there. I want my joto brothers to break the silence. First, we need to examine ourselves and develop a language. Then, we can return home and talk with a new language to our families. We can also talk to our white queer brothers and inform them of our needs. We can create alliances with our lesbian sisters and strengthen the activism. We can build bridges where new generations of activists can be born. We can take care of each other and reward each other with peace. We will stop lamenting martyrs, and begin celebrating the heroes in this world.

I want more bridges to be built and I want new beginnings. I want the spirit of change to affect all peoples. I want the silences to cease. I want energy to explode out of repressive molds. I want the written words to call forth change and activism. I want the spirit of collected words, such as those in *This Bridge Called My Back*, to rise once again and activate change. I want all this to be a collaborative effort. From this point, we can erase fear and guilt. We can celebrate by—as Alarcón's poem illustrates—

extending our arms to one another. When we touch and run through one another, we are saved and born on and through bridges. I wish to begin building and forming *now*.

Note

1. "Puente," in *Ya Vas*, (San Francisco: Humanizarte Press, 1985), is reprinted with permission from Francisco X. Alarcón.

five

Engaging Contradictions, Creating Home . . . Three Letters

Alicia P. Rodriguez and Susana L. Vasquez

To My Beautiful One,

That's what I called you soon after you were born. Having you I felt a love that I never felt before. Your dad said that he never saw me as happy as when I was pregnant with you. I guess it was because I always wanted children. Through your birth I realized some meaning to my life that was lacking in my struggles to complete a dissertation that I never dreamed I would pursue and that I considered not finishing. Around the time of your conception and birth I was doubting the course of my life and my decision to pursue a degree, an academic career. Having you motivated me to complete that portion of my life causing me so much anxiety. I remember commenting to a former graduate student friend about how your birth motivated me to finish the dissertation. She felt that motivation should come from the love of the subject, the love of the field, the love of the career. I didn't agree with her, although I don't remember if I expressed my disagreement. She seemed worried that I was losing my academic drive, which I probably was.

As I look back on her comments and expereince a second stage of doubts or, more positively put, deep thinking about my career goals, I understand her response. I've seen many academics with very compartmentalized lives, separating their career life from their personal life. I've realized that I can't compartmentalize very well, and may not want to. And now as I'm going through another major turning point. I really want to work on achieving a more integrated life—a life where I can be a good mother, good partner, good worker, good person. Now with the birth of your baby sister I've decided to do the mother/career woman thing my way and not succumb to the pressures to sacrifice family over career.

When I was young I was very driven. Most everything I did, I did with intensity. I remember often being told by family and friends, "Alicia, you're too serious." When I was about nine years old I decided that I wanted to be a doctor, a pediatrician to be exact. I don't remember if that desire came from only me. I suspect that my father had a lot to do with it. In school I worked hard in my studies, did well in my classes, and went on to become a doctor of a different type. I was always passionate about sports as well. I loved and excelled in numerous sports and realized later in life how important sport and exercise are to me and my mental health. Although I had dreamed of competing in the Olympics, I did not seriously continue my athletic interests after high school.

Throughout my youth and now adult life I always desired to have a family, too. I just didn't know where to fit it in, given my other interests. I tell you this to explain why my life has progressed in the way it has and why, now, I'm at a turning point. I've realized that during my youth I was much more confident in my abilities and more in control of my life than I have been as an adult. Many of the choices I've made as an adult were done without much foresight. You were my one true choice.

Before you were born, I chose to pursue graduate studies beyond a master's degree even though my heart wasn't truly in it. I chose to accept jobs that satisfied my economic needs at the time but not my intellectual desires. I chose to stay in Illinois for much longer than I wanted. I chose to pursue a career and postpone motherhood. In many ways these were not choices but accommodations to my circumstances. The decisions came from not knowing what I really wanted and from being stuck in a pattern of pleasing others rather than pleasing myself. I forgot who I was. I forgot my dreams. And never being much of a risk taker, I rarely fulfilled my fantasies.

I hope that your fantasies will become reality. I hope that your future will be much more open and accepting than the society we live in now and the one I lived in as a child. And I hope that all the hang-ups that people have about race, gender, sexuality, religion, etc., will lessen and allow you to grow in wonderful ways. I want you to be free to realize your dreams and be who you are, without constraints. People would say that you're the product of an "interracial marriage." You probably don't think about it too much now, other than noticing that my hair is much kinkier and wavier than yours and your father's, but it may become an issue later.

In the United States many people think I'm Black/Black Latina and in Cuba I'm a mulatta, and racially that's how I see myself. But your classmates will probably look at me and say to you, "You have a Black mom." When you were born I could only be Black or White, because that's what the hospital form allowed under "Cuban." I made a decision I don't feel comfortable with. I marked "White," even though I'm also African, indigenous, and Chinese. Now, with your sister, I've marked "Black." I hope that by the time you have children you won't have to choose.

I know that you will not always be able to do what you want and be who you want to be. But I hope that you'll be more deliberate about your life than I once was. Don't let social expectations prevent you from living the life you want to live. Be yourself. I am confident that your open and inquisitive nature will continue to flourish. Like you, I want to visit all the countries in the world. I hope we can visit at least a few of them together. I love you, sweetie.
Mami

Dear Papi,

It has been many years since I have written you, several months since I have spoken to you in my heart. I want to share with you the woman I have become. You gave birth to me when I left Chicago looking for a new life in Ecuador. I was twenty-one. I was tired and broken. My public life and private life were worlds apart. I could not forget my first love. I could not forget my mother's anger. At the university, my public self was affirmed as smart, articulate, a student leader. To my family I was the bright one, the responsible one, the political one.

To you I was simply your daughter. A well-known stranger that you were so proud of. I landed in the dark mountains thinking I would begin my journey sola. But you were there, having magically received my letter that should not have arrived in time. You loved me. Boasted to anyone who would listen of your daughter from the United States who was going to be a lawyer. (I changed my mind, Papi, but I know you'd still be proud of me.) I asked my cousin, in my broken Spanish, Why does my father love me? She gave me what would become a constant look of befuddlement. Because you are his daughter, she answered. So simple. I am your daughter and you gave me unconditional love. You asked about my first love. What went wrong? I don't remember what I said, but you listened.

I have a wedding picture I have stolen from my mother: the moment you are placing the ring on her finger. My mother's face is angel white. Her eyes are looking at you, but they are seeing heaven. She loved you. You loved her. You abused her. Three children later, you left her. I always wondered how you could abuse someone you loved. You returned to your home, thousands of miles away. When I came to live with you, I wasn't even the one to raise the question. You did, haltingly. You shared how you spent ten years alone, mending your life.

I was blessed to get to know you as a father who had changed, and who now was a loving husband and father of two young children. But you did not forget us. And you did not forget my mother. You married a woman with the same face and name as my mother. And you had two children. One shares my name. You built a small house with rooms for each of your three U.S. children. Your family laughed, thought you a fool to waste your money on a house for ghosts. But before you died, we had all come to stay under that roof.

You showed me pictures of my great-grandmother. She looks like Sojourner Truth. Black as night. You shared how she ran away from her abusive stepfather when she was six years old. She walked many miles till she arrived in Ibarra and was taken in by a kind woman. You shared how you grew up poor. But everyone knew your mother, the woman who cleaned their clothes and cooked the best food.

Walking down a quiet street one night, I explained my mother's anger. It all began with me trying to explain the challenges of racism in our private lives. She is white and I am brown. How it felt growing up different. How it felt when she explained to me that she had always wanted a blond-haired, blue-eyed baby and that was why she had my little brother. It led to me sharing my beliefs on race, class, and sexuality. For, as a young feminist, I thought I understood how they are connected. I shared my belief that women can love other women and men can love other men. It was too much for her and she grew angry, told me I could not see my little brother again until I changed my beliefs. You listen, surprised. You tell me that love is not wrong, no matter who it is with. It is always this simple.

On a bus one night I try to ask what you think about us getting to know each other. I am choking on my words, because they are the only words I can form to ask about your love for me and express my love for you. Did I ever say I love you? My time in Ecuador is spent reflecting on my life, writing about my thoughts, reading your books. You give me Nietzsche, but tell me I'm smart enough to read his arguments and still know God exists.

After three months of labor, I am reborn. I return to Chicago, brown and smiling. Life quickly moves forward. I am working as a community organizer in a Puerto Rican neighborhood. I still struggle with my Spanish, but know enough to be angry when the housing campaign I am working on has not translated all the materials I need to educate my community. Anger drives me. I work with low-income tenants. They are all Latino and African American, mostly single mothers. I grow frustrated with the inability to create change with weak laws. I write you about my work. You are proud that I am working for the community. As for my frustration, you share a line from a poem, *la vida es un sueño*. Life is a dream. We do not know what is real.

What is real? I fall in love. He is so different from me and so much a part of me. A year later I come to visit you. You are cautious when you listen to me speak of him. You finally say, We must limar our differences, smooth them out now before we hurt each other. I leave thinking this is best, slow down. I return to Chicago and to a proposal of marriage. I say yes. Two months later I get a phone call. I throw the phone and scream. My fiancé tries to comfort me. You, the man who traveled to Egypt to learn the secrets of the pyramids. You, the man I planned to visit every year for the rest of my life. You are dead.

I expected you would visit me in my dreams. And after reading so many Latin American writers, I think I have failed as a Latina for not being able to receive your spirit. I remember your words. You also did not know your father. But you would comfort yourself with your own circle of thinking. Who is your father? God. Who is God? Your father. Always so simple.

So who is my father? God. Who is God? God is my father. I marry in a church. And although my partner has shown me boundless love, I immediately feel I have entered a strange room. It does not last. And I learn very quickly how cold anger is and how weak I truly am. I let go of a house, a family, a church. I return to my sister, who lets me be a little child again. And I begin a new role in my work.

But my private life continues to need mending. You are not there, Papi. But you helped me renew my faith in God, and He is always with me. I find a Black Catholic church that speaks to me, and I take my dream trip to Italy to bury my wedding ring. I am reconciled. I have woven together working in a Latino community, worshipping in an African-American community, and living in my intimate community of family and friends.

I have created a community of relationships that very much reflects the lives of those in *This Bridge Called My Back*. This book that served as my bible in college. The only difference is, in my community there are gay men and straight men, devout Christians and devout atheists, people who participate in international political movements and people who would laugh to hear me call myself a feminist. This is my world, Papi. I hope you are proud of me. I love you.
Susana

An Open Letter to Our Readers,

In writing this piece and coming to understand how feminism has shaped us and how we have shaped our feminism, we realized that *This Bridge Called My Back* was an affirmation of our identities. We were able to see ourselves more completely in this collection of writings than in any other feminist text. *This Bridge* spoke to us as young women who have never neatly fit into the dominant definitions of ethnic and racial affiliation. We always have served as bridges between people who would otherwise remain apart. *This Bridge* acknowledged our contradictions as women of mixed racial/ethnic backgrounds. We were our own audience. We became the center of our own debate.

For a certain time and space, *This Bridge* served as our identity road map. As we continued to experience our lives and travel with the contradictions of our relationships, we struggled to move beyond the written word and create a feminism, a strong womanism, that truly felt like home.

We did this through the close friendships and professional relationships we built, but most important by embracing our own contradictions. Alicia's relationship with her son and Susana's relationship with her father have made the challenges of feminism more real and meaningful than words on the page or in our women's studies classes. *This Bridge* helped break open feminism, creating an internal dialogue about the contradictions feminists faced among other feminists around issues of race, class, and sexuality. We wanted to expand upon this dialogue by sharing the contradictions we experience around the personal choices we make as women.

Throughout our lives, throughout our journey to understand ourselves in relationship to others, we have been trying to find our community, our home. Writing letters to two people we love and to feminists seemed the most intimate way to express our thoughts.

What impact does the written word have on our lives? The writings in *This Bridge* had a lasting impact on us because they reflected, challenged, and stretched our life experiences. Giving voice to the contradictions we have faced (and learned to embrace) is what we sought to accomplish in our two separate letters. One speaks of choice, the other of reconciliation. Both speak of journeys.

We've lived with many contradictions around racial identity, motherhood and careers, and domestic violence. How can feminism embrace these contradictions? Can we conceive of choice as something that liberates rather than constrains? Can choosing to be a mother be as powerful as choosing not to? As multiracial/ethnic Latinas who are often seen as only Black or only Latina, we realize that we have little control over how others perceive us racially. However, when it comes to those aspects of our humanity that we do have control over, such as how we live our lives and how we love, the decisions we make may be contrary to our "feminist training."

By writing to her father, Susana wished to challenge the belief that "once an abuser, always an abuser." Although she knew that her father had abused and left her mother, Susana made the choice to get to know her father, to be reconciled, and to gain a new life with him. She also acknowledges how faith has helped give her strength. For Alicia, deciding to choose motherhood as primary to a professional career has not been easy, but in the end it has been liberating. She realized that this choice does not mean that one is less feminist by succumbing to gender role expectations. By embracing our contradictions we have found reconciliation. Our best choices have been those made from our hearts.

As we celebrate *Bridge's* impact on feminism and in our own lives, we must continue challenging ourselves to build upon the stories, theories, and poetry both told and untold. We continually struggle with the expectations of asserting a politicized, gendered, classed, racialized, sexual, linguistic, spiritual identity and are more at peace when we do not meet those expectations. Complexity is our reality. Our life struggles have taken us across the bridge of feminism and back home again to a fuller understanding of who we are.

With Respect,

Alicia and Susana

six

Bridges/Backs/Books: A Love Letter to the Editors

Jesse Swan

Dear Editors,

Your back is my mother's back, a back, as your volume indicates, despised by the sexist, white supremacist, classist, heterosexist dominating culture of the United States. Your back, my mother's back, is a back I learned early in life to turn my back on. Now, though, after reading your book for years, reading that has helped me outline some of the contours of the hate and tyranny I had childishly internalized and so directed against my mother/my self, and reading that has encouraged me to move ahead on the strength of your book, your back, I have bridged my way back from the grim terrain of white hate to my mother's vibrant alluvium of iridescent love.

Love. Everyone loved Vangie—the scores of people sobbing and dumb at the funeral was amazing, though entirely predictable. Everyone loved her, I used to think until a couple of years before the funeral, except me. Like daddy, whom no one but my Aunt Belia would defend, I couldn't understand Vangie. I wondered why mother had to visit family and friends in Mexico so much, why she had to read cards and do so many novenas, why she had to be quite so tenacious in publically denouncing white supremacist clerks and cashiers: *This Mejicana's not leaving without speaking to your manager.* Why did she have to take my brother and me, I would further wonder in a state of crazed incomprehensibility, into those restaurants that didn't like us without daddy? Why would she make the grotesquely fat, greasy, pallid, T-shirted man come at us yelling, "Now look here you dirty mess-kin, you're gonna git outa here one way or the other"? Why, I wondered increasingly angrily when tired of wondering anxiously, would my mother make such scenes? I understood, in those moments, so I thought, daddy's angry frustration with this woman.

For crying out loud, Vangie, stay home. What d'you need going to Monterey again. Don't you see enough Mexicans here? Like me, daddy did love mother, but he was always hurt by her because he wanted what no one can give, but what, in a sexist white supremacist and patriarchal culture, women, especially women of color who are wives, are supposed to naturally give: absolute and utter capitulation in their unidirectional and constant attention and service. Such requirements are stingy with love and kill it, even as they claim that they provide the only true life for love. This mother seemed always to know. Wanting to love others and to be loved by others, at home and abroad, mother didn't want to kill love, I now understand, she wanted to, needed to, quicken and expand it. "For women," Audre Lorde says, "the need and desire to nurture each other is not pathological but redemptive" (98). However, daddy felt that such need and desire violated the sacred bonds of (white) matrimony and (sexist) maternity. That is, in Lorde's words again, mother's need and desire was the "real connection, which is so feared by a patriarchal world" (99). Daddy lived that fear. As a patriarch who sympathized with the speaker's passion in Robert Browning's poem "My Last Duchess," daddy did often feel that mother didn't really love him. Certainly, he felt that her love of others—and their love of her—threatened and detracted from his dignity and his due, especially if the lovers were dark others with familial claims: *La familia is going to be the end of us.*

As further evidence of my father's and my own victimization at the hands of such a potent, sonorous figure as Vangie, I would insistently and incessantly rehearse one of her angry retorts to daddy, a retort I made into her motto: *I didn't marry you to stay home with you. I gave you two sons who look like you: I've done my part.* I don't know if "love" makes any sense in such cultural contigencies—that is, in the American nuclear family, of which ours was a terribly toxic example. The white supremacist and male supremacist economy of values and way of being assumed by my father and learned by me made our "love" for Vangie the cause of our victimization, bondage, and sorrow, while they simultaneously made mother unworthy of such affection, since she incorrigibly violated the economy's role for her, which was to serve white, male others in the forms of husband and son. The economy further encouraged us masculinist victims to see Vangie as unnatural and even wickedly cruel, which is why I repeated her rash, defensive expressions to myself so very often and made them serve as clear, unequivocal evidence of her selfishness, her self-centeredness, and my own pathetic status as simply one instrument, one means to things she really wanted. In this way, I, and my father, saw her use of our "love" as a discursive weapon against us to win what she really wanted. Of course, the discursive weapon of our white and male supremacist "love" was a discursive weapon aimed perpetually at her at the closest range possible. Somehow, she learned to shield herself against it. Seeing her apparently unaffected by our love, I "knew" daddy was right, and that we were both Hamlets, even if he expressed himself as a Lear.

Although we tried to make mother a Gertrude, Regan, or Goneril, she was actually much more a Catalina de Erauso, that rough, cross-dressing Basque contemporary of Shakespeare who roamed Spain's new world as a gambling quick-tempered soldier rather than staying confined to a convent close to where she had been born. How mother managed to maintain her integrity and achieve so much that she desired, as de Erauso had, with so much pressure to abandon her integrity and her dreams— that is, to stop being Evangelina and to submit to being Mrs. Swan, as I came to call her for several years—amazes and instructs in many of the same ways de Erauso's story and your bridge/back/book do. There's injustice—*My counselor* [at "Fox Tech" high school] *told me,"Little Mexican girls can't be doctors. Some can be nurses, but you look better as a secretary"*—there's anger—*I know you think you're white and so better than me, but you're mine, too, and so remember you're just a Mexican, too—* there's passing—*This is Mrs. Stanley Swan. We need to negotiate some acceptable alternative to Pee, Eee for my Jesse: I cannot have him in such programs, as you, no doubt, can understand"*—there's betrayal—*I'm your mother, mi hijito,* [sob] *please stop calling me "Mrs. Swan"*—there's some attempt for rational justice—*Yes, okay, I do love your brother more, but only because he needs it more*—there's genuine respect for humanity—*Mi hijito, you know, not all boys like girls . . . like Ricardo, you know, my hairdresser, he doesn't like girls. You don't have to. I mean, you know, like that*—there's abiding love—*mi hijito*. If I had not come across your book—quite nervously in that huge used bookstore on Broadway in San Antonio—and only consulted furtively because I was too afraid to buy it from the tall, cute white guy smoking and affecting a loitering demeanor at the cash register (I was afraid that he'd recognize the book and all that it meant to me and realize that I was a fag and a Mexican, a realization I was afraid would ruin all my chances of getting him to fall in love with me, since, in my bizarre, childish, self-hating yet desiring dream-mind, he'd only fall in love with me if he thought I was another straight, white guy like he appeared to be), I may never have been able to know or understand my mother's back, my mother's bridge, my mother's greatness, my mother's open, redemptive love for everyone, including for herself, including for those who hate, including for me.

I haven't crossed the bridge that is your back, my mother's back, though, because it seems that the bridge that is your back, my mother's back, needs to be made wider and wider and longer and longer. This bridge, it seems, needs never to be crossed. Instead, it needs always to be inhabited so as to "be the bridge to nowhere / But my true self" (xxii), as Donna Kate Rushin sings. This bridge of backs and books needs to be, perhaps, a bridge into a delta instead of across a fluid flux from one hard terrain to another. The bridge, the water, and the sediment comprise the world I see in your book, a better world than the rock-hard you-I, I-you world of terra firma. "There is," as one of you notes, "an enormous contradiction in being a bridge" (206). That contradiction expands as the bridge expands more and more to nowhere but our true selves.

To this bridge to the nowhere of learning and loving others in ourselves and outside ourselves, I have begun to offer my back, brown once again as it always has been, indistinguishable from my mother's back, your back, or even really my father's back, if it were relieved of its white armor. Of the several ways in which I've begun to lay down my back for this bridge, this book, one is to offer the unlearning you have helped me achieve, an unlearning crucial to being able to love my mother again, to love myself for the first time. "But it's taken over thirty years," to borrow the words of another part of this bridge, "to unlearn the belief instilled in me that white is better than brown—something that some people of color *never* will unlearn. And it is only now that the hatred of myself, which I spent the greater part of my adolescence cultivating, is turning to love" (202).

Thank you, editors and contributors, and thank you, mama.

Con cariño,

jesse

seven

Bridging Different Views: Australian and Asia-Pacific Engagements with *This Bridge Called My Back*

Helen Johnson

Complacency is a far more dangerous attitude than outrage.
     —Naomi Littlebear, This Bridge (168)

As an English adolescent emigrating with my family to Australia I needed to adapt to a white-settler society very different from the overt cosmopolitanism of Hong Kong (at that time a British colony), where I had lived for some years. However, I now know that my adolescence was formative to my current life passion: working toward the construction of international coalitions that celebrate cultural diversity and allow women's many capabilities to blossom. I have fashioned the concept "international coalition" from Chandra Mohanty's "'imagined community' of third world oppositional struggles." Her community is "imagined" not because it isn't "real" but because it suggests potential alliances and collaborations across divisive boundaries" and because "community" refers to the idea of "horizontal comradeship" ("Introduction," 4). Her proposal's appeal retroactively linked with my reading of *This Bridge* when I was at university in 1984. The contributors' narratives captured my imagination, then enthralled and fostered my political interests in social justice issues involving women across cultures. They diminished some of the boundaries between "self" and "others" that were shaping my consciousness in a new country. And the individual women's voices articulating the pain and power of *their* emerging social and self-awareness also questioned the powerful discourse of white western feminism, which had jarred with my memories of cross-cultural friendships at school in Hong Kong.

This Bridge Called My Back continues to have meaning for me as an educator through its introduction of the concept of pluralism among women and its presentation of social biases' effects on women's sense of self. Unfortunately, the work is out of print in Australia, but my university's single copy is kept on reserve during the semester I use it as a key text.

One of the first feminist women-of-color texts I encountered as an anthropologist, *This Bridge* provoked me to consider the processes by which white ethnographers "allow" other women to speak, and then to question whose points of view frame knowledge production in a globalising environment. Its varied range of voices, heritages, and styles of self-presentation shaped the critical consciousness I used in my doctoral field research in France and postdoctoral work in the South Pacific with New Caledonian women, suggesting to me the technique of interweaving the voices of friends and field informants into my publications. The narratives continue to provide themes for a second-year university course I teach to white-settler Australians and people of color from Asia-Pacific countries. Combined with later works, it offers students a sense of social and historical process; enhances their awareness of how identities are constructed and articulated as racialised, sexualised, and classed representations; and brings a deeper understanding of "women" to students' work.

More generally, the collection has also been formative to Australian intellectual life. It combines with contemporary discourses about "white-

ness" as privilege and discussions on possible futures for a country invent-
ing itself as culturally pluralist. Allusions to the authors' stories enter the
discussions of female graduates from the 1980s who now perform mana-
gerial and/or volunteer roles in the community. The text has indeed
helped Cherríe Moraga and Gloria Anzaldúa to achieve their aim; it is "a
revolutionary tool falling into the hands of people of all colors" (xxvi).

The authors' narratives have also helped to fill gaps in feminist analyses grappling with the different experiences women can encounter (especially those perceived as minorities in their host countries), and suggest
that, rather than "ghettoizing" women of color's work, cross-cultural
women's issues should be located at the center of existing courses. Their
portrayal of the power relations that frame who generates knowledge
about whom has driven my evolving feminist pedagogy to guide students
away from being, as Clare Bright describes it, "compliant recipients"
(128) to active creators of knowledge. Happily, I can use *Bridge*'s concepts, theories, and methodology to challenge students' existing thought
structures. Their ideas are reflected in and constructed through static
monolithic conceptions of race, class, and gender promoting stereotypes
of women as asocial individual agents or as passive patriarchally determined victims, and ideas about white privilege. The text also unsettles
students from financially comfortable backgrounds, whether white-settler
Australians or international, through depictions of class and racial deni-
gration. The intense emotional descriptions can provoke students to
change their relaxed perception that racism has "died out" because their
friends and family do not articulate overt racist ideologies.

Further, the text helps breach the barriers of students' received ideas
and the "rampant relativism" of subjective knowledge (Dunn). For example, one Malay student perceived the work to present an effectively politicised but nonetheless philosophically monolithic notion of oppression
that did not fit with her daily reality of strong, confident, educated women
contributing to an Islamic women's movement in Malaysia. She consequently used her female relatives' narratives to critique "oppression" as an
unexamined political concept. She reconfigured Malay women as active
subjective agents who are shaped and inscribed, but not determined, by
international capitalism's social and political dynamics. She illustrated
how students engage with the text to create their own knowledge in fluid
interaction with a complex, changing, and politicised reality.

I chose *This Bridge Called My Back* to frame one of my courses
because it links with my passion for international coalitions by fostering a
global perspective on issues of race, gender, ethnicity, and power. Audre
Lorde's compelling observation that women can use the tools of patriarchy against other women allows students to perceive power's subtle

practices within and across cultures. The work also decenters Euro/U.S.-centric feminisms and envisions change as dialogic process. I ask students to reflect upon the inherent privilege of western-based education and to identify how women of color (whether from non-Australian countries or Aboriginal women in Australia) are routinely underestimated and rarely heard. Building identifications and coalitions across nation-state and racial boundaries helps students learn that "rather than locking ourselves into static identities, many of us may become able to identify . . . with a range of purposes, values and cultural ways we appreciate from sisters (and brothers) elsewhere" (Essed, 244). In working toward new ways of identifying and creating alliances students can move beyond *my* utopian vision to *their* potential to initiate a different, more egalitarian political reality for *their* futures in localised yet globalising arenas.

Teaching *This Bridge* had broadened my own views. While anthropologists have been trained in a discipline that, at its best, celebrates and elucidates cultural difference and the creative aspects of cognitive dissonance, as a white-settler teacher I also frequently engage with material that dramatically challenges my sense of received knowledge. Reading around and beyond the authors' issues has sensitised me to the international relations of power operating through and intersecting with racist and sexist policies, particularly in terms of western, neo-colonial, authoritarian efforts to limit nonwestern communities' movements toward self-determination. doris davenport's argument—that white women's "infatuation with the word 'power' in the abstract . . . mainly means external established power or control. They have minimal, if any, knowledge of personal power" (88)—is also pertinent. Her assertion provoked my research into the many forms of manifest power, such as resistance, overt confrontation, and subtle compliance while strategising for the future. The research, in turn, shaped my teaching, community politics, and personal demeanour in the field.

Interactions with Asia-Pacific students taught me that they view white feminist politics' utopian ideal of universal sisterhood as antiquated, though they perceive its philosophy to have been inclusive in intent. Due to their relative youth, many also situate themselves as never having participated in a white feminist movement. It has become anachronistic for them because, as young cosmopolitan women with an internationally acknowledged education, they perceive new opportunities that do not rest upon their prioritisation of white Australian values. From their family's lived experience and their country's heritage many recognise the quite obvious existence of cultural difference, and they prefer to move beyond the limitations generated by twentieth-century sociopolitics. Others perceive white feminism to be a thing of the past, in that they have moved beyond its intellectually Euro/U.S.-centric and middle-class aspirations toward the construction of feminisms more pluralistic in perspective and more intellectually aware of the diversity of women's politics, ambitions, and personal histories. Nonetheless, both white-settler Australian and Asia-Pacific students acknowledge that *Bridge* authors were affirming their commitment to their *own* feminism, at that particular historical moment. In addition, Anzaldúa's (202) profound expression of positive emotional change and psychic purpose provides students with a sense of the intrinsic humanity of U.S.-enculturated "minority" women.

Reading *This Bridge* induces compassion in students' development of a twenty-first-century social and cultural consciousness of regional and global dynamics. Many become aware that recognising and acting against political and economic oppression is a continuous struggle and a primary purpose of education. They accept the need to move beyond universal sisterhood in order to understand the historical circumstances that have produced powerful divisions between women of color and white women. From listening to their parents' experiences of colonisation many Asia-Pacific students commiserate with the ways American women of color may harbor "understandable resentment and repressed rage about racial oppression [and] the overwhelming absence of sympathy shown by white women" (hooks, *Feminist Theory,* 96). Their empathy moves them beyond their family's local experience to an appreciation of other peoples' harsh tragedies, allowing *This Bridge* to work as a cultural and political reference beyond the United States.

In what other ways has *This Bridge Called My Back* been useful for Asia-Pacific students and my vision of creating international coalitions? Mitsuye Yamada's discussion of Asian-American women's invisibility is pertinent also for international and Asian-Australian students. As Yamada wrote, Asian-Americans "are finally . . . demanding that they be included in the multicultural history of our country" (36). Many Asian-Australian women, in response to course material, have discussed their sense of exclusion and invisibility. Yamada's allegation that "not only the young, but those who feel powerless over their own lives know what it is like not to make a difference on anyone or anything" (39) articulates a sense of disempowerment that particularly resonates with young female students from cultures where self-effacement is constructed as the most socially appropriate "femininity." Many Malaysian students have remarked that they felt excited yet fearful when reading Yamada's words, wishing to break with the strictures of family and religion to become autonomous intellectual women, yet fearing the consequences of being labelled "western." I've watched some students evolve a different sense of self as they realise how their received ideas have been formed by knowledge constructed and propagated through relations of power. One student, for example, developed sufficient confidence to return to Malaysia and organise a women's cooperative among the minority Dayak in her home state of Bornea. In subtle distinction to her measured evolution of self, other women (especially Singaporean and Hong Kong Chinese) maintain a distinctly individuated position, recognising the authority traditionally inherent in their family but developing a "modern" way of being on their return home.

Many young Asia-Pacific women's need to traverse between home culture and host education can produce a hybrid sense of self, a "nomadic subjectivity" (Braidotti). *This Bridge Called My Back*, when read in conjunction with poststructural theories of subjectivity and identity (particularly Chris Weedon's classic *Feminist Practice and Poststructuralist Theory*), enables students to diminish their confusion and sense of fragmentation. Drawing their attention to testimonies from *This Bridge,* I encourage them to recognise that they are not alone. Poststructural theories are also effective in illustrating how female and feminist scholars have moved from the notion of universal "woman" to the incorporation of "difference" into anthropological and women's studies courses.

This pivot in focus from "woman" to "women" enables students to reflect on "difference" in constructing politically effective international coalitions that recognise diversity because, as Moraga asserts, "within the women's movement, the connections among women of different backgrounds and sexual orientations have been fragile, at best" ("La Güera," 30). Her assertion has dramatically shaped my teaching as I work to overcome many young people's socially constructed fear of difference. I use the authors' narratives to show students how divisions have been generated, for example, in traditional pedagogies that deny or diminish "the fountain of non-european female strength and power" (Lorde, "Open Letter," 95). Demonstrating how socially constructed divisions may be negotiated, *Bridge* narratives assist my desire to promote strategic alliances and challenge students to work beyond their possible need to victimise others through their own fear of difference.

The combination of *Third World Women and the Politics of Feminism* with *This Bridge Called My Back* has launched debates about how relations between white women and women of color have often been constructed to reinforce differences in social and institutional status founded on race, as well as the truth of Moraga's argument that "women of color do not have [the power to implement racist ideology], but white women are born with it and the greater their economic privilege, the greater their power" (*Bridge,* 62). I use the text's analysis of the fear that supports power, coupled with examples from my field research, to teach students of the status differences constructed within and between ethnic communities and peoples of color. Challenging students to recognise that all women's voices must be heard, not just those of the most powerful or privileged in any racial/ethnic grouping, I remind them of Yamada's caution: "we must remember that one of the most insidious ways of keeping women and minorities powerless is to let them only talk about harmless and inconsequential subjects, or let them speak freely and not listen to them with serious intent" (40).

To emphasise the need to listen to women's diverse viewpoints I structure sex tourism in the Asia-Pacific region as a contemporary social and cultural issue demonstrating that other women's psychological and physical realities can be dramatically different from their own. We consider the connections between the use of women and children as sexualised commodities in "developing" countries with the rise of contemporary mass tourism. The students analyse the bizarre phenomenon to assess how "women's experience" can be gendered, embodied, different from, and similar to, that portrayed in *This Bridge Called My Back*. Because sex tourism is a social phenomenon that has grown from the intersection of male power with the rise in global capitalism, it substantiates Yamada's assertion that women rarely believe "that the political and social forces affecting our lives are determined by . . . a group of persons, probably sitting behind a desk or around a conference table" (39). This topic also shows educationally privileged students how they must look beyond class and racial difference to grasp the sociocultural reality of others, and it provides an appalling but necessary example of the intellectual and social complexities inherent in constructing international coalitions.

Significantly, the visceral way many students encounter the issue resonates with Moraga's proposition that a "theory in the flesh means one where the physical realities of our lives . . . bridge the contradictions in our experience" (*Bridge*, 23). Students have told me of their confusion as they intellectually and psychically work through Moraga's observation that one must first "emotionally come to terms with what it feels like to be a victim. If . . . anyone . . . were to truly do this, it would be impossible to discount the oppression of others, except by again forgetting how we have been hurt" ("La Güera," 30). Because I believe that feminist cross-cultural teachings can facilitate international and local students' perception of alternative ways of being, I explain the different values, beliefs, and perceptions that people may bring to their "rational" actions.

Indeed, many students learn of others' lives through small-group tutorial discussions. Aboriginal-Australian women have spoken of their histories and communities, Asia-Pacific students have compared their parents' sexist perceptions with their own and those of their white-settler

Australian friends, Asian-Australians have articulated their distress when faced with openly racist insults, and white-settler Australians have talked about their sense of confusion when encountering political issues presented through racist and sexist terminology but glossed with the rational aura of "common sense." Yet many international students find racism difficult to explore; their experience reflects that of Barbara Cameron, in terms of their "own racism toward other people of color, and because of a complex set of 'racisms' within [their] community" (49). Cameron's clarification of the psychosocial difficulties encompassed by notions of difference from "whiteness," and differences between "self" and "other," complements her assertion that "racism among third world people is an area that needs to be discussed and dealt with honestly" (49). While my students would justifiably contest their categorisation as third world, I link her insights with class anxieties in Australia that stereotype indigenous peoples as "dirty," unkempt, and incompetent. I provoke students to investigate class anxieties so they can recognise how the intersections of racist, sexist, and classist perceptions act as powerful sociocultural frameworks for oppressive political practices. Their recognition can then facilitate alliances *within* their society as well as coalitions that are international in scope.

The authors' celebration of diversity has both framed and generated aspects of my experience as a female anthropologist and white-settler feminist teacher. Their insights have significantly stimulated my desire to construct international coalitions between young white-settler Australians and Asia-Pacific students. Their perceptions and politics work to compose and maintain local and international cross-border dialogues through the creation of the mutual respect required to establish frame-breaking alliances and friendships among all women (and men).

eight

Thinking Again: *This Bridge Called My Back* and the Challenge to Whiteness

Rebecca Aanerud

This Bridge Called My Back. A glance at its table of contents rekindles in me a sense of its strength, its urgency, its groundbreaking—and groundbuilding—articulations. As I walk across campus to teach an introductory women's studies class, my feet feel the solid, sturdy support of *This Bridge*, and I review the comments I plan to make and the questions I plan to pose on this first day of class. I know from experience that students take this class for a variety of reasons. Some come out of curiosity, some on the recommendation of a friend, some because the class meets at the right time and provides the needed distribution credits. Others, like myself many years ago, enroll because the gender system has worked with a crushing and pervasive force in their own lives often enough for them to want to arm themselves with the tools of knowledge. Others come with a far more complex understanding that an oppressive gender system *cannot* work without the collaboration of other systems of power and oppression. Such range creates a challenging, stimulating, and enriching classroom environment. I know that, when asked to define feminism, the students will generate an impressive, if not at times disheartening, set of ideas and definitions. I also know that the definition of feminism I'll give to them will be taken from *Bridge's* pages. Barbara Smith's words— "Feminism is the political theory and practice to free *all* women: women of color, working-class women, poor women, physically challenged women, lesbians, old women, as well as white economically privileged heterosexual women" (*Bridge*, 61)—provide the framework not only for the course I am about to teach, but for my own writing and research commitments.

I first read *Bridge* in an Introduction to Women's Studies course in 1986. Still fresh in my memory is the excitement I felt looking at its cover and reading the titles of its entries. Perhaps I sensed the energy, vitality, and commitment of the women who made sure that *Bridge* found its way to a second printing. Perhaps I sensed that *Bridge* would play a significant role in my own intellectual and personal development. I was very new to any form of feminist thought or policy and didn't realize that *Bridge* represented voices and perspectives too often silenced in western feminism. I was reared in a large Catholic family, and the Women's Movement took place largely outside of my purview. I had few personal attachments to a universal or hegemonic feminism that failed to recognize the ways in which gender was always already articulated along with race, class, sexuality, nationality, and so on. Of course, as I would come to understand, as a white, middle-class, heterosexual female with U.S. citizenship, I certainly did and do maintain structural attachments to hegemonic feminism. Indeed, *Bridge* proved instrumental in helping me to theorize these attachments.

Considering *Bridge* now, thirteen years later and as it nears its twentieth anniversary, I am struck by how my own growth as a feminist, particularly one whose research commitments center on interrogations of whiteness, has been fundamentally impacted and shaped by this text.

At its best, whiteness studies—a fast-growing field in recent years—

analyzes how whiteness as a socially constructed category of racial and cultural identity maintains and reproduces its hegemony. However, long before whiteness studies entered the academy, women of color—including many *Bridge* contributors—articulated cogent critiques of whiteness and white feminism. In this essay, I examine the challenges *Bridge* posed and continues to pose for white feminist theory. These challenges provide the seeds for the formation of a white anti-racist subjectivity. I begin with a brief discussion of its reception in feminist theory, then examine how *Bridge's* structure and organization de-center whiteness while simultaneously granting agency to white anti-racism.

A number of years ago, prompted by comments such as Teresa de Lauretis's statement that "the shift in feminist consciousness that has been taking place during this decade may be said to have begun (if a convenient date is needed) with 1981, the year of publication of *This Bridge Called My Back*" (10), I began to think about *Bridge's* impact in feminist writings. Clearly *Bridge* is seen as a monument, a signifier of the focus on difference, especially in terms of race. But has this status perhaps masked the ways in which *Bridge* was marginalized within feminist theory? My questions led to a project analyzing *Bridge's* citation history. Working from social science and arts and humanities citation indices, I compiled a complete citation list. Through the 1980s and into the 1990s *Bridge* was cited widely and often in journals as diverse as *Signs*, *The Black Scholar*, *Critical Inquiry*, and *The Yale Law Journal*. In fact, *Bridge* is one of *the most* cited books in feminist theorizing. However, authors do not discuss *Bridge's* content and specific arguments. Rather, *Bridge* serves as a marker of change, often cited along with other feminist-of-color titles like bell hooks's *From Margin to Center*, Gloria T. Hull, Barbara Smith, and Patricia Bell Scott's *All the Women Are White, All the Blacks Are Men, But Some of Us Are Brave*, and Barbara Smith's *Home Girls*. For white feminists, *Bridge* and these other titles made "difference" an issue no longer possible to avoid. And yet, paradoxically, its inclusion—without textual engagement—in citation lists reproduces the very same marginality that *Bridge* so succinctly critiques. As Norma Alarcón has noted, *Bridge's* citation use tends to be "cosmetic. . . . Anglo feminist readers of *Bridge* tend to appropriate it, cite it as an instance of difference between women, and then proceed to negate that difference by subsuming women of color into the unitary category of woman/women" ("Theoretical Subject[s]" 357–58).

It is perhaps no great mystery why so many white feminists failed to fully engage with *Bridge's* writings. After all, seeing oneself as racist is highly disagreeable. Our popular discourse does not permit a nuanced understanding of racism: either one is or is not racist; there is little room for a more complicated understanding of a subjectivity opposed to, yet complicit with, racism. In large part, this limitation has its source in the popular discourse depicting racism as individual not structural. In this framework, a plausible response to racism, particularly for one who is white, is to simply distance oneself from racist expressions and people. If *Bridge* was to be read as a book primarily about white women's racism, disengagement would be a predictable response.

The irony, of course, is that *Bridge* is not primarily about white feminists or their racism. Only one of the six sections focuses directly on this issue. *Bridge* is a book of writings between and among women of color. While race difference and the fact of racism in the women's movement are common themes, they are by no means the only or even the dominant themes. Heterosexuality, homophobia, classism, nationality, belonging, borders, and bridges are also central themes. Moreover, *Bridge* offers no single and unified statement on racism. Some writers, like Rosario Morales, argue that all people regardless of race can be racist (91). Other writers, such as Chrystos and doris davenport, locate racism specifically in white people and white institutions. Some writers, like Nellie Wong, write of the pull toward whiteness: "I now know that I once longed to be white" (7); others, like mary hope lee, write of the desire for darkness: "She never wanted / no never once / did she wanna / be white / to pass / dreamed only of being darker / she wanted to be darker" (9). If a singular articulation can be found in the pages of *Bridge*, it's that racism (along with heterosexism, classism, ageism, and so on) works in conjunction with sexism. Gender absent race might be theoretically tidy, but it is not nor can it ever be as specific and accurate as is necessary for the lives of all women—it can never be a theory in the flesh. One of the challenges *Bridge* poses for white feminism, as Alarcón has written, is to engage with a theoretically more complicated feminist subject.

A second and perhaps more vexing challenge was that of a de-centered whiteness. Unlike other woman-of-color anthologies, which centered on a singular racial identity, *Bridge* was unique in bringing women of color's writings and ideas across racial differences. In many *Bridge* pieces the authors clearly specify that they're writing to other women of color. White feminists were relegated to the sidelines by a text that sought to forge, as Cherríe Moraga wrote, a unified U.S. Third World Feminist Movement. While *Bridge* began as a response to racism in the Feminist Movement, it soon became "a positive affirmation of the commitment of women of color to our *own* feminism" (xxii).

Bridge was ahead of its time. Whiteness studies and the language of "de-centering" had not yet entered theoretical circles. For white feminist theory, *Bridge*'s "subject reassignment" was read less as an important, necessary, and invigorating challenge and more as a threat. Reminiscent of the rhetoric of "expediency" associated with the First Wave Feminist Movement, many responses to *Bridge* imagined a failed social and political movement in which "divisiveness," not "sisterhood," would define U.S. feminism. Regrettably, this claim of divisiveness provided an easy justification to under-theorize difference. Moreover, because *Bridge* posited difference as something between women of color themselves, it questioned a monolithic and ahistorical representation of women of color or Third World women. While women of color may share the experience of being a target of racism, they also have many experiences that divide them. As Moraga wrote in the preface to the second edition:

> The dream of a unified Third World feminist movement in this country as we
> conceived of it when we first embarked on the project of this book, seemed
> more possible somehow, because as of yet, less tried. . . . In the last three
> years I have learned that Third World feminism does not provide the kind
> of easy political framework that women of color are running to in droves.
> We are not so much a "natural" affinity group, as women who have come
> together out of political necessity. There *are* many issues that divide us. (n.p.,
> author's emphasis)

This acknowledgment—that all women must find ways to build alliances across difference—is one of *Bridge's* most significant contributions to feminism.

How does one build alliances? For me, as a white feminist, *Bridge's* greatness lies not in its challenges to white feminism, as important as they are, but in the tools it offers to meet those challenges. *Bridge* does not merely de-center whiteness, but repositions it. This new position is a space of agency for white feminists yearnful of a viable anti-racist position. While many white women read *Bridge* and felt defensive or guilty, I read *Bridge* and felt invigorated and enabled. It's not my intention to demonize the former response and champion the latter. (There's nothing more destructive to anti-racist work than competing for the coveted spot of least racist white around.) Instead I'm far more interested in investigating why *Bridge* opened that space for myself and others. Our ability to forge successful and strategic challenges to racism in its many forms relies on understanding the formation and maintenance of anti-racist subjectivities. In the remainder of this essay, drawing from selected poems and essays I demonstrate how *Bridge* creates this space of anti-racist agency. Specifically, I highlight three key concepts: (1) racism as a white problem, (2) naming racism, and (3) self-education.

To understand how *Bridge* can be an emancipating text for white women as well as women of color involves an analysis of subject position or location. While my upbringing in a suburban socially liberal family located in the U.S. northeast positioned me to abhor racism, it also taught me to locate it elsewhere: in the south, in the cities, in the past. The fact that I was white seemed of little significance. Whiteness was, as Richard Dyer would later put it, "the natural, inevitable, and ordinary way of being human" (44), not a site of structural privilege. This instruction carried with it two implications. First, it defined racism as the singular and intended expression of prejudice between individuals. The imagery that accompanied this definition—evil, nonenlightened whites versus innocent, honorable blacks—reinscribed my own position of innocence while simultaneously casting African Americans as victims, lacking a history of resistance or agency. Second, it taught me that because I was innocent of racism—as a northerner, as a person who did not engage in individual and intentional acts of prejudice—I did not need to challenge it. All I need do was adopt the well-worn expression of liberal humanism, "They're just like us," an expression that, although alluding to the commonality of all people, nonetheless keeps in place the us/them binary of colonial discourse. It's unlikely my mother would have inverted the phrase to tell me "We are just like them," thus situating her blond-haired, white-skinned daughter as unknowable and Other in the racial hierarchy. Challenging racism was left to benevolent white authorities and the brave, nonviolent actions of southern Blacks who, in keeping with my misinformed perspective, were embarking on their first organized resistance.

Two decades later, I questioned these childhood lessons. I could clearly see that racism was alive and well, yet I remained woefully misinformed about its complexities and bereft of a theory or a politics of antiracism. Reading *Bridge* helped me break through these obstacles. It taught me that racism was indeed my problem as much as it was anybody else's. As Moraga asserts in her introductory comments to the section on racism in the Women's Movement, "As Third World women we clearly have a different relationship to racism than white women, but all of us are born into an environment where racism exists. Racism affects all of our lives, but it is only white women who can 'afford' to remain oblivious to these effects" (62). *Bridge* began to map out a new geography of race for me. Within this new terrain I recognized that racism had been and would continue to be a fundamental influence on my own personhood.

Barbara Cameron's "Gee, You Don't Seem Like an Indian From the Reservation" further complicated my understanding of racism. Cameron's acknowledgment that the topic of racism is difficult "because of [her] own racism toward other people of color, and because of a complex set of 'racisms' within the Indian community" (49), contradicted what I'd been taught. No one, it seemed, was immune to the overwhelming misinformation about race. Cameron writes: "I've grown up with misconceptions about Blacks, Chicanos, and Asians. I'm still in the process of trying to eliminate my racist pictures of other people of color. I know most of *my* images of other races come from television, books, movies, newspapers, and magazines" (49, author's emphasis). Never before had I encountered a person writing about her own racism in terms that did not position herself as "bad" or "guilty." Instead, Cameron recognized her racism as the inevitable result of living in this culture. Her frank discussion gave me a new paradigm: opposing racism did not and could not mean simply claiming a self free of racism. There is no site free of racism. A framework that defines racism in terms of intentional acts between individuals may afford a degree of comfort and perhaps a sense of righteousness for those who do not make racist comments. However, it does little to actually challenge racism because it fails to recognize the subtle, complicated ways racist societies shape subjectivities. I began to realize that racism's proximity was not a function of my evil, but rather a function of my interaction with my culture. Contrary to what I had been taught, racism *was* my problem.

This recognition created new avenues for opposing racism. Before reading *Bridge* my opposition to racial inequality was philosophical; I opposed racism on the grounds that it was inconsistent with the tenets of liberty and equality. Because racism did not have anything to do with me, my opposition signaled my charity and enlightenment—my commitment to the ideal of racial equality, not necessarily to actual people. Repositioning me, *Bridge* gave me new reasons and infinitely more complex obligations to challenge racism. First, I had white privilege, which could be strategically deployed. Second, even as I use that privilege to challenge racism, I remain complicit with racist structures; an oppositional stance to racism did not and could not mean I was somehow "not racist." Third, sustainable white opposition to racism could not be forged exclusively on idealist terms or altruistic motives; we all pay a very high price of living within racist structures. While I do indeed benefit materially from racism, in all other ways—intellectually, emotionally, spiritually, socially—I, like all people, am damaged by racism.

Bridge also taught me the subtlety of racism. Jo Carrillo's poem "And When You Leave, Take Your Pictures With You" speaks to a racism of appropriation masked as admiration and inclusion. The speaker notes how "our white sisters radical friends love to own pictures of us" (63). These pictures of an imagined global sisterhood, united in the struggle for gender equality linked to issues of production and reproduction, are reassuring to white feminists. Such romanticized images deny lived experiences of imperialism and exploitation, and position desirable difference across national borders. In the flesh, however, women of color are not so welcome and loved. "We are not as happy as we look / on / their / wall" (64). Carrillo's poem exposed the ways in which exoticizing the Other is a form of racism. Like so many of the writings in *Bridge*, the poem asks white feminists to "think again." This directive emphasizes introspection as crucial to anti-racist work. Only through rigorous and exhausting examinations of motives and impulses—many of which may appear as symbols of unification—can we begin to recognize and resist racism.

Mitsuye Yamada's essay "Asian Pacific American Women and Feminism" explores nationalism—another name racism takes. She writes: "When I hear my students say 'We're not against the Iranians here who are minding their own business. We're just against those ungrateful ones who overstep our hospitality by demonstrating and badmouthing our government,' I know they speak of me" (75). As a Japanese-American woman whose family was forced out of its home and into the internment camps during World War II, Yamada knows the precarious status of being Other. Although her students were not hostile to her, she saw in their comments the same justifications for fear and hatred that targeted Japanese Americans a few decades earlier. Yamada's essay gave me a far more complex understanding of racism as mobile, transferable, and highly invested in notions of whiteness and national belonging.

Entries such as Wong's poem "When I Was Growing Up" and Moraga's essay "La Güera," indicate another name racism takes, that of internalized racism. Moraga explores its subtlety, noting that even without intention she learned to privilege whiteness: "No one ever quite told me this (that light was right), but I knew that being light was something valued in my family (who were all Chicano, with the exception of my father)" (28). Like Cameron, both Wong and Moraga internalized racism as a cultural phenomenon—something learned in the movies, on television, or in the family. Although never overtly taught that whiteness signaled superiority, I began to see that indeed this was precisely what I'd been taught. My reaction was one of deep sadness and anger. I had been misinformed; I had been lied to. And yet, I also felt a tremendous gratitude to the *Bridge* authors who articulated so honestly their own battles with racism in its many forms. By doing so, they gave me a sense of agency and courage. If they could delve into that "deep place of knowledge," so could I.

Perhaps the most significant tool for creating spaces of white anti-racist subjectivities stems from *Bridge*'s insistence that white women must educate themselves. Throughout *Bridge,* in all its sections, we see this absolutely fundamental assertion. "The Bridge Poem," by Donna Kate Rushin, makes self-education a primary theme: "Stretch or drown / Evolve or die" (xxii). With great passion and frustration the speaker outlines her sheer exhaustion with explaining, translating, mediating, legitimizing, and connecting people across difference. Audre Lorde, too, writes of the oppressive energy-sapping strategy: "Now we hear that it is the task of black and third world women to educate white women, in the face of tremendous resistance, as to our existence, our differences, our relative roles in our joint survival. This is a diversion of energies and a tragic repetition of racist patriarchal thought" ("Master's Tools," 100). Such articulations were pivotal in demonstrating to me white supremacy's subtleties and particularly my own inscription within certain power relations.

As *Bridge* pushed me to examine and theorize this inscription, it did so with clear direction. In her essay "—But I Know You, American Woman" Judit Moshkovich writes: "I don't usually hear, 'Hey, what do you think of the work of such and such a Latin American feminist author?', but rather, 'Teach me everything you know.' I say: *read and listen*. We may, then, have something" (80, author's emphasis).

Read and listen. Or, as Yamada wrote, quoting Moraga, "What each of us needs to do about what we don't know is to go look for it" ("Asian Pacific," 72). Educating oneself, searching to make sense of that which seems incomprehensible, is of course not the copestone of white anti-racist subjectivity; it is the cornerstone. It is the beginning. *Bridge*, with its eloquent and incisive critiques, its honesty, and its generous spirit, allowed for this beginning.

nine

The Spirit of *This Bridge*

Donna Hightower Langston

When I think of the influence *This Bridge* has had on feminism, I am reminded of my grandmother's saying, "Eagles don't need to be crows." The writers of *This Bridge* fed our spirit by offering a vision of feminism as it was, and as it could be. *This Bridge* was a role model for those who watched. It said to those of us from backgrounds other than white, middle class that you are not just important, you are essential. It addressed the invisibility, which Patricia Williams has termed spirit-murder, the toll covert racism and classism take in our daily life ("Spirit-Murdering," 234). This book held a special place in our lives, which we must never lose touch with, or let future generations forget.

Younger generations of feminists must recognize those who went before, those who gave us the opportunity to stand on new ground. Elders in any community do not last forever. We must recognize the *Bridge* editors and writers, as they made us ready to do something we hadn't dreamed possible. Their words are written on our hearts. Yet a troubling question remains: Did we take the spirit of their words to heart? Many women are still missing from the feminist movement. Have we done something that has kept the place beside us vacant? Has feminism remained willfully determined to cling to distances between us, incapable of having the right priorities or knowing what is important, dependent on language and words that degrade those without privilege?

This Bridge remains one of the most quoted works in women studies. Academic publications benefitted greatly from the groundbreaking theory, but seldom seemed to take to heart the spirit of the original volume. Part of that spirit was expressed in its immediate, direct, accessible language. *This Bridge* was one of the first feminist collections written primarily by lesbians of color from working-class backgrounds. It was also one of the first feminist works readily available in Spanish. While centrally reshaping U.S. feminism, its authors also reached beyond geographical borders/fronteras.[1]

This Bridge engaged audiences beyond academia. There was a power in seeing practical, concrete language combined with sharp political insights on a printed page. I first read *This Bridge* while working on an oil refinery crew. I had tried to make my way through previous feminist anthologies attempting to address class issues, but the texts were so incomprehensible that I would underline words anytime I understood what they were trying to say. There wasn't much underlining in these volumes. *This Bridge* remains the most underlined and re-read volume on my shelves, marked-up with a dozen different pen colors denoting different times in my life when I have returned to re-read it. I related to the language; I related to the stories and the women. For example, Gloria Anzaldúa wrote about her mom being sixteen when she was born, the same age of my mother when I was born.

This Bridge was a tonic for the writer's block of many previously silent voices. Here were women who not only talked and thought like us, but also put it down on a printed page. It gave us permission to write by offering a model of real-life language, and validating a wider range of voices and political consciousness. Anzaldúa's "Speaking in Tongues" led my life in very different directions as it encouraged me to claim the courage to take my writing seriously.

Who gave us permission to perform the act of writing?
—Gloria Anzaldúa, "Speaking" (166)

This Bridge provided a publishing outlet for working-class women of color, a group traditionally excluded from publishing opportunities. The lack of material written by working- class women of all colors arises from a variety of conditions, including the priority economic survival takes, lack of access to education, and socialization that tells us, as Anzaldúa states, that "writing is not meant for women such as us" ("Speaking," 166). Class identity affects one's choices and actions. Undertaking activities deemed inappropriate for your class is difficult even to imagine much less achieve. Working-class women are seldom encouraged to develop intellectual skills or recognized as possessing them. Lack of education and early marriage shape our opportunities. We become mothers at younger ages than do middle-class women and are more likely to hold multiple jobs. Even if we could begin to view ourselves as serious writers, the time needed to devote to the process is hard to come by. Class is still largely unaddressed in U.S. feminism.

> *I lack language. The language to clarify my resistance to the literate.*
> —Cherríe Moraga, Loving (62)

Many works of the past twenty years owe a debt to theoretical breakthroughs made by *This Bridge*.[2] Some of this contribution was repackaged in academic jargon with little apparent relevance to women outside universities. Yet it was theorists possessing multiple identities and the gift of using nonexclusionary language who produced genre-challenging work that changed the face/cara of feminism as we know it.

Academic women disproportionately publish feminist theory. How do our particular backgrounds shape the body of work we produce? Some abstract theoretical writing is like designer clothing, nice to look at, or sometimes just plain silly, but who wears it in real life? We need a range of writing styles, including designer packaged, but it has often been more of a challenge to find publishers for "nonscholarly" feminist theory, and to make our theory available and accessible to the majority of women not connected to academia. Scholars must realize the impact of our language choices. We have a right to speak our minds, but must recognize the tremendous responsibility our words carry, act in ways that are careful of others, speak straight, use our words to express practical wisdom and show respect.

U.S. education has served as a great divider. Our language indicates conscious decisions about whom we want to speak to. Patricia Williams has criticized the process of theory mystification, which makes most works inaccessible to the overwhelming majority. She calls for theory written in animated language, which could serve as a form of "witnessing"

("Alchemical Notes"). Nancie Caraway makes a similar point about "talk story" or story sharing in Hawaiian communities.

A variety of language forms have historically been censored from public voicing and publication. Aida Hurtado has noted that working-class women's languages have been omitted from public and written records. Yet languages that have been viewed as deficient have an empowering effect when they are voiced; as Anzaldúa recalls, "When I saw poetry written in Tex-Mex for the first time, a feeling of pure joy flashed through me. I felt like we really existed as a people" (*Borderlands*). Language plays a central role in the ability to claim consciousness. I began thinking about my racially mixed background after reading *Bridge* writers like Rosario Morales and Judit Moschkovich. I am a one-quarter blood, tribally enrolled Cherokee. When I grew up unless you were full-blood, lived on a reservation, and were tribally enrolled, you did not identify as American Indian. Our generation had followed our parents' model of assimilation. My Chicano friends in school also thought of themselves as white—as Spanish and therefore European. I also have a great-great-grandmother, Della Hanley, who was called mulatto, mixed African American and white, so I most accurately identify as being racially mixed. Racial purity is a myth. Most American Indians, Latinos, Hawaiians, Filipinos, and African Americans, among others, are racially mixed. I imagine younger generations will begin to acknowledge this reality in their language and actions.

Is academic feminism the graveyard of radical ideas?
—Dawn Currie and Hamida Kazi

Although *Bridge*'s direct, accessible language is one of its most most radical aspects, this radical sprit was often translated into academic debates with little relevance to nonacademic women. When feminist theory occurs within the province of academia, incomprehensible texts and language often emerge. If feminist theory is not concerned with accessibility, what distinguishes it from other dominant bodies of theory? Becky Birtha has argued that writings that use language that excludes most women isn't feminist writing. Does feminist theory have a political responsibility to speak to women other than those who are academically trained?

Academic language can become a tool of domination rather than a way to communicate ideas. The impact of exclusive language usage may be unintentional, but its outcome is still the same. Why not write in formats that engage rather than exclude? As Nancy Hartsock notes, just as the theoretical significance of work by women of color emerged, academic women flocked to a new abstract body of theory, postmodernism. Barbara Christian finds that most theory has become self-indulgent and disconnected. This "race for theory," as she calls it, has muted racial voices and created writing blocks in those unable or unwilling to engage in incomprehensible language exchanges. A core of academic elites has been established. Who are we speaking to and for? What is the responsibility of academic women to the larger mass of women outside the academy?

It's an easy way out to write for the academic crows; it's a far more difficult task to write for the common women.

—*Gloria Gyn*

Many *Bridge* writers did not choose academic language as the vehicle of communication and thus they were able to speak to an audience beyond academia. They communicated through poetry, letters, and conversations, in addition to more analytical pieces. It was theorists who possessed multiple identities that produced genre-challenging work. How do we bridge the privilege of higher education with political responsibility? The Cherokee have traditionally viewed education as the ability to sift through experience for wisdom and knowledge. According to this worldview, we show wisdom and knowledge through the ways we choose to communicate it to other people. *This Bridge* remains a model of wisdom worth following. We are indebted to its writers; feminism is the better for it. Its spirit should serve as a guide to future generations.

Notes

1. *This Bridge* was one of the books Las Entiendidas, the first lesbian group in Central America, asked me to buy for them.

2. In the mid-1980s I co-edited an introductory women studies text, *Changing Our Power*, which acknowledged our debt to the writers of *Bridge*.

ten

Remembering *This Bridge,* Remembering Ourselves: Yearning, Memory, and Desire

M. Jacqui Alexander

In March 2000, the Department of Gender and Women's Studies at Connecticut College organized an event honoring a multiracial group of six women poets of distinction and marking the twentieth anniversary of

This Bridge Called My Back. Poets on Location was a way to bring back to memory an earlier historical moment when the vision of a pancultural radical feminist politics seemed more vigorous, more visible in the United States of North America. All six poets combined the search for beauty with the struggle for social justice in their life's work. We wrote in the program notes: "These women poets have scrutinized their lives, wrestled with their different inheritances of geography of place, race, class, sexuality, body, nationality and belonging, and molded it all into sources of insight and wisdom. Among them they have lived 363 years, spanning continents, threading dreams, holding visions." Honored were Chrystos, Dionne Brand, Cherríe Moraga, Sonia Sanchez, Adrienne Rich, and Mitsuye Yamada, three of them original *Bridge* contributors. Audre Lorde, Toni Cade Bambara, and Pat Parker joined us in spirit. Donna Kate Rushin read "The Bridge Poem," and on the night of the honoring, nestled between the overgrown stems of the most radiant sunflowers, she and Papusa Molina recalled the names of all thirty-two women who had put their pens, as Audre would have said, in the full service of their beliefs. The moment was electric: songs on drums, no land to light on, the heat of fire changing the shape of things, reminiscences of the desert and the promise of oasis, listening for something, dreaming of a common language, moving radiance to trace the truth of history. On that evening, a "terrible beauty" had soaked the cadence of playful flute and solemn drums, and a not-so-silent hunger of a crowd, determined to smell the taste of a past now brought present. Yearning, memory, and desire. A powerful combination.

My own earliest memory of *This Bridge* was planted fourteen years ago as I was giving birth to myself in the summer of 1986. I navigated the passage in the waters of *This Bridge, Home Girls, Cancer Journals,* and *Sister Outsider,* yearning, without knowing, for the company of lesbian women to help me swim in those gray Maine waters on Greenings Island, which seem strangers to their turquoise blue-green sisters thousands of miles away, but merely seven hours by plane. Unrelated on the surface only. Down in that abyss, their currents reach for each other and fold, without the slightest tinge of resentment, into the same Atlantic, the rebellious waters providing the path for a more violent passage, many, many centuries, but not so many centuries ago. Secrets lie in the silted bottom of these waters. In that summer of a reluctant sun, incessant waves, and what seems now like an interminably full moon, I remember how much I have forgotten of that daily awakening. Stark outlines remain, but the more tactile reminders have receded. No notes on my dissertation indicate that as I wrote those slow pages heavy with the weight of the costs of medicine and the disproportionate brunt workers bore at the hands of corporate and state managers, my heart was moving to a different rhythm. But I remember how my passion and love for a woman and a distant memory of a deep and necessary transgression folded into a joy I felt upon meeting the *Bridge* authors for the first time—women like me—bound in a collective desire to change the world. The experience of freedom in boundary-crossing. I later went in search of *Zami*, but when these women "who work together as friends and lovers" announced a new spelling of their name in jet black letters on a thin blood-red spine snuggled under the section "Women of Color" at New Words Bookstore in Cambridge, my fingers became tentative with a memory of the harsh sound of the word *Zami* in Trinidad, and the whispers about two women whom my furtive friends and I had climbed over a fence to see, on the way home, from the convent high school.

I couldn't live Caribbean feminism on U.S. soil and Caribbean soil had grown infertile. Caribbean people had docked one ship too many. Waved one goodbye too many to women recruited for the war in Britain or for work as domestics in Canada or the United States. Grown one banana too many, thin and small—not Chiquita, not Dole—that would turn to manure before being eaten. Heard one demand too many to smile for tourists because they presumably provided your bread and butter. I was not in Jamaica with Sistren, documenting the rage of women who worked in the sugarcane fields (*Sweet Sugar Rage*), using theater to score the unequal vicissitudes of their lives. I would read much later CAFRA's inaugural discussions.[1] Nor had I joined the droves of women who left the Caribbean and the metropolis with equal discontent to build the revolution in Grenada. I was not in Boston in 1979, as the bodies of black women fell, twelve in all, at least that time, the same year the People's Revolutionary Movement came to power in Grenada. Blood that defied insistent rains and vowed to leave its mark on the harsh concrete, on the cluttered, winding, dark alleys. Not in Pine Ridge, South Dakota, as the "red blood full of those arrested, in flight, shot," flowed as Sioux and Lakota alike occupied Wounded Knee.[2] Or part of the "primary emergencies" confronting different women of color: living on the other side of structural inequities: of violence within the false safety of home; of the imposed invisibility's unnatural disaster; of passing across color lines, different shades of light and brown, wearing "exhausting camouflages"; negotiating the pathologies of racism.[3] I missed Nairobi completely, hidden away in the stacks in the basement of Widener Library, and was forced instead to go in search of my blood sisters at one of the many post-Nairobi reports back to the community, sponsored by Boston Women's Health Book Collective. There I met Angela Bowen for the first time, sister traveler come to sojourn only four blocks away from where I lived in

Cambridgeport. We have walked these dusty tracks before. By the mid-
'80s, then, when at least twenty thousand people had read *Bridge* and
shared it with at least another twenty thousand of their friends, I had only
begun the journey, and then only in text. For me, *Bridge* was both anchor
and promise: I could begin framing a lesbian-feminist woman-of-color
consciousness and move my living in a way that would provide the moor-
ings for that consciousness. Neither anchor nor promise could have been
imaginable without the women in *Bridge* who gave themselves permission to write, to speak in tongues (Anzaldúa).

I was not a part of the sweat and fire giving shape to a U.S. woman-
of-color politic in the '70s and '80s, and this is why I want constantly to
remember that I have been shaped by it, why I am indebted to the
women who literally entered the fire for me, on my behalf. I found compelling the plain ol' courage and determination of a bunch of different
women, still tied to some kind of cultural inheritance, sometimes at a cost,
sometimes isolated from it, at times yearning for it. They were my age,
many younger than me, saying so much about so many different things,
gesturing to me about a forgetting so deep that I had even forgotten what
I had forgotten (Walsch, 15). I had not known that a love letter could still
be a love letter, to one's mother no less, and deal with betrayal and
wounds. I read Merle Woo's "Letter to Ma'" with my mouth open—and
covered, of course. After all, I could not be caught staring at something,
or someone, so impolitely, with open mouth. I couldn't imagine speaking
in this way within my family, where speech was such a scarce commodity
and the trade in silence was valued. A system of silence, my uncle calls it.
How do I come out to family? To my five brothers? No sister to tell. She
closed her eyes for good nine days after opening them, when I was only
four and could barely see the eyelet bonnet caressing her soft face in the
coffin. To my mother? For years I would think that as a lesbian I had a
cosmic duty to perfect my relationship with my mother. My father by then
had died alone. Months afterwards, in one of those early hours before
dawn, he visited me as a wraith, propped up on a walking stick. He saw
my partner and me lying in bed, but said nothing. At least he knew. Later,
I would see that my own hesitation about "coming out" in Trinidad was
laced with a dutiful daughter's fears of jeopardizing middle-class
respectability. Anti-colonial nationalism had taught us well about heterosexual loyalty, a need so great that it reneged on its promise of self-determination, delivering criminality instead of citizenship (Alexander, "Not
Just (Any) *Body*"). And yet my father's death released a different desire:
a different form of loving and a new kind of politic that I found first in
Bridge.

In Barbara Cameron's "Gee, You Don't Seem Like an Indian From the Reservation," I saw reflected much of my first-year undergraduate experience in this country, where for the first time the majority of people around me were white. Accented, foreign, and seen as friendly in this predominantly white environment, I had not yet known that I was being compared to black students (*African-American* was not used then) and positioned in relation to the "unjustifiably angry" black American. I had not known until the slave auction, when white male students thought they could have fun by "hiring" white women as slaves for a day. The campus exploded. Amid sit-ins and teach-ins, I was forced to confront the utter silence of white students who had previously befriended me, and the sudden shift to being a stranger. It was my most tactile experience of what I had only read about and seen on television that would begin to instill a *daily* awareness of seeing myself as black—and equally important—to begin thinking about what white people were seeing/thinking as they saw me. Growing up in Trinidad within an apparent black majority I had not negotiated the daily assignment of racial superiority and inferiority, or its most egregious costs (Alexander, "Not Just (Any) *Body*"). It would take me six more years and a walk down the streets of Williamsburg, Virginia, with my friend Beverly Mason to really understand how racism distorts and narrows the field and scope of vision. "Do you see how they look at us, Jacqui?" "No, no," I insisted, not knowing even intuitively. I had not yet felt double consciousness although I knew of its existence, mainly from Fanon's *Black Skins White Masks,* which implicated French colonialism in the psychic splitting so evident in Algeria and Martinique, and by extension other parts of the colonized world.[4]

Nor had I known that the texture of identities could be made into a theory of the flesh, as Cherríe Moraga outlined. It echoed consistently throughout *Bridge*: "The most general statement of our politics at the present time would be that we are actively committed to struggling against racial, sexual, heterosexual, and class oppression and see as our particular task the development of integrated analysis and practice based upon the fact that the major systems of oppression are interlocking. The synthesis of these oppressions creates the conditions of our lives" (Combahee, 210). I had to work to understand how our lives are shaped daily through structures, and even how to use flesh-and-blood experiences to concretize a vision. I did not know how precisely the personal was political, since I had not yet begun fully scrutinizing much of what was personal. The mid-1970s mobilization of Black Power in the (english-speaking) Caribbean spoke to our subordinate economic position in the world economy, but much of the contextual history of slavery and colonization, how we came to be there and got to be who we were was largely missing from an educational system (nationalism notwithstanding) that tracked smart students to learn the history of imperial might—British history, U.S. history and geography—nothing of Caribbean history. All of Dickens, Shakespeare, Chaucer. None of Jean Rhys, George Lamming, Louise Bennett, Ismith Khan. It gave no clues about the connections between systems' operations and people's behaviors, no clues about our social sexual selves, or at least how we could be agents in it.

The processes of colonization in *Bridge* wore a face different from those I knew. Articulated by Chicanas, Puertoriqueñas, and Native women, it spoke to the reservations' internal colonies; the barrios; the labor regimes of the Texas cotton fields; Malintzin's contentious inheritance, and the confusion between devotion and obedience usually cathected unto women or otherwise collapsed into the religious figure of the Virgin Mary who had accompanied me throughout my thirteen years of Catholic school. I had longed to become a nun. Chrystos learned to walk in the history of her people, coming to know there were "women locked in [her] joints" ("I Walk," 57). Where does one learn the stories and histories of one's people? Who were we? As Trinidadians we did not all come on the same ship as the national(ist) myth held. Some of us, Indian, had been captured/brought, under indenture to work on plantations evacuated after the "end" of slavery, with the broken promise of return to Calcutta, Bombay, Madras. A colonial betrayal pushed under the surface, constantly testing Indian loyalty to Trinidad, the home of forced adoption. Some Chinese, also smuggled/brought as contract laborers, also to work on sugar plantations (Powell). Some blacks captured/sold from a geography so vast the details would daunt memory and produce a forgetting so deep we had forgotten that we had forgotten. Missing memory. Who are *my* people? How will I come to know their stories and histories? With Chicanas and Puertorriqueñas, I shared a non-belonging to the United States. Like Mirtha Quintinales—Cuban lesbian, a Caribbean lesbian—I did not belong in the U.S, and while I was not Cuban, there was a family link since my father's brother had left Tobago to search for home in Cuba, Oriente, where the roots of trees travel without the need of a compass to the deep forests of Mayombe, Kongo; to Dahomey, Da ha homey; and to New York. Trees remember and will whisper remembrances in your ear if you stay still and listen.

Charting the Journey

This sensibility of a politicized nonbelonging with its capacity to fuel an imperative about self-determination persisted in *Bridge's* sister companion, *Charting the Journey*, undertaken by black women in Britain navigating a different set of waters. Immigrant waters. Colonial waters. That nation's borders were made porous long ago; when black women organized one of the campaigns, "we are here because you were there," they stood at the confluence of historical forces tying together a politics of dislocation and migration (which made ample room for solidarity with politics "at home" in Ireland, Palestine, Eritrea, Chile, Namibia, and El Salvador), a consistent critique of state practices, of Zionism, and systematically folded it into the praxis of what it meant to be black women in Britain.

In one sense this transnational intention is but implicit in *Bridge*. *Charting* made room for a dialectic of intersecting forces, splintered, as they constituted both the local (several localities simultaneously) and the global, across and within inherited maps. The bridge, in its first incarnation, is internal, crossing into different experiences of colonization, to be sure, but assuming that the very borders of the American nation are intact, an assumption later dislodged and reimagined as a desire to be more explicitly international.[5] As Moraga stated in the preface to the second edition, "the impetus to forge links with women of color from every region grows more and more urgent as the numbers of recently-immigrated people of color in the U.S. grows in enormous proportions." These metaphors of links, charts, journeys, bridges, and borders are neither idle nor incidental, however, as we come to terms with the different cartographies of feminist struggle in different parts of the world; our different histories; where they change course and how they diverge (Mohanty, "Introduction"). We must come to terms with, and engage, that confluence of the local and the global in order not to view the transnational as merely a theoretical option. Our standard of living, our very survival here, is based upon raw exploitation of working-class women—white, black, and third world—in all parts of the world. Our hands are not clean.[6] We must also come to terms with that still largely unexamined, undisclosed faith in the *idea* of America, that no matter how unbearable it is here, it is better than anywhere else; that slippage between third world and third rate. We eat bananas. Buy flowers. Use salt to flavor our food. Drink sweetened coffee. Use tires for the cars we drive. Depend upon state-of-the-art electronics. Travel. We consume and rely upon multiple choice to reify consumption. All those things that give material weight to the *idea* of America—conflating capitalism and democracy, demarcating "us" from "them."

What might it mean to see ourselves as "refugees of a world on fire" (Moraga)? "What if we declared ourselves *perpetual* refugees in solidarity with all refugees?" (Jordan, 94). Not citizen. Not naturalized citizen. Not immigrant.[7] Not undocumented. Not illegal alien. Not permanent resident. Not resident alien. But refugees fleeing some terrible atrocity far too threatening to engage, ejected out of the familiar into some unknown still to be revealed. Refugees forced to create out of the raw smithy of fire a shape different than our inheritance, with no blueprints, no guarantees. Some die in flight: Palestine. Afghanistan. Rwanda. Kongo. Bosnia. Haiti. Some live a different death: Alejandrina Torres. Susan Goldberg. Silvia Baraldini. Leonard Peltier. Mumia Abu Jamal. Marilyn Jean Buck. Linda Evans. Political prisoners. And women and people of color shackled, in disproportionate numbers, at the height of their creativity in a privatized system of imprisonment. Many undergo daily trials by fire: since 1941 women in Vieques, Puerto Rico, have lived with the U.S. Navy's aerial bombardment and military maneuvers, and now live with more carcinogens and cancers than their neighbors. Some die a different death: 46,000 of us in the United States, every year, of breast cancer (Jordan, 159). The continuing deaths of African Americans from HIV/AIDS, in the face of reduced rates of infection in every other racial group. The stunning increase in HIV/AIDS-infected babies to whom immigrant women give birth. A preventable phenomenon![8] And a general globalized violence producing rapid dispersals of people, some 100 million, mostly women and children seeking asylum. What are the different intolerables from which we desire to flee? How do we distinguish between those sites to which we must return and those from which we must flee entirely? To wrestle with these questions we must adopt, as daily practice, ways of being and relating, modes of analyzing, strategies of organizing in which we constantly mobilize identification and solidarity, across all borders, as key elements in the repertoire of risks necessary to see ourselves as part of one another, even in the context of difference (Freire, *Pedagogy*, 31). We must disappear the idiocy of "us" and "them," and its cultural relativist underpinnings, the belief that "it could never happen to 'us,'" so that our very consciousnesses become shaped by the multiple and not the singular—multiple histories and events, multiple geographies, multiple identifications.

And yet we must remember fire's character, its paradoxical dimension: it provides sustenance and warmth; and it can destroy, it can kill. The difference between those of us who fear fire and the "the welder" is her knowledge that she must become intimate with this danger zone in order to re-create, to create anew—to enter the fire not figuratively or metaphorically, but actually, that is, in flesh and blood (Moraga, Clarke). The difference between the welder and those who fear fire is the attentiveness she brings to the process of entering fire: this consciousness cultivates the intelligence to discern, embrace, and live that important yet malleable relationship between destruction and sustenance. Fire can kill, but without it we *will* die. Can we see that a lotus can bloom in the furnace without losing its freshness?[9] We must learn to make peace with contradiction and paradox, see its operation in our own lives' uneven structures, and learn to sense, taste, and understand paradox as the motor of things—what Marxian philosophy and political economy *and* the metaphysics of spiritual thought systems share. Dialectics of struggle. Paradoxes of the Divine. Still, we know that living contradiction is not easy in a culture that ideologically purveys a distaste for contradiction and an apparent attachment to consensus (Morales, ". . . And Even Fidel"). But living contradiction is necessary if we are to create the asylums of identification and solidarity with and for one another, without which our lives will surely wither (Jordan, 95).

We Have Recognized Each Other Before

Who are we as women of color at this moment in history? Where is the political movement calling itself a woman-of-color movement? Who mobilizes within it? On what terms? At the original writing women puzzled these questions even while linking themselves to the emerging politic. Mirtha Quintanales got to the heart of the paradox of naming:

> Not all Third World women are "women of color"—if by this concept we mean exclusively "non-white." And not all women of color are really Third World—if this term is only used in reference to underdeveloped . . . societies (especially those not allied with any superpower). Clearly then it would be difficult to justify referring to Japanese women. . . who are women of color, as Third World women. Yet if we extend the concept of Third World to include internally "colonized" racial and ethnic minority groups in this country, the crucial issue of social and institutional racism and its historic tie to slavery in the U.S. could get diluted . . . .The same thing would likely happen if we extended the meaning of "women of color" to include . . . women . . . who are victims of prejudice . . . but . . . nevertheless hold racial privileges and may even be racists. . . . [M]any of us who identify as "Third World" or "Women of Color," have grown up as, or are fast becoming "middle-class" and highly educated, and therefore more privileged than many of our white, poor and working-class sisters. (151)

Fractures of class and skin color, the different economic and cultural positions to which our countries of origin adhere in the capitalist hierarchy: these objective and lived conditions add considerable contention to this category woman of color. At this historical juncture, it is structurally larger and more internally differentiated than at the moment of its inception over two decades ago. The ongoing fact of "immigration" and its transformation of racial politics' complexion, often jeopardizing relationships between indigenous and "immigrant" women of color, underscores the weight *woman of color* is called upon to bear. Yet, these are the very nonidentical conditions, the objective conditions, what Avtar Brah calls the "entanglements of the genealogies of dispersal and those of staying put," that daily shape our consciousnesses *as* women of color, even as we negotiate the very different elements constituting that consciousness (*Cartographies*, 242). As in all matters of racialization both our identity (social, cultural, and historical location) and consciousness (the experiences, interpretations, and knowledge we use to explain that location) are constantly thrown into contestation.[10]

The challenge of "woman of color" and the question of whom the category can contain at this moment comes not only from the massive dislocations in women's labor (by now a permanent feature of capitalism) but also from the destabilizing effects of capitalism's underside which communities of color and white working-class communities disproportionately suffer. This is partly what makes it politically, emotionally, and spiritually necessary for women of color to return to their geographies of origin. Additionally, the movement that gave rise to *Bridge*, as well as *Bridge* itself, may well have helped build passage to the specificities of women's particular histories (Moraga, "Tuna"). Many women of color have returned home, not necessarily to the homes once vacated, but to a new temporality and urgency, to the cultures we had not fully known— partially reflected in the growth of many culturally specific grassroots organizations, in aesthetic expression, and in more recent anthologies.[11]

Clearly a new moment has emerged, producing the need for a different kind of re-membering—the making of different selves. I shall not call it nationalism here, although I felt it as such as a Caribbean woman at the 1994 Black Women in the Academy Conference, when a small group of African-American women asserted their need to sort out their own identity, alone, before considering solidarity politics. I have grown sensitive to the taste of exclusion which as a girl I have sucked from birth. You see in my face neither sister, ally, nor friend. Only Stranger. Not even in my eyes can you read your yearning, nor mine. A loss so great, there is no safety in home. To whom do I flee and where? To whom do you flee? I had made home among and with African-American women. Where was my place in this new map of identity? Who were its cartographers? Had I not already earned the right to belong? How do we remain rooted in the particularities of our cultural homes and simultaneously committed to a collectivized politics of identification and solidarity, and its different historical complexions? There is a difference, for instance, between black consciousness and woman-of-color consciousness. At the very least the latter requires collective fluency in our particular histories; an understanding of how different gendered racisms operate, their old institutionalized link to the histories of slavery and their newer manifestations which partly rely upon the "foreignness" of immigrants who have not been socialized into the U.S. racial/racist geographies (Brah, *Cartographies,* 154); and the conscious act of framing our analyses, politics, sensibilities, and being, through the chasms of those different, although overlapping, temporalities. We are not born women of color. We become women of color (Alexander and Mohanty). To *become* women of color, we would need to become fluent in each other's histories, to resist and unlearn an impulse to claim most-devastating, one-of-a-kind, defying-comparison oppression; to unlearn an impulse allowing mythologies to replace *knowing* about one another; to cultivate a way of knowing in which we direct our social, cultural, psychic, and spiritually-marked attention upon each other (Brah, "Scent"). We cannot afford to cease yearning for each other's company.

The expression at this 1994 conference was but a small episode in an ongoing choreography between African Americans and Caribbean people, oftentimes captured in fiction, all the time lived in the raucous seams of a predictable meeting, the ground for which was set at the time of that earlier Atlantic crossing. Predictable and more pronounced at this moment, four decades since the British, for instance, "announced" independence for certain parts of the (english-speaking) Caribbean region. They buried their antipathy for the United States without a single gunshot—a gentleman's agreement, the perfect foil, conceded its imperial role to America, setting the stage for global capital to operate more fully, disregarding national sovereignty or boundaries. In keeping with its logic, it expelled large numbers of Caribbean people in successive waves, the majority joining the ranks of an already disgruntled proletarian class on U.S. soil, with its own peculiar brand of racial antipathies.[12]

Not far beneath the surface lies a mirror, refracting the twin companions of colonialism and slavery, their psychic and material legacies, the historical antecedents making this contemporary meeting possible. Neither one nor the other, but both, mutually aiding and abetting each other. The memory of slavery has receded in Caribbean people's lived experience; colonization has greater force. The memory of colonization has receded in African-American people's lived experience; slavery has carried historical weight. There is a cost to this polarized forgetting in the psychic distortions both thought systems have produced: the hierarchies of inferiority and superiority and their internalizations; the internecine struggles in a gendered, racialized political economy of global capital with its intrepid mobilization of race, gender, and nation as it manages crisis after crisis in this late stage of its evolution. Racial polarization and contradictions: the face decolonization now wears in the United States.[13] As black people and people of color in this country, we are *all* living witnesses to the largely unfinished—some say failed—project of decolonization, in the United States, Britain, the Caribbean, Asia, and Africa.

Decolonization's failure rests upon at least four axes. First, a forgetting, on the part of some radical folk, that it is an unfinished project in which we are all still implicated; in other words, we still have work to do. Second, the avid embrace (by both third-world and first-world elites) of new structures of colonization, privatization, and structural adjustment policies of NAFTA, the World Bank, and the IMF making it almost impossible for most third-world people and working-class and communities of color in metropolitan countries to live with dignity. Third, a fierce denial on the part of the state and other institutions, including the academy, that its own contemporary practices of racialization have been shaped by a refusal to admit and confront its historical complicity in racism against indigenous people of color on these shores. Fourth, the fierce revival of ethnonationalisms. Part of our own unfinished work, therefore, is remembering the objective fact of these power systems and their ability to graft themselves onto the very minute interstices of our daily lives. We are all defined in some relationship to hierarchy. Neither complicity (usually cathected unto someone else) nor vigilance (usually reserved for ourselves) is given to any of us *before* the fact of our living. They are learned in this complicated process of determining who we are and whom we wish to become. The far more difficult question we must collectively engage concerns the political positions (in the widest sense) we come to practice, and not merely espouse, the mutual frameworks we adopt, as we live (both consciously and unconsciously) our daily lives (Brah, "Scent," 13). No matter our countries of origin, decolonization is a project for *all*.

It is no longer tenable for Caribbean people—it never really was—to continue seeking immunity from racialized internalizations. Caribbean people of African descent may well have claimed a premature victory and comfort of a black majority without sufficiently wrestling with the racial inequalities in our own countries of origin, the positions of Indians, for example, in Trinidad, which I came to understand as second-class citizenship, only after experiencing U.S. racism. This is perhaps why sometimes we continue reenacting within metropolitan Caribbean organizations the same dominant repetitions positioning us as most targeted vis-à-vis Indians and Chinese (now defined as Asians), whom we believe benefit more from the U.S. racial hierarchy than we do. Given the fact that this advanced capitalist colonial nation constantly redraws its own national borders, creating insiders and outsiders, African-American claims for citizenship can no longer be undertaken as if the nation-state's borders are fixed.[14] Like third-world states, this U.S. of Northamerican state is redrawing borders all the time; these gestures become more transparent with the destabilizing effects within communities of color. Immigration policies are another face of racism.

Additionally, are there not fissures of class, skin color, shades of yellow and brown within our respective nation/communities? Linguistic and regional differences creating their own insiders and outsiders? At what historical moments does heterogeneity become homogeneity—that is, the moment to create an outside enemy? Neither African-American nor Caribbean people created those earlier conditions of colonialism and Atlantic slavery.[15] Yet we continue living through them in selective forgetting, setting up an artificial antipathy between them in their earlier incarnation, behaving now as if they have ceased to be first cousins.

We have recognized each other before. Blood flows, making a mockery of biology, of boundaries—within individuals, within families, within neighborhoods. One drop of blood is not sufficient to mark where one line begins and the other ends. Boundaries are never discrete. We have recognized each other before: in the streets of Harlem when we believed, along with 6 million black people worldwide, that Garvey's Black Star Line would sail clear to the continent above the objections of black middle classes who believed that they had arrived by distancing themselves from Africa. Or in the heyday of Panafricanism when, as Baldwin elegantly framed it, "we were concerned with the immensity and variety of the experience called [Black]" (56),[16] by virtue of both slavery *and* colonization, but not only because of them. Neither movement was entirely free from exclusions, sexism, the contradictions and intrigue of class and color, xenophobia. But they kept alive an idea which for all its fractiousness lent public visibility and legitimacy to our humanity. We have recognized each other before. We agreed with Audre Lorde when she said that we are part of an international group of black women "taking care of business all over the world" (*Burst,* 109). We have been neighbors, living in the raucous seams of deprivation. We have healed each other's sick, buried each other's dead. We have become familiar with the swollen face of grief growing large in that stubborn space between love and loss.[17]

To be African American and exiled on the spot where you were born (Baldwin 404; Phillips, 252). To be Caribbean and exiled on foreign soil, producing a longing so deep that the site of neglect is reminiscent of beauty. We have grown up metabolizing exile, feeding on its main by-products—alienation and separation.[18] We walk these foreign caves crouched in stealth, searching for the bitter formations of betrayal and mistrust, seeking answers to who has betrayed whom. Crumpling expectations and desire unto half-written notes of paper, barely legible, which lie now in overstuffed baskets, never delivered. Hieroglyphic markings to an estranged lover.

What kinds of conversations do we as black women of the diaspora need to have that will end these "wasteful errors of recognition"? Do we know the terms of our different migrations? Each other's work histories?

Our different yearnings? What is to be the relationship with Africa in the term *African-American*? Our different relationships with Africa . . . on this soil, New Orleans, New York, or reincarnated in Cuba, Brazil, Haiti? Shall we continue reading Edwidge Danticat while Haiti remains, like the Pacific, on the rim of consciousness? To which genealogy of Panafrican feminism do we lay claim? Which legacy of Panafrican lesbian feminism? These conversations may well have begun. If so, we need to continue them, meeting each other eye to eye, black women born in this country, black women from different parts of the continent and from different linguistic cultural inheritances of the Caribbean, Latin America, and Asia, the Pacific. Nothing can replace the unborrowed truths that lie at the junction of the particularity of our experiences and our confrontation with history (Nhat Hanh, *Fragrant*, 89).

Are you sure, sweetheart, you want to be well?
                                        —*Toni Cade Bambara, Salt Eaters (1)*

Women of color. Who are we now, twenty years later? Have we lived differently? Loved differently? What has become of the thinking that linked the internal colonization of women of color born here with women of color who experienced colonization elsewhere, and either remained in their countries of origin or became refugees—exiles on these shores? Where does one come to consciousness as a woman of color and live it, at this moment? Have we developed a new metaphysics of political struggle? Did *Bridge* get us there, as Toni Cade Bambara believed before she moved into timelessness and probably still believes. Did it coax us into the habit of listening to each other and learning each other's ways of seeing and being (vii)? Have we made the crossing? In what shape have we reached shore? In whose company? With what in hand? Do we remember why we made the crossing back then? Other crossings before and since? Or had a desire to do so? Who are we now, twenty years later? Why do we need to remember?

Remembering is different from looking back. We can look back sideways and not bring things into full view.[19] One can look back to a when, to some past perceived to be wholly retrievable in the present, or some mirage, a nostalgic gesture that can gave rise to different fascisms. We live in a country apparently bent on inculcating a national will to amnesia, to excise certain pasts, particularly when a great wrong has occurred. The recent calls for this American nation to move ahead in the wake of the 2000 presidential election rest on forgetting. Forget intimidation at the polls and move on. Forget that citizenship is particular and does not guarantee a vote for everyone. Forget that we face the state reconsolidation of conservatism as the fragile seams of democracy come apart. Forget that law and order can be invoked so that a court can act with supreme expediency and not supreme ethics. Forget that as media make the U.S. presidential election *the* only news, Palestinians continue struggling for a homeland and Haitians for a democracy. Forget that in the midst of a "booming" economy, there are more people hungry in New York than they were ten years ago. Forget that capitalism does not bring democracy. "Once a great wrong has been done, it never dies. People speak the words of peace, but their hearts do not forgive. Generations perform ceremonies of reconciliation, but there is no end."[20] And this is partly why the desire to forget does not rest only in one place.

At times forgetting stands in for never having known or learned something, the difference between staying in tune with our own wisdom's source and relying on borrowed substitutes, fleetingly fulfilling. As Audre Lorde says in "Solstice," "we forgot to water the plantain shoots when our homes were full of borrowed meat and our stomachs with the gifts of strangers who laugh now as they pass us because our land is barren" (117). But plantain shoots are tricky: the young can choke out the mother, or the mother can choke out the children, as *my* mother has instructed me. How do we learn the antidote to barrenness? It may be not so much that we had never known about keeping things fertile and watered, the ancient sources of wisdom, but that at times the forgetting is so deep that forgetting is itself part of what we have forgotten. What is so unbearable that we even forget that we have forgotten?

"The scent of memory (our own and that of strangers)" can become faint, as faint as the scent of dried roses, when things become unspeakable, unbearable, when the terms of belonging get reshuffled. This was the case in the white working-class community of Southall, London, where waves of South Asian immigration upset "origin stories" of white belonging, producing violence of different kinds.[21] The memory of the turbulent crossing, some of which still lies in the silted bottom of the deep, is a site of trauma and forgetting. Traumatized memory, Elizabeth Alexander calls it. Such a memory of violence and violation begets a will to forget the innards of that violation. I remember Morrison's Beloved who went to the depths of that silt. Her mother Sethe did not dare remember why she sent her there, until it was safe to do so, when Paul D returned (*Beloved,* 38). To trust and remember. Love inspires re-membering. It caused "floods and floods of blocked memories" to break when Barbara Cameron returned to the reservation after an eight-year absence and rediscovered herself, "walking on the Lakota earth," looking at the "cragged faces of her grandparents" (52).

So much of how we remember is embodied: the scent of home; of fresh-baked bread; of newly grated coconut stewed with spice (we never called it cinnamon), nutmeg, and bay leaf from the tree (not from the bottle); when we see ourselves squinting, arms akimbo, frowning, adopting the same intonation, especially when angry, or running from the rain in the same way that our mothers and grandmothers did. Violence can also become embodied, that violation of sex and spirit, which is why body work is healing work is justice work. Assimilation is another kind of violation that can be embodied, assimilating alienation, one's own as well as others' (Fonesca, 281). We have to be sure we want to be well. "Are you sure, sweetheart, that you want to be well?" Minnie Ranson tests Velma Henry in the opening scene of *The Salt Eaters*, a necessary question, "just to caution folks . . . and not waste . . . time" (3–4). A question that makes conscious the yearning to be healed. Conscious and practiced. Conscious and embodied. "A revolution capable of healing our wounds" (Morales, 56). Healing wounds by touch. Touching is part of the work of decolonization. Practicing again and again the ways in which we want to be well.

Women don't want to forget in the pages of *Bridge*. Barbara Cameron "will not forget Buffalo Manhattan Hat and Mani." "When some lonesome half-remembered place" is reawakened in a sweat, Valerio remembers a past, before colonization (43). What brings us back to re-membrance is both individual and collective; both intentional and an act of surrender; both remembering desire and remembering *how* it works (Morrison, *Beloved*, 20). Daring to recognize each other again and again in a context that seems bent on making strangers of us all. Can we *intentionally* remember, all the time, as a way of never forgetting, all of us, building an archeology of living memory which has less to do with living in the past, invoking a past, or excising it, and more to do with our relationship to time and its purpose. There is a difference between remember *when*—the nostalgic yearning for some return—and a living memory that enables us to re-member what was contained in *Bridge* and what could not be contained within it or by it. What did it make possible? What else did we need? All are part of this living memory, of moments, of imaginings, which have never ended. And they will never end so long as we continue to dare yearning for each other.

For me, remembering *Bridge* is a way of remembering myself, for, even as I write, I am aware that memory is not a pure act of access. I had not imagined when I began "Remembering Bridge," and named it after writing only three sentences, that it would require such excavation, such remememory of deep forgettings. Feeding hungry ghosts (Nhat Hanh, *Touching Peace*). As I bemoaned the travails of this writing, my friend Chandan posed his version of Minnie Ranson's question to Vilma Henry: "What archaelogies have you undertaken, Jacqui?" "And I had promised myself,"

I continued without answering, "that I would begin to write in a different voice. But it is excruciating to keep that promise in the midst of impending deadlines." "You know, Jacqui," Chandan offered, "sometimes we can only authenticate our voice when we are up against a wall; if not, we are only an impostor in a new language, speaking in the name of populism." Authenticating voice comes through rediscovering the underbelly, literally unearthing and piecing together the fragmented members of existence.

Remembering the unrelenting vision of *Bridge* in the multiple ways remembering occurs is crucial in these times. It is a generous vision which was gifted two decades ago. I want to insist upon its generosity, for in the midst of uncovering the painful fault lines of homophobia, culture, and class within different communities of belonging, advancing critiques of racism within the women's movement, it did not relinquish a vision of interdependence, of interbeing, if you will. Not a transcendent vision, but one rooted in transforming the dailiness of lived experience, the very ground upon which violence finds fodder. Vision can only be as effective and sturdy as our determination to practice, emphasis on the practice.

Daily practice will bring about the necessary shifts in perception that make change possible. Vision helps us to remember *why* we do the work. Practice is the *how*; it makes the change and grounds the work. A reversal of the inherited relationship between theory and practice, between how we think and what we do. As Mab Segrest has argued, these components of what we do, who we are (ontology), how we know (epistemology), and how we act from within our interpretations of reality (metaphysics) are all part of *engaged action*—engaging us at the deepest, spiritual level of meaning in our lives. It is how we constitute our humanity.

El Mundo Zurdo and the Ample Space of the Erotic

Moraga: If the gun and the cross have been used as instruments of oppression, we must learn to use them as instruments of liberation.

Anzaldúa: And yet to act is not enough. Many of us are learning to sit perfectly still, to sense the presence of the Soul and commune with Her. We are beginning to realize that we are not wholly at the mercy of circumstance. . . . We have come to realize we are not alone in our struggles, nor separate, nor autonomous, but that we . . . are connected and interdependent.

Lorde: [T]he dichotomy between the spiritual and the political is false resulting from an incomplete attention to our erotic knowledge, for the bridge which connects them is formed by the erotic, the sensual, those

physical, emotional and psychic expressions of what is deepest and
strongest and richest within each of us being shared: the passion of love in
its deepest meaning.

For three years now I have been participating in ongoing meetings and discussions among a group of women and men—lesbian, gay, bisexual, transgendered, and heterosexual, of different nationalities and ages, with different cultural and spiritual affinities, including those with close relationships to the institutionalized Christian church, to learn what sex and spirit, what sexuality and spirituality taken together, might tell us about who we are. Early in this work, we found that many "secular" activists were reluctant to come out spiritually. Some reluctance came from the historical ways the Judaeo-Christian church, in particular, operated as an instrument of colonization: enforcing heterosexuality and nuclear family as the moral norm; attempting to erase the connection between sexuality and land—in Hawai'i, for instance, splitting apart the ontology of mind, body, and spirit into the particularities of (white) manliness, colonized "other," and (christian) religion, respectively. A more contemporary religious right had mobilized globally to advance an anti-human agenda, mistakenly attributing its authority to God. But this dominant mythologized collapse of spirituality into religion was also operating among us, another indication of the subtle internalization of dominance. We found that we had a great deal of practice coming out politically, but many were timid about coming out spiritually *as* (radical) political people. It seemed that in combining the two we were on the brink of committing heresy of a different kind.

As we moved to unite these powerful forces of sex and the spirit, we identified another kind of shared internalization. Grappling with the inherited division, we understood that it is sustained in part by an ideology steeping sex and sexuality in sin, shame, and general disavowal of the sacred. Simultaneously, this very ideology has attempted to contain all spirit and the spiritual within the structure of religion, with predictably devastating consequences. We named this process of fragmentation colonization, usually understood as a set of exploitative practices in political, ideological, and aesthetic terms, but also linked in minute ways to dualistic-hierarchical thinking: divisions among mind, body, spirit; between sacred and secular; male and female; heterosexual and homosexual; in class divisions; in divisions between the Erotic and the Divine. We saw its operation creating mono-thinking: the mistaken notion that only one kind of justice work leads to freedom. Presumably, organizing for a decent, just, living wage is not connected to anti-racist work, to anti-homophobia work, to organizing against the U.S state in Vieques. Such thinking is always premised in negation, often translated into singular explanations for oppression. Breaking down these divisions and hierarchies, indeed making ourselves whole again, became our work throughout our entire journey.

Since colonization has produced fragmentation and dismemberment at both the material and the psychic levels, the work of decolonization must make room for the deep yearning for wholeness, oftentimes expressed as a yearning to belong, a yearning both material and existential, both psychic and physical, which, when satisfied, can subvert and ultimately displace the pain of dismemberment. Because anti-colonial and left liberation movements have not understood this sufficiently in their psychology of liberation, they have not made ample political room for it. This yearning to belong cannot be confined only to membership or citizenship in community, political movement, nation, group, or belonging to a family, however constituted, although important. Indeed, we would not have come to the various political movements in which we have been engaged with such intense passion had it not been for this yearning. With the help of Bernice Johnson Reagon we recognized in this yearning a desire to reproduce home in "coalitions": our political movements were forced to bear too much of a longing for sameness as home, the limits of nationalism. But we needed to wrestle with that desire for home a bit longer, examining more closely the source of that yearning we wanted to embed in the metaphysics of political struggle, the metaphysics of life. Its source is the deep knowing that we are in fact interdependent, neither separate nor autonomous. As human beings, we have a sacred connection to one another, and this is why enforced separations wreak havoc on our souls. There is great danger, then, in living lives of segregation. Racial segregation. Segregation in politics. Segregated frameworks. Segregated, compartmentalized selves. Our oppositional politic has been necessary, but it will never sustain us; while it may give us some temporary gains (themselves becoming more ephemeral the greater the threat, which is not a reason not to fight), it can never ultimately feed that deep place within us: that space of the erotic, that space of the soul, that space of the Divine.[22]

"To sense the presence of the soul and commune with her" is what Gloria Anzaldúa has said is required in this job of excavation, this job of changing the self. It is a job. It requires work. It requires practice. It cannot be someone else's excavation easily appropriated as our own. It cannot be done as spectator or ventriloquist. It requires the work of each and every one, to unearth this desire to belong to the self *in* community as part of a radical project—not to be confused with the self-preoccupation on which individualism thrives. Self-determination is both an individual and collective project.

There is an inevitability (not passivity) in this movement toward wholeness, this work of spirit and the journey of the Soul in its vocation to reunite us with the erotic and the Divine. Whether we want it or not, it will occur. Do we dare to undertake this task of recognition intentionally, as self-reflexive human beings, open at the very core to a foundational truth? We are connected to the Divine through our connections with each other. Yet no one comes to consciousness alone, in isolation, only for oneself, or passively. It is here we need a verb—conscientize, which Paulo Freire used to underscore the fact that shifts in consciousness happen through active processes of practice and reflection. Of necessity, they occur in community. We must constantly envision this as we devise ways to practice building communities (not sameness) over and over again. We can continue holding on to a consciousness of our different locations, our understanding of the simultaneous ways dominance shapes our lives and, at the same time, water the erotic as that place of our Divine connection which can transform the ways we relate to one another.

Oftentimes when we have failed at solidarity work we retreat, struggling to convince ourselves that this is indeed the work we have been called upon to do. The fact is that there *is* no other work but the work of creating and re-creating ourselves within the context of community. Simply put, there is no other work. It took five hundred years, at least in this hemisphere, to solidify the division of things that belong together. It need not take us five hundred more years to move ourselves out of this existential impasse. Spirit work does not conform to the dictates of human time. But it needs our courage, revolutionary patience, and intentional shifts in consciousness allowing us to anchor the struggle for social justice within the ample space of the erotic.[23]

One of feminism's earliest lessons is that the personal is political: some of our lives' most infinitesimal details are shaped by ideological and political forces much larger than our individual selves. During a pitched battle to transform the curriculum at the New School University, where I taught five years ago, I came to appreciate another shade of this insight as the school's administration sought to make me *the* entire political struggle. With a great deal of help and a deep level of self-scrutiny I learned how a single individual could ignite a political struggle but ultimately had to be subsumed under it, simply be within it, if that struggle was to be successful. This interior work is indispensable in the journey to wholeness. Through the task force's conscious attention to the reknitting of sex and spirit and the spiritual-political work I have undertaken in my life, I have come to see that an inside change in the personal is not entirely complete if it remains at the level of a shift in ideas, or even in practice, although both are necessary. Desire is expressed most fundamentally where change takes place: at the root of our very souls, the base of the internal source of our power and yearning. Yearning and power we have been taught so much to fear. When Anzaldúa asks us to commune with the Soul, or Lorde urges us to find something our soul craves and do it, our first task is to become attentive to the soul's desire and to place ourselves in its service. It is a necessary and delicate undertaking in spirit-based politics, this joining of the sacred and secular, "to have," as Sharon Day imaged it, "the ethics of spirituality inform daily life." It requires intention, a revolutionary patience, courage, and, above all, humility. Once this work begins, the temptation to cross narrow boundaries becomes irresistible; connections, once invisible, come into full view. And I am assured that when the practice begins to bear fruit, the yearning itself is transformed.

An old man has etched himself into an ancient slab of rock deposited in a park at the end of my street in Harlem. His face comes into view only from afar, with distance, with perspective. Close up, he simply folds himself back into the stone, disappearing—pretending, perhaps, not to be there. When we do not see him does it mean he does not exist? Unlike the figures of Davis, Lee, and Jackson—patiently chiseled into the Mountain of Stone in Georgia, now pasted on the tourist bus stationed opposite the park, figures that announce themselves from far and near—this old man works in stealth, through years of weather, bringing himself into my field of vision only by the angle of my gaze and the distance from which I stand. Although I have lived for seven years on this same one-way street leading directly to this slab of stone, I had not seen him before. And yet, he is there. The challenge for me is to see him in the present and to know he's there even when I cannot see. Rocks hold memory.

Land holds memory. This is why the land and live oak trees rooted in the Georgia Sea Islands whisper in our ear when we allow ourselves to listen. The Ibo of Nigeria were captured and brought to these islands. When they arrived and saw the conditions of their capture and homelessness, they turned around, walked on water, and drowned themselves. The place, bearing the name Ibo Landing, holds the memory of that moment which still lives in the heart of every Gullah child and in the oaks' solid trunks. The live oaks will tell us these stories when we listen. And the mountains of Hawai'i will echo the ancient Kanaka Maoli belief that they are stewards, eyes, children of the land. Deep within their undulating folds draping themselves with the ease of velvet around the opulent embrace of mist and cloud, we will feel the land's ancient power to heal. Ocean will reveal the secrets that lie at the bottom of its silted deep. She requires no name before her. Neither Pacific. Atlantic. Arctic. Southern. Indian. She is simply her watery translucent self, reaching, without need for a compass, for her sisters, whomever and wherever they are. She will call you by your ancient name, and you would answer because you would not have forgotten. Water always remembers.

Notes

This essay is in honor of Cherríe Moraga and Gloria Anzaldúa, who bore the original vision. It is dedicated to Gloria Wekker. Much gratitude to AnaLouise Keating for her insights and for staying close throughout this process; and to AnaLouise and Gloria Anzaldúa for their gentleness. Angela Bowen, Gloria Joseph, Gail Lewis, Mab Segrest, Jerma Jackson, Linda Carty, and Gloria Wekker have all accompanied me throughout this process and have read different versions of this essay. I relied upon them for the their astute eyes, their commitment to sisterhood, their critical engagement, their desire to make our world intelligible in order to change it, and their perpetual generosity and love.

1. See the video documentary *Sweet Sugar Rage* (Sistren Theatre Collective, Kingston 5, Jamaica, 1985). See also Sistren's *Lionheart Gal*. Since its inception in 1986, CAFRA (Caribbean Association for Feminist Research and Action) has been explicitly committed to examining "the relations between men and women in capitalist and socialist societies; to use a framework inclusive of race, class and sex; and to demonstrate the ways in which exploitative relations between men and women are facilitated maintained and reproduced by exploitative capitalist relations, and how capitalism itself benefits in the process."

2. Chrystos, "I Walk," 57. The 1973 occupation by the people of Pine Ridge and members of the American Indian Movement lasted for sixty-nine days. The conditions leading to the occupation still continue. Conversation with Sharon Day. See Brown.

3. Quintanales, 151; Yamada, "Invisibility," 35; Morales, "We're All in the Same Boat," 92; davenport, 85.

4. Du Bois's earlier analysis of double consciousness is pertinent here. These formulations lie at the heart of the concept of internalized oppression used within feminism.

5. The politics of black women in Britain have always been infused with a more systematic critique of state practices than U.S. women-of-color politics. The claim for black women's citizenship was anchored on a subjectivity as colonials, hence the notion that the British nation's borders had never been fixed. Gail Lewis, one of *Charting's* original editors, believes that this is a new moment: black women are posing questions of belonging in ways that fundamentally challenge and change the character of Britishness. We need a fruitful set of transatlantic conversations between black women in Britian and U.S. women of color. See Lewis and Brah below.

6. Taken from the text of a song by Sweet Honey in the Rock, reproduced in Enloe.

7. We must distinguish between wealthy refugees fleeing to protect privilege—for instance, lightskinned/white Cuban refugees who fled to Miami with communism's triumph in Cuba, Asian Ugandans expelled by the 1972 edict of Idi Amin who had business interests in different parts of the world (Brah, *Cartographies*, 35), and the comprador classes of many third-world countries who flee to metropolitan countries partly out of a refusal to rebuild civil society in their own countries of origin. This latter insight came from Chandan Reddy in conversation. See also Bhattacharjee.

8. See Cohen, *Boundaries*, 123. I learned of these disturbing data and their implications (referring primarily to African and Brazilian women in Massachusetts) in conversation with Barbara Herbert. African-American women who have had this disease since it became visible in 1981 still have disproportionate mortality rates, even with the advent of new medications. Clearly the question of our political interventions to make breast cancer, HIV/AIDS, and other diseases central parts of our organizing is urgent.

9. From eleventh-century Vietnamese Zen monk Ngo An: *"The jade burned on the mountain retains its natural color / The lotus, blooming in the furnace, does not lose its freshness."* It is the epigraph of Thich Nhat Hanh's *Vietnam* that traces the history of Vietnamese Buddhism and its engagement in the conflagration called the Vietnam War. I thank Mab Segrest for this reference.

10. For an exceptional analysis of dominant postmodernism's premature theoretical abandonment of social location and identity, see Moya.

11. See, for instance, Latina Feminist Collective, Women of South Asian Descent Collective, Kadi, and Harjo and Bird.

12. There are of course different class migrations, in turn linked to the categories and quotas deployed by the Immigration and Naturalization Service. See Bhattacharjee for a comparison with South Asian migration to the United States (210).

13. I thank Chandan Reddy for this point. This polarization is also reflected in a theoretical schism between postcolonial and ethnic studies. A larger analysis—which should also entail an analysis of the academy's hiring practices—is warranted.

14. Our understanding of this social formation would benefit enormously from analyses that do not automatically imagine a democratic U.S state. Such a refusal could reduce the anomaly of positioning the state as democratic at home and interventionist abroad. See Jaimes Guerrero for an understanding of how the American state negotiates advanced capitalist *and* colonial relations, particularly with Native peoples; Cohen's *Boundaries* for an astute reading of the "advanced marginalization" of African-American communities; and Lewis for an exceptional formulation of Britain as postcolonial social formation.

15. The fact of African complicity in the Atlantic slave trade is a different point from the one I'm making here.

16. Of course Baldwin's conflation of Panafricanism with royal manliness is not be missed.

17. I recall here the shared mobilizations in New York City around the death of Galvin Cato, the police brutalization of Abner Louima, and the police shooting of Amadou Diallo.

18. See this most important essay by Lorde, on which I lean very heavily: "Eye to Eye," in *Sister Outsider*.

19. Dionne Brand, talking here about the sidelong glances Caribbean people give to slavery.

20. Epigraph taken from the Tiv of West Africa (Marshall, *Chosen Place*).

21. Brah has simply done a brilliant analysis demonstrating how to think about identification across difference, which everyone should read. The analysis plays on *The Scent of Dried Roses*, an autobiographical account by a son, Lott, of his mother Jean's suicide in Southall. Brah reconstructs his family genealogy in this white working-class community in the context of interviews conducted earlier with Lott's contemporaries, analyses of South Asian migration, and the attendant violence against South Asians (which interrogate "origin stories" of belonging), in order to understand how Jean was implicated in her world and she in Jean's.

22. Chela Sandoval's original formulation of an oppositional consciousness remains very important.

23. I borrow the term *revolutionary patience* from Gloria Joseph.

eleven

Seventh Fire

Joanne DiNova

For a time we forgot
The sounds of ghost
      dancers
On the plains, drums
Ancestral, resolute
Converging in the distance
For a time we forgot
      the Voices
For a time we believed
The tinny pulpit voices
      instead
Could see only their pink
Fisted bibles
Raised as if poised
      to strike
And for a time we were afraid

But now I believe the sounds grow large
And now I see the Northern Lights gone wild
And between the shivering folds of pink paranoia
I hear the Voices, softly now:
      Tear down their fences
      They can't think without lines

ii.

"still struggling with the boxes people
try to put me in" . . . resisting the labels

twelve

Interracial

Amy Sara Carroll

thirteen

Los Intersticios: Recasting Moving Selves

Evelyn Alsultany

*Ethnicity in such a world needs to be recast so that our moving selves can
be acknowledged. . . . Who am I? When am I? The questions that are asked
in the street, of my identity, mold me. Appearing in the flesh, I am cast
afresh, a female of color—skin color, hair texture, clothing, speech, all
marking me in ways that I could scarcely have conceived of.*
                                                            —Meena Alexander (66)

I'm in a graduate class at the New School in New York City. A white
female sits next to me and we begin "friendly" conversation. She asks me
where I'm from. I reply that I was born and raised in New York City and
return the question. She tells me she is from Ohio and has lived in New
York for several years. She continues her inquiry: "Oh . . . well, how
about your parents?" (I feel her trying to map me onto her narrow cartography; New York is not a sufficient answer. She analyzes me according to binary axes of sameness and difference. She detects only
difference at first glance, and seeks to pigeonhole me. In her framework,
my body is marked, excluded, not from this country. A seemingly
"friendly" question turns into a claim to land and belonging.) "My father
is Iraqi and my mother Cuban," I answer. "How interesting. Are you a
U.S. citizen?"

I am waiting for the NYC subway. A man also waiting asks me if I too
am Pakistani. I reply that I'm part Iraqi and part Cuban. He asks if I am
Muslim, and I reply that I am Muslim. He asks me if I am married, and I
tell him I'm not. In cultural camaraderie he leans over and says that he
has cousins in Pakistan available for an arranged marriage if my family so
desires. (My Cubanness, as well as my own relationship to my cultural
identity, evaporates as he assumes that Arab plus Muslim equals arranged
marriage. I can identify: he reminds me of my Iraqi relatives and I know
he means well.) I tell him that I'm not interested in marriage but thank
him for his kindness. (I accept his framework and respond accordingly,
avoiding an awkward situation in which he realizes that I am not who he
assumes I am, offering him recognition and validation for his [mis]identi-
fication.)

I am in a New York City deli waiting for my bagel to toast. The man
behind the counter asks if I'm an Arab Muslim (he too is Arab and
Muslim). I reply that yes, I am by part of my father. He asks my name,
and I say, "Evelyn." In utter disdain, he tells me that I could not possibly

be Muslim; if I were truly Muslim I would have a Muslim name. What was I doing with such a name? I reply (after taking a deep breath and telling myself that it's not worth getting upset over) that my Cuban mother named me and that I honor my mother. He points to the fact that I'm wearing lipstick and have not changed my name, which he finds to be completely inappropriate and despicable, and says that I am a reflection of the decay of the Arab Muslim in America.

I'm on an airplane flying from Miami to New York. I'm sitting next to an Ecuadorian man. He asks me where I'm from. I tell him. He asks me if I'm more Arab, Latina, or American, and I state that I'm all of the above. He says that's impossible. I must be more of one ethnicity than another. He determines that I am not really Arab, that I'm more Latina because of the camaraderie he feels in our speaking Spanish.

I am in Costa Rica. I walk the streets and my brown skin and dark hair blend in with the multiple shades of brown around me. I love this first-time experience of blending in! I walk into a coffee shop for some café con leche, and my fantasy of belonging is shattered when the woman preparing the coffee asks me where I'm from. I tell her that I was born and raised in New York City by a Cuban mother and an Arab father. She replies, "Que eres una gringa."

I am shocked by the contextuality of identity: that my body is marked as gringa in Costa Rica, as Latina in some U.S. contexts, Arab in others, in some times and spaces not adequately Arab, or Latina, or "American," and in other contexts simply as *other*.

My body becomes marked with meaning as I enter public space.[1] My identity fractures as I experience differing dislocations in multiple contexts. Sometimes people otherize me, sometimes they identify with me. Both situations can be equally problematic. Those who otherize me fail to see a shared humanity and those who identify with me fail to see difference; my Arab or Muslim identity negates my Cuban heritage. Identification signifies belonging or home, and I pretend to be that home for the mistaken person. It's my good deed for the day (I know how precious it can be to find a moment of familiarity with a stranger). The bridge becomes my back as I feign belonging, and I become that vehicle for others, which I desire for myself. Although it is illusory, I do identify with the humanity of the situation—the desire to belong in this world, to be understood. But the frameworks used to (mis)read my body, to disconnect me, wear on me. I try to develop a new identity. What should I try to pass for next time? Perhaps I'll just say I'm Cuban to those who appear to be Arab or South Asian. A friend suggests I say I'm an Italian from Brooklyn. I wonder if I could successfully pass for that. Ethnicity needs to be recast so that our moving selves can be acknowledged.

*They would chop me up into little fragments and tag each piece with a label
Who, me confused? Ambivalent? Not so. Only your labels split me.*
—Gloria Anzaldúa, "La Prieta" (205)

This Bridge Called My Back revolutionized how we saw ourselves as women of color. Our experiences—unacknowledged by the dominant culture and by feminist, ethnic, and/or queer movements—were finally named. *This Bridge* insisted on a theory of the flesh through which to bridge the contradictions in our lives: "We do this bridging by naming ourselves and by telling our stories in our own words" (Moraga, 23). *Bridge* authors powerfully addressed the multiple displacements women of color often experience, or what Gloria Anzaldúa calls "los intersticios: 'Alienated from her mother culture,' 'alien' in the dominant culture, the woman of color does not feel safe within the inner life of her Self. Petrified, she can't respond, her face caught between los intersticios, the spaces between the different worlds she inhabits" (*Borderlands,* 20). Many multiethnic women identify strongly with this experience of being alienated in different ways from our various communities, trapped in a space of dislocation. Our complex selves can't be acknowledged as unified and whole.

When we're not acknowledged as complex unitary subjects, we become caught in los intersticios, haciendo caras to get by. Lisa Suhair Majaj, born to a Palestinian father and a white American mother, growing up in Lebanon and Jordan, has spent much of her life in los intersticios: "I learned to live as if in a transitional state, waiting always for the time that we would go to Palestine, to the United States, to a place where I would belong. But trips to Iowa and to Jerusalem taught me that once I got there, 'home' slipped away inexplicably materializing again just beyond reach. If a sense of rootedness was what gave life meaning, as my parents' individual efforts to ward off alienation implied, this meaning seemed able to assume full import only in the imagination" ("Boundaries," 71). Majaj's lived experiences are not mapped out; there are no ready frameworks to understand her identity as complex and simultaneously Arab and American. She never felt like she fully belonged anywhere and found herself searching for "home," a space of belonging. Yet she recurringly experienced belonging as deferment: "In my experience cultural marginality has been among the most painful of alienations. My childhood desire, often desperate, was not so much to be a particular nationality, to be American or Arab, but to be wholly one thing or another: to be *something* that I and the rest of the world could understand, categorize, label predict" (79, author's emphasis).

We carry this pain with us as we live in los intersticios. To "belong," we must fragment and exclude particular parts of our identity. Dislocation results from the narrow ways in which the body is read, the rigid frameworks imposed on the body in public space. At the end of the day, I'm tired of wearing masks, being misunderstood, projected upon, otherized, erased. "I am tired of being afraid to speak who I am: American and Palestinian, not merely half one thing and half of another, but both at once—and in that inexplicable melding that occurs when two cultures come together, not quite either, so that neither American nor Arab find themselves fully reflected in me, nor I in them" (Majaj, "Boundaries," 68). Identity must be reconceptualized so that we can speak our own identities as we live and interpret them in multiple contexts. But how can we create a space for the articulation of multiethnic identities as unitary and whole rather than fragmented and dislocated?

If we change the reading/framework/lens, we can transform dislocation into location. We must reconstruct "belonging" to embrace the experiences of all human beings. As Adrian Piper (a light-skinned African-American woman who grew up in los intersticios, alienated from the black community for her light skin complexion and alienated from the white community for her blackness) has stated, "the racial categories that purport to designate any of us are too rigid and oversimplified to fit anyone accurately. But then, accuracy was never their purpose" (110).

Racial categories' purpose has usually been geopolitical. In "Dislocated Identities: Reflections of an Arab Jew," Ella Shohat discusses how today's dominant frameworks do not account for her identity as an Arab Jew and illustrates the ways in which these categories have been recently constructed as antithetical. Such frameworks have a political function. For her grandmother's generation and for hundreds of prior generations, Jewishness was inextricably linked to Arabness; they were not binary categories but logically linked: an Arab could be Muslim, Jewish, Christian, or any other faith. It was when she arrived in Israel from Iraq (as a refugee) that her grandmother had to learn such imposed constructed distinctions. New cartographies were created within which her identity became dislocated: "For Middle Easterners, the operating distinction had always been 'Muslim,' 'Jew,' and 'Christian,' not Arab versus Jew. The assumption was that 'Arabness' referred to a common shared culture and language, albeit with religious differences." In the U.S. context this binarism between Arab and Jew operates, allowing for the narration of "a singular Jewish memory, i.e., a European one."

Shohat's experience points to the political nature of categorization. Meanings attached to identities shift not only over time and space but also according to political circumstance. That such meanings change indicates that we can alter them. We can create a new cartography. An inability to conceptualize multiethnic persons reflects a colonial ideology of categorization and separation based on a "pure blood" criteria—a system constructed for the white colonists to maintain power. Rigid racial categories keep us separate. Multiethnic identity comes as a surprise and a danger within this framework as people attempt to place us, to make sense within the schemas available for understanding people and the world. Our identities transgress the constructed categories and become threatening. As Piper explains, "These incidents and others like them had a peculiar cognitive feel to them, as though the individuals involved felt driven to make special efforts to situate me in their conceptual mapping of the world, not only by naming or indicating the niche in which they felt I belonged, but by seeking my verbal confirmation of it . . . [an attempt to] locate me within the rigid confines of [their] stereotype of black people" (83).

I seek to decolonize these essentialized frameworks, so that I can move through public space without strategizing a performance, selecting a mask for each scenario. I want to expand los intersticios, creating a space for us all in our multiplicities to exist as unified subjects. It is a nonessentialist way of relating that creates a space to articulate multiple identifications and unlimited interpretations of those dimensions. This new space begins with a question: Ask me who I am. Don't project your essentialisms onto my body and then project hatred because I do not conform to your notions of who I'm supposed to be. There is no essentialized blueprint. Opening up the possibility of articulating the variety of ways we experience and negotiate our identities benefits everyone, not just the multiethnic. Recasting our moving selves begins with an openness and a willingness to listen, which leads to dialogue.

Notes

I would like to thank Marisol Negrón, Alexandra Lang, María Helena Rueda, Ericka Beckman, Karina Hodoyan, Sara Rondinel, Jessi Aaron, and Cynthia María Paccacerqua for their feedback in our writing seminar at Stanford University with Mary Pratt. I would especially like to thank Mary Pratt for her invaluable feedback, and AnaLouise Keating and Gloria Anzaldúa for their thoughtful editing.

1. Although such episodes are not exclusive to "public space," I will not be dealing with the complex dynamics of "private space" in this piece.

fourteen

Gallina Ciega: Turning the Game on Itself

Leticia Hernández-Linares

In the large lot full of weeds and dust, where the tree that sometimes gave us shade watched us play, we would spin. ¡Gallina! ¡Ciega! ¡Gallina! ¡Ciega! When my friend from down the street would tie the scarf around

my eyes, all I could see were patches of dust on the sides of my shoes.
Hands stretched out looking for an arm, the edge of a shirt—not knowing
exactly where I might step, I learned early that if I tried to lift my lids,
purple and black spots would poke through my lashes and map out the
darkness in which I had to find my friends.

You have to lunge toward the sounds. When you play Gallina Ciega
(Blind Hen), you are blindfolded and spun around, and then you try to
catch the other kids singing out "¡Gallina! ¡Ciega! ¡Gallina! ¡Ciega!"
Behind the noise of the Hollywood freeway, I remember, girls, boys, running around me, light, dark, black hair, red hair, migrants, speakers of
more than one language. We saw our differences, but more important to
us as children were the things that brought us together: escaping the day,
the neighborhood violence, and the economic struggle around us. Close
your eyes and learn to see through your mind, through your other senses.

I later played this game as an adult during a summer of bilingual
recreational activities with girls from migrant Mexican communities and
working-class white families. At a K–6 community center in Santa
Barbara, these girls ran with me in those same circles. Barely aware of the
categories "migrant," "Mexican," "bilingual," "monolingual," "white," into
which they were being molded, these girls broke out of their familiarity to
learn new words and games, and make new friends. This game that urges
us to look for each other's voices, to seek others in their words and not
simply in their color, culture, gender assignment, helped these girls move
toward a bridge, a common meeting ground. As for myself, the game's
simple lessons have been difficult to appreciate. I am still trying to open
my eyes in the purple darkness of my blindfold and my steps are slow and
unsure.

La Gallina Ciega Plays Hide and Seek

In 1994, while I worked with the girls in Santa Barbara, I was living a huge
contradiction. I played a different kind of game with myself, and tried to
fit into a mold that made me just like everyone else. I mainly interacted
with Mexican and Chicana/o communities, and my work was exciting, but
difficult, as I was often silent about my Salvadoran-ness for fear it would
change people's attitudes toward me. Only when asked, which was almost
never, did I explain that no, I was not Mexican. I dreaded the confusion,
surprise, suspicion, alienation which claiming that difference often
unleashed. Too many times I had been forced to contend with folks
entangled in the cracked mirror games of "who is the most authentic of
them all." I didn't care to fight about identity issues, but I did allow the
narrow-mindedness of a few to keep me silent. It was important for me
that the Santa Barbara community know that shared experiences had

brought us together. As long as I could do the work with youth that I wanted to do, I didn't explain my difference when I didn't have to.

These experiences helped me recognize what Andrea Canaan describes as the danger of becoming too preoccupied with terminology. The tendency to "stereotype and close off people" into categories of "brownness," "whiteness," "Chicano," "Latino" had us running around in circles, but hardly innocent ones. By silencing myself, I was complicit in my own alienation; I gave in to the requirement that I check a box. While I understand the specificity and importance of the history behind the term Chicana/o, for my generation of Central Americans born or raised in the United States, this term also has a particular significance. More than a category we're placed into by others, it is an identity that many of us have entered into, and have begun to expand.

When I was growing up, and even in college, I was aware of my difference: my Spanish, the color of the beans my mother cooked, the reason for my presence in the United States, the blank looks on people's faces when they asked where in Mexico I was from and I mentioned El Salvador instead. Yet I also grew up speaking Spanglish; running around East L.A. while my father played music with a Chicano rock band; eating black beans and lengua out of flour tortillas; relying on Chicana/o support services and academic programs in college; being mistaken for and held accountable as a Mexican. In college, I was adamant about not being subsumed under the category "Chicana/o," but I have also come to understand the many ways that my experiences align me with a Chicana/o cultural context. It's also important for Central Americans to excavate our specific histories as we are beginning to do now with the first Central American studies program under way in Los Angeles. As the writings in *This Bridge* and *Borderlands/La Frontera* have helped me understand, my home and culture are not one but many.

Splitting

Nine years after I first read *This Bridge*, I find myself still struggling with the boxes people try to put me in. Nine years ago, words like *Chicana, Latina, Salvadoran, feminist, working class* were extremely important to me. While discovering the meaning behind these identifications has been necessary for me and will continue to be necessary for others, I feel confined by having to pick one and claim that "I am_____" as each adjective by itself is so insufficient and invites the assumptions and conclusions of others. Constructing my own names and communities has been about letting go of the importance of fitting into neat categories that only serve to divide us.

Maybe new ways of identifying will emerge, maybe it won't even matter. When nationalism arises between the Mexican/Chicana/o and Salvadoran sides of the room, I have no desire to pick sides. As I write this, I share the fear Anzaldúa describes in "La Prieta" of expressing critical words, yet I know it's time to own my difference, to come out as a Salvadoran who grew up Chicana; a pocha who grew up speaking Spanish; a Guanaca fluent in Spanglish; a Salvi who doesn't want "hyphen-American" in her last name. While I understand the limits of these categories, I also acknowledge my relationship to them.

I flow through and between these markers, and in my usage, I do not allow them to restrict me. To a certain extent, in order to communicate, we have to function in the existing system of language that depends on constructions such as "race," and "gender," and "nation," but we also have to continue dismantling it. Perhaps the anger and enlightenment I found in books such as *This Bridge* afford me the luxury to ask people to question these categories. It was in those pages that I began to see this challenge to language. And certainly, I am still negotiating my way around the Borderlands and contending with what Anzaldúa describes as the limitation and stigma caused by the labels that split us.

This splitting can be quite literal. The endless list of "isms" is based on an interconnected linguistic and material violence that fails to recognize identities, and purposely erases racialized bodies. On a large scale, in the interest of what Cherríe Moraga calls a "total vision," we must always work to flip the script that translates such language systems physically and hence violently. These material manifestations—the illness and bodily abuse—were discussed in the first *Bridge*, and continue marking the unseen, ignored, abused bodies of women, immigrants, sweatshop workers, young girls. As the erasures in language work themselves out on the material body, the importance of being heard becomes even more urgent.

¡Gallina! ¡Ciega! ¡Gallina! ¡Ciega!

Few of us have escaped the physical and psychic heridas caused by the boxes that close us in, cover us. In 1993 when I moved to Pennsylvania and entered graduate school, I almost suffocated in my self-imposed feelings of shame and guilt. I had so internalized people's expectations, or lack thereof, that I questioned and berated myself: What was I doing there? Who was I to be the one Latina in the English Department at UPenn? Where did I get the audacity, the right to get a Ph.D.? These questions were ridiculous, but I had become my own worst enemy, especially in the isolation of graduate school. Philadelphia street encounters presented me with daily questions about what I was: Spanish? Indian? Foreign? Something? A neighbor, reading the inscription below a map of El Salvador, C.A., on my wall, asked if I was from El Salvadorca, or El

Salvador, California. Feeling alien and homeless took on a whole new meaning after that incident. It was also around this time that the Philadelphia police department officially dropped the classification terms "Hispanic" and "Latino" from their list of racial identification options. Arresting officers were bestowed the power to decide whether people were European, African, Asian, or Indigenous—check only one.

I was unidentifiable not only at the school, but in the entire city. Easy explanations became my strategy, but the constant need to define myself wore me down. Simply stating my name invited questions about my citizenship and origin. One professor asked me where my "nominal" preoccupation came from. In translation, that meant when did I begin to demand people pronounce my name correctly, you know, was it a "p.c." thing? I explained—as my job in Philadelphia was to explain—that it was when I first went to school and heard the difference between what my mother called me and what some of the teachers called me. "Letisha" was a different name, to which I didn't know to respond. And then came people's reaction—their tremendous surprise and defensiveness—when I, Salvadoran or Mexican or whatever, named "Leteesha," or "Letisha" or whatever, would explain that I am a Ph.D. candidate. My impatience and exhaustion began eroding my resistance, and eventually stress-related illness overpowered my body and mind. I decided to take a leave from school in order to heal from the "disease of powerlessness" to which I had become an accomplice and that had left my body literally struggling to defend itself. I was guilty, as Anzaldúa bravely charges, of acting out on myself society's ideas of who and what and how I was supposed to be.

Back to School: Please Bring Glue, Erasers, and Pencils

To survive the oppressive forces inherent in the education process, especially as a person of color, I have spent the last nine years working in various educational settings. I've taught art to kindergarten-age girls, tutored bilingual elementary students, counseled "at risk" middle school youth, and taught university-level writing courses. Every city where I've worked has its share of disempowered folks power-tripping on each other. My experiences, especially those with K–12 youth services, have taught me that education is a priority preceded by the politics and whims of administrators, teachers, community-based organizations, and parents who have too little resources, acknowledgment, and hope. Yet it is here, in education at all levels, that a crucial part of the work for change begins.

Once I made it to college, I was surprised and frustrated by the pointless, ridiculous authenticity game in which those around me engaged. Worse yet, beyond college campuses, similar kinds of power struggles impede the education and liberation of disempowered communities, young girls in particular. When people of color who have not challenged and healed themselves try to help youth, they perpetuate misogyny, homophobia, and prejudice. I see those of us who are supposed to be joined in liberation struggles fighting each other. We're blindfolded, dizzy, trying to catch those running around us, but the difference in this version of Gallina Ciega is that we are afraid, or unable, to take steps; we aren't playing the game right. The game doesn't ask us to be color blind, it just demands that we learn to expand our ways of seeing.

While the intricacy of language and the process of naming continue to be important aspects of the work for change, sometimes such issues create unproductive power struggles among women, people of color, the poor. All too often, we focus on fitting into the boxes and preserving the shape, the lines, the contents. But before we can support others, we must be honest with ourselves. The analyses we formulate about the systems we oppose must also apply to the systems we internalize and enact. The coming generations look to us for guidance, and we are responsible for them. My current stead in a San Francisco after-school program has reminded me of how we fail this responsibility; when middle school youth don't get the benefit of a summer program because of the petty politics, territorialism, and egos of staff and administrators, we have all regressed many steps.

I keep hoping that the little bit of innocence some young people still retain can teach us and offer an entering point for remembering, relearning, and modeling openness—as the girls who played together in Santa Barbara taught me. All liberation efforts, whether they focus on one specific community or group or on several, are necessary. When we're honest and respectful about the positions that we occupy in each context, we don't need to choose between remaining within "our own communities" or participating in larger ones. I have focused here on myself and on people of color's internalization of and complicity in oppression, but it goes without saying that at whatever place one occupies positions of privilege, it is always imperative to exercise self-conscious self-criticism.

Solidarity continues to be crucial, and I know that I'm still working on opening myself to such efforts. What does solidarity look like? It's more about what it sounds like—like people dialoguing. Identity, language, labels are all parts of the game, and we need to learn how to play and turn the game on itself. We all wear the blindfolds; we don't have a choice in that. But rather than blind us, the blindfolds can teach us how to see in alternative ways—instead of through preconceived static notions of how people should act, look, be. All the players should take turns being the gallina ciega and learning to follow the voices.

It's important to continue creating forums on the page and in the day-to-day for reviewing how far we have come with the goals we have set. There we can remind ourselves that solidarity is not about fighting each other over funds. It's not about "white" women and men running the organizations, adopting and mimicking stereotypical and trendy notions of coloredness. Solidarity requires the recognition of multiplicity, without the loss of specificity—that is, keeping in mind our privilege and experience. Can we learn to separate the identities that we wear, that we act out, from our complexity, which can't be conveyed in easy terms? Lunge toward the sounds.

When I first discovered the bridge and the Borderlands, the anthologies that described and deconstructed these spaces were safe places to express anger and criticism. In that vein, I offer my words as a call for all of us to make better use of our blindfolds, reinvigorate solidarity, and get to work. If we keep moving our feet to the sound of the voices, we can gain momentum for our words-

¡Gallina! ¡Ciega! ¡Gallina! ¡Ciega!
¡Hey! no peeking.

fifteen

QUE ONDA MOTHER GOOSE: THE REAL NURSERY RHYME FROM EL BARRIO

Berta Avila

NURSERY RHYMES, RAZA IN THE STREETS OF EL SEGUNDO BARRIO
    EL PASO, TEJAS . . .   JUAREZ, CHIHUAHUA

        QUE ONDA "MOTHER GOOSE"

JUAN BE NIMBLE
JUAN BE QUICK
JUAN DIED FROM A NEEDLE STICK

ONE POTATO, TWO POTATO, THREE POTATO, FOUR,
TERESITA HAS BECOME THE BARRIO WHORE

TINA CRANKED COKE, AND SHE DON'T CARE
CORINA CRANKED COKE, AND SHE DON'T CARE
SUSANA CRANKED COKE, AND SHE DON'T CARE
. . . AND THEY'RE NOT COMING BACK NO MORE

WHAT ARE LITTLE BARRIO GIRLS MADE OF
BROWN SUGAR AND SPICE, OPPRESSION AND CRIES
THAT'S WHAT LITTLE BARRIO GIRLS ARE MADE OF

ONE, LITTLE TWO LITTLE THREE, LITTLE INDIOS
FOUR, LITTLE FIVE, LITTLE SIX, LITTLE INDIOS,
SEVEN LITTLE EIGHT LITTLE NINE, LITTLE INDIOS
TEN LITTLE INDIOS . . .
    DIED DAILY IN THE VIET NAM WAR

    R.I.P. Ruben Avila

LITTLE MISS TUFFIT
WORKED THE LATE NIGHT SHIFT
KEEPING HER DREAMS AT CLOSE BAY
THEN ALONG CAME THE PALE FACED RIDER
AND FRIGHTENED MISS TUFFIT'S DREAMS AWAY

sixteen

The Hipness of Mediation: A Hyphenated German Existence

Mita Banerjee

Nobody ever told me I was different. And yet maybe their denial was actually proof. For some reason, though, shedding my difference and walking around in the skin of sameness is a dream more soothing than anything I can imagine, for one minute not to identify—emotionally—with all the ethnic minorities discriminated against in this country. Class privilege was to absolve me from this emotional identification: as the daughter of a German mother and an Indian father, both academics, no one has ever been "openly" racist to me. Yet the subtlety of the racism I felt was much harder to address let alone challenge. My father's silence when once again complimented on his German after thirty years of studying, lecturing, and writing in German only made my sense of helplessness more acute.

I decided to study "postcolonialism" as a way to express these feelings. Suddenly, my very identity was hip; it seemed fitting for a person of "mixed ancestry" to study a literature by migrants, books in which all protagonists happened to be "hybrid." Yet the transvaluation of hybridity made me uneasy: a hyphenated existence was the thing to be; yellowness was not inauthentic but instead better than the dullness of being either (simply) black or white. I began to suspect this consensus on the new palatability of difference, a toned-down difference, an enjoyable exoticism. Enjoyable for whom? As "postcoloniality" has become historically and culturally indefinite, mediation is said to be no longer a burden but an asset. A fusion of both cultures, I'd become a bridge in its own right, a token hybrid since negotiation between the cultures making this hybridity was no longer attempted.

Suddenly accepted as future norm in this fusion of cultures, I began to closet this anger that in the multiculturalist consensus seemed out of place. Rereading *This Bridge,* the anger I find there soothes me. I'm afraid that I'll lose this rage, settle for less: for the subtle fetishization of a particular brand of cultural difference, for well-meant investigations into the reason for my tea-colored skin, and for the reassurance that I need never identify with the non-hybrid and hardly privileged Nigerian who doesn't even speak German.

In Germany, I've never been non-white. Mine was a whiteness of privilege; class has somehow enveloped me in whiteness. In academia, my father's Indianness was an exception, the living proof that brown men can think. Yet my class privilege is always disrupted by my knowledge of its contingency, its arbitrariness: Why do all the people who clean the university where I work look like me? I went to a carnival event last year; the only people in the sold-out town hall who looked like me were waiting tables. A shock of recognition on both sides; I would have preferred to spend the evening with them, waiting tables; my privilege was something I had somehow usurped.

Born in Germany, I speak the language, German, the only language I can speak perfectly, if there is such a thing as the perfection of a native speaker; in Germany, your language is your passport. Or is it? Every time I'm at Frankfurt Airport, people insist on addressing me in English. As I strive to shed the accent I don't have, my language suddenly sounds artificial, thus confirming their prejudices—I don't look German. Spanish, more likely. Mediterranean. Exotic. In my quest for Germanness, I yearn for authenticity. My language betrays me, and I try for the authentically authentic: German dialect. Surely, I must be a native (German) given this perfect regional dialect I adopt. The person at the counter, however, continues speaking English. I babble on helplessly.

In Germany, my toned-down cultural/racial difference is not meant to be deciphered. As Portugal, Spain, and Italy, precisely in their meaning as Mediterranean, are mutually interchangeable to begin with, the riddle thrives on the pointlessness of its resolution: the provenance of this dash of cultural difference mixed with "our" sameness is of no interest here. I am enticing, then, mostly as the object of speculation. Because this speculation is couched in the politically correct terms of a (well-meant) interest in cultural difference, I can't expose this multicultural guessing game as a fetishization of a generic difference.

My gender furthers this exoticizing project. At conferences, the same people who benevolently comment on the assets of postcolonial studies as a discipline, sitting opposite me at dinner, then discuss the assets of my nose-ring. Where, exactly, do the politics of race and gender intersect? Would they have discussed parts of my body if I'd been white? Would people ask me to prepare Ceylon tea for them in a university setting if I were a man? In this context rereading *This Bridge* comforts me, for it articulates the pain inherent in these contradictions, in these intersections of race and gender, and the solace of not having to resolve them.

Even as I begin writing this essay, its structure starts falling apart—fractured by all the connections and contradictions. Connections emerging with a vengeance, it seems to me, because I never explore my feelings about these issues, issues that overlap with but cannot be completely contained in academic theory, the postmodernist and postcolonialist theories I deal with every day as an Americanist in Germany. However, being an Americanist does put me in touch with a discourse on culture and hyphenation only beginning to establish itself in Germany. This essay is part of my closet agenda, an experience that I know is true, authentic, as close to authenticity as I can get—never the authenticity of culture or language, but that of experience. It's this authenticity of experience I find in Donna Kate Rushin's poem: "I must be the bridge to nowhere / But my true self" (xxii).

But of course, I've become too diplomatic to mention this authenticity to anybody, even to my father, whose experience in Germany, I assume, is similar to (or even worse than) mine. He tells me to be diplomatic; don't be "militant," don't accuse people of racism. I understand that he doesn't want me to get hurt, but his words are a betrayal. His silence frustrates me.

Diplomacy. As I write these words, the anguish I feel is somehow reassuring, tells me I have not quite lost track of this authenticity of experience that must not be mentioned theoretically, ever. Authenticity is an essentialist term that has become unspeakable. I am aware of this contradiction; I silence myself. It scares me that I'm getting better at diplomacy;

I know exactly what the other person wants me to say. Whenever I state that Germans can be racist (a racism that they'll acknowledge only if someone is physically injured, pushed in front of a train, beaten to death), I am quick to say that of course racism exists in other countries too. They are so predictable. In Germany, the uniqueness of German experience, after the Holocaust, must never be implied. In this diplomacy, I silence my own anger by relativizing the atrocious reality.

I wear my diplomacy like a mask (though sometimes it slips), a mask whose strategic necessity I sometimes forget by forgetting about the anger it hides. In a way, this relativization of German experience is also a diplomacy of translation, a translation that, twenty years after *Bridge's* publication, has become the be-all and end-all of multiculturalism. I am hip because, as Salman Rushdie has told us, "translated beings" like myself are always preferable to the narrow-mindedness of cultural belonging. What I've called inauthenticity, I am told, is the actual, true state of (postmodernist) being. It is in a spirit of revenge, of subversion, that I return to this anger at translation in Donna Kate Rushin's "Bridge Poem": "I've got to explain myself / To everybody / I do more translating / Than the Gawdamn U.N. / . . . / I'm sick of it / . . . / Stretch or drown."

I'm asked to sit next to the German consul general in Toronto at a reception at York University. His name connotes both German nobility and an origin in a part of Germany notorious for its racism. I tell myself not to be prejudiced. What's in a name? The following hours are a nightmare of racist predictability. The clumsy obviousness of this discourse. Oh, you're a vegetarian—of course you would be, he smiles at me. Even as I open my mouth to say that my vegetarianism has nothing to do with my ethnicity, these words are transformed, in mid-air, into speech bubbles, silent gestures incomprehensible to him: everything will be reduced to stereotypes of culture. As he leers at me, I wonder at the intersection of racism and sexism: Which box should I check now? I console myself by thinking that he acts as if he had come out of a theory book; I want to inform him that this is what I do for a living, argue about or against people like him. In his small talk I'm subsumed under the generic category of cultural difference: Indians all like colorful clothes; Cambodians are childlike; gypsies should settle down and stop thieving. He uses the German term for "gypsy," *Zigeuner*, whose etymology denotes "traveling con-men," language being inextricable from racism here. I tell myself that people like him are why political correctness will never lose its urgency.

My silence is suffocating me, the language of diplomacy only makes things worse. I finally escape, seize on the only non-white person (by German standards) in the room, a Turkish-German woman, and tell her, exasperated, what happened. They're so predictable, she says. In such instances it's less ethnicity than non-whiteness that matters; ironically, as I share my nightmare with this Turkish-German woman, we assume the sameness that racists project onto us to begin with. As Nellie Wong writes, cultural difference, to the racist, is always generic, interchangeable: "when I was growing up, people would ask / if I were Filipino, Polynesian, Portuguese" (8).

We arrive at a familiar deadlock: I repeat the consul general's gesture of my generic difference because I cannot help identifying with all these peoples he rallies against: Sintis and Romas, Cambodians, Indians—I now feel I'm one of them, feel the non-whiteness of my own skin. I willingly become a native informant. Even in this absurd conversation, if I do not try to rectify the historical ostracizing of Sintis and Romas as uncivilized because of an inbred itineracy, who will? The burden of non-whiteness I carry not only beneath my own skin but on my shoulders, on my back— the burden of having to represent so many non-white peoples. I blame myself for knowing so little about these cultures, for not being a more informed informant. Latching onto the easy excuse that their ethnicity or culture has very little to do with mine except for the near-sightedness and narrow-mindedness of racism blurring our faces into one would have been irresponsible in this context. And yet my sense of responsibility confirms his prejudice that of course I would be able to represent my fellow "ethnics."

At the same time, I'm aware that in this conversation with a racist consul general I am both inside and outside his discourse: paradoxically he speaks to me only because I speak the language, his language (German), and speak it well enough to follow his sophisticated (he thinks) and dubious (I think) argument. Racism has never been sophisticated; it is so predictable in the constellations it takes. I wonder if he thinks, for one minute, about the possibility of my identification with "them," my resemblance to them being the reason why he latched onto this topic to begin with. Or does my class and academic privilege prevent this insight on his part? Sometimes I wish I could take refuge in this class privilege, and preclude my identification with the Pakistani colleague a white bus driver complains to me about. Yet losing this identification would be losing one of the few things I like about myself.

I want to wear this interchangeability of cultural difference like a mask, want to confront them in the guise of their own stereotypes only to drive home the point that culture is not predictable. I join Amnesty International as a safe space where surely no one can be racist. An older member whose opinion I truly value wants to share an anecdote with me, an anecdote that to him is precious, about his past; he is drawing me into an inner circle of sameness, of Germanness, of belonging. The anecdote centers on his mother's war memories of African-American soldiers who were so childlike, always playing games. It's in their nature. I'm speechless. Disappointed. I tell him that culture can never be reduced to any innate qualities, let alone qualities like playfulness, rhythm, or happiness. So much for safe spaces.

Being both Indian and German, German and Indian, I want my face to be unreadable. Where does the Germanness begin and where does the Indianness end? And yet at times I am unreadable to myself, as my face seems to be neither Indian nor German. Maybe people are right after all, and I really am Portuguese. Sometimes I look Italian to myself. Conversely, this unreadability is precisely the point: as marginality and ethnicity (always in the sense of difference) have become fashionable, hip, unreadability has itself become an asset. My face is all the more mysterious because so many cultures—races—can be read into it, an ethnic or postcolonial puzzle where origin is not the point, but speculation is. Yet in embracing cultural difference of any kind whatsoever, because of its subversion of white German standards, I myself seem to be making the identical move: I scrutinize strangers' faces, trying to divine the origin of their difference, trying to recognize my own difference in their faces. Is my obsession any better because it arises from identification rather than exoticizing fascination?

There is yet another meaning of masking: I long for a time when, trying to imagine a German face, Germans will be able to close their eyes and see nothing, a blur, because Germanness can no longer be conceived in ethnically definite terms. I long for a time when any face can be German and people looking like me will never again be complimented on their fluency in the German language. Thus I long for the solace of sameness, of walking around in a white German person's skin and sitting back when the news is on. The luxury not to identify with an asylum seeker clubbed to death by angry skinheads whose transgression, again, is never part of a pattern of xenophobia but a (never-ending) series of isolated youthful errings.

I watch a talk show on the political resistance to bi-nationality, to granting German citizenship to bicultural citizens while letting them retain the passports of the country they initially emigrated from. A Turkish-German actress, Renan Demirkan, accuses German politicians of racism. Her tone is emotionally charged; the politicians she addresses seem to be ashamed of her immaturity, her lack of diplomacy. I feel both elated and depressed. Elated that someone is saying out loud things I have known to be the case all along; depressed because as an actress she can say the things I can't. I have learned to couch my feelings in academic language, the language of postcolonial theory, that will offend no one.

The postmodernist provisionality of postcolonialism seems to reflect my own mixed heritage. Postcolonial theory stresses in-betweenness in all its manifestations, in Homi Bhabha's dictum that it's theoretically non-productive to retain the division between colonizer and colonized; in the (postmodernist) assertion that the opposition between previously opposed political parties on the right and on the left has evaporated; and, above all, in its privileging of hybridity. For hybridity involves acts of translation, a relativization of cultural difference in order to enable its blendability. Even more disturbingly, this penchant for hybridity also holds true on the level of race: time and again, I wonder why all fictional protagonists in canonized postcolonial fiction are racially hybrid and living in western metropoles. Cultural difference, I fear, is meant to "spice up" the sameness or even the self-avowed dullness of white privilege; but this difference can only be incorporated in its toned-down form—exotic rather than threatening. In my mixed cultural/racial ancestry, I have become the epitome of hipness. Yet mine is a difference in which the norm of whiteness can still recognize itself; because of this recognition my skin color is never quite as threatening as my father's.

This fashionable notion of hybridity is also the epitome of bridging. Bridging, in turn, seems to be what my academic life is all about. How to explain my experience without offending anyone, an explanation that, most of all, depends on my ability to learn *their* language. Even as I try to speak about racism, a racism that permeates the way I see the world, I have to somehow aestheticize it, strip it of its vulgarity. On good days, I tell myself that perhaps my message is nevertheless subversive; I bridge the gap between their experience and mine by coding this message in a way they may or may not understand. My only comfort: although in coded language, I keep on speaking. Reading Rushin's poem, I am suddenly aware how sick I am of constantly having to bridge, a bridging that seems to start in my very body, its racial ambivalence or in-betweenness; the desire to finally shed the mask of this strained non-offensive coding. If they knew what I'm really talking about. The power of *This Bridge*, twenty years after its publication, is inherent in its courage to disregard the code of academic propriety if this propriety presupposes the repression of the personal, of the alleged triviality of racism; the courage to argue for a revolution of the academic sphere instead, to enlarge the academy until, like Maxine Hong Kingston's universe referred to at the very beginning of *Bridge*, it will be large enough for contradictions: "I learned to make my mind large, as the universe is large, so that there is room for paradoxes."

I turn to *This Bridge*, also, for another reading of hybridity that acknowledges the pain of in-betweenness. It seems to me that postcolonial theory's blindness to anything but the assets of unbelonging arises from its focus on reforming mainstream culture—only by subverting the dividing lines of racism can in-betweenness be celebrated. In my own life, I've experienced in-betweenness more in terms of a longing for authentic Indianness; it's this longing that I find in mary hope lee's poem: "not yellow / not no high brown either / . . . / she prayed / for chocolate / semi / sweet / bitter / sweet" (9). I find myself wanting to delve into the depth of an Indian culture that postcolonial theory tells me does not exist; and perhaps it does not exist except for hyphenated, quasi-Indians like me who don't even speak an Indian language. The nostalgia for something I have never quite known remains. Whenever I see a "real" Indian woman, an Indian-Indian woman, I find myself staring at her, wanting to look like her. And inevitably, the (white) people I talk to about this fascination tell me these women are too ethnic, too different—hyphenation being the more attractive *look*.

Thus in the context of cultural difference as the "enriching" of white sameness—an enriching predicated on the possibility of assimilation into this sameness by virtue of toned-down foreignness–it seems absurd for me to long for the solidity of deep brownness that lee addresses in her poem. To shed the sense of in-betweenness appears absurd. At the same time, this deep brownness is itself a sign of a less hybrid cultural belonging—cultural belonging that has come to be seen as an idea of bad faith, since hybridity, in its racial or cultural sense, is always more enticing than any semblance of homogeneity.

Writing this piece has been immensely difficult. Above all, I am afraid of losing my own sincerity because whatever I say has its echo in postcolonial theory, a fashionable discourse, but it's an echo in a different key. It celebrates the hyphenation I experience as disorienting, even painful, as being hip, normative; it declares essentialist, even potentially chauvinist, a longing for culture, for a darker skin as the marker of unmediated, non-hyphenated ethnicity. But something about this search for sincerity is even more disturbing to me: if ethnicity, if talking about hyphenation and interculturality in all its guises has suddenly become fashionable, I am afraid I will start using phrases for their mere sound, knowing they will fit into a jargon I can no longer escape; that I'll substitute jargon for essences. Perhaps in this sense also, given the hipness of hyphenation, I've become unreadable to myself, not knowing whether the things I am writing are sincere, really personal, or a show of sincerity. The use of the personal only as a footnote or anecdotal illustration of the academic. At the same time, I hope that my awareness of the jarring accord of real experience and its fashionable discursivization in postcolonial studies will at least be some kind of safeguard. But maybe not.

Finally, *This Bridge* reminds me that the personal is so much more than an embarrassing footnote to a sophisticated academic discourse. This discourse only makes sense if it can be traced back to the personal from which it abstracts but which it must never dismiss. I've learned to trivialize the personal. Even as I write this essay, I feel the urge to slip into a more academic discourse, to support these everyday experiences with something more substantial. At the same time, I want to stress my racial/cultural difference in an academic context so contented with itself, with its own multicultural tolerance: I want to jeopardize my own token position in this discourse by making them see that benevolence can never be enough, that nothing short of a revolution of the entire discourse will do. Again, I am shocked at how being steeped in postmodernist theory makes me police my own thoughts. Revolution, how vulgar a term, smacking of a passé materialism and an obsolete belief in political change. In this context, then, my return to *This Bridge* feels like exuberant defiance. Cherríe Moraga and Gloria Anzaldúa write, "We named this anthology 'radical' for we were interested in the writings of women of color who want nothing short of a revolution in the hands of women—who agree that that *is* the goal, no matter how we might disagree about getting there or the possibility of getting there in our lifetimes" (xxiii–xxiv, author's emphasis).

These thoughts remain fragments that I cannot seem to connect into a more coherent order. Yet this fragmentation is soothing; it betrays that I have not quite been numbed, lulled by the benevolence of a current academic consensus on the hipness of my existence. Maybe this fragmentation is as much a sign of my helplessness as of the anger I may have sustained after all. This anger I will try to keep alive, trusting in the solace that *Bridge* provides—a solace which tells me that this anger, as much as the reality of racism it stems from, is anything but dated, and can help us revise the easy exit of hipness.

seventeen

Living Fearlessly With and Within Differences: My Search for Identity Beyond Categories and Contradictions

Shefali Milczarek-Desai

> *People keep asking me where I come from*
> *Says my son.*
> *Trouble is I'm an American on the inside and oriental on the outside.*
> *No Kai*
> *Turn that outside in*
> *THIS is what American looks like.*
>
> —Mitsuye Yamada, "Mirror Mirror"[1]

People who live at the margins of categories provide an especially valuable starting point for exploring all the ways that identity can be deconstructed or reconstructed.

—Mary Coombs

Growing up in Phoenix, I did not know I was different until the girl behind me at the drinking fountain line called me a nigger. I was in the fifth grade. The eldest daughter of Indian immigrants, I was forced to think about my identity at a young age. At school I tried to be as "American" as possible: I wore western clothes and carefully monitored my pronunciation. Conversely, within the Indian community, I was not "Indian" enough: I did not stay indoors, babysit, and serve food to the *uncles* like other "good" Indian girls. The *aunties* shook their heads and whispered, "That girl will never get a good boy, her skin is too black and she is too *Americanized*."

I have often wondered what this term, *Americanized*, means. To my white friends, it is positive—a sign that I have succeeded in "fitting into" U.S. culture. For Indians, it is an insult—to be bestowed upon brown girls who think they are white and call themselves *feminists*. The idea of being *Americanized* taught me that there was a rigid distinction between Indian and American (this view was reinforced by both the Indian immigrant community and my American peers). It also taught me to believe that I could either be Indian or American, but not both at the same time. I attributed my feminism and my disdain for the rigidly defined gender roles prescribed by Indian culture (or what I had been led to believe was "authentic" Indian culture) to being *Americanized*. On the other hand, when diversity, multiculturalism, and ethnic food fairs started becoming a fad in the early 1990s, I claimed my Indianness so that I could believe the exotic picture of myself that was being painted all around me. Although I had some sense that my identity was not singular—indeed, I always felt uneasy whenever someone asked me where I was from because I knew the expected (and legitimating) response was to name some far-off place instead of the mundane but truthful answer, "I'm from Phoenix"—I thought I had to choose to be either Indian or American and that I could not be both at the same time.

The project of integrating the brown girl who spoke a bizarre Gujarati-English language and ate with her hands, and the woman who called herself a feminist and had been raised in the Arizona desert, unconsciously began when I went to college and read Bharati Mukherjee's *Jasmine,* and *This Bridge Called My Back.* Through the pages of Mukherjee's book, which portrayed "Third World" women in their native countries and as western immigrants, I became aware that women of color were *other* in two respects: as women and as people of color. For the first time, I began to wonder if western feminism could apply to all women because the feminist discourse I had been exposed to in my women's studies classes employed the figure of a western woman as its model for all women. What was and was not considered feminism depended upon western women's notions of terms such as *oppression* and *liberation,* and women of color who chose to follow certain cultural customs and traditions were looked upon as "oppressed" and in need of western feminist "liberation." The feminism I learned did not allow for a two-way dialogue with women of color because women of color were not viewed as equals who could provide western feminists with important insights and lessons of their own.

And then it occurred to me that Mukherjee's characters weren't the only ones made invisible by western feminism because the feminist essays and icons I had studied did not prepare me to understand women like my own mother. Western feminism taught me that Indian women were weak because the great importance they placed on their roles as daughters, mothers, and wives led to their oppression by their families and their culture. And yet my mother left her homeland to find work, unmarried and alone, when she was very young. And she, in turn, was raised by a woman whose husband abandoned her with four children and one still in the belly so that my mother and her siblings were brought up by a household of strong, independent women. Thus, the feminism I knew did not seem to take the lives of women like my mother and grandmother into account when it defined "oppression" and "liberation," and this same feminism created an either/or choice for women of color such as myself: forcing us to choose between our cultures and our struggles as women in patriarchal systems.

The women I found in *Jasmine*, on the other hand, were different from the feminists in my women's studies texts because they redefined the very idea of what it meant to be a feminist, a woman of color, and an American. These Indian immigrant women accepted both their Indian identity and their newborn American selves: they were intimidated by America and they embraced America; they were altered by America and they altered America. In short, they found ways to live with and accept their many identities and, in the process, showed me that there was more than one way to be a feminist—a lesson my mother and grandmother had often tried to teach me.

Eager to find new ways of understanding feminism and my identity, I read *This Bridge Called My Back*. I felt an immediate solidarity with Nellie Wong's "long[ing] to be white," Rosario Morales's frustration with categorizations, and Cherríe Moraga's refusal to split the white from the brown. I learned that I was not alone, nor was I the first woman of color to feel the contradictory pulling and tearing created by simplistic invocations of words like *culture, tradition,* and *identity*.

And yet, there was something missing in both *Jasmine* and *Bridge*. I am an Indian woman, but not in the same way Mukherjee and her heroine are: I have no accent, I carry an American passport, and I have never lived in India for more than a few months. I am a woman of color, but not in the same way many of the authors of *This Bridge* are: my parents are immigrants from the other side of the world; I do not share a sense of history with women of color who can point to their roots in this country; I have known privilege through my upbringing in a middle-class family, my membership in one of the "model minorities," and my heterosexuality. Thus, although *Jasmine* and *Bridge* taught me that I had to redefine my notion of identity, they did not address the problems I would face in effecting this task. For instance, I felt "white" much of the time—I speak perfect English and I know how to "fit in" with the dominant, middle-class U.S. culture. Many of the voices emerging from *Bridge*, though they struggled with their "white" identities, seemed further removed from the dominant paradigm and I envied their ability to identify with their respective cultural groups. Additionally, many of the women of color represented in *This Bridge* found solidarity with other women of color both within and outside their respective cultural groups. I, on the other hand, had found it difficult if not impossible to find a community of American-born, Indian women similarly plagued by questions of identity, cultural meaning, and the adequacy of western feminism.

Realizing that I would have to embark upon my own journey and create an identity for myself, I traveled to India. I did this for many reasons: First, I knew what "American" culture was (it surrounded me) and I knew what Indian immigrant culture was, but I did not know what it meant to be

"Indian" outside a western context. Second, although I knew my identity was different from both those Indian women who are immigrants and those who live in India, I wanted to know how to think of myself in relation to them. Finally, I journeyed to India to re-think the feminism with which I had been indoctrinated and, perhaps on an unconscious level, to seek forgiveness for the narrow western feminist light in which I had, until recently, viewed Indian women, including my grandmother and mother.

My first destination in India was the home of my maternal grandmother. When I was twelve, Ba (the Gujarati word for grandmother) had come to live with us in Phoenix. I vividly remember watching a small, wiry woman wrapped in a light-gray sari step off of the airplane. My siblings and I had expected a plump, gift-giving, cookie-baking grandmother like the ones we had seen on television. Instead, Ba seemed more interested in making sure we completed our chores and homework. For a long time, I resented this foreign woman who scolded us for our "American" ways. Since I didn't begin to appreciate Ba until the end of her stay in the United States, I was determined to visit her in India, and, this time, to really hear what she had to say.

When I went to see her, Ba lived in one of India's many burgeoning towns, once peaceful villages surrounded by forest now taken over by developers capitalizing on the insatiable needs of an overpopulated country. Ba lived with my uncle, his wife, and their son. Every morning I hauled water up four flights of stairs for the day's cleaning, cooking, bathing, and drinking needs since there was no running water in the building. Once a day, Ba and I ventured out to the local open-air market to buy fruits and vegetables for the evening meal, the leftovers from which constituted lunch the following day. I spent the rest of the day helping my aunt and Ba to clean the tiny flat, cook for my uncle and cousin, wash clothes and hang them to dry, napping when the hot Indian summer sun was at its brightest and relaxing after dinner by listening to Ba weave stories of people and places that had long since ceased to exist.

Through her memories, Ba took me to the small village where she was born and spent the first few years of her life—a place without cars or electricity, a place where the women would go to the river each day to bathe and wash their families' clothes. When Ba reached school-age, she and her sisters were sent to a convent school in India because her family valued education for girls as well as for boys. Ba confided in me that she had wanted to be a doctor but when she was eighteen, Ba met a young man who told her she was pretty and that he would die if she did not marry him. Despite her mother's advice that she stay in school and pursue her education, Ba, naive and unaccustomed to being flattered and wooed by a man, chose to abandon her would-be medical career and married my grandfather.

After her marriage, Ba moved to the big city of Bombay to live with her husband's parents in a joint-family home. When Ba was pregnant with her fifth and last child, my grandfather left her for his mistress. Ba's in-laws denounced their son's actions and offered to take care of Ba and her children. Although Ba remained with her husband's family for a brief time, she ultimately chose to return to her hometown. There, she raised her children with the aid of her widowed mother and her two unmarried sisters. Together, the four women worked to earn enough money to support the entire household. When Ba recounted her struggle to raise her five children, I marveled at my grandmother's courage and found, in her personal narrative, feminist acts of strength and defiance. Ba's "feminism," though, had little to do with overthrowing oppressive, patriarchal systems and more to do with survival. And yet, Ba's stories *were* about Indian women coming together, making their own choices, and collectively fighting to preserve their families and their freedom. The difference between the feminism I knew and the feminism I witnessed through Ba's stories was that the Indian women in these stories did not ultimately reject their cultures or the customs that upheld their cultural norms and values. Instead, they worked within their cultural framework as both traditionalists and revolutionaries. This point is illustrated well by my grandmother's views on marriage.

Despite Ba's unfortunate marriage and subsequent departure from the traditional joint-family structure in which she was expected to live, my grandmother had no repugnance toward the institution of marriage. In fact, Ba actively encouraged her daughter, my mother, to get married even though she simultaneously encouraged my mother to excel in her studies and be independent so that she would not have to rely on a man for her survival. Ultimately, Ba told me that my mother left India in order to avoid the pressure to marry. For me, Ba's desire to see her daughter married was a contradictory message because, while Ba had succeeded in living most of her life as a strong, single, independent woman, she wanted her daughter to assume a traditional role that had brought my grandmother much sorrow. Furthermore, Ba's contradictory message—praising her daughter's individual achievements while upholding traditional gender roles within the family—was the same contradictory message I struggled with in my relationship with my own mother.

My mother, perhaps desiring to do what her mother never could, wanted to become a doctor as well. But it was not a man who stole my mother's opportunity to fulfill her ambitions; my grandmother did not have enough money to pay for medical school and my mother earned her degree in physical therapy instead. When there was a shortage of nurses and physical therapists in North America, my mother decided to apply for work in Canada. When she was twenty-six, my mother left India to work as a therapist halfway across the world.

My mother arrived in North America in a sari with a single suitcase. She took a cab to the Toronto YWCA, where she was given a small room to sleep in and told she could use the communal kitchen. Today this story seems rather benign, but at the time it was almost unheard of for an unmarried Indian woman to leave India by herself and to live and work so far away from her family and homeland. My mother continued to trailblaze by not marrying until she was in her mid-thirties and, even then, it was a man of her own choosing, not someone chosen for her by her family. Even after she married and had three children, she continued to work full time. Like her own mother, my mother encouraged me and my sisters to pursue their dreams, to study hard, to be independent thinkers, and to stand up for what we believed. I learned those lessons well. The lessons I did not learn were the contradictory messages acted out on a daily basis: she came home after working twelve-hour days to cook large Indian meals for us, always serving my father hot rotis and waiting to eat until everyone else had finished. She covered her head and played the part of the quiet, loyal wife whenever we traveled to India and attended events within the Indian community. The most contradictory message, however, was my mother's wish that my sister and I would marry Indian men and have "Indian" families of our own.

In *Dislocating Cultures: Identities, Traditions, and Third World Feminisms*, Uma Narayan writes that "our relationships to our mothers resemble our relationships to the motherlands of the cultures in which we were raised. Both our mothers and our mother-cultures give us all sorts of contradictory messages, encouraging their daughters to be confident, impudent, and self-assertive even as they attempt to instill conformity, decorum, and silence seemingly oblivious to these contradictions" (8). I felt that my mother, by deviating from established cultural norms in her own life and supporting my independence, encouraged me to decide for myself whether or not to follow certain customs and traditions. At the same time, she warned that I would "lose" my Indian culture and identity if I refused to comply with cultural expectations. I found similar contradictions during the time I spent in India with Ba and in conversations with other Indian women who, despite their independence, intelligence, and ability to challenge existing paradigms, continued to value their roles within their families and their communities even if this "interfered" with their individual goals.

And then I began to see that the contradictions I found in Indian women (including my mother and grandmother) highlighted the very difference between western feminism and what I have come to think of as "Third World" feminism. While western feminism creates the illusion that I must either choose to be a strong, independent woman or play a role in my family and community, Third World feminism allows us to embrace and express several identities. For example, my grandmother taught me about the importance of self-reliance and individual courage while upholding traditional values of family, community, and marriage. Likewise, my mother's feminism (her independence, her determination, her ability to sidestep convention when it did not fulfill her needs) coexists with her traditional roles as Indian daughter, wife, and mother.

I should add, however, that what I am calling Third World feminism is not synonymous with Indian culture. In other words, the mixture of rebellion and conformity I found in so many Indian women's lives is not, I think, an inherent or even sanctioned component of Indian culture, which is largely defined and controlled by Indian men. In this way, Third World feminism shares common ground with western feminism because both strains of thought contain women who subvert and distort dominant discourses. The difference between the two lies in western feminist beliefs that there is only one "correct" way to do this: by denouncing marriage, rejecting communal/familial structures, and refusing all traditional roles. Third World feminism, on the other hand, seems able to balance western feminist values of individualism and independence with more "traditional" values of family and community because it recognizes that women can express both sets of values/identities and still challenge dominant discourses. Perhaps most important, Third World feminism recognizes the importance of what Chela Sandoval, in her essay "U.S. Third World Feminism: The Theory and Method of Oppositional Consciousness in the Postmodern World," terms "differential consciousness." According to Sandoval, "differential consciousness" refers to the ability to "read the current situation of power" and "to self-consciously [choose] and [adopt] the ideological form best suited to push against its configurations" (15). As Sandoval astutely points out, "differential consciousness requires grace, flexibility, and strength: enough strength to confidently commit to a well-defined structure of identity for one hour, day, week, month, year . . . if readings of power's formation require it" (15). Thus, Third World feminism gives expression to our ability—largely born out of necessity—to move/travel/flow in and among our many selves.

Coming to an understanding of Third World feminism not only expanded my definition of feminism, but also led me to expand my definition of identity. What I am calling Third World feminism is not a categorization in which I would place certain women, but a labeling of certain *actions*. The contradictions I witnessed in my mother's and grandmother's lives questioned my existing notion of identity, shattering what I had previously viewed as rigid and inevitable categories. Thus, Third World feminism not only destroyed western feminist categories separating "oppressed" women from "liberated" ones, but also blurred the distinction between my American and Indian identities: If what mattered were my actions and not the categories themselves, then I could resist certain traditional norms and still be Indian and I could embrace certain roles as an Indian woman and still be American. By practicing Third World feminism—that is, by acknowledging that my many identities existed simultaneously and allowing each its own expression—I finally saw a way to escape my lifelong dilemma of having to choose between selves.

When it was time for me to leave India and say goodbye to my grandmother, Ba demonstrated what I would call an act of Third World feminism. Early in my visit, Ba told me that she had melted two gold bracelets she received at her wedding so she could give two smaller bracelets to each of her granddaughters at each of our weddings. Disturbed by Ba's assumption that I would one day marry, I asked her what would become of my pair of bracelets if I never married. Ba answered by reiterating that the bracelets were wedding presents and if I did not get married, there would be no reason to give them to me. On the day of my departure, my grandmother startled me by assuring me that I would receive two gold bracelets regardless of whether or not I eventually decided to marry. Clearly, Ba had thought about our initial conversation and had decided for herself that in this instance it was necessary to break with tradition. In doing so, she had not denounced all tradition, but she had decided that it need not apply in this circumstance. At that moment, I felt as if Ba and I had overcome a sixty-year age difference, thousands of miles, and the divide separating East from West.

I did not leave India with a perfect and complete understanding of what it means to be an Indian woman or how to define Indian culture. On the contrary, I returned to the United States thinking that Indian culture, just like my identity, is a composite of many different values, customs, traditions, and viewpoints. No one could prescribe certain guidelines I would have to follow in order to be Indian; indeed, my grandmother and mother explicitly rejected certain hegemonic guidelines for Indianness yet they remained Indian. Being in India and learning about Third World feminism taught me that what my parents and the Indian community in Phoenix touted as "Indian culture" was merely one narrow definition. I arrived at Los Angeles International Airport determined to simultaneously embrace my Indianness, my American upbringing, and my feminism.

Thankful that I did not have to wait in long lines for non–U.S. citizens at the port of entry, I headed toward a young-white-male Immigration and Naturalization officer at the station labeled "U.S. Citizens ONLY" in bright red letters. I braced myself for questioning—not only because of my brown skin, but because I was wearing traditional Indian clothes and my hands were decorated with intricate patterns of henna. To my surprise, the officer merely glanced at my passport, smiled, and boomed loudly, "Welcome home!" Dazed, I walked into the August sunshine wondering if America was my home and if I was an American.

My first reaction was, I don't want to be American: the word *American* doesn't convey my complexity, it doesn't embody my ability to speak fluent Gujarati or my ties to my Indian family or community and it sure as hell doesn't demonstrate that I have spent hours in hot little kitchens cooking with other Indian women until our sweat and laughter and tears became part of the spices and sauces with which we nourished our families. American translates into white, the eradication of culture, the homogenizing of identity.

But if I did not call myself American, how would I refer to myself? Did I prefer to string a long list of adjectives after my name so that I would introduce myself as an Indian-American-heterosexual-feminist? Wouldn't this also serve to reinforce categorized identities that, in reality, cannot be neatly separated from one another? And then I remembered what Bharati Mukherjee had told me about calling herself an American as a way to "sabotage the hyphen" in *Indian-American* because, she explained, each time one of us becomes American we change the very definition of that word and change everyone else who refers to themselves as American as well. Might I not, by referring to myself as American, be resisting categorization of my many identities? And wouldn't calling myself American while displaying my cultural heritage and background challenge any singular view of American culture (by challenging that America is blond-haired and blue-eyed) as well as any singular view of Indian culture (by challenging the notion that to be Indian I must renounce my American upbringing and feminism)?

I am aware that there are those who will say, have already said, that if I call myself American, I will lose my cultural identity, my Indianness. I think they are right if they view cultures as being separate and discrete entities, each in its own individual box with well-defined boundaries. As a child of two cultures, I cannot view culture in this way; Indian and American have both been spilling over into me for as long as I can remember. One might ask why, if my identity contains both Indian and American, I would choose to call myself "American" rather than "Indian." I think there is a very simple answer to this question: America is my homeland. Chandra Talpade Mohanty, in "Crafting Feminist Genealogies: On the Geography and Politics of Home, Nation, and Community," writes that "how one understands and defines home . . . is a profoundly political [question]" (487). In declaring America as my homeland, I have defined America in a way that is as multiple as my identity. In calling myself American, I re-create what it means to be American.

Finally, by insisting that all of my identities are included in the identity "American," I refuse to view the different parts of myself as contradictions. As Third World feminism has taught me, not viewing the "contradictions" as contradictions destroys the categories that would have me choose from among my many selves, which are, in reality, inseparable.

I am still learning how to live with my many identities and how to resist the categories others would place me in. This is not an easy task. I have begun to think of Tucson as my home since falling in love with the Sonoran desert: its melt-in-your-mouth, cotton candy, pink and purple mountains at sunset; clear azure skies and replenishing monsoons falling like big, wet, sloppy kisses in the summertime. I have also fallen in love with a white man who, I sometimes think, is as foreign to my feminist friends as he is to my Indian immigrant parents. The categorizations continue and I am a "straight" girl within the feminist community, and while I recognize the privilege accompanying that category, I feel its stinging connotations as well. And some days I wonder if I will ever be able to convince them that my heterosexuality does not contradict my feminism. To my parents and the Indian community I am the rebel Indian girl abandoning her roots and heritage to assimilate into what they consider to be "white" American culture. And some days I wonder if they will ever see that my marriage to a white man does not destroy my Indianness. It seems that everywhere I go I am defined singularly: I am a law student in the women's studies department, a radical feminist within the sterile corridors of the law school, an Indian in America, an American in India, a brown woman surrounded by whiteness. Some days I wonder if anyone sees that I am all of these at once, and other days it doesn't matter what anyone sees because I am comfortable being a contrary, existing at the margins of categories.

This, then, has ultimately been a story about how I have come to define myself and my home through the evolution of my understanding of feminism, the lives of my mother and grandmother, their motherland, and my Indianness. It has also been a story about how I grew up segregating my Indianness from my *Americanized* self, and how I have spent the last several years of my life trying to become whole again: it is a story about choosing identities without even knowing that I had the choice not to choose, and realizing that identity—like each and every one of us—is multitudinous, gyrating, and ever-changing.

Note

1. Mitsuye Yamada, *Camp Notes and Other Writings*, copyright © 1992 by Mitsuye Yamada. Reprinted by permission of Rutgers University Press.

eighteen

A Letter to a Mother, from Her Son

Hector Carbajal

Querida Mamá,
I am a sea with outstretched islands
reaching the shores
of a destiny.

Estudiando the Anglo way y
aprendiendo para trabajar,
I have read countless pages
but still haven't found the complete me.

Being dual, I'm only half.
Folded and ripped in two.
I'm still trying to recover the other side,
thrown away and lying in misery.

Me dices:
"Cuando acabes la escuela,
puedes trabajar para que compres tu propio carro.
Te casas y asi no me preocupare de ti."

Meanwhile, I'm building the armor
as a shield from rocks that deform
and hurt when breaking family rules.
Remember your hurt when grandpa chose to leave?

I have been stoned.
I have cried the tears of deformity.
Now, I choose to throw the stones back
through these words—so I can survive.

Ma, you have given me everything
and you have put me on a pedestal.
But I choose to fall and build my own mountaintop
Where you can see *all* of me:

a beautiful prieto
a proud joto

a loving son
a faithful Mexicano

Undivided, unruled, and understood.
I close this letter with a gift: An island called love.
You can locate it on a map without
dividing lines and see it as a whole.

n i n e t e e n

Young Man Popkin: A Queer Dystopia

Marla Morris

Brought up as a poor and deserving girl in a milieu that was almost exclu-
sively feminine and religious, Herculine Barbin, who was called Alexina by
her familiars, was finally recognized as being "truly" a young man. Obliged
to make a legal change of sex after judicial proceedings and a modification
of his civil status, he was incapable of adapting himself to his new identity
and ultimately committed suicide.

—Michel Foucault

Suicide is enfleshed. Queer bodies are enfleshed. More queer kids commit suicide than straight kids. Teenage suicides are highest among queers.
More queer kids are attacked than straight kids. Kids who survive the
teasing and the attacks grow up. Queer childhood haunts. Grownups
internalize these sufferings. Queer bodies suffer from othering.
Herculine Barbin/Alexina lived in what Foucault calls a "happy limbo of
non-identity." A neither here nor thereness. But heteronormative desire
cannot stand ambiguity, androgyny, shifting borders, slippery parameters.
Heteronormativity demands freeze-frame sexuality. Herculine
Barbin/Alexina was finally determined to be "'truly' a young man." What
is at stake here, Foucault remarks, is Truth. "Do we truly need a true sex?
With a persistance that borders on stubbornness, modern societies have
answered in the affirmative" (xi–xiii).

The question of truth and sex is raised not only around hermaphro-
ditism (as in the case of Herculine Barbin), but around every kind of gender and sexuality. Jokingly my lover Mary comments that I am "truly"
young man Popkin. This is not a literal claim of course. It's a joke. I am
not young man Herculine, nor am I young man Luther, but I am young
man Popkin. "What is a 'popkin'?" you might ask. Well, I don't know

exactly, but whatever it is, it is me. I am not exactly a girl, not exactly a boy, but a Popkin, kind of an in-between. A straddlin-man. Not only do I look like a cross between a boy and a girl, but my scholarship straddles. Like William James and the Buddha, I always take the middle position between this and that. A straddlin-Popkin. But this kind of in-between identity comes at a price. As Foucault points out, "the intense monosexuality of religious and school life" (xiv) has made queer existences somewhat miserable. It is to my misery that I would like to turn. Misery or melancholy is embodied—brought on, in part, by being othered. I find it rather amusing and disconcerting when others cannot figure out "what" I am. Witness the double take. The look. The looking back, and back again. Sometimes I forget and say to myself, "What are they looking at? Do I have horns on my head?" I am alerted that these double-lookers are uncomfortable with androgyny. At once amusing yet also unsettling.

This Bridge Called My Back beckons me to do queer "theory in the flesh" (23). Doing theory in the flesh is not doing theory in the head only. Theory in the head is detached, Cartesian, simple(minded). Stuck in the mind. Theory en-fleshed leaks, oozes, swells. Fleshy theory is embodied, in the body, through the body, the feet. It is the hand that writes queer theory, the hand that feels, the hand that moves the pen over paper and over keys. The hand feels the theory and so too does the gut. The gut and the hand work together through the ears, not the eyes. To listen to queer theory being sounded is crucial. The eyes see Plato's Enlightenment and want to see light outside the cave. The ear listens/in embodied ways, connected, ambivalent. Feeling the pain (an embodied pain) takes its toll. No matter how much I laugh about it, the stares and "sirs" I get creep into my skin and up out of the depths of my unconscious in the form of nightmares. Nightmares are fleshy. Residues of battering queer-a-phobia have settled in my flesh, my heart, my soul, my spirit, in my mirror under my "I," under my psyche.

Toni Cade Bambara says "we will discover [ourselves] in the mirror, in the dreams, or on the path across this bridge" ("Foreword," v). In the mirror: I look but I do not know who I see. I see my dead father's face; I see the face of a young man. But queerly, I am not my dead father and I am not a young man. Thus, I cannot discover myself in the mirror, for the mirror is a monster. Go to the mirror and smash it. Mirrors = a con-fusing re-presentation of my con-fused identity. So I suffer nightmares. I can uncover more about who and what I am in dreams, but these dreams are not pleasant. I often wonder if others suffer nightmares all the time. Giant snakes attacking. Falling. Falling elevators. Beds crashing through third-floor apartments. Ghosts. Biting dogs. Getting attacked. Tidal waves. Whitemen with knives. Flooding. Barges carrying poison. Going mad. Depression is brought on by internalized hatred. Othering kills. Swinging in a tree, naked, mad. The dreamer dreamt. How to escape othering. I ask my psychoanalytically-oriented therapist: "What is wrong with me?"

There is nothing wrong with me, she says. It's the world. The world has gone mad. Queers get thrown into the space of heteronormative policing, always-already a product of a reactionary culture. This United States of America. This reactionary culture. What are we to think? There is nothing wrong with us, with queers, but there is something wrong with reactionary creeps who succeed in making us illegal, abnormal, and contemptible. But it is not only the USA. My lover Mary frames a scene we experienced while in Paris. (Queer-a-phobia is alive and well there too!) "A moment in the Musée d'Orsay. I was standing with my partner [that's young man Popkin] on the second floor of that vast train station made over into a museum, admiring a Rodin statue. . . . A guard approached me. . . . 'Your friend,' he said, 'jeune fille ou jeune homme?'" Does it really matter? What's the curiosity about anyway? Why is difference so shocking? Why should we all look the same, why should we be gender-polarized? Difference should make a difference. Riding on the Magazine Street bus in New Orleans, two whitetrash junkiemen threatened to kill me because they thought I was a "fag." Nobody bothered to help. The bus bible readings continued. Two young streetpunks playing hoops outside our door yell at me "hey fag." Young man Popkin, however, is not a man, not a fag, and not that young anymore.

No matter what our scholarly disagreements concerning queer theory might be, one thing remains clear: We do this work as a path toward social justice. We're called to respond to violence both outside and inside the academy. William F. Pinar stresses that we do queer theory "[i]n memory of those who have been murdered and beaten in gay bashings, those exterminated in the Holocaust, those who struggled to survive in families whose 'values' justify sadism, for all those who have died of and are living with AIDS, you are here with us" (2). So I do queer theory in the flesh to flesh out the notion that this call is a social one. Socially engaged queer theory is also a form of praxis. This theory = praxis is done in the flesh and on the front lines. Being out is being queer. Hiding in the closet is not queer. I do not think queer means anything goes. Queer, for me, means in your face, out in the streets, out in the academy, out to our students, standing on the front lines and taking risks. The queer bodypolitic demands that we show forth, bring forth and fight for our rights, fight against all forms of violence. It is not enough to fight for the self; we must fight for others, too. One way we can do this is through sisterhood, developing sites (cites) for conversations, conferences that allow for queer expression, writing letters to Congress to help pass laws that will make us legal, granting us the same protections our straight friends have. Social justice is a call to build community-in-difference, a community based on the idea of difference and perhaps a community where we can voice our feelings of alienation. To gather together in spaces where we can talk and share our ways-of-being, our alienated knowledges, our troubled worlds. It is to our individual and collective sufferings that we must turn. Still, the notion of collectivity needs to be qualified.

The notion of community might signal some kind of unity that in fact undermines individuality and idiosyncratic identities. Community must be rethought to stress that the self is radically other from the other and the other is also posited within the self. I am other to myself, as the mirror re-presents someone who I am not. I am a site/cite of liminality and so too is the other. Judith Butler asks, "[Does] unity [or community] set up an exclusionary norm of solidarity at the level of identity that rules out the possibility of a set of actions which disrupt the very borders of identity concepts, or which seek to accomplish precisely that disruption as an explicit political aim?" (15). We have a choice. To create yet another "norm" of queerness, or to act out of the site of difference and idiosyncratic identities that admit of shifting, changing parameters. Continually dis-rupting the idea of a core identity and community, de-constructing and dis-mantling the idea of community as consensus, resulting from the stable, core Aristotlean foundation of selfhood.

Community building is difficult, because people do not agree on basic issues and community should be built on the notion of agreeing to disagree, yet paradoxically we must agree on certain basic issues: to fight for our freedom, to fight for queer rights, to fight to stop the violence. A community should be built on what Simone de Beauvoir called the "ethics of ambiguity." Here de Beauvoir argues that ethicality is based on actions that have aporetic consequences. We can never be too sure, or too arrogant, to think that good intentions will lead to good things. Even when we think we are doing good things, our acts have multiple reactions and can inadvertently harm others. This is why queer theory in the flesh, as a mixture of theory = praxis, is risky. Coming out can also get you killed. Being out means taking risks.

One of the risks academics can take is creating academic positions for scholars who do queer theory, making sure that when we come up for tenure our writings are considered legitimate. But then, in reactionary America, not all academicians value scholarship about queers; many do not even know what queer theory is. Many do not care. Those who say they care often hide their homophobia. But it all comes out in the wash.

Social justice is also about making it queer (clear) to our assimilationist friends that we are hurting out here on the front line. Assimilationists live off the fruit of our labor. Now, some argue that there is nothing wrong ethically with assimilation. Some choose to take this path as a way to survive. For assimilationists, too queer means too dangerous. Ethicality demands living dangerously. Cowards live on an easy path. The easy life is not queer. What kind of a life would you prefer? A shopping-mall life, where things are plastic and cheap? Assimilation is cheap. So you are a consumer of others' work. Cheap grace. The easy path, or the difficult one? I do not want the last remaining moments of my life to be a reflection of the easy path, the path of assimilation. Perhaps these are existential questions. Some may say they are beside the point. But I do not think so. Questions like these *are* the point.

These queer sufferings are situated in the body. These sufferings caused by oppression and hatred manifest as melancholy, depersonalization, splitting, dissociation, numbness, and detachment. Melancholy: a time that knows no duration, a time that stops and turns stony. Melancholy caused by othering gets into my body. Moments frozen in time. This freeze frame has been introjected from without and remains buried and pressed into my unconscious.

It wasn't always this way. There was a time (I was about five) when I was happy. But then I don't remember anyway. Yet I dream that at the age of five I was free of the freeze frame. I probably felt in transit, fluid. As Homi Bhabha comments, "we find ourselves in the moment of transit where space and time cross to produce complex figures of difference and identity, past and present, inside and outside, inclusive and exclusive" (*Location*, 1). These are queer spaces, fluid and undefined. Why is heteronormative culture so invested in freezing the frame of desire?

To live a frozen identity is to live a false identity. Race, class, gender are all nicely separated in the freeze frame of false identity. But these complex and contradictory sites are messy. Unlike the call in *This Bridge*, I cannot "[b]ridge the contradictions" (23) of my identity, if bridging suggests a smooth relation between different sites of identity. Bridging contradictory sites is only possible if lived experience is felt in jagged ways. I live out these contradictory sites without attempting to link up neatly my whiteness and my Jewishness. The only thing that bridges my identity is ambivalence and liminality.

Of course whiteness and Jewishness are not essentialist categories. They are shifting, unstable signifiers. Being white and Jewish seems paradoxical because Jews have not historically been considered white in the United States. But since we're considered white now, I must think about and combat white privilege. Is my whiteness complicit with the oppression of non-whites? If so, what must I do to fight it? There are many ways of being Jewish. I suppose that whiteness and Jewishness are, at least for me, liminal states. Reconciling my queerness and my Jewishness is always tricky. Judaism is a patriarchal tradition, a het tradition. I see this quite clearly when I attend synagogue. I find these visits at once comforting and yet alienating. So I stand in the middle feeling othered. Straddlin-man. Straddlin-Popkin.

My Jewish queerness is complexified by the fact that I am and always will be working class. But I cannot easily make sense of my working-class-ness while inside the academy, which is clearly not working-class. My Steel City mentality is always there (read: born in Pittsburgh, home of the Steel Hunk). I put my silverware down on the plate incorrectly, Mary tells me. I drink beer out of a bottle, never a glass. Anathema at university dinners. Young man Popkin.

Young man Popkin dreams of studying and becoming as famous as Richard Rorty. But Rorty is clearly not working class. Can I achieve this kind of status as a queer Jewish woman? Can I achieve the status of, say, a Derrida if I continue putting my silverware down incorrectly? When asked in a *New York Times* interview if he watched TV, Derrida said that he watched it all the time. But does he watch MTV (clearly working class)? He probably watches public television and the Independent Film Channel. You know, he probably watches film, dahling. Quite honestly I don't know what or who I am. This is queer. But perhaps such queeries are misguided. Perhaps the question is "whose am I," as my dear friend Bill Pinar puts it. With the recent death of my father (August 22, 1999), I realize very strongly that I am my father's daughter. I look like my father. These are his hands, his intellect, his humor. Symbiosis perhaps. I am myself too. But not really. I am who I am, young man Popkin.

I take courage from Gloria Anzaldúa, who teaches us to "[t]hrow away abstractions and the academic learning, the rules, the maps and compass. Feel your way without blinders" (*Borderlands,* 173). Academic identity, though, mitigates against this thinking. It too can become a freeze frame for writing. It too can stifle identity. Who made up the rules anyway? Deadwhitemen no doubt. Judith Plaskow and Carol Christ warn that when we speak our voices we risk careers. "To choose to violate standards of scholarly objectivity by writing in a way that speaks to the whole self rather than the head is to run the often costly risks of scholarly deprecia-tion or academic dismissal" (6). What counts as scholarship in the first place? Who decides and why? What counts as queer theory? Well, some good ole boys in the academy do not think personal testimony important or relevant. But how do we write anything honestly or meaningfully with-out writing lifestories into our texts? Writing, detached from lived experi-ence, is flat, dull, lifeless, meaningless.

Embodied, fleshy theory is what I do when I talk queer theory. Yes, I've published highly abstract and academic articles. Reaching a small number of specialists in my own field of curriculum theory I wonder if I'm doing any BODY any good. Am I doing the work of social justice or fooling myself? Can I help stop the hate? Do I really speak my pain? Or perhaps I've become what I dread. Perhaps I'm nothing more than a middle-class, sort of, academic hiding behind concrete walls, trying to be rad? "So how do you know when you're being dissident?" Anne Middelton asked in a seminar at Berkeley: "When they come at dawn, take you away, and lock you up" (quoted in Sinfield, 53). Well, I've never been locked up. They haven't taken me away yet. But I do fear that the whitecoats will be coming soon. But maybe I'm not dissident enough.

The personal is the political. The life and writings should be testimony to social justice. Walking the walk. Walking out when not being listened to. Or perhaps we should walk with a hammer. Hammering home our alienation. Walking the walk. Talking the talk. Talking not just of abstractions, not just talking about sealing wax and kings, but talking about issues that make a difference, that dis-mantle the same-as-usual status quo homophobic discourse. Social justice comes in many packages. Facing up to someone's sexism, telling them to their faces: get real, get lost, get out of my face. Owning up. When feeling squashed by queer-a-phobia, let them own up. Tell them off. Act up and act out. The personal is the political. Being queer is being there. Be there in ways that make your voice heard. Let your voice be heard loudly!! Shout!! Be there in quiet ways. Quietly facing your opponents, but with ever the firm hand. This is the hand that uses the pen, signs the document, writes the letters, writes the scholarship that writes the literature, the poetry, that brings down oppression. This is the hand that quietly makes the difference.

Doing queer theory is about subverting the genre considered appropriate in the scholarly community. What are we living this life for anyway? If I spent my whole life imitating this frozen genre, this frozen writing style, my life would be wasted. Frozen writing is an extension of frozen identity, frozen sexuality, and frozen desire. The ways in which we write about queer theory are political. The politics of style tell much about how one negotiates one's body-in-the-world. Recently finishing my dissertation, I feel suddenly released. This "scholarly document" has taken its toll. It has proven to be a heavy burden. We go against the grain of our bodies when writing style is dictated to us by others. It is a relief to know that Anzaldúa and others encourage subversive styles in *This Bridge*.

But can queer theorists really change the academy? Can we flesh it up? Can we be truly "revolutionary" anymore? Or are these times, these postmodern times since *Bridge* hopeless? Like my father, I am a pessimist, but not a nihilist. Young man Popkin straddles between hope and doom, but mostly young man Popkin is a doomsday prophet. I don't feel very hopeful about radical change inside the academy. I suggest that utopian hopes are misguided. Toni Morrison eloquently teaches this message in her novel *Paradise*. We live in a dystopic condition. We are othered. The othering will continue. Kids will continue to be attacked, killed.

Kids will continue to commit suicide. Those who survive the teenage years will grow up to be queerdults, suffering the battering ram of queer-a-phobia, internalizing hate. The cycle continues. Liberals in the academy will talk the talk but not walk the walk. Conservative gays, lesbians, and transgendered people who choose assimilation leave radical queers on the front line, alone and in danger. When will queers be fully recognized as human beings in these United States? Probably not in my lifetime and I am young still. I am young man Popkin but I don't feel very young anymore. Being queer, being on the front line, makes me feel old.

I offer up what I term a queer dystopia. Queering the personal, the institutional, and the social through critique, skepticism, and a bit of laughter is my aim. I am not advocating nihilism. Rather, I advocate doing the work of social justice, the work of the prophets, the work of subverting the academy's norms, the work of continually undermining frozen identity and frozen desire. A dystopic condition does not draw clear lines between the psyche, the unconscious, and the social. Dream work is important for queer identities. It is crucial to think about why nightmares take over. Battering rams of queer-a-phobia seep into dreamtime. Perhaps this cannot be undone. The internalized hate is too heavy.

Giving in to the nightmare is not the answer. Giving up will not do. To close the chapter on one's life is to give up. The book of life must remain open, even if tattered, worn, and yellowed by the years. "Closure is always inadequate. The complexity of the social formation and the multi accentuality of language combine to produce an inevitable excess of meaning" (Sinfield, 37). A dystopic condition queers language and meaning because it is a site of excess and ingress. It is a straddlin place between here and there, now and then, first and second. A dystopic condition is not a resolution. I do not offer a utopian plan. As I write elsewhere, utopias historically have served to other (Morris). Utopias lead to sameness, blueprints, plans, final solutions. Utopias, from Plato's Republic to Rousseau's Social Contract, from futuristic to backward-looking romantic vision, do not sound happy endings for those of us who have traditionally been marginalized and othered. In fact, they make our place in the world even more marginalized. The notion of the new, the not yet, the perfect place yet to come, will not come because we are always already thrown into the old, into the traces of tradition and culture. The new can happen in the midst of the old, and I believe only slight change will occur. If one believes that radical revolution is possible in queer spaces, disillusionment is bound to set in. But perhaps it is at the site of disillusionment that the work begins. To become disillusioned with great/revolutionary changes will allow us to start at local sites, with particular, situated, idiosyncratic notions and goals. We change things one step at a time, one walk, one talk, one paper, one piece of poetry, one novel, one film, one conference at a time. My pessimism does not spring from nowhere. I am a product of, perhaps, a pessimistic generation. I am a third-generation Jew after Auschwitz. Hitler had his utopia.

This bridge across my back is heavy. The burden of fighting against the hate is heavy. Why can't I just "live in a happy limbo of non-identity?" (Foucault, *Herculine Barbin,* xiii). Young man Popkin did at age five. But then the "truth" of my sex had to be known. My happy life came to an end. I was "truly" an enigma. Now I am "truly" young man Popkin.

twenty

Transchildren, Changelings, and Fairies: Living the Dream and Surviving the Nightmare in Contemporary America

Jody Norton

The only thing worth writing about is what seems to be unknown and, therefore, fearful.

—*Cherríe Moraga*

In *Trans Forming Families*, a collection of life writings by and about transgendered people, Florence Dillon recounts her attempts to come to terms with her female-bodied son's masculine identity. Unable to understand why his grandmother gives him a pink velvet, lace-trimmed dress for his third birthday, the boy decides, shortly after, to change his name from Sarah to Steve. While his parents support him (reminding him, at the same time, that he has a girl's body), Steve's school is less accepting, and Dillon eventually embarks on a well-intended but disastrous feminist acculturation of Steve. Assuming that it is not really Steve's sex he objects to, but the traditional gender role prescribed for middle-class girls, Dillon seeks to reeducate Steve to a more contemporary understanding of his (birth) sex's capacities. Stressing the *agency* that educated, middle-class women (if by no means all women) have achieved through historical struggle, Dillon repeatedly points out girls' and women's achievements in exaggeratedly glowing terms. But this rhetorical strategy, carefully engineered to reinforce sex/gender congruence in her son comes, at last, to a painful end: "One day, after years of exposure to our 'women can do anything' message, my seven-year-old turned to me with tearful eyes and said, 'Mommy, you only like girls.' Suddenly, I realized that everything I'd been doing to help my child feel good about herself had instead made him feel that I didn't accept or love who he really was. My child was Steve, a wonderfully creative, articulate, and very patient boy who had been waiting his whole life for his parents to see him" (7–8).

Tracing my lineage of selves back to childhood, I find a boy through whom flowed a deep river of femininity. I was not a "sissy," and I didn't consciously feel that I was a girl. I had, instead, a very powerful identificatory bond with my mother, even to the point of symbiosis; a great affinity for the "femininity" of nature (lakes, mist, birdsong, grass, trees, solitude); and a very deep and delicate sensitivity to people and the world. And I was powerfully erotically attracted to boys and their bodies. In another time and culture, I would have been, or lived as, a girl. And in other places and other lives, I did.

Through working with female healers and therapists, I have learned many things: in the days of the matriarchy, long before written language, I was left to die on a hillside, an unwanted male infant; through many of my lives, my mother and I were strong women together; in my present life, I felt the (never-expressed) need to apologize to my mother for the male body I couldn't help having. I have learned that I cannot heal my mother, who has endured a lifelong struggle with depression, by destroying myself. Self-sacrifice is not the way to spiritual health, because self-sacrifice, even when it derives its energy from love, leads inevitably to victimhood and despair, on the one hand, and to guilt and resentment, on the other.

I know now that my fairy self flies with hir own wings. That s/he is magical, and has great power to love hirself selflessly, and to love others from that giving place of love. S/he is transformational, a healer, and a poet—but s/he is able to change, heal, and sing only in the manner that *all* animals, children, and grownups are able to change, heal, and sing, if they become free. Often, I wish that the circumstances of my life and health did not prevent me, for the time being anyway, from transforming more materially toward my woman self. I wish that like a girl Peter Pan, I could remain forever twelve, forever in bloom, forever loved by fairy and human boys. But growing older, I appreciate those diaphanous selves and relations, the shadows and pools of the woods, just as acutely as I did as a preconscious child, and with far more recognition, far deeper understanding.

Trans is as trans does. I have survived my lack of knowledge; it played itself out as heroin addiction, alcoholism, suicidality, drug overdoses, self-mutilation, hepatitis, and cirrhosis. I am lucky. And I'm grateful for my degree of recovery. I write this to help other gender-variant children— and all children—love themselves more easily and more fully, so that self-destruction does not seem the only way.

In the years intervening between *This Bridge Called My Back* and *this bridge we call home,* the mid-century work of sexologists John Money, Robert Stoller, and others, distinguishing gender from sex; poststructural theory; discourse theory; psychoanalysis; and the panoply of second-wave feminist discourses combined, enabling the conceptualization of the social construction of gender, most prominently in Judith Butler's work. At present, we are witnessing a correction of the radical social construc- tionist view, according to which sex and gender are mythic effects produced entirely out of the confluence of particular historical/environmental condi- tions, systems of representation, and cultural ideologies, toward a more balanced perspective that tries to include genetic, hormonal, and other biological and psychosocial factors in a holistic view of sex/gender devel- opment and change. For example, feminist biologist Anne Fausto- Sterling reminds us of "the embodied nature of identities and experience" (4). She writes: "There *are* hormones, genes, prostates, uteri, and other body parts and physiologies that we use to differentiate male from female, that become part of the ground from which varieties of sexual experience and desire emerge. . . . [V]ariations in each of these aspects of physiology profoundly affect an individual's experience of gender and sexuality" (22).

In my own theoretical work, I suggest that to understand gendering at the individual level we should devote less attention both to gross anatomical characteristics *and* to culturally sex-stereotyped behaviors, and look much more closely at patterns of affinity and affiliation (identi- fication and group belonging) as signs of materially influenced, but situa- tionally enacted, social identities.

In the vast majority of world cultures, of course, sex has historically been understood as determined by reproductive anatomy, and gender has existed not as an independent concept but as the identity, role, and per- sonal style common to one's sex. However, there appear always to have existed some children who have been either unable or unwilling to be "boys" or "girls" in the conventional ways their bodies suggested they should. For instance, Elagabalus, proclaimed emperor of Rome in 218 C.E. at the age of fourteen, frequently dressed in women's clothes; invested Hierocles, one of his male lovers, "with the title and authority of the emperor's, or, as he more properly styled himself, of the empress's husband" (Gibbon, 115); and "was said to have requested castration so that he could be a true woman" (Bullough and Bullough, 39).

Many Native American cultures included fully developed alternative gender roles for male-bodied and female-bodied persons who did not identify as boys or girls, men or women, respectively. Such persons are loosely referred to as "two-spirit." The alyha role among the Mohave Indians is exemplary (Devereux). A boy who was to become an alyha would demonstrate his gender atypicality by age nine to twelve, often showing little or no interest in learning his sex role and its functions. After consultation among the boy's relatives, a test/initiation would be arranged, without the boy's knowledge. Walter L. Williams retells an account first published in the 1930s: "[A]fter the ceremony, the boy is carefully bathed and receives a woman's skirt. He is then led back to the dance ground, dressed as an *alyha,* and announces his new feminine name to the crowd. After that he would resent being called by his old male name" (24). Mojave hwame, or male-identified girls, "played with boys, refused to learn women's work, and demanded a loincloth instead of a woman's skirt" (Lang, 274). Cocopa warrhameh showed an inclination to play with boys and to hunt in childhood. A "young man might love such a girl, but she cared nothing for him, *wished only to become [a] man*" (Gifford, 294). Significantly, unlike most dominant-culture gender-variant children today, two-spirit children have traditionally been accepted in most Native cultures, and often have been honored for the unusual spiritual, healing, or other socially important abilities attributed to them.

In his biography of the novelist Stephen Crane, John Berryman relates an 1894 anecdote about Crane and his friend James Huneker's encounter with a transchild sex worker on the streets of New York: "they were on their way to the Everett House when a kid came up to them in Broadway, apparently begging. Huneker gave him a quarter but then as he tagged along saw that he was really soliciting. Crane, 'damned innocent about everything except women,' did not understand till they emerged into the glare of the hotelfront and could see the boy was painted, with big violet eyes like a Rossetti angel. Huneker thought his friend would vomit. Shortly, Crane became interested, took the boy in with them and fed him. . . . Told he was diseased and wanted to be treated, Crane rang up Irving Bacheller and borrowed fifty dollars to give him. He now began a novel about a boy prostitute. . . . His book started in a railway station, with a country boy running off to New York—a scene that in Huneker's view Crane never surpassed. It was going to be called "'Flowers of Asphalt'" (86).

Transchildren have existed in ancient and modern societies, across cultures and races, in preliterate and literate communities, amid great wealth and in dire poverty. Many have been less fortunate than the alyha child above. Elagabalus, for example, was assassinated at the age of eighteen, and although the motives were political, the killing and subsequent degradation—Elagabalus's mutilated body was dragged through the streets of Rome and dumped in the Tiber—were justified on the grounds that Elagabalus's femininity was a moral disgrace. And it is doubtless no accident that Crane's young acquaintance was a street prostitute, in all probability suffering from syphilis or some other sexually transmitted disease. Many transgendered children and adults in the U.S. today sell their bodies as a means of survival, since relatively few employers will tolerate public violation of the gender taboo—and many transgenders pay with their lives for this "survival" strategy (Ordoñez; Pettiway).

While transchildren turn up in all classes and races, the poorer, less educated, and darker skinned you are, the more likely you will find it necessary to resort to prostitution, with all the risks of violence (by others on the street, by tricks, by police), arrest, drug involvement, and disease that accompany street life. But transchildren, whatever their race and class circumstances, do not, for the most part, willingly choose the street, either in the United States or elsewhere. Many come from families in which they have been sexually and/or physically abused, or from which they have been cast out. Others leave to spare their parents, brothers, and sisters public shame, humiliation, and censure—choosing, out of love for their families, to bear the entire burden of communal transphobia themselves. In *Travesti: Sex, Gender, and Culture among Brazilian Transgendered Prostitutes*, anthropologist Don Kulick records the stories of a number of travesti—born-male, transgendered sex workers who inject industrial silicone into their bodies to enlarge breasts and hips, and who live as women. Typically, the future travesti leaves home in early adolescence. "Keila . . . left at age thirteen, because she felt that if she stayed, her 'homosexual tendency . . . would shame my father and mother.' . . . When Adriana finally 'came out' as a travesti at age twelve, 'I was thrown out. *Ave Maria*, that was one of the saddest moments in my life,' she told me, crying. 'This is one of the greatest remorses I have because I was put out, thrown out, with just a plastic supermarket bag with my clothes'" (59–60).

These children rebegin their lives as sexual and economic adults, never experiencing the period of youth enabling most preteens and teenagers to acquire the education, experience, emotional growth, and self-confidence to move into the grown-up portion of their lives with some chance of happiness and success. They must leave their hometowns, taking their legacy of guilt with them, and find a city large enough to swallow them in anonymity. The family, and the community, are "healed" by forgetfulness; and the child goes forth, in loneliness and pain, to find hir way as best s/he can (*The Transformation*).

See, we're coming out of the shadow.

—Gloria Anzaldúa, This Bridge

In 1983, when the second edition of *This Bridge Called My Back* was published by Kitchen Table, transchildren did not exist. That is, most people didn't realize, or behave as if, such a kind of child existed. Nontraditional or variant gender behavior in children, to the extent it was noticed at all, was understood as play or, if it recurred in a patterned way, as individual peculiarity or pathology.

Today in the United States, transchildren of all races are still, as a rule, nameless and homeless: silenced (in their schools), disciplined (in their families, and by doctors, therapists, social workers), privately concealed, and publicly effaced. Virtually no elementary, intermediate, or secondary school teacher can or does teach about them. And extra-curricular gay clubs and gay/straight alliances that might offer them a community have recently come under attack by school boards from Florida to California. I've never seen any reference to transgendered children in the mainstream national press or on network television news programs. Transchildren, then, do not exist in their schools or in the national news media—the two foremost sources of recognition and modeling of approved (or even disapproved) cultural identities.

Gender oppression of transchildren, whether overt or covert, limits all children's freedom to discover themselves, to realize themselves as richly and subtly as possible. While relatively few children are intensely cross-gendered or disidentified with their bodies, *all* children display both "masculine" and "feminine" attributes and behaviors, to some extent, in some contexts, as these are defined within the cultures in which they live. Fears about gender adequacy, in the bipolar terms under which we operate in western dominant cultures, not only cause many children much anguish but are an important factor in limiting the mobility of spirit, the playfulness, and the imagination that children need to develop their capacities for joy, wonder, love, and connection.

We do not need a revolution, in the '60s sense, to make positive change. Assuming we have our own houses in order (a situation rather, indeed, to be assessed than assumed), we need only teach differently (in the sense that all the elders—in age, experience, and/or knowledge—teach all the youngers). *We teach first by sharing ourselves: who we have been, who we are, who we are becoming; how we have lived, how we live, how we are coming to live.* We teach through our behavior, speech, spiritual practice, affiliations, work, and play; and through the systems of representation we create and use, in speech, in performance, and in all the myriad forms of personal writing from the case study to autoethnography, to diary and journal, to memoir and autobiography, to autobiographically-inflected fiction and poetry. In sharing ourselves, we also share *our* models: those people and events that have shaped and influenced our sense of our own possibilities (whether those people and events are historical, mythical, or imaginary).

Secondly, we teach by activism, seeking to promote social justice and facilitate public acceptance of alternatively gendered people. In *Bridge,*

Anzaldúa writes of "*El Mundo Zurdo, the left-handed world,*" composed of the marginalized, the abused, and the oppressed—people who need help. But it is also a social, political, and spiritual Way. In her words, "El Mundo Zurdo path is the path of a two-way movement—a going deep into the self and an expanding out into the world, a simultaneous recreation of the self and a reconstruction of society" (208). And it is a form of alternative community, "a network of kindred spirits, a kind of family" (209)—versions of which include the kind of queer alliance Minnie Bruce Pratt writes of in *S/HE*, or the transgender community Leslie Feinberg envisions at the end of *Stone Butch Blues*. The oldest adage of community organization is that there is strength in numbers. When we join together in communities of affinity, forming strategic coalitions with other legally disempowered, socially stigmatized groups, we build a political force to be reckoned with. *Bridge's* creation out of the articulate voices and energies of many women of color, working together to free the spirits, voices, and energies of other women like, and unlike, themselves, is a powerful example of educating for social justice.

We teach, finally, by demonstrating the multiple confluences in the lives of conventionally gendered children and transchildren, illustrating samenesses and shared interests, and emphasizing the importance of securing all children within cherishing, comforting patchwork quilts of connection, affiliation, and acceptance. One strategy for normalizing the transchild, even as we recognize his or hir difference, is narrative. So far as I know, there are no children's stories about transchildren. I am writing one. But until it and other such stories are published, we need to transread the stories we have: we need to interpret *narratives* of difference specifically as *metaphors* of gender difference, so that gender-variant children can see themselves as present in their culture's literature, and conventionally gendered children can understand that everyone is not the same, and that difference is not inherently wrong. Often, a text invites transreading, through its details and the latitude of its form (a latitude always more generously afforded by oral traditions).

I do but beg a little changeling boy, / To be my henchman
                                                                    —*William Shakespeare*

When I was little, my mother, now and again, would refer to me—with love, but also with a mixture of sadness, wonder, and incredulity—as a "changeling child." Changelings have often been thought to be fairy children left to deceive parents when a human child is stolen away. Thus, a changeling *resembles* a normal child, but is crucially different: somehow inhuman, monstrous, even vaguely diabolical, but also magical. According to the Reverend Robert Kirk, writing in 1691, fairies "[A]re said to be of a midle Nature betwixt Man and Angel, as were Daemons thought to be of old; of intelligent studious Spirits, and light changeable Bodies, (lyke those called Astral,) somewhat of the Nature of a condensed Cloud, and best seen in Twilight. Thes Bodies be so plyable thorough the Subtilty of the Spirits that agitate them, that they can make them appear or disappear att Pleasure" (5). But Fuller writes, in 1642, "A Changeling . . . is not one child changed for another, but one child on a sudden much changed from it-self" (quoted in *OED*, 378). It is this sense in which my mother used the term, and this sense, perhaps, that can allow us to read Hans Christian Andersen's classic fairy tale "The Ugly Duckling" not simply as a metaphor for maturation or the search for one's sociobiological order, but as a more subtle, complex parable of the misleadingly embodied transchild, who must set out on an arduous journey, suffering physical pain and the traumas of undeserved scorn, contempt, and exclusion before discovering hir being and hir community.

"The Ugly Duckling" lends itself to such transreading in that it involves a male "child" both censored and praised in language that quite clearly privileges femininity. When the Ugly Duckling finally cracks his shell, he is described as "large and ugly" (277)—quite unlike his siblings, whom his mother calls "the loveliest ducklings I've ever seen" (276). He is assaulted by one of the ducks simply because "he's so gawky and peculiar" (280). And the grande dame of the barnyard declares that the Ugly Duckling "doesn't seem right" (280).

The first step in the Ugly Duckling's discovery of self comes when he catches sight of a flock of swans, "beautiful birds, all glittering white with long graceful necks" (289), about to set out on their southward migration. The Ugly Duckling "felt so strange as he watched them" (290). Here Andersen creates, in a few rapid strokes, an intense drama of affinity, precursory to self-recognition. The Ugly Duckling is drawn to the birds' whiteness, grace, and beauty, but with admiration, not envy. Just as a masculine boy feels awe, admiration, allegiance, and an identificatory kinship in relation to an older male "hero," so the Ugly Duckling can be understood here, parabolically, to admire the feminine beauty and grace of hir sisters, and to feel an intense, unconscious identification with, and affinity for, them.

The Ugly Duckling's accession to a valued and satisfying place in hir social world depends on a new vision of hirself and a transformed identity created by a dialectical interplay between hir own emergent sense of self and this self as perceived by others. As a swan (girl?) s/he bears hirself, joyfully, as s/he. Only then can s/he be accepted, through concentric circles of ritual behaviors, public language, and symbolic situating, as *s/he*, the beautiful, rather than *he*, the ugly. The Ugly Duckling's new social identity, in turn, is marked by, and expressed in, an appropriate language of feminine beauty. S/he is now "the loveliest of all lovely birds" (295).

We can take from this little transparable the implication that our twofold task is to nurture the emerging selves of all our children, and to educate our societies to a new understanding of the "changeling." The idiosyncratic, the strange, the wandering ("deviant") child does not have to be responded to with fear: myths of abduction, fantasies of loss of control (of family, of genealogy, of identity), and nightmare linkages to the demonic serve only to stigmatize the child, setting him or hir up for hysterical retribution.[1] When, instead, we become familiar—with a land, an animal, a culture, a person—we become more knowing, more understanding, less fearful. We see the beauty of a transchild who seems transformed anew by the transformation in our own perception. And when we open ourselves, allowing ourselves to feel the Godgivenness of the spirit to whom the body is home, we can begin to love, and to celebrate each ugly duckling as the swan s/he is.

A more contemporary children's tale that lends itself to a transreading is Anzaldúa's *Friends from the Other Side/Amigos del otro lado*. Both the preadolescent heroine Prietita and her new friend Joaquin are unconventional in their gender performativity, partially due to circumstance (construction, culture) and partially by choice. Prietita, a strong young Chicana, meets Joaquin, a recent immigrant from Mexico, when he comes to her house selling firewood. Observing his shame of the sores on his arms, she recalls the curandera, or herb woman, who is a healer. Shortly, Prietita intervenes in Joaquin's behalf with her cousin Tete and his friends, who are bullying the "mojadito" (little wetback). Joaquin thanks Prietita, admitting his fear, and she walks him home. At home (a three-walled shack), Joaquin and his mother bemoan the lack of work on both sides of the border, and Prietita promises to "tell the neighbor women about you. Maybe they'll have some work." When Prietita leaves, she invites Joaquin to play with her the next day. Sure enough, Joaquin comes the next day, in his pink shirt and matching pink sneakers, and every day after.

One day the Border Patrol—white officer, Chicano subaltern—come in search of undocumented Mexicans. Once again Prietita rescues Joaquin, and this time his mother as well, from male domination, taking them to the curandera, who hides them. Joaquin is trembling with fear, but Prietita and the curandera are angry and resolute, despite their anxiety. Once the Border Patrol is safely gone, the curandera calls Prietita and Joaquin to go with her to gather herbs. She will show Prietita how to make a paste to heal Joaquin's arms. The book ends at this moment of symbolic entry into womanhood: Prietita will learn the special knowledge of healing, just as she has already acquired the knowledge of feminist resistance. As the curandera puts it, "It's time for you to learn. You are ready now."

While the story does not directly represent Joaquin as feminine, a trans-reading of the text shows that Joaquin moves from a passive, diseased, fearful, spiritually etiolated boyspace, through a process of recovery, into an evolving community of activist women including Prietita, her mentor the curandera, and Joaquin's mother, whose strength of character has enabled her to make the dangerous crossing into the United States in search of a better life for herself and her son. The book is not a "story," in the traditional sense, as much as it is a role play: this is how you protect those made sick by poverty and oppression; this is how you form feminist communities; this is how you learn to heal others and yourself. Prietita's apprenticeship to the curandera will prepare her for a compassionate, politically conscious womanhood and, in doing so, mark her precisely as a "sister." Perhaps slight little Joaquin, in his pink shirt and sneakers, protected from the bullies and secure in a community of strong women, will learn these secret, credentialing knowledges as well. And perhaps, as he grows to adulthood, he will find that his desire is for men, but that his affinity is for women.

Perhaps, or perhaps not. The project of such a reading, particularly when children make up part or all of the audience, is to point out gently that variant interpretations/reimaginings, and variant lives that do not conform to the usual conventions, are both possible (thinkable) and okay. Not all boys need to dream of being heroes. And some boys dream of being heroines. In this story, the aggressive males are depicted as the problem, not the solution. As for Prietita, on the other hand, she may decide that gathering herbs is kind of boring. Clearly a leader, and an activist, Prietita may choose to become a social worker, labor organizer, or even a good cop (though never, one feels, a member of the Border Patrol).

Let us all, then, avoid becoming Border Patrolmen of identity. Let us not police the borders of racial, ethnic, sexual, and especially, in this instance, gender dichotomies, enforcing the law that every human being should be, and behave, as a *male* or a *female,* however those words are locally defined. Let us free our children from the shackles of gender (clumsily and inaccurately conceived as the congruent binaries male/female and masculine/feminine) so that they can use their own fairy wisdom to enjoy their always transitioning beings to the fullest, and so that they can help the little ones coming along beside them—who look up at them with such love and admiration—to be free in their turn, and in their turnings.

Note

1. Compare the myths of fairies' abduction of children with the persistent American fear of homosexual recruitment.

twenty-one

The Real Americana

Kimberly Roppolo

I am the American Woman,
and I am every bit as dangerous and wonderful
as the singers have said.
You may have more important things to do
than spend your time going on with me,
but even if I've been married fifteen times,
you'll still love me anyway.
I am democratic in my loving—
men and women,
Indian, Italian, Irish, Chicano, Chicana,
Black, Jewish, Cuban,
and even straight-up Redneck White Boys,
I have been egalitarian about
these things, about where
I have allocated my affections.
Sisters and Lovers and Friends and Brothers,
I have a hard time being selfish with.
American Women get a good dose
of the desire to be a martyr
at a
very
young
age.
I have conceived children in the
back of a green '79 Ford Thunderbird
and in my German great-grandmother's
hand-me-down bed.
I have nursed them in tipis
and in shopping malls.
I have raised them
with men by myself
and
by myself by myself.
And I even, on occasion,
have allowed others
to help.

I can fry chicken,
make jerky,
cook a mean chili,
a serious stew,
and make
the
world's
best
frybread.
My children have drunk enough
Kool-Aid to dye them permanently red, yellow, orange, green, and blue.
The identities of their fathers affects the color of their skin less than
what I weaned them on.
I've been a brunette,
a blonde,
a redhead.
And I've discovered that
all it takes to snag a man is
the irresistible
aroma of
estrogen
and
hairspray.
A checkbook
to pay for the pizza
is simply
a bonus.
The things I can do with
bacon
are mere parlor tricks.
I can
catch a fish,
clean a deer,
write a love poem,
perform emergency
C-sections,
tracheotomies,
vasectomies,
and acrylic
my best friend's
nails.

If it means feeding my children,
I can sell you anything,
and you'll pay my price—
wisdom, dope, lipstick,
a beer,
or a plate of food,
even my body.
But you'll never,
never own
my spirit,
never
put a UPC on
my soul.
But I'll feed you
if
you're hungry,
shelter you
if
you're cold.
I'll fix
your broken heart.
And I'll break it
in two
again
if
necessary,
because
my children
must survive.
It's the first commandment
of my Great Mother.
You can call me
a bitch
if
you want to.
Just don't call me whore,
Christian, or capitalist
because
if
you think
I'll be

your sucker,
you're dead
wrong
mister.

twenty-two

Shades of a Bridge's Breath

Nathalie Handal

"Who are you?" we are often asked. Who are you, if you have to struggle to answer? Who are you, if you answer and *others* still find it necessary to redefine your identity without your permission? Who are you, if you know who you are yet still struggle with the boxes *others* put you in? How do you define yourself when you're hyphenated, or maybe even bi-hyphenated, when you exist in the incessantness of in-betweenesses? Does cultural multiplicity condemn us to complicated, unsettling identities or does it liberate us from set cultural definitions that too often confine us and elevate us to a place of never-ending possibilities?

My grandmother's family left Armenia during the Turkish occupation and went to Palestine. The holy and majestic little town of Bethlehem became her home and there she married my grandfather, Nicolas, a Bethlehemite. But in the early half of the twentieth century Palestine became a dream of return. They took a boat to the unknown. Landed in France. Continued. Landed in the Americas. Continued. Landed in the Caribbean. But soon enough, political instability led them to yet another departure, this time to the United States. Meanwhile, my grandparents' children were in schools in Europe, Chile, Mexico. By then, Palestine was occupied and my grandparents' families became exiles within their own homeland. Today we are a large family, displaced, scattered all over the world.

My grandmother knew who she was. She had emigrated, yes, but her identity had a steady anchor. My mother was disoriented: she claimed her heritage but was very European despite her severe insistence on preserving our ancestry. Reading was her way to meet herself. But my sister Alexandra and I, who were we? Who are you, when you grow up listening to Francis Cabrel and the Police, Michael Jackson and Merengue, Farouz and Armenian duduk? Can you bridge easternness and westernness when they stand so far apart, when they do not know how to live together? And how can you accept what is expected of you when it seems impossible to build a bridge from Bethlehem to France, France to America, America to the Caribbean? When what is expected of you and what you expect of yourself, what others insist you should believe and what you actually believe are not only generations but also cultures apart?

It was difficult enough trying to weave all those elements into one coherent pattern and even harder to face the unweaving of ourselves by others. I think that *others* created dilemmas inside us. We know who we are; others have a problem defining us. Many Arabs considered us Americans or Europeans. Many Americans did not consider us *real* Americans because of our looks, accents, or mannerisms. Many Caribbeans considered us Turkos (since many Arabs had Turkish papers when they immigrated due to Turkish colonization). The Arabs integrated well among Latinos—becoming very much part of their society politically, economically, and socially. This integration is partly due to the parallelisms between the two cultures, from common family traditions to common living conditions to similar weather. Also, physically, the Arabs could assimilate easily. In France, we were considered French but with origins elsewhere—that *with* preventing us from fully integrating. We had to free ourselves from external definitions to find—or rather reclaim—ourselves. How could others define us according to their formulation—weren't we allowed to name our identity?

This question of identity has exasperated me for so long, and I've often wondered if I would ever really liberate myself from the boundaries others set. But today, I say who I am, and those who are not satisfied— that remains their issue. Unfortunately, many people still continue to impose their definitions.

I used to think that in my family, everything you did was wrong, until I met other Arab families, Armenian families, Latino families, communities with strong cultural ties. I admire their struggle—to believe so much in their past, their tradition, their homeland, that they would go as far as possible to preserve it. There is great beauty even in the silence of that struggle. Yet when faced with certain beliefs—like cultural separatism and exclusiveness or the notion that one should marry from his/her cultural background—proceeding becomes a mouth of unbearable pain, for we must accept societal change, or, at least, accept choice.

I used to think that my family was more restrictive than others. But as I became part of other Mediterranean, Latino, and Black societies, I found common grounds. Women in these societies had similar experiences of prejudice, displacement, in-betweenness, oppression, double-consciousness. When I started to read Maxine Hong Kingston, Gloria Anzaldúa, June Jordan, I discovered a comforting parallelism as they too dealt with issues of homeland and identity politics, hyphenation, marginalization, fragmentation. I found courage and hope that Arab-American women could take the steps our ethnic sisters had taken.

As I journeyed, trying to explain myself to myself, I found voices like mine when I heard or read other hyphenated ethnic women writers; they enlightened my understanding of my own multiplicity. I discovered that I would never find myself solely in the Arab or the French or the American or the Latino community. I could never belong exclusively to any one group but I should never feel foreign to them, for I'm a part of them all. As long as I am myself, whole in each identity, I've found who I am. I became more and more confident that any alienation came solely from those who, themselves, had not reached self-harmony.

I've learned that you are the sole definer of yourself. Within my own family there are French, Americans, Spanish, Mexicans, Palestinians, and so forth. Whatever their origins, they've chosen to be or simply are culturally any of the above. A German friend told me that many Turkish people in Germany want to be German and reject their Turkishness. But if they are raised or have adopted Germany as their country, aren't they Germans? If they choose to continue to preserve their heritage then that is also their prerogative. However, if those Turks did not participate in German life, Germans would view them as immigrants abusing the system. So can you really win when you stand in-between? Cultural marginality is one of the most difficult of alienations; and worlds don't always want to understand each other, remaining convinced of their cultural righteousness. However, as we enter the twenty-first century "there are no more cohesive societies," as Edward Said says. We're becoming more and more multicultural. In this changed light, we as ethnic women, as women, as feminists, we who have histories rooted in occupation, oppression, alienation—must continue remembering, acting, speaking, and writing. In the past twenty years, we have (re)constructed ourselves as women, and have translated our cultures—not rejected them but re-adapted them according to our times and our new histories. It's an endless negotiation of difference, but as long as these negotiations are articulated, adapted, and tolerated—no matter how many times they continue to shift—we women continue to participate in positive transformations.

Throughout my life I've watched my Siti make Arabic pastry. Once, not too long ago, Siti was visiting my mother and although she was welcomed in the kitchen my mother's kitchen had to be constantly cleared up, for there, food was cooked for a colony of men—my father, his brothers, and their sons. The new generation of women were away—living in the United States, Europe, Mexico, anywhere else but under this male roof in Santo Domingo. In fact, they were more perseverant intellectually and culturally—seeking beyond themselves, beyond the traditional curves. And then again, the women had to go away to become themselves; the men could be who they were—they had less walls to break, less bridges to cross.

"Na'th'alie," Milagro called me, adding a Spanish flavor to my Franco-Russian name. She was the Dominican cook who helps my grandmother make pastry. I did not answer immediately, my words held back by the view—a perfect silhouette of green leaves against the light blue sky, the sun hiding its light yet opening all the colors of nature, opening the shadows, allowing new images to exist behind those familiar to our eyes. Those who live in cities tend to forget the shape of the clouds, that trees elevate the soul, that rainbows of flowers tell us a little more about the world, that the sea is an endless floating wing, that not looking at the river beneath bridges is like walking life without ever knowing what a single breath sounds like. I heard my name again, turned around, and responded, "Si, Yo vengo." This is how the island welcomed me, as I left the cold winds of New York in the back pockets of my mind. This is what happens in the Caribbean—imagination has a twist of fate.

I heard my grandmother's footsteps follow her voice as she repeated, "Ya Allah, ya Allah," and then, as if she remembered something from the past, "Ya Allaaaah." I grew up with those two words—O God—in Arabic. The echoes of a collective Palestinian ache traveled across the rooms of those two words, through its windows, across its skies, through different houses, new homes. This longing, an endless *A* expanding itself, was the pressing feeling my grandmother transmitted to my sister Alexandra and me in our childhood.

"Siti," I screamed out joyfully and opened my hands to hug her, as I usually did whenever I saw her for the first time after a long absence. Her blue eyes met mine and we held each other. I looked at her and wondered why this ninety-year-old woman had so few wrinkles. Was it the food? She sat elegantly with her auburn hair combed in the back, her reddish orange lipstick, and her porcelain skin covered of a light pink blush. She still worked, traveled, played cards and dominos with her friends—she was everything anyone would hope to be at that age. And of course, she had a memory that I sometimes wish she didn't have.

"Ya Nathalie, did you find a husband?" she asked. It was only the second day of my visit so I still had a lot of patience and kindness stocked inside. "O Siti," I said nicely. How could I be entering my thirties without a husband or children? It was unheard of, although all her children and grandchildren had stepped out of eastern tradition and were *real* Americans—living deep in the south, Georgia, or in the west, Nevada. Except, of course, for my mother and one of her sisters, who lived partly in the Dominican Republic and partly in Florida (but then again, Miami is not *really* American; it's a Latino city). All the burden of family tradition was pressing on us, privileged with many cultural coats yet unable to wear any of them properly.

My mother followed the poetic echoes of *aaa* with yet another tune, a French passion—sometimes violently beautiful, sometimes exhausting, always grabbing—as she carried the words of Jacques Brel and Charles Aznavour with her. She grew up in French schools, French lands, and transmitted to us this culture. Alex and I were thus left trying to bridge our Arabic words with our French words while also belonging to the shadows of *Grease*, roaring for our basketball and baseball heroes, and surrounded by the Caribbean islands' exotic smells; while eating grape leaves and kebabs, foie gras and steak au poivre, black beans and white rice, tostones verdes o platanos maduros fritos, griot, tassot, poison sauce Creole; while listening to Patoit tunes, compas, or lamenting songs of the suffering and poverty of the Black man in radio FM, Port-au-Prince . . . and wondering what these things had to do with the corridors of my mother's French European cities or the ruins of my grandmother's Bethlehem. From one island to yet another island, merengue or salsa, Juan Luis Guerra or Tito Fuentes, the music making our bodies move with the hesitation of the waves—Santo Domingo dancing in the pulses of our hips. All this, while always carrying the American dream in our pockets—and believing in Madonna. It was the wonderful old streets of Boston that got to know us, the New England breeze that we adopted. Through it all, my grandmother's voices never ceased to penetrate the spaces between my exiles. Yet generations separate us, many stops, many exits, home after home. But home is different for all of us.

"Why you don't find a nice man to marry?" my grandmother asked me, her heavy accent pressing on her r's. And so, it all continues, even beyond university degrees; it all continues like in old villages—every step a statement. The telephone rang and my mother answered. She was mostly silent, listening intensely. My grandmother took advantage of my mother's diversion and told Anite, the cook from Haiti, "S'il vous plait chérie, pote dattes et mamoules, pote toute mange'a et Cola Cola et chi, khooran." Anite kindly said, "Qui Ma'dan Nicolas." It always seemed strange to me how Arabic and Creole could exist together in one sentence. Although Anite was not literate she could count perfectly in Arabic, knew the most common Arabic greetings in a Creolized Arab, and knew how to cook Arabic dishes wonderfully. Our Siti usually mixed three, four languages in one sentence and it sounded just right. Her knowledge of each language was fragmented, and she created her own language by picking words from each language that, she decided, had the best word to describe that object, place, or feeling. I doubt that it was conscious on her part, but it worked, at least for those of us familiar with all the languages or simply accustomed to the co-existence of different languages in speech.

She was feeding us again—that was simply sacred. If you look at the history of Arab immigration, among the main things they preserved were food and marriage within the same community. The language was practically lost, for many reasons: when they arrived in their new homes, language was not their preoccupation during difficult economic times; they did not want their children to be marginalized; or they were illiterate and at the time there were no schools that taught Arabic. Those who emigrated after the 1950s were more likely to transmit the language.

My mother hung up the telephone and told us, "Albert is getting a divorce. . . . He almost beat Myriam to death." I feel particularly betrayed when such things happen in our culture, for we are constantly reminded to believe that people from our culture could only protect us. Had I heard the same story from a noneastern friend, although it would revolt me, I would understand that such things occur and we must fight against them. But in this case, it should never have happened—it was not allowed. How could something like this have happened? We knew these people our entire lives. I suppose one never really knows anyone. Had Albert been a foreigner, it would have been an even greater story. Our families would use this incident endlessly to prove to us that we mustn't look beyond our backyard. But since he was not from outside our society, tragic as this event was, it would be considered an exception.

Similar incidents happen continuously, but only today are people speaking about them. I felt revolted and happy simultaneously—angered that violence was so present in our communities and happy that Myriam had left. I felt a sense of relief that there was more awareness and acceptance of these dark unjust realities since all tended to be veiled—(our families) often living on the edge of an invented reality, under false pretenses of perfection. As someone who respects the Arab culture, I used to feel that saying anything negative about it was a betrayal. As a feminist, as a woman who wants to participate in positive, necessary changes, I have learned to acknowledge the injustices as a point of departure—to eradicate inequality and violence and to create balancing grounds. I now understand that these issues are universal, not an Arab problem but a gender problem. I know women from many cultures who have experienced such abuse. The greater problem is to remain silent, to believe that our culture is flawless.

We ate while waiting for this story to find a bench to sit on inside of us—surely we each experienced it differently, approaching truth with different levels of honesty. Can we change what we have been brought up to believe in? Can we erase the guilt because we want something different? Can we accept ourselves as someone other than who we were told we should be? My grandmother says, "What a shit he is." And my mother asks, "What will she do now?" Alex looks at her and responds, "Mom, who cares? Now she's safe." But it was not worth discussing philosophically, for there is no real logic—not in the structure that cultures have created and not in the consequences of those structures. We continue eating, and I think of how little we knew of what awaits us—an incessant in-betweenness—between cultures, nationalities, languages, countries, mentalities. Yet if we want freedom, everything must exist harmoniously within us, for they're all part of us even if the extremities found very small land to stand on.

We ate, ate. My sister turned to me and told me that things were finally changing; women from the new generation do not expect to live in the margins of happiness. Things have changed thanks to the women's movements, to spokeswomen, feminists, activists, researchers, writers, and books bridging experiences.

I know that everyone judges according to their experiences, that my grandmother and mother had changed despite the fact that they often had to force themselves to do so. Through their granddaughters and daughters, their mentalities were altering. It's difficult, for finally we understand a place better when our feet touch its ground than when we merely read about it or see photographs of it. They had also participated as cultural workers—my grandmother, through food, taught us about hard work, demonstrated the courage women need to survive and exist on their own despite the odds; her husband passed away when she was very young. My mother, by insisting we learn and acquire as much knowledge as possible, participated in our evolution, in bringing more independent women to the world. She also transmitted to us the love of travel and adventure—maybe we did what she dared not venture. We are free from others' judgments, but she has remained enslaved by what society says. Perhaps it's this that makes her such a contradiction: she worked all of her life, is educated, smart, strong but still feels obliged vis-à-vis the rules her society dictates although they often overshadow her. Perhaps her lack of independent experiences (she married so young), does not allow her to comprehend our experiences. Because her formula for happiness is exclusively outlined in a traditional context, she often finds it difficult to understand our views. I looked at my Siti, my mother, my sister—we have different shades on our tongue, but we are one long breath weaving one familiar bridge.

After eating, I made coffee. I love coffee's aroma, how it awakens your senses and invites you to come to it. I enjoy putting my hands in the coffee beans—they remind me of all that I am, many flavors but all still coffee. As we drank, all was silent. It was the coffee stealing us away from ourselves. I looked at my mother's Palestinian embroidery and remembered when I used to stare so intensely at grandmother's embroidery that the design patterns would start dancing in my vision. The tones live in my eyes, defining themselves—different tones of red . . . apple red, blood red, silver red, blue red, golden red, orange red, and an elegant black weaving between the spaces. How lovely the framed embroidery, hanging on my grandmother's wall beside old black-and-white pictures. Old pictures of my mother's childhood days. I watched her growing up, picture after picture. I could hear her footsteps and knew when she stopped in front of a book vendor. Old books, torn books, new books, out-of-print books, colored books, stained books—I knew their different smells, the dustiness of unopened books settling in my nose; the paper from new books like fresh paint or clean silk sheets calling you to inhale. Books after books, that is how I have come to best describe myself—a place where words have no boundaries and titles change. A place with many places, different names, endless endings, and beginnings . . .

Notes

Siti: Grandmother.

Tostones verdes o platanos maduros fritos: Fried green plantain bananas and fried ripe plantain banana (a common food in the Caribbean, especially in Cuba, Puerto Rico, and the Dominican Republic).

Griot, tassot, poison sauce Creole: Creole dishes—fried pieces of pork; fried pieces of beef; fish dried in salt for days then poached and served with Creole sauce (usually tomato based).

Compas: A typical Haitian merengue.

S'il vous plait chérie, pote dattes et mamoules, pote toute mange'a et Cola Cola et chi khooran: Please sweetie, bring the Arabic pastry, bring all the food and Coke and tea, thank you.

Qui Ma'dan Nicolas: Yes Mrs. Nicolas.

twenty-three

Nomadic Existence: Exile, Gender, and Palestine (an E-mail Conversation between Sisters)

Reem Abdelhadi and Rabab Abdulhadi

We are sisters despite the different spellings of our last names—a function of translating names created in a colonial space into the language of that space's dominant empire. We were born in different places: Reem in Amman, the capital of Jordan; Rabab in Nablus, now under the control of the Palestinian Authority but then under Jordanian rule—another prob-

lematic aspect of nomadic existence. We received different educations:
Rabab in the United States and Reem in Britain. Our partners also illus-
trate the diversity of Palestinian diasporic existence. Rabab's partner,
Jaime Veve, is a Puerto Rican born and raised in New York, outside the
geographical space of his ancestral land; Reem is married to Mahmoud
Derbas, a Palestinian born and raised in Beirut, Lebanon. Nour is Reem's
son and Rabab's nephew. In the following e-conversation, we explore
Palestinian displacement.

From: Rabab
To: Reem
Cc: AnaLouise
Sent: Thursday, June 29, 2000 16:46
Subject: BRIDGE book activists/feminists/scholars/exiles

Habibti Reem,
AnaLouise suggests that you & I do an email dialogue for inclusion in
the book. She suggests that we focus on our experiences as
activists/feminists/scholars/exiles. Which memories come out?
Here's a thought!! What does it mean to be in exile: uprooted from
where you were born, from your family & friends, from the smell of
Zeit ou Za'ater,[1] from the sun which comes out early & sets with all
colors of red, purple, & lots of orange? Of course we were not
uprooted like the Palestinians in 1948. We did not lose all our belongings & our identification papers, leave behind a land, an orange
orchard, a hill of old olive trees, pack ourselves & our little ones &
travel to nowhere—like Khaltou (auntie) Samiha & 900,000 other
Palestinians—to a life of misery & humility where dignity is an expensive commodity & respect nowhere to be found. Sympathetic people
want to embrace you but pity you & never think of you as an equal—
after all, now you have become a refugee.

The other day, when Jaime & I were in Boston, we had a heated
discussion with Fatmeh, Mansour, & George about what it meant to be
exiled. Fatmeh said we were nomads in the sense that we did not
belong anywhere; we must recognize our condition & move on. What
do you think? In my mind, there are different senses to this nomadic
life. On the one hand, and I think this is what Fatmeh meant, we can
no longer belong to whatever we conceive of as "back home." Yet we
never fully belong here either—whatever "here" may mean; we are not
comfortable anywhere but we can make homes everywhere. On the
other hand, is anyone who leaves one place to live in another for
many years really comfortable in this new place or the previous one?

For me, living in exile is not so bad at this point. I like it much better than living at home. I am much more comfortable with not having anyone interfere in my life, tell me what to do or how to think. But I am so envious of people with a peaceful serenity of belonging. With 100% certainty they would tell you, "But of course, this is who we are," as if this were the most natural thing in the world. Although many of us did not choose life in exile, nomadic existence can be OK. I like not having to always say that I only enjoy Arab food, because frankly this is not true: I do not crave Arabic food more than I crave Chinese, Thai, or Puerto Rican food. Someone may read this & think, "Aha! a postmodern moment par excellence; a cosmopolitan existence." Fine, but let me say two things: (a) I am really not trying to impress anyone by this; I just like all these foods & I do feel that to praise Arabic food only out of a sense of loyalty would be a lie; (b) I have serious problems with this juxtaposition of "us," the "cosmopolitan modern beings," and "them," the "provincial backward creatures"—an implied assumption of belonging to a "superior culture."

To me, this immediately brings to mind the question posed in certain liberal quarters: "What is the big deal about falafel being called Israeli falafel?" Why do we become so upset because humus is served as Israeli food or cucumber-tomato-onions-mint-parsley-olive oil-lemon-juice-salt-salad is called "Jerusalem salad," which, to anyone in the U.S. who follows restaurant reviews, does not refer to the Jerusalem we know: the old city with the Palestinian women who seat themselves on the ground outside Bab el-Amoud and set up their portable makeshift vegetable stands to sell meloukhiyya, spinach, & other freshly harvested vegetables? The Jerusalem salad on restaurant menus is precisely meant to invoke images of the Wailing Wall, the Israeli flag, the "modern" hardworking & professional Israeli women (as if there were one single image of Israeli women) who know exactly what they want & how to get it—an image so in-focus, so unlike the image of the Palestinian peasant woman (I am intentionally using the singular here & the plural to refer to the multiplicity of Israeli women's experience to undermine the problematic nature of such constructs) who fades away from human imagination & whose image invokes thoughts of "backwardness," illiteracy, misery, & pity. Ironically, when this image is deployed, it does not enlist feelings of compassion & sympathy stirred by similar images of indigenous women in other parts of the world. This has a lot to do with our invisibility as people—we are denied the victim status.

I am wondering whether I should just delete this discussion. But this is for a women-of-color anthology; where could we discuss these uncomfortable issues if not here? Besides, while some Jewish & Israeli intellectuals would rather we did not raise these uncomfortable issues, our friends (Ella Shohat, Simona Sharoni, & Ros Petchesky) who are very conscious on issues of representation & appropriation would welcome & insist upon this intervention. And, of course, you want to be polite & considerate; you certainly do not want to be labeled an anti-Semite. It is ironic for a Semite to be labeled anti-Semitic. But, regardless of how much theorizing has been done on the specificity of anti-Semitism in Europe, the discussion still boils down to the need for a more nuanced understanding of Zionism, anti-Semitism, discrimination, racism, & prejudice work; where we apply certain terms; & how we produce a complex analysis of these labels' particular flavor & context. Then we must ask why the powerless are always expected to be polite & considerate while dominant groups never subject themselves to the same rules of etiquette they demand. I have to go now; my hands are killing me & this discussion is taking too much energy!

Love to Mahmoud & Nourrabab, Rabab

From: Reem Abdelhadi
To: Rabab Abdulhadi
Sent: Saturday, July 01, 2000 01:11
Subject: Loyalty, Being British & Arab

Habibti Rabab,
I do not like the smell of Zeit ou Za'ater. It is too poignant a reminder of childhood & the safety of my family home. When you left home, you were so eager to find a new life. As a child, I felt that you were never homesick because you were so eager to leave. But when my turn came, I felt truly uprooted & still feel so. I have adapted pretty well to living in Britain. In fact, I feel very much a British-Arab. It is not a question of loyalty. Why do they always insist on that? As if who you are is based solely on which side you would take in a state of war.

Do you remember Peterborough, when I came to spend a weekend with you? You stood in the hallway with open arms & a beaming smile. I greeted you with icy English coldness, as if I had never been an Arab. I had withdrawn into myself, vowing that I would not show my emotions so that I would not be accused of emotionality or worse still, "irrationality." I never told you, but I felt it was the only way to cope with living in a boarding school which produces upper-class English ladies. I had to "assimilate." I thought that if I adopted their accent & manner, I would fit right in & they would stop their racist harassment.

But I never denied my Arabness. I wrote in my diaries, "I am an Arab through & through." I was proud to be an Arab, but I was too withdrawn—far too withdrawn. I was a child uprooted from her family & her town, totally unprepared. I was so homesick, I still feel nauseous when I think about it. It took me years to come to terms with who I am . . . culturally. I knew I was an Arab, but what is this memory of British things? Even now, I say things like "we used to do this when we were small," but I was not here when I was small; I came as a teenager. It is something like cumulative memory. Why do I know English nursery rhymes, old customs, & superstitions? Why do I know things that other British people would not know? It is not just the years I have spent here, or the fact that I came here at a relatively young age but because I have embraced "Britishness" (whatever that means); I have immersed myself in this culture. Britain has become my second home.

Being an Arab was never in question. I loved being an Arab, looking like an Arab, reaffirming my culture and my origin. I developed quite a liking for Arabic as a language & took a great interest in Arab & Muslim civilization. I used to write my homework about Arab contributions to science & other disciplines. But something was always missing. I was not totally comfortable in my skin as an Arab. In fact, Mama unwittingly helped me. She could not understand why I found expressing myself in English terms easier than "naturally" thinking of the Arabic alternative. I used to get agitated, simply because I had no answer. I would ask myself, "But I am an Arab, so why is it easier to speak in English?" Then it dawned on me: I have actually spent more time in this country than I have ever spent at home in Nablus. I shared this with Mama & we talked about it. Then I started thinking seriously about it. This nagging memory, the basis of which I do not understand, is in fact part of my British self. I am British. I am as British as they come. I am a British Arab. This is who I am. I was equally influenced by Omar Khayyam and by Shakespeare. I was at home in two very different parts of the world. As soon as I came to that realisation, I started wearing my skin with much more comfort. I love my skin colour, my black eyes & black hair, my accent, & I love coming up with a reference so British as to make an Englishman loosen his stiff upper lip.

But you know what, Habibti, if I was not involved in politics from an early age (I still remember Mama telling us about our history when we were four or five), I would not have become who I am today. This inner pride in my Arabness is definitely due to our parents. The slow adoption of Britishness is because I followed political developments religiously & became involved in British political life. I became an activist in the late '70s. As soon as I had some control over my life, I began taking a serious interest in the world around me. I was involved in many campaigns—local, national, international. This, I think, is part of being Palestinian—part of your experience whether you like it or not: being a Palestinian sensitizes you to others' suffering.

Of course whatever I do, I will not be accepted as British, simply because I am not white. I am not striving for this acceptance. I am a Palestinian Arab who has been greatly affected by the many years spent in this country.

What do you think uprootedness means for us since our family has not been displaced? There is a certain feel to displaced families—don't you think? They/we deal with things in a totally different manner. We live in the security & comfort of a safety net. Because our family is not only still living in Palestine, but has been living in the same area for hundreds of years, this sort of long-standing rootedness is important. But I agree with you about being nomadic. Only I am not sure whether I feel it; I certainly do not feel that I "belong" here, nor do I feel that I "belong" back there. In a sense, then, I belong nowhere, or perhaps I do belong everywhere—well here & there only.

Why do you question what makes other Palestinians similar? It is easy: we all eat Zeit ou Za'ater or so they say. But seriously, as a social psychologist, this is my answer: we share a culture & a history. Here is an anecdote for you to chew on: A large group of us, all women in our twenties & all Palestinian, were walking along the Thames one mild night. One of us started singing & the rest followed. The group was comprised of two women from Lebanon, two from Palestine, one from Switzerland or another European country, one from London, one from the Gulf, one from Jordan/Saudi Arabia, & one from Jordan/Kuwait. With such diverse backgrounds, how did we all know the same songs, songs not heard on any radio station! I think it is culture. We share the same culture.

For me, living in exile is not so bad at the moment either. But I recognize that I came here by choice. Thousands never have the right to choose. An immediate example from my own personal life: Mahmoud is not able to live in Palestine nor am I able to live in Lebanon. This situation has forced us to continue living in this country. Our case shows that even in choice, there are degrees.

Although it is healthy & tasty, I do not crave Arabic food at all. I agree with you about the images Jerusalem salad, falafel, humus, & kibbutz salad are meant to invoke. It robs us of our culture. Falafel was eaten by Egyptians since God knows when—perhaps since the time of the Pharaohs. Israel was created only 52 years ago & European Jews did not have these dishes in their cuisine. If it is Israel-born then it was "born" well after the Arab people of the region (Muslims, Christians, & Jews) had been serving it for hundreds of years. To call it "Israeli" is not only another example of cultural appropriation but is also not true.

I do not understand what you mean about victims: Are you saying that we deserve the victim status? We are strong women. Our rights are still denied & we have a long struggle ahead of us, but we are not passive victims: Palestinian women have always struggled against oppression as far back as recorded history allows—not to mention oral history. In the least, we know they struggled against the Crusaders & the Ottomans, fought the English & the Israelis, & they/we still had some leftover energy to fight patriarchy in our own society. The unfortunate truth is that this struggle does not elicit the compassion it merits. Instead, I find only contempt & condescension from some British feminists who see Arab women as less deserving of understanding than other women. What is it about liberal feminism that allows these things to continue?

I do not want to be polite. I want to write about any & all uncomfortable issues. It is late. Have to go. Will talk to you later. Love to you & Jaime.

Reem

From: Rabab
To: Reem
Sent: Friday, July 3, 2000, 13:43
Subject: Identity in Exile, Falafel, Gendered Morality, Memory

Habibti Reem,

I'm struck by how different our experiences have been even though we were raised by the same parents in the same home. But I also felt the pressure to conform. Some Palestinian activists, with whom I worked to build a Palestine solidarity movement in the U.S., pressured me to go along to get along. Here you had these smart, radical, & politically astute activists who did not live the internationalism they advocated. This was extremely disappointing, especially when their discomfort with my relationship with Jaime was translated into questioning my commitments to the Palestinian cause & whether our relationship meant that I would shift my solidarity work from Palestine to Puerto Rico. This troubled me as it implied that two causes of colonized people were in opposition to each other. Also, it made me question the extent to which we, as a movement, practiced what we preached.

I do not think that we, or anyone else for that matter, have a franchise on victimization. But I am not saying that we deserve the victim status. Rather, I tend to agree with Edward Said, who said in one of his talks during the Intifada [popular uprising] that we, Palestinians, are denied the label of victimhood because we are victims of the victims & thus must prove that we were, in fact, victimized. The same analogy applies to women: imagine then being marginalized on the basis of your gender, without resources because you are poor, & further dispossessed as a result of the Nakbah [Palestinian catastrophe in 1948]. This compounded condition makes it very hard for Palestinian women to lodge a long-lasting and effective movement for change. Yet they/we do. The fact that this struggle is not recognized as a feminist struggle by mainstream U.S. or British feminists has to do with the sort of struggles we wage & the particular model they know. It immediately raises a question concerning the legitimacy to differ & whether people really respect differences. We note certain omissions on the part of these feminists who are precisely enabled by their privileged position, which gives them some sense of entitlement to know & judge. Did you notice that most radical women of color never walk around with this air of elitist entitlement? Those of us who have been less privileged than others, either because of race, gender, sexuality, class, nationality, or any other system of marginalization, tend to be more humble in professing our views & make tentative conclusions.

You raise the example of the Palestinian song you & your friends all knew, despite growing up in different places. But this, Ya Habibti Reem, is the fascinating thing about how people construct their identities in exile, especially when this identity is constructed in opposition to the status quo—in defiance of what is proper & acceptable. For the Palestinians in particular, we somehow constructed our Palestinianness as a home in the absence of a homeland: we have been shaped by a colonial legacy & the heritage of resistance. This is why when something close to a state came about, we began witnessing diverse manifestations of identity, or an identity crisis as you social psychologists would call it.

Your reference to the English nursery rhymes you "remembered" reminded me of childhood events I remembered but later began to question. I clearly remember the time our parents took us to Haifa after 1967 to see the house that belonged to our grandfather but was occupied by an Israeli family. I was so certain that the Jewish woman living there, hanging her laundry to dry, had refused to let us in. This mem-

ory seems so clear in my mind, but it was shaken when I read an article criticizing Rigoberta Menchú's biography as fictitious. The critic, an
anthropologist, suggested that Menchú patched up different stories of
Guatemalan struggle & presented them as her own. After reading this
account, I began doubting my own memories: Was I only drawing upon
the Palestinian people's collective memory? You know how it is: they
doubt you so much that you begin doubting yourself. How do we make
sense of this paradox? It might be ulterior malicious motives on the
part of critics with their own political agendas. Or perhaps Rigoberta
Menchú and her U.S. critics have different sensibilities concerning the
boundaries of the individual/collective self. Two interrelated things
occur simultaneously; 1. In colonized spaces, there's a collective sense
of self less individualized than in the Empire. 2. The dispossessed are
constructed by their dominators as a single homogenized entity, which
then leaves very few possibilities for expanding the individual self's
boundaries. The outcome is a more collective & relational sense of the
individual self. Does this make sense? It is not that some memories are
not true, in the sense that they did not happen. We all know they did.
But it becomes irrelevant really to determine to whom exactly this particular incident happened & to whom it did not. This realization was so
clear during the events marking 50 years of Palestinian Nakbah, or
catastrophe. When I interviewed little kids in the streets of Nablus, they
told me with unambiguous certainty that they remembered Palestine.
How could 12–year-olds remember things that happened before they &
perhaps their parents were born? But finally it dawned on me: they
remembered in the same manner we all seem to remember historical
narratives that may have never happened personally but that, nonetheless, nourish a people's determination to struggle. Collective memories
then become a powerful tool, a strategy for resistance. To forget is to
abandon one's struggle, to give up. Tell me what you think!

    Got to go Habibti. Love to Mahmoud & Nour.

    Rabab

From: Reem Abdelhadi
To: Rabab Abdulhadi
Sent: Tuesday, July 04, 2000 14:43
Subject: Gradual Exile, Memory

Habibti Reem,

    Talking of exile, there is an important point to consider: it did not
happen suddenly. For both of us, it happened gradually. We did not
set out to be exiled. Indeed, I did not feel I was "exiled" until only a

few years back, when the decision to stay had become more of a fait accompli than a freely made choice. I cannot imagine what it was like for "real" exiles. The Israelis once confiscated all my cassette tapes; most I could buy anywhere, but a few were of sentimental value. They refused point blank to let me have them. 15 years later I still pine for them. They are only cassettes—not someone's life or limb. How would someone deal with having all their possessions taken? How would they deal with the sudden uprootedness? You know, in the "west" when a government has a case involving application for residency, an applicant's lawyer may say "but this is the only home they have known for 10 years." Why don't they apply the same argument to the hundreds of thousands of Palestinians forced—many instances at gunpoint—to leave their homeland? I know that we, Palestinians, are meant to understand the suffering, but I am afraid I do not. I cannot claim to begin understanding how the dispossession is felt. What I do feel, however, is how fortunate I am to have remained on Palestinian soil throughout my childhood. It taught me to appreciate the sense of security having a homeland gives. In a sense, you cannot take these things for granted. I cannot even begin to imagine what it feels like to have a place one calls a homeland. Do you think people in such situations appreciate what this means? I used to cherish my Israeli Travel Document because I thought that "if worse came to worst," I could always be deported to Palestinian soil as if experiencing deportation was an OK thing. On the other hand, traveling on a Jordanian passport, to which I was entitled, made me so afraid that if this "worse come to worst" situation occurred, I would be sent back to Jordan with no hope of ever seeing Palestine.

Habibti Rabab, this will be my last e-mail in this exchange. I think we have enough for now to contribute to *this bridge*. I want, though, to continue these exchanges with you. Not only do they give me the freedom to express my thoughts without the tedious requirements of a "traditional" academic paper, but they allow me to think through with you certain issues that have been on my mind for a while.

Love to you & Jaime.

Reem

Epilogue

At the time of the submission, our living conditions have drastically changed. On a personal level, Rabab has moved to Egypt for a teaching position at the American University in Cairo. Reem has begun researching the experience of Arabs in Britain and is now expecting twin girls. On a general level, the continuous wounds inflicted on Palestinians make it impossible for us to focus solely on our academic careers (assuming such a venture is even possible). News from back home takes a different and more central place in our lives, psyche, and feminist theorizing: situating the imagining of "back home" within the persistence of what's occurring "back home," then, sharpens our identifications with the homeland and further brings into focus the deepened alienation of the exiled condition in its relational intimacy with "back home." Reem's son, Nour, has nightmares about "the Israelis coming to kill sidou [grandfather]." The almost four-year-old boy wakes up crying, wanting to go to Nablus, Palestine, to defend sidou. Our nieces and nephews, more fortunate than many Palestinian children because they are still alive, are suffering from all sorts of psychological problems; some hide under the bed at night in fear for their lives, teenage girls are petrified of being violated, and younger children are beginning to wet their beds again. Regardless of whether their fears are founded or not (latest statistics on casualties among children speak for themselves), the next generation of Palestinians has been marred by the scars of inhumanity. Statements such as those made by the Queen of Sweden, who questioned whether Palestinian mothers loved their children, further deepen Palestinian feelings of abandonment and alienation. The back-and-forth contemplation and choices we all make and the constraints under which we make them compel us to revisit our initial discussion on the politics and poetics of nomadic existence. This dilemma—situating the knowledge we produce about nomadic existence—continues simmering quietly in our minds. No categorical conclusions can be reached at this point; only a tentative tapping on the surface. We are, therefore, grateful to have this hospitable environment in *this bridge,* which allows us to grieve for all those who lost loved ones, to recognize our humanity, the complexities of our lives, and the shifting sands of our respective experiences without being forced to engage in the arrogant exercise of categorical conclusions.

Note

1. Zeit ou Za'ater: olive oil and thyme—a daily staple of Palestinian cuisine, consumed usually in the morning with toasted Arabic bread. When bread with Zeit ou Za'ater is baked in a brick oven, the special aroma intoxicates the exiled and provokes feelings of yearning for a land lost.

twenty-four

(Re)Writing Home: A Daughter's Letter to Her Mother

Minh-Ha T. Pham

April 30, 2000

Dear Mother,

Twenty-five years have passed. I wonder how you are. More than that, though, I wonder who you are. Here in America, I have heard many stories about you and it becomes more and more difficult to untangle the stories from the lies. Your silence has not helped. The soldiers tell me that you gave me up, you grew tired of fighting for me, you let go when keeping me became too troublesome. My brothers and sisters say you had no choice. The years of fighting and defending yourself would have worn out anyone. You fought valiantly but it was an unfair fight. You were outnumbered and overpowered. You bowed before our fate because refusal to do so was not a choice.

What is the truth, Mother? What is the Truth?

I absorb my days with words, struggling to begin where rumors of you leave off. Where your stories are cut off. I write this narrative struggling with words that are as unfamiliar and as intimate as a new lover. A writing that is mediated by an Other language, inescapably another sensibility. I struggle with a language that is not my own and a narrative that is but an extension of yours. I struggle with words that remind me that I am still ill-literate. Sick with the loss of your words. Dis-eased by assimilation and the ideologies of grammar, syntax, and punctuation. My story is earmarked by the tear of your absence.

Where are you now? Are you dead, Mother?

The death of parents . . . is a trauma that causes an invisible tear in our self-identity (Miller, x).

I wanted to write you to let you know that I'm OK. Life is OK here in America but it has not always been easy. In America, everyone needs their own name, their own Identity. This is important in America. An American identity is important. A trauma that causes an invisible tear *No matter what they say.*

One day you raise the right hand and you are American. They give you an American Pass port. The United States of America. Somewhere someone has taken my identity and re-placed it with their photograph. The other one. Their signature their seals. Their own image. And you learn the executive branch the legislative branch and the third. Justice. Judicial branch. It makes the difference (Cha, 56).

I tell them that I am Vietnamese, that my name is Minh-Ha. A name thoughtfully bestowed onto me. It is not mine but mine nonetheless. It means bright river, bright in a dazzling way. I am proud of such a life-giving name. A living gift. Fluid as a river, running north to south. Just like me. North to South Viet Nam. But that will never do, they say. Not here in America. "Why don't you change your name to Michele? Michele is a nice name, sounds like yours but it's easier to say. No complications. No discomfort. No hyphen." One day you raise the right hand and you are American.

But that little hyphen answers a challenge, I tell them. The hyphen does not need to be there but that space will always be. The challenge of living with the chasm is inescapable. And the hyphen is comforting. It is a gesture. A bridge. A scaffold offering passage but not passing so that I might cross over and back again, always back again. Thirteen years of I-pledge-allegiance cannot close that gap. Ten years of documentation cannot suture that chasm. Vietnamese-American, post-colonial, post-war, post-memory.

That is why I am writing you—but I don't want to carefully peel away layers like wet rice papers. I am hungry, Mother. I want to penetrate your stories the way I eat a thousand-layer cake. I will not stop until it is inside of me, making me full. Making my story full. Do you remember me? Do you love me? Was I wanted?

What does a daughter want from a mother, what does a mother want from a daughter? One and the same thing: recognition (Miller, 58).

According to some of my brothers and sisters, I am a traitor. They call me Viet Kieu. It means that I have betrayed you, Mother. It means that I am a girl, a disloyal daughter. It means that I am a chapter of a story few remember. It is too old, too long, too meandering to memorize. But you knew me by heart. Read me from memory, re-imagined me every time. I began in the back of your throat, on the roof of your mouth, rolled off your tongue like a good ng sound.

This sound is not assimilable; it stands on the rim. Teetering on the Pacific Ocean, always threatening to jump in.

You wanted to forget me.

You gave me up . . . didn't you?

*I am writing to tell you that I am alive. That I am OK. I have not forgot-
ten you. You will always be my mother* what does a daughter want from
a mother *but I am unsure if I am your daughter* one and the same thing.
Have you forsaken me?

*Mother, I tell everyone that I am yours. I tell them that the Documents lie.
The documents amputate my legs, burn and slash my tongue so that I
can't move or scream when they erase me. The documents unravel the
intricate knots of your hair, your stories, your secrets, annulling them to
the trivial. Making them powerless. They make a clarity of me. yes no
black white asian american english only.* Clarity is a means of subjec-
tion, a quality both of official, taught language and of correct writing, two
old mates of power: together they flow, together they flower, vertically, to
impose an order (Trinh, *Woman*, 16–17).

*They say that I am a war orphan. I am marked by these documents that
declare: Parents—deceased/dis-eased by communism and the memories of
agent orange. But I know who my parents are. Mother—Me Viet Nam
Father—Co Vang Ba Soc Do.*[1] *And I know who I am: the child of a dragon
and granddaughter to an angel. Con rong, chau tien. I tell them how
beautiful you are. I tell them about the silk that threads your words
together, the silk that you taught me to make, to adore.* This chant that was
once mine, given me by my mother, who may not have known its power
to remind (Kingston, 20). *I tell them that this silk thread connects us; this
thread senses movements. You and I are connected by these.*

Motion is the thread of narrative. Motion is the threat of Narrative.

*I can feel your sadness, your exhaustion, your age. This silk thread res-
onates with you. I wrap myself into the silk and am warmed and protected.
But silk does not provide totality. It breathes. It lives. It reminds me that I
am always at risk of disappearing. Too much silk and and I am oriental,
not enough and I am invisible.* It is as if everywhere we go, we become
Someone's private zoo (Trinh, *Woman*, 82). *It is fragmented stories and
forms, at once a defining difference and a confining difference. It is a fractured heirloom. But it is ours. And though it grows more ragged with each
hand it passes through, I know I will pass it down to my children.*

*From the stories your children tell, I have come to know you. I recognize
your voice because its echoes sound in the breakbeats of my mind and res-
onate off my thoughts. its power to remind its power to change minds I
know your language even though you are multilingual. (Are we still multilingual when learning an other's language is compulsory?)*

I know your favorite foods because they are my soul foods. I eat them and am comforted by the smells, the warm, soft feel of them on my tongue. I swallow them and am returned by the sharp sting of lemongrass. Refreshed by the salty sweet of a dried plum drink, your secret home recipe that everyone knows. I know the sounds you make as you eat. Makes me hungry to hear you. I know your face because I am your face. "Face" is the surface of the body that is the most noticeably inscribed by social structures, marked with instructions on how to be (Anzaldúa, "haciendo caras," xv). *I am the first thing people see when they see you. I am you.*

From the stories your children tell, I have come to piece you, I have come to speak you, to rearticulate you to me.

I open my mouth, breathe deep, prepare to answer your call but my tongue is domesticated. Housebroken in a stranger's home. Accented. The outlandish sound scratches the echoes. The breakbeats jump. Thought, in [her], took the visible form of a foreign language (Thiong'o, 17).

Can you tell me who I am? Can you tell me who, in the family, I re-assemble? Am I like a headstrong aunt or a storytelling cousin? A timid child who cannot be held by a stranger? Where do I fit into the story? I know that I am the first daughter second born to a first son and second daughter but where does this narrative fit into the larger story? Was my birth significant enough to make it into your diaries?

A parent's history is a life narrative against which the memorialist ceaselessly shapes and reshapes the past and tries to live in the present (Miller, 5).

I am sure that I was conceived in love. The North and the South joining in an epic moment, joining without subsuming each other. Without a canceling out. Together and opposite but not opposing. Conceived in the Year of the Rat and birthed in the Year of the Ox. Born on the anniversary of your liberation. Born in a memento of your arrest. A French hospital next to the South China Sea. A home birth with foreign records. Their signature their seals.

Irony is the essence of the hyphen.

I am sure that I was conceived in love because the bonds between a mother and daughter, once established, do not loosen. I tell myself stories to help me understand you.

[A] self portrait of a son or daughter emerges in complex counterpoint to the portrayal of the parent (Miller, 3).

You were brave and strong but the father's power prevailed, as it customarily does. You were raped and gutted, put in your place. Made common. You sacrificed me because you did not want me to live in silence and in fear of the father. You gave me up out of love. It was the best you could do. You miss me.

I tell myself stories to help me understand myself.

[A] self portrait emerges in complex counterpoint to the portrayal of the parent.

I am stubborn because of you. I am captivated by the poetic because at the heart of your story is a poem. I write often because your story seduces me into representation. Into translation. Into a third nation.

I believe you are still there, alive and waiting.

I want to go home.

Con nha Viet Nam

A child of Viet Nam

As soon as we learn to be "Asians in America"—that is, to come to a rest in a place supposedly always there, waiting to be discovered—we also recognize that we can't simply be Asians any longer (Trinh, *Moon*, 160).

Note

1. "The yellow flag with three red stripes" is the democratic flag of Viet Nam. It was used prior to May 1975, the fall of Saigon to communism.

twenty-five

IN THE END (AL FIN) WE ARE ALL CHICANAS (SOMOS TODOS CHICANAS): *pivotal positions for change*

A textual collage of cross-cultural exile stories
by Susan M. Guerra

Who am I, a poor Chicanita from the sticks, to think I could write?
—Gloria Anzaldúa, "Speaking in Tongues" (166)

to think I could travel?
to think I could understand?
to think I could see?
to think I could speak?
to think I could think?
to think I could . . . ?

1. Marginality as a Place of Power

backyard games
a universe locked inside
chainlinked
backyard fence
lined with double-dare you drought daisies
brown-tipped and strawberry cream pinked

stalking ears of corn mock the alamo tree
playing snow with its drop of cottonseed in the spring
and cracked cement porch
trips bicycle tires and rollerskate wheels
round and round
and nobody goes

the torn wires
worn
chickens coop
behind a sappy plum trunk

rusted nails, that ol'sour
mop or two
inviting as barbed wire

exhausted, as we, thrown against the
house paint-chipped wall

our lean paradise,   our phantom scream
our nightmarish
kinder palace, daddy left . . .
and we, no lap to sit on, no stories good bedtime
to hear, in there
the three p.m. sun, waves of dripping air
pitchfork hot, caught, a rotten peach hangs
too hot for us to know,
no breath left for a skip through the ages,
jump the rope, nor other cool, savvy
survival games
just the hide, the seek
tag, you are it.

Of four sisters, I am the only Chicana. Hey! But one of my sisters speaks better Spanish than I do. Anyday! Grammar, pronunciation. Very suave. Studied
in Peru, muy academica y real down-to-earth. We always wanted to send her
to *Jeopardy!*, she's-so-smart-can-learn-anything-sister. But Chicana? I don't
know. She talks more about the Dalai Lama than La Virgen. Do you think
she would mind? La Virgen, I mean. Or what about the Dalai Lama? What
he doesn't know is that my sister paints him gathering roses and his robes
bear sequins on satin of red, white, and green, con gold sandals on his feet.
    Then there is the city planner who plans bike trails in urban American
cities. She doesn't even know how to ride a bike! Left for the northeast con
un Ivy League boyfriend (rubio) and, well . . . sometimes makes comments
as if she disdains "Chicana"/"woman of color"/"Latina" talk. Said something once about "send those . . . back where they . . ." The telephone lines
between us on fire, and both of us, so far away from Texas. I *think* sometimes our brain gets as bent as a mother's back. Bent with the histories of
poverty, of how wars change a life. Of houses of broken glass, neighborhoods of kids taking a piss on sidewalks and how this makes some mothers
keep their children chain-linked in the back, behind a bush; makes a daddy
disappear; teenage guys leave their hearts and throw knives. A drive-by on
Calle Chihuahua or, was it Morelia Street? That's when dad said "Basta!"
In NYC, the city planner tries not to look, because like it or not, it still
hurts. A drive-by memory shoots the gut (or is it the heart?). Memories of
what is real yet unaccounted for. Including the days of alegria, with laven-
der/yellow pansies on Easter dresses, hand-sewn with chiffon ruffles,
laced-trimmed socks popping up in somersaults dangerously near the cac-

tus and rock garden, the kitchen full of steam from the pot of mole simmering on Thanksgiving day; invisible stories of our history. Today, the city
planner and I can almost afford DKNY sleek to mask the stories of broken
pieces of glass in a mosaic beneath our breasts and across our backs. The
heart and body are poor editors with these stories we'd like to leave
behind, or better yet, wouldn't we like to send them *all* back?

The third sister, the oldest one, the beauty, *Helena, hermosa (she
doesn't even know I see her in this way),* hmmm; I don't know what happened to her. La movie star once a wildcat doing *Tommy* and *Hair* musi-
cals. The spikes and red streaks of punk, blueblack nail polish, or glitter
green lips, in a white mustang '83 Zoommmmm. Lesbiana y lista. That
September at the Santa Rosa hospital waiting room after my mother lost
a leg because of the gangrene (she hated los doctores), *Helena, hermosa*
left us and entered a psychological space behind armoured doors all her
own, swallowed the iron key and to this day sifts through biographies of
St. Maria Goretti and Helen Keller. Amen.

Exiles. Forced to leave the dear and the wicked. Forced to re-arrange
the blueprints of experience. As I take on the position of slayer of contorted
histories I discover myself in the position of the slayed. To re-shape my
heart, I must change the subject, while collecting myself as the object. I am
the pivot for transformation, the axis of what I choose as the end and what I
choose as the beginning. But help me, sisters. Al fin, somos todos Chicanas.

2. Living Round-Trip

(A Chicana has nothing to lose?)
"Where do you come from?"
Voices from a backyard locked with a mother's fear and love.
Snapdragons, daisies, sweetheart roses, stalks of corn, peach tree sap stick-
ing to our knees. Lightning bugs. *The mexicans. You are mexican. Fill out
the form at school, little girl with the Spanish surname (the knot in your
stomach tells you: you are not like the others). Early childhood removal
from the home to learning programs in the official monolingual world.*
"I'm from Texas," I tell the Scandinavians.
"Oh! But then you're an American!"
This was the first time someone ever called me an American.
"From *Texas!* John Wayne, bang bang, horses. We know about *Texas.*"
Hearty laughter. *The only image of my home. Bang bang.*
"But *(on second thought with a squinted look at my face),* from where?
Where do *you* come from?"

I left the backyard of San Antonio in 1972. I proclaimed myself as an official Chicana after I'd lived outside of the U.S. a couple of years. Going

back home and attending COPS (Communities Organized for Public Service) rallies in Pablos Grove (now called Mateo Camargo Park). I heard speeches, saw men and women who looked like my parents and grandparents, my neighbors and relatives. Like Mexicans. *Speaking up* about neighborhoods and backyards that I knew something about! Mops, unpaved streets, shotgun houses. People acting from that place I grew up in. Poder. My heart was home. I knew I was also a Chicana.

Not everyone in my family liked this.

"Why that word, m'ija. Que cochino! Why associate yourself with . . . ?"

"Con quien, mami?"

My grammo, mami's mama, refused. To become an American citizen. Lived in Texas for over fifty years. From one shotgun house to another on the same unpaved street. With the hum of her fanicos inside and rows of okra outside. Her husband (at least that's what they told us) with plenty of longneck Lone Star beers and a feed store with pigeons and rabbits for sale and girly calendars on the bathroom wall. Her life with the flutter of dim blue light from los bullfights on TV Saturday night. Una vida de lime and salt. Like a Mexican with a Spanish surname. "C'mon, you can apply now, after so many years?" Grammo. Un poco arrogante, her scent of *Tabu* perfume. She refused any other option. Flat. "Quitate!" she'd scowl, "con tus preguntas!"

3. Langu-edge

Ellos no saben. They don't know that it's possible to grow up with two. Simultaneously. Putting one to rest while you use the other. (m)Other tongues. The researchers, the experts, the teachers. Keep saying, *Speak Norwegian*! A national politician here has just made an official statement to the press (election year '99) that immigrant parents in Norway who do not ensure that their children speak fluent Norwegian by the time they begin school should be reported for child neglect to Child Protective Services! Had this guy been on the Internet to California?

My friend Malika knows what the experts don't. Her kids learned Arabic and Norwegian from birth. With all the attachments to the langu-edges too! Couscous filling their nostrils, steam in their dark brown curls as they hear mama Malika talk that dynamic language sounding like cinnamon bark and whole clove stems being crumbled into a casserole. Hearing her speak her language is the taste of cardamom in thick espresso coffee and the crunch of sweet almonds between your teeth. And the Norwegian papa setting knives and forks on the dinner table, joking and laughing in that language of tonal hills, snowy slopes, deep icy fjords, and red apple orchard valleys. His langu-edge, right alongside the Arabic. The children's underwater voices toss sounds from one system to another. The bubble ball of words floats off the tongue and rolls and rolls and rolls. A tex-mex twin. A nor-abic duet to contemporary cues. Every other night every other langu-edge to sing your family and friends good night.

4. Refugees of a World on Fire[1]

"I will speak for myself as a Third World person" is an important position for political mobilization today. But the real demand is that, when I speak from that position, I should be listened to seriously; not with that kind of benevolent imperialism, really, which simply says that because I happen to be an Indian or whatever . . . .A hundred years ago it was impossible for me to speak, for the precise reason that makes it only too possible for me to speak in certain circles now. I see in that a kind of reversal, which is again a little suspicious.
—*Gayatri Chakravorty Spivak,* The Post-Colonial Critic

Chicana. You are not a third-world person. You come from America.

Politics does something to people. My friend Nasreen from Pakistan knows. My friend Sita from India knows. My friend Murvete from Kosovo knows. Our survival games have brought us to the fat side of the world. We are it. We know.

Our bodies inhabit a portion of earth. We taste the sky know the stars see the waters, roots, and breathe in the wind. Outside of my body, there are other peoples' wars, documents with signatures of men and noble families, canons, guns, poisons, and rigid ideologies. Long before I ever was. Long before my father and mother.
Did you grow up knowing who inhabited your land before you? Did you grow up without knowing?
War ravaged a man. Hunger ravaged a woman. Religion ravaged a soul.
Refugees of a world on fire.
Bare feet. Backs and hands of labor. Artists. Thinkers. Communities tied together, knots of love and necessity. Or is it? Are our communities tied together only out of bare necessity, without the privilege to love affluently? Love luxuriously? Survival games trick us into assuming particular identities. "South African Black" identity saves a Capetown mother throughout her twenty-seven years in exile. But she forgets to inform her twelve-year-old daughter that there is so much more than just survival. An Iraqi mother keeps her daughter under the scarf so she won't turn out like . . . . "con quien, mami?" Family stories. Border stories showing no way out for communities threatened by owners of guns, writers of documents, holy holders of the word. Where does exile begin and where does exile end?
Refugees of a world on fire.
I knew nothing of my past. Stories told around the kitchen table, pressed out as secrets and shame, revealed to me one by one; the contours of his-

tory and family. For every new bit of knowledge, I learned to see. Feel. I tasted the coarse salt, caked clumps of South Texas red dust. Northern Mexican clouds gathered from what I already knew in my heart. A boy child has had to grow up alongside the stench of death. The child never even knew living could smell any other way. When a man kills another man on the Texas border to Mexico, when a woman is raped on the Kosovo border to Albania. Families live for generations to build peace. Hunger strikes first the stomach then the heart, even before a child is born. I know.

Refugees of a world on fire.

We have inherited lives of separation, histories of fragmentation. Inherited the hearts of our fathers, haunted and scarred. Exile is also a search for emotional reconciliation, even if it means a geographic and cultural distance. Go mi'ja, go.

That's why they let me go. She must go to create the key we need to unlock ourselves from the harm of the faceless and furious past. Re-create our legacy, m'ija. Re-do what needs to be re-done so we can die in the appreciation of who we are, the histories we were unable to honor and know about while we lived. We did not have the luxury of intellectual distance. Our poverty, our brutality, seeped into our pores. We did not learn about it from books, or from other people's stories. The third world was our only world. Go m'ija. The way your great-grammo crossed her own territory, now the border, into dusty south Texas. There were wars. There were people. There was a portion of earth our bodies inhabited. Politics and wars changed names and papers, monies. We remain the people of this portion of the earth. You are the ones we let go. Our daughters. You are the ones to reshape our legacy, return honor, and bring us all back home. The spirit of your grammo lives in you. You and the other scattered people.

Refugees of a world on fire.

Zanele in Capetown knows.

Antonia in Buenos Aires knows.

Gloria in San Antonio knows.

5. Looking at the Scandals of Our Production

So what I'm interested in is seeing ourselves as namers of the subaltern. If the subaltern can speak then, thank God, the subaltern is not a subaltern any more.

—*Gayatri Chakravorty Spivak*, The Post-Colonial Critic

Our collective consciousness can work to transform concepts of power, from hierarchical to relational approaches to power. We are accomplices of each other. Accomplices in the circle of different ways of Be-ing. *I am because we are.* (voice of South Africa) *You are the we of me.* (voice of Carson McCullers)

I seek an orbital path for a broad distribution of knowledge. The poets know this is possible. The poets create scandals of vision. Intellectuals, what is the scent of your knowledge? What color is your theory? Am I a Chicana theorist? Whose books do I read? Whose books do we read? How do we define, and not delimit, our community?

It is in the position of the "other," the "marginal," the"diaspora," the "theories of resistence," "identity politics." The only thing they still won't read or listen to is "class." The poverty (and Karl Marx) still taboo.

I am round-trip. I inhabit a piece of earth, leave no part of me behind, al fin. Dance in cultural landscapes. Del sur, del norte, encompassing temporal and spiritual crossroads of eastern and western thought. *Cultural codeswitcher? O cultural codegiver?* Soy una mexcla de poesia y trabajo, pensamientos y amor. Mujer.

I am known to have androgynous qualities, which I flaunt con mi Humphrey Bogart look in the Nordic autumn weather. Felt hat y trenchcoat. A Somalian hot dog vendor in Oslo once asked me, "*Where* do *you* come from? Must be Paris, cuz that's the only place I've seen women dressed like *you*." His eyes lit with his passion for life, larger than the endless gray horizon. He'd never heard of San Antonio, pero *Texas*? Yeah. Bang. Bang.

Androgyny can go a long way. Don't you think so, my accomplices? Let's place androgyny out there . . . como Virginia Woolf, you know, help her in her project, which maybe has been simmering too long on the same spot waiting for us radical Chicana U.S. Third World feminists to finish our formal education and then dig in.

(fingers flip through *The American Heritage Dictionary of the English Language*)

Androgynous: adj. 1. Having female and male characteristics in one; hermaphroditic. 2. Botany. Composed of staminate and pistillate flowers. Said of the flower spikes of certain sedges. (Latin androgynus, from Greek androgunos : andro- + -gynous.) Androgyny, n.

Open territory. Open borders. So I want to put the word out there as a conceptual tool for our theories and knowledge, even our existence. (Jacques Derrida, contemporary French philosopher, used the *HYMEN*, yes, *our* body part, as a conceptual tool!)

Learning that the political is personal is political and back again is to be brave enough to leave security and live through the fire of experience, round trip, and find out that home looks like someplace else. Todo, todo cambia. The Chicana imagination continually builds a new creative framework to step into, and away from, in order to love the larger picture of change.

What is a poor Chicanita doing thinking she can think?

What does this woman, who for eighteen years only knew the backyard, chainlinked, *do* now as a woman with acquired theories, increased subjective and theoretical knowledge, where does she go with this? What does a woman with third-world poverty branded onto her skin do with the knowledge once set aside for the privileged, now that she has access to it? Now that we have access to positions we choose, but did not originally define? Is it less difficult today to bring our integrity and honorable humility to the tables of power? Tables we have not set. Do we get sucked into a system that is not the system we would have created for our stories? If it hurts, do we retreat? Must we leave again? Tu casa no es mi casa. Este casa es nuestra casa.

Remembering those conversations and her grandmother's last and final words, Denver stood on the porch in the sun and couldn't leave it. Her throat itched; her heart kicked—and then Baby Suggs laughed, clear as anything.

"You mean I never told you nothing about Carolina? About your daddy? You don't remember nothing about how come I walk the way I do and about your mother's feet, not to speak of her back? I never told you all that? Is that why you can't walk down the steps? My Jesus my."

But you said there was no defense.

"There ain't."

"Then what do I do?"

"Know it, and go out the yard. Go on."

—Toni Morrison, Beloved

6. To Think I Could . . .

Pivot: a person or thing that chiefly determines the direction or effect of something; the essential component.

—The American Heritage Dictionary, 1981

My love of spinning tops. Purple, wooden, high tech, shiny, striped, red, metal, plastic with whistles or silent. A mad twist just to observe how long it can spin spin spin spin until some outside force of physics makes it stop. The potential energy lies in its design. Like the design of a Chicana. With assistance (the community), con ganas (interactions of love), a curious twirl of a thumb and forefinger (our own individual power), the top can spin spin and spin (our work). Landing just about anywhere (our Be-ing).

Chicana spirit is in everyone. I always tell my *first-generation-immi-grant/refugee/minority* friends here in Oslo that I am their daughters and sons, perhaps more their grandchildren. Because of my long-term running identities such as mexican/little-girl-with-the-spanish-surname/mex-

ican-american/set-the-X-in-square-for-mexican-race/hispana/chicana/
spick/texan/latina/tejana/american/minority/immigrant experience; because
of the pakistani-norwegian hyphenations just beginning; because the generation of young, bi-cultural voices in Europe are yet in the bud but coming; because brown Norwegian faces appear as commentators on
television programs; because my friend Agnieska is allowed to make free-
lance radio programs even though "chee haz an ahccent"; because after
twenty years but already at the age of forty-three, Latin-American political refugees are beginning to dare to look back at the past; loss and ale-
gría pressed out like secrets around a kitchen table with friends, to open
up a history from which they have not had the luxury of being intellectually distant. Because I've heard so many times the story of so many
women like Nesret crossing borders, once a republic, then a province and
now a war-torn region in the Balkans. I place the wanderings of my great-
grandmother Catarina next to hers, next to those of my grandmother, next
to the people scattered over territories of Northern Mexico once a republic, then a province, then a new border between countries. Al fin?

Fazel, an Iranian artist, forty-eight years old, has lived in exile for six
years. A short term compared to so many minorities like Chicanas in Texas,
Albanians in Kosovo, Kurds from Turkey. Nevertheless, as we sit at a café
table across the museum gift shop, he tells me about his acquired life of
minority status. "I've never done this before. Lived someplace where I did-
n't know the language or cultural codes and customs. I can do it, yes, but I
often still cannot grasp this as *my* own life. I often have a feeling which
strikes me as an unexpected flash of white light and I brutally wake up from
this life of continually coping, . . . *this is me now*. I haven't lived a Chicana
life as you have. I begin from scratch, but I am still an Iranian artist."

Alejandro, my colleague, in exile from Argentina since the early eighties, *shoots the bull* with me in my office before we start the work day; "You,
Chicana, Swedish television did an interview with two young people who
were born in Chile, but came to Sweden as very young children with their
parents, who were forced to flee their country at the time of Pinochet's
coup d'etat in 1973. So they've grown up for the most part of their lives in
Sweden. They spoke about themselves feeling like Swedes, growing up
with the Swedish culture and language, schooling, todo. As they spoke, I
felt they *looked* like Latinos; but then again *something* in their mannerisms, the way they wore their hair, these small details hard for me to
explain, made them appear like Swedes, too. Chicana, you should have
seen this! Later, their parents came into the studio, and wham! As they
spoke with their parents, they *were* Latinos. Young people transformed.
When they turned to the Swedish television reporters again, it was like
they could switch, de repente, and there they were in their Swedish mode.

It was amazing to see these kids switch like that and know how to carry on from the one cultural mode or the other. What capacity, no?"

Un poco arrogante, and with memory of the scent of *Tabu*, I say, "Claro. Just wait, Alejandro, in the end, somos todos . . ." As my thirteen-year-old son, Aksel Albert, says, "An American passport. A Norwegian passport. I must be 200%!" His healthy choice.

My family of round-trip. I have painfully discovered that the true colonization-of-the-mind is when I allow my ethnicity/identity to act as my limitation rather than my take-off point. I am *it* and I want always to be a beginner with new choices. I choose these cultural, spiritual, geographical, politcal states of exile as a liberating process. My decision to choose Chicana as the pivotal point of my other positions is my political choice and my politics comes from the heart. Spirit *and* power.

Refugees of a world on fire.

These are my survival games. *I am because we are.* Without expecting *sameness.*

Community survives when it is the result of acts of love. What I choose now sets the direction for someone else in future generations. My great-grandmother Catarina, Murvete's mother Nesret, my colleague Alejandro, l'artisto Fazel, l'escritora Gloria, mi amiga Zanele . . . chose to walk off the porch of exile into a world of political color, a world the color of red and burnt truths. No matter which portion of the earth I inhabit, I face unfinished promises of reconciliation. We will choose different paths. In the end, we are all Chicanas.

Chicana, I take your name in honor.
Ever since I first heard your name, a story surfaced which was me. I am
because we are. My link to a universal Chicana spirit is not only born from
my backyard, but of who I am in the political picture of Texas and of the
world. I gained insight to the history of my family, my neighbors, the
cousins I lost because of a war and a poverty. As you took from me my illu-
sions, you also had something to give. I have expanded my family across
continents. You gave me both the barbed wire and the daisies from which I
choose to re-shape my legacy.
I had to leave to find you and I have found you in many faces.
This has been my path. And you have always been with me.

Notes

I dedicate this work to my sons, Martin, my star; and Aksel Albert, my sun. Also to Maria Antonietta Berriozabal, who ran for a congressional seat from Texas in 1998 and whose persona and campaign fed my hope that democracy is an act of love by a community of people.

1. Cherríe Moraga

iii.

"locking arms in the master's house"...
omissions, revisions, new issues

twenty-six

Burning House

Liliana Wilson Grez

twenty-seven

"What's Wrong with a Little Fantasy?" Storytelling from the (Still) Ivory Tower

Deborah A. Miranda

I found *This Bridge Called My Back* at the local library when, at age thirty-three, I was finally beginning to write again, and write honestly. I had also recently reconnected with my Esselen Nation family, from whom I had been separated by both history and my parents' divorce. I was just beginning to trust my own interpretations about what it meant to be a mixed-blood Indian woman in a colonizing culture that fetishizes "purity" and privileges whiteness, to hear and question the intricate layers that make up my psyche: silences about rape, abandonment, desire, loss, the gift of memory. *Bridge* was full of the voices of women of color, inspiration, and story; food for the soul of a lonely Indian woman.

But it didn't satisfy me—though at the time, I was not sure why. Now I know that I was looking for that moment of resonance, the lightning strike of identification that comes when we see our struggle, our story, in someone else's words. There were Indian voices in *Bridge*, a few poems or personal narratives that moved me, but which barely began to represent our astonishingly diverse Native communities. Only Chrystos had other published work available to me, and even her well-known collections were difficult to locate. I wanted more. I wanted to belong to this book, own this book, I wanted my struggles as an *Indian woman* to be present and *part of* this beautiful, incredible book! It took me a while to admit, but that interaction didn't happen. I felt like a traitor because of it.

In many ways, the book was somebody else's story. I felt that in order to have some claim to the book's power, I needed to become a generic woman of color, lose my Indianness. The radical differences between my own story and the stories in *Bridge* are illustrated by this amazing quote from Joy Harjo, poet and musician of the Muskogee Creek Nation: "The literature of the aboriginal people of North America defines America."

Think about this. Not the literature of Mather, Hawthorne, Emerson, Thoreau, Alcott. Not even the literature of Nora Zeale Hurston, Rita Dove, Audre Lorde, Maxine Hong Kingston, Sandra Cisneros, Alice Walker, Naomi Shihab Nye, Helena Maria Viramontes, Bharati Mukherjee, Hisaye Yamamoto, Janice Mirikitani. Try to follow Harjo's line of thought: *the lives, history, and voices of Native people on this continent define "America."* Yes, others have come to this continent by choice, kidnapping, force, necessity—but this continent (are you tired of hearing this?) was not empty of human culture, life, richness. And those

First Peoples are not gone! My question here, then, is not only *who has been silenced?* but *whose ears have been denied sound and song?* What has been hidden even from you, my sisters of color? What do you not know about the land you stand on? Why don't you know it? How can you learn it? How has it formed you as a non-native woman of color in North America?

If you do not examine Native experiences and voices, you agree to live in, and help construct, a culture of erasure, invisibility, lies, disguise.

There is something intrinsically different about being an Indian woman in the Americas which the work of other women of color cannot express: we inherit *and still live* histories and oppressions designed to legally enforce Indian identities as not just disempowered, but genetically incapable of autonomy; we carry and still live out generations of human rights injustices such as the denial of documented treaty rights and the deadly form of literacy wrought in Indian Boarding Schools, meant to further enslave rather than empower. Our bodies and hearts carry a deep sting, an engulfing shame, and a contrary assertion of survivance, which all stem from the fact that our identities and cultures—our hearts— sprang from this land, from a place stolen, defiled, yet still present beneath our feet every day of our lives.[1] There is no metaphor for such pain.

The voices in *Bridge* are not inadequate or inarticulate. Those voices helped save my life. But I craved the indigenous voices that knew the paradox, pain, and deceit of a colonized homeland beneath my feet—and beneath the feet of every American.

As I was to find out, the underrepresentation of Native women in *Bridge* is by no means an anomaly.[2] In four years of graduate school, I haven't found Indian women's voices to be truly present in most publications or forums, academic coursework, readings, conferences, or critical analyses of American literatures and culture (including projects by and about women of color). I know that this erasure is part of a larger, cultural amnesia surrounding the foundational crime that North American educations, governments, and national myths are built on. But I am always disappointed to find so few works by Native women available, much less read, utilized, and acknowledged by other women of color. Everywhere in feminist discourse is the "new" voice of Third World Women, frequently included under the catchall label *transnational*. Yet the Third World Women in your own country are rarely, if ever, acknowledged as such.[3] This omission holds the U.S. women's community locked into the strange position of championing causes for those who are silenced without accounting for the use or history of the land from which they launch those causes.

Women of color still need to talk about what it's like to be an indigenous person alive in her contemporary, colonized homeland; someone who sees few traces of an indigenous presence—and yet *knows that indigenous presence is there because she is it*. What does this do to our sanity? What does it do to the other cultures and communities living in this homeland? What does it do to the ways that our relationships with one another are formed—especially, for Native women, issues of feminism and a women's community? What does it tell us about how non-native women, as "North Americans," face and deal with a criminal act of a colonization that has never ended?

I have struggled to find words for telling this. Perhaps the best way is through my own story as an Indian woman in academia in the late twentieth century. It certainly isn't "traditional" in the way most people in the United States have learned to see "Indian" stories; but it's my story nonetheless.

The time: end of the twentieth century. The scene: My university. The context: A graduate seminar, Theories of American Literature. The plot: student facilitation of a class session using a book called *The Ethnic Canon*. My responsibilities are to Jana Sequoya-Magdaleno's article "Telling the *Differánce*: Representations of Identity in the Discourse of Indianness." I look forward to the day of my seminar with less and less enthusiasm, even as I obsessively read and re-read the article.

Differences raise fear in the classroom. Attorney and professor Patricia Williams, speaking of a white student who objected to certain readings because the work made the student feel guilty, depicts a typical confrontation: "I am very angry and it shows. I can feel how unprofessorial I must seem; looking into her eyes, *I know I'll have to pay*" (*Alchemy*, 21). Williams, an African-American woman, witnesses the intersection of race and rights in her own classroom because of who she is, and what she is teaching: an "alchemy" that has potential to become explosive. Likewise, in my American literature seminar, it is the Native American portion of the syllabus and my encounter with it that arouses fear and bitterness in my classmates.

I know that as leader of my particular seminar discussion, my own response to tensions will need to be informed, rational, and articulate—more so than anyone else's. It is my job to maintain a professional demeanor even if that "class discussion . . . threatened the deeply vested ordering" of a particular student's world (22). Like Williams, I know that if I lose my composure, I will have to pay.

I am responsible for this juggling act in part due to my assigned role as facilitator. But I am also aware that as the sole Native American woman in my classroom, and, more often, the sole "minority" student, I am perceived as *the* representative of all Indians or even—incredibly—all people of color, sexual minorities, and disabled populations! I'm supposed to tell other students what "we" want, how we "Others" enter this discourse. Further, I am responsible for somehow presenting my "unique" academic contributions and myself in a conformist manner. If I respond to a racist or ignorant comment (let alone respond heatedly) I play into a stereotype: the undereducated, inadequate, incorrigible savage who is unable to master her own passions, much less the English language and a classroom full of students. Displaying a passion for one's culture is a radical risk for people of difference within the academy: passion—or anger, fear, pleasure, commitment—becomes synonymous with "primitive," and that "primitive" voice is then okay to discount, deride, or even turn against itself.

This assignment is no simple course requirement for me. It is my life on display.

Discussion starts with the question hovering behind Sequoya-Magdaleno's article: namely, who is "Indian"? Native Americans are legally required to be "card-carrying Indians"; that is, members of federally recognized tribes must have an ID card proving that recognition, complete with a photo, name, tribal affiliation, and enrollment number. No other nonwhite group of people in the United States needs such identification to "qualify" as disempowered and receive reparation services.[4] (Is it accident that this legality applies only to indigenous people?) Such identification techniques have been less concrete within ongoing Native literature criticism about "who is Indian" and *what* is Indian, which Sequoya-Magdaleno teases out in her article. Academics want to pigeonhole Native literature, make "authentic" writing fit preconceived standards of Indianness. However—one argument goes—it might be that this very authenticity cannot be morally shared outside their tribe by Indian writers, for fear of violating cultural boundaries that are too sacred to reveal: in other words, a "real" Indian wouldn't "tell." Thus, the battle about "authentic" Indians feeds on itself.

I field a comment from a student who says, "Oh, it's obvious to me that [authenticity arguments are] blatantly economic—there are scholarships I'd love to get, but *I* can't because I'm white, not Native American." Sitting at the front of the classroom, I feel my skin tingle with adrenaline: I had received a tuition waiver from the Office of Minority Affairs. In this university's culture, taking a tuition waiver based on minority status is comparable to welfare fraud, and this student calls me on it. He is male, white, blond, and blue-eyed to boot, clueless to the privileges that his physical appearance entitles him—or that benefitted the lives of his ancestors. He feels he has worked hard to get here, receiving no help along the way—being, in fact, pushed further down the line by minority students cutting in ahead. Limited by life experiences, physical attributes, gender, a reduced capacity for compassion, and fear, my classmate makes an uninformed, irrational argument. He believes every word.[5]

I point out that Indian students receive academic funding so that they may make their mark as Indian scholars, teachers, scientists, lawyers, or doctors—frequently working for the benefit of their own tribes or other Indian people, thus eventually reducing dependency on financial assistance. But I wish later that I had also pointed out that scholarships don't magically make up for historical and current economic and/or educational situations that leave us very underprepared for the rigors and culture of academia.[6] Perhaps, in my own first hesitant quarter of grad school, this point was too close to the bone to admit out loud.

Another detour—"I don't see what the big deal is about appropriation of culture," this same student objects, "I'm white, and somewhere, someone, sure as I'm sitting here, is appropriating *my* culture right now, I guarantee it!" He is flushed, angry—passionate. I don't mind his passion. What I can't stomach is the violence behind that passion. I describe for him the connections between *appropriation* of a cultural object or person—such as Disney's portrayal of a cartooned Barbie-dolled Pocahontas—and *exploitation*, which is akin to *violation*. "There's no truth there," I argue, "it's pure fantasy!" My classmate asks, "What's wrong with a little fantasy?!"

Throughout the room, we rock back in a collective, stunned pause. I look out at the confused graduate students, the silent professor, the three women of color who, like myself, have hardly spoken up all quarter and do not speak now. *What's wrong with a little fantasy?* I don't know how to argue that *whose* fantasy is what's wrong; that your fantasy backed by power is *my* reality. I have not yet read Robin Morgan's celebrated aphorism, "pornography is the theory and rape the practice" ("Theory," 88), so I can't rip back with, "Pocohontas is the theory and Wounded Knee the practice." I don't think fast enough to say, "The problem with little fantasies is that they grow up to be big fantasies." Anyway, those responses would be too passionate, too emotional, too "Indian"—not a neat, theoretical response. It doesn't matter that my classmate is being racist; his privilege gives him that right without loss of position. But if *I* respond passionately it will let this student, these classmates, my professor, know that I live in my body, an Indian woman alive and vulnerable. Unable to compete at an academic, intellectual level. Unable to perform that surgical separation of body from mind, culture from intellect.

I crack a joke: "You mean, a fantasy like the naked Indian hunk running through the forest with a torch for the first five minutes of [the movie] *The Scarlet Letter*?" Everyone laughs, a little loudly (earlier, we had agreed this scene was purely gratuitous New Age "ceremony" as created by Hollywood). I endeavor, briefly, to describe the consequences of "a little fantasy"—abuse of power, disenfranchisement, racial and sexual stereotyping . . . as if those words mean anything. The session ends, and we all go our separate ways. We've run out of time, never return to that discussion—taking place, as it does, in one of the last days of the quarter. But at least I'd extricated myself from a tricky moment—hadn't I?

Late that night I try to take refuge in the last chapters of Patricia Williams's book. I read, "At a faculty meeting once, I raised several issues: racism among my students, my difficulty in dealing with it by myself, and my need for the support of colleagues. I was told by a white professor that 'we' should be able to 'break the anxiety by just laughing about it.' Another nodded in agreement and added that 'the key is not to take this sort of thing too seriously'" (*Alchemy*, 166). Stunned, I realize that this was exactly what I had done that afternoon: laugh off the racism in my classmate's remark, try to relieve the tension by giving him—and myself, our classmates—the easy way out. I still operate by rules of behavior long ago laid out by white men.

For me, the hardest texts to grapple with in grad school have been the subtle, ever-present canons of racism and classism. My own contorted adaptations to life as an Indian woman are the texts within the texts, and inside is still another text about my relationship to non-native women of color. I'm not sure that even now I can articulate it. I've become accustomed to certain maneuvers, negotiations, that are necessary to my comfort zone—and to the comfort zones of the dominant culture and other women of color. These contortions often arise from my own need to negate or obscure racism and difference. But to deny that difference exists or racism happens—and the various insidious ways I have helped to deny both—erases *me*, and the justification of reparation and change. It's painful to contemplate; there's a complicity there I don't want. As Emma LaRocque (Plains Cree, Metis) writes, "As a child, I never spoke up in classrooms or in playgrounds. As an adolescent, I felt shame and confusion. But in my late teens, I began to talk back. . . . To those whites I considered friends, I made special attempts to explain. *Years later I came to understand that, like many native individuals before me, I had been forced into the position of being an apologist for 'my people'*" (367–68, emphasis added). The role of apologist —to make "special attempts to explain"—is no less damaging to indigenous women than other institutionalized methods of colonizing; like English itself, the need to explain reifies the subordinate role of the speaker. Indigenous women who try to explain "indigenous women" end up "negotiating," criticizing ourselves and our cultures in order to minimize or apologize for difference.[7]

Of course, if everything you try to explain about yourself results in condemnation or silence because it is uncomfortable for your listener, yet you can't stop *being* what it is that makes them respond so, then you've got some serious internalized shame going on. In "haciendo caras," Gloria Anzaldúa's words speak to the ways people of color translate this shame and apology into their relationships within the academy: "I wanted students-of-color to become aware of, and get out from under, conditioned subservience; I wanted to call attention to the dynamic of avoidance among us, of not acknowledging each other—an act of dehumanizing people like ourselves . . . to emerge from 'blank-outness' and openly combat the dominant groups' denial and erasure of ethnic subjectivity" (xix–xx). Four years of academia later, I am only beginning to bridge the gaps found here, to see the complexity of Anzaldúa's "dynamic of avoidance" in the relationship between Indian women and other women of color. More radically, I imagine a bridging between us done *without* breaking our own backs in the process.

This does not mean that I reverse power plays, demand explanations from white and non-native women-of-color peers and/or professors (at least, not always!); it does mean that I am learning to demand dialogue, active conversations in which I am one of many people working to cross gaps. It also means that demands for dialogue come with a price. Often I am discouraged, exhausted, and depressed, especially by Indian-specific racism that targets all Indians as enemies for refusing to live inside Disney's hand-inked frames. Here in Washington State, vicious anti-Indian racism has flared up in the aftermath of the Makah tribe's decision to assert their treaty rights and resume whaling now that the gray whale is no longer endangered. "Save a whale, harpoon a Makah!" read bumper-stickers in the UW student parking lot; bomb threats are called in to Chief Leschi, a K–12 school on the Puyallup Indian Reservation (far from Makah lands); as I drive into Seattle on I-5, radio call-in shows feature openly anti-Indian slurs and threats from both DJs and callers. White acquaintances tell me they are shocked, but when I hear the same venom echoed in the library, restrooms, and walkways of the UW—the supposedly open-minded bastion of liberalism—by people of color and whites alike, the general public's hatred doesn't surprise me in the least. Instead, I fear that anti-Indian sentiment goes so deep into the bones of the United States that it spreads to every cell.

Being an Indian woman in the Ivory Tower at the beginning of the twenty-first century is not just a financial drain, or an intellectual challenge. Academia is a soul-breaking endeavor. Every university in this country is built on Native land that was stolen with great loss of indigenous life. Within those universities, Indian people are presented with professors, peers, and syllabi that accuse us of stealing someone else's entitlement. In the library we are fantasies—vanished, invisible, quaint. When, by some miracle, a judge upholds the law and "allows" us our treaty rights, our acts are viewed as tantamount to treason, barbarous cruelty, savagery.

This story is larger than just one seminar. My graduate school doesn't have a Native literature program in the English department. In fact there is not even a single Native American lit course at the graduate level, nor is one planned for the future. Now, just because I'm Indian doesn't mean I was born with an innate knowledge of Native literature. This hole in the program means I must construct my education about Native literature, and the scholarship around that literature, from scrounged sources: a course in American literature (two articles on "Indians"), a course in "post"-colonial women's literature (Rigoberta Menchú the sole indigenous author studied), "Women's Love Poetry and Erotics" (all-white reading list). I benefit from the generosity of colleagues and friends in programs at other universities (let's hear it for e-mail!) and read endlessly, but I have never studied with another American Indian scholar or author at the university, never had an American Indian professor or advisor, never taken a course in which Native American literatures were the focus. I've had a Native scholar/writer in one of my graduate classrooms exactly once. I've learned to make waves about these issues, but I am not nearly up to Menominee poet Chrystos's brilliant repartee: Chrystos, who in her brief career as a college student told a racist professor "fuck you!" to his face and exited the room—and college—with a grace I will never possess.

This lack of coursework affects me daily, hourly, deeply. But what this absence in the English program means to other, non-native graduate students, both white and non-native people of color, is far more damaging. What I have tried to communicate here are the dangers we face as members of a culture based on lies. Even within the "us" of the women-of-color community, I still feel like a "them," *and there are historical, cultural reasons for this sense of alienation.* Educated within anti-Indian institutions and U.S. culture, women of color learn the same deafnesses to Indian voices that white graduate students and professors absorb and pass on. There is a peculiar relationship between women of color and Indian women, with solidarity on the one hand, silence on the other. Given the story I have just told you, can you think of a good reason why American Indian experiences are still absent from a communal discourse about racism, representation, academic life, or literary theory in projects led by "women of color"? I know I am not the only Indian woman/scholar/author who feels marginalized this way in a roomful or bookful of women of color. I also know that the same Indian women have told me that sharing this sense of marginalization with women of color is hideously difficult.

I feel presumptuous, foolish, nervous saying to women of color, "Wait! We're not done yet!" But I don't claim that indigenous women are somehow more special, or more important, than any other women of color. What I *do* claim is this: in the violence and trauma of a genocidal colonization and in conjunction with the erasure of indigenous presence that is part of an omnipresent, long-term colonizing policy, Indian oppression and resistance are both less easily seen or heard than even other women of color might suspect. This erasure is not because we are completely silenced, but because U.S. women of color, like everyone else, have been subjected to a pervasive, vicious cultural education of erasure. Twenty years after *This Bridge Called My Back*, there is no shame in recognizing and pointing out the work yet to be done.

What do I ask of you, sisters of color? I ask, remember the differences between indigenous and diasporic; between indigenous and exile; between still-colonized native and freed slave; between *choosing* education as a way to speak, and having literacy shoved down your throat in a boarding school far from home, beaten into you. Don't assume we are not interested or unavailable if no Indian woman responds to your CFP; advertise outside the academy! Ask us to edit, read, review, speak. When teaching theories of literature, remember to find out about and compare the concepts of indigenous aesthetics—theories of knowledge based on a North American origin rather than diasporic, immigrant, colonizing, "post"-colonial or transnational emergences.[8] Remember that even as I write this, legal motions are being made to strip us of our sovereign rights, our status as indigenous peoples. Has anyone told you to legally stop being Chinese American, African American, Chicana? Remember that our oppression is different—not better, not harder, not deeper—but physically *different*, present, a wound re-opened each time we awaken, a battle we fight in which genocide is never apologized for, adulthood is never legally granted, and land can never be separated from the nations of our own bodies.

Indian women are not entirely alone, nor forgotten, and we don't want to compete in the Oppression Olympics. But listen up, women of color: some indigenous wounds have become yours. Because you live on this continent, our lives and souls connect in much the same way that the webs of our planet's ecology simultaneously depend on and support a whole entity. The erasure of American Indian literatures from the academy is not simply the chance squeezing-out of one ethnic literature. Remember Harjo's words: *The literature of the aboriginal people of North America defines America.* This means that the *erasure* of aboriginal literatures defines *you*. You are constituted by an erasure; you negotiate not just your own histories and oppression, but a huge national fantasy on which those histories and oppressions rest, a fantasy that surrounds you in every detail of your daily life.

As I write and revise this essay, I keep looking at the cover of *Bridge*: a woman on her hands and knees, bearing the weight of misunderstanding and hatred on her back. Bearing even fantasy. Just out of sight are her sisters, also bent over, spines aching, shoulders trembling. In my mind, I wonder: What would happen if those women stand up, face one another, make many bridges of arms and hands, fingers interlaced at the center?

Please listen, and pass it on: welcome the depth and reality of difference in this country. It's a start; it's a different kind of crossing altogether.

Notes

1. For more on the idea of Chicanas as representative of indigenism, see the following e-mail exchange, "Footnoting Heresy."

2. The absence did not go unnoticed by the editors of this current retrospective collection, either: one of the reasons I responded to the call for papers was that AnaLouise Keating wrote to me, acknowledged the underrepresentation of Native women, and asked me to contribute. This kind of conscious inclusion by the editors crosses many communities and perspectives and is, perhaps, the most noticeable and admirable difference between *Bridge* and this new anthology.

3. The term *fourth world* has been coined to define cultures that fit typical Third World constructs but exist within the First World. To avoid complications, I leave that discussion for another time. An excellent starting point for more information is the website http://www.cwis.org/fwdp.html.

4. Though this sounds like a simple arrangement for distributing reparations, it is not. In addition, there are many nonfederally recognized tribes (like mine, the Ohlone-Costanoan Esselen Nation) spending every penny and ounce of energy they can to fulfill the complex legal requirements to become "recognized"—not for lusted-after aid, but for tribal well-being, and strengthened intertribal relationships.

5. My classmate's comment elaborated his ongoing complaint that Affirmative Action was an unfair and outdated program. Although his vehemence and wronged arguments made no sense to me, I knew that he was far from alone. (In fact, two years later, passage of I-200 in Washington State—the initiative that reversed Affirmative Action—validated this.) Inherent in this argument is truly a selective and dispassionate memory: too many Americans do not want to remember our recent history of colonization, slavery, and theft, and do not acknowledge the dirty work of covering up that history and its consequences. Resentment about minority scholarships goes right to the heart of that denial: if the past injustice didn't happen, or didn't happen recently enough, horrifically enough, then reparations are not only unnecessary, they are *unfair*. It is a small, blind, damaging leap of logic that ignores how our culture *now* is constructed around those same *past* injustices. Anti-Affirmative action legislation denigrates the lives of every minority person in this country, in very personal ways.

6. In 1995, Louis Owens reported that, "Among all Ph.D.s granted in 1989–90 in all humanities fields, 9.2% went to minorities, while only 0.3% went to American Indians. In the field of English and American literature, the figure for Indians was 0.1%." Among Native American scholars, an incomplete degree often signifies choices we make about survival rather than ability.

7. One need only examine the criticism received by so-called angry Indian women writers such as Chrystos, Paula Gunn Allen, Lee Maracle, and Leslie "Almanac of the Dead" Silko to see how quickly and efficiently we are labled *difficult* for one reason or another—too honest, too dykey, too feminist, too vengeful—when we bypass negotiations.

8. I refer here to distinctly indigenous ways of knowing the world and self. For example, Gerald Vizenor has asserted that indigenous art and literature are a kind of postmodern affirmation—or that postmodernism is indigenous—by virtue of how Native traditions embrace and live by change and movement rather than static definition. The theory that all Native art is based not on an aesthetic of beauty, but of use, is another such idea: "art for art's sake" would not only be ridiculous, but unthinkable and possibly sacrilegious within such a framework. See Leuthold, Ortiz, Womack, and Allen, and Maori Linda Tuhiwai Smith's excellent manifesto for indigenous survival.

twenty-eight

Footnoting Heresy: E-mail Dialogues

Deborah A. Miranda and AnaLouise Keating

Date: Tue, 01 Aug 2000 08:41:30 +0000
To: dmiranda@u.washington.edu
From: AnaLouise Keating <zami@mindspring.com>
Subject: "what's wrong w/ a little fantasy?"
hi deborah,

i've read your new essay draft & again, let me say, i'm so happy you're writing it. you make many important points that need to be heard. it's funny; another contributor mentions, almost in passing, the overlooked differences between those identifying as "women of color" & those identifying as "Indian." when i asked her to consider expanding this statement (because it *is* so often overlooked), she pointed out that this vital issue is really a paper in itself . . . & now you're writing about it! synchronicity?

i'm going to share w/ you some of my reactions to your essay. do w/ them what you will. i'll try to make sure gloria reads the essay next week when i'm in santa cruz & i'll get back to you w/ her comments.

i think one of the things gloria will ask about is the place of chicanas (especially those like herself who work hard to claim their indigenous ancestry & connections) in the context of the distinctions you draw between native women & others. i know (or think i know) that gloria connects very strongly w/ her indigenous elements & the land. where she's from, in texas, was part of mexico before seized by the U.S. the land & her family were divided in two & from her writings & conversations i know that she has a sense of living in colonized territory, of having her language & land stripped away, of living (in your words) w/ "the fact that our bodies & souls sprang from this land, from a place stolen, defiled, & yet still beneath our feet every day of our lives." Would you be interested in addressing this issue?

thanks again. let me know if you have any comments/questions about the above.

contigo, AL

Date: Wed, 9 Aug 2000 16:40:18 -0700 (Pacific Daylight Time)
From: "deborah a. miranda" <dmiranda@u.washington.edu>
To: AnaLouise Keating <zami@mindspring.com>
Subject: Re: gloria's comments on "What's Wrong . . ."
Hi AnaLouise,

I've been wrestling with the comment about Chicana indigenism, & how that can be interpreted as representation of Indian women. As I'm sure you realize, the issue of indigenism is complex! I've given it a lot of thought. I began to carve out some notes in my reading journal about the similarities & differences between Chicanas & Indian women. I've developed some of these thoughts to come up with the passage below, which is currently designated as a "footnote." However, I still feel that there is something indescribable or at least difficult to describe that I am not expressing. Perhaps you & Gloria could read this passage over, & give me some feedback? I realize it is "only" a small point or footnote to the essay, & yet omitting any discussion of it would be a sin in my book. Deborah

Footnote [attached to the line ending ". . . a contrary assertion of survivance which all stem from the fact that our bodies & souls sprang from this land, from a place stolen, defiled, yet still beneath our feet every day of our lives."]

Here, I am tempted to include Chicanas as members of the indigenous peoples of North America; among these women is, for example, Gloria Anzaldúa, who acknowledges, embraces, and wrestles with her indigenous heritage in articulate and painful ways. There are good reasons to include Chicanas as indigenous women, and complex reasons for my hesitation to commit what many Indians would call the heresy of inclusion. At the risk of attempting to write a second paper into a footnote, here is my train of thought about my final, "Chicana-less," version.

1.) It seems clear that many Chicanas share the visceral connection to land that indigenous women feel: la raza is mestiza, a mixture of the indigenous and the (Spanish) colonizer. But if most U.S. Indian women writers—and I include Erdrich, Harjo, Hogan, Silko, Bird, Gould, Bell, Blaeser, Hale, Allen, Tremblay, Chrystos, LaDuke, Rose, Endrezze, Brant, myself, and many more—are actually mixtures of the indigenous and the (English, French, Russian, Spanish) colonizer, then U.S. mixed-blood Indians should not claim an "Indian" identity at all, but a mestiza identity. Why don't we? Why this insistence on essentializing an "Indian" identity for U.S. Indians but not for mixedblood Indians from south of the border? I know that Ines Hernández-Ávila touches briefly on this idea in her essay "Relocations upon Relocations," commenting wryly that including Chicanas/Chicanos in the definition of Indianness "disrupts" the more common definitions of that identity, and is "unsettling" to scholars. She attributes the "unpalatable" aspects of this idea to "the internalized racism and historically regulated animosities that have obstructed the si(gh)ting of both communities with respect to each other." But aren't these two obstructions very real, very powerful, in how U.S. Indians construct our Indian selves?

2.) Yes. In short, we essentialize because U.S. and Mexican national mythologies have been constructed around the same issue—colonization of indigenous peoples—in two very different ways. In the United States, being Indian is haunted by the idea of a Manifest Destiny which demands the colonization of land and destruction of any "primitive" inhabitants. In the United States, genocide depends upon negatively racializing and dehumanizing the Other: nonhuman animals that compete with colonizers for food or resources may be killed. In Mexico, colonization was not just about the taking of land but of souls; Spain saw the mestiza offspring of Indian and Spaniard as a benefit: more people, more converts; more converts, more slaves; more slaves, bigger Church; bigger Church, more power. But English Protestant conquest, in order for the noble and racially pure mission of Manifest Destiny to be perpetuated, needed "Indians," not mestizas; "Indians," not children of rape.

3.) Also, note the difference between the mythologies surrounding the U.S. Indian Princess—Pocahontas—and the Mexican royal, La Malinche. Pocahontas serves the European John Smith with her purported compassion and mediation skills, saving him from bloodthirsty male savages; but she does not have sex with him. La Malinche also mediates, serving Cortez as a translator and, not incidentally, saving his bacon as a conquistador. She is also his consort. Each woman serves the colonizer in ways that ultimately come at the expense of her people. Yet the representations of the two women could not be more different. Pocahontas is deified in American history as an Indian woman who protected an important white man. La Malinche's name means The Fucked One: she is defined purely by her sexual relationship with the Spaniard Cortez; she is a wanton native woman who betrayed her people. Pocahontas eventually marries a different white man, travels to Europe, and dies young. Her mixedblood son grows up to be a soldier against Indians, and assimilation effectively vanishes whatever Indian identity is left. Assimilation is made relatively painless in this story; being mixedblood is a temporary problem, part of the "progress" in which Indians diminish and fade away. "Real" Indians—the "purebloods"—are safely preserved on reservations, mythologized like Pocahontas. But La Malinche's children not only don't fade, they become reified as a third race, neither Indian nor Spanish: La Malinche is sex, is ugly, is mestiza—but real. She's nobody's Barbie-doll cartoon. Pocahontas, her vanishment and the disappearance of her child, is the fantasy.

4.) In large part, I agree with Hernández-Ávila that we (U.S. Indians) have bought into this classification system and have too often refused Chicanas their indigenous ties to the land. We have heard the U.S. government's definitions of Indian so many times, so many ways, that we can no longer envision ourselves outside of those definitions. We accept the borders given us, but the border between Pocahontas and La Malinche is, like the U.S./Mexico border, a false one. We—United Statesian Indians—are not Malinche's purer sister. We are Malinche's children.

5.) Yes, but—despite all genetic logic, U.S. Indians still deal with the social reality of being treated differently than any other people of difference in this country, and much differently than Chicana/os. Three things seem to define the construction of Indian in the United States: reservations, treaties, and paternalism. Chicana/os never had a reservation system. While this means they have not been legally restrained to certain patches of land, it also means Chicana/os do not "own" even a portion of their homeland as token recognition of indigenous rights. Being Indian means growing up on, or with the idea of, "the Rez." Even urban, non- or off-reservation Indians, like it or not, have this construction of being internally boundaried, or interned within our own homeland. The idea of the Rez has both restrained and connected U.S. Indians to the idea of homeland. Further, Indians were initially recognized as sovereign nations and entered into treaties with English, Spanish, and U.S. governments. Holding the United States to these treaties gives Indians a great deal of power that may not be manifested in economic terms, but is certainly an emotional and communal strength. Chicana/o indigenous ancestors do not have treaties, and again, ties with their homeland are in some ways obscured and damaged by this lack. Finally, U.S. Indians' lives are guided by paternalistic rules and regulations at every step of the way: we must register with the government, measure up to blood quantums, carry racial ID cards—all this in order to receive the "reparation" services (health care, academic scholarships, for example) owed us. Chicana/os do not have to qualify as a minority. Lands and monies are held in "trust" for Indians by the U.S. government, but are frequently frittered away; still, the United States is held responsible to Indians by its own legal documents. Also falling into the category of paternalistic behaviors is the idea of anthropology: Indians are a separate race to be studied, used, documented, and filed away. I have not seen many dissertations on the ceremonial uses of Chicana/o artifacts, or the differences between contemporary and traditional Chicana/os. In these ways, U.S. Indians learn to essentialize our Indianness because to do otherwise is to vanish completely, legally erased. Because there is no "official" category for mixed-bloods, to deny our "Indianness" is a heresy that would ensure the futility of any fight for justice or repatriation or reparation; and that, we will not allow.

6.) In addition to being socially constructed as "Indian," U.S. Indian writers seem to have simultaneously resisted this construction by moving away from a genetically pure definition of Indianness (meanwhile, New Age representations of Indians usually tend toward full-bloods—preferably old and wrinkled—whose role is to "train" white women as medicine women). Instead, mixedblood Indians who acknowledge their hybridity yet choose to identify as "Indian" paradoxically emphasize the ways that Native cultures are about change, or as mixedblood-Anishinable poet and scholar Gerald Vizenor says, "motion [serves as] nomadic survivance." By adapting and moving *with* their own mixedblood culture, mixedbloods bring the core of Indianness—survival and change—back into native culture itself. Rather than perpetuating the static, stuck image of "Indian" that the U.S. national mythology needs, mixedbloods present themselves as Indians who have merely adjusted to new circumstances, Indians who won't stand still for the camera. By identifying as mixedbloods, mixedbloods establish themselves as Indian.

7.) This train of thought, of course, is my own theoretical rambling. What we have in this essay is the reality of Indians who must constantly "prove" their Indianness to a government that holds tremendous power. Thus, as I see our situation now, U.S. Indians can accept the indigenous lineage and hearts of Chicanas, but still resist embracing our own mestiza identity until we are more assured that our indigenous survival is provided for. When we omit Chicanas from the "Indian Rolls," then, what we are also doing is resisting our own coming out as Mestizas.

8.) And by using the word *Mestiza*, I suddenly realize that it is much larger than simply blood or genetics: "Mestiza" is even larger than gender, despite its gendered origins. Mestiza means that which does not obey or even see boundaries; that which blurs sharp distinctions in favor of what is best or most appropriate; that which thrives in ambiguity because ambiguity means survival, creation, movement. Mestiza is all that is transgressive to "the norm," all that breaks the rules of male/female, white/not-white, normal/abnormal. Mestiza is richly fluid, deeply strong. Thus, all people who engage in breaking boundaries are engaged in what I would call "mestiza acts." *Mestiza* may have originated as a racial term to indicate mixed-race, but the ways that I am seeing that word and that way of being now are much more about self-directed identities, a personal, historically, psychically informed and aware construction of self that resists static definitions, craves the joy found in constant, organic, positive change.

After all this time! I am finally beginning to understand what Gloria meant by the term "mestiza consciousness." We are just beginning to form the Mestiza Nation that she saw twenty years ago. That's got to be the ultimate in heresies. No wonder I wanted to footnote it!

Date: Fri, 11 Aug, 2000 02:38:33 +0019
To: deborah a. miranda
From: AnaLouise Keating <zami@mindspring.com>
Subject: RE: gloria's comments on "What's Wrong . . ."
hi deborah,

thanks for your e-mail, & for your thoughtful comments. believe it or not, gloria & i had a similar discussion about these issues 2 days ago. your "footnote" deals w/ a very important issue, one that many people haven't thought about. you also negotiate between commonalities & differences in an important way. but really, it's a topic for another paper & detracts from the points you're making in yours. *but* what you say must be said, so here's our suggestion. it's rather innovative, let us know what you think: 1. keep the essay as is, w/o the note; 2. after your essay, we could include a version of my previous e-mail to you, where i ask about the issue, followed by 3. your email (you could, of course, revise & tighten it); 4. the e-mails would stay in e-mail format.

here's why we like the idea:
* it mixes a conventional genre (the essay) w/ a newer genre form (e-mail)
* it gives readers more of an idea about the process that went into writing your essay & into editing the anthology
* it gets the ideas out there & demonstrates that you're not gloss-

ing over the issue, that you're not making simplistic divisions between groups.
* it creates a mini-dialogue, & really, when you think about it, dialogue is a vital component to writing.
what do you think? let us know.
take care, AL

Date: Fri, 11 Aug 2000 05:03:42 -0700 (Pacific Daylight Time)
From: "deborah a. miranda" <dmiranda@u.washington.edu>
To: AnaLouise Keating <zami@mindspring.com>
Subject: RE: gloria's comments on "What's Wrong . . ."
Hi AnaLouise & Gloria,

This is a FANTASTIC idea! Let's go for it! What tortured me—even more than the heretic nature of my footnote—was the idea of appearing to have solid, inflexible answers; of needing to follow the convention of the academic or even most personal essays in coming to a conclusion; of wrapping up all loose ends at the cost of severing whole lives. Ignoring that dialogue that *is* the whole basis of Bridge. And keeping our dialogue in e-mail format is, again, fantastic. Several pieces in the original Bridge were written as letters to Gloria or Cherríe, & this continues that more intimate connection, while highlighting the fact that the radical women of color behind Bridge are not sitting around our communal cornfields tapping out our writing in traditional petroglyphs. LOL You mean they actually use e-mail??? !Viva la e-mail!
Deborah

twenty-nine

Memory and the New-Born: The Maternal Imagination in Diaspora

Shirley Geok-lin Lim

There is a will resisting resistance. We inhabit
Those spaces given up by ghosts we disinherit.

—Shirley Lim, 1980 (53)

Modern power-relations are thus unstable; resistance is perpetual and
hegemony precarious.

—Susan Bordo, 1993 (28)

The 1981 appearance of *This Bridge Called My Back* achieved a major and substantive transformation in U.S. cultural discourse; that is, it affirmed the presence of women of color writing in U.S. feminist consciousness.[1] However, the tendency among readers, critics, and students to construct "ethnic" American women as totalized entities persists. Such "ethnic labeling"—rather like designers' labels—threatens the loss of much that is vivid and particular about women of color's individual positions. The privileging of theory as a more compelling intellectual enterprise, with its corollary critique of "experience" and "narrative" as grossly reductive, has also strengthened the tendency to read women's writing abstractly and thus to ignore crucial distinctions in subject positions that *This Bridge* had set out to make visible.[2] A better acquaintance with "Chinese-American" women's cultural productions will show that Chinese-American racial and gender formations cannot be reduced to one notion of Chinese-cultural-descent ethnicity.[3] Totalizing categorizations are inadequate to explain the multiple, heterogeneous, even conflicting, historical formations of "Chinese-American," let alone "Asian-American" feminist consciousness.

Cherríe Moraga observed, in her 1983 foreword to the second edition of *This Bridge*, that, had the volume been conceived in 1983 instead of 1979, "it would speak more directly now to the relations between women and men of color, both gay and heterosexual," and "it would be much more international in perspective" (n.p.). For this daughter-volume, I aim to insert a particular notion of an international perspective; for, as an FBA, a Foreign-Born American, I carry certain dreadful markers of unassimilated alterity, such as a non-American accent and the propensity to decenter the United States and to insert the Asian as a subaltern in a global and diasporic, postcolonial, late-capitalist, and postmodern society, diplomatically recognized as the United States of America. The end of the twentieth century saw the emergence of "diaspora" and "global" studies that take into account radical changes in population and capital flows, the increasing impact of globalized corporate structures on nineteenth-century notions of national sovereignty, and the transformations, not always desirable, of local, indigenous, and environmental agents. At the same time, I aim to add another dimension also absent in the 1981 publication of *This Bridge*, the perspective of women as maternal figures. Although Anzaldúa and Moraga dedicated *This Bridge* specifically to their mothers, and generally "to all our mothers," the only two contributors who were known to have been mothers then, Rosario Morales and Audre Lorde, did not identify themselves or speak as mothers. Indeed, the narrative of the daughter, almost always American-born, or at least American-assimilated, dominates the anthology, as it does much of ethnic women's writing.[4] I offer a different narrative; not simply a mother's story, but a story coming from a maternal imagination in diaspora.

The diasporic Chinese American, a subject whose representations are contiguous with representations of émigrés, transnationals, and first-generation American immigrants, has only recently been recognized. The *Aiiieeeee!* editors' 1975 manifesto had attacked Asian-born Chinese Americans for being too "Americanized"—that is, too assimilated into white American norms. Frank Chin, Jeffery Paul Chan, Lawson Fusao Inada, and Shawn Hsu Wong, labeling foreign-born writers as "Americanized Chinese," argued that foreign-born Chinese Americans had "consciously set out to become American in the white sense of the word, and suc-ceed[ed] in becoming 'Chinese-American' in the stereotypical sense of the good, loyal, obedient, passive, law-abiding, cultured sense of the word" (xii). According to this thesis, "Americanized Chinese," or "model minorities," accept "[b]ecoming white supremacist [as] part of their consciously and vol-untarily becoming 'American'" (xii). In contrast, real Chinese Americans, native-born, reject white cultural norms and resist "white supremacy."

This early insistence that Chinese-American identity can be recog-nized—and rewarded or critiqued—for inauthentic or authentic content suggests the politicization of representations of ethnicity. More, it made visible internal resistances within Asian-American communities to the "foreignness" of new immigrants from Asia, resistances ironically influ-enced by and rhetorically similar to anti-Asian, anti-immigrant, nativist discourses in the United States. Aihwa Ong has argued that when Asian Americans take "a defensive posture in being 'real' Americans, they unwittingly reinforce the public perception of Asian Americans as 'for-eigners within.'" "The strategy of Asian Americans to distance themselves from the new Asian transnational publics," she notes, "although logical within American racial politics, nevertheless discloses an ongoing political vulnerability that merely reifies the ethno-racial divide between Asian Americans and white Americans while studiously ignoring the objective reality that a majority of Asian Americans are now linked to transnational family networks" (180).

Strategies of distancing within Chinese-American communities have been memorably scripted as simultaneously gendered and classed in David Henry Hwang's 1979 play, *FOB*, which satirizes the second-gener-ation Chinese Americans' virulent prejudice against freshly disembarked immigrants from China through the character of Dale. Dale, "dressed preppie," denounces the FOB as both sex-driven and masculine-inept; yet, ironically, the FOB manages to steal both the limelight and his girl: "F-O-B. Fresh Off the Boat. FOB. What words can you think of that char-acterize the FOB? Clumsy, ugly, greasy FOB. Loud, stupid, four-eyed

FOB. Big feet. Horny. Like Lenny in Of Mice and Men. . . . High-water pants. Floods, to be exact. Someone you wouldn't want your sister to marry. If you are a sister, someone you wouldn't want to marry" (6).

But Hwang reverses the moral and creative ascendancy of the newly arrived Asian dramatized in *FOB* to skewer foreign-born Asian Americans as superstitious, irrational, and violent in his 1981 play *Family Devotions*. This play introduces three generations of Asian Americans: American-born teenager Jenny; her second-generation (Nisei) Japanese-American father, Wilbur; and Ama and Popo, Joanne's (Jenny's Philippine-born mother) mother and aunt. Ama and Popo, China-born, arriving via the Philippines, are imagined as colonized Asians not adverse to lynching in the cause of Christianity. In contrast, their freshly-landed brother Di-Gou, displaying a materialist decolonized mentality, takes on American identity in the space of a heartbeat: "Now that my sisters are gone, I learn. No one leaves America. And I desire only to drive in an American car— very fast—down an American freeway" (145).

In comparison to earlier FOBs, the immigrants whose lives under the Asian Exclusion Acts have been recorded and imagined in histories, autobiographies, memoirs, and novels, a contemporary foreign-born Asian American, protected by Civil Rights amendments, school and housing desegregation, and so forth, may be said to enjoy an improved legal and social status. Nonetheless, this status is ambivalent and vulnerable to geopolitical contingencies. The criticism of the FOB/FBA as not sufficiently American or as incorrectly assimilated American explains some of the confusion that greets my work in the United States. Unlike second-, third-, and fourth-generation Asian Americans, I live and write in more than one culture, and I speak and write in more than one English register and dialect and sometimes in more than one language. I move frequently across different national and geographical spaces, between American and Asian societies. More complexly, however, I write from strata of experiences that can be glimpsed wherein the subject often operates simultaneously in or strung on interconnected planes composed of more than one cultural and language world. If American culture and the English language form the singular norm by which an Asian-American identity has been recognized, then clearly I am insufficiently American, possessing as I do a personal history of multiple cultures and languages. At the same time, academic success in the U.S. marks me as "model minority," occupying an unstable, outcast position in an Asian-American collectivity prescribed as working class and unassimilated into U.S. institutions.

These, however, form extreme readings of the FOB/FBA. A counter-reading of the Asian American as a diasporic or transnational subject, one fresh off the Boeing 707, a first-generation immigrant from an Asian territory, will exhibit Asian—or foreign, if you will—frames of references that inevitably provide that subject with another consciousness different from American-national. But, unlike Hwang, who satirizes the alien belief systems of his foreign-born characters in *Family Devotions*, I do not represent my out-of-America perspective as violent, gross, primitive, or irrational. However, neither am I that obedient, passive white supremacist "Americanized Chinese" that the *Aiiieeeee!* editors had characterized. The subjects of my work, as well as the subject constituted through my work, are embedded in multiply complicated contexts, including Asian-American contexts, within traditions of diasporic and immigrant literature; and also the contexts of other national canons, including Anglophone writing from postcolonial Southeast Asia.

Writing the First-Person Immigrant Mother's Story

A first-generation Asian-American author, I do not write a daughter's story in the way that Maxine Hong Kingston and Amy Tan have done. Asian American women's writing has been dominated by a mother-daughter thematics (Lim, "Tradition"). The point of view of the discourse of maternality almost always originates in the American-born daughter. Jade Snow Wong, Monica Sone, Hisaye Yamamoto, Maxine Hong Kingston, Wakako Yamauchi, Velina Hasu Houston, and more: these are American-born daughters whose memoirs, fictions, and plays reproduce the Asian immigrant mother in subtle, complex variations.[5]

The daughter-narrators' reinscriptions of "mothering" scenes move from the harrowing—as in the birth of the illegitimate daughter and the suicide-murder described in Kingston's "No Name Woman" chapter (3–16)—to the painful—for example, the scene where the Issei mother, Tome Hayshi, in Yamamoto's short story "Seventeen Syllables," confesses to her horrified American-born daughter, Rosie, that she had a premarital affair and a loveless marriage (18–19). In these scenes the daughters are almost always resistant to the Asian-born mother's culture and values; they have moved from Asian maternal origin to present-time U.S. society, with its own history of race and gender relations and conflicts.

In contrast to these mother-daughter narratives, in moving into U.S. citizenship I am writing the story of the immigrant mother, the story of the one that the second generation writes against. To write this immigrant mother's story I offer the irreducible, ineradicable weave of personal history that is entangled in and itself entangles the subject of my writing and my identity. Writing from a diasporic maternal imagination I offer a particular illustration of a belated Asian-American presence; belated as a first-generation Asian American entering an ethnic literary history that is already filled with second- and third-generation voices.

The Female Gaze as the Maternal Gaze

Drawing upon Lacan's essay on the mirror-stage, which theorizes the infant's gaze as initiating the intrapsychic separation and entry of the subject into the Symbolic World of the Father, Laura Mulvey argued that the spectatorial gaze in film is male. This male scopic desire breaks the objectified female body into parts to be consumed. Later critics asked how and when to insert a female gaze. A number have argued that a female desiring gaze can only come into being through representation that offers the possibility of another form of productive gaze, one that breaks, and breaks free of, the mirror structure. That is, the female gaze may be conceived as not simply a reversal of the male gaze but as an other kind of exchange of desire.

Is there, moreover, a distinction to be made between the female gaze and feminist consciousness? Is there ever a position from which a woman might see herself without feeling herself seen through the male gaze, and, if so, where is it? These questions are related to feminist literary theory, for they suggest reading practices for a different form of writing, in which it is possible for the woman writer to dislodge the dominance of a patriarchal culture. These tantalizing questions were taken up but not resolved in the 1980s debates over interpretive methods that Elaine Showalter had termed "gynocriticism." Gynocriticism did not succeed as a reading practice because it was seen to deploy foundational or essentialist assumptions about the nature of woman as a category operating outside of history and social constructions. Gynocritical readings have usually been critiqued for ignoring other signifying categories of race, class, ethnicity, sexuality, religion, and so forth.

Gynocriticism's attempts to read the female into a subject's gaze, however, may be well worth recuperating, albeit with a more modest claim to authority and with cautionary digressions. For example, we may begin with Michel Foucault's concept of a "technology of sex," which critiques discourses developed after the eighteenth century by the western bourgeois class to support state power and which focused on the family. Adrienne Rich, in an associated argument, noted that surveillance and control of women's bodies as disempowered items of desire and exchange go together with and should not obviate the individual's empowering experience of her body as flesh and pleasure (*Of Women Born*). Pulling together these and other insights, Joan Kelly, in her 1979 essay "The Doubled Vision of Feminist Theory," argues that gender has to be read through interconnected sets of social relations, and that women are affected differently in different sets. Gender as a signifying ideology, therefore, is both a positive and negative force, depending on which set of social relations we find ourselves in. Moreover, as Teresa de Lauretis pointed out in *Technologies of Gender*, because "the social representation of gender affects its subjective construction and . . . vice-versa, the subjective representation of gender—or self-representation—affects its social construction, [and] leaves open a possibility of agency and self-determination at the subjective and even individual level of micropolitical and everyday practices" (9).

Together, Kelly's (on the interaffective sets of social relations through which gender is constructed and that affect women differently) and de Lauretis's (the possibility for individual subjectivity to act upon social constructions of gender) points can be said to compose a double insight. This double insight can be used to re-write the question of the female gaze as a maternal imagination capable of bringing into convergence complex particularities in which instantiations of race, nation, class, history, and so forth are present. On the possibilities of a female gaze that will also have feminist significance, we may look for a specifying female gaze in that of the mother upon the new-born. The moment of birth appears in many histories and societies as deliberately excluding men who saw women immediately after birthing as polluted or fearfully endowed with procreative power. In the mother-infant dyad, I imagine a relational space where the distinctly female gaze, the woman who has birthed, looks upon what she has brought forth intently and intimately, with the infant's gaze mirroring her position as desiring mother.

My imagined birth scene is far from a universal abstraction, for not all women are mothers, nor will all mothers affect similar gazes. Sarah Hrdy's 1999 *Mother Nature: A History of Mothers, Infants, and Natural Selection* makes a case for the bio-social paradigm of mothers across species as flexible, manipulative opportunists, responding to provisional, circumstantial, environmental (including cultural), and social pressures. Given socio-cultural differences, one cannot assume a universal maternal gaze operative in women's experiences. Indeed, in the scene of a mother's gaze upon her new-born, the gaze may be for a brief moment, or, under some conditions, may be impossible, conflicted, or absent. Constrained to bear male heirs, the new mother may already be ruled by patrilineal, patrilocal law. Or a slave woman may be gazing with the deeply disturbing consciousness of bringing forth another worker for the master's plantation.

For this occasion, however, I wish to narrate a phenomenology of relationship between mother and child different from, and imbricated in, the social and political constructions of institutional motherhood. Rich had postulated that motherhood is embedded in separate analytical categories, the public/institutional and private/experiential. However, insofar as the personal is the political, we cannot separate ideas of motherhood into a public domain and a private domestic sphere of emotion, affect, and family. Instead, we must allow for interconnectivity between the two, a condition of simultaneity that can be described and narrated rather than abstracted and theorized.

Mother in Two Cultures

The Nonya-Baba community into which I was born in Malacca, Malaysia, only partially affected by British colonialism, displayed many characteristics that cultural studies theorists today foreground as multicultural. According to Chin Kee Onn in the introduction to his 1984 novel *Twilight of the Nyonyas*, this community was formed by pioneers from southern China who "married native women or women of mixed ancestry who had absorbed Siamese and Indo-Malay customs and habits. . . . The result was a new synthesis: the emergence of the 'nyonyas' and the 'babas'—a phenomenon in the alchemy of mixed cultures: Malay, Siamese, Indonesian and Chinese" (n.p.).[6] Western medicine, pedagogy, and economics were making in-roads into my parents' society, but they were distant confluences, more confusion than enlightenment in their daily lives. My mother had three babies after I was born, so as a young girl I was steeped in the folk practices of childbirth and the familial values that ruled Nonya-Baba society of the 1940s and 1950s. A westernized child trained in the British imperial educational system, I understood my early struggles as my resistance to social conformity, parochialism, hypocrisy, and the misogyny and gender-ruled strictness of my parents' community. As I wrote in my memoir, *Among the White Moon Faces*, I could not get away far enough, fast enough, from Nonya society.

Such resistance is also a personal legend; for even as I was rebelling against that community, another subjectivity within the resistant individual inevitably was interpolated through the cultural representations of the initial all-encompassing folk society. I could and have approached this first cultural subject, formed before the intervention of colonial education, through nostalgia; a sickness for an unrecoverable first home, inasmuch as infancy and childhood are always realms of the lost. As Jonathan Steinward memorably defines it, "nostalgia as an imaginative forgetfulness perfecting memory with its supplement" (10).

The maternal gaze on the new-born, generating a genealogical sentiment, is not, however, a matter of nostalgia, the longing for origin, for the new mother's old mother's home. The infant interrupts and breaks the recursivity of nostalgia. The new-born is about the future, not the past. Taking its direction from a feminist location and paying attention to interconnecting sets of social relations, this essay examines the subject of and subjectivity immanent in the experience and condition of diasporic motherhood. It offers a phenomenological accounting of BEING, on the site of a doubled, interconnected vision of transformation. The autobiographical materials address aspects of maternal experience that were culturally constructed in a Southeast Asian gender regime and provide an account of both the subject of transformation and the subjectivity on whose body the processes of multiple interconnected interpolations play out their psychic and material compulsions.

Putting into focus the experience of being (born) in one culture and observing and participating in its disappearance while moving actively, even urgently, into an entanglement of hybridized, mixed, increasingly westernized cultures, this essay considers briefly the shape of that experience. Examining this change across a fifty-year span, from Asian to western base, from "tradition" to "modernity," I hope to discern a pattern that earlier lay indistinct, as if age has foreshortened vision and a shape has emerged that was invisible when vision was lengthened toward the horizon. Instead of looking out toward a future and a horizon, I now shift my focus and angle of sight, so that what was backward and grounded may come into view.

Genealogy as Wreckage

What comes into view looks very much like the wreckage of a culture and society. What had happened, not simply to my parents' generation but to the world in which they lived and into which I was born? In the encounter between modernity, which in Malaysia and Singapore was viewed as practices, values, and structures drawn from Britain and the west, including the United States, and tradition, those spiritual beliefs and religious rituals, social practices, and organizations founded on Asian culture and oriented inward toward family and community, tradition inevitably has been the loser. Nonya-Baba society was changed and left behind by the forces of colonialism and Asian modernization, and, as a rebellious, English-educated daughter who left for the west, I had done my best to help change and abandon it.

I did not understand this colonial-made, self-complicit devastation until I became a mother. Gazing at my infant, born in an antiseptic theater in an expensive, suburban New York hospital, my position shifted from daughter to mother, and with that, my location in history; that is, in a generation narrative subsumed under the trope of "genealogy." According to Foucault, "Genealogy is gray, meticulous, and patiently documentary. It operates on a field of entangled and confused parchments, on documents that have been scratched over and recopied many times" (*Language*, 139). Foucault argues that genealogy must record the singularity of events outside of any monotonous finality; it must seek [these events] in the most unpromising places, in what we tend to feel is without history—in sentiments, love, conscience, instincts; it must be sensitive to their recurrence, not in order to trace the gradual curve of their evolution, but to isolate their different scenes where they are engaged in different roles. Finally, genealogy must define even those instances where [these events] are absent, the moment when [these events] remain unrealized. (139–40)

Taking a cue from Foucault's subtle conceptualization of genealogy, my narrative will draw together "discreet and apparently insignificant truths," while steering as far away as possible from the search for "origins."

At the moment of becoming a mother, I felt the weight of the infant in my arms, and also the weight of something new, which, for want of a better term, I will call maternal memory. For a diasporic subject, arriving alone in the United States, maternal memory encompasses a timeline that is not linear. In the rupture between two radically different territories and cultures, possible linkages may be invented, constructed, suffered, and absented, within the sole subjectivity of the diasporic individual. For me, then, what comes before does not lie flat along the same history with what comes after. The birth of my child marks, in what must be differently constructed ways from those of American-born mothers, my realization of entry into a different and new history—personal, social, and national. My child forever has my history, my communal and national past, foreclosed to him, in a way that children born to non-diasporic subjects do not.

Food Craving

At the moment of coming into motherhood, I understood the enormous barbarity of my past actions as a daughter, an understanding that came through the sensations of a longing that could not be satisfied. For a time I believed that the longing was merely a craving for certain types of food. Growing up in Nonya society, I had learned that pregnant women experienced strong food cravings; the desire for pork cooked in soy, ginger, and wine, for example, or for things extremely salty or sour or bitter. Some food cravings were bizarre: for pig's heart, duck webbed feet, or English toffees. Pregnant women, however, were to be indulged, and families tried their best to gratify these food longings.

I also had a food craving. As the summer grew hotter, into June and July, and I grew heavier—thirty, forty, then fifty pounds over my normal weight—I longed for the ice kachang from my childhood in Malaysia, the syrup-sweetened shaved ice concoction heaped over sugared red beans, canned corn, and pink and green gelatin strips. My American version was crushed ice cubes over a pretty close approximation of the caloric mess.

The day I brought my son home to my Jewish American husband and a split-level house in upstate New York, I was struck by an overwhelming craving for popiah, a complicated stew of bangkuang (jícama as it is called in California), tofu, napa cabbage, bean sprouts, diced pork and shrimp, onions, shallots, garlic, all wrapped in rice pancakes smeared with chiles and hoisin. Still hurting from the cesarean I had endured only three days ago, I minced the mass of vegetables and meat to be stir-fried, stewed, and wrapped into those rolls that my stepmother had prepared as a treat on special occasions. After hours of slicing and cooking, I was overcome with fatigue and nausea. Unable to take even a bite of popiah, I went to bed with the baby, and my husband ate the entire dish himself.

What does this incident say about maternal memory as it manifested its power on my body? For one thing, maternal memory is deeply subterranean, a force over which I had little understanding and even less control. Among its more overt manifestations is the attempt to reproduce a remembered past. As a child, I had observed that motherhood was a social rather than mere biological event in Nonya society, and the social was expressed through acts of cooking and eating. My mother's birthing events were accompanied by special foods: the scents of ginger, wine, ginseng root, red dates, and star anise simmered with the smell of chicken or pork ribs for days when a child was born. These dishes were intended to assist the mother in recovering her vigor and youth, and to ease her into the demands of nursing. Returning from the cold efficient hospital to the nuclear family home, I was unconsciously trying to reproduce the food scene of motherhood in my memory.

The attempt failed because I had not understood that food was not the central referent in that maternal homecoming; the missing referent was the extended family, particularly the female community. Those mothers, grandmothers, sisters, aunts, grand-aunts, sisters-in-law, cousins, neighbors, friends that made up Nonya society were the cooks and servers my memory had failed to recall, because the rebellious daughter had rejected them as conventional, constraining, restrictive, narrow, boring, out-dated, and unnecessary. I had left behind this women's community, many of them illiterate, superstitious, suspicious of people outside their immediate family, moralistic, and judgmental—or if good-hearted, ignorant and powerless. Just as my mother, raised to be a traditional Nonya, had abandoned her children for employment in the big city of Singapore, I had also left even the acquaintance of Nonya aunts and cousins. There was nothing to be learned from them, I had decided at an early age, and so went on to an English education, to the university, to the United States, and to my home in New York.

But maternal memory in the body is without ambition; involuntary, determined by neural networks laid down long ago, it raises the dead that the individual believed she had buried a long time ago. What my personal experience gestures toward is not simply the acknowledgment that motherhood is a socially constructed condition—in Rich's term, motherhood as social institution—but that it is exposed in the individual as a culturally specific experience, embodied as intrapsychic and psychological drives.

Matriarchal History

Inasmuch as women see themselves living in or supported by women's communities, among the earliest of these communities are those formed by mothers, sisters, aunts, and peers. Birth is one of several moments in which the transmission of a female legacy is strongly apparent. Cutting across cultures and classes, women have traditionally gathered to welcome the infant with gifts, rituals, songs, chants, and prayers; to nourish the mother to health with strengthening foods, drink, massage, purification rites, and praise songs.

For diasporic women, immigrants or refugees who find themselves in the United States alone, a sharply felt deprivation is the loss of their women's community, a socius that offers life-affirming rituals and sentiment. My husband, sisterless, had lost his mother years ago. Pushed in a wheelchair by a nurse with my baby wrapped in a blanket on my lap, then driven by my husband back to our split-level house, I was also a nuclear-family mother in a culture and society that lay outside my memory. More, what was stored in memory was not just another country that a plane ride could bring into view. It was a history barely remembered, so successfully had colonialism and globalization done their work of modernization in Malaysia and Singapore, and I my work of resistance to Nonya kinship ideals.

Let me cast back to this involuntary memory of what surrounds newborns and new mothers. The first image that comes to mind is of other women welcoming the mother and child. Then the offering of special foods to help the milk appear and the uterus contract, hushed intimate talk about how to get the body back into shape, with tight swaddling around the waist and hips, special massages on the belly and back to ease postpartum aches. The language of this community, a mixture of Baba Malay and Hokkien Chinese, is murmurous, laugh-filled, infant-cooing. Women come and go throughout the days until after the first month, when it is finally safe to present the baby to the world. Then a group of women appear to work in the kitchen: plucking chickens and ducks; chopping lean and fat pork; mashing garlic and slicing ginger; boiling eggs and staining them a bright red; steaming pulot, the sticky rice that glows with turmeric and is garnished with crispy dried shrimp and fried shallots.

The men and the children are underfoot, shooed away, for mother and infant are to be protected from loud noises and violent movements.

This re-creation, idealized and distant, emerging as craving for the foods of that community and event, was later substantiated by and became the motive for my research into Nonya history and ethnography. Coming from indigenous matriarchal societies such as the Batak, as Chin Kee Onn notes in the introduction to his novel *Twilight of the Nyonyas*, the community modified the Confucianist kinship structures that their husbands had brought from China. In Chin's novel, the sons' education in the west and their unhappy contact with British colonialism and racism resulted in their turning back to Chinese patriarchal customs, and so in undermining the indigenous mother's matriarchal rule. When the eldest son, for example, "exerted his authority, claiming that by right of traditional Chinese custom, he, the eldest son, was now the head of the family . . . [t]his humiliated the mother, for according to the nyonya code, the mother is the head of the family" (250). Having evolved an indigenous matriarchal regime, the nonya family suffered devolution to Chinese patriarchal norms as a form of Asian male empowerment in resistance to British racism.

Traditional Nonyas disciplined their children to a prescribed code of conduct and for clearly formulated social ends. The contract between mother and son was unambiguous: "All she fondly thought of and dreamed of, was that he would become an engineer, come back to Malaya, make a lot of money, build up a family of his own, and make her life in her old age, a happy one. He was an obedient and a filial boy—that was why she was prepared to slave for him, so that he could go to England and fulfill his ambition, and be of benefit to her and the family" (222).

Born to such a family before World War I, Chin locates his narrative of the collapse of this matriarchal community between the two world wars. A son and grandson to such women, he places the nonya widow as the central character in a generation narrative in which she gradually becomes marginalized. The novel is that strange bildungsroman in which it is the older character that develops emotionally and intellectually in response to the increasing loss of her social and familial authority. Inasmuch as her achievement as matriarch rests on her children's professional and economic progress in the British colony, the mother is forced to learn from her children as they master the English language and adjust to the changes brought about by the contact with colonial administration and modernity. Ironically, her children's upwardly mobile entry into the modern world, a success she schemes and works for, also signifies the diminishment of her traditional power. Chin's novel offers very little criticism of this matriarch; the male authorial voice privileges and valorizes her maternal power, foregrounding devotion to the family as the primary good.

Resistance and Cost

Chin's imagined Nonya family represents the kind of matriarchal society of my early years in Malaysia that I did not want for myself, for it placed maternality as a primary value, found its satisfactions in female separation from men and their interests, and constituted its power through cooking, rituals, prayer, and control of the female and infant body, all within the domestic sphere. So why at the moment of my return from the hospital bed to my home did the overwhelming longing for this community come upon me?

It was perhaps then that I recognized that the rupture between mother and daughter, and between the daughter-turned-mother and her child, a three-generation transmission, was not as severe or damaging for other women as it had been for me. What do we call daughters like myself, who rejected our mothers' and grandmothers' pre-feminist world, for whom women's place in patriarchal history poses an intolerable constraint, a backward location that holds terror and degradation, and what kinds of maternal memory can we bring to our children, once we have wrecked our mothers' worlds?

Maxine Hong Kingston expresses this peculiar dilemma of the daughter in the aftermath of resistance to her mother's values, values that included models of strength and endurance but also mystifications demeaning of female abilities. The narrator Maxine carries with her the burden of a mother's voice that says, "'I don't see why you need to go to college at all. . . . Everyone else is sending their girls to typing school. 'Learn to type if you want to be an American girl.' Why don't you go to typing school? The cousins and village girls are going to typing school'" (203). But resistance to the Chinese mother, the revolt against an Asian mother's presence that is coexistent with patriarchal devaluation of females, brings with it a psychic cost. As Kingston warns: "Be careful what you say. It comes true. It comes true. I had to leave home in order to see the world logically, logic the new way of seeing. I learned to think that mysteries are for explanation. I enjoy the simplicity. Concrete pours out of my mouth to cover the forests with freeways and sidewalks. . . . Shine floodlights into dark corners: no ghosts" (204).

Resistance "comes true." It achieves its end, and so carries the loss of what is resisted as well as the cost of that erasure. Pregnant at the age of thirty-five, I had not thought either to write to my mother for advice or to bring her from Singapore to New York to assist me. Instead, I steeped myself in Dr. Spock and other self-help books for new mothers. There was something reassuringly sanitary and sane about the language and attitudes in these books; they offered such superior medical knowledge that it never occurred to me I should want my mother's help, a mother, moreover, whom I viewed as irrational, helpless, and pathetic. For a bookish academic woman, the Nonya mysteries surrounding birth had long been vanquished in the struggle between tradition and modernity.

But books are not surrogates for community. It was only at the moment of my initiation into motherhood that the spectral presences of mothers and births past seized me as a craving for a food that is so labor-intensive that it is usually only prepared communally. That I did it alone, that I could not eat it after such hard labor, and that my husband then was its lone consumer: these are materials that perhaps only imagination can explain, as the mysteries of diasporic maternal memory rising in response to the mother's gaze on her new-born.

Genealogy takes on urgent sensory shape for the diasporic mother as she gazes on the infant who is both her child and not her child, born into a society in which her past has no material existence. Her self as a history-saturated subject is triply threatened: first, as universally, past vanishes from present; second, as a history that has no place in but lies outside of U.S. history; and third, as social relationships and beliefs that have disappeared from Asia itself, an Asia in which western modernism, late-twentieth-century globalization, and feminism have effectively destroyed traditional female communities. The maternal imagination in diaspora gazes into the future in her new-born, even as she is traced over by sensations coming from pre-western, pre-feminist social organizations; by beliefs, tastes, and desires that lie, not beyond, but before and within Asian-American subject formation.

Notes

1. Teresa de Lauretis marks the shift in feminist consciousness in the United States "with 1981, the year of publication of *This Bridge Called My Back*." According to De Lauretis, it was such books "that first made available to all feminists the feelings, the analyses, and the political positions of feminists of color, and their critique of white or mainstream feminism" (10).

2. Barbara Christian, in her landmark 1988 essay, was one of the first to contest such binaries that placed Black women's writing especially under question. This debate took center stage during the early 1990s; see, for example, Sara Suleri's critique of bell hooks's "anecdotal" criticism in "Woman Skin Deep: Women and the Postcolonial Condition." But the devaluing, subtle or confrontational, of narratives of experience appears to have tapered off as more and more U.S. literary feminist and nonfeminist critics have rushed into writing memoirs and "engaged" criticism.

3. Many Asian-American critics and commentators on Asian-American communities have noted this heterogeneity; among them, see Elaine H. Kim's 1982 *Asian American Literature*, my 1989 introduction to *The Forbidden Stitch*, and Lisa Lowe's 1991 "Heterogeneity, Hybridity, Multiplicity: Marking Asian American Differences." See also Michael Omi and Howard Winant's study on racial formation in the United States, which adopted Stuart Hall's thesis that racially or ethnically characterized divisions "can be attributed to or explained principally by reference to

economic structures and processes" (25). That is, the class paradigm establishes "the roots in exchange relationships of racial inequality" (25).

4. Two examples of such daughter discourses are Moraga's poem "For the Color of My Mother" and Merle Woo's "Letter to Ma."

5. See Jade Snow Wong, *Fifth Chinese Daughter*; Monica Sone, *Nisei Daughter*; Hisaye Yamamoto, *Seventeen Syllables*; Maxine Hong Kingston, *The Woman Warrior*; Wakako Yamauchi, *Songs My Mother Taught Me*; Velina Hasu Houston, *Tea*.

6. An alternative and usually preferred spelling is *nonya*.

thirty

The "White" Sheep of the Family: But *Bleaching* Is like Starvation

Nada Elia

Consider your own sky on fire
your name erased
your children's lives "a price worth paying"
                —Lisa Suhair Majaj, "Arguments Against the Bombing"[1]

Ever since I first bought the book as a graduate student instructor in women's studies, I have consistently used This Bridge Called My Back, *and not only in classes about women-of-color feminisms. Indeed, I have never found any reason to leave issues such as "minorities" and "sexual orientation" to the end of the semester, or classes focusing on multiculturalism, but have instead foregrounded them throughout the semester, even in such supposedly anodyne classes as Introduction to Women's Studies, or Non-Western Literature, which frequently fulfill a university requirement and are therefore peopled by students who would really rather not know much about lesbian separatism. Alternative modes of living have been pushed to the margins too long, and I center them every chance I have. I have centered them in every syllabus I designed, every lecture I gave, and every discussion I led, as instructor, faculty, guest speaker, or unwelcome audience member.*

The 1981 edition of This Bridge *has not helped me, however, with regard to what may well be the most invisible minority group in the United States, namely Arab-American feminists. But it does not stand alone in this shortcoming. In fact, judging from the various available anthologies, one can safely conclude there are no Arab-American writers, thinkers, scholars, or artists, for multicultural anthologies that claim to be alternative, to remedy and shatter the silence and invisibility surrounding minorities, do not feature us. We are ghettoized, published in volumes on Islam, or the Middle East, such as* Middle Eastern Muslim Women Speak *(Fernea and Bezirgan) and* Opening the Gates: A Century of Arab Feminist Writing *(Badran and Cooke). More recently, the voices of Arab-diasporan feminists, as distinct from Arab women, have appeared in* Food for Our Grandmothers: Writings by Arab-American and Arab-Canadian Feminists *(Kadi) and* Bint Arab: Arab and Arab-American Women in the United States *(Shakir). However, with only one exception that I am aware of,* Third World Women and the Politics of Feminism, *Arab-American feminists have not appeared in "general" anthologies featuring the diverse experiences of women, of whatever shade.*

Yet I take this chance to express my feelings about This Bridge *specifically, out of hope and conviction that it is a highly influential, change-promoting, knowledge-creating, empowering book. Twenty years ago, it had that potential. It made an impact. The ripples are still felt today, and I want to throw my own pebble into the pool, contribute my culture's concentric rings, and watch them cross over, merge with the other shimmering curves . . .*

For the "multicultural" anthologies never truly represented our experiences. We fight our own forms of patriarchal traditions, religious fundamentalism, and western intolerance. We may not be allowed into the streets without a veil in some Arab countries, and we are vilified for wearing the veil in the U.S. Yet I sincerely doubt that many Arab or Arab-American women would name the veil as their greatest inhibitor, even though it may be the most outwardly obvious one. Nor are our problems restricted to clitoridectomy and polygamy; indeed, the majority of Arab and Arab-American women are unaffected by these manifestations of cultural violence against women. But how are American feminists to know that, if our voices remain unheard? Multicultural anthologies don't seem to be helping much, yet surely, surely, multicultural anthologies cannot be one more disguise of the master's tools?

To this day, I am not sure which is greatest, my pain or my rage at a colleague's suggestion that I not tell members of interviewing committees that I am Palestinian "until after they've hired you." She was a well-wishing white feminist, who herself probably didn't know I was Palestinian until after she befriended me. Clearly, to her, being Palestinian is negative, can be held against me, and she was suggesting means to deal with my "handicap." Echoes of W. E. B. Du Bois's haunting, unformulated question "How does it feel to be a problem?" (3) as well as another well-wishing war veteran's advice to a black person, quoted by Frantz Fanon in *Black Skin, White Masks*: "Resign yourself to your color the way I have resigned myself to my stump; we're both victims" (140) reverberated in me. And like Fanon, who revolted against the advice that sought to amputate him, I revolt against advice that requires me that to silence a defining aspect of my identity. The most recent, official version of such silencing is President Bill Clinton's policy of "Don't ask, don't tell" about homosexuality in the U.S. armed forces, with its implicit request that gays engage in their own erasure. In fact, as I think of it, I am impressed by the number of my "friends" who insist on forgetting that I am Palestinian, as if they can deal with all the other aspects of me except that one.

But I am not writing this essay to reinvent the wheel and denounce racism in the white women's movement. This essay is addressed instead to those who write/speak out against invisibility, even as they refuse to acknowledge my existence. Another colleague also explained to me that the reason I was having difficulties finding employment in my field was that I was a "white" person researching the experiences of people of color. That colleague was black, and had probably forgotten that I'm Palestinian . . .

Apparently, while white people see me as a person of color, members of the latter category view me as white. No side of the "divide"—if we are to go by the convenient binary, "white" versus "people of color"—claims me as its own. I am Arab-American, which may be one of very few instances where being hyphenated does not imply duality, Du Bois's "twoness," but a lack of belonging on either side.

I suspect that women of color (minus Arab-American women) have tended to ignore the very existence of their Arab-American sisters because they have not sufficiently challenged the categories and labels designed by the dominant discourse. According to that discourse, people of Middle Eastern origins are white. I have been told that the inclusion of Middle Eastern peoples into the "white" category was indeed an achievement in the crusade against anti-Semitism, as it merged Jews and Christians in one category, thus ending the official designation of "Jews" as "Others," a designation and scapegoating that, in Europe, culminated in the traumatic Holocaust, while it translated, in the U.S., into restrictive quotas lasting into the middle of the twentieth century. But as they proudly contribute to the national culture, American Jews today certainly do not seek to become invisible, to "pass," nor has their culture been erased. The U.S. president's lighting of a menorah for Hannukah, as well as the U.S. post office's issuing of Christmas, Kwanzaa, and Hannukah stamps for the 1999 holiday season, bear testimony to the respect granted the Jewish community. On the other hand, the Muslim holy month of Ramadan, which also coincided in 1999 with these other cultural moments, remained uncelebrated on a national or official level.[2] Indeed, the losers in the equation of Middle Eastern with "white" have been the

Arabs, whose forum of expression was usurped before they could gather the necessary momentum to articulate their identity.

Consequently, women of color can ignore Arab-American feminists, and progressive, proactive groups that consciously seek to diversify themselves, hoping to hire, publish, or otherwise feature members of under-represented minorities, still do not see that they are perpetuating the invisibility of one group by not reaching out to its disenfranchised members. When I argue that Arab-Americans are possibly the most under-represented U.S. minority group, I am told that Arab-Americans are not a "recognized minority," and therefore can neither be "represented" nor "under-represented" to any degree at all.

However, the acceptance of pre-established categories, even if it is in order to reclaim them positively, is not sufficient in itself, but must be accompanied by a challenging of the various assumptions that went into the making—or denial—of these categories. "Ain't I a Woman of Color" must be an experiential question, not one determined by Affirmative Action forms. Having experienced countless incidents of racist prejudice, I know which side I'm on. The insults in my career have ranged from a student walking out of my French classroom upon realizing that I am Arab, not French, because he was not there "to learn Swahili," to students, too many to be counted, who were offended at my "arrogance" in presuming to correct their English, because I am not a native speaker of *their* language. In my personal life, I have often been directed to the welfare lines at various government offices, even as I protested that I did not qualify. Recently, I inquired about our town's "Food Project," where I was hoping to drop off excess vegetables from my overflowing garden, and I was told to feel free to help myself to whatever is on the table, whenever I needed it. When I take my time reading the fine print on various forms before signing them, someone generally volunteers to explain them to me. White women do not need to walk around with a banner confirming their literacy, and a source of income, but I have to insist I do have a Ph.D., thank you very much, I am just a conscientious reader . . . All these experiences confirm to me that I am a woman of color, a Majority World woman. Not having internalized racism and self-hatred, I am most at ease with darker people. But I have not experienced sisterhood. To the dominant discourse, I am the abject other, demonized without apology, to people of color, I am "the white sheep of the family," someone people of color need not reach out to.

I am Arab-American, *ergo non sum*. The absence of Arab-Americans from "women-of-color" forums suggests, if only by default, that we are white. But "white," according to dominant and subordinate discourses, means European. Why then are Arabs—that is, Asian and African peoples—included in that category?

Our invisibility occurs at all levels. Courses in American Ethnic Literatures rarely feature Arab-American writers, yet there are some excellent texts available, like Suheir Hammad's *Drops of This Story*, Diana Abu-Jaber's *Arabian Jazz*, and Rabih Alameddine's *Koolaids: The Art of War*. Multicultural anthologies do not feature us. To cite only those of women of color, *This Bridge Called My Back,* as I mentioned above, does not include us, suggesting that there are no Arab or Arab-American radical women. Gloria Anzaldúa's *Making Face, Making Soul/Haciendo Caras: Creative and Critical Perspectives by Feminists of Color*, "dedicated to all mujeres-de-color," has sixty-two contributors, none Arab.[3] Tracy Denean Sharpley-Whiting and Renée White's *Spoils of War: Women of Color, Culture, and Revolution* seems to indicate that Arab women have not suffered from military fighting. In fact, we are only featured in *Third World Women and the Politics of Feminism* (Mohanty, et al), an anthology edited by then-students at the University of Illinois, which has long counted Arab-American feminist Evelyne Accad among its active faculty. The anthology itself is the published proceedings of a conference Accad helped organize, and at which she presented her article, hence her exclusion would have been unthinkable. Yet when Mohanty, now a professor, joined forces with M. Jacqui Alexander to edit a second anthology, the token Arab was dropped: *Feminist Genealogies, Colonial Legacies, Democratic Futures* does not feature Arab women.

Thanks to the formidable efforts of feminists of color over the last few decades, an ever greater number of social constituencies are now being represented in various media. By the same token, because of our absence from the work of such women, the invisibility of Arab-Americans has been compounded and the problem has already infiltrated the younger generation. I have a six-year-old son, and like many mothers I have occasionally relied on that ever available, ever affordable babysitter, the television set. I have monitored every program that my son watches and, to the best of my knowledge, at the moment there is not a single program that has an Arab- or Muslim-American character. *Sesame Street* has "all" the ethnicities (like *Hacienda Caras* represented "all *mujeres-de-color*"), and various degrees of ability, ranging from the wheelchair-bound to the deaf and the blind, but no Arab- or Muslim-American. *Puzzle Place* has Native American, Jewish, Latina, White European, Asian, and African-American characters, but no Arab- or Muslim-American. *Magic Schoolbus* has Euro-Christian, Jewish, Latino, Asian, and African American children, but no Arab- or Muslim-American. *Barney* has children representing European, Latina, Jewish, African, and Asian heritages, but not the Arab or Muslim. After watching a *Barney* show on "breads of the world," featuring pumpernickel, tortillas, bagels, chapatis, and so on, my son asked me which of these is ours. None, I had to respond. The flat pocket bread known here as pita is the starch staple of twenty Arab countries, but was presented as Greek. Another time, he watched a show on cultural celebrations from around the world, and again he asked me which one was ours, and again, I had to say none. One day, he simply asked me: "When will they show something from our home?" Maybe when you're older, I said. And it hurt me to say it, but I will not lie to him, and know better than to suggest it's tomorrow, or next week. And it will only happen when he's older if we start remedying the problem today. We have already lived through five hundred years of invisibility, five hundred years of solitude . . .

Indeed, it is at once painful and fascinating for me to observe the dilution of all Arab culture as it enters the American mainstream: pita and shawarma ("Gyros") are known by their Greek names, stuffed grape leaves are referred to by the Turkish "dolma," while hummus and falafel are "Jewish," despite the fact that the very word *hummus* is Arabic for chick peas, while *falafel* means "spicy fritters," also in Arabic. One program on health food claimed that "the Mediterranean people eat garlic, garlic, and garlic," promoting that bulb as infallible panacea, and I thought to myself that garlic sales and consumption would probably come to an immediate full stop if the wording of the claim was slightly modified to "Arabs eat garlic, garlic, and garlic." Funding for educational children's programs is "America's investment in the future," to quote the National Science Foundation, which sponsors many of these programs, where there are no Arab-Americans. And these are the "good" programs, the only ones I let him watch. The "bad" programs are unfortunately very likely to feature us, but always as dangerous, hostile foreigners, never as fellow Americans with a culture to celebrate.

Is it any wonder the overwhelming majority of Americans have no idea that the second-largest religion in this "Judeo-Christian" country is Islam, not Judaism? Of course, this invisibility is extremely convenient for the master, for if Islam were to be recognized as one of the country's main religions, accommodations would have to be made at various levels, including, for example, the possibility of college students carrying a full-time load without Friday classes.[4] Much more seriously, if Islam were to be recognized for what it is, the second-largest religion in the United States, the division between "us" and "them," "civilized" versus "barbaric," "modern" versus "reactionary," would not be so clear. For now, once we are "in," "naturalized," we are bleached, Arab-American culture gets obliterated, and we might as well forget about having our needs or contributions acknowledged. As Shakir writes in the introduction to *Bint*

Arab: "Once they [Arab women] come to this country, a great silence descends." Indeed, it seems as if the existence of Arabs can only be tolerated as an entity outside of the xenophobic United States, always and only as foreigners. As such, we offer the ideal scapegoat, the one that can be vilified with impunity: we are terrorists who must be kept at bay, denounced for the national threat that we present. And the myopia of U.S. feminists, including women of color, is such that they can see Arab and Arab-American women only as victims of Islam, so that, whenever we are mentioned, it is as victims of the veil, or of circumcision. Ugly as those manifestations of cultural violence are, I am convinced that I am not alone in wishing they were our only source of oppression.

At the NWSA annual conference in Boston in June 2000, flyers were handed out at the well-attended Thursday plenary session, announcing that a protest was being planned for Saturday morning against Secretary of State Madeleine Albright, who had been invited as commencement speaker at Northeastern University, one small block away from Simmons College, where the NWSA was meeting. Various health and human rights organizations have long documented the disastrous effects of the U.S.-imposed, Albright-defended sanctions on the Iraqi civilians, the majority of whom are women and children. Women in Iraq today have the world's highest rates of psychological traumas, and wife abuse has skyrocketed in that country since the imposition of the sanctions. *Of all the NWSA members who had converged on Boston that week, I was the only one who joined the anti-Albright protest.* I know that, because I had a copy of the hefty NWSA conference program with me, and I showed it around, asking if any other NWSA members were there. Did no one from NWSA feel the need to join the protest because these Arab women are not the victims of Islam, but of U.S. policy? Let me put it bluntly: Had the NWSA members been informed at a plenary session that a protest was being planned against female genital mutilation, or the Taliban, would not a large delegation have spontaneously formed, grateful for the fortuitous coincidence, and headed toward the nearby site of the protest? Was the lack of action due to the fact that Albright is a woman, and if so, by what logic do we refrain from criticizing a woman whose policies very seriously endanger the lives of tens of thousands of women, and lead to the deaths of more than 250 people a day, 150 of whom are infants and toddlers?[5] Is it because Albright is of Jewish descent, and if so, by what logic do we refrain from criticizing someone because they are Jewish, when their policies endanger the lives of tens of thousands of innocent civilians? In April 1996, Albright appeared on the television show *60 Minutes*, and the reporter asked her what she thought of the fact that the U.S.-imposed sanctions were killing more children in Iraq than had died in Hiroshima and Nagasaki. Her response was that "the price is worth it."

"Consider your own sky on fire / your name erased / your children's lives 'a price worth paying,'" writes Arab-American poet Lisa Suhair Majaj, and I shudder as I know it is my own sky on fire, my own name erased. My son's life, had he been born in Iraq, like me, instead of Illinois, where I was working at the time, would have been "a price worth paying."

The list of "erased" Arab-Americans, as well as the fora where they are erased, is so long it may bore you, but the harm it inflicts on us is far greater than mere boredom. By creating among us the illusion of utter loneliness and isolation, the feeling that we are absolutely alone in a nation numbering almost 300 million, it leads to attrition and severe alienation. As each one of us fails to see herself as a member of one of this nation's various communities, each one feels her voice is puny, bound to get lost in a hostile wilderness. And, whatever we may think of identity politics and special constituencies, if we believe we are a negligible quantity, so few we really need not be counted, we will refrain from demanding basic rights, visibility, or representation, preferring to join forces instead with a greater group, which dilutes our intrinsic needs, alienates us from our guttural knowledge of who we are.

Living at one remove from oneself is indeed a handicap. From my experience as an activist, I know I have frequently refrained from participating in marches for visibility for groups who could not see me for who I am—an invisible Arab-American, preferring to think of me instead in one of the already existing slots: feminist, anti-war activist, vegetarian, mother. The master's tool was at work, isolating, silencing me. But I have also grown to realize that we must reverse that course. As women of color insistently denounced white feminism, and dissociated themselves from the white women's movement, Arab-Americans must today denounce the myopia of women of color, minus one shade. We must denounce it, and not keep our bitterness to ourselves, contained in anthologies of Arab-American writing, even as we welcome such anthologies, delight in their publication, proudly display them on our coffee tables, and subversively offer them to our best friends, our local women's resource centers, and libraries.

As Arab-American feminists, we have no support network outside our own community. Yet coalition building is vital to our visibility, to our very survival. Special sessions allow us to articulate the myriad differences within. We can speak about the problems of inter-religious or inter-cultural households, the effect on Arab-Americans of the negative portrayal of our home culture, resistance to Islamic fundamentalism, our boredom with the western/Orientalist voyeuristic focus on the veil, polygamy, and clitoridectomy . . . However, such private spaces also perpetuate our isolation. How many, besides the already converted, would buy a book such as *Bint Arab*, or *Food for Our Grandmothers*, when there are numerous excellent multicultural anthologies, minus an Arab-American contribution? How many would attend a session on Arab or Arab-American diaspora feminism at a conference where there are concurring sessions on women-of-color feminisms, minus one shade?

As I already said, I have no desire to reinvent the wheel: some excellent essays have already been written about invisibility. I merely wish to point out that Arab-American women constitute a significant group of their country's gagged and censored people, and that this is occurring at the hands of women who are supposed to be our allies. White men have not opened the door to multiculturalism. White women have not either. Women of color, indefatigably chipping away at the armor of white privilege and supremacy, are to be credited for the more representative media and academic curricula that now exist in the United States. The flip side of their wonderful efforts is the erasure of Arab-Americans.

Our bleaching will not protect us, it will only allow for a continuation of our misrepresentation, our erasure, our silence. Cherríe Moraga wrote, in *This Bridge*, that "silence *is* like starvation" (29). As the "white" sheep of the family, I must add:

But *bleaching* is like starvation, too.

Notes

1. This poem first appeared in *Al Jadid* (Winter 1998) and is reprinted here with the kind permission of Lisa Sahair Majaj.

2. The Muslim calendar is lunar, and the dates of holy days vary annually, by a few weeks. In 1998 and 1999, Ramadan began in December, which would have made it convenient to include Islam in the "spirit of the season."

3. Paula Gunn Allen, although part Lebanese, has written very little, and only very recently, about that aspect of her cultural heritage. Her poem "Some Like Indians Endure," included in *Haciendo Caras*, addresses her Native American heritage, and her ethnicity is given, in the book itself, as Laguna Pueblo/Sioux, although her entry in the contributors' biographies, most likely provided by the contributors themselves, does indicate Laguna/Sioux/Lebanese.

4. The majority of Arabs are Muslim, hence the occasional overlapping, in my discussion, between Arab cultures and Islam. Even when members of a community are not "believers," they tend to celebrate their religious holidays: secular Christians celebrate Christmas, secular Jews celebrate Hannukah and Passover, and secular Muslims celebrate Ramadan. Seven percent of Americans are Muslim, as compared to 3.5 percent Jewish, and Islam is the fastest-growing religion in this country.

5. For information on the impact of U.S. sanctions against Iraq, see www.iraqaction.org.

thirty-one

Lesbianism, 2000

Cheryl Clarke

Preface

This Bridge Called My Back: Writings by Radical Women of Color is a powerful presentation/representation of multicultural expressivity–one of the earliest and one of the best. *This Bridge* offered direction to so many women-of-color writers, predominantly lesbians in the successive years of lesbian-feminist publishing, and still remains a life-changing text. My deepest and long-overdue thanks to its editors, Cherríe Moraga and Gloria Anzaldúa. You gave me the opportunity to write and publish the endlessly popular "Lesbianism: An Act of Resistance" back in 1979. From its very beginning, the essay took on a life of its own and caused contention within, among, and across diverse communities of women— queer, of color, white, straight, and otherwise, particularly college students. Every year since its publication, I have been invited to either a women's studies, black studies, queer studies, or cultural studies class to answer up to the assertions studding that essay. (The most recent class in which I "answered up" was held at New York University on November 11, 1999.) A writer could have no greater accomplishment than that her work gets read and talked about by many of the people for whom it is intended. That's what happened with "Lesbianism: An Act of Resistance," and I am having a ball.

> *Have you complexitized your ideas since you wrote this essay? I was turned off by them, because I'm excluded. I'm biracial and bisexual. What's in it for me?*

Five or six years ago (at this writing) a young woman student confronted me with this question. She objected to my characterizations of bisexuals and mixed-"race" people as impostors, poseurs, and passing as dominant. The passage to which the student refers follows and is one in a series of several complicated and problematic analogies of "lesbianism" and "blackness" assayed in "Lesbianism: An Act of Resistance": "There is the woman who engages in sexual-emotional relationships with women and labels herself *bisexual*. (This is comparable to the Afro-American whose skin-color indicates her mixed ancestry, yet who calls herself 'mulatto' rather than black)" (130).

The irreverence is absolutely intentional. Besides, who would want to call herself "mulatta/o" rather than "black" anyway? The student did not care for being the brunt of my Malcolm-X-Leroi Jones/Imamu-Baraka-type signifyin(g). She believed I was advancing a purism about identity, sexuality, and race that contradicted the mestizo-ism of *This Bridge*, enunciated by the late Toni Cade Bambara in her 1979 "Foreword" to the first edition: ". . . . Blackfoot amiga Nisei hermana Down Home Up Souf Sistuhsister El Barrio suburbia Korean The Bronx Lakota Menominee Cubana Chinese Puertoriqueña reservation Chicana campañera . . . Sisters of the yam Sisters of the rice Sisters of the corn Sisters of the plantain putting in telecalls to each other. And we're all on the line" (vi).[1]

And I suppose the student was also wondering what makes me a "radical" woman of color if I cannot get beyond the racialist and monocultural norms of everyday life in U.S./North America. But that was 1979 and I was "coming out"—not as "black" or as "lesbian"—but as a "black lesbian writer," and brash spoken and written declamations of identity were the primary tools I used to "break the silence(s)"—as they had been used to break so many other silences. "You hadda be there," I cajoled. "It was a stage," I continued to retort. The student was still not convinced of lesbianism as an act of resistance. I encouraged her and the rest of the class members to read the essay in the context of the full *This Bridge* text. *Bridge* letters, journal entries, poems, essays—"telecalls"—were flowers of declamation and contamination, shouts of multiplicity, fire-words challenging all our notions of identity, oppression, struggle as fixed modes of action. But in "Lesbianism: An Act of Resistance" I chose the poetics of reification—a strategy used so successfully by black arts movement practitioners (roughly 1963 to 1975) to advance black nationalist practices. This paradox-of-sorts critiques its practices of exclusion, sexism and homophobia in black communities, and racialist judgmentalism among black lesbians, and falls short of "theorizing" a multicultural lesbian-feminist future. Make no mistake, I am not going to "theorize" that here now.

Twenty years later I can say I don't give up *black* for African-American, don't give up *gay* or *lesbian* for queer, and I want to reaffirm my lesbian practice: "I am a mannish dyke, muffdiver, bulldagger, butch, feminist, femme, and PROUD."[2] I don't give up *feminist*, which is a doppelganger for lesbian and always gives me a way to move. I do not wish to be a lesbian without feminism. Feminism still means—roughly, that is: *the revolution that will liberate all women (and men) from patriarchal oppression.* Lesbians need to be feminists, as do any really serious progressive people, and struggle to take on hybridity, to take on queer, to take on diasporas, to "work across" sexualities,"[3] and to admit the always-already unready.

As much as I deplore the insertion of the self into the self's essay, I do feel the need to qualify. I have gone back and forth on the angle of this piece. Do I talk about the life of the essay "Lesbianism" over the last twenty years? Do I call this current essay "Lesbianism: An Act of Resistance 20 Years Later"? Or do I pick up where I left off twenty years ago—talking about loving ourselves as "the final resistance"? (No, no, I won't pick up from there.) Or do I "complexitize" the ideas presented in the original, as the young bisexual, biracial woman recommended. (Others have already done that; e.g., Cathy Cohen, Evelynn Hammonds.[4]) Do I cop to my "put downs": of light-skinned people of color, bi people as the "niggers in the woodpile" of heterosexuality, black lesbians who "castigate" other black lesbians for sleeping with white lesbians, black men who are "rabid heterosexual[s]," and heterosexuals enthrall to an institution that is the foundation of the "master-slave relationship between white and black people in the United States."[5] No, I don't *even* want to take myself on. What I wrote stands on me as I stand on it.

Lesbianism has emerged at this time in my life as more of a strategy and less of a hard-and-fixed-identity-politics-that-I-am-going-to-be-no-matter-how-it-gets-deconstructed. One never knows how one may have to "live as a lesbian" trafficking in conservative-family-maniacal U.S. capitalist hegemony, do one? Lesbianism and feminism are mutually instrumental practices. In fact, I said earlier—they are "dopplegangers." Each stands in for the other. I prefer what dykes are putting down. (Dykes are feminists too.) But not every feminist has to prefer it, do it, or be it. *Any* woman cannot be a lesbian (or a feminist, for that matter). Dig it? Dig it. Everybody ain't able. But everybody needs to be a feminist for her own good. I believe this more than ever, particularly since battering, rape, and other forms of violence against women (and children) are no less frequent—only less unheard of—than they were twenty years ago. Be feminists—it may just save your lives. Be feminists—and you may just save some other women's lives.

When *This Bridge* was being put together by its editors—more than twenty years ago—I was living a double life in the suburbs of New Jersey with a very suburban white feminist lover, her two daughters, writing sometimes, doing graduate work, and trying to be a black lesbian feminist. Read my biographical statement in another classic text of the period, Bulkin and Larkin's 1981 *Lesbian Poetry*. I'd attended several black feminist retreats and meetings in Massachusetts, Connecticut, New York, and New Jersey, organized initially by black feminists in Boston.[6] The twenty or so of us who joined together at those retreats had histories in black civil rights, women's liberation, new left, black nationalist, black women's studies, black church. I'd been involved in one of the New Jersey defense committees for Assata Shakur. All of us had learned from the black power movement that we had to speak directly and publicly to our communities.

We'd learned that we had to hold accountable all our people for our collective justice. We knew that a larger body of writing had to be created. We'd learned the power of words, angry words. We believed in the power of "mothers" and "sisters"—that is, the power of recovering the words of black women writers—past and present—'live and dead. Audre Lorde was one of those sisters, amazons, warrior women we extolled; and she was very much a poet—"out there," in the street, hanging tough, palpable, reading her liberatory work, standing up and in for freedom, being a lesbian, being a feminist. Reread her 1978 collection of poems *The Black Unicorn. Unicorn* is certainly a critical context and crucible for *Bridge,* as it throws down Lorde's challenge in "Solstice" to "never forget the warning of my woman's flesh" (118).

Some of us are not brave.

However, we recovered, discovered, and paid long-overdue homage to others: Angelina Weld Grimke, Mae V. Cowdery, Alice Dunbar Nelson, Zora Neale Hurston, Nella Larsen, Toni Morrison; and appropriated their characters: "Irene Redfield"/"Clare Kendry," "Big Sweet," "Sula" and "Nel," "Meridian," the "Ladies in Red, Yellow, Green, Brown, and Purple." Alice Walker gave us "Celie" and "Shug Avery." (Defying the behavior codes of straight black womanhood in U.S./North America, Ntozake Shange and Walker took a lot of heat for their gifts.) We felt they belonged to us, and we had the right to read "lesbian" into the motive of every black woman writer and imagined black woman, including Morrison and "Sula."[7] Morrison didn't like it one little bit.[8] Also, some of us felt we should require allegiance to lesbian expressivity of all black women writers who claimed black women as their subjects. And we created quite a stir when we thought anyone was hedging or getting *it* wrong. As evidence, see the following excerpt from a 1982 taped conversation of fledgling black feminist critics about *This Bridge,* on the dilemmas of only writing homage:

> L: The search for perfection is something which also affected my view of *This Bridge Called My Back: Writings by Radical Women of Color.* With all the "hooplah" which attended its publication, one would have expected it to be the definitive work on the issues of women of color in the United States. I suppose I also resented being defined as a woman of color, because I feel my blackness is subsumed. I guess I took that resentment out on the book. . . .
>
> J: I don't feel blackness is subsumed in the "women of color" designation. . . . I would have liked more space devoted to women as artists and political beings. . . .
>
> E: I feel *This Bridge* would have been much stronger had class and economics been addressed . . . [but] I'll go on record about *This Bridge.* It is a valuable beginning.

B: Then I'll go on record about [*All the Blacks Are Men, All the Women Are White, But Some of Us Are*] *Brave*, since it was the first composite of black women's studies. . . . [When I reviewed it] I wanted people to look at it themselves. I wanted . . . to say: "You have to look at it. Don't think it's wonderful in the world, but you need to look at it."

C: Sometimes I can't see my own value judgments getting in the way. Audre Lorde confronted me. . . . She said, "How come you criticize what isn't there? It's like you put the burden of the whole world on me." And my response to Audre was, "Well, now, Audre, you know we expect you to be perfect." (Clarke et al.)

In 1973, after four years of reckless heterosexuality, I collided high speed with lesbians and lesbianism. I spoke of this as an epiphanic moment in "Lesbianism: An Act of Resistance": "For me personally, the conditioning to be self-sufficient and the predominance of female role models in my life are the roots of my lesbianism. Before I became a lesbian, I often wondered why I was expected to give up, avoid, and trivialize the recognition and encouragement I felt from women in order to pursue the tenuous business of heterosexuality. And I am not unique" (134).

But now I am inclined to embellish this narrative with the fact of my relationship with a jazz-loving, freaky, myopic white boy that helped me cross over the burning sands of group disapproval/dissension. I always wanted to be wild, after my sheltered petit bourgeois black upbringing, and the "interracial" and the "lesbian" put me right out there. Then that same year, 1973, Assata Shakur burst on the scene after the notorious "shoot-out" (ambush) on the New Jersey Turnpike, just up the road from where I lived in New Brunswick, N.J., Assata, more revolutionary than Angela Davis, and whom Angela supported, became the symbol of resistance against racist, capitalist, imperialist patriarchy for which all progressive women longed. When Assata became pregnant by one of her New York codefendants while awaiting arraignment on one of the many bogus charges the government rigged up against her, I, for one, was disappointed. I wanted her to "come out," like Susan Saxe, as a revolutionary black amazon. Of course that wasn't going to happen, because black natonalist organizations policed her loyalties, marginalized her female lover, and ferociously guarded her image as a black heterosexual revolutionary. None of that would matter by 1977, when Assata escaped from Clinton Prison, a minimum-security facility for women in New Jersey, and finally to Cuba. You go, girl!

So, I came to appreciate how far out there lesbianism could send one—erotically and politically. I opted for above-ground agitation, lesbian visibility, and theoretical decentering of whiteness, maleness, hetersoexuality. I was not crazy (or courageous) enough to be a warrior, and I was too nonconformist to be a soldier. By the time I was writing "Lesbianism: An Act of Resistance," I had become convinced that there existed multicultural bevies of lesbian communities just waiting for the words of lesbians. As a dyke prison activist once said to me, "So little has been said to us, everything is appreciated"; or as a well-known dyke organizer said quite recently at a public event, "To get applause from a lesbian audience, all you have to do is walk onto the stage." So, here was my moment to take that stage, to be the writer I'd always wanted to be, since my days of apprenticeship to blackness, to do it for lesbians about lesbians with lesbians. I could signify-on the black intelligentsia (a favorite and frequent target of black writers), expose some funky little truths, and air some dirty laundry. These were the strategies that came together in "Lesbianism: An Act of Resistance" as well as its nearly as well known companion piece, "The Failure to Transform: Homophobia in the Black Community." The time was *then* to illuminate the failures of one's groups. The time is *now* as well.

I learned from the black arts to be direct, relentless, and mocking. Plus, if I could cop as pompous a tone as, say, Baraka, Larry Neal, or Nikki Giovanni—a form of what my sister calls "beration therapy"—I would have struck a black blow for lesbianism and feminism, as Audre Lorde and June Jordan had been striking for years. Oh, to be in that company!

This performance of black arts style catapulted my message all over black queer communities. And I have been thanked over and over by black queer people for the performance of this style. What was this "style" a performance of? Anger. Anger—the righteous "eye to eye"— projected at the sources of one's people's woes—racist, hetcrosexist, capitalist patriarchy (i.e., homophobic, misogynist, woman-destroying patriarchy); at one's own communities when they submit to cooptation, assimilation, or self and self's groups' destruction; at self for self's collusion in all the aforesaid. Anger as instrumental as lesbianism, as feminism, as blackness; as fluid as sex; as essential as fire. "How to train that anger with accuracy rather than deny it has been one of the major tasks of my life," poses Audre Lorde.[9]

Anger is the challenge I should have ended "Lesbianism" with, instead of that corny "love" thing. Anger and rage are heavy challenges in *This Bridge*, directed at white feminists who won't check their racist ways, social and cultural institutions that exclude and damage, mothers who won't accept daughters' differences, and legacies of powerlessness. And anger, a still relatively unexplained and unexplored phenomenon, has to become a tool of action, correction, and reflection. We need to reread

Lorde's "Uses of Anger: Women Responding to Racism" (written in the same vein as her blockbuster essay, "Uses of the Erotic"): "Every woman has a well-stocked arsenal of anger potentially useful against those oppressions, personal and institutional, which brought that anger into being. Focused with precision it can become a powerful source of energy serving progress and change."

Go from there, project it out again to shock women into checking themselves out even as they still deny what they see: capitalist hegemony, perilous enmeshment of church and state powers, global colonization, global genocide, global violence against women, murderous homophobia. White people—including white feminists—still do not want to be held accountable for their history and their privilege. With the exception of black gay men, black men have still not affirmed their solidarity with black women—and even black gay men must continue to check their masculinist tendencies and male privilege. The homophobia of the black middle-class community is still prevalent and most telling in the lingering silence surrounding AIDS/HIV, except by some of the most conservative black policy brokers and faith healers in the country and by diverse under-funded grassroots organizations in urban areas hardest hit by the disease. Straight black women are still afraid to reject the trappings of conventional heterosexuality and be feminists.[10] Bisexuals as a political constituency still do not hold themselves accountable for their heterosexual privilege. While some lesbians and gays are redefining and revolutionizing same-sex unions and childrearing, too many liberal lesbians and gay men seem content to reproduce bankrupt heterosexual institutions—weddings, commitment ceremonies, and showers.

Anger, yeah. Use it. Be used by it. Or lose it.

Notes

1. Bambara's own 1970 *The Black Woman: An Anthology* was the model for *This Bridge*.

2. This assertion is taken from flyers posted all over New Brunswick, N.J., in 1991 at the time of the Fifth National Lesbian and Gay Studies Conference, which was held at Rutgers University. This flyer, among others with similar expressions of queer vernacular, was a subversive welcome to conference attendees detraining from New York, walking back to hotel rooms, or strolling/cruising the campus between sessions. Campus officials, at first nervous about the three-day event, mistook the flyers as hate messages. I also used the statement at the beginning of an article I wrote for *Theorizing Black Feminisms* in 1993.

3. Lorde advanced the strategy of "working across sexualities" in "I Am Your Sister: Black Women Organizing across Sexualities." A signifying essay/speech directed at political black women—like those at Medgar Evers College in Brooklyn whom she was addressing—"I Am Your Sister" advances not only a theory of intersectionality but also a theory of coalition building that challenged black heterosexual women not to allow homophobia to rob them of the resource and power that would come from building coalitions across sexualities.

4. Cohen's *Boundaries of Blackness* is an illuminating and rich political science text that uses the Afro-American response to the AIDS pandemic as critique of and testament to Afro-

American history of survival and resistance. Hammonds's early work illuminates Cohen's. As early as 1986, Hammonds emphasized the invisibility of black women in AIDS research, treatment, and education. Four or so years later, we begin seeing grassroots work with black women, indeed all women living with AIDS/HIV.

5. From "Lesbianism," 132–35. I still believe this.

6. Barbara Smith, Demita Frazier, M. Okazawa-Rey, Evelynn Hammonds were among them, though the latter two did not attend retreats or meetings.

7. Barbara Smith's much-noted and oft-published "Toward a Black Feminist Criticism" states: "Despite the apparent heterosexuality of the female characters I *discovered* in rereading *Sula* that it works as a lesbian novel not only because of the passionate friendship between Sula and Nel, but because of Morrison's consistently critical stance towards the heterosexual institutions of male/female relationships, marriage, and the family" (33).

8. In the first question of a late-seventies, early-eighties interview by Claudia Tate, Morrison is asked, "How does being black and female constitute a particular perspective in your work?" In the advancement of her heterosexist project, Morrison quickly disposes of any queer intentionality: "when I wrote *Sula*, I knew I was going to write a book about good and evil and about friendship. . . . Friendship between women is special, different, and has never been depicted as the major focus of a novel before *Sula* [Clarke notes: This is highly suspect] Nobody ever talked about friendship between women unless it was homosexual [Clarke notes: This is more highly suspect.], and there is no homosexuality in *Sula* [Clarke notes: This depends totally on who is reading *Sula*, which is the argument Smith was making]."

9. "Eye to Eye: Black Women, Hatred, and Anger" in *Sister Outsider*. According to Lorde's note, this essay appeared in an "abbreviated version" in *Essence*, October 1983. "Eye to Eye" is one of Lorde's longest, most complex, richest, and sometimes most enraging articles; and it teaches us so much about the rigors of self-reflection and its uses for life-changing action. One of the most useful passages to me is: "Theorizing about self-worth is ineffective. So is pretending. Women can die in agony who have lived with black and beautiful faces. I can afford to look at myself directly, risk the pain of experiencing who I am not, and learn to savor the sweetness of who I am. I can make friends with all the different pieces of me, liked and disliked" (174).

10. In the spring semester of 2000 on campus, a black graduate student approached me after a public talk on feminism, shook my hand, and said, "Yes, I'm just here to see what it's [feminism] all about. I'm not one." Note any recent issue of *Ebony Magazine*, *Essence*, or *Black Enterprise*—and check out contemporary black women's role options.

thirty-two

"Now That You're a White Man": Changing Sex in a Postmodern World— Being, Becoming, and Borders

Max Wolf Valerio

In *This Bridge*, as Anita Valerio, I wrote: "At age seven I had a wild crush on a girl a year younger than myself that lasted a whole year. I would stare at her picture in the second grade yearbook and cry. I drew her pictures of dragons and gave them to her. It seemed a bit odd to me, but I wanted to marry her? I felt as though I was the only girl who'd ever felt these things. Perhaps there had been a mistake. I decided it would be better to be a boy and I stayed awake at night praying to turn into one. If I was a boy it would be easier to be a super hero and to be president. Finally—I decided to remain a girl and make the best of it" (43–44). How did I get from that decision, to where I am today? An ostensibly "straight" man who is often asked (usually by lesbian or feminist-identified women who meet me for the first time), **"Now that you're a white man, and have all that male privilege—how does it feel?"**

In my *Bridge* essay I explained away my early feelings of gender discomfort by linking them to lesbianism and a yearning to take on traditionally male gender roles. Reading my essay in front of a large crowd of (mostly) women at La Pena in Berkeley, 1981, I felt extremely uncomfortable when I reached this section. There was a charge in that short, confident explanation, a hidden part of myself that felt revealed by my testimony while remaining submerged in dark and unreachable fear. After *This Bridge*, I did little autobiographical writing—partly because I am a poet who generally writes non-narrative/experimental poetry not centered in a stable "I" voice or location. Yet there is another reason: I was not yet in touch with a self authentic enough to write about. The autobiography had not yet emerged.

It would be a lie to say I always knew, or knew with a constancy defying my circumstances. I didn't. I buried my male gender identity pretty thoroughly for many years, particularly when living as a lesbian. I believed, as I wrote in *Bridge*, that unhappiness and feeling at odds with biological femaleness were directly a result of a Patriarchy that had created narrow, stultifying roles for women. For a long time, I thought that almost all lesbians had those feelings. When I searched far enough back, I began to recover a sense of myself that did know.

I sift through my memories, focus:

Stretched out on the bed, watching the ceiling, a tree bends outside my window. It's quiet, late afternoon, time moves sluggishly toward evening. I'm in a world of shifting time, reflection. Memory animated by a sense of discovery.

Childhood feelings elongate into adolescence, feeling male inside my body, standing and screaming "I'm not a girl" . . . at the age of three over, over, and over again "I am not a girl!" in tears, desperate for someone to believe me. My mother tells me I'd stand, crying and screaming. Where did those feelings go? Thinking back now as an adult at thirty-one, I feel a chill, remembering their ferocity, clairvoyant and lucid. Sometimes, there's a voice in my head now that screams, "I'm not a woman!" This voice isn't disembodied. It's a part of myself, barely articulate yet breaking out into awareness.

I ponder a monster figurine I've retrieved during a Christmas

visit to my parent's house. This monster, with its lightning-streaked helmet, is identical to the kind I drew in second and third grade. Its lingering fascination provides a clue. I study this blue-green monster, caught at the moment of impact as he steers or brakes into a delirious crash, wild-eyed. I know this monster is the real thing.

My girlfriend at the time, Roxanne, thought this little toy remarkable for a singular reason: "It's so phallic," she smiles. This embarrasses me a little; I'm not supposed to like "phallic" things. I mean, I'm a lesbian. Lesbians imagine themselves to be outside of the phallic male world jutting out all around, ubiquitous. A facade of raw impulses welded into a landscape of skyscrapers, porno magazines, action movies, corporate structures like power-drunk circus tents. We are indifferent. Or so we think. But am I really indifferent?

Why had I loved that monster so much when I was a child? Why had I drawn him and others like him over and over? Some secret is encoded in the monster's slender form. I see suddenly—with recognition and joy—his primal, anarchic male qualities: long bloodshot eyes bulging out, haphazard tongue hanging down in a sneer or defiant leer, his wild racing in an oblong car with big wheels oblivious to danger, cranked on adrenaline, smashing with a defiance of force and willfulness—the sheer artful adventure of virility. The long stick shift jammed up into his tiny hands like a kamikaze erection! He is a messenger. This is my male self!

It was becoming clear to me–I am never a woman in my fantasies or in the image of myself that I hold in my mind. I am a man. *I feel like a man. That feeling . . . Walking into a roomful of women and feeling as though they are talking about me when they're talking about men. Reading books about men describing their fantasies about women and feeling as though I shared those exact same fantasies. I'm beginning to become aware of a faint memory of another way of naming myself, hanging at the back of my head.*

I become aware of the fact that my issues are deeper than a concern about the confines of traditionally defined gender roles; they concern my actual female body.

The night before I leave New York, in bed with Tama, the TV screen light flickers gently on my body. Prone, I look down at my breasts. For once, I am naked, my skin moist in the humid night air. My entire torso shines softly, taut, resilient, elastic stretch of flesh. My slender arms rest parallel to Tama's. Nude, our bodies seem congruent. Contextualized in erotic closeness, I become hyper-aware of my physicality. The way my body is motivated through its flesh. I yearn to embody a physical presence that feels more substantive. Stronger, larger. My arms feel too slim, almost fragile, my skin too soft. I want my body to contrast hers, to be muscular, firm, hard. It isn't simply a matter of becoming well-muscled, of attaining the sculpted physique of a female body builder; I yearn for my body to have the texture, smell, and look of a man's body. To possess a physicality I don't completely comprehend, but at that moment, I instinctively know this physical self is male.

Perhaps I wasn't really a lesbian after all.

The maleness I learned to hide as a child, to be embarrassed about, was the same maleness I'd hide and be embarrassed about in my adult life as a lesbian. As a feminist, I attempted to put away the feelings, tastes, and fantasies I viewed as "male." Maleness became "bad," the "other," the "oppressor." I had to disown my penchant for superhero action figures and Big Daddy Roth monsters with bulging eyeballs. I had to quiet down my taste in music, and for a while actually tried to like folksy-sweet "women's music" and not the black leather and punk rock that would eventually win out. I made failing attempts to imagine I was an emanation of the goddess, that two women making love were the apex of erotic feeling. The fiercest of these attempts lasted only a few years. In time, I was spiking and dying my hair black or bleaching it, dressing in black leather and chains, strapping on a dildo, and listening to loud, fast-and-hard testosterone-drenched music. Look what happened then.

My outlook was, for the late seventies and eighties, quite possibly, ahead of my time. Often when my Punk Dyke friends and I attempted to enter a lesbian bar, we received harassment at the door, sometimes asked to come up with more than one ID. Once inside, there were long blank or frightened stares from the women and a silent treatment so startling we wondered if they were going to call the police. Now, of course, lesbians listen to Punk, Goth, Hip Hop, Techno, any "alternative" music, while looking pretty much any way they choose. Tastes have changed. The palette and spectrum of lesbian fashion and sexual expression is larger and more diverse. What has not changed is that, essentially, lesbianism is a world of femaleness, even if some lesbian women are actively questioning their gender identity and hesitate to call themselves "women."

To take this leap, to become part of a class of people I had once believed were in some sense the "enemy" was an enormous risk—like stepping into the path of an oncoming tornado. In time, all I knew or thought I knew was altered. I was consumed. The transition from female to male completely and entirely changed not only my physical body, but also my most closely held values and deepest perceptions.

How Does It Feel?

Disappointment is what I feel the most when I hear the questioning accusation of male privilege and the inevitable, resentment-filled "So, how does it feel?" Disappointment that this is the most urgent question that these women can come up with—a response dredged from an essential poverty of imagination. How can they reduce my amazing experience to this rote question? It is an interrogator's question, not a real inquiry. I immediately sense they believe they already know the answer before even asking. They have a cartoon-character image of my life and my current identity, and want me to respond to their fantasy as though it were real. This stiff-necked question about privilege surfaces at odd times: at a party, a theater outing where I'm reunited with old friends and meet new lesbian acquaintances, and especially when I speak to feminist audiences about my transition.

In 1998 I was invited to speak long-distance by phone to a class on transgender and transsexuality in Toronto. The course was taught by a transsexual woman, Mirha-Soleil Ross—Quebecois, a performer and filmmaker, an avowed vegan, a longtime proud-and-out prostitute, and a tireless, inspired transsexual activist. She warned me before the class to expect some difficult questions and attitudes inimical to what we both regard as the realities of lived (not theorized) transsexual experience.

Making my experience more difficult, some women in the class apparently identified in some way as FTM. I refer to these individuals as "women" since they were still in the biological female state, having not undergone any medical transition—and to emphasize that I experienced their presence as being the undiluted presence of women; their "transgressive" male gender identity could not have felt less substantive. They were women taking on a maleness they appeared to know little about and were openly hostile to. Rather like the countless white people I have met who adopt American Indian ancestry, claiming a standard-issue "Cherokee great-grandmother" who is often, naturally, a "Princess." Generally these white people are not hostile to Indians, although they usually know next to nothing about the actual lives of flesh-and-blood Native people. We are all "spiritual," one with sacred Mother Earth, walking in the ways of our ancestors with the four directions. Often these same part–Indian Princess white people cannot even recognize a person with significant American Indian ancestry when they see one, often asking me—"Are you part Asian?"

These "FTM" women were not on testosterone and, with one exception, did not plan to use hormones or surgery to accomplish transition. They are part of an emerging group that identifies as "transgender," self-

identifying variously as "boy," boy dyke," "FTM butch," "transgender lesbian FTM," or other evolving and complex hyphenations. Let me emphasize, I have nothing against anyone exploring any identity. Although I
don't actually believe that gender is "fluid," I do know that identity can be
multiple, complex, and dynamic. However, as a transsexual who has
undertaken medical transition, I find these individuals a very particular
and tedious challenge. Because of their self-identified "transgressive"
gender identities, many of these women believe that we have a great deal
in common. They have strong expectations about what my behavior and
attitudes should be. They are often caught up in the fantasy or belief (take
your pick) that they're engaged in a battle with the "bipolar gender system," and want everyone else, especially me, to participate in this battle—
on their terms.

Sex Roles and Queering Gender

After viewing "Max," (Monika Treut's short documentary of me, and part
of her larger feature, *Female Misbehavior*), the class phoned me, and the
invisible audience began hammering out their questions. Thousands of
miles away, I listened and shivered as I registered the shrill, resentment-
filled anger. It had been a long time since I had heard *that tone* of voice,
a tone I remember and might have used myself many times, when I was
a lesbian feminist. "Here we go," I thought. I took a deep breath and tried
to answer each question as patiently, as thoroughly, as I could.

My every move was weighed and monitored. It would be up to me to
prove that I was now a man who suited their tastes and met their standards, a "sensitive" feminist (to their definition), possibly "queer-identi-
fied" man. A man who was as nearly like a woman as a man can be. I knew
right away from their tones that I had not passed the test.

Initially, I was bewildered by such hostile reactions. Now, I have
come to anticipate them. I am no longer an innocent. It is never enough
to be honest and to present your experience with as much accuracy and
insight as you can muster. It must also fit the outlines and regimens of
feminist expectations. The angriest questions often concern my statements about testosterone and its effects, or the scenes that don't match
expectations of proper "gender transgression."

One woman asked a perceptive question, "Were you told to box the
camera by the Director, or did you do that on your own?" I responded,
"That's smart. I was asked to do that by Monika, but I was not forced, I
did it because I wanted to. It felt right, it came out of who I am. It was
energetic, an outburst of joy and uncontainable energy. It was great how
she interspliced that scene with my voice saying, 'Is *this* how men feel?'—
my observation and astonished question when I took testosterone and

experienced an incredible increase of energy. And I actually like boxing you know." I was smiling unseen a thousand miles away, hoping to interject some levity into an all too serious discussion. "*Raging Bull* was one of my favorite films." There was silence. "I know that everyone would be much happier if I was knitting," I quipped into the tension. This actually got a laugh.

I understand the enormous suspicion and seething resentment beneath these questions. Rigid sex role expectations have hurt women and damaged men. We all want to reinvent our lives free from gender stereotypes' binding constraints. However, real life always intervenes in utopian landscapes. The truth hurts. I wasn't knitting, and I would rather be boxing the camera. My sex drive did go up when I took testosterone, as did my energy level. I experienced great changes in my emotional volatility, my sense of smell, even an alteration in my visual sense. The stereotyped differences between the sexes that I've resisted my entire life do make more sense to me now. As for boxing versus knitting, that might be personal taste. However, I actually understand men's fascination with sports much more now that I have a hormonal experience of maleness (although I have yet to get into team sports!). I have more energy, am physically a great deal stronger than before, and generally less inclined to "have a good cry" and more inclined to "take a long walk" or do push-ups to "burn off steam." This doesn't mean that women aren't athletic, of course; I certainly was before the testosterone, but there is a reason why the "male" hormone testosterone but not the "female" hormone estrogen is banned from Olympic competition. This was the great shock: the testosterone changed me physically *and* psychically, and in dramatic ways I hadn't anticipated. I began to question whether many other things I had believed about men and women were also incorrect.

As the class continued, boxing the camera led to a larger arena of concern: How did I feel about holding up "stereotypical" sex roles? This is a typical charge. Now that I am a man, even a transsexual man, or possibly especially because I'm a transsexual man, I am expected to be above or beyond expressing traditional male sex roles. However, there are things about me that *are* "typically" male—masculine. These attributes were there before I did the change, and they're still present. Before, these gender role expressions were charming and rebellious; now they might seem "sexist" or "macho." In other words, if I'd boxed the camera while I was still Anita, most of the class would have been delighted.

How do you feel, I might have asked, when you wear lipstick or a dress, or cook dinner for a partner, or are unable to fix a mechanical device and ask for help, or nurture an infant, or talk on the phone about your feelings, or sit in a circle to process—that is, anytime you do anything considered "typical" of women? Would you only be filmed doing things that women are never supposed to do, or haven't typically done? Do you think about these issues all day long, and monitor your actions and thoughts to prevent slipping up and "buying into the bipolar gender system?" Probably not. Then why expect me or any other transsexual to?

I do not hold the gender role expression of people I meet every day up to this scrutiny. I don't expect them to fit into a cookie-cutter fantasy of being somehow magically outside the "bipolar gender system." I expect most people to be multidimensional, to be male and female in both typical and atypical ways. I would never attempt to second-guess their gender expression by holding it up to expectations that feel nearly utopian.

But I go further. It is my belief that masculinity is actually something to celebrate. There is an exuberance, a bursting id-driven joy. Masculinity doesn't have to be power-over, although it is power: the increased propulsive intelligence I feel in my body, the white hot sexual drive that exists on its own terms, without emotional clutter or sentiment. Being male is not something that transsexual men or any man should have to apologize for.

Privilege

My greatest privilege in life is to live in North America, during a time when I can accomplish my medical, legal, and social transition. First, the question of my "whiteness": I am, as those familiar with the first *Bridge* will remember, not actually "white." My mother is from the Kainai or Blood band of the Blackfoot Confederacy and I'm a registered Treaty Indian in Canada. My father is Hispanic from Ranchos de Taos, New Mexico. I'm descended from an isolated (until recently), idiosyncratic people extremely proud of their Spanish heritage, and my genealogical and historical research has uncovered a strong Sephardic Jewish ancestral link, which I'm now exploring. Forced to convert to Catholicism or leave during the Spanish Expulsion in 1492, and in a similar expulsion from Portugal a few years later, many who converted (the Conversos/New Christians) journeyed to New Spain (now Mexico). Often, they fled to avoid the fires and tribunals of the Spanish Inquisition, instituted primarily to identify and punish any Converso practicing Judaism. The Hebrew term for these reluctant converts is *Anusim*, or the forced ones. Following them, the Inquisition was then established in New Spain. Those suspected of practicing their Jewish religion in secret ("Crypto-Jews") were burned at the stake, imprisoned for life, buried alive, or tortured. Many fled to even more remote regions, including northern New Mexico where so-called New Christians were allowed to own land—in contrast to the "clean blood" laws forbidding them from owning land in many other Spanish territories. Apparently, before they arrived in the Americas the

Valerios had already fled from Spain to Italy because of religious persecution, changing their name from the Spanish Valero to the Italian Valerio along the way, retaining (like Sephardic Jews the world over) their Spanish language and culture (Gitlitz, Santos).

Of mixed race, and the lightest person in my family, I appear to be any number or combination of ethnic groups or races, depending on who's observing me. Rarely do people get it right, or even close. Apparently, I inherited all the recessive genes in my family line for hair, eye, and skin color, having been born with blond hair and blue eyes that got darker as I got older. My eyes became a blue/green/hazel, my hair a golden reddish brown (unless I'd colored it for Goth/Punk effect). My mother, although brought up as an Indian on the reserve,[1] is actually one-quarter Dutch/German and French Huguenot. She didn't know him, but over time we've traced the ancestors of my lone northern European great-grandfather, Fred Kanous, all the way back to the Revolutionary War. I like to joke with my mother that she could join the Daughters of the American Revolution! Privilege aside, and contrary to what some may assume, I never liked being so light, and only accepted it with great effort over time.

I've lived in the border regions of racial/ethnic identity my entire life. There's an enormous energy in being more than one kind of person, although it can be confusing. Since some people view me as a "white person," it would be fair to say that I must sometimes have "white skin privilege." However, when I am taken as white only, I feel invisible as a nonwhite person, and unseen.

And what of this male privilege? This question is valid, although it carries with it certain underlying assumptions that are slippery and subject to evaporation on close scrutiny. I usually have to think hard to tally what privileges I have now that I didn't have before; in others words—being a man isn't all it's cracked up to be. Transsexual men do not accomplish their change for male privilege. At least I didn't, and I don't know anyone who has. In my experience, anyone attempting a sex change simply to gain male privilege would inevitably be disappointed.

However, there are certainly some advantages. I am listened to more, at least by the world at large, if not by lesbians (although even lesbians and feminists give me more air time than previously). Women are raised to be congenial, as well as to defer to men, and even lesbians are not entirely exempt. I take up more air time, since I possess more energy and it's harder to hold myself back. This change in energy level is primarily hormone-driven. A male voice does appear to carry a greater authoritative resonance, especially one in a deeper register, like mine. I don't worry about being raped or sexually harassed on the streets. This is not a small privilege—to walk without the fear of rape or sexual assault shadowing my moves in the night. However, it surprises many to learn that I've actually been threatened with physical violence more times as a man than I was as a woman. I have been kicked and punched, spit on, and threatened. Now, the violence and threats are man-on-man, and I am expected to fight back as an equal. The violence is territorial and of a different nature than before.

I am still poor, and becoming a man in the eyes of the world didn't automatically confer upon me the phallic scepter of commerce or industry. I have worked at a variety of jobs, from lead generation/telemarketing to content pouring for Internet portals. At the time of this writing, I live in a single room in a residence hotel, paying over $700, a bargain in San Francisco. Neither an academic nor a professional, I scrape by and attempt to find time for my writing and other artistic pursuits as best as I can. It is not easy; the struggle is enormous each day simply to survive and continue to create. I don't always know how to identify or take advantage of whatever privilege may accrue to being male, so it is possible that I have let opportunities slip by. People expect more of men, and it is more difficult to distinguish oneself—success is assumed and its lack is judged more harshly. Women, even feminists, have more of an eye on my earning capacity.

I always remind audiences that, as a transsexual man, I could have all male privilege could be taken from me if it is discovered that I was not born into a biologically intact male body. Undoubtedly, all transsexuals live with this threat, layered just beneath our conscious awareness as we go about our daily lives. Actually, this hovering threat goes beyond the loss of "male privilege" to include, more ominously, the loss of *nontranssexual privilege*. The sudden discovery that I am a bona fide weirdo who's had a sex change could toss me right out of the category "member of the human race"! This loss of "privilege" could be lethal.

Nontranssexuals have the privilege of taking their gender for granted. They don't have to constantly defend and explain it. They don't live in the constant insecurity that they might be discovered and therefore have their gender identity discounted and stolen from them.

The Movement Has Been Hijacked

Transsexuals' gender role expressions are rigidly scrutinized by people who don't share the same life experiences, or the same profound and specific medical-social alteration of biological sex. While this discourse—carried out in "queer" or "gender" studies departments and conferences—is certainly making the careers of a handful of feminist (trans or not) academics more profitable and durable, the feeding frenzy's effects on the lives of real-life transsexuals are not necessarily positive. Increasingly, transsexual people tell me that academia's theories have little bearing on their actual lives. In fact, they often find much of queer theory to be annoying and pretentious. For some, the encounter is more than a source of irritation, it devastates an emerging sense of self.

Ironically, queer theory does not always offer positive, validating concepts to those attempting to understand and negotiate what some have come to consider a "queer" gender identity. Further, the conflation of genderfuck into the transmovement has confused and eroded authentic transsexual voices. Although there's nothing inherently wrong with gender-bending, gender-fuck, and the assorted hyphenated identities becoming common in the queer world, I must ask: What does it really have to do with my life? The answer, increasingly, is nothing.

Although transsexuals enjoy an unprecedented attention, the thrill wears thin. The party is entrancing, but the results might be devastating. Recently, I saw an article in *The International Journal of Transgenderism* that made me feel a rising panic. It predicted that the "transgender" movement's recent liberatory gestures might liberate us out of the legal framework and protections that transsexuals have labored so hard to create (Swartz).

While certain strictures regarding entrance into transsexual medical programs should be relaxed or redefined, and the language and/or classification of the GID (gender identity disorder) reformed or changed, the legal framework enabling transsexuals to alter ID and birth certificates, get passports, have protection under civil rights laws, and obtain medical providers held to high standards needs to continue. If anything, legal provisions should be enhanced and strengthened to protect our rights further, ensuring timely, quality, and *insured* medical care. A wholesale destruction of the established legal and medical provisions surrounding and defining transsexual care is not in our best interest. It benefits only the most privileged among us, those who can afford quality care no matter what.[2] Many of the most ardent supporters of the GID's destruction fall into one or more of the following categories: they have had their surgery; they identify as transgender, not transsexual, and don't want medical intervention; they are white, well-educated, from upper-middle-class backgrounds, and relatively financially secure (O'Hartigan).

If all legal provisions are thrown to the wind, what happens to transsexuals in prison, those working as prostitutes, poor transsexuals, and the many transsexuals without health insurance? Outside my door here on the border of the Tenderloin, I see mainly Latina, African-American, and Asian transsexual women, many of them recent immigrants, selling sex often with the hope of earning their surgery money. If jailed or imprisoned, they will need to obtain hormones, which will be more difficult without an actual diagnosis. Many transsexual men are also on an economic edge since we lived for so long as gender-incongruent women, and have the resumes to prove it. We were often the last hired or the first fired, felt extreme discomfort in the workplace due to our inability to conform to gender role in matters of dress or general comportment, and often lack social skills owing to our extreme gender role and body distress. I know transmen who have waited years for their top surgery (I did), and would have benefitted greatly from some type of comprehensive health insurance program.

Without legal provisions, the battle for health insurance to cover transsexual surgery or medical care will never even begin or will be reversed, since it will only be considered "cosmetic" and not medically necessary. Also, if universal health coverage becomes available in the United States, transsexuals will certainly need a diagnosis to obtain medical benefits.

But the eradication of the GID could lead to far greater problems. Ken Morris, a transsexual man, did an informal survey of surgeons now doing transsexual surgeries. When asked whether they would continue to perform surgeries if the GID were eliminated, the vast majority answered that they would not—period. Surgeons do not want to be liable, in this lawsuit-crazed country, for radical life-changing surgeries that don't have a medical basis on the books. Also, it will be difficult to obtain a legal prescription for hormones. You can't treat something that doesn't exist.

The clash of the goals and vision of a Utopian Social Movement and a more pragmatic Civil Rights Movement cannot be more clear. Certainly, we have the right, and even obligation, to theorize, dream, and hope for a complete expansion of human capacities (the transcendence of the limitations of "bipolar gender or sex"). However, to paraphrase Buddha, our liberation begins by touching our hands to the earth. Working with what is in front of us, a confrontation with our ordinariness, a lack of pretension that goads us to make our lives better in ways we can actually testify to—let's *get real*.

Finally, the ideologues, who bore us with their stale ideology, while making a name for themselves analyzing, citing, or eulogizing transsexual experience. Leslie Feinberg is one of the most egregious. While she has contributed some context and historical background to the Transmovement, and is certainly a decent chronicler of the world of masculine women, her overly sentimental prose and Marxist harangues are hard to bear. She is, unbeknown to most lesbians, who adore her as the avatar of transgender, one of the most unpopular people on the planet among transsexual men who have undergone medical transition. *Stone Butch Blues* reads like a negative, stereotyped rendition of our life journey: a lesbian fairy tale about a botched sex change endured chiefly to obtain the benefits and protections of male privilege, followed by a renunciation of her brief, tragic male life and identity, and an eventual retreat and tearful homecoming to the lesbian community. She warmed up for this book by first writing, as Diane Leslie Feinberg, a little-known volume, *Journal of a Transsexual*—a narrative hostile to medical sex change (CaiRa). Later, after she dropped her first name and identified as a transgendered person, other activities harmful to transsexual interests have ensued. Feinberg has taken it upon herself to attempt to eliminate our diagnosis, one with no bearing on her present life. She didn't want any more surgery, but she nearly made it impossible for us to get ours, even petitioning NOW to come out against the GID. So much for "Transgender Liberation."

Queer feminist academic Judith Halberstam has written, "I suggest that butches and FTMs alike think carefully about the kinds of men or masculine beings that we become and lay claim to: alternative masculinities, ultimately, will fail to change existing gender hierarchies to the extent that they fail to be feminist, antiracist, anti-elitist, and queer" (306–307). While on the surface this statement appears benign, even copacetic in its compelling urge to overturn gender inequity, the actual ramifications for transsexual men are insidious and undermining. Most transsexuals I know, men and women alike, agree that rigid "gender hierarchies" should be destroyed or transcended, but an important question remains. The end phrase, "feminist, antiracist, anti-elitist, and queer"—although evoking a crescendo of righteous fervor—must be interrogated. Although Halberstam calls for rigorous self-interrogation and self-policing among FTMs (and butches), in my experience the sharpest edges of this interrogating voice generally originate from a source outside transsexual experience. This outside, nontranssexual perspective renders my own very real commitment to gender equity invisible, simply because I appear to be a gender-congruent man. I ask, who is going to measure whether any FTM transsexual masculine expression is "feminist," "anti-racist," "queer," or "anti-elitist"? Who gets to vote, and what measure are they using?

In my experience, transsexuals are often scrutinized by people with little knowledge or empathy for our life experiences. The life project of "queer," although it holds possibilities for anarchic and inventive identities, is too often used as a bludgeon, robbing authentic vital transsexual life experiences of their unique intelligence. Our voices stopped up before we even speak, when we do speak, we're viewed through a grid of judgments belittling the integrity of our perceptions. I have been asked if I'm "queer," and I'm never sure how to answer. Although I am definitely a "freak," and therefore a member of the general "queer" family of perverts, I am also heterosexual and appear to be relatively gender role congruent as a male.

Possibly, there is another way to express my odd conflation of apparent normality and completely nonconforming, bizarre, and "unnatural" freakdom. As one perceptive transmale friend of mine, Will, stated in response to the idea of transsexual men as "gender bending"—"We aren't bent, we're broken." I'm so "straight," in such an absolutely twisted—paradoxical and trickster-like way—that *I am way too far gone*. So are other transsexual men who have undergone at least some medical transition and live as men twenty-four/seven—regardless of their sexual orientation. We soar in an arena defying easy interpolation or assimilation by a nontranssexual-originated "queer" label, or even the values and rhetoric of the feminist movement. Transsexuals are only beginning to explore and express what that arena contains: the wounds, the provocative, mischief-making possibilities, the high-velocity sensations and dream-images that lightly hold our lifeforce, the way we are not subject to explanation, the dynamic tension between male and female that won't be reduced to a series of political cliches. The moralistic, confining preachiness of feministic academics like Halberstam can't even begin to know us—we are completely out of her line of sight, she is looking in the wrong place.

For too long I have been attempting to communicate with people who cannot even hear me, whose value system is corrosive to my existence. Many transsexual men share these experiences, although many are reluctant to talk about them publicly for fear of recrimination from either the lesbian feminist community or the emerging community of "genderqueers" who are increasingly indistinguishable from it. It occurs to me that the movement has been hijacked.

Although I will always support women's complete and total equality in law and emancipation in gender expression, I believe that feminism must stretch toward an unseen place. As a transsexual man, I feel that it is time to break from feminism (as we have known it), if it doesn't enhance our life experience, clarify and intensify our perceptions, or serve our needs. It is time to break from queer theory, if it doesn't speak to transsexuals' daily issues or enable us to expand our vision of what our lives are and can become.

For all transsexuals, particularly those not easily defined by current "queer" standards of behavior, but ultimately for each of us, a huge risk must be taken. For each transsexual person, another deeper way, a newly generative source must be uncovered.

Glossary

I have chosen to use these terms according to the following definitions. Most are fairly standard, although some may be open to dispute or used in slightly different ways by others.

Boy dyke, transgender FTM lesbian, TG lesbian, transgender butch: These terms are coming into vogue as more people in queer communities take on various identities concerning gender role expression. Some may experiment with hormones or take hormones on a limited basis; however, the majority live as gender-variant women/people in their daily lives, not doing sex change on a full-time medical, legal, or social basis. They may not consider themselves "women," since many feel that gender is only a social construct. Their life project appears to be at variance with the majority of transsexual life projects, although there is some intersection.

FTM: Female-to-Male.

MTF: Male-to-Female.

Nontranssexual: This term, originated by transsexuals, simply means people who are not transsexual. I use it in lieu of "genetic" or "biological," since some evidence emerging (although tentative) indicates that transsexual identity may have a biological basis. Also, transsexuals do take on many biological characteristics of the sex opposite to their birth, because of hormones and, to some extent, surgery.

Sex and Gender: *Sex* in this essay refers to biological sex, as in the primary and secondary sexual characteristics of male and female. *Gender* refers to an individual's legal, social, or subjective characteristics, which may or may not correspond to physical sex.

Transgender: Originally a term used by MTF crossdresser Virginia Prince to describe male crossdressers who do not take hormones or have surgery, it has expanded to include nearly anyone who is gender different or transgresses traditional gender roles. It's also an umbrella term for transsexuals, crossdressers, butch lesbians, intersex people, drag queens, and other gender/sex-variant people. I use *transgender* or *TG* to describe people with a gender expression that is not congruent with their biological sex; however, I do not include transsexuals. See below.

Transsexual: A person undergoing medical and legal transition from their original biological birth sex to the other sex.

Transsexual Man, Transman, FTM: I am a transsexual man—a man born biologically female who lived as a female person until I decided to undertake the process of sex change. This process includes the male hormones testosterone, and "top surgery" or a female-to-male chest reconstruction (bilateral mastectomy for FTMs). Complete hysterectomy is often done. "Bottom" or genital surgery is optional because of its difficulties and imperfections, although many people have these procedures. I use *transsexual* as a modifier for *man*; together, they describe my biological sex and gender identity in a complete way. I identify as a man sometimes, as a transsexual at other times, but the entire term is most descriptive.

Transsexual woman, transwoman, MTF: A woman, born biologically male, who has undergone medical transition or "sex change" from male to female, and lives as a woman all the time. Medical transition and maintenance include female hormones, estrogen and sometimes progesterone, and may or may not include "bottom" or genital surgery.

Notes

I would like to thank all the wonderful transsexual men and women who have made this essay possible with their support, subversive thinking, irreverent wit, perseverance, and illuminating discussion (in print, in person, or both): Mirha-Soleil Ross, Viviane Ki Namaste, Ken Morris, Xanthra Phillipa MacKay, Trish Salah, Beryl Dean Kotula, Ray Rea, Henry Rubin, Kevin Horwitz, Margaret Deirdre O'Hartigan, Jayson Barsic, Will Power, Carlos Gonzales, Gianna E. Israel, Ann Ogborn. I also would like to thank two sage, perceptive, and enormously wonderful nontranssexual friends for their feedback: Anthony (Tony) Raynsford and Judith Zoon.

1. Canadian term for American Indian reservations.

2. Gender Identity Disorder, or GID, is the American Psychiatric Association's official diagnosis for extreme gender dysphoria used in the DSM-IV. This diagnosis allows mental health and other medical providers to identify transsexuals, enabling them to receive competent, standard-

ized medical treatment. Those attempting to delete it use the model of the Gay and Lesbian liberation movement (which lobbied successfully to remove homosexuality from the DSM) and argue that it "stigmatizes" transpeople with a mental disorder, and that gender-role-defying children have been institutionalized and subjected to psychiatric abuse because of its existence. Those who don't want it deleted often want the definitions or parameters reformed; however, they argue that transsexuals are different from gays and lesbians: we require and desire ongoing medical treatment, and therefore warrant a viable diagnosis to insure standards of care, treatment, and, eventually, insurance. Psychiatric abuse involving this label is just that—abuse, and no one has ever been hospitalized using only this diagnosis. This debate has polarized the transcommunity in the recent past, but so far the GID has not been removed.

thirty-three

Poets, Lovers, and the Master's Tools: A Conversation with Audre Lorde

mary loving blanchard

I have finally learned enough to miss you, Audre. Sometimes, knowledge demands trial, then repays accomplishment with grief. By both has my knowledge of you been wrought. As a poet, I was just a kid when you died. Then, I didn't know enough to feel the loss of your passing. Now, I am compelled to keep your words alive by coming to them in silence. Knowing that my silence, although framed in respect, is little more than a mask to hide my fear, you mock the silence that cloaks me; you protest my very act of hiding: *"What are the words you do not yet have? What do you need to say? What are the tyrannies you swallow day by day and attempt to make your own, until you will sicken and die of them, still in silence?"* (*Sister*, 41; my italics).

I first came across you in the '70s—*that black lesbian poet.* Your words reached out to me from the mouths of so many other women—Sonia Sonchez tried to introduce me to you, as did Alice Walker. Nikki Giovanni invited me more than once to break bread with you and her, but I declined. I was afraid, Audre. I searched about for other, more acceptable models; but no matter where I searched, your words pierced their stories, their experiences, to reach me. Audre, you must know that being a lesbian is counterrevolutionary. If you hang out with lesbians, read about lesbians, you must be one.

The Black man saying this is code-warning every Black woman present interested in a relationship with a man—and most Black women are—that (1) if she wishes to have her work considered by him she must eschew any allegiance except to him and (2) any woman who wishes to retain his friendship and/or

support had better not be "tainted" by woman-identified interests. (Sister, 47;
my italics)

In spring 1998, a white woman who is about twenty years younger than I am assigned your work to me. A woman I have come to love. But then I felt left out, a little jealous because she knew you and I did not. With her assignment came acceptance, for I could run from you no longer, Audre. So I kept still. And from that place, I reached outward, toward your light. I set about ordering the place where I found you so that I might come to know you. Now, grief undergirds my knowledge because the work I have to do places me in disagreement with you.

But you command me to speak, so I dare not keep quiet any longer. A poet who loves me says that I remind her of you and I wonder how she means that. Maybe she sees a lesbian. Maybe she sees a poet. Maybe the two are inseparable if you are a woman who loves women and words. As poets, you and I share a bond beyond gender and race. As poets, we have in common our use of a set of tools, poetic devices, that were passed down to us from writers like Homer and Lucy Terry. Because all writers use the same set of tools, Audre. Okay, sure, we each have a set of our own specific tools—our own cultural designs, to appropriate one of Jane Tompkins's tools—but we are all working with the same set of tools. All of us—black, white, and free and slave and Asian and English and African and male and female and gay and lesbian and the rich and the poor—are invested in the same set of tools. Because if we are not using the same basic tools, Audre, then how do we explain Phillis Wheatley's use of Alexander Pope's tools, or Mary Wollstonecraft's use of tools from the slave narrative genre. Or my use of Jane Tompkins's tools to explain myself to you.

Still, Audre, I need you to know that but for your making clear the differences in writers' tools, I might not have been inclined to make clear their similarities. What is important is that we are both making clear and for the same reason: to (re)integrate our black female self(s) into the intellectual history of the world; to upset the master's house: "*For the master's tools will never dismantle the master's house. They may allow us temporarily to beat him at his own game, but they will never enable us to bring about genuine change*" (*Sister*, 112; my italics).

As a black woman scholar, I understand the frustration you must have felt when you made that statement. Often the academy, despite its objections, is vested in viewing the term *black scholar* as an oxymoron. Insert *woman* and the possibility becomes, in some corners, a sure sign of affirmative action diluting the genius inherent to a white male institution. Knowing all of this, you responded out of your own grief-stricken knowledge, a knowledge that reveals all too clearly how women become deft players in patriarchy. For some of us—black and white sisters alike—are not immune to the general attitude that still exists among gatekeepers of western intellectual history. Some of our white sisters are so vested in patriarchy that they perpetuate the myth of why we were accepted into graduate school in the first place. They discourage our research efforts, not in any real attempt at helping us focus our scholarship, but rather to safeguard the sanctity of current thought. They relate to us through an old pattern of patriarchy, and they don't hear us, Audre, whether we scream or whether we whisper: *"The history of white women who are unable to hear Black women's words, or to maintain dialogue with us is long and discouraging. But for me to assume that you will not hear me represents not only history, perhaps, but an old pattern of relating, sometimes protective and sometimes dysfunctional, which we, as women shaping our future, are in the process of moving beyond, I hope"* (Sister, 66–67; my italics).

And we black sisters buy equally into the myths perpetuated in this fishbowl called the academy. We celebrate our own genius only if there is one of us, thereby allowing us to imagine ourselves the lone soldier descended from W. E. B. Du Bois's talented tenth. We play quick and loose with each other's survival to ensure our own. We are embroiled in an inner conflict, brought on in part by our own acquiescence to the games of patriarchy. Worse, *"We do not love ourselves, therefore we cannot love each other. Because we see in each other's face our own face, the face we never stopped wanting. Because we survived and survival breeds desire for more self. A face we never stopped wanting at the same time as we try to obliterate it"* (Sister, 155; my italics). And because we women, black and white, become vested in the master's tools, it may appear as though the only thing left is to get rid of the whole toolbox.

But I'm here to tell you, Audre, that getting rid of the toolbox isn't necessary. Because here we stand—you and me and Lucy and Phillis and Mary and Sonia and Alice and Nikki and Jane—locking arms in the master's house. In our hands, the master's tools have become ammunition in the dismantling of his house, as we set about adding an extra room or two. We have taken his tools and with them made tools that fit our individual hands, as each of us sets out to do the work we have to do. And we will use these tools to read in ways that include us. We can do this with these tools of reading that we have inherited because we are already vested in, and for the most part, trust them. They are the same tools we have used to read Pope and Oliver Wendell Holmes and Shakespeare and T. S. Eliot and Ezra Pound. We have used these tools to read William Faulkner and

Wayne Booth and Ovid and Carl Jung. And once we've learned to use these same tools to read Wheatley and Wollstonecraft and James Baldwin and Harriet Jacobs and Julia Alvarez and Lucille Clifton and Richard Wright and Charles Johnson and Jean Toomer and Alice Walker and Carson McCullers and Flannery O'Connor and George Moses Horton and Maxine Hong Kingston, we'll realize that those tools didn't belong to the master, after all. Well, they didn't belong to him all by himself. They are our tools too. And they have been so all the time. And that is one way that we gain agency, by adapting the tools we have rather than by reinventing the wheel; although the wheel is reinvented along the way. And each new reinvention becomes part of the whole because the whole keeps expanding, you see, based on input from all its parts.

Gaining agency through my specific use of the master's tools is important to me in part because, most times, it seems I have to make a choice between making new tools, or retooling these old, worn-out tools of patriarchy and having time to write really necessary poetry and love really necessary poets. And each day that I find myself beating on that wall built to exclude me, I do so knowing that once that wall has been toppled then I must set about resurrecting it because it was beating on that wall that kept me from silence. It was beating on that wall that taught me to adjust and adapt the master's tools to my own hand. And it just may be that part of becoming, part of gaining agency, has to do with tearing down the master's house and rebuilding our own house(s) to our own specifications.

And that's where I am with you, Audre. Keeping some of your tools as they are; retooling others so that they fit my hand. Somehow, I don't think you would be upset with me. I think you would understand completely. Because poetry is not a luxury, and being able to retool saves time for poetry in the end. Besides, your words have been encouraging me all along in that direction: *"The quality of light by which we scrutinize our lives has direct bearing upon the product which we live, and upon the changes which we hope to bring about through those lives. It is within this light that we form those ideas by which we pursue our magic and make it realized"* (*Sister*, 36; my italics). The magic I must now make realized has been aided by your words, and by your fight to keep those words in front of me even while you waged battle for your life. I stand now in the light made possible by your work. Thanks for the light, Auntie. I love you.

September 2000

thirty-four

"All I Can Cook Is Crack on a Spoon": A Sign for a New Generation of Feminists

Simona J. Hill

During the 1998–99 academic year, I served as faculty-in-residence for a housing program devoted to understanding women's issues on a small, rural, elite campus. Being one of a few women of color on campus helped to create a visible agency of diversity that was important. I considered myself fortunate to nurture some burgeoning ideas about what it means to be a feminist for the twenty-first century. But I had no idea when I hauled my belongings up to my room that September how much I would learn from a cryptic slang phrase adorning the door across the hall.

"All I can cook is crack on a spoon" read the sign I passed every day for weeks in the mornings when my eyes were not quite open and late at night when I returned from a day filled with the hustle, joy, and exasperation of life. What would *your* reaction be to such a sign? At first glance, I chuckled mildly and dismissed the sign as a reflection of someone's derisive outlook or cry of mock desperation. "Everyone is entitled to his or her opinion," thought my politically correct persona as I walked by the small (in size) and seemingly unassuming (to me at the time) sign. Admittedly, in fact, I did not pay much attention to the sign's hidden meanings. However, repeated exposure to such a potentially controversial choice of words wears on a feminist. I believe that we must question and carefully examine the images and symbols (some of our own choosing) that attach themselves to our surrounding environment, infiltrate our senses, and can unwittingly challenge our definitions of self by their very presence. For me, this is fundamental to being a productive activist and change agent. So I began contemplating the broader meaning of "All I can cook is crack on a spoon" for women, feminists, and young feminists engaged in the third wave of feminism in particular. As my understanding of the phrase increased, I saw the "All I can cook is crack on a spoon" poster as a sign for a new generation of feminists. Many of these "grrls" are in the process of creatively adapting feminist ideology and making it relevant to their unique location within the movement.

The third wave of feminism began between the late 1980s and the early 1990s. Composed of the "Gen-X" feminists, this movement seeks to build from the groundwork laid by earlier movements. Although appreciative of the second wave's gains, third-wave feminists have their own expanding agenda. To add to the next level of structure for people aiming to gain full access to the public sphere, this generation must work through contradictions in society. They accomplish this by "attempting to fit the legacies of and lessons from the women's movement of the 1970s into their own lived experiences" (Orr, 30).

The third wave tends to be inclusive of all races, religions, colors, sexual orientations, and genders. Inspired by earlier feminists such as Audre Lorde and Gloria Anzaldúa, young feminists seek to "eradicate the image of feminism as a rich woman's club" (Tobias, 253). Most important, members of this third wave redefine feminism so that it includes themselves (Drake). On the pulse of a computer age, third-wave feminism is comfortable outside traditional academic constructions. Cyberspace and 'zines get the message out.[1] Although third-wave feminists may not have experienced forms of oppression as overt as those experienced by their predecessors, they are encouraged to talk about their experiences through popular media.

Place a hand to your hip, if it pleases you, and say, "All I can cook is crack on a spoon" out loud a few times with attitude. I encourage you to examine your own reactions. This essay is about the deconstruction of the phrase "All I can cook is crack on a spoon" and how it is a potent metaphor laden with contradiction and ambiguities that often mirror the internal struggles young women of the third wave face in a rapidly changing postmodern world.

Traditionally, the Women's Studies House where I lived has attracted writers, scholars, and activists invested in keeping the tenets of the women's movement alive. In their direct and inimitable ways, these students (and those from supporting campus organizations who frequented the house) tend to push the envelope on issues and gradually jar the institution into new levels of consciousness. As the only African-American woman living in a four-bedroom Cape Cod with four to six other women over the span of two semesters, I quickly realized that we came from unique intellectual places and diametrical environmental spaces. These undergraduates for the most part were very unlike me at their age: white, upper middle class, suburban, privileged. Some were lesbian or bisexual, others were not.

In our polite ways, we agreed to disagree. I would not venture to say that we were a bonded family, but neither were we strangers in a dead-end alley. Recognizing what joined us, however, was easier if we remained focused on some common grounds of experience such as coming of age, equality between the sexes, and the longing for retribution for various acts of female oppression. From my perspective, our most significant resource was mutual respect, tentative earlier in the year, but always present in some form.

Our generation gap could be measured not so much in years (there was about a fifteen-year difference in our ages) as in ideological postures. For example, I see the challenge for women, particularly those who are young and of color, as an odyssey to find authentic "cultural shelters"[2] within the constraints of pre-existing -isms: racism, sexism, classism, and heterosexism, to name a few. As anthropologist Leith Mullings notes, "some aspects of culture, while perhaps initially responses to inequality, now facilitate the reproduction of domination and are an obstacle to progress" (192). Importantly, these shelters offer points of entry for third-wave feminists to identify with the aspects of feminism that are appealing, relevant, and boldly speak to their issues. Given time, personal owner-ship, and attention, cultural shelters are transformed, at their best, to comfortable homelike settings where risk is not only possible, but also expected and encouraged. Neglecting any part of the process of building a substantial homeplace is detrimental to individual sanity, relationships, and collective integrity.

In *Yearning*, bell hooks reminds us that homeplace is a primarily inside safe haven where women have "the opportunity to grow," to develop and nurture spirit, and, most important, to create a shared "com-munity of resistance" within the outside culture of white supremacy (42). Homeplace evolves into a core site of being where purpose, courage, truth, and testimony converge along a dynamic axis. Stationed firmly within the binding safety of homeplace and the necessary crises of char-acter it creates, the truths of relationship are allowed to flourish. Ideally, for me, the task of constructing viable cultural shelters is equivalent to that of making hooks's homeplaces. And what this means on another level is a "return in the rediscovery of connection, in the realization that self and other are interdependent and that life, however valuable in itself, can only be sustained by care in relationships" (Gilligan, *Voice*, 127).

In terms of historical process, today's social reality is different from the social reality of tomorrow. For my housemates, woman's place is as much a reality as is combining high-maintenance careers with the com-plexities of contemporary family life. Superwoman is questioned for what she is—superhuman and not a normal state of activity or prize hard won (Christopher Jones). The need for choice in decision making is a pre-mium not to be bartered away. Homeplace seems to be an accepted right rather than struggle. It is inviolate, standing without apology for its being. To this end, homeplace is a non-negotiable entity that exists regardless of prevailing structures and oppressions.

College-age women's beliefs and attitudes about feminism will deter-mine feminism's value to the future (Alexander and Ryan). Their experi-ences now shape how feminism's ideals will operate in their lives. They have the opportunity to take up the fight, make it their own, and ensure that feminist thought progresses to the next generation. Perhaps this is the legacy of earlier times to these daughters and granddaughters of women's movements. Regardless of the source, I remain amazed by an intrinsic joie de vivre reflecting a genuine sense of entitlement and access to the freedom to create and to be that their understanding of homeplace confers.

It was somewhere during the middle of the second semester, a few weeks before Spring Break, when I noticed that new computer-generated sign on the door of one of my housemates. She was a graduating senior who had an early case of "senioritis." At the bottom of the words "All I can cook is crack on a spoon" was a clip art drawing of a silver spoon.

Just as in hardcore, inner-city crack cocaine dependency, presenting pseudo–crack-addicted, out-of-bounds behavior crosses territorial lines. It generates awkward destruction to social conventions and causes a multitude of problems within small groups such as families and peers, communities, neighborhoods, and society at large. In campus parlance, to be a "crackhead" is a sardonic colloquialism. It can mean that others regard your behavior as crazy, out of control, and otherwise "off the hook." "Are you smokin' crack?" is a question posed when someone demonstrates blatant inconsistencies fraught with indecisiveness, hyperactivity, anxiety, and/or chaos. The derisive question usually promotes laughter. Crackheads are persons, male or female, who demonstrate a mental break from reality. They are generally disconnected from homeplaces either temporarily or permanently.

At second glance, I realized that the student's sign could even be a coarse allusion to the so-called crackheads on campus: students who do the bare minimum academically but tend to soar in the social pursuits of frequent binge drinking and riotous parties. Probably hung for laughs rather than for philosophical discourse, the sign annoyed my feminist sensibilities with its continued presence. Moreover, as a woman of color, how could I ignore the implications of such a sign for so many in urban settings blighted by crack cocaine?[3] It was a huge problem in the mid-1980s and remains so for many communities today. At $5 to $20 per rock, crack is a much cheaper alternative to powder cocaine and because it is so concentrated it gives users a more intense "high" (Gest). The National Household Survey on Drug Abuse (NHSDA) estimated the number of current crack users to be about 604,000 in 1997, which does not reflect a significant change since 1988. Crack is commonly found in black communities, and powder cocaine is more popular among wealthy whites. An astounding 83 percent to 90 percent of those convicted of possessing crack and sales are convicted (Fields; Bivins). Since I come from Philadelphia, a city plagued by the aftermath of the easy availability of crack cocaine (and heroin), I failed to see the humor in an "All I can cook is crack on a spoon" poster.

But the phrase was provocative not only because the connotations of crack were evident but also because it challenged traditional roles for women. Are stereotypes supported, unilaterally destroyed, or merely muddled in the cavalier remark? As one of my teaching assistants later pointed out, such an expression can conjure in women deeply held fears about incompetence and self-worth, and about impossible standards of beauty, sexuality, strength, and weakness.

To reconcile these questions and the others that follow in this chapter, I needed to translate the sign into a language I could understand. I decided to explore the statement's deeper meanings—first with myself and then with my students. In fact, the sign became part of the take-home portion of the final examinations in both my Minorities and Introduction to Women's Studies courses.

Initial student reactions ranged from perplexity to anger, from disgust to frustration. One young woman saw "All I can cook is crack on a spoon" as a response from a society awash in decades of exposure to feminist rhetoric. She continued to declare that the woman who says that she cannot cook anything except crack is renouncing the submissive specter of the "housewife" image still haunting patriarchy's ideal of femininity. Truly, this is a substantive reformation that challenges oppressive, hegemonic constraints of the modern world and demands that women have real—rather than phantom—choices. A few students shared a sense of betrayal that feminism had abandoned those who seem to squat on the outskirts of society—those caught in a fixed downward death spiral of chemical dependency and other self-destructive behaviors, those most powerless to break free of oppression. Some expressed the hopelessness that women and feminists might feel in their efforts to live within or change the social order. Hardly exclusionary in tone, "All I can cook is crack on a spoon" has meaning and implications for many depending on personal history, location within feminist thought, and circumstance.

Backhanded and backbiting statements slap across the faces of women who want more in a society that demands all and gives little in return. A sister, not necessarily biological in form, is a woman who shares in the struggle as well as the triumph. She is a steady support in the ghostly face of powerlessness and self-loathing. Despite any bewilderment, sisters model the belief that things are never quite what they seem and the hope that a "change is gonna come." Placing hand to hip and declaring, "All I can cook is crack on a spoon" can be a lighthearted yet revealing motto. Subtle and overt meanings reflect class distinctions and racial/ethnic loyalties. Differences among interpretations can have equally pessimistic and optimistic overtones with the power to both unify and divide. In some ways, it is a skewed attempt for the woman to examine how she is trapped (or believes she is) by a society over which she has no control. Has her "homeplace" now imprisoned her? If so, there is a need for an immediate expansion of possibility within her cultural shelter.

Airing difference can have a chilling, sometimes paralyzing, effect as women strive to recognize connections and build bridges over stormy waters. For example, a woman's individual needs may require her to look like "Barbie," the all-American standard of unattainable, plasticized beauty, while at the same time be a traditional wife, mother, chauffeur, caregiver, accountant, teacher, broker. You get the idea. Women who buy the "Barbie" limited warranty are expected to be seen and not heard, just like their children. "All I can cook is crack on a spoon" women who believe that they have no power individually will continue to be like "Barbie." At great cost, they keep their mouths shut tightly, allowing neither food to enter nor voice to exit. In this light, the statement indicates a sense of deep failure and defeat. Women can say, "All I can cook is crack on a spoon" but do not literally mean that they are crack cocaine users or producers. They may only be unsure of their choices in the absence of healthy, functional environments. They may believe that they have little potential or ability to succeed and to reach life goals.

Likewise, clinically depressed women may say, "All I can cook is crack on a spoon," near the point of giving up on themselves, their lives, or their ability to parent. Quite paradoxically, they may have conflict over fulfilling social roles as mothers while trying to control their substance abuse (Sterk, 118). A woman who says, "All I can cook is crack on a spoon" to another woman in the same position may find a sympathetic shoulder to cry on or a friend with whom to laugh. She may be referring to a domestic situation putting incredible demands on her time and pressure to perform based on unrealistic expectations. She may be "tired of being tired" of serving her family or fighting the battles of her everyday existence. She is now the Barbie with swollen ankles and perpetual PMS. Sometimes when women say, "All I can cook is crack on a spoon" to other women, they are not only pulling themselves down, but dragging other women down as well. They are reinforcing the self-hatred and ignorance of genuine feminine power. It is a self-fulfilling prophecy realized. Crack kills!

Feminism has liberated many women from the domination of men in their lives (at least in some respects). It has not fully liberated women from the domination of heavy social expectation, glass ceilings, and concrete floorings that keep woman in her place. The sarcasm embedded in the phrase puts women in a negative light, implying that women are victims rather than survivors of choices and conditions.

"Crackheaded" women, if I may coin a term here, are icons fulfilling convenient stereotypes—hindrances to the cause of feminist thought. "All I can cook is crack on a spoon" figures of speech, perhaps slightly humorous to some, imply an internalization of defeat that only magnifies failure on other levels. The ability to motivate and generate pride, self-esteem, and worthiness among those who succumb to the lure of their drug of choice is a virtually impossible feat, an uphill endeavor. Hence the cycle of self-destructive (addictive) behaviors is repeated and interpreted as feeling safe. If the woman continues this pattern, she will die. If not a literal death, then most assuredly a spiritual one with slight likelihood for resurrection. Literal and metaphorical crack-addicted women are slowly starving away their willingness, power, and truth. Crack is a temporary, blind safety net that is frayed and causes women to disintegrate by degrees and disappear completely without fanfare or remembrance.

On a surprising note, perhaps what is ultimately at stake for "All I can cook is crack on a spoon" women is freedom. One student, a campus activist, interpreted it as a positive statement about freedom. "Women will not be seen as domestic animals," she writes. "We will no longer be barefoot and pregnant, and cooking meals for our good, breadwinning husbands." This universal "kiss-my-ass response" indicates that a woman no longer concedes to her subservient status.

Metaphorical crack-cooking bestows the freedom to take care of one's own needs without stumbling through the mire of guilt, obsessive-compulsive behavior, and restriction. Crack-cooking women within this context have a heat-seeking device that targets peace of mind over perfectionist standards. The price for this transformation is that "All I can cook is crack on a spoon" women, real or hypothetical, must want change and rebirth.

Claire E. Sterk's fascinating account of women who cook crack cocaine discusses the "Queens of the Scene," the women who cook crack cocaine. These "Queens" belie the general stereotype that women addicted to crack have low status. Cooks are proficient in the complicated process of transforming powder cocaine into crack and as long as their own drug habits do not interfere with their "kitchen" skills, they're valued. They are *least* likely to be poor. These are the women who tend to achieve power, control, and independence in the drug hierarchy. However, if drug dealers perceive them as threats, patriarchal rules, harassment, and sexist behavior are used to keep them in place (53–59). Women on either end of the violent world of the crack industry—from the street-bound prostitute to inside, high-status cooks—are not equal to men and must appeal to men's sympathetic predilections.

Just Saying No: A "Crack" Attitude for Third-Wave Feminists

Cultural shelters, homeplaces of safety in the midst of oppression, are always dynamic, never static. Such shelters help us to move forward, shift perceptions, and grow beyond the work of previous generations. I believe that interpreting an "All I can cook is crack on a spoon" sign helps third-wave feminists see differences of opinion as well as common grounds of persuasion. This type of statement brings feminists together regardless of race, nationality, ethnicity, or origin. The underlying principle is not to accept what is given to you or expected of you. "All I can cook is crack on a spoon" becomes a warning to all that this person will not compromise. It is a firm commitment to strength, to rebellion, to power.

Returning to the sign on that student's door, I wonder how much of its meaning is a tribute to the women who marched, protested, formed companies, climbed corporate ladders, struggled to clear paths in academia, and kept home fires burning. From what I know of the student who made the sign, she has a steel obstinacy and the boldness to claim empowerment. She does not relate to a "crack" mind-set of victimhood or passivity. She lives out loud and loves it. This "grrrl" has the voice of her convictions and the yearning to be heard in her own right.

I agree with Jennifer Drake that this is where hope is the crest of the third wave: it is a kind of faith, in and of the everyday, unruly like anger (97–108). My concern remains whether the issues important to the second wave will be diluted or lost in my housemate's generation. Do third-wave feminists realize the magnitude of issues of equality, equity in pay, discrimination, and political ideology transmuted into social and government policy? On what level do they recognize that gains for women are at risk of systematic erosion, especially for women of color, those living in poverty or in a Third World country? The mere suggestion that crack cocaine is recreational does more to impede the progress of the next generation of feminism than young women like these are probably willing to acknowledge.

If those of the next generation of feminism are to be the well-grounded, dynamic, productive activists that we hope them to be, then images and symbols must continue to be analyzed. Dialogues and, yes, even signs in dormitories need to be questioned for what they are and the meanings they can generate. Audre Lorde foretold of this new generation, cautioning:

> Sometimes we drug ourselves with dreams of new ideas. The head will save us. The brain alone will set us free. But there are no new ideas still waiting in the wings to save us as women, as human. There are only old and forgotten ones,

new combinations, extrapolations and recognitions from within ourselves, along with the renewed courage to try them out. And we must constantly encourage ourselves and each other to attempt the heretical actions our dreams imply and some of our old ideas disparage. (*Sister,* 127)

This dreaming takes rebellion, action, and for Lorde the return to a poetry of the dark soul. It is the knowing spirit (which is woman's most honorable legacy to woman) that can see the hidden meaning of "All I can cook is crack on a spoon" signs. As our recent encounters in both the wars on drugs and the battle for homeplace attest, just saying "no" hardly ever works in the manufacture of a compelling ideology that transforms the world.

Notes

I would like to thank the students in my spring 1999 Minorities and Introduction to Women's Studies classes for their contributions to this discussion. I appreciate my sister-colleagues Susan R. Bowers, Kamika D. Cooper, and Michelle D. Durham for their patience, fiery support, and vision.

1. For one example of a website, visit the *3rd WWWave!* It describes itself as "a group of women who feel passionately about women's issues . . . [who] decided to put up a site that would reflect the unique view of women's issues and feminism in the generation of women who came of age in the 80's." http://www.io.com/~wwwave/.

2. I use the term *cultural shelter* to refer to physical as well as conceptual space. It is a place of safety as well as a point of tension in which ideas, identity, and perspective can be formed and nurtured. For example, the Women's Studies House was a conceptual idea, a programming opportunity, which allowed those who often felt at risk or were marginalized in other parts of the campus community to come together and share who they are in some meaningful ways. The house itself was a physical extension of conceptual chasms on a campus where feminism is not easily understood or embraced.

3. Between late summer 1985 and 1986 a hurricane of destruction swept through large urban cities (New York City, Philadelphia, Washington, and Miami) and unleashed a potent new form of cocaine called crack that ravaged the streets of America. Crack, a nearly pure type of free-based cocaine, is a stimulant that causes a short-lived feeling of euphoria. Crack cocaine is manufactured by dissolving the chemical cocaine hydrochloride (powder cocaine) in a solution of water and ammonia or sodium bicarbonate (household baking soda). The solution is heated to remove the hydrochloride and the final product dried. The crack cocaine is then cut or broken into small "rocks" weighing only a few tenths of a gram. It is called "crack" because it snaps and cracks when heated and smoked. The process of transforming powder cocaine to crack is rather complicated and demands expert "cooks," most of whom are female. Crack is used by placing the rock in a three- to four-inch glass pipe, heating it, and inhaling the vapors. The vapors are quickly absorbed into the lungs and give the user an immediate rush that lasts anywhere from ten to thirty minutes. Whereas powder cocaine must be inhaled or injected, or smoked (with the risk of dangerous flammable solvents), crack has none of those drawbacks; it is cocaine for the masses. Although technically the crack for cocaine is smoked rather than "cooked on a spoon" by its users, it is habit forming and can be related to life-threatening medical emergencies. One does not have to overdose on crack to die from it.

thirty-five

DON'T TOUCH: RECUERDOS (SELF-DESTRUCTION)

Berta Avila

PLEASE, I PLEAD, DON'T TOUCH MY FACE
I DON'T REALLY BELONG IN THIS PLACE
DON'T WHISPER YOUR PASSION IN MY EAR
IT BRINGS TO MY HEART TERROR AND FEAR
DON'T TELL ME MY HAIR SMELLS SWEET
LET ME GO, LET ME RUN OUT TO THE STREET
DON'T TOUCH MY LIPS OF TENDER RED
HOW I WISH YOU WERE DEAD
DON'T TOUCH MY SHOULDERS, DON'T TOUCH MY HAND
YOUR VERY PRESENCE I CANNOT STAND
DON'T TOUCH MY THIGHS OF TANNED BROWN FLESH
YOU ARE, MORE THAN I, TRASH
DON'T LET YOUR VOICE CALL OUT MY NAME
I'M ONLY TRYING TO PLAY THIS SICK GAME
DON'T TRY TO STOP ME WHEN I MUST GO
DON'T YOU UNDERSTAND... IT'S THE END OF THIS SHOW

For All My Sisters Still on the Streets . . . Still Lost

El Paso, Tx.
1979

thirty-six

Premature

Donna Tsuyuko Tanigawa

I am pregnant.
I am pregnant.
I am pregnant.

—Morning mantra

I am trying to have a baby. Like all lesbians, I had to find inventive ways to get the sperm to meet my egg. No amount of my lover's love or her spit or the fluids that pass between us in private could, in the end, impregnate me.

I knew that someday I would find myself writing about this experience. Like any passage, I learned how gender, sexuality, race, and class
give structure to my life. Superstitious as I am, I thought that I would wait
until after I had the baby to write about the process. It has been three
years since the first thawed-out specimen made its way through my cervix
and into my uterus but there is still no baby and now the words, the
words, are pushing themselves out.

"Oooh, bay-bee, bay-bee."

> The Accidental Pregnancy
> Did you know that there are no accidental pregnancies?
> Each one is intentional and deliberate. "The condom
> broke," my lover's mother told her, "that's how you came."
> "I forgot to take the Pill," my friend explained to her hus-
> band. "The timing sucks," she added. "Accidents do hap-
> pen," my mother consoled herself the moment she
> discovered that her eldest daughter, my sister, was four
> months pregnant and in her senior year of high school.
> My seventeen-year-old niece conceived on Valentine's
> Day. According to her, she got pregnant while on the Pill.
> "It must have been the antibiotics," the doctor supposedly
> said, "that counteracted the birth control." "Stranger
> things have happened," my mother explained to us.

I always wanted to be a mommy. Throughout my childhood I moth-
ered over a dozen Drowsy Dolls. As soon as the pink flannel polka-dotted
pajamas frayed at the seams, revealing the small plastic box that housed
Drowsy's voice, my mother would buy me a new one. Pull the string and
Drowsy would say, "I'm hungry" or "I want a drink of water."

> I am trying to get at not having a baby.

I lie to my mother.
Mom, I'm pregnant. I know you said to wait until after I finish graduate school and settle down and find a secure job and start putting away
money and move out of our cramped one-bedroom apartment and catch
up with the bills (and didn't you say, "find a man"?), but it was an accident.
Really. Lee-Ann and I didn't mean to do it, but it just happened, you
know? It's just one of those things.

> Saying the F-word aloud: Fertility.

Sensing the Presence of Sarah's Spirit: A Docufiction

Interview Date: December 12, 1997
Location: 2734 Nako'oko'o Street, #7, Honolulu, Hawai'i
Interviewees: Two Asian females in their early thirties

Interviewee 1: I didn't need the alarm to get me up. I usually slap down the snooze bar one or two times before I fully open my eyes, but that morning I sprang up and found myself talking. I remember saying, "Hello, Sarah." I could sense her. I felt a current of energy near me. Next to me. Attached in a way to me. Near my left hip. It was alive and busy. It was Sarah and she had chosen us.

Interviewee 2: I guess we both were afraid that if we named it, it would go away. When Donna was asleep, I'd sometimes talk to her. "Hi Sarah, it's me, Daddy." But then one evening while Donna and I were making love, she pushed me. "Did you feel that?" I blurted out. And then we looked at each other and knew: our baby girl was with us.

Interviewee 1: Children choose their parents. Parents don't choose them. To confirm things, we asked our spiritual teacher. "Yup," she said. She could see the spirit within my aura field. "It's definitely a girl." A few days later our teacher took us to the beach at five in the morning, before sunrise, to perform a fixing ceremony. "Sometimes the spirit changes its mind," she said. "This is to help her know that she's loved and wanted." We offered three white flowers and watched as the sun kissed the surface of the ocean for the first time.

Interviewee 2: In the spirit world there is no sense of time. We had to tell Sarah, "Now, sweetie. Not later, but now." A friend of ours had a miscarriage at five months. Her doctor told her and her partner that the fetus was genetically imperfect. What he didn't say, and probably didn't know, was that the spirit had changed its mind. A spirit can change its mind up until the last moment, the last stretch through the birth canal. It happens. I hope Sarah doesn't change her mind.

Interviewee 1: I'd find myself talking to Sarah, especially when I passed the toucan family at work. She loved being at the zoo every day. I worked in a playground, I guess she thought. Whenever I'd approach the enclosure, the birds would squawk louder. Sarah loved it when the toucans ate their green grapes from the metal tray.

Interviewee 2: It's not very hard to sense a spirit. We found ourselves buying a few children's books and reading them aloud to Sarah. We knew that pregnant women are encouraged to read to their fetuses, so we thought that we were just getting a head start. She loved Akiko Tamura's *Miss Takuan* the best. . . .

Interviewee 1: But each time we tried another insemination at the doctor's office, it didn't take. My periods continued coming. So when our spiritual teacher told us, "Don't say anything. Make like she no stay 'cause she getting too comfortable," we ignored Sarah.

Interviewee 2: Some well-intended people told us, "Relax. If it happens, it happens." How the hell is it going to fucking happen if we don't make a point to go to the goddamn doctor's office?

[Interview ends.]

My acupuncturist helps me balance my energy.

"Too much yin," she says. "Too much female energy not good for making baby." She places strategic needles on my palms and at my feet and near my navel. I am put on a remedy of Chinese herbs, bee pollen, and Vitamin F and told to stay away from ginger in all forms.

After several failures at the doctor's office, I go to see a numerologist. I give her the date and time of my birth and she quickly tells me, "You have not-so-good numbers through 1999." I am in my yakudoshi year, the time in which a person's spirit and body are reborn. Calamities and bad luck run rampant during this time. A daughter (not son) born during a woman's yakudoshi year is often considered the "devil's child." But what she tells me that I do not know is this: "You've got your mother's guilt draped over your back. She is strong and you are not." "But can try," she says. "No hurt trying, yeah?"

I ask the universe for a Tiger. My lover and I check the astrological charts to confirm that a child born in the year of the Tiger will be highly compatible with Fire Horse parents. I try to get pregnant, but by May we realize that any child conceived here on out will be born not as a Tiger but as a Rabbit. Later that year we adopt a five-month old puppy. "This is our Tiger baby," I tell my lover. "I should have specified the species."

The day I turn thirty-two I go to the Shinto shrine for blessings. The priest writes both my name and my lover's name into his ledger (she tells him her name is Yuki and passes for a man) and gives me a white paper doll, a wooden arrow, and two cloth amulets. He instructs me to take the doll and rub it down the entire length of my body and then place it under my pillow when I go to sleep that night so that the doll will catch all of my misfortunes and illnesses. I am told to burn the doll in the morning.

One of the amulets is for safe pregnancy. I take a safety pin and fasten it onto my underwear each morning. On New Year's Day, I respectfully return the charms to the shrine to be burnt.

I go to my Buddhist monk friend for prayers. He lights two small candles, places a stick of incense in a ceramic bowl, and then proceeds to chant for forty-five minutes. "Chanting will help strengthen the spirit," he tells me. "Birth is painful not only for the mother but for the spirit. They are born into the physical realm at a specific frequency of vibrations."

He tells me in counsel, "You cannot change the world. Accept things as they are." I say "yes" but fight his words. I think he means I must accept my infertility. A few days later I realize that my monk friend is talking about my protestations to heterosexism.

I write my mother. I tell her my period is three days late this month. Three days later, my period arrives. The next month, she encloses five packages of maxi pads and two boxes of tampons bought on sale at Target in a "care package" along with ginger spice cake. I think back to what the numerologist said: "She is strong and you are not."

I go to the Roman Catholic cathedral to light a candle in front of the Virgin Mary and the Baby Jesus. I ask them to help me. I look for the statue of Saint Jude, the Patron of Desperate Cases, but find out that he is at the shop being cleaned. I purchase a seven-day candle and take it home. My lover and I set up an altar in the living room. Each week I light a new candle and ask the Virgin Mary and Baby Jesus to burn into light all the negativity surrounding my having a child. Each week my candle holder forms a black film around the top of its plastic rim.

I have kept a candle burning for over three years now.

This year for Valentine's Day my lover gives me a soapstone-carved statue of Kwan Yin. Through this female Buddha I learn to say, "No fear."

I rely on signs. My niece gets pregnant the month that my lover and I first try to have a baby. Our male friend's wife gets pregnant a month later. She tells us that it was SOOOO easy. "It happened the moment I went off the Pill." "She's SOOOO het," we complain to each other. Our lesbian friend gets pregnant on her doctor's table during her first insemination. In three years, I have had a total of four single, very pregnant students give birth during the semester. This spring semester, two of my students drop my class after two months because of morning sickness. I throw a baby shower for a student expected to give birth next month. Yesterday my friend called me up to say, "We're both mommies!" Her lover gave birth to a healthy baby girl. Each time a sign appears I try to find my way.

I know not how to read the signs, though. On days when I feel strong, I think the signs appear to give me hope. On other days, they only serve as salt to be rubbed into my womb.

> The term *artificial insemination* is odd.
> *Artificial* as opposed to *natural*?
> *Natural* meaning *normal*?
> *Normal* meaning *heterosexual*?

How many people does it take to help two lesbians have a baby? One regular ob/gyn, a local Japanese woman, who scribbles down for us the names of several well-known "specialists" in town (we ask if there are any female specialists and she partly tells us, "Nope"). Two white male infertility specialists, Drs. Earl Borden and Bill T. McNeil. Their staff of female nurses. One extremely nice, conscientious local male ob/gyn. (Although he refers to himself as "just a regular ob/gyn, not a specialist or anything," he helps a friend of ours get pregnant twice through artificial insemination.) Five or six anonymous sperm donors at the California Cryobank, a reproductive tissue service (plus the speedy folks at UPS shipped the frozen specimens in nitrogen tanks). The efficient young female technicians who thaw and count the sperm at the Reproductive Biology Laboratory. Two willing and fertile male friends (and one wife and one girlfriend). A circle of about twelve women and three men who send fertile thoughts my way each month. An acupuncturist/massage therapist. A numerologist. A Buddhist monk. A Shinto priest. The Virgin Mary. Baby Jesus. Saint Jude. Kwan Yin.

A friend of mine tells me that she went to see Dr. Glenn K. Tanaka, a fertility specialist and friend of her pediatrician stepfather. The doctor performs an IUI (intrauterine insemination) ten days after her first doctor's visit. I call his office for an appointment but his receptionist tells me that he does not take new patients.

The next person I see is Dr. Fenton K. K. Chang, another fertility specialist. I tell his receptionist, "I'm a lesbian and I want to have a baby and need some help." She puts me on hold for what feels like ten minutes and then a middle-aged-sounding nurse promptly tells me, "We don't do *those* kinds of procedures." I tell everyone I know not to go to Dr. Chang (and this is a small island).

I call Dr. Borden's office and repeat my spiel to his receptionist. She politely recites for me their standard package plan: a regular ob/gyn exam; a uterine biopsy; two estrogen-level blood tests; an x-ray of my reproductive system (a painful procedure that includes having viscous blue dye shunted up my tubings while Dr. Borden and the male radiologist talk about the renovation delays at the hospital); a five-day supply of Clomid, a "safe" fertility drug; several AIs (artificial inseminations); vaginal ultrasounds to check the size and growth of the follicles; and an occasional HCG injection to stimulate the follicles' release. The receptionist tells me that only the initial exam is covered on my medical insurance. I do my homework. Under the State of Hawai'i laws, a married heterosexual couple is entitled to medical coverage for a single artificial insemination so long as one of them is diagnosed "infertile."

Simply the facts. 11 viable menstrual cycles. 30 clinical inseminations: 25 with Dr. Borden, 1 with Dr. McNeil, and 4 with the really nice ob/gyn. 30 vials containing approximately 72 million motile sperm, some washed, some unwashed. Quarterly storage rental at the laboratory. 55 tablets of Clomid in dosages from 50 to 100 units. 110 progesterone suppositories. 26 applications of Crinone. 9 HCG injections. 31 ultrasounds. 11 boxes of LH-surge (ovulation) kits. 6 estrogen tests. 9 early pregnancy kits. 11 progesterone (pregnancy) tests at the laboratory.

There are few seeds and my lover cannot sow.

We call the California Cryobank and request a donor catalog. I ask my lover to take care of the orders. She narrows down the selection to seven possible donors. She reads somewhere that babies resemble their fathers more than their mothers. She sends a photograph to the sperm bank so that the matching counselors are able to determine which donors have features most similar to my lover's face.

We order several twenty-page profile reports and audiotaped interviews. The three-generation medical and genetic histories tell us everything from birth defects to balding. The profiles also tell us the donors' mathematical, mechanical, athletic, musical, and artistic skills, as well as their religion, hobbies, favorite pets, SAT scores, and physical characteristics. We choose from different hair and eye colors, heights, weights, blood types, and academic majors. The Cryobank assures customers that most donors are recruited from UCLA, USC, MIT, Stanford, and Harvard.

After a few unsuccessful attempts, we change donors. My lover scans the monthly catalogs for Asian donors. We change donors again. We change again. And again.

I learn what it means to be female in the most expected of places: the exam table. There I was, naked from the waist down with only a pink floral paper blanket to cover me, when I caught on to what was going on with the men. Dr. Borden was out of town and so his colleague Dr. McNeil would do the insemination. While looking through my chart Dr. McNeil muttered, "Why nine cycles on Clomid?" Before he was done pronouncing the "d" in "Clomid," my lover and I jumped all over him. Caught off guard, he told us that normally he doesn't let a patient go more than five cycles on Clomid without trying something different. Dr. Borden had done the same thing for each of the nine procedures. "I'll confer with Earl" was all he added.

Once Dr. Borden came back into town, he phoned me and said the next step would be a surgical procedure to check for scar tissues in my uterus or fallopian tubes. When I asked about potential risks, he said, "It could cause scarring." There was no mention of the Clomid treatment or of Dr. McNeil's comment. When I called Dr. McNeil's office, his nurse told me she would give the doctor my message. When I called other specialists, they told me they do not give second opinions.

I never return to Dr. Borden's office. When I take stock of his practice, I notice that all of his staff—receptionist, office manager, and nurse—are white. He is white. Many of the patients in his waiting room are white. I am not.

Artificial means made by man.

I learn the meaning behind the clichés "You can't put a price on life" and "Life is priceless." For over six years, my lover and I had put money into a "baby fund." The money has all been spent and we have closed the account. I am still afraid to sit down and figure out just how much we spent on trying to have a baby. I only admit to myself that each doctor's visit ended with handing over a personal check for roughly six hundred dollars and each order at the California Cryobank added about four hundred dollars to our credit card statement. I keep on telling myself that once the baby comes I'll total up all our expenses.

The cliché is true because at no time did any of the doctors affix a set price to their work.

Some well-intended people have told us, "Why don't you just adopt." I ask them, "When was the last time you met an adopted kid whose parents were two Asian women in their thirties who make well under $40,000 a year?" This usually shuts them up. Occasionally it doesn't, so I add, "And are lesbians."

There is another cliché: "Some of the best things in life are free." After nine unsuccessful doctor visits, my lover and I try to do the inseminations at home. We purchase specimen containers and a syringe from a medical supply store. Later we pick up a glass turkey baster from a gourmet shop. After two attempts, the tip of the baster chips away and cuts the crease of my lover's palm.

I ask one of our male friends to help us. He says okay, but later changes his mind. He tells me rather apologetically, "I don't think I can handle the possibility of having a little me running around." I say I understand, but wonder how many men think of this before they have unprotected sex.

Our friend, father of a one-year-old baby girl, volunteered to donate his sperm. When my lover and I went over to his house to pick up the specimen, his wife invited us into their living room. She offered us drinks and asked if we wanted to stay for dinner. We told her perhaps another time. After about forty minutes of playing with their daughter, our donor-friend came into the house from doing yard work (we thought he was producing the goods) and said to his wife, "Honey, you never give them the stuff?" "Nooo," she yelled from the kitchen. He then added, "It's sitting on the shelf in the bathroom." My lover looked at me and I looked at her and in our heads we exclaimed, "S-i-t-t-i-n-g o-n t-h-e s-h-e-l-f! The sperm has a freaking shelf life!" She answered her husband, "Oh yeah, I forgot." When we finally brought the specimen home it was gummy and smelt like mildew.

Another friend offered his sperm. He told us, "Most of the time it's only going to waste anyway." His girlfriend helped him produce the goods and even drove it over to our apartment. As I laid on the futon in the living room with my butt propped up in the air, I heard my lover yell, "Fucking shit!" I asked what was behind the "shit" but instead she replied to our cat, "Get away from that!" Finally after a minute or two she told me, "It's on the floor." "What is on the floor?" was all I could muster. It left a stain for three weeks.

After several months of home inseminations, we stopped. My friend's wife told me, "This is getting too hard on us. It's nerve-racking waiting for your period."

We found a really nice local male ob/gyn late last year and he performed two inseminations for us. Perhaps when we recoup our losses, we'll try again.

Well-intended advice: Maybe it's not the right time.
More well-intended advice: There will be time later.

Time has no place to sit in our lives. Four years ago my lover was involved in a near-fatal motorcycle accident. If not for her helmet, she would be dead. Lying in the hospital bed she tells me that there is no later, only now. I say, "Yes, honey," but only fully live these words for myself this year when I am diagnosed with tongue cancer. As I nurse a chunk of crushed ice to try and bring down the swelling, I understand that there is no later, only now.

My cancer is surgically removed. My otorhinolaryngologist tells me in the recovery room that oral cancers are hard to get rid of. He suggests I undergo radiation implants, but my lover tells him we are trying to have a baby. He nods and says he'll just have to watch my tongue "like a hawk." Later I sneak a look at my chart while waiting for him to return: I find among the documents a note scribbled that I have an "alternative lifestyle."

My spiritual teacher reminds me, "Your will ends at the point where another person's begins." I think about Sarah. I recite from the Karaniya Metta Sutta, "Seen or unseen, living far or near, those who are born or are to be born, may they all, without exception, be well and happy."

I have been sad. I have been frustrated. Angry. Depressed. Disappointed. Hopeful. Zazen sitting has helped me to understand myself. "I am pregnant, I am pregnant, I am pregnant," I recite aloud.

Taking Part

This is on my mother's side. She had a hysterectomy. Uterus and ovaries, tubings taken from her, taken out. "It wasn't painful," she told me over the phone from a hospital bed in Carson City. "I'm fine. Really." No more scrapings. No more unexplained bleeding. No more drenched pads. No more hardened polyps and rigid cysts. She is in her mid-forties.

My grandmother gave up her parts to no one. She kept them with her until the end. Dying of ovarian cancer in her early fifties, she kept them nonetheless. Maybe back out in Hanapepe no one thought the need or had the nerve to take such things from anyone. No hearts taken, no livers, no kidneys, no sex organs.

I want to keep mine until the end.

Last week I had an ultrasound. The doctor stuck his wand up my vagina and *poof* I saw an image of a uterus and ovaries. *I saw my uterus.* I think back to when my mom would take my older sister and me to the crack seed store to buy abalone. The shop owners hung the abalone from metal hooks which dangled slightly above our heads. This was a delicacy. Once home, my father would take a small paring knife and whittle out thin strips for all of us to eat.

My uterus looked like that abalone.

I imagine that my mother is allowed to take her parts home. She would soak them in alae and then lay them out to dry in the sun. She is like the deep sea diver who harvests the abalone, only it is not she who pries open the shell but her doctor. The point: who gets to harvest and who gets to pry and who gets nothing.

This week I undergo a biopsy. I bend my knees and spread my legs and two pairs of duck bills descend. One enters my vagina, the other goes through my cervix. "The procedure will feel like a mosquito bite," the doctor tells me. "According to the tests, you seem to never something-and-another-technical-term-and-something-else." I sit, stunned. My sensibilities help gather me up. I clamp down these thoughts: I have no eggs. He has just told me that I have no eggs. I think back to the abalone at the store and how it was dried and I wonder if mine is the same.

My uterus looked like that abalone. A callused, curved, closed fist.

I like the way my lover can feel my parts as if they are guppies in a fishbowl when she dips her hands in. For her there is no protective shell. Only wet, breathing surface. I feel them moving. Swimming, too. My ovaries swum, I murmur. She rubs my belly as if I am the wise and benevolent Buddha herself. We lay and wonder if my eggs have hatched and which ones will turn into beautiful lotus blossoms to prick her fingertips. We wonder.

thirty-seven

The Reckoning

Joy Harjo

Everyone has their own version of the world I tell myself as I wait on the Central Avenue sidewalk while Larry disappears behind the Starlight Motel to take a piss. The vacancy sign flashes on and off. Closing hour traffic jams the street. I imagine everyone taking off for the forty-nine, squeezed into cars and pickups with cases of beer under their legs heading in a caravan to the all-night sing on West Mesa. Each direction is a world and each world has its own set of rules, its own hierarchy of gods and demigods, its own particular color. I am painting a series based on the four directions but I am stalled. It has been months since I've painted.

When I was five my mother began standing me on a chair to wash dishes after dinner because I couldn't otherwise reach. The front of my dress was usually soaked when I finished. "Don't get your dress wet like that, it means you'll marry a drunk." Yet night after night after dinner she would drag a chair to the sink and my dress would soak no matter my efforts otherwise. Every morning when I wake up with a hangover after trying to keep up with Larry, I remember the wet stomach of my dress. I then promise I will let him go. I know I cannot save him, but to let him go feels unbearable.

This morning Larry mentioned that his cousin was coming into town from California and wanted to have dinner before heading out to the pueblo. Would I like to go to Alonzo's for pizza with them? A wedge of tension cut the air between us. I tried to ignore it. Last night he said he was going to quit drinking again and Alonzo's is one of his favorite bars. I watched as he fried the bacon and stirred the eggs, as he placed them in a perfect arrangement on our plates. He cooked as deftly as he honed out an argument or turned a piece of silver into the wind. I poured Joe Junior a glass of milk and wrapped a sandwich for his lunch. He fidgeted, running his Hot Wheels cars up and down his chair, across the table, faster and faster in response to the tension. "Stop it!" I yelled, surprised at the vehemence in my voice. He put his head down on the table and began slowly kicking the table leg. I told myself then that I could use a break.

That night after cleaning the house and walking guiltily by my easel I took Joe Junior to the babysitter. He liked going to Larry's sister's house because she had twin boys his age so I didn't mind leaving him for the night. When I handed him over with his pack of clothes, toys, and snacks I hugged him close, savoring his freshly shampooed hair. I felt bad for yelling at him this morning. He saw the twins peeking around the corner and wriggled free. Larry's sister was roasting chiles and had just pulled out of the oven a fresh batch of those little fruit pies her people make. She offered me some. "And take some for Larry, too," she said. When she said her brother's name worry flickered across her forehead. I was worried too, but to entertain all the reasons would cause an avalanche. I would prefer to stay here with Joe Junior in Larry's aunt's warm house, to wash dishes and set the table and visit, but the zigzag of anxiety went way back, over tortuous territory. If I followed the source it would slam me back into childhood, to my father staggering in drunk, beating my mother, the shame and hate in him burning, burning. Then he'd hit my brothers. And then me whom it was said he loved most. He'd save me for last, when his anger was ashes, when the fire was hottest. And then he'd hold me, "Sugar, sugar," he'd croon, the tears so thick they made a lake on the linoleum floor.

There is a world of mist in which my father now lives. It is beyond the Milky Way but it is also as close as my voice to your ear. I have often seen my father in the middle of the night when I am painting. Or when I have tucked his grandson in after he has fallen asleep. He is just the other side of the spin, the same frequency as moonlight. He's held here by disappointment, by the need to speak. He tells me he loves me and asks if I will forgive him. I do not say anything. "You're a dreamer," my mother says when I tell her, "just like your father. And you won't ever get it together until you decide to deal with the real world." She is an elected tribal official and she teaches Sunday school every week. She has a mission in her small world. She wants to make sure there are rules and that they are enforced.

The first time Larry hit me was on a Saturday night like this one. We hadn't been together long. We were still amazed we had found each other. We were partying away not at Alonzo's but at the Feathered Dancer on the other side of town. He was talking politics with his buddies while I played pool with my best friend Jolene and some other students in the backroom. I kept feeding the jukebox with quarters, playing the Rolling Stones, "Wild horses couldn't drag me away," over and over again. He was down about the anniversary of the death of his best friend a few years ago. That should have been a warning to me. This man had been his idol. He had been the only man from his pueblo to finish law school and he fought the U.S. legal system by any means possible, including his fists. But he couldn't fight alcohol. He was taken down by drink, his body found in a field weeks after his death. His grieving brothers were honoring him by drinking to oblivion and they were getting rowdy. I tried to ignore them and kept shooting the solids into the pockets, just as I had ignored my father when he and his friends partied, argued and played. I knew the routine. There was a high and then there was a low.

Every small hair on my neck was on alert. "Fuck you," I heard Larry yell. We ran in from the pool tables to see what was the matter. Larry aimed a pitcher of beer at his cousin Leno's head. It missed and smashed into the bar mirror. There was a terrible crash. We all scattered as the bartender called the police. Larry refused to go; instead he decided to climb the fence to the roof of the bar. Leno and I tried to stop him. He punched me and I went down. He climbed to the roof and jumped, then stood up like a defiant child, without a scratch, and walked away, the sound of approaching sirens growing loud and shrill.

I should have left him then; instead I caught a ride back with Jolene, who tried to convince me to stay at her place. "No, I want to get the sad good-bye over with," I told her. The next morning he apologized profusely. This will never happen again, he promised as he made us breakfast of his specialty: chorizo and eggs. He came back from the 7-Eleven with a newspaper and a bouquet of wilted flowers. I told him to pack his bags, to get out. "No," he said. "How can we make a better world for the people if we cannot hold it together in our own house?" I convinced myself that we owed it to ourselves to keep trying. I found excuses. He was taken over by grief for his buddy, I told myself. And most of the time he wasn't like that, I reasoned. I took him back.

The next few weeks were tender and raw. Carefully he planted a garden in the small yard behind the apartment with my son. He worked obsessively. He held fire in his hands and he crafted a bracelet to bridge the hole in our universe. I believed he didn't mean to lose control. I believed that he loved me. "So did your father," Jolene reminded me. "You've gone and married your father." I didn't want to hear her and after that I talked to Jolene only when I had to, at rallies, at Indian center meetings. She was a distant reminder of prickly truth, a predictor of trouble. I watched her disappear on the horizon as I turned to tend to my shaky world. When he asked me to marry him, I said yes.

We were nervous the day we headed up to Santa Fe in a borrowed car to get married. I had never planned to marry anyone and this would be my second. The first had been to Joe Junior's father. Larry had gotten grief from his parents for shacking up with a girl who wasn't from his tribe. Marriage would make me one step closer to acceptable.

It was a perfect spring day as we headed north. Joe Junior stayed at Larry's sister's place and was excited about getting to help make the wedding cake. A small reception was planned for the next day. We'd just passed the city limits when the Ranchero Bar came into view, poised on the reservation line. All the windows were painted and broken glass mixed with gravel in the parking lot. Larry pulled the car over and parked. "Let's go in, just for a beer," he said. "To celebrate." It had been a few months since he had stopped drinking, after the punching incident. He already had enough jewelry for a show and had attracted a dealer who talked New York and Europe markets. We had been happy. "No. You can't drink." "One drink will not hurt me, or you either," he said as he opened his door. "We have a lot to celebrate." "Okay, you promised," I reminded him. "I promise," he said.

One beer turned into a pitcher because these were his brothers, he announced eloquently to the bar. The pueblo farm workers sitting around him smiled at me and nodded their heads. "It's time to go," I urged him under my breath, all the while smiling at his new friends. "I can't turn down a drink because I would offend them," he whispered, looking at me sharply because I should know better. Obviously he wasn't afraid of offending me.

I sipped my beer and felt my heart sag in disbelief. This was my wedding day. If I had another drink I wouldn't hear the voice telling me to get out, to get out now. I poured myself another beer from the pitcher, matching Larry drink for drink to the delight of Larry's new friends. The day stumbled into oblivion. I have a faint memory of dancing a rancheria in front of the jukebox with a cowboy, and of a hippie girl coming into the bar and sitting on Larry's lap. "It's part of my job," he told me once after I had yanked a blond girl off him and demanded he come home with me. He had pocketed the girl's phone number as he slid off the stool and followed me. He had a reason for everything.

We didn't make it to Santa Fe to get married. I tore up the marriage license and tossed it like confetti over him and his drinking partners, confirming that I wasn't the kind of girl his pueblo parents wanted for his wife. His mother would never embarrass his father in that manner no matter what he did to her. I left him with the borrowed car and hitchhiked back. I called Larry's sister and told her the wedding was off and I'd pick up Joe Junior tomorrow when I could pull myself together. I could not think; I could not paint. I looked up the women's center in the student directory. What would I say to them? Do you have a crisis center for idiots? I missed Jolene and my friends, but I had too much pride to call them now. I dialed my mother's number and hung up. She would just say, "I told you so."

It is now two-thirty in the morning and the avenue is quiet. Larry should have been back by now. The small desk light in the motel office makes me feel lonely. I feel far away from everything. There's that ache under my ribs that's like radar. It tells me that I am miles away from the world I intended to make for my son and me. I imagine my easel set up in the corner of the living room in our apartment, next to Joe Junior's box of toys. I imagine my little boy asleep in my arms. I imagine having the money to walk up to the motel office to rent a room of my own. I know what I would do.

First I would sleep until I could sleep no more. Then I would dream. I fly to the first world of my mother and father, locate them as a young married couple just after the war, living with my father's mother, in her small house in Sapulpa. I am a baby in my mother's arms, cooing and kicking my legs. Then I am a girl on my father's shoulders as he spins and dances me through the house drunk on beer stolen from the bootlegger. I hold on tight. I hear my mother tell him to be careful, let me down. We are all laughing. He spins until I am in high school and I have won the art award. Then I am a teenage mother. "A new little Sugar," he says as he holds his grandson and sings to him. Then I am standing with my mother at my grandmother's funeral, singing those sad Creek hymns that lead her spirit to the Milky Way. My father can't be found in time for the funeral. Then he's next. The centrifugal force of memory keeps moving through the sky, slowly sifting lies from the shining truth.

My mother told me that if you go to sleep laughing you will wake up to tears. My father's mother told me that to predict the shape of the end of something take a hard look at the beginning. "I'm not interested in marriage or finding yet another man to break my heart," I remember telling my friend Jolene as we stood in the heat in front of the student union the day I met Larry. The tech people were making a racket while they set up the microphones and tables for the press conference. I had just gotten over Joe Junior's father. He left me before the baby was born, even took the junk car, drove off dragging it behind his cousin's truck to his mother's house in Talihina.

"Well, there are always women," she said nodding toward a table that had been set up by the women's resource center. They were passing out information on their services. I walked by the women's center every day on my way to work at the Indian center after classes. Once I stopped to visit on my way to an organizational meeting. I had heard a speaker from their center address students on the mall about women's rights and it occurred to me that our centers could link up in an action. But the day I walked in with my son in hand I got the distinct feeling that Indian women with children weren't too welcome. I had never gone back.

"Women would certainly open up our options," I agreed with Jolene and we laughed. We thought it was funny, but we agreed that as women we spent most of our time with each other, took classes together and cried on each others' shoulders in the shifting dance of creation and destruction.

It was a fine-looking contingent from the National Council on Indian Rights who made their way to the makeshift stage. They were modern age warriors dressed with the intent of justice in their sunglasses and long black hair. "There is my future," I said lightly and nodded to the Pueblo man whose hair was pulled back in a sleek ponytail. I watched as he balanced his coffee and unclasped his shoulder bag of papers. He felt familiar at the level of blood cells and bones though I didn't know him. I had heard him holding forth before at meetings and had seen him in passing on campus. "Who is he?" Jolene knew everyone because her father was a name in local Indian politics. "His name is Larry. He's an artist," she said. "A fine artist. He makes jewelry. Be careful. Women love him and are always chasing him." I could see why and I could not stop watching him as he read the press release demanding justice and detailing how it could occur. He was as beautifully drawn as he was smart.

As we stood in the hot sun listening to the prepared statements I was suddenly aware of the fragility of life, how immensely precious was each breath. We all mattered—even our small core fighting for justice despite all odds. And then the press conference was over. That day would become one of those memories that surfaced at major transitional points like giving birth and dying. I would feel the sun on my shoulders, hear the scratch of the cheap sound system, and feel emotional. I would recall a small Navajo girl in diapers learning how to walk, her arms outstretched to her father. I would remember picking up my son at the daycare across campus, his bright yellow lunchbox shaped like a school bus.

That night at the impromptu party after the strategy meeting I watched from the doorway of the kitchen of Jolene's cousin's apartment as Larry easily rolled a cigarette with his hands, then licked it. His hands were warm sienna and snapped with the energy of his quick mind, his ability to shape metal. He lit a cigarette and blew smoke through his perfect lips in my direction. The lazy lasso hung in the air between us. I passed him a beer as I was the end of a brigade passing out beer from the cooler in the kitchen.

"So who are you skinny girl?" I kept passing and throwing beer to the rest of the party as he talked, pretending to ignore him. "You must be one of those Oklahoma Indians," he said. I had been warned that he was used to getting what he wanted when it came to women. "Come on over here and sit next to me, next to an Indian who is still the real thing." I considered hitting him with a beer for that remark. These local Indians could be short-sighted in their world. "Why would I want to?" I retorted. "Besides, you look Mexican to me." His eyebrows flew up. His identity had never been challenged, especially by a woman he was interested in. "We're fullbloods. We haven't lost our ways." "And what does that mean? That my people have?" I questioned. "Then why do you have a Spanish last name?" Of course I knew the history but he had pissed me off, still I couldn't help but notice his long eyelashes that cast shadows on his cheeks. I caught the last beer and opened it, stood close enough for his smell to alert my heart. "All tribes traveled, took captives and were taken captive." I emphasized "captive" and leaned in to take a puff on the cigarette he offered me. Jolene waltzed over and grabbed my arm, dancing me to the living room in time to the music in order to save me. I didn't talk to him again until I headed out the door with my ride, two other first-year students. We were buzzed on smoke and flying sweetly. "Hey girl," he shouted from the corner as I reluctantly made my escape. "I'm going to get you yet."

It happened quickly. When I got home that night there was a message that my father had died. Joe Junior and I left for a week. When we returned Larry met us at the bus station with flowers and toys. He took us for breakfast at the Chuckwagon and then we went home together. It wasn't long after my father's death that I dreamed a daughter who wanted to be born. I had been painting all night when she appeared to me. She was a baby with fat cheeks and then she was a grown woman, with a presence as familiar as my father's mother. She asked me to give birth to her. I was in the middle of finals and planning for a protest of the killing of Navajo street drunks by white high school students on weekends for fun. They had just been questioned and set free with no punishment. "This is not a good time," I said. "And why come into this kind of world?" Funny, I don't remember her answer but her intent was a fine unwavering line that connected my heart to hers.

I walk behind the motel to look for Larry. He isn't anywhere but I find his shoes under a tree where he has taken them off. And ahead of them like two dark salamanders are his socks. A little farther beyond is his belt, and then a trail of pants, shirt, and underwear until I am standing in the courtyard of the motel. My stomach turns and twists as I consider all the scenarios a naked and drunk Indian man might get into in a motel on the main street of the city.

I hear a splash in the pool. He's a Pueblo; he can't swim. I consider leaving him there to his fate. It would be his own foolish fault, as well as the fault of a society that builds its cities over our holy places. At this moment his disappearance would be a sudden relief. Strange that it is now that I first feel our daughter moving within me. She awakens me with a flutter, a kick. I don't know whether to laugh or cry. I never told Larry about the night she showed up to announce her intention, or how I saw her spirit when she was conceived wavering above us on a fine sheen of light. Behind her my father was waving good-bye. The weave pulled tighter and tighter, it opened and then he was gone.

iv.

"a place at the table" . . . surviving the
battles, shaping our worlds

thirty-eight

Puente del Fuego

Nova Gutierrez

thirty-nine

Vanish Is a Toilet Bowl Cleaner

Chrystos

Here's the popular image
of a slumped over Indian
with 2 pathetic feathers
on a horse who should have bucked
the poor guy off years ago
Gives me a migraine
Myself, I've never seen anyone Indian
sit like that unless they were past
3 sheets to the wind drunk
Next we know that there should be
two or three figures at least
because we don't ride alone
The guy has no supplies & no robe
so apparently he is planning to commit suicide
by freezing and/or starving to death
whichever comes first
The popularity of this drooler
in Indian Country
may reflect how badly we feel
but is no excuse
to take on a white man's lie
Witness, for example, African Americans I know
who collect Aunt Jemima images
or like to be whipped
or call each other the N word
Embracing racist doggerel
does not give us the last bite
I have big plans for this wimp
First off, we're getting him
a Fredrick's of Hollywood chin-up support
We're adding parfleches filled with good food
rolled up blankets
& tucking a loaded rifle under his hand
Now he's looking over his shoulder
at the advancing white savages
kneeling his pony
to get the hell out of Dodge

heading home to his people
where he'll be warm no matter
what slop syphilization cooks up
The end of the trail
stops here

forty

Yo' Done Bridge Is Fallin' Down

Judith K. Witherow

To quote Audre Lorde, "The Master's tools will never dismantle the master's house." With all due respect to Ms. Lorde, I wish she had continued on and said, "Nor use those tools to build on rooms and a glass ceiling for yourself. Don't hone your skills with power tools and leave your sisters out of sight in the cellar." Unfortunately, this is exactly what has happened. Some women have gotten a place at the proverbial table, while others are left to endure belly-touching-backbone hunger. I angrily watch as lawmakers shred entitlement programs. Where are my sisters? How long will they wait before organizing numerous others to join in this heartless fight?

Twenty-five years ago, when I joined the women's movement, I was constantly assured that after we worked on the ERA, abortion rights, pay equity, credit, sexual preference, etc., etc., we would put our energies into poverty. Countless times I was told, "Be patient, Judith." Patient? I've come to realize that *patience* is a word used to stifle dissent. It's also a word I hear when someone doesn't have a clear understanding of the magnitude of a problem. *Welfare* was another word that many others didn't want to hear. It was a four-letter word then. It is a capitalized four-letter word now. With the dismantling of entitlement programs, time has virtually run out. When are feminists going to take up the battle cry and come out in the same numbers as they did for every other cause?

Some are doing what they can—like the Welfare Warriors located in Milwaukee, Wisconsin. Their slogan is "We are mothers in poverty working to make a difference for all of us." The key word is ALL. Coming from the poorest of the poor—Native American—I understand this concept of a group or tribal effort. It's hard to focus on any one issue. Through experience I've found that poverty has its greatest effect on health. Here's what happens when culture, poverty, and racism collide on a personal level.

Below the Bottom Line

There was a time when I had a bottom line concerning my health. No experimentation. Never. Decades of watching how the medical community treated my family instilled this belief in me. Now, too much has happened to keep me from rooting around in their guinea pig pen. I'm willing to try treatments that have the barest chance of helping. Perhaps they will hurt, but what if they help? What I know for certain is that I live in this body alone. No one knows what my diseases feel like. Even the women who share this same bed of illnesses do not know.

Well-meaning feminist friends believe they know what is best for me. Many times they get upset when I choose to make my own decisions and ignore their advice. This matronizing attitude leads me to believe that we are not so equal after all. If my decisions are not respected, then what is the definition of equality? Has twenty-five years of fighting for every woman's right to choose counted as naught? A lot of the time the answer is, sadly, yes. For many years I took the advice of those I thought were wiser. Wiser because they had degrees to prove their wisdom. My partner of twenty-two years has always told me that degrees prove privilege, not wisdom. I believe she can say this because she has a number of degrees and a job that people respect. If careers and education aren't important, why is it that they are the first two subjects discussed at many gatherings? Try entering these discussions with "high school" and "disabled." Heads swivel faster than that girl's from *The Exorcist*.

The generations of female bodies who breathed life into me were silenced by my arrogance of assimilation. Perhaps with age I've gained the knowledge that no teacher, preacher, or book could provide. It's of no comfort to realize that what I was seeking was among my own people. The ones who need the most help are all around me. That is where I can see the most progress or decline taking place firsthand. Coal mining companies and various factories polluted the land and water of my birthplace. Because of this environmental assault, my large family has many health problems. When you add generations of poverty, illiteracy, and abuse by the system, you don't need a crystal ball to determine your destiny. What you do need is a nation willing to provide health care to everyone regardless of his or her ability to pay.

Perceptions. You will have to accept mine as you would another's life work of research. If not, you will need to lay wide my brain with a scalpel and poke around inside until my truths become evident to you. Scoop out what useful fact or figure you need to support your theory or belief. What I know about illness, cures, and addictions comes from experience and firsthand stories. I believe myself to be intelligent enough to help others understand a way of life that might not be theirs. Sharing some of the information gained with someone else like myself is of even greater importance.

I've written a number of articles about my life of poverty and ongoing illness. But I'd rather get whipped with a keen switch than answer an oral question about my health. This same feeling of being invaded applies to giving out information about my family—majority Native American—and friends. For the purpose of this article, I will do both. (What I won't do is name specific tribes.) A combination of sadness, anger, and embarrassment fills me as I consider what details to discuss.

While I appreciate my friends' and family's concern regarding experimental treatments, fear is not enough to still my longing to learn some truths. If I choose to enter an experimental program, I do it with as much knowledge as possible. Who should this research be done on? Less-educated uninformed women who have no other option? Common sense tells me that the testing needs to be done on those who have the disease being researched. Don't I have the absolute right to choose to volunteer for testing? I need answers. I'm weary of being randomly served up like a tennis ball. My humanity cannot be bought, taught, or tested out of me. And yes, many times I am fooled. The will to live and be free from pain can cloud the senses and turn research into regret.

I strongly dislike seeing new medical people. The first thing they want is your medical history. That is to be expected. What isn't expected is my long list. It's like naming ex-lovers. Someone thinks they want to hear the answer, but you'd better not have a very long list.

My list is very long—the medical one. Some of my diseases and surgeries: systemic lupus, multiple sclerosis, endometriosis, cancer, tapeworm, Bell's Palsy, fibromyalgia, vasculitis, osteoporosis, peripheral neuropathy, heart disease, kidney disease, gall bladder surgery, hysterectomy, left and right oophorectomy, appendectomy, osteoarthritis, etc., etc.

I take eighteen different medicines daily. Do they help? To quote my deceased father, "I'm not about to stop any of them to find out." Many of the illnesses listed cause considerable pain. Some days I spend curled up in a knot because it hurts too much to move. When this happens, the treatment I use is not prescribed or bought over the counter. Mother Earth supplies the relief to temporarily deny the demons. This down time is used to relive mentally how malnourished I was in childhood. I lay and fantasize about whether getting free lunch at school would have made a difference. The answer is always yes. It would have helped me concentrate on my schooling instead of the loudness of my belly's growling. I know that I would also be a healthier adult today if more emphasis had been placed on the feeding of my body. To begrudge any child food is an unspeakable evil. Many politicians have used this as a way to save money. Little or no fight was put up when it happened in the early eighties.

Whenever some politician or newscaster talks about "those people" on SSI, welfare, or Medicaid, it intensifies the pain. Are they so ignorant that they don't know that an underfed child without health care will grow up to be someone like me? It shouldn't take a college degree to figure out that you will require more services as an adult if your needs were ignored in childhood. Society needs to call it what it is—death on the installment plan. High premiums and low percentages. (The median life span for a Native American is forty-five years.)

Whenever a medical problem occurs, I try various methods of treatment. The list is as long as what ails me, from "traditional" treatments to "experimental." Some of the medicines and procedures prescribed for me are not FDA approved. This is allowed, while other things that might be tried for muscle wasting and pain, such as marijuana, are illegal. In an effort to find relief, I've tried Pow-Wows, acupuncture, meditation, wailing with the wolves, numerous herbs, Healing Circles, massage therapy, Holistic Healers, trigger injections (a combination of lidocaine, Novocain, and cortisone injected into the muscle spasms in my skull, neck, and shoulders), Wicca, three tattoos—a wolf (canis lupus) on my left forearm, a Celtic knot on my right wrist, and a dream catcher around my ankle.

My first tattoo was done when I reached the age of fifty. I dreamed what each tattoo should be and when it should be done. Doctors aren't impressed by my body art. This does not surprise me. A lot of people don't understand the significance of this art form. The tattoo artist who did each tattoo is a daughter-in-law. She protected me against infection and other problems that might occur. Everyone should visualize her own bottom line for surviving.

Reading the medical treatments my family used might give a clearer understanding of my attitude toward trying different things. If you stepped on a nail, you greased it and placed it over the doorway. If any evil Spirits came in, they would slip back out. This protected you from infection. My mother was protected from getting whooping cough because her parents had a black stallion blow its breath in her face. The treatment doctors suggested to keep my tapeworm at bay was kerosene or turpentine mixed with a tablespoon full of sugar. (I have no idea what long-term poisoning this did to my system.) You stopped the sting of a bee by using the dirt from under an apple tree as a poultice. Your own urine was used to treat an earache, as was cigarette smoke blown in the ear. Camphorated oil was also a remedy; it has now been taken off the market. The FDA said people were mistaking it for castor oil, drinking it and getting poisoned. This fall I made a batch of it for my family. A cousin—who also shared other remedies I had forgotten—gave the recipe to me. (She has multiple sclerosis; her sister has systemic lupus.) The oil has many uses: from treating swollen glands and joints to chest colds. You heat unsalted pork fat in camphorated oil and tie it around your neck. Leave it on overnight and it will draw out the congestion.

Some of the older ones say the stems of marijuana soaked in rubbing alcohol will work for joint pain. Though it is widely known that different forms of marijuana can be used for pain control and weight gain, very few doctors will prescribe it. The government grows marijuana for a select few in an ongoing drug trial. When these people die, the government will stop growing it, and the experiment will be considered finished.

Making marijuana illegal doesn't solve the problem, though. Too often drugs and alcohol cause more pain than they relieve by contributing to ongoing poverty and disease. I say this like some backslapping, hand shaking, statistic seeker. Maybe I say it because I feel it's expected of me. It is truth and tragedy smeared like clay on an unbaked pot. My truth doesn't involve pointing the middle finger of blame at anyone. Some of us try to overcome the environmental poisoning. Others find no peace except that of a momentary nature followed by a lifetime of payback.

"Slammin," "Huffin," and "Champagne" are names that whisper and scream the words addiction and despair. Just writing about these deadly "highs," I fear someone will try something new she might not have heard about before. A "sister" described to me the practice of "Slammin." I had asked her why I saw so many empty quart beer bottles lying around the reservation. (It is illegal to sell alcohol on a reservation. Reservations still have more overseers than the largest plantation ever had.) She said beer was injected into the veins of the nose and neck by the younger ones for a quick high. Many Native Americans are diabetic. Needles are borrowed from diabetic relatives and replaced without the owner's knowledge. AIDS is spreading because of this practice.

"Huffin." Inhaling substances from a paper or plastic bag to get high. If you see a young one with paint around her mouth, you will know the evil name of her poison. The names of other inhalants are too numerous to mention. Too numerous, and too dangerous to risk the responsibility of writing down their names.

"Champagne." A drink like none other. A bottle of household cleaner, cleaning fluid, or a similar item is used. The higher the alcohol content the better the binge. The damage this "champagne" does to the liver, kidneys, etc. can only be imagined. The consumption, and desire for this liquor, fills the eyes with unceasing tears.

Whether our health has been damaged by the poisons that have contaminated the air, land, and water or by our need to find an escape from the pain of daily life, we are all searching for a way to survive. These are my thoughts on getting by medically. Some illegal things I hesitated writing about. But what is the state going to do? Give me another illness? Get in line.

The most important piece of advice I can offer is don't be afraid of questioning your medical treatment. Don't allow anyone to blow off your questions. If it's bothering you, it's worth having an easily understood answer. When medical personnel stand up—the international signal to "hit the bricks"—stay seated. It's your life. It's their job. If they whip out their big words like some pervert in the park, don't sit there feeling ashamed and exposed. Ask them to use words that you do know.

Do your own investigation of any diagnosis or treatment. When you are given a prescription, look up its use and side effects in a pill book. If you can't afford to buy one, page through the books they keep at the pharmacy counter. Medical information can also be found at the library. Discuss your prescriptions with the pharmacist. Double-check her or his answer with a pharmacist who didn't fill your prescription. Get all of your medicines at one pharmacy so an ongoing record of what you are taking is kept. It will lessen the chance of getting something that might conflict with another drug you are already using.

While writing this article I have been having a "lupus flare." The amount of steroids I am taking has been raised three times. The pain medicine has also been doubled. A drug that is used for leprosy, pneumocystis pneumonia, and lupus was started. I'm trying Plaquenil because the steroids aren't healing the lupus lesions covering my body. My joints are so painful that the thought of placing my fingers on the keyboard is enough to keep the words piling up like snowflakes for days at a time. Something is also happening to the connective tissue between my ribs. It feels like my ribs are crushing together when I sit down at the computer. I feel the need to tell you what I am experiencing because it's as big a part of this chapter as the words are.

Equally important are some of the medicines I am taking: Plaquenil, Flecainide, Klonopin, Percocet, Macrodantin, prednisone, Tylenol, Miacalcin, Dapsone, Flonase, Clobetasol Propionate, Fluori-Methane spray, Vicon Forte, 50,000 units Vitamin D weekly, Miacalcin Nasal spray, Muro 128, Patanol, Mycelex, Prevacid, Lasix.

Today, Sue came home from work to drive me to the neurologist. She knew the pain was so out of control that I wouldn't be able to express my medical needs. This doctor said the problem was the systemic lupus, not multiple sclerosis, and I should call the other doctor.

I waited until the next day to call the other specialist. The rheumatologist agrees that what "we" are trying isn't working. He told me to double the amount of steroids again, and gave me a schedule to follow. Each time the steroids are lowered my auto-immune system rebels with a vengeance. This is the fourth schedule change within two months. I remind him of this. We also discuss the sixty pounds I've lost. Neither of us knows when, or if, the wasting will stop. He is very kind when he tells me that during my next visit we need to discuss the use of IV Cytoxan. This is one of the chemotherapies, an experimental medicine used to try to put systemic lupus into remission. He explains that it will be a two-year program. I'm also very calm and kind during our discussion.

After talking to the doctor, I call Sue and tell her about the latest treatment being considered. The silence between us smothers and covers the dreaded word *chemotherapy*. This conversation has to wait until we are close enough to touch each other while we are talking. After twenty-two years together we can't bear not sharing everything. If there were a way to protect her from this I might try. But, no, she and me are we. During the phone silence she too heard the thud of me striking that place far below the bottom line.

Note

A previous version of this essay appeared as "Below the Bottom Line" in *Sojourner* (March 1996).

forty-one

Council Meeting

Marisela B. Gomez

I sit in council meetings with these guards of the Ivory Tower, working toward diversity. I must constantly remind myself of why I am engaged in this caricature of equality. Around this table, we pretend we are all equals; all races, colors, sexual orientations, physical abilities, genders, religions. We participate in the daily farce of similar perceptions of "diversity." We are the microcosm of academic power (deans, doctors, faculty), setting the standards of our society as we intellectualize and contemplate the meaning of diversity.

I oftentimes preach that my many years of schooling were to gain me access to places I would otherwise not enter as a poor woman of color. Places like this board room, housing the respectable few capable of making policy decisions that influence laws of this and other lands. Now the time has come for me to "practice as I preach" and discover if the preparation for this war has been sufficient for victory.

"Victory over what and for whom?" you ask. Assuredly it is not simply for the outsiders to trade places with the insiders, duplicating hierarchical systems without change in power redistribution.

Meanwhile, it is this sham of egalitarianism that maintains many of the oppressive forces in place and keeps the wall surrounding us elite protected from the "community" outside. I find solace in my role as outsider—though I am perceived as insider, sometimes. The credentials (Ph.D., M.D.) buy me a place at the table, my rhetoric allows me to participate in the conversation, my passion keeps me alive in this den of chaos. But I am not fooled by their superficial acceptance of my place here. Nor do I ignore their perception of me as a tool and a product of "their" diversity struggle; the poor little brown girl from an underdeveloped country.

The issue on the table today is how to celebrate the white liberals within the institution, who have "struggled" on the inside, on behalf of the poor folks on the outside. Never mind that the opinion of the outsider has not been sought or listened to when voiced. And we cannot forget the sacrifices the white man has endured at the cost of academic mobility. Sacrifices that have placed them at similar disadvantages "as the poor, black woman in the street who continues to suffer the legacy of slavery." All heads, like puppets, nod in agreement. My stomach boils, bile bubbles its way upward, as I try to feign interest and mild disagreement.

Excitement rises as they make self-congratulatory remarks about the liberal whites sitting at this table. Calmly, I paste on a smile and spit out words shrouded in jargon; "it is dangerous to compare the struggles of whites and blacks in this country" and "we should not categorize good and bad whites." The response is one of much irritation. Why can't I understand that the struggles of the "good" white and the poor black are similar? "Why can't you accept this and shut up for just once?" written on their faces. Fleeting glimpses of suspicion travel the faces but soon depart to be replaced with condescension; "Who are you anyway?" Another meeting adjourned in silence. No eyes meet mine as I leave another board room, framed with portraits of great white men. Outside one person seeks me out and agrees that these conversations must be had, in private!

That meeting will cost me an evening of physical weariness, emotional fatigue, and hours of work as I replay it several times and critically disassemble and reintroduce different scenarios. I will analyze each response and contemplate all comments. Finally, I will sleep restlessly, and reconfigure a council meeting in my dream. Around the table will be snakes, dressed in Guatemalan garb. There will be one rat in a snake costume, waiting for the moment of discovery when she will become a snake or be eaten alive by snakes.

forty-two

For My Sister: Smashing the Walls of Pretense and Shame

Anonymous

I carry this photograph of us—me as a baby, you as a toddler. I separated it carefully from the many pictures in which your eyes are looking my way, your mouth scowling. In this one, however, your face—turned toward me—only reveals that you have questions: "Who is this girl?" "Can I love her?" The image reminds me that we belong together. "I wish I'd never woken up. I wish the pills had killed me!" you yelled desperately to our father one morning. Him, pleading for you to take back your words. Me, afraid to open my bedroom door and get involved. "Don't let this affect your studies," our parents cautioned me. Young Indian friends and family on Zoloft, Prozac, drinking 'til drunk—a common occurrence. We must look very good, even when feeling very bad. Me, afraid to open my bedroom door, to face you, to show you I'm with you, to say, "You don't have to die to show us how bad you feel." Back then, I hadn't yet figured this out for myself: I don't have to die, leave, silence myself to show the world how bad I feel from oppression. But maybe I do have to scream a little.

I've been thinking about you for the past six years, since the last time you tried ending your life, and I wonder what it would be like for us all to speak more openly of the most secretive things about our own communities. It is time to smash the walls of pretense, shame, and silence to really show ourselves—and not just as victims of oppression, but with the motivation of communicating great feelings of caring for others and hopefulness about organizing for change, about letting our true power and brilliance guide our movement in order to recapture our full humanity in an oppressive society. Sister, I want to share my thinking on the suicide problem and present a possible solution. Suicidality and the feeling of hopelessness among South Asian American youth are heavily interconnected with oppression—systematic mistreatment from the outside—and its internalized effects.

There is something irrational in our elders' and our own notion of home. The mentality goes something like, "The United States really isn't my home. You see, I'm an immigrant (or child-of-an-immigrant), a 'visitor.' My cultural values tell me that my family and South Asian countrymen come first. Therefore, I don't have to treat you like my neighbor. I don't have responsibility toward you." There seems to exist a general lack of priority among class-privileged South Asian Americans regarding the building of a sense of solidarity and community with people in the working class and other people of color. This lack of community hurts us all, sister: we lose contact with a piece of our own humanity in the process of playing the capitalist game. The suicides of our young adults, people who are newcomers to the "game," testify to this loss. However, many of our people seem comfortable in their isolation, in not considering class-based struggle, attributing offensively different living standards to the "laziness" of the non–South Asian working class. Given our already-existing Asian patterns of pretense, shame, and terror, our high level of productivity and separation from other communities completely numbs out and further isolates us in our despair.

Sister, I have also been thinking about how you might have been hurt as a young person and as an older sister. The systematic mistreatment of young people (meaning under age twenty-one) is barely recognized; however, it is key to understanding the hold any other kind of oppression has on us. The mistreatment we all experienced as young people was a training process for all other types of oppression, when we first learned to be oppressors (of those younger than us). Additionally, we learned powerlessness as young people: we learned to accept the role of being oppressed when we did not get enough caring attention; when we were mistreated after showing emotions such as fear, anger, excitement, and the desire for intimacy; when we were forced to attend schools that were not set up adequately to support our development; when we were not given the choice to vote and denied adequate pay for our work; when we were humiliated, threatened, and sometimes even physically brutalized (Sazama).

Our relationship as sisters became laden with internalized young people's oppression in the form of meanness and highly critical attitudes toward each other. Additionally, as the older sister you got tagged with the heavier sense of obligation. Our family expected you to make sacrifices and serve as caretaker for me, your younger sibling. You took persistent responsibility for making things go well in many areas. You also internalized sexism in a way that moved you to create an external image of flawlessness; at the same time, you hid your difficulties. The week before you took poison, you were a vision of such "perfection" at a community party. You looked beautiful, offered help wherever needed, socialized with the young people and elders, and wore a smile the whole time. I had no idea you felt so terrible.

Not only have we all experienced oppression as young people, but by the age of about twenty-one, we began the experience of young adulthood—a gateway into another kind of systematic mistreatment also connected with the terror and despair in our community's youth. As young adults (between the ages of twenty-one and thirty), we often experience extreme pressure to conform, to succeed, and to give up on our dreams. We internalize these expectations, becoming extremely competitive about jobs, relationships, salaries, and appearance. We're very hard on ourselves and have a deep reluctance to ask questions because the expectation is "now that we're adults, we're supposed to know everything." Yet we are still often treated like we do not have enough experience to have real responsibility in the adult world. The resources available to us are gravely lacking, and our oppression is often invisible, even to ourselves (Sazama, 89).

Now, factor in another form of internalized oppression: self-criticism hammers in and maintains the feelings of victimhood, so that we feel even more powerless to end the oppression against us. The internalization is harsh. We congratulate each other for successfully competing but avoid discussing how hard this competition actually has been on us. However, we are eager to gossip about how hard it has been on others who've been less "successful." We are eager to criticize anyone who doesn't carry on the appearance of being "perfect" and criticize the efforts of anyone who attempts to take leadership within and outside of our community. Whenever uncooperative, destructive behavior is directed at another person of one's own identity group, the action has at least part of its base in internalized oppression. Period.

Without effective strategies to transform our relationships with each other into a place of complete respect, we really haven't freed ourselves from the oppressions that limit us. However, the internalized patterns are tricky. While most of us are quick to understand external oppression as reprehensible, the internalization is often viewed as "just the way we are" and therefore not recognized as existing *distinct from* our fully caring, competent, intelligent, and powerful selves. I'm in India right now and getting a better sense of what we'd look like without the internalized racism that comes from living on the same land as the oppressor. Although imperialism has certainly made its mark here, Indians in the subcontinent just don't carry the "ugly-dirty-brown-person" complex that many of us grew up with in our predominantly white neighborhoods, and this makes such a difference. Living here for the past year has given me a chance to laugh every day with other Indians without the resurfacing of my internal recordings of "white boys don't want me"; "I'll be picked last on the team, again"; "I'll just 'drown' myself in my studies"; "keep far away from the other people of color, including Indians, so I won't be targeted"; "assimilate and blend in with the white folks." This time in India has been useful for seeing the impact of white racism in greater detail: it's clear that feeling ugly and inadequate was just not a part of the way we were before the oppression hit us.

So how do these different types of external and internalized oppression relate to youth suicides? Our patterns of shame and pretense (common to Asian heritage people in general), racism from the model minority myth, and our classist oppressor patterns isolate and numb us out. The experiences of young people's oppression, and all subsequent oppressions, make us feel too powerless to push up against and change difficulties in our lives. Eventually we believe that any pain we're feeling is the result of our own inadequacies and that we "just need to work harder." (Young adult oppression digs this message in deeper.) The presence of internalized oppression makes it seem even more impossible to counter the oppression. Consequently, we are left feeling that there's no alternative; we must "make do" or die. I assume that, as the older sister, this feeling was especially magnified for you.

To address this problem means ending *all* oppression—external as well as the internalized effects. We can be so creative in developing ways to do this. We must persist even when we make mistakes; and it's highly likely that we will make mistakes! The key is to keep thinking, clean up the mistakes, and continue the work. For instance, I've tried countering our family's classism by asking our parents why they never contributed toward a health insurance policy for the black woman who has been coming to clean our house every week for over twenty years. I tried talking with cousins about the racist events on my college campus and the subsequent organizing of people of color (with the participation of very few Asian heritage people). These early attempts didn't go so well, as you may remember. I was too quick at blaming our community members for their assimilationist and oppressor patterns and didn't listen enough to their fears.

A considerably more successful experience was my performance piece about pushing through my own internalized racism to get closer to our grandmother. Asian Americans in the audience, as well as people of many other races, were moved to tears and seemed to be touched by the story's honesty and perhaps even by the commonality of our struggles. When I shared this experience with our mother, she cried and even had enough attention to ask me about my other experiences of racism. It is during such times as these that I am able to remember the fine details about our community. There's *so much* to like. I like the sound of roaring laughter when we get together; I like our emphasis on family; I like the languages we speak; I love it when we dance—Indian folk, western, and fused forms of both—because there's a place for three generations on the floor, and these are times when I am clearly able to see that we are beautiful together. Even if you've already decided to survive, sister, I want more of you, and more for you, than merely your survival. The same goes for all our people. I want the good things about our community—our humanity—to be apparent to us at all times so that we choose to act completely powerfully, lovingly, intelligently. I've identified five areas below in which our community in the United States could really tackle the youth suicide issue.

Ending the Despair

1. *Don't criticize or attack other South Asians.* We must remember and act upon the belief that every person of South Asian heritage is a perfectly likeable and intelligent person apart from his or her harmful, annoying, or otherwise bothersome behavior, which is only a reflection of his or her distress from the outside. (a) Figure out where we get hooked into being destructively critical of someone else without being able to appreciate him or her. In other words, what about *you* keeps you from supporting others to be more rational? (b) Find ways to end other South Asian Americans' critical patterns.

2. *Seek closeness with all other groups of people.* We need committed and caring relationships in which we *fall in love* with each other, and I don't mean this in a romantic sense. (a) Find ways to build relationships with people who differ along lines of race, sex, class, sexual orientation, physical/mental abilities, and so on. Importantly, we must not act like the superior model to other groups of people. Nor should we play into our destructive assimilation pattern (by "hanging in there" with someone who continues to mistreat us), subjecting ourselves to a lot of harsh treatment. (b) Challenge others' incorrect notions about us without going victim so that we can still develop the relationship. Instead of treating others simply as "oppressors," we must re-envision them as people who must have been badly hurt themselves to have made the choice to behave hurtfully toward us. What if we were to interrupt anti-Asian oppression, for instance, from the standpoint of being an ally to the person espousing the oppressive sentiment in the place where she or he was hurt?

3. *End our community's oppressor patterns.* We must stop considering ourselves "visitors," only "immigrants" and "not U.S.-ers" and refuse to be oppressors of the working class. Let's take on all of our community members' prejudices and challenge them *always*, fiercely and lovingly. Let's remember that our elders *are* flexible enough to change their oppressor patterns, just as they were flexible enough to immigrate to a completely different country as adults.[1] (a) From now on, let's *make* the United States

our complete home: where we're at is what we call home. This doesn't mean we cannot simultaneously see our parents' country as ours, too; both can be ours. (b) Actively encourage all South Asian Americans who are in or seeking leadership positions to take a significant stand against oppression. We don't need to agree with all they're doing or rationalize hurtful decisions they've made. Rather, we find ways to assist them in leading effectively with non-oppressive attitudes and policies.

4. *End young people's and young adults' oppression.* Those of us who are young people and young adults should not "play small" in the presence of elders. We should show our brilliant, powerful intelligence to them in ways that make sense for the development of our relationships across age and *never hold back in using our own thinking.* (a) We should spread information about young people's oppression. (b) We should interrupt all mistreatment of young people and young adults.

5. *Build up a strong support network so that each of us does not end up working for the above points in isolation.* We need people whom we care for intensely, to whom we can show our biggest secrets and our deepest feelings of hurt, shame, powerlessness, anger, grief, and terror. We need people who can help us overcome destructive patterns of pretense and isolation. This network will assist us in moving beyond the pain that prevents us from acting rationally in all situations. It will also help us create brilliant solutions to end our people's despair.

You know, I do have a personal fantasy about what could happen following a couple years of persistent work on this matter. In 1998 I went to a talk given by Al and Jane Nakatani, a Japanese-American couple who at the time were traveling all over the country to stop homophobia in Asian-American communities. Their three sons had all died—one, a heterosexual, of murder, and the other two, gay men, of AIDS. During the first few minutes of hearing them talk about their love for their sons, as well as their homophobia and internalized Asian oppression that kept them from being closer with their two gay sons, I was touched and felt a sudden burst of emotion. Just as the Nakatanis were standing before a large group of Asian Americans, I immediately pictured our parents standing before an audience of South Asian Americans, biting down on the shame that they might initially feel, to say, "Our daughter tried to die but didn't. We care too much about each human in our midst to let another one of us die, so let us tell you our story, and let's strategize to end this pain."

What would it take to actually get to this point? What would it look like for our people to cherish and treat each other in light of our complete goodness? What if our people actually believed and remembered that all non–South Asian people (in the United States and beyond) could be close and dependable allies to us? What if all of us took on leadership with integrity; interrupted injustice firmly, every step of the way, wherever we saw it; *always* acted on the principle that we would only look for solutions to community problems in ways that *didn't* perpetuate the oppression against us and others? To feel such a sense of responsibility and commitment all the time from our people and allies would, I think, keep all of us human enough so that no one's feelings of powerlessness would have a fighting chance to survive for very long.

Note

1. Personal correspondence with Dr. Benita Jackson.

forty-three

Resisting the Shore

Nadine Naber

My parents immigrated to the United States from Jordan in the mid-1960s for the American dream. My family climbed the economic ladder by running our own business, by believing in capitalism, and by believing that anyone could become president, even an Arab. Climbing the economic ladder meant moving out of our urban, working-class multicultural neighborhood to a so-called enlightened California suburb that believed in "democracy" and "equal rights."

I entered grammar school in the '70s during the U.S.-Arab oil wars. While my parents happily upheld the U.S. census's classification of Arab-Americans as white, my best friend's parents greeted me by imitating my parents' accent (laughing) when I entered their home.

At school, some students called me towel head and camel jockey. They asked me questions like, "So, does your dad own a 7-Eleven or an oil well? Do you have camels in your backyard? Does your dad beat your mom?" During my sophomore year of high school, my friends and I made a music video. We created a skit to the song "Killing an Arab," by a band called The Cure.

We filmed the video at my parents' house since it offered us an "authentic" Arab setting. Each of my friends played undercover U.S. policemen and FBI agents while I played "the Arab." My friends wore "American" clothes, like jeans, plaid shirts, and black leather jackets, while I wore a gallabeya and kuffiyai according to a commonly portrayed stereotype of an Arab or Muslim.

For the opening scene of the music video, I (the Arab) sat under a palm tree sipping Arabic coffee from a small brass coffee cup while smoking fake hashish from an argilah (Arabic water pipe). My white American girl friends (the undercover cops) sat behind popular open-face American magazines like *Rolling Stone, Newsweek,* and *Cosmopolitan* and disguised themselves before the kill. The music played and the chase began, around the backyard and through the house. The American cops chased the Arab (me) up the stairs and eventually threw me over the balcony to my death. The scene ended with the Arab (me) lying face-up on the ground, dead, and the white American cops raising their arms in victory. Together, my friends (and I) joined in laughter as we watched and re-watched the video with larger groups of peers throughout the years.

I remember Killing an Arab (me). I remember turning down the volume of the Arabic music that I love so deeply on our car stereo when my mother dropped me off at school so that none of the other kids would hear it. I remember the isolation. But where was the anger and where was the pain? Was the pressure to become "American" so powerful that the price of denying my history, language, and culture was worth it?

Maybe I practiced silence because I was occupied fighting on the front lines of a different war at home, with my mother, and my culture, or the culture that my parents' generation manufactured after immigrating to the U.S., in the name of protecting us. Perhaps, as a young warrior, I was not yet prepared for multiple battles.

Sometimes, the cultural war would begin on the couch. Mama would be watching TV, holding the remote control, and flipping through the stations. Station after station, a similar picture of an Anglo-American man and woman embracing each other in some sort of sexual way would appear. Mama would make comments like, "Sleep-Slept, Sleep-Slept . . . that is Amerika!" She would say things like, "el sex il hum, zay shurub al mai" (sex, for "them" [the Americans], is as easy as drinking water). At home, "Al Amerikan" (the American) was always referred to negatively. It was the trash culture, and anything associated with it was degenerate, morally bankrupt and not worth investing in, while "Al Arab," (the Arab) was always referred to positively, with references to Arab family values and hospitality, and the ways that "'banatna' ma bitlaau fil lail ['our' daughters don't go out at night]." In our home, it was black and white, good and bad, Al Arab versus Al Amerikan, as if there were a boundary, or a box, created around everything associated with being Arab. The assumption was that if you do "these things" you will be in the circle, and if you don't, then you're out. And "these things" only applied to daughters. And so it was that controlling my sexuality became the means toward maintaining our Arabness, and my virginity became the shield that would protect Mama from losing me to the "Amerikan."

That was when my resistance began. I committed myself to dismantling the Arab/American virgin/whore split and crafting my sexuality on my terms. I simply wouldn't tell Mama about my life outside the boundaries of our home. Silence became my resistance. Without speaking, without revealing, I relied on myself for answers to who and what I was going to be.

But freedom always has a price. Mama's pain permeated my sleeping and waking existence. The same person controlling me (Mama), was raising me, holding me, and loving me, while Baba worked at his store from 4 A.M. till evening. So my defiance meant betrayal, guiltpainlove (it's one word), and yearning for her acceptance. "You're crazy, wild, too free!" she would say. "No boundaries and no control! Unbrushed hair, messy-clothed girl, put on a dress! Patch up those clothes! Embarrassing your brothers on the streets with your jeans. Take those earrings out of your holes. What man will ever want to marry you?" While rebellion provided my strength, it also brought my psychological isolation from Mama and my so-called enlightened California suburb that didn't understand me, or the ongoing cultural wars within our immigrant family home.

In college, I finally grasped the connection between my personal isolation and U.S.-Arab political relations. I finally understood the link between U.S. government policies that kill and displace hundreds of thousands of Arab people and Killing an Arab/me/falling off the balcony to my death. At last, memories of childhood, coupled with scenes of the Gulf War's fire and bombs on my TV screen, inspired my transformation.

I adopted the struggle against all forms of oppression. I began working with my Arab and Arab-American sisters who are combating Arab and Arab-American women's isolation in the United States while increasing the visibility of Arab women writers, activists, and artists among U.S. feminist movements. We're building bridges with our feminist sisters and challenging racism within our communities.

Today I turn up the volume of my Arabic music that I love so deeply. I dance to the beat of Um Kulthoum, who united Arab people, made history just as history made her, and sang, "Demands are not met by wishes; the world can only be taken by struggle." Today, I swim the waves of white, black, olive, green and borders diasporas stones and guns. Earringed, short-haired, turbaned, veiled sisters, we're surviving the oceans and redesigning the shores of Arab/American virgin/whore.

forty-four

Standing on *This Bridge*

Chandra Ford

I doubt I'll ever forget the attacks I experienced in the summer of 1989. A newspaper clipping about the first one still sits in my old copy of *This Bridge Called My Back*. I was beginning to learn then that we who are victims of racism, sexism, homophobia also internalize it. As a "sistah" active in a political movement that denounced both femininity and homosexuality, even as it uplifted black male masculinity, I had been living an absurd contradiction. Through this collage of journal entries, newspaper clippings, personal reflections, and excerpts from *This Bridge Called My Back*, I revisit the events from that period. I share this story to help complete my own healing process, and hope that in my so doing, other lesbians of color are reminded of their own unique capacities for tremendous growth in the face of adversity.

Journal entry, date unknown

There can be no peace
when in my dreams
I can only relive it,
the nightmare, of you
ramming your hard, thick pole
    into my skinny,
    straddled
    body . . .
when,
even in my silent moments,
my body
 is rocked to the wild rhythm of rape
    upon a concrete floor
    beat me
        then pump and pump and pump and pump me
    and slam me
        against a door
        a bed railing
        a desk
        an open window on the sixth floor
There can be no peace
when I know within my heart—

though I've not
had the courage to proclaim it to the world—
that it was not I
who was wrong for
being,
but you,
wrong for doing
and insisting
that you were justified...

Journal entry, 19 July 1989

. . . I'm so ashamed, embarrassed and hurt and humiliated. I feel very violated . . . it wasn't very much of a fight since he's so much bigger and stronger than me . . . .I kept yelling "NO" and "STOP" and "leave me alone!" But it didn't help at all . . .

. . . M. and I fought for a long while, he trying to take my shirt and bra off. It was a t-shirt I had just bought two days ago with T. from the PSU bookstore, "Special Olympics" for $3.00. He eventually won the battle. He sat on my back and put one arm under his leg and took the shirt and bra off one arm at a time. I still struggled, making it at least difficult to do . . . he mocked and ridiculed me since I evidently was presenting very little of a challenge to him. But to me it was the principle of the whole thing that mattered. I wasn't just going to sit there and *let* him (or anyone) fuck me. I felt so helpless. He threw me around in his room and ridiculed me and touched every single part of my body even though I was yelling and adamantly telling him not to. Then, he rhetorically asked me filthy questions ... and when I said no, he would proceed and do it saying, "You mean you're not having fun at all? You can't tell me that you're not enjoying yourself, etc." How insulting. Eventually I just started all out crying.

He just kept pumping my body so hard that my sore breasts were bouncing hard and that is so painful ... he abused my breasts, pulling them ... and squeezing them and sucking and biting them so hard. I was scared the nipple would come off (as I had once read about how some crazy man in a sex frenzy bit a prostitute's nipple right off and, needless to say, she went into shock and there was blood everywhere). . . . . Both breasts are still bruised, but the left breast has a *really* big bruise on it. I've never seen anything like it. I'm not sure if I have bruises elsewhere on my body because I haven't had the time or privacy to examine my body. Another humiliating thing is he kept staring . . . at my face and my body and if I made any movement, he would attack me or do something awful to me. That *hurt* so much. The main problem I had was that he was so much bigger, stronger, heavier. He could manipulate me without any major expenditure of his energy whereas I would struggle and squirm and fight and often not even prevent him from doing whatever he was trying to do. My breasts took the most beating. My nipples have been erect for more than the past 24 hours just from the sores. They took the most abuse because somehow (I don't know how, but I'm just glad it did) I managed to keep my pants up most of the time. No one came to help me. I wanted S. or somebody to help me so bad, but no one came and I was all by myself.

I identified as a black nationalist in the late 1980s and defined all aspects of my life—including my womanness and queerness—through an afrocentric lens. I was the only out black lesbian on a campus with tens of thousands of students, but being a lesbian was not nearly as important to me as displaying a unified black presence on our racially hostile campus. Our community of black activists was a warm one in which black men and women dedicated our lives to one another and to our shared vision of black power. Having lived my entire life in the shadow of the myth of white supremacy, I thrived in what felt like a rare, albeit nostalgic, black utopia.

[T]he system of patriarchal domination is buttressed by the subjugation of women through heterosexuality. So patriarchs must extoll the boy-girl dyad as "natural" to keep us straight and compliant. . . . Against that historic backdrop, the woman who chooses to be a lesbian lives dangerously. (Clarke, 130)

In the hours after he released me, I wandered in circles through the streets of State College, Pennsylvania, my mind in an emotional daze. It was almost daylight, and I had been locked in his room since just after dinner the night before. I was exhausted, very upset, and afraid. Random memories from that evening into morning remain with me still. The most visual memory is of the poster in his room that showed a big black warrior bowed before a petite, African queen. It was a striking depiction that seemed to restore high regard to the daughters of slavery and masculinity to slavery's emasculated sons. As the night wore on, however, the eyes of the queen and warrior became more prominent and I felt like they were watching each moment of the assault in silent approval. I became increasingly embarrassed in their presence and resented the fact that I had so foolishly believed black men thought of me as an African queen.

I remember being glad that it was so hard for M. to get my jeans off of me. What he didn't know was that since the zipper was broken, I always safety-pinned the bottom of the fly to make sure it never came open. Even though M. eventually did stick his nasty prick through my partially ripped down jeans, I took some comfort in the fact that at least I had not spent the entire night with my ass and vagina fully exposed. I spent most of the evening with my face either pressed up against something or looking only directly into his eyes, so it wasn't until he was chasing me that I actually had the chance to see his penis. I remember amusing myself afterwards by thinking about how pitiful he looked scuttling around the room, his white cotton underwear tangled around his knees and erect penis bouncing in front him. I remember seeing how long and thick it was, and thinking "No way! That thing is NOT going inside of me."

What I recall most, though, are the cruel mind games he played. Several times he pinned me down while twisting my arms and legs hard behind my back, and then forced me to look into his eyes. Laughing at me, he'd ask me questions like "Are you a lesbian?" There was no right answer, for when I said "Yes," he physically assaulted me, and when I said "No," he sexualized the assault, telling me I enjoyed what he was doing. He repeatedly contorted my body into bizarre configurations then threatened me with, "Stay still! If you breathe you're gonna get it," or "You like this, don't you? You want me to do it to you again, don't you?"

I also remember how the physical pain of him hitting me, shoving me, and twisting my body never really diminished through the night as I had assumed it would. Each time he wrestled me down I could feel my joints pressing into the cool, tile-covered concrete floor or my face squished against some item of stationary furniture. I remember realizing how heavy he was while I struggled to get out from underneath him. I remember being unable to breathe while he sat on my chest, sometimes bouncing on it, often kissing me or pretending to get ready to spit on me, nevertheless asking me the same dirty questions.

> It is hardest to see my enemy as brown men yet in order to see myself clearly I must face the closest threat to my survival for it is he who most rapes me, batters me, devalues my strength, will not allow my weakness. I love him, I glory in his maleness and agonize in his degradation. I must refuse to allow him to oppress me while I must be concerned for his survival. (Canaan, 235)

Within a few days of that incident, a group of about ten brothas from our shared circle of black activists barged into my dorm room and mock gang-raped me. They didn't undress themselves nor did they take off my clothes. They knocked me back onto my roommate's bed and, while several held me down with my legs spread-eagle, each took turns jumping on top of me and "raping" me. Even through my clothes, I could feel their bulges pounding against my vagina; it made me so aware of my own vulnerability. When they all finished, they muttered lewd comments and abruptly left the room, raucous and loud. I felt so humiliated and repulsed that I never told anyone about it and certainly did not press charges against them. I never wanted to think about it again.

Journal entry, 21 July 1989 (Friday)

> I wonder if the reason he did it is only because I'm lesbian. He used to like me
> a lot but I told him I was lesbian and he couldn't accept it. This was two years
> ago.

In fact, M.'s exact words were "I forgive you for that." I was insulted
by his assertion that who I am was something that required forgiveness,
and, furthermore, that someone like him could offer me redemption. It
seemed like my attraction to other women was less a threat than the fact
that I chose to identify as a lesbian. At the time, my desire to fit into the
black community and my understanding of what it means to commit oneself to a movement made it difficult for me to blame them for the pain I
experienced as a result of their actions. It seemed more appropriate to
blame myself.

Years later, a bisexual friend from a different state told me without
even realizing it the brothas' side of my own story. She described how
she'd heard that during the summer of 1989 brothas at my university
raped a black lesbian to teach her a lesson. That's when I realized these
attacks had actually been a conspiracy.

Journal entry, date unknown

> . . . A brotha raped me once
>   in the name of a revolution
>   he claimed would set our people free . . .

For a long time I thought M. would apologize to me, but he never
did. In the months that followed those incidents, the black community
ostracized me. Even so, I continued to align myself more closely with the
black attacker I would eventually send to prison than with the women,
most of them white, who claimed to care about survivors of sexual assault.
I retreated into a closet of silence where my fears kept me in what felt like
patriarchal checkmate.

Journal entry, date unknown

> *Oppression*
> ...How frustrating to be alone
>   without friend or peer
>   when Sisters are unwilling
>   to put a foot down
>   or raise a point
>   for fear a brother may disagree

How isolating and sad it is
>to be Sisters
>>and yet to have never really shared
>>or cared
>to be living and fighting and working
>daily for our brothers
>but not understanding
>>Ourselves.

Journal entry, July 1990 (Wednesday)

I'm feeling extremely depressed today. I found out that M. is now a certified rape counselor at the women's resource center. S. and T. said he's putting himself in positions where people depend on him similar to the way Ted Bundy did, where he abuses those who most rely on him. I'm getting really, really scared of him.

I left the women's movement utterly drained. . . . Perhaps white women are so rarely loyal because they don't have to be   There are thousands of them to pick up & discard   No responsibility to others (Chrystos, 69–70)

Ten months after the assaults, I found myself calling the women's resource center basically to confirm that M. was not becoming a rape counselor. But when I called, I found out that, in fact, he was nearing completion of the certification process. Still emotionally unprepared to discuss the incidents, I told the program manager simply that he had sexually assaulted me almost a year ago. She contested my disclosure immediately, explaining that she and other women at the center really liked him. Within a few days, she called me at home and informed me that if I took the case to court, she would testify as a character witness on his behalf. Part of what I had appreciated about the insulated circle of black nationalists was that on some level they celebrated black femininity. As I interacted with the "feminists" at the center, however, I realized I was in the familiar position of begging white women to acknowledge black female vulnerability.

And when our white sisters
radical friends see us
in the flesh
not as a picture they own,
they are not quite as sure
if
they like us as much.
We're not as happy as we look

on

their

wall. (Carrillo, 63)

Journal entry, summer 1990

...How can I live

in a community where you are free

and your eyes greet me

through the haunting eyes of every man I meet?

Centre Daily Times, Thursday, August 9, 1990

Man faces trial on attempted rape charge

By JOSEPH GRAF

Times staff writer

A man was ordered to stand trial for attempted rape Wednesday from an incident that took place more than a year ago.

A Penn state student told police two weeks ago that she was attacked last year by [M.], 23, of Philadelphia, in his dormitory room on campus.

. . . After an hour-long preliminary hearing, District Justice Clifford Yorks ordered [M.] to stand trial on charges of attempted rape, indecent assault, false imprisonment and simple assault. . . .

Penn State police interviewed [M.] July 25 and he told them he "forced himself upon her," . . .

The woman said in court that another reason she waited before speaking with police was because both she and [M.] were involved in the same student groups on campus, and she feared retaliation from [M.] or his friends.

I never imagined that I would one day find myself turning to the racist criminal justice system to press charges against someone I considered a strong black man. The decision I faced was either press charges against him—and, in so doing, turn him over to the very system I held responsible for the destruction of black communities, one defendant at a time—or accept the fact that M. would likely assault other women, especially black lesbians. I still recall the district attorney's haunting counsel to me, that M.'s chances of conviction were strongest not because of the evidence, but because he was both a dark-skinned and a big black man. Maybe M. had counted on my distrust of the system to keep him out of prison. After all, I identified as a black nationalist. But I also identified as a feminist. And, as a feminist, was I not morally bound to advocate for the well-being of women?

When it became clear to me that no one, not even the women's resource center, was willing to do anything to protect other women from him, I felt like I had no choice but to file charges. And that's when I was labeled a traitor in the black community. I understood and, on some level, even empathized with the hostility expressed toward me. Essentially, they thought of me in the same way they would have thought of any Uncle Tom. Given my previous work in the community, however, it was disillusioning that they so quickly considered me a sellout. What hurt most deeply was that except for one sistah, who called me sobbing and upset late the night before the first court date, I never received what I longed for more than anything else: some semblance of compassion from women who claimed to be my revolutionary sistahs.

Ray Gricar
District Attorney
Centre County District Attorney

March 5, 1991

Ms. Chandra Ford
Re: Commonwealth v [M.]
Dear Ms. Ford:

This is to inform you that the above-mentioned defendant was recently sentenced and received the following sentence by the Court:

pay the costs of prosecution; pay a fine in the amount of $1000.00; to be incarcerated in the Centre County Prison for a period of 4 months to 23 1/2 months, credit for time served on this charge; to be evaluated by the Base Service Unit and attend counseling as recommended by that agency; to attend counseling sessions in the Centre County Sexual Offenders Program . . . .

Sincerely,
Dawn G. McKee
Victim/Witness Advocate
for
Ray Gricar
District Attorney

We believe the most profound and potentially the most radical politics come directly out of our own identity, as opposed to working to end somebody else's oppression. . . . We reject pedestals, queenhood, and walking ten paces behind. To be recognized as human, levelly human is enough. (Combahee River Collective, 212)

I survived that period by relying upon the written words of warrior women who understood the challenges that surface when we choose to Stand in our communities of origin and Be across identity borders.

I am not trying to reify lesbianism or feminism. I am trying to point out that lesbian-feminism has the potential of reversing and transforming a major component in the system of women's oppression, viz. predatory heterosexuality. (Clarke, 134)

I won, not because M. went to jail, but because I spoke when he and others counted on my fear to silence me. I still feel empowered today when I recall what it felt like to look directly in his eyes in the courtroom as I pointed him out to the judge, and uttered my truth in his presence. I won then when I chose to embrace my identity as a lesbian of color, rather than to partition myself into categories and only permit the acceptable ones to be recognized.

> You believed once in your own passivity, your own powerlessness, your own spiritual malaise. You are now awakening in the beginnings of a new birth. Not born again, but born for the first time, triumphant and resolute, out of experience and struggle, out of a flowing, living memory out of consciousness and will, facing, confronting, challenging head-on the contradictions of your lives and the lives of people around you. (Wong, 180)

Through reading volumes like *This Bridge*, I began to see myself as part of a powerful albeit oppressed community, if accessible then only through those texts. As a budding young feminist, I took pride in my new definitions of woman, black, and lesbian. I pressed charges against M. because of my sense of responsibility to other women, especially lesbians-of-color. As I saw it, the lesbian-of-color community, through me, had to respond in order to assert its worth. But not unlike my mother's own tendency toward self-sacrifice, I had overlooked my personal right to dignity and never even thought to vindicate my self.

Through introspective work in therapy I am learning that I tend to define myself only in terms of an oppressed collective. I am working toward a fuller understanding of my own humanity; simply, the self-worth of Chandra that was too invisible for me to fight for in 1989, even as I fought for the identity and rights of a whole group of women with whom I identified. The sexual assault of lesbians is political, but it is never only political. For the survivor, the violent experience is also very intimate and weaves itself into her life in many intricate ways: her thoughts, dreams, and emotions, the well-being of her body, the relationships and forms of self-expression that she chooses. Identifying as a lesbian of color gave me the courage to stand when I was first afraid. My process of healing now demands that I face my most private and subjective fears. I find that not all of them can be easily interpreted as the terms of a collective experience.

My strength grows
rooted in the Truth that I live
And I take pride
      in being
      and in understanding
Chandra—
      whom few will ever know

Note

The author wishes to thank Lisa Coxson and Perrianne Davis for careful readings of the manuscript. The author also expresses deepest appreciation to Kara Keeling for her loving encouragement through all the phases of the project and for her careful reading of numerous drafts of the project.

forty-five

Stolen Beauty

Genny Lim

Rage is the python
which swallows the heart
I am the woman who makes no apology
Love and hate spring from me

A good woman bears her cross with humility
She is a paragon, a virgin of invisible flight
Her name is pity

If you cut open a frog
It will bleed to death
Everything inside will stop
But its muscles will contract
and its heart will continue to beat

Rage is the revenge of the heart and
I am the queen of hearts
Durga's nemesis

forty-six

Looking for Warrior Woman (Beyond Pocahontas)

Joanne Barker

In June 1998 while reading through my monthly subscriptions to *News from Indian Country* and *Indian Country Today* I came across an ad soliciting job applications for the U.S. Secret Service.[1] I am going to call this ad Warrior Woman. Centered at the top, in bold-faced print, the ad seeks "*a new kind of* WARRIOR." Below, an American Indian woman stands direct in a black suit and white buttoned-up dress shirt. Behind her left arm a detail of the Secret Service's badge shadows her in gray outline. In her right hand, she holds a spear garnered with feathers and wrapped in cloth (you almost forget to notice her polished nails, matching lipstick, and silver ring). Around her left ear, dangling into the inside of her jacket's lapel, is an almost transparent ear-piece. On her lapel, there is a small silver pin in the shape and colors of the U.S. flag. The first button on her jacket is large and silver, bearing a design of four arrows pointing out. Framing the bottom of the ad is the main text, overlaid another U.S. flag. The badge centers the "Secret Service." Below appears the following text: "Everyday the U.S. Secret Service battles to protect our nation's leaders and financial systems. We are looking for young Americans with diverse skills and backgrounds who are interested in a challenging career in federal law enforcement. To find out more, give us a call (202) 435–5800 www.treas.gov/treasury/bureaus/usss."

It is a stunning ad. The image is bold; the textures and lines are sharp; the woman is proud and powerful. For one quick moment, you actually consider a career in federal law enforcement. And for any woman of indigenous citizenship, that is one very long, richly complex moment.

To Find Out More, Give Us a Call

I ask around. According to family, friends, and colleagues, Warrior Woman seems to circulate for a few months in various newspapers, magazines, and journals. Tribal colleges receive her in full-poster form with no accompanying explanation or information. Many end up in the trash. Meanwhile, I make some phone calls. My first round is to the Secret Service public relations department. I want to know the advertising agency, photographer, model, and any other details, as well as a list of publications where the ad has appeared. But I am unable to obtain any information. The Secret Service is hardly forthcoming. So, I take a different approach. A friend in Los Angeles works as a researcher for a

Japanese production firm that makes commercials and print ads for U.S. companies to be shown in Japan. He tells me of a Midwest company that, upon payment of $150, will track down all of the details about specific ads. I call the company, but they can find out nothing. Nothing at all.

So I take another track. I call the Secret Service at the *to find out more* number, but the receptionist is more than flustered. Apparently, Secret Service ads for jobs usually have reference numbers; when you call for information you are sent a packet that includes detailed guidelines regarding qualifications, application procedures, and test dates (for some jobs, there is an intensive two-year security background check). I tell the receptionist that the ad I am looking at does not mention a specific job or include any reference numbers and that I am making a more general inquiry into the kinds of opportunities for Indian women that the ad is referencing. To say that I confused her would not say enough. "What job is it that you want to apply for?" "Do you have any unique skills or interests?" "Do you have secretarial skills, for example?" Like typing or shorthand. "Accounting skills, perhaps?" No. "Janitorial skills? Something like that?" Not exactly the type of stuff I believed this *new kind of* WARRIOR Woman was doing nor that the ad wanted me to emulate.

After I tried to explain that I just wanted to know what opportunities the Service had for Indians, the receptionist became suspicious and belligerent. She demanded to know my name and from where I was calling. When I told her I was a student at the University of California, Santa Cruz, her tone relaxed somewhat but I could tell that she still found me suspect. After several minutes, she relented and promised to send me a brochure—which I have never received—and told me I could call back if I had any further questions after reading it. She also referred me to the website and said that I could learn more there. (Truly a waste of time. The page is an Internet version of a glossy brochure—telling you everything and nothing all at the same time.)

My crass investigation confirmed that the ad did not really want Indian women to apply. It merely wanted to reinvent its image among Indian communities, or perhaps more generally, to confirm the Service's commitment to anti-racism and anti-sexism in the context of recent debates about Affirmative Action policies. (Like Chevron's environmental awareness TV ads in the wake of its own destruction of U.S. reserves.) Maybe the Service was hoping to instill reassurance among Indian communities that any Indian person working for a U.S. federal law enforcement agency is trustworthy, proud, and deserving of respect? Maybe they hoped for more cooperation given their affirmation of all the "skills and backgrounds" Indian people have to offer? In any case, the ad is most decidedly *not* a solicitation for applicants. So, what's it advertising?

A *"new kind of* Warrior" Woman?

There are as many versions of the story of Pocahontas as there are representations of her in U.S. popular culture. It would be impossible to sort
through all these images and the ensuing questions about their factuality
and significance here. Were she and John Smith in love? Did she save
Smith from her father? Why did Smith only write of the scene in his draft
of the *Generall Historie of Virginie* (1624) after Pocahontas had gained
notoriety in England as the famed "Indian Princess"? Why did
Pocahontas spend all of her time at the fort? Why did she marry John
Rolfe, convert to Christianity, change her name to Rebecca, leave for
England? Why was she returning home? (And why did Thomas Rolfe
later lead U.S. troops against his mother's people?)

I do not mean to minimize these compelling questions' importance.
Several scholars have pointed out the necessity of understanding the historical and cultural context from which Pocahontas came, for it informed
the political agenda of her father, Powhatan, concerning their respective
relations with Smith and the colony. Indian women have cared very
deeply about what Pocahontas's story tells us about the history of Indian
women's roles generally and Pocahontas's role as a Powhatan woman
specifically. Was the famed salvation scene actually an enactment of a
Powhatan adoption ceremony that would have brought Smith under
Powhatan's authority? Is it possible that Pocahontas spent so much time
at the fort because estranged from her own community following an
alleged rape? Was she spying for her father, carrying out an elaborate
scheme to obtain intelligence on the colonists and their plans?

My efforts are not to recover "the facts." Rather, I want to try to understand how the narrative works. It is a different strategy that cares about the
way "facts" are put to use rather than, say, deconstructing the plausibility of
particular fact-claims in understanding what histories still need to get told.

In "The Pocahontas Perplex" Cherokee scholar Rayna Green suggests that the persistence of Pocahontas's story has been its utility within
U.S. nationalism's mythic structures, particularly in (re)enacting the inferiority of Pocahontas's culture and the dominion of Smith's in what was to
be figured as America. Pocahontas's alleged defiance of her father, her
choice to save Smith, her attention to Smith and the other colonists' survival, her marriage and conversion, her Christian renaming, and her move
to England are made evidence that she knew that her own culture lacked
the qualities valued by Smith's and the New World (Berkhofer). Stripped
of any vestiges of her own political agenda and her own cultural affiliation
and identity, Pocahontas is made to speak to that new world, to that
America, as heroine and ancestor.[2]

These interpretative practices transfiguring Pocahontas into a quintessential American hero are insidious: such inventions render her insignificant outside her heterosexualized relationships to men and erase her affiliation as a Powhatan. Dispossessing Pocahontas of her sovereign identity, culture, and history—and thus political concerns and agendas other than those serving U.S. colonial men and interests—makes it impossible to consider that she might have spoken for or to other issues, such as those addressing her father's powerful position, her people's autonomy and survival, and the colonists' treatment of Indians. Instead, Pocahontas becomes merely everybody's great-great-grandmother, resolving conflicted problems of dispossession and genocide that characterized her and her nation's history with an all too easy and hypocritical "affirmation of relationship" (Green, 20).

Warrior Woman is more than coincidentally (in)formed by the representational practices of Indian women as icons of U.S. nationalism. These practices are registered in the very moment Warrior Woman is dispossessed from her own history, culture, and identity and invites Indian people to identify with and emulate that dispossession. The ad's call for recruits is juxtaposed with the text soliciting *a new kind of* WARRIOR." But what exactly does it mean by "new"?

Given its timing and location, the ad anticipates applications from recent high school and college graduates. The first response to the ad, then, is to conflate the "new" with the "young" American Indian students it seeks out. I think a more purposeful reading is to understand how the "new" works in junction with "diverse skills and backgrounds." There, the ad implies Indian Warriors with culturally unique abilities and understandings who could employ those "skills and backgrounds" to the more "challenging" ends of the Secret Service. So, just what is "new" about the Warrior the Secret Service is soliciting?

The feather-adorned spear is a generic ornament, a too-easy signifier for the warrior in the Warrior but without any of the stuff that would mark it culturally relevant (indicating, for instance, that it is used in fishing or in conflict or identifying which specific culture it is employed within [not all Indian nations use spears of that kind]). In other words, while the ad offers its recognition of Indian Warriors' "diverse skills and backgrounds" it does not refer to any specific culturally relevant skill or background or any specific culturally defined Warrior, such as members of Lakota Warrior societies or Cherokee "red town" councils. Neither does it make reference to Indian Warriors who have already proven their service to other kinds of acts of "federal law enforcement," such as the Diné Code Talkers of WWII or the thousands of Indian persons who are serving and have served in the U.S. military and police forces throughout the United

States and around the world ever since (Nielsen and Silverman). Instead, the ad makes an Affirmative-Action-sounding acknowledgment of the "diversity" of Indian "skills and backgrounds" in reference to the other kinds of warriors already in its legions.

Given the non-exclusive reference to the relevancy of Indian cultural knowledge to the Secret Service, the "new" is more in concert with the reference to the Secret Service's particular needs in its search for applicants. Since the ad specifically announces that it "battles" "everyday" to protect U.S. national leaders and financial systems from outside threat and corruption, perhaps it is asserting that something about the Indian Warrior's "skills and backgrounds" would serve those ends in a "new" way. Perhaps the ad means to suggest that the Indian Warrior's "diversity" is the skill and background in defending as opposed to threatening those leaders and systems. In its very celebration of this possibility, the Indian Warrior's spear implies that this emblem is somehow a remnant of a past when the Indian Warrior was successfully trained in fighting against the very U.S. military and economic structures that the Service now firmly maintains. In other words, the "new" would be using those skills and backgrounds in service *to* the United States. If this is the case, then the Indian Warrior's "skills and backgrounds" are understood as going unchallenged in Indian people's contemporary world. What is "new" is the opportunity the Secret Service provides to Indian Warriors to remember and re-employ their otherwise seemingly outdated abilities in a challenging and meaningful way.

That the Indian Warrior is a woman is central to how the ad carries out its signifying chain from the old to the new to the old again. The Warrior Woman wants us to believe that what would be "new" is neither the idea of Indians in the Service nor the relevancy of their "skills and backgrounds" to the Secret Service but rather the very notion that the Warrior would be a woman. The *"new kind of* WARRIOR" *is a Woman* is the jingle that I believe the ad invites its audiences to sing. The Secret Service wants to foreground its acknowledgment of "diversity" by extending it from Indian to woman—from race to gender— in one sweeping Affirmative Action gesture. It wants us to believe that the Secret Service counters the often hyper-masculinized and racist notions of U.S. patriotism, particularly those associated with the growing incidence of Euro-American militia activities in the United States, with the very radical idea that the Secret Service already recognizes and reveres Indian women's heroic loyalty. In circuitry, of course, that quality is an invention of the very U.S. nationalism on which the Secret Service stands.

The "new" erases a multitude of historical and cultural sins from the pages of U.S. history. The fact that Indians continually transformed their "skills and backgrounds" in order to defend themselves against U.S. military, economic, and cultural aggression; that anywhere from 60 to 95 percent of the Indian population in the U.S. died by disease and armed conflict in the 1800s alone (Stiffarm with Lane); that Indian people have been systematically removed from their lands, communities, beliefs, and languages in efforts to eradicate Indians from everything Indian; and that U.S. national leaders and economic systems have had an instrumental hand in directing and implementing these policies in practice are all shaken from the ad's apparent affirmations of anti-racism and anti-sexism as if Indian-U.S. history were an Etch-A-Sketch drawing that could be turned upside down and started anew when the lines got too messy.

The Warrior Woman suggests that what is "new" about herself is that a woman could be a warrior (like there weren't ever any Indian women warriors!) or that the service of Indian women as a whole in the Secret Service has been unnoticed until now. But I believe that she is fooling herself. That the Warrior is a Woman is as much a precondition of the erasure of the history of the role of U.S. national leaders and economic systems in carrying out U.S. imperialism as it is a reconfiguration of it. The Warrior Woman simultaneously constructs an Indian woman removed from her own histories and cultures, as a detribalized Indian generically adorned, as a deterritorialized warrior without a nation of her own "to protect and to serve," as she constructs those erasures to be lived within. The cost of her ability to serve the secret intents of federal and economic policy is displaced from the very scene that celebrates the possibility of that service.

Enough Is Enough

In "Thoughts on Indian Feminism," Assiniboine (Nakota, Fort Peck Reservation) scholar Kathryn Shanley argues that American Indian women have too often been made into "tokens" for a "white feminist movement" that has ignored the historical and cultural specificities of their own particular struggles and beliefs (213–15). Shanley posits that the concerns characteristic of the "white women's movement" over the economic and social oppression of the mainstream workforce and "nuclear family" have little translation into contemporary Indian women's lives and concerns. For Shanley, sovereignty and cultural tradition are the basis for any reformulation or understanding of Indian women's epistemologies and politics, informing the range of their activism concerning environmental, resource, and land rights, domestic violence, language retention, education, health care, and a myriad of other issues.

In "Relocations upon Relocations" Chicana/Nez Perce scholar Inés Hernández-Ávila argues that Native American women's writings are situated within their commitments to their unique *home(lands)* and shared histories of (re)location, within their own communities' struggles for political and cultural sovereignty. She also maintains that Native women's epistemologies are informed by an emphasis on homelands; while *home* generally refers to a domestic sphere of familial relation and responsibility, *homelands* refers to the historical forces that have very publicly relocated Native peoples from their territories, cultures, and identities. In this way, Hernández-Ávila demonstrates that Native women's writings pivot on an axis of political sovereignty and cultural autonomy.

Drawing from Shanley and Hernández-Ávila, I suggest that an oppositional reading strategy for the Warrior Woman ad could start from an understanding that Indian women are first and foremost situated within and concerned about the struggles of their own unique nations for sovereignty and cultural autonomy as well as that of all indigenous people in the Americas—North and South. This methodological perspective takes sovereignty and cultural autonomy as the primary frames of reference for understanding the politics of representation for/of/about/by American Indian women. This is not to suggest that all Indian women have experienced histories of relocation, dispossession, and genocide in the same way, nor that their ideas and goals about how to accomplish the repatriation of their histories, cultures, and identities are the same. Rather, by insisting on sovereignty and autonomy as the primary frames of reference for a hermeneutics of Indian women's representations, the strategy emphasizes the embeddedness of Indian histories, cultures, and identities in meaning systems that are discrete *and* related. National and cultural survivance, concepts of membership and belonging, and socially defined roles and political agendas provide the context from which to interpret representational practices of/by Indian women (Kauanui).

In the case of Pocahontas, this approach would fundamentally impact understandings of her significance and use as an iconographic reference for U.S. nationalism. Her representational significance would be understood in the context of how she has been made not only receptive to but solicitous of the colonizing man/colonial project, continually made over as giving herself, her people, and her lands to him/it. Her role within her nation as Powhatan's daughter, possible motives for spending so much time with the colonists and marrying into their community, the cultural traditions informing her seizure of the alleged execution attempt: these issues resituate analysis of her representational significance within her own historical and cultural experiences. The point would not be to romanticize her as an anti-hero—maybe she was a sellout, maybe she did give up, give in, but maybe not. (An analysis beyond the scope of this essay but certainly worth fuller consideration.)

What happens when we read the Warrior Woman, insisting on sovereignty and autonomy as the frames of reference? Unlike Pocahontas, Warrior Woman is not a historical figure per se. Believing that agency is something you do and not something you are or are not given, I suggest that Warrior Woman's political and cultural agency is located within her self-determining history, culture, and identity. The challenge, of course, is that the image does not identify her Indian national affiliation; the codes provided by the term *warrior* and the emblematic spear are far too tribally generic to be helpful. So I'll have to look elsewhere to enact the reading.

In "Rosebuds of the Plateau," Rayna Green suggests a story for the two Indian women lounging on Japanese-American photographer Frank Matsura's fainting couch (*Two Girls on Couch*, 1910). Though I would never presume to speak for Warrior Woman, I would like to take my cue from Green and make up a story that might fill in her confused dress, proud stance, and role in the Secret Service. Because at some level I can not quite explain away, I like her. I am transfixed by her. I am deeply troubled by her. From the moment I ran across this ad, I wanted to cut it out, frame it, hang it on the wall. I mean, there she is with her matching polished nails and lipstick, her MIB (WIB!) suit and silver adornments, her spear, and that wonderfully suggestive ear-piece. I don't know, maybe I've watched too much of *The X-Files*, but I like this woman.

So I've decided that the story I like best for her is that she is a double agent. Perhaps I am informed by the readings of Pocahontas's role and historical significance that suggest that her presence at the fort and salvation of Smith from execution were part of some wider political strategy by Powhatan to take in the colonists like he had taken in so many Indian villages in the building of his empire. Or perhaps I am informed by Joy Harjo's remembrance, in her poetry collection *In Mad Love and War*, of Anna Mae Pictou Aquash—the American Indian Movement member assassinated and dismembered in the 1970s by, most likely, FBI agents or others doing their bidding (Mattiessen; Churchill and Vander Wall). Or perhaps I'm still waiting for that "great American novel" or weekly TV drama staring an older Indian woman like Tantoo Cardinal as a PI solving mystery after mystery without one tired old reference to Indian tracking skills or night vision. In any case, the story I like best is that Warrior Woman is a double agent—that the *secret* in her *service* is that she is an informant *to* and not *of* federal law enforcement activities. How delicious is that?

From the seemingly endless reserve of data banks, filing cabinets, and musty ill-numbered boxes in Pentagon basements and Nebraska warehouses, Warrior Woman is passing to her people information that she has finally been made privy to after years of loyal and quiet service. So loyal and quiet, in fact, that she is almost unnoticed. Almost invisible. Even now. And who could doubt the likelihood of that scenario? A woman too dark, too smart, too competent to be seen by the hyper-heterosexualized patriarchal structures in which she works; appearing in conference rooms and department meetings only on year-end personnel review and employment statistic forms filed before they're really read; seen only as a satisfaction of a quotient for "race" and "gender" diversity, as if that's what Affirmative Action was about.

So she decides to take advantage of her invisibility. Unbeknownst to any of her colleagues in one of the world's most infamous intelligence agencies, the dust-ridden secrets hidden away in encryption codes and storehouses are brought out of their hiding places and passed on to those who can decipher their significance, break their codes, and unseal their overdue warnings for "confidentiality" and "national security" to assist them in their struggles for sovereignty.

On the day this picture was taken, Warrior Woman had scheduled a rendezvous with one of her contacts. She has discovered a password for *www.treas.gov/treasury/bureaus/usss* that allows the user to enter all *usss* files at will and she is anxious to pass it on.

She has been well placed at the front of the president's caravan in a parade for some misconstrued national holiday down New York City's main street—the perfect Kodak moment. She resisted carrying the spear, arguing that it would get in the way if there were trouble, but her superior had had it specially dug out of a box of supplies in the oldest part of a Nebraska warehouse. Marching through the heat, stopping occasionally to pose for pictures, she imagines the spear's history.

She has decided that the spear was used in the special "citizenship ceremonies" developed by Secretary of the Interior Franklin Lane in 1916. Lane made the delivery of land patents and the commensurate status of U.S. citizenship under the provisions of the General Allotment Act of 1887 a ceremonial event, probably because he thought he knew how important rituals were to Indian people. In the ceremony, Indians were to solemnly step out of a teepee and shoot an arrow across an assembly, to signify that they were leaving their Indian way of life behind for the responsibilities of U.S. citizenship. (Possibly the presiding official, for those tribes that did not use bows and arrows, carried around a supply like so many Edward Curtis props. On one day, perhaps, his supply got left behind and the Indians had to use their own spears, confiscated by the agent in the confusion that followed. So that, instead of shooting an arrow, the Indians had to fling their spears across center stage. I am sure, at any rate, that it could have happened that way.) Moving slowly away from their teepees, the Indians were to place their hands on a plow to demonstrate that they had chosen the responsibilities and demands of a farming, tax-paying life. Given their allotment and citizenship, they would have to earn a living for their families by "making use" of the lands that they were being "given." With hands on plow, Indians were handed a purse by the presiding official to remind them to save what they earned that they might fulfill their new responsibilities. At the ceremony's closing, they were presented with an American flag and directed to repeat the following phrase: "Forasmuch as the President has said that I am worthy to be a citizen of the United States, I now promise this flag that I will give my hands, my head, and my heart to the doing of all that will make me a true American citizen" (McDonnell, 95). To conclude the ceremony, the presiding official pinned a badge decorated with an American eagle and the national colors on the recipient to remind the Indian to act in a way that would honor the flag and the privileges of U.S. citizenship that had been afforded to him/her that day. (These ceremonies were first performed on the Yankton reservation in South Dakota in 1916, and were conducted by Lane himself [McDonnell, 95–96]).

As Warrior Woman carried the spear down Main Street, she wondered about those who participated in the citizenship ceremonies. She is sure that many of them went through the ceremony half-heartedly, even mockingly, but that probably many more were *interpolated* into the life it enacted. Participation didn't have to mean compliance, but it would be hard for a spectator to tell the difference. Those watching her march down Main Street like an emblem of the president's Affirmative Action prowess, a symbol of Secret Service loyalty and patriotism, would probably believe her a modern-day Pocahontas—a hero, a traitor, depending. They wouldn't know that she had switched the frequency of her radio over to a station playing Buffy St. Marie's "The Universal Soldier." That she had flipped over the pin on her lapel so that the flag was upside down. That she was waiting for her contact to bump into her through the crowds so that she could pass on the small notepad hidden in her left coat pocket. But that's all okay, she thought. She knew.

When All Things Old Are New Again . . .

American Indian women, while sharing experiences with other "women of color" in the context of ongoing histories of U.S. nationalism, are not another "ethnicity" in the rainbow of American cultural difference. Identifying as Indian is not quite the same thing as identifying, for instance, as "Black" or "Chinese American" or "Chicana." To identify or mark indigeneity is to claim oneself as a member of a people—a "collective nonstate entity" (Wilmer, 164) with internationally recognized legal rights to political and cultural sovereignty and autonomy. This is why so many Indian people insist on their national or tribal identities in opposition to being identified as Indian. In fact, the very processes of racialization as *Indians* has been integral to the political processes that have sought to undermine Indian sovereignty and autonomy. To the extent that Indians have been counted as "minorities," "under-represented," and/or as making up an "ethnic group" within the larger U.S. polity, the notion that they are citizens of their own unique nations has been undermined, displaced. This has important and immediate consequences to self-government, land and resource rights, juridical autonomy, and cultural survivance. In other words, the *ethnicization* of Indians and the representational practices that employ it have been extremely useful in the systematic negation of Indian people's sovereignty and autonomy (Barker).

Of course, issues of dual citizenship and the more slippery concepts of membership and belonging for mixed-race and mixed-tribal Indians complicate matters even further. There are Indians, for instance, who want to be recognized as U.S. citizens and consider themselves patriots; there are those who have not recognized themselves as citizens of Indian nations at all; and there are those who believe themselves to be citizens of two countries. Further, the identities and memberships of "mixed-bloods"—those of mixed racial and/or mixed tribal descent—make it impossible to render a simple notion of what it means to identify or be identified as Indian within the context of representational practices. I do not mean to dismiss these complexities but rather to suggest that for Indian people in the United States the erasure of the sovereign from the Indian has been a particularly strategic goal of dispossession, genocide, and assimilation. This goal is encapsulated by the Warrior Woman: denationalized, detribalized, an emblem of diversity within the "our" of U.S. politics and economics.

The issues Warrior Woman embodies are foregrounded by the way the ad sets up a tension between U.S. nationalism's hegemonic knowledge practices and American Indian women's oppositional strategies. It is not a natural tension. It is very much a construction of the kinds of power imagined within colonialism, capitalism, and patriarchalism. Pocahontas as a historical figure is enigmatic of these troubles, her dispossession and death the precondition of her usefulness in maintaining the mythic structures of U.S. nationalist discourses. Warrior Woman indicates that these troubles have been carried forward in the continued possibilities for making Indians speak to/for the very political and economic agendas that have undermined their struggles for sovereignty and autonomy. It follows that the precondition of her service is the erasure of their own unique and diverse histories, cultures, and identities. I have tried to show how it might be otherwise.

Notes

This paper was conceived and written for *Beyond the Frame*, a collection of essays examining the relationship between the politics of (self-)representation and the category "women of color" in the United States (Angela Davis and Neferti Tadiar, editors). Part of the collection's process was a workshop held in March 1999 at the University of California, Santa Cruz. Over thirty women of color participated as reviewers and mentors. I am particularly indebted to Jennifer Gonzáles, Valerie Soe, and Theresa Harlan for their feedback on the version of this paper presented at the workshop. I'd also like to acknowledge the editorial board of *Beyond the Frame*—Victoria Banales, Luz Calvo, Ceclia Cruz, J. Kehaulani Kauanui, and Keta Miranda—as well as the members of the *Women of Color in Collaboration and Conflict Research Cluster* at UC Santa Cruz who planned and hosted the workshop. A warm thank you to Luana Ross for providing me with a color copy of the ad.

1. See inserts, *News from Indian Country* (June 11, 1998, 9A) and *Indian Country Today* (June 8–15, 1998, B8).

2. As Green shows in "The Pocahontas Perplex," the Pocahontas image is troubled further by her twin, the squaw/whore, who shares her one-dimensional referentiality to colonial men and colonial processes.

---

forty-seven

So Far from the Bridge

Renae Bredin

Technology will redeem us; technology will ruin us. The problem with this particular contemporary contradiction is that the technology that might redeem or ruin us has been and continues to be under the control of primarily white heterosexual male elites. So, if technology winds up in the hands of radical women with a vision, perhaps it can transform us. In fact, when *This Bridge Called My Back* was published over twenty years ago, the voices of women of color, men of color, and lesbians of all colors were more than just difficult to hear, they were nearly inaudible in the cacophony of mainstream discourse. Gloria Anzaldúa, Cherríe Moraga, and the amazing collaboration of radical women who came together to speak out created an astonishing conversation among women of color, a conversation that readers were then welcomed to join. The very fact that such a conversation would take place was radical—a dialogue about who "we" are and how "we" came to be. The potential for radical change opened by the book seems both endless and truncated.

Much of the writings in *This Bridge* explored what it meant to be on the outside of the paradigm, excluded from participation in the discourses of the dominant. The assertion of an identity that was powerful and transformative, at the same time without voice in U.S. cultural practices, was a dangerous act, a radical conversation, a revolutionary act. This book got into college classrooms and the revolution was afoot. In some ways, this act of conversation in print became a transformative act, but it was also often an act of voyeurism and appropriation on the part of teachers and students in women's studies classes, feminist theory classes, literature classes, ethnic studies classes, and even composition classes. From *This Bridge Called My Back* came voices that moved us, transformed us, condemned us, redeemed us. By "us," I mark out the territory betwixt and between identity politics and the personal—an us that did not, does not, cannot, and will not exist, because we are all caught in the spokes of the machinery of differences. And by "us," I mark out the territory of women speaking on their own terms, women who had been silenced, ignored, denied, or patronized by women not like them. Us is the impossible but necessary sign of "woman," inclusive of all who wear the sign, but nonetheless impossible. Speaking, in many ways, to those very women not like them who had done the silencing. Patrice McDermott describes the project of *This Bridge Called My Back* in this way: "Moraga and Anzaldúa designed their text as a political strategy to lay down the ideas and voices—rather than the bodies—of women of color as a means of bridging 'the river of tormented history' separating women" (407). And in these ideas and voices lies the potential transformation toward unity for women in their differences

So how has the conversation turned in twenty-plus years? There is nothing about *This Bridge* that is no longer relevant—the claims staked, the oppressions exposed. We have come so far; we have not come far at all. The issues remain the same, but the possibilities for ways of addressing the issues have expanded. Who we are as women is still at stake, and alternatives to heterosexual, white, masculinist representations of these identities are still subject to violent silencing and aggressive marginalization by both men and other women. So the need to speak, to hear, to listen, to understand remains, even as we do so in new ways, with new tools and new approaches.

Shakti Butler in her 1998 interactive documentary film *The Way Home* takes up the radical, revolutionary conversation of women staking a claim to invisible identities that was initiated in *This Bridge Called My Back*. Moving from print to film, Butler presents voices of women seeking a more complete sense of self within a racist and sexist world. Eight councils of women of different ethnic and racial backgrounds came together to talk about the everyday texture of oppression by way of one's raced and gendered "categorical" definitions. The councils include the following: Indigenous, Latina, African American, European American, Jewish Council, Multi-Racial, Asian Council, Arab. Like *This Bridge*, the discriminatory practices that confront each woman become a point of exposure, a raw nerve, a lesson to be heard and learned. The women in each council speak of the pain of growing up, of living on the margins, of being different.

The councils, however, remain segregated safe spaces for women with apparent common ground to expose their pain. There is, within each council, confrontation and comfort, agreement and dissent. The Multi-Racial Council's women of mixed ancestry describe the pain of being outside every group, and the places in which they were able to find love and acceptance. In the mix of this dissent/agreement, Butler's text is committed to inclusion. This model of inclusive, individual, parallel conversations about race, class, gender, and sexuality is a new model, made more possible within the context of technologies previously unavailable to "the masses."

Perhaps something radical, something altogether revolutionary, becomes possible in the new digital economy, where representational technologies are no longer inaccessible to all but a few. It is here that the roots of *This Bridge* and *The Way Home* are similar. Within an economy of publication that favored the elite with access to expensive and "complex" printing equipment, mainstream presses silenced voices that failed to speak in harmony with their own sense of the world, those not like them. Persephone Press, a small white women's press, was the first publisher of *This Bridge*. Kitchen Table Press, publishers of the second edition, was born out of the commitment of Audre Lorde, Barbara Smith, and Cherríe Moraga to exclusively publish work by women of color. It was, at the time, the only press to make such a commitment (Short, 4–8). Today, Third Women's Press is the only press to continue in this tradition.

Through the eight councils, Butler expands and includes many women's voices, in "real-time" dialogue. Seeing the dialogue, the person speaking, and what happens between and among the women on the screen is powerful and moving. Like Moraga and Anzaldúa, Butler, through a grant from her organization World Trust, makes visible the conversations that we have read/heard in *This Bridge*, and she does so within a similar economy of publication to *This Bridge*, outside of mainstream film production. World Trust, the sponsoring group for *The Way Home*, was founded in 1987 as a nonprofit educational organization, using "media as a catalyst for dialogue as a way to address critical social issues" (*World Trust*, screen 1). *The Way Home* is at the heart of this Heart-to-Heart Conversation Program. It appears that Shakti Butler, who produced and directed the film, is the executive director, and possibly the founder of World Trust. However, few other names appear on the World Trust website as associated with the organization, although many people are credited in the film for their work. It would seem that while these two texts use slightly different models of publication, they have similar radical births. They illustrate how people from outside the mainstream of publication/media/film get their hands on the means of "production" and articulate alternative visions and identities, creating revolutionary new paradigms, inflecting the psyches of people inside and outside of the mainstream with potentially transformational ideas.

Sohail Inayatullah and Ivana Milojevic, in "Exclusion and Communication in the Information Era," articulate clearly the current conditions of global power regarding computer and information technologies, and offer a set of challenges concerning the future possibilities of the uses of these technologies. However, in order for the current conditions to be transformed, people committed to social justice need to "imagine and design" new models for information and communication within institutions, and to re-model "ownership, funding and public accountability" that will serve the needs of "cultural pluralism" (Inayatullah, 81). And this is precisely what Butler, and before her Anzaldúa and Moraga, do. They imagine and design alternative "arrangements for information and communication technologies," proposing new structures that not only accommodate but enhance the requirements of cultural pluralism.

But there are limits to film as a recursive dialogue. Dipping in and out, rereading Audre Lorde's letter to Mary Daly, or combing through Mitsuye Yamada's poetry in *This Bridge Called My Back* is not possible with *The Way Home*. This is inherent in the differences between the technologies of print and film. Print is a medium that allows the reader to return easily at any given moment, without the aid of special equipment beyond a good pair of eyeglasses. It is always on and connected; thus anyone at any time with access to the book can draw from it. Film is much more elusive for such returns. We do come to know the women in the film, learn something of who they are, were, or hope to be. They share their intimate pain and self-loathing, their cultural pain and anger, as well as their individual strengths and personal desires, but to quote one woman's voice or words is difficult, because we don't know their names for most of the video. In fact, we never have the opportunity to put names and faces together.

However, as Inayatullah and Milojevic assert in regard to computers, "these technologies are developing in the context of a world-view still fixated on progress which, in the words of Foucault, 'make us an object of information, never a subject of communication'" (81). I would argue that this assumption applies to film and print media as well. Information as a one-way street fails to transform the social contract. Communication, becoming the subject, rather than the object, is at the heart of the transformation. Inayatullah and Milojevic propose that transforming information into communication is the means to undo the relations of power in an information age (86). Butler refuses the traditional documentary of "expert" heads talking at us, a model that offers a one-way path of "communication," and performs this transformation using film. She records the conversation and includes the viewer/audience in the experience through the workshop and workbook component. I first saw *The Way Home* in the context of a gathering in which several of the women from the councils participated in a question-answer dialogue with the audience, and Shakti Butler conducted a powerful and transformative workshop on anti-racism. The VHS video version includes a carefully thought-out set of exercises much like the workshop I participated in at Cal Poly, Pomona, a very sophisticated, updated consciousness-raising guide of sorts. This type of participatory filmmaking is precisely the shift from information to communication called for by Inayatullah and Milojevic.

The technology of film is not new, but the ability to make use of film with the intense power of visual images has long been available only to those with access to the incredibly expensive, incredibly complex apparatus of film. And that access has been controlled by a small group of elites (read: men with capital) who doled out the money and the knowledge of production that made filmmaking possible for only those like them. If technology is to be redemptive, access to and control of technologies—old and new—must be wrested from the control of the elites, whoever they may be.

While the possibilities of film in the hands of radical women are endless, they are also fixed within the context of current relations of power exercised in the control of the means of production. Technology will reify and reassert current relations of power unless something revolutionary is done. The means are still difficult to come by to make films that might undermine or even undo the control of white, particularly male, elites even using new and more accessible digital video. Reliance on grants and loans from large non-profits, and fund raising from those who already have little to spare is a difficult and time-consuming project in and of itself. The potential for social transformation, for the voices of radical women of color to be heard, resides in the collective model of groups like Kitchen Table Press, Web Grrls, and the Guerrilla Girls of the art world, as well as Shakti Butler's work in film. With computers, CDs, and digital video, the means of communicative production has become more affordable, ubiquitous, and accessible. The potential resides in the act of women sharing with other women how to use the new technologies—how to write computer code, how to frame a film shot, how to create text using desktop publishing software, and how to write the grants that will make these new skills deployable.

Nevertheless, in this act of sharing, in this collective model, the original goals of *This Bridge* and *The Way Home* cannot be lost. Both seek to expose racism and sexism, and their relationship to each other and to each of us (the troubled "we"). And so the sharing, the conversation—in print, on film, with computers, and at conferences, workshops, and gatherings—will continue to be about identities, power, oppression, racism, sexism, homophobia, and exclusion. It is not only that the dialogue takes place, but that the conversation continues exploring the stories of who we are and how we came to be, as well as what we want to be and what the world should be. As with *This Bridge Called My Back*, the possibilities of *The Way Home* are both endless and truncated—endless if we are willing to be changed, truncated when we refuse to hear each other—despite the voices of transformation all around. We have come so far from the bridge, only to find that the way home is a return across that same bridge.

forty-eight

The Ricky Ricardo Syndrome: Looking for Leaders, Finding Celebrities

Rosa Maria Pegueros

"Lucy! Would you 'splain something to me?!" Ricky Ricardo's Cuban accent punctuated many of the harebrained schemes hatched by his wife in the classic television comedy show *I Love Lucy*. Desi Arnaz's Ricky Ricardo was flustered yet suave, elegant, and talented, a band leader wearing full white shirts that evoked pirates of the Caribbean. His on-screen persona masked his deep involvement in the production of the weekly series, possibly the most successful show in television's history. He talked funny, his appearance was exotic, and he had a glamorous job in New York City during the pre-Castro "good old days" when his home-town, Havana, symbolized licentiousness and general decadence. Lucy, played by Lucille Ball, was the classic screwball comedienne: a cross between a redheaded clown and Hollywood's dumb blonde, but oh, what timing! In moments of frustration with Lucy, Desi would break into a torrent of Cuban Spanish that was hilarious even if you could not understand the language.

Aside from Ralph Cramden, the bus driver character in *The Honeymooners*, Ricky Ricardo may have been the only TV husband of that era who worked; we never knew what most screen husbands did for a living. Unlike Ralph Cramden and middle-class husbands like Robert

Young (*Father Knows Best*), Ward Cleaver (*Leave It to Beaver*), or Ozzie Nelson (*Ozzie and Harriet*), whose relationships with their wives were so sanitized that audiences might wonder where their pesky children came from, Ricky was the Latin Lover. While the other TV husbands began as married men with ready-made families, Ricky and Lucy had a television pregnancy and were shown in their bedroom—albeit with twin beds—breaking TV taboos in both instances. Despite his essential role in the *I Love Lucy* plotline, ultimately Ricky was expendable, and so was Arnaz. After their real-life divorce, Lucille Ball went on to make two more TV series without him—though she never found a foil as effective as Desi Arnaz.

Ricky Ricardo offers an excellent metaphor for Latino intellectuals, particularly those engaging in the vociferous and often poisonous discussions of racial and ethnic equality. Like Ricky Ricardo, they come from a rich culture and, although deeply involved in U.S. culture, remain secondary to the main characters on the stage: the whites of European ancestry who have been the majority in the United States through most of its history and the African-American descendants of the slaves forcibly brought here during the seventeenth, eighteenth, and nineteenth centuries.

In public debates over race, the term *people of color* includes Americans from many racial and ethnic backgrounds, but the only intellectuals of color seen on television (the most universally accessed medium) are African Americans like Jesse Jackson, Henry Louis Gates, or Cornel West. Latino/as[1]—when they participate *as Latinos* in the discussion—tend to be the few who are "acceptable" to mainstream America—like Richard Rodriguez, who appears regularly on the *Jim Lehrer Newshour* (PBS), and Linda Chavez, a regular on *To the Contrary* (PBS)—those who in theory and practice call for assimilation into mainstream America, for leaving behind our language and customs. Every African American knows who Jesse Jackson is, but most U.S. Latinos wouldn't recognize Chavez or Rodriguez if they tripped over them. This is not to say, however, that there are no other high-visibility Latino celebrities. Actors Hector Elizondo, Jimmy Smits, and A Martinez are all well-known figures.

Neither Desi Arnaz nor his Ricky Ricardo would have considered himself a "person of color," since he had coloring that reflected his Spanish heritage rather than that of the mulatto or Afro-Cuban groups constituting perhaps a fifth of the population in pre-revolutionary Cuba. Like Ricky, the members of Florida's Cuban emigré community (from the middle and upper classes who rejected Castro's revolution) do not consider themselves people of color. Their "whiteness," their higher class status, and their conservative political leanings (because Republican administrations have traditionally been seen as anti-Communist) set them apart from other Latinos in this country. Two Cuban refugees, Gloria Estefan and Andy Garcia, attained high visibility during the shipwreck survivor Elian Gonzalez's sojourn in the United States, castigating the actions of both the U.S. and Cuban governments. Although they did exploit their celebrity status to highlight their Cuban community's desires, these Latinos can't be regarded as leaders.

If Latinos were to drop out of the national discussion, no one would miss us. When experts appear on television to give an opinion on an issue of the day, whether they come from the political right or left, they are (with the exceptions of Rodriguez and Chavez) always black or white. This polarization demonstrates U.S. culture's unwillingness to recognize its growing cultural pluralism. Moreover, it reflects a stubborn resistance to acknowledge the shift from a predominantly white populace to one in which the population of non-white minorities together will be larger than that of whites, and in which Latinos will thus be in the majority.

Each minority has a small group of conservatives who advocate alliance with the right wing. This alliance is mystifying until one reflects on the slow progress of change for anyone in the United States who is not white, male, and middle or upper class. In the last three elections, Democrats have moved ostensibly to the political center, but actually to the right. Both Bill Clinton and Al Gore are conservative Democrats. Black U.S. conservatives include Clarence Thomas and Alan Keyes; the anti-abortion movement has Norma McCorvey ("Roe" of the 1973 U.S. Supreme Court decision legalizing abortion, *Roe v. Wade*); the women's movement has Phyllis Schafly. We Latino/as have Linda Chavez and Richard Rodriguez, the dynamic duo of Latino ambivalence. In practice, we—Latino activists on the political left—have demonized them for their apparent lack of commitment and identification with our vision. Yet to the segment of educated Americans who watch public television, they represent Latino culture. Unlike high-profile African Americans like Myrlie Evers, Vernon Jordan, Charlayne Hunter-Gault, and Benjamin Hooks, they do not represent the commitment to civil rights. They are not confrontational like Jesse Jackson or Cecil Williams; not brilliant, well-educated, and committed to racial equality like Angela Davis, Patricia Williams, Lani Guinier, or bell hooks. Chavez and Rodriguez declare that they are more like mainstream (white) America than they are like the black civil rights activists, and complain openly of being lumped together with such troublemakers. Why are there strong black voices for change, but the Latino community has no nationally recognized leaders speaking out against the assimilationists?

Recently, I revisited Rodriguez's and Chavez's writings when a student asked me to direct her independent study on Latin American identity. This was a bit unusual for me. My field is Latin American history, but I don't teach about Latin Americans in the United States; keeping track of twenty countries and over five hundred years keeps me quite busy. However, since there was no one else she could ask and she was a good student who had taken several classes with me, I agreed.

I was struck by the explosion in Latino/Chicano literature and fiction during the last fifteen years. Cuban, Mexican, and Dominican Americans, Puerto Ricans, and Nuyoricans are producing a literature of identity—that is, works that highlight one's coming to terms with being Latina/o in the U.S. There are also theoretical works: from *This Bridge Called My Back, Loving in the War Years, Borderlands/La Frontera,* and *Making Face, Making Soul/Haciendo Caras,* to philosophical writings by María Lugones, history by Rudy Acuña, José Gomez-Quiñones, and George J. Sanchez, among many others. I had an embarrassment of riches to choose from, and I could dismiss Rodriguez and Chavez out of hand. Yet I couldn't adequately address the breadth of Latino concerns without grappling with them, if for no other reason than their recognition inside and outside the Latino community as representing a particularly Latino perspective.

Technically speaking, neither our academics and public intellectuals nor the duo can be considered *leaders*. In the late twentieth century and early twenty-first century, heroes, sports stars, movie stars, celebrities, and leaders/spokespersons are those obstreperous enough to call attention to themselves. The word *leader* implies that someone is following, that there is a movement or a community of some kind and the leader is at its head. A leader has a vision that inspires people to follow; she or he has goals or objectives and a strategy with which to carry out those plans. Those identified by the media as leaders or spokepersons generally bear little relationship to a real leader. One example of a media-anointed feminist leader is Gloria Steinem. While Steinem has had a lively career as a gadfly, writer, and magazine editor, she has never held herself up as a leader or claimed to speak for the "feminist movement." Yet when a woman's issue arises, she is often asked for her opinion, which is then presented to the public as the voice of feminism—not just the voice of one white, middle-class, middle-aged feminist. A better example of a leader is the Reverend Jesse Jackson, whose lifelong commitment to civil rights coupled with his activism as the head of PUSH and later the Rainbow Coalition reflect his vision of a multiracial, pluralistic, non-violent society.

There are three major obstacles to nationally recognized Latino leadership in the United States. First, there is not one Latino community, but many. The Cuban emigrés in Miami, the Chicanos in East Los Angeles whose families were in California before the United States annexed the western states, and the new Central American refugees in Washington, D.C., have vastly different needs and concerns, and they are only three of the many Latino groups in the U.S. Second, Latinos do not have the network of educational institutions (such as the historically black colleges) to support and strengthen Latino identity. Our leaders' development is very diffuse. Finally, the continual immigration from Latin America in response to political conflicts, natural disasters, and economic uncertainty means that Latino communities are always in flux. At this writing, Latinos still rank below African Americans in successful completion of high school, bachelor's degree programs, and doctoral programs. The diverse cultures, political backgrounds, aspirations, and economic classes make the idea of a strong figurehead like the Reverend Jesse Jackson for Latinos highly unlikely. In a word, Ricky Ricardo and the late Farm Workers Union president Cesar Chavez would have little connecting them besides language and religion.

How then did Richard Rodriguez capture the attention of the media and white U.S. intellectuals? His books *Hunger of Memory* and *Days of Obligation* were graced with a stunning writing style. These books elegantly detailed the journey of the child of migrant farm workers through America's educational system. A contemporary Hamlet, Richard began to realize that his brilliance won scholastic opportunities for him that were denied to his less intellectually gifted peers. By the time he finished his Ph.D. in British literature, he claims that he was no longer able to speak his native tongue and his relations with family members were reduced, in his words, to polite interviews. Worst of all, when he was courted by a number of top-ranked universities, he was overwhelmed by guilt when he realized that his non-Latino friends did not have the same opportunities. When one of them confronted him, attributing his success to affirmative action and the color of his skin, he declined the job offers and left academia. His choice haunts me.

If every Latino academic quit because of attacks by classmates for the opportunities given to us or because we could not bear to be associated with affirmative action policies, there would be no Latino academics. As for every person of color who has tried to make his or her way in academia, the waters have been filled with other, sometimes bigger, fish, vying for the same few morsels. In abandoning the chance to do what he really loved—teaching and writing about British literature at the university level—and instead pursuing a career as a writer of popular culture, Rodriguez achieved what few Latinos have: media as a public spokesman for the Latino community. Ironically, he is an occasional essayist on the *Jim Lehrer Newshour*, a program distinguished by the participation of a true civil rights heroine, Charlayne Hunter-Gault, the first black woman to desegregate the University of Georgia. Yet Rodriguez would be unlikely to consider himself a Latino leader. His tortured ambivalence does not invite followers. His commentaries are distinctive for their thoughtful and idiosyncratic qualities; his identity is that of a citizen of the world, beholden only to his own intellectual development.

Linda Chavez's connection with the Latino community is even more tenuous. Growing up in Colorado, the daughter of a white mother and Latino father but raised by her mother alone, Chavez seems determined to put as much distance as she can between herself and the Latino community, even championing the English-only movement. She has not forgotten how to speak Spanish; she never knew how. She has not rejected the community of her childhood; she was never part of a Latino community. Her book *Out of the Barrio: Towards a New Politics of Hispanic Assimilation* echoes the beliefs of those who think that Latinos should disappear into the mainstream as quickly as possible. *"Out of the barrio"*; *"new politics"*; *"Hispanic"*; *"assimilation":* even the title pushes her away from the family table. Latino culture's rich vitality is apparently lost on Chavez. Her political conservatism is not conserving anything of value to us. Quisiera decirle ¡no vez que tienes el nopal en la frente![2]

Both Rodriguez and Chavez call to mind the famous letter from the late federal judge Leon Higginbotham to Clarence Thomas during the Senate Judiciary hearing: "You call yourself conservative but what are you trying to conserve? The legacy of slavery, hatred, and bigotry? The political inequality of your own people?"

It is a well-worn complaint that the U.S. government and society treat Latinos as if we were monolithic. Latin American communities in the United States are many microcosms of the twenty countries from which we came. While many Latinos are first-generation immigrants fleeing civil unrest or extreme impoverishment, millions have been here for generations. Indeed, the western third of the contiguous United States was the northern half of Mexico until 1848. In terms of race, the situation is even more complicated: in appearance, some Latino/as are as white as the first Europeans to arrive in this hemisphere; a large number—particularly those from the Caribbean and Brazil—are mulattos, that is, of mixed African and Iberian (Spanish or Portuguese) descent; in Mexico and the Andes, of mixed indigenous, African, and Spanish ancestry; and in a few other countries, of mixed indigenous and Spanish stock. Our Latino/a heritage is varied, multicultural, religiously pluralistic, and syncretic. I have only begun to realize how little community we actually have, how splintered our interests are, and how damaging to our future this fragmentation is.

Benedict Anderson, in his famous book on the origin and spread of nationalism, defines a nation as an imagined community. Anderson's nation is *imagined* because it exists only in the minds of members who will never actually meet all their fellow members or even hear of them. It is *limited* because it exists within certain boundaries, and there are others outside its boundaries. The number of members, though large and elastic, is not infinite. While U.S. Latinos are part of only one culture within a nation of many cultures, we lack the cohesiveness and mutual empathy needed to claim a single Latino community.

Nor can Latinos claim sovereignty, another characteristic of nationhood. Indeed, any discussion of Latin American countries' sovereignty must include an examination of the United States' hegemony in the region. Whether it has supported brutally repressive dictatorships such as Manuel Noriega's in Panama or the kleptocracy of the Somoza family in Nicaragua; the overthrow of democratically elected leaders such as Jacobo Arbenz of Guatemala and Salvador Allende of Chile; the U.S. Marines' attempts to hunt down Pancho Villa in Mexico or Agosto Sandino in Nicaragua; or the embargo against Cuba and the assassination attempts on Fidel Castro, the United States has not allowed the Western Hemisphere's southern countries to be completely autonomous. Puerto Rico, until 1898 a colony of Spain, passed into U.S. hands as a territory when Spain lost the Cuban-Spanish-American War. Finally, nation is imagined as a community because, regardless of the actual inequality and exploitation that may prevail in each, the nation is conceived as a deep horizontal comradeship.

Whatever the vast numbers of people of Latino heritage may be, we are not a single community. *We are too diverse, and we keep insisting on our diversity.* From the stubborn Cuban emigrés in Miami's "Little Havana," to Gloria Molina's Los Angeles, we see little inclination or desire to join in common cause or to imagine ourselves as part of one community. There are too many different communities with particular interests and class divisions. And while it is well-known that the original Cuban emigrés set themselves apart from other Latino communities for economic and political reasons, they are not the only ones to do so. On my own campus, I've witnessed tension among the Puerto Rican, Dominican, and Colombian students. When I was a graduate student at UCLA, I saw similar difficulties between recent Salvadoran, Guatemalan, and Mexican immigrants and the older established Mexican community. While some groups may see themselves as part of a single community with a common interest, the class, racial, and ethnic differences among us are quite profound and will not easily bend to a notion of community. Latinos are not the only ones with this problem. Asian Americans, with their old Chinese and Japanese communities, the second generation of Korean immigrants, and the waves of new Hmong, Cambodian, Laotian, Thai, and Indian immigrations face similar difficulties. America can handle anything, it seems, but complexity.

For me, the paradox is that at the historical moment when Latinos are about to achieve the critical mass needed to have a real impact on U.S. society, when we will have the greatest political and economic clout we have ever had, and when the backlash against our very existence is the greatest, we are not only fractious and divided, but we have no recognizable leaders and little motivation to find common cause with other Latino communities. Cesar Chavez is dead, and middle-class Latinos might have had some difficulty identifying with the leader of a migrant farm workers' union; he is honored more since his death than he was in life. Henry Cisneros is in disgrace and lying low. Only New Mexico's Bill Richardson maintains a high profile, first as U.S. Ambassador to the United Nations and now as Secretary of Energy. Until the security breaches at the Los Alamos nuclear research facility (regarded to be within his purview) ruined his chances, he was touted as one of Al Gore's possible choices for vice president. Representative Loretta Sanchez, a Democrat from California, slayer of Tyrannosaurus rex Robert Dornan, may be the last Latina ever to win a congressional race if the Republicans keep throwing money into the efforts to unseat her.

Chavez and Rodriguez are distinguished by their deliberate refusal to identify with any kind of a Latino community. While not willing to go as far as singer Michael Jackson to mask the color of their skin, they have clearly staked a claim on the area outside Latino communities and concerns, beating the drums for Latino assimilation. Few who continue to identify with Latino communities can break into the mainstream discourse as Latinos. Latina intellectuals who use both languages in their writings, such as Moraga and Anzaldúa, are even further from the discussion. The only visible Latinos are accomplished individuals who happen to be Latinos. Could it be that our numbers and diversity defy the popular American desire for simplicity?

There are only two high-visibility Latinos in the news media: Ray Suarez, late of NPR's *Talk of the Nation* and now a co-host of the *Lehrer Newshour*, is a new face on television, while the other—ubiquitous with his cable and network television shows—is one I have a very hard time claiming: Geraldo Rivera. Rivera began his career as an investigative reporter in 1970 for New York's WABC's *Eyewitness News*. Eventually, he became the host of one of the most irresponsible, sensationalistic, and almost pornographic television talk programs. Rivera earned my grudging respect during the O. J. Simpson trial. In his nightly coverage, while he did not sympathize with Simpson, he doggedly brought up issues of racial discrimination with his interviewees. It was clear from his reactions that he was shocked by the depth of racism in this country.[3] Recently, he expressed a desire to run for mayor of New York. His employers at MSNBC quickly intervened, telling him that a mayoral campaign would interfere with his job. Rivera withdrew his name from consideration.

Mentioning Geraldo Rivera in the same breath as Gloria Anzaldúa and Cherríe Moraga seems almost sacrilegious. If Latino intellectuals could vote for a spokesperson, there is no question in my mind that one of these women would win the vote. But we are dealing with a much larger forum, in which Rivera is a star and probably the only Latino opinion-maker known to the general public; being known, however, is not the same thing as being liked or trusted. But few Latinos have *any* national standing.

In a recent Internet poll on Latino.com, the "Latino Link," readers were asked to identify the one hundred most influential Hispanics of the twentieth century. Leading the list were: (1) Cesar Chavez, (2) Che Guevara, (3) Edward James Olmos, (4) Gloria Estefan, (5) the recently deceased bandleader and Latin jazz star Tito Puente; (6) the murdered Latin rock star Selena; (7) Ricky Martin, the swivel-hipped rocker; (8) movie star Jennifer Lopez, and (9) Latin Tropical and Salsa star Marc Anthony (10). The next ten nominees included Emiliano Zapata, Pancho Villa, Fidel Castro, Rigoberta Menchu, Frida Kahlo, and several movie stars and musicians. Many readers nominated their parents, uncles, aunts, and grandparents. The web master highlighted the president of the Southwest Voter Registration Project (SVREP), Antonio Gonzalez, recently selected by *Hispanic Business Magazine* as one of their one hundred most influential Hispanics.[4]

At a time when we could have real clout, the ambivalence between the desire to maintain our customs and language and the desire to assimilate runs very deep. It makes Latinos hard to pin down and hard to define. We must find a way to break free of the stereotypes and marginalization that prevent us from being the movers and shakers of U.S. society. I have no answers, but in raising the questions I hope that a clear-eyed generation of Latinos responds and helps us to find the way to the future—and to center stage.

Notes

1. I use *Latino/a* rather than the more limiting *Chicano/a*, which refers only to U.S.-born Mexican Americans, or *Hispanic*, an official U.S. government term used in the census and other government statistics but without universal acceptance among the residents to whom it refers.

2. *Can't you see the imprint of a Mexican cactus on your own forehead?*

3. While his father is Puerto Rican, his mother is Jewish. Geraldo Rivera was once known as Gerry Rivers, a fact usually mentioned to discredit him and imply that he is trading on his Latino roots.

4. See www.latino.com/community/heritage/#countdown.

forty-nine

Survival

Jeanette Aguilar

i / come / from a long line / of

        healers
        curanderas
        jotos / jotas
        mujeres-hombres
        y hombres-mujeres—
        queers.

Proud, accepted, honored
Then they came
Colonization, genocide, catholicism
Came with the Spaniards, and etc.
          etc.
             etc. . . .

on every continent
    every nation
        they raped us
        they burned us
        they killed us
        they colonized us—
        and *still* we survive.

All through out history
we have been here—
everywhere
in every movement for liberation,
every struggle for freedom
i have marched through *his*/story
with fist raised high
and voice unleashed

'69
i was / a faggot / marícon / marímacha / jota / dyke / butch / femme / drag
queen / queer.
we were / colored queer
we were / colored queens
"perverts" & queerz / transgender warriors
in heels w/ bricks in hand

'69
police riot
fires burned for 5 days
i was / *beaten* by the pigs
i was / *arrested* / *raped* / *dehumanized*
they tried to break me, my spirit—
yet we made revolution that night
they oppress us
and *still* we survive.

In every culture, every history, every city
we exist / we live / we work / we struggle / we fuck / we love
and *still* we make revolution
w/i and w/o
they're still trying
to silence us
jail us
burn us
rape us
kill us
tell us we are sick
          unnatural
             against "god"
that we have no right to even exist / to LIVE
and *still* we survive

so remember this—(like Michael said):
      "you can't pay for culture
          it can only be experienced"
(and like Gloria said):
      queer is not just a sexual life
      it is a political life
      it is a social life
      it is a revolutionary life / force

they got us down—
but we *will* survive

Thanks to Michael Franti and Gloria Anzaldúa for their inspiration.
6/5/99

fifty

Imagining Differently: The Politics of Listening in a Feminist Classroom

Sarah J. Cervenak, Karina L. Cespedes, Caridad Souza, and Andrea Straub

The threat of difference has been no less blinding to people of Color.
—Audre Lorde

For us the statement that "life is complicated" means that the process of sharing knowledge about our lives is also complex.[1] Writing this chapter has been complicated because we examine our experience in a class on U.S. Latina feminisms in the spring semester of 1998 at a northeastern university. All of us, separately and from different social locations, found ourselves questioning class dynamics as it became fraught with various contradictions regarding its goals and those of U.S. Latina feminisms.[2] This essay arises from our frustrations about class members' failure to listen to each other, and about the larger sociopolitical and cultural practices further challenging our claims to voice.[3] We each came to this class with a particular commitment to feminist theory and praxis emerging from and responding to the complexities of engaged living.[4] As a feminist educator, Caridad's goal has been to facilitate the emergence of learning communities and support a learning process that is both critical *and* pleasurable as intellectual engagement.[5] She envisioned the class as a space where participants could share knowledge and strategies for feminist praxes in a supportive, noncompetitive way. For Andrea, the class was a way to explore feminism, the meaning and construction of a feminist identity. She was interested in talking with other women about transnational, multicultural, and multiracial alliances, and thought the class would attract women with similar politics willing to explore these ideas. Karina was seeking the work and insights of feminists of color, hoping to find a language through which to express and explore the complexities of liminality, of being always-already an outsider within. Sarah's commitment to feminism always requires a consistent analysis of the complexities of people's psychic and material lives, and acknowledges that each is nurtured by the intersectional nexus of race, class, gender, and sexuality. For her, the class became a potential space to engage the work of feminists of color at the forefront of articulating those complexities and the in-between moments of schizophrenia they imply.

It was among the pages of *This Bridge Called My Back* that each of us first encountered a blueprint for dialogue across the boundaries of difference, one that could "coax us into the habit of listening and learning each other's ways of seeing and being" (Bambara, iv). We each experienced multiple moments of cross-identification with the complexities *Bridge*'s contributors have described.[6] The book also became an important catalyst for the contradictions in class discussions. Since in our opinion one of *Bridge*'s most important messages is that we attend to and critically examine internal differences along with those across groups, we decided to collectively think through how the homogenization of experience through narratives of authenticity and binary ways of thinking operates among people who want to develop oppositional practices that challenge the status quo.

This chapter is further complicated by our attempt to critique existing cultural nationalist and hegemonic feminist paradigms of listening and learning in order to develop new ways of understanding solidarity. Contrary to some class members' perception, we all came to that classroom with different ways of speaking and different theoretical paradigms that helped us make sense of our past(s) and our hopes for the future. The narratives of authenticity that circulated in our class maintained an understanding of Latinidad as oppositional only through an allegedly nontheoretical posture where visibility was synonymous with demonstrating "experience" as a group member.[7] Framing Latinidad in this way excluded Latinas and African-American and white women who questioned the terms of that authenticity by raising concerns about the different sites, including the classroom, where power operates and difference is ultimately suppressed. Our experiences demonstrate how even subordinated people often misrecognize themselves and each other through rigid understandings about who people are and their potential for change.[8] Misrecognition took the form of cynical glances, snickering, occasional laughter, and a resistance to the insight that there are multiple ways of articulating the pains of oppression and exploitation. Yet those of us who resisted attempts to homogenize experience were tagged as unapologetically operating in collusion with the State's efforts to silence people of color.

Writing this essay has required that we approach the laughter and interrupted conversations critically to explore both what they hide and what they show. It has challenged us to unearth those hidden components referred to by Lorde as the dark spaces of paralysis and possibility housing a potential for change. Our attempts to imagine "something else," a shared utopic space where difference is recognized not only between and among established categories of race, class, gender, and sexuality but also *in-between* those categories, have made us incomprehensible to our colleagues.[9] That is, we were not understood, not recognized for what and who we are and how we define ourselves. These shared moments of incomprehensibility led us to question how it is that some bodies and lives become more readily understandable or "real" while those of others remain unintelligible. We have also had moments of "craziness" that result from trying to imagine that "something else" in the gap between the so-called margin and center. We reside and mobilize somewhere within that gap, which we envision as the place between what goes unsaid in cultural nationalist and hegemonic feminist discourses and our hopes for sustained material change. Only beyond these formations can we regain our sanity.

We propose that recognizing each other's complex personhood initiates the process of listening and learning that opens us to new visions of solidarity from which new political praxes can emerge. We also want to reveal the various problems within oppositional practices, feminist or otherwise, that limit our understanding of difference by reproducing the very homogenizations and binaries these practices set out to critique. Some readers will experience discomfort from our attempts to disrupt the binaries they may (however unconsciously) perpetuate. Our hope is that these readers will risk venturing along with us and come to appreciate our struggle to discern alternate political practices. Others may even recognize something about their own condition in this telling, something about their own search for new ways of seeing and being in the world. We offer these musings as a way to affirm that even for those who stand outside established frameworks of comprehensibility, spaces for clarity do exist.

The Complicated Terrain of One Feminist Classroom

To more precisely understand the operation of what Avery Gordon calls the "eccentric traces of power's presence" (25) we turn to the feminist classroom. As an oppositional site within the academy, a feminist classroom's location within the State reflects the very complexities we want to nuance. It also allows us to highlight the muddled contradictory workings of power that might include, for example, the capacity of any class member, whether student or teacher, either to further a state agenda or to work against it. Opposition to the educational system's norms grows out of early confrontations with racist, sexist, and elitist assumptions in that education. The U.S. educational system positions subordinated people into a counterstance since, outside the Family, school is one of the first places where subordinated people learn rituals of control through the arbitrary exercise of power. As hooks notes, instead of being a place where learning is pleasurable, education becomes a place of punishment, confinement, and control (*Teaching,* 4). Prevailing educational models still promote authoritarian hierarchies that position teachers/professors as the only legitimate transmitters of knowledge. To be a critical thinker, one who questions established assumptions and mores, is to be a threat to authority. For education to have possibilities beyond intellectual subjugation, it must engage alternate ways of conceptualizing what and how we learn. That is, pedagogical approaches must encourage the development of learning communities that sustain efforts to promote excitement about a collective process of learning. Members play an active role in discovering and evaluating information, creating cultural and social facts, and producing knowledge. They question *all* received categories and assumptions to transform their personal anecdotes into critical reflections by *connecting* them to larger sociopolitical, historical, and economic contexts. Ideally, an engaged learning environment supports respectful and sensitive explorations of cross-cultural/racial inequality and difference informed by a theoretical and empirical base that also attends to current reality.

Our class's structural and social power valence made it different from other women's studies courses in some important ways. As an elective in an ethnic studies department, two-thirds of the students were Latinas of various classes, colors, ideologies, and sexualities. The other third included women of African-American, African-Caribbean, non-Latina mestiza, and European descent. Only one (queer) Latino took the course. While many class members were ethnic studies majors, many more were not. As often happens in ethnic and women's studies departments, students have a wide range of educational and intellectual preparation and interests. One important course goal was to explore whether U.S. Latina feminists' critical and creative writings might be useful for our feminist praxes outside the classroom. The course reading list self-consciously included a variety of narrative genres from the social sciences and humanities.[10] This reading list was not a comprehensive approach to U.S. Latina feminist thought since that experience is still largely undocumented. Instead, it was meant to guide the class toward Latina feminist thinkers, and situate their work within their appropriate feminist and national/ethnic contexts in order to elicit comparative insights about how different Latinas produce feminist theory and praxis.

As the instructor, Caridad proceeded from the notion that all class members bring personal and specialized knowledge from their academic, intellectual, occupational, and life experiences to bear upon a particular subject. Everyone has some type of knowledge that adds nuance to what we read, think, and discuss. A secondary goal was to create the type of learning community allowing all participants to develop a vision of feminist praxis that reflected the historical and cultural moment of class members in a collectively written document. Assuming a connection between biography, history, and social structures, the course attempted to connect the theoretical ideas discussed within the readings to people's everyday lives, and vice versa. Such a process requires that, as students, we take seriously the questioning and cross-referencing of analytical and experiential codes, and the theorizing of empirical work to rethink our approaches to and assumptions about contemporary cultural and economic worlds.

"We/They" Binaries and Other('s) Narratives of Authenticity

Although we understand the feminist classroom as a site for oppositional thinking and learning that potentially mitigates against state narratives, it is not without its own inherent contradictions. Perhaps because our class was located within an educational institution emphasizing upward mobility based on a corporate model, there was a bias toward notions of identity consistent with corporate understandings of the world. Along with these more commodified notions of identity grounded in consumption practices, many people entered the class with ideas about identity also informed by families, national/ethnic communities, the media, and campus student organizations (Greek and non-Greek). Specific choques developed, resulting from some class members' desire for an uncomplicated sense of unity believed possible through engaging in a national/ethnic, and presumably feminist, counterstance. Class members expected instant unity based on a notion of Latinidad that perceived others through the lens of homogenized experience and ignored difference. Some class members (authors included) objected to how these attempts to establish unity erased the multiplicity of difference.

One way binary thinking occurred was through the discourse of Sisterhood, a term fraught with various political difficulties. Both hegemonic feminist and cultural nationalist ideologies draw the line around liberatory personhood by excluding racialized ethnic, economic, and queer identities.[11] Second-wave feminism, for example, has rhetorically marked gender as the only site where struggle occurs. Sisterhood became a rallying cry for political mobilization, leaving a powerful narrative of white-normative authenticity unchecked. Such calls for unity under the rubric of gender identity ignored how we can become women in ways other than in opposition to men (Alarcón, "Theoretical Subject(s)"). In this instance, Sisterhood meant the exclusion of marginalized women based on race/ethinicity, class, sexuality, age, and/or physical ability. Similarly, "Sisterhood" among cultural nationalists invokes racialized claims to authenticity that valorize a "connection" with an imagined, national/ethnic community along the lines of sameness based on oppression and common interests. Sisterhood in this context is grounded in bourgeois, masculinist notions of family, and promotes communal modes of engagement recognizing race or class struggles while excluding (female) gender, (homo)sexuality, and nonfamilial modes of experience. Both ideologies homogenize in ways that reproduce the coercive and repressive mechanisms of the state narratives they resist.

Feminists of color have challenged hegemonic feminists and cultural nationalists by marking the complexity of the multiple differences they live. Sometimes this challenge entails a critique of the exclusively white female body constructed by second-wave feminist homogenization of the category "woman." Other times it might mean confronting sexism or homophobia within class- and/or race-based political collectivities. Such multiple contestations provide the type of spaces from which works like *Bridge* emerged. However, despite its contributions to the dialogue about political engagement across difference, many of us remain locked in oppositional practices preventing the mode of listening and learning that *This Bridge* advocates. Moving beyond this practice necessitates looking inward to excavate the master's face within each of us. For the condition of subordination does not prevent us from reproducing similar dynamics of power. Put differently, "even those who haunt our dominant institutions and their systems of value are haunted too by things they sometimes have names for and sometimes do not" (Gordon, 5). The haunted do not readily have names for their own abuses of power, nor do they always provide self-representations that critically address them. Instead, they rely on a "we/they" binary where the "we" functions as an undifferentiated group and "they" becomes all those whose separateness from the group somehow entails collusion with the State. Such representations render the two opposing sides recognizable through simplistic understandings of social existence that dehumanize those labeled "we," those labeled "they," and those who remain outside or resist this homogenizing gesture.

Unraveling the relations of power among and between whites and people of color means critiquing narratives of authenticity that homogenize—or make same—"experience" in the name of unity. According to Lorde, "the need for unity is often misnamed as a need for homogeneity"

(*Sister,* 119). Sisterhood in our class drew on an essentialized notion of Latinidad that assumes it is natural, innate, and easily recognizable. One class member, for example, stated: "I was looking for sisterhood in the class. If we are all Latinas, we share similar interests, similar oppressions. Why can't we connect?"[12] Such an uncritical use of Sisterhood invokes hierarchical and bourgeois familial ideologies that disavow the complex differences shaping Latina identities. While it is important to recognize how Sisterhood may provide an alternate space of self-loving and appreciation in the face of state repression, violence, and coercion, it is simultaneously a complicated haven that reproduces its own power dynamics.

In this case, "Latina Sisterhood" was premised on notions of groupness established within the larger context of Latina/o student life available on campus. One class member described her expectations about the course in the following manner: "I entered the classroom on U.S. Latina feminisms expecting to see a class full of Latinas. Of course, I'm going to feel a connection to a Latina more so than to someone who is white. There's a *culture* that connects us" (speaker's emphasis). This statement ignores color, class, sexual, linguistic, legal, regional, and national/ethnic identifications and differences, and assumes that a connection exists between Latinas with few or no prior affiliations. Such interpretations were challenged by class members who cautioned against assuming solidarity organized around one type of difference at the expense of other, equally important differences. They objected to the homogenization of what "unifies" Latinas or what connects "us." These objections were interpreted as hostile criticisms against the alleged unifying principle of Latinidad, and those class members were labeled incomprehensible in ways that stifled and halted dialogue. While the impulse toward this pan-ethnic unity did not succeed in creating a context for "connections" among us, it continually surfaced as a tactic of political engagement that imposed criteria for claiming group status.

For cultural critic Waneemah Lubiano the construction of "groupness" functions in contradictory ways in which both state and group agendas are intertwined to undermine the political efficacy of its oppositional strategy. She notes that "[Black] people who consciously think of themselves as part of a [Black] group often think of themselves as oppositional *at the very same time* as they are internalizing precisely the state's most effective narratives, narratives that are the mediums by which the state dominates the group in ways the group does recognize" (73; emphasis ours). Our class's construction of various disparate individuals into a "Latina group" shows how, in the very process of opposing them, we internalize state narratives created to dominate us. As our class polarized around two "self-consistent, but habitually incompatible frames" of "we" and "they," it became increasingly difficult to listen to and learn from one another. About such counterstances, Anzaldúa reminds us that "it is not enough to stand on the opposite river bank, shouting questions, challenging patriarchal, white conventions. A counterstance locks one into a duel of oppressor and oppressed; locked in mortal combat, like the cop and the criminal, both reduced to a common denominator of violence. . . . Because the counterstance stems from a problem with authority—outer as well as inner—it's a step toward liberation from cultural domination. But it is not a way of life" (*Borderlands,* 78). As a position of political opposition still determined by the reasoning and concerns of the originating stance, the counterstance can become mired in reactionism.[13] Although an important political necessity in the disruption of the normative logic, it should not be an end in itself. Power in such homogenized contexts operates through claims to authenticity that limit our ability to imagine new knowledges and resistances. Moving beyond the counterstance requires an excavation of our internal differences; once we begin to understand how we are different we are in a potentially better position to critically, but non-judgmentally, assess how another's difference shapes our own.

Ironically, some students used *Bridge* in their attempts to prevent this movement. Those most invested in automatic unity drew on *Bridge*, their personal experiences, and an understanding of theory as "white" to challenge those of us who advocated for a more nuanced understanding of difference.[14] *This Bridge* became an imperative for voice and testimonio, and was held up as an example of "true feminism" in ways that violated the spirit of its message. It was valued for its testimonial aspects with little regard for its profound theoretical insights about politics, boundaries, and difference. *This Bridge's* appropriation became a way to sanction a specific kind of Latinidad that some of us found contradictory. Such contradictions throughout the semester revealed how Latinidad could be performed as a complicated form of identity politics.

How Theorizing Is Not a Luxury

Coming to comprehensibility in our course also demanded that we maneuver an in-place theory/testimonio binary, one whose framework of inclusions and exclusions ultimately drew the line between the audible, recognizable "frontline" and the unreadable, inarticulate, and incomprehensible background. This conflict occurred around the uses and abuses of theory and testimonio. One class member began the day's discussion by questioning why others remained silent throughout much of the course, explaining her fear of speaking: "Theoretical works still confuse me. The terminology goes beyond a point where I can really grasp it." The ensuing discussion erupted in a conflictual session in which those interested in engaging the course material on its own terms with the texts' language were labeled "discursively exclusive." The readings were "too theoretical" and "a lot of people don't talk [in class] because . . . for some of us to understand theory we have to change to fit ourselves into [those ways of thinking and speaking]." Underlying this statement is the assumption that those remaining silent did not participate in any ideological or binary thinking. Yet the very maneuver to oppose "theoretical" works through silence, for fear of tainting or contaminating presumably more authentic ways of thinking and speaking, was itself very much grounded in theorizing about the presumed effects of theory. Theory became an essentialized category that inferred elite European male thinking.

Here, the idea that a "common language" makes us comprehensible emerged to counter discomforts regarding some course readings. Counterarguments suggested that we already use multiple language forms in our daily lives, and that the basis of everyday misunderstandings and miscommunications occur because we assume that we understand the meaning of everything spoken, when we often do not. Misunderstandings and miscommunication in our everyday lives necessitate listening more closely as well as asking questions that elicit the speaker's meaning. They require that we evaluate others' responses according to the meanings we hold about the particular words we use when we speak. Understanding the "theoretical language" of the Latina feminists' writings requires a similar commitment and process, in which you read closely to decipher and evaluate meanings within a particular context. The class's social dynamics demonstrated how although its members mouthed a respect for difference, their practice, in fact, masked an impulse toward sameness that felt coercive and surfaced in class members' hostility toward each other.

Academe devalues personal experience as a way of knowing while emphasizing the knowledge of "high" theory as the only "real" route toward making sense of the world. Such theory is used against people to silence, censor, humiliate, and devalue. Yet arguments that advocate throwing out all theory support a false dichotomy between theory and practice. Although there is nothing inherently liberatory about theory— for it does only what we ask of it—theorizing helps us discover "a place where one can presumably find a sanctuary, can imagine possible futures, a place where life [can] be lived differently" (hooks, *Teaching*, 61). While it has been used as an instrument of domination, "the production of theory as a social practice can [also] be liberatory" (65–67). Theorizing occurs in different contexts, in different ways, and toward different goals. When we internalize binary ways of thinking about theory, we understand it as collusion with the State and do not acknowledge its liberatory possibility.

Our perspective here resonates deeply with how Lorde understands poetry as "a vital necessity of our existence" that "forms the light within which we predicate our hopes and dreams toward survival and change, first made into language, then into idea, then into more tangible action" (*Sister,* 36). Theorizing is not a luxury for those of us who remain outside the comprehensibility of white-supremacist-capitalist-patriarchal narratives. In fact, historically theorizing has proven *vital* for thriving despite white-supremacist-capitalist-patriarchal State agendas. For queer, colored, and other disenfranchised people, theorizing is a crucial aspect of survival. "How else have we managed to survive with such spiritedness the assaults on our bodies, social institutions, countries, our very humanity?" (Christian, 336). Such spiritedness is especially crucial for working-class women of all backgrounds who have historically been prohibited from intellectual production by structural and cultural conventions locking them into particular life paths. Anzaldúa notes that writing "compensates for what the real does not give me . . . to record what others erase when I speak, to [rethink] the stories others have [misrepresented] about me, about you" ("Speaking," 169). We take a similar position about theorizing, especially from and with those works produced by U.S. feminists of color, which are often written against Eurocentric theory. Rendering ourselves comprehensible requires that we connect how we theorize in our everyday lives to theory's testimonial aspects. Such theorizing connects our feelings to our thoughts so that we can "transpose them into a language" and share them. Indeed, what such a process "makes more evident is the bond between the two—that ultimately reciprocal process wherein one enables the other" (hooks, *Teaching,* 61). Through listening to and respecting our feelings and our thoughts (as well as those of others), we can make the transformations in our behavior possible. Thus, our suggestion that theorizing is not a luxury should not be understood as promoting the sterile wordplay so often understood as theoretical work. For it is only through knowing our feelings and thinking about them critically that they "become sanctuaries and spawning grounds for the most radical and daring of ideas" (Lorde, *Sister,* 37).

During the course, attempts to express how theory and testimonio might inform each other were rejected as empty intellectualism and Eurocentric elitism. In a context in which reimagining the possibilities of political praxis required a critical dismantling of the counterstance, thinking about theory and testimonio as shaping and shaped by each other became impossible. Theory, hence theorizing, became something completely unrelated to lived experience, something "unreal" to those who spoke in "common" language. Whiteness was equated with the ability to theorize as a result of educational and institutional privileges. For instance, one person remarked, "I expect white people to speak theoretically." Implicit in this statement is the premise that Latinas, or other "non-whites," either do not or should not speak theoretically. The course readings, however, included a variety of theoretical languages (prose, poetry, and so on) and positions taken up by U.S. Latina feminists that demonstrated the many ways they theorize. Those class members interested in engaging the course material in relation to lived experiences by analyzing systemic, historical, and conceptual ideas were considered vendidas (sellouts) and deemed too "theoretical" in ways that whitened/lightened them within the classroom context. Among these were various straight, queer, working-class, and middle-class Latinas, African Americans, and white women. Literary critic Barbara Christian has argued that people of color have always theorized but in forms quite different from the western form of abstract logic (336). We prefer to think of theory and theorizing as processes alive and vibrant in us all, or as similar to what Lorde calls "poetry as illumination." Viewing theory as something only white people do accommodates those state narratives that associate thinking with people of European descent and body with the rest of the world. Neither binary is very useful and both lack complexity and nuance. Marxist philosopher Antonio Gramsci helps us understand the danger in relegating all intellectual production the sole domain of elite Europeans when he writes that "All [people] are intellectuals, one could therefore say: but not all people have in society the function of an intellectual" (9).[15] In other words, while not everyone functions socially as an intellectual whose primary job it is to theorize social reality, we all theorize our experience in some form.

Universalizing claims to knowing and understanding life, and how all of "us" sharing particular identifications experience it, encourages distrust of folks who offer alternative visions. In the classroom, the "authority of experience" becomes a way to assert voice that affirms presence and the right to speak. However, it simultaneously animates a power play of authoritarianism and hierarchy. In "Essentialism and Experience" hooks critiques the claim that the "authority of experience" is simply an essentialist move within classrooms used by people from historically oppressed groups (*Teaching*, 81). We agree with hooks and yet believe that the very discursive practice of "authority of experience" replicates, however oppositionally, the politics of state domination. Both the personal and the theoretical always complicate each other and serve as lenses for one another to reveal new possibilities for "truth/telling." And testimonio and experience alone are not enough to make solidarity among women/feminists of color possible. We must oppose those practices that construct experience in monolithic, essentialist ways without surrendering the power of experience upon which to build analysis or formulate theory. Theorizing is valuable in the search for new modes of interaction. It facilitates the process of coming to know feeling and experience and also allows experience to remain open to its endless possibilities—performative, written, and imagined—as a social and cultural text. As Henry A. Giroux argues, we must situate experience "within a theory of learning" because the combination of the analytical and experiential makes knowing richer (quoted in hooks, *Teaching*, 88–89). Otherwise, difference gets derailed, opening us to uncritical assumptions about facile allegiances and unities.

Respecting Difference: Toward a Politics of Engaged Living

Acknowledging that life is complicated (Gordon) means respecting differences across and within groups by recognizing the divisions already existing among us, and analyzing how they get produced. These divisions have real, material effects that show up in our interactions with each other, the respect and loving perception we show each other, and the arrogant perception and rudeness we mete out to those who don't conform to our sense of "reality," to sameness. Respect and appreciation for the integrity of difference allow us to love in complicated ways, acknowledging that our love for ourselves and each other is circuitous, growing deeper with the introduction of new knowledge. If we begin by embracing conflict and contradiction for what they can teach us, the elusive goal of unity becomes less important than the process of learning to listen.

We can move beyond the hostility and arrogant interactions we encountered in the classroom by activating what feminist philosopher María Lugones refers to as loving perception. A set of processes guided by our movements and by those who inhabit the worlds around us, loving perception encourages active listening and a willingness to grow ("Playfulness"). As a new way of seeing and thinking about the complexity of identification, loving perception respects the integrity of difference within and among identities otherwise rendered uncomplicated and readily comprehensible by white-supremacist and patriarchal-capitalist forces. As a loving praxis, it is deeply tied to the recognition of each other's complex personhood, "conferring the respect on others that comes from presuming that life and people's lives are simultaneously straightforward and full of enormously subtle meaning" (Gordon, 5). Complex personhood presumes that

> all people (albeit in specific forms whose specificity is sometimes everything) remember and forget, are beset by contradiction, and recognize and misrecognize themselves and others. Complex personhood means that people suffer gra-

ciously and selfishly too, get stuck in the symptoms of their troubles, and also transform themselves. Complex personhood means that even those called "Other" are never never that. Complex personhood means that the stories people tell about themselves, about their troubles, about ther social worlds, and about their society's problems are entangled and weave between what is immediately available as a story and what their imaginations are reaching toward. Complex personhood means that people get tired and some are just plain lazy. Complex personhood means that groups of people will act together, and that they will vehemently disagree with and sometimes harm each other, and that they will do both at the same time and expect the rest of us to figure it out for ourselves, intervening and withdrawing as the situation requires. (4)

Taking seriously "the stories people tell about themselves" and the ways they tell them opens multiple spaces for self-recognition, and carves out loving worlds structured by the creative and critical practice of listening and learning. In our course on U.S. Latina feminisms, complex personhood depends upon the possibility that Karina's working-class, liminal, pro-revolutionary Cubanness ruptures nation in ways that help Andrea's Irish/German working-class south shore Long Island's discomforts about un/conscious racialized class privilege teach Ana's Cuban/Mexican middle-class self something about solidarity. Complex personhood means that Sarah's Irish/Slovakian, working-class, central Jerseyness doesn't need to fill Caridad's ears with narratives of air mattresses, velour couches, and impostor sneakers for Caridad to know what Sarah *means* when Sarah speaks about feeling the beauty in Chela Sandoval's utopian manifesto. Complex personhood taps into and extends our visions of utopia through its rendering politically significant the smiles and nods, the shady glances, and the inarticulate moments. It illuminates the overlapping contours of our dreams that comes from the labor of "know[ing] where we live in order to imagine living elsewhere [and] imagining living elsewhere before we can live there" (Sandoval, "U.S. Third World Feminism," 5). If we refuse to engage our imagination's productive potential we stifle its growth, allowing ourselves to disavow "those people" outside both dominant and oppositional frameworks of comprehensibility. This disavowal reflects a commitment to not see, hear, or acknowledge the potential for those rendered unintelligible (unhearable, unseeable) to tell the truth. Before we can make change that registers as psychically, materially, and socially meaningful, we must realize how complex personhood, and how those moments of incomprehensibility, exist for us all.

The recognition that our lives are filled with "enormously subtle meaning" occurs as we slow down the pace to really listen and learn, discovering with each inhale and exhale that there is nothing absolutely "straightforward" about our being in the world. Such realizations are always work, and require that we take the time to carefully examine our dreams and the "stories people tell about themselves" in order to arrive at this complexity. This mode of knowledge production is not about solving a problem but about remaining open to pursue new ways of thinking about "what it *means* to be a problem" (Du Bois, emphasis ours). What does it mean to traverse the hostile institutional demands of resolving and managing diversity, reaching a place where the complexity and integrity of differences can be valued? What might it mean to arrive at a place beyond the pressures of having "the answer," a place where we can create meaning among landscapes of uncertainty? What would it look like if we were to tap into the lifeforce that confers upon us the right to live and work toward possibility as opposed to remaining paralyzed and dissatisfied with the falsities offered as answers and solutions?

The dark space of possibility (Lorde), as part of the creative lifeforce within us each, opens us to new understandings about ourselves, each other, and our world(s). We are taught to ignore and fear the dark space within us, to understand the lifeforce as something outside and alienated from us. The violence produced through state narratives meant to dominate us becomes echoed in those oppositional positions that eclipse the potential for creating new knowledge through these dark spaces. Such strategies of engagement and communication keep us (and kept our class) from that inner knowledge and disconnect us from the source of our creativity. As we begin tapping into this source of power, living becomes not something to conquer or have dominion over, but something to experience and engage. Here, we have in mind a politics of engaged living similar to what Lugones means when she writes about playfulness:

> The playfulness that gives meaning to our activity (world-travelling) includes uncertainty, but in this case the uncertainty is an openness to surprise. Rules may fail to explain what we are doing. We are not self-important, we are not fixed in particular constructions of ourselves, which is part of saying that we are open to self-construction. . . . We are not wedded to a particular way of doing things. So, positively, the playful attitude involves openness to surprise, openness to being a fool, openness to self-construction or reconstruction and to construction and reconstruction of the "worlds" we inhabit playfully. ("Playfulness," 401)

Engaged in living and traveling with each other, we can self-consciously accept change—internal movement involving a radical evaluation of how one's mobilization of identity acts on people who identify similarly. Productive forms of mobility do not depend upon silencing or quieting (immobilizing) folks who are not you. Mobility is not always seen or aboveground. It can take place underground, in the dark spaces, thus making life complicated. Complicated and engaged living requires not only that we learn to cherish our feelings but also that we respect those hidden sources of power where new knowledge is birthed, felt, and embodied. It is from this space of recognition that we begin to appreciate each other enough to listen and learn.

Notes

This chapter is dedicated to Barbara Christian (1943–2000), an inspirational teacher and thinker who gave us the gift of her pioneering work on Black women writers and Black feminist thinking.

The authors thank the editors for their patience, comments, and support throughout this process. Thanks, also, to Adriana Garriga-Lopez for her work on the initial stages of this paper. Shona Jackson and Tara Mattarrazo read and commented on earlier drafts. Manolo Guzman cued us in to pleasure, and gave us some wonderfully sensual comments. Gina Perez was most encouraging in her request for more information on the class. Ralph Watkins and Miriam Jimenez Roman commented in helpful ways. Katie Straub helped us during a moment of technological chaos. Rod and Bison put up with our taking over their space through their gracious hospitality. We'd also like to thank Coatlicue for all the gifts she put in our path—polar bears, smoky rooms, crooked glasses, disheveled hair, and all. Finally, we'd like to thank the participants of the course on U.S. Latina feminisms for their presences, their absences, and the ensuing dialogue.

1. We draw on Avery Gordon's use of this phrase; Gordon, in turn, draws on the work of Patricia Williams.

2. See Zavella on the concept of social location.

3. Assuming the "we" here is a dangerous position that requires a continual guard against understanding those people who are marginalized in a seamless, unified way that does not differentiate among all of the many types of people who may fall into this category. Since *Bridge* already successfully debunked the uncomplicated "we" implicit in second-wave notions of Sisterhood, we want to build on its contributors' efforts by framing our use of the "we" here as both facile and contradictory, and with the acknowledgment that such a deployment is always work. It requires an investigation into its history within nation-formation and oppositional coalition-building since using "we" after the fact and in the midst of this investigation is at once possible and impossible.

4. Engaged living requires a particular commitment to speaking truths about ourselves that acknowledges and attends to the complexity of the worlds we come from and those to which we aspire to belong. This kind of truth-speaking is always a risk and, as such, makes compromised practices of listening all the more complicated to grapple with.

5. hooks discusses how to achieve a learning space open to deconstructing traditional notions of education (*Teaching*, 8–9).

6. Muñoz defines cross-identification as a mode of identification across difference, a way of being in the world shared between and among people from different sociocultural and economic locations.

7. The term *Latinidad* emerged as a way to challenge imperialist notions of Hispanidad. Derived from the more popularly used self-identificatory term *Latino*, it has, as Aparicio and Chávez-Silverman note, "contestatory and contested, fluid, and relational" meanings that both "valorize seemingly authentic cultural practices that challenge both colonial and imperialist U.S. ideologies in North and South America" and "describe the sets of images and attributes superimposed onto both Latin American and U.S. Latin subjects from the dominant sector."

8. *Subordinated* is used here to acknowledge that while everyone is subjected in some form within U.S. society, specific classes of people are politically, economically, and culturally placed in asymmetrical relations to others. Instead of using terms like *minority* or *subjugated* we use

subordinated to signal how domination is something done to others and that those others resist and contest domination.

9. See Kaplan, Alarcón, and Moallem, especially the introduction, for a more developed discussion about the in-betweenness of women's relationship to nation.

10. The course reading list included Pesquera and Segura; Romany; García; Zinn and Dill; Trinh's "Difference: A Special Third World Women's Issue" (*Woman* 79–116); Hurtado, "Relating to Privilege"; Moraga and Anzaldúa; Alarcón; Quintanales; Sandoval's "U.S. Third World Feminism"; Lugones and Spellman; Lugones's "Playfulness" and "Hablando"; Trujillo's introduction to *Chicana Lesbians*; Moraga's "From a Long Line of Vendidas" in *Loving*; Emma Pérez; Alarcón, Castillo, and Moraga; Castillo's "La Macha"; Ortega; Cofer Ortiz; Lorde's *Sister Outsider*; and Behar.

11. By hegemonic feminism we mean what Sandoval calls the legitimization of "certain modes of culture and consciousness" that "systematically curtail the forms of experience and theoretical articulations permitted [to] U.S. third world feminism" (6).

12. We recognize that these comments are rendered through our memories and responses but have tried to approximate them verbatim. The speaker's identity is omitted since we believe that privacy should be observed.

13. A distinguishing feature of the counterstance is its one-dimensional ideological reasoning that inevitably becomes stifling, inflexible, and inhibiting as the normative logic it defines itself against.

14. We would like to thank AnaLouise Keating for putting into words these ideas. Personal communication, April 2000.

15. For Gramsci, "When one distinguishes between intellectuals and non-intellectuals, one is referring to the immediate *social function of the professional category of the intellectual* . . ." and although "there are varying degrees of specific intellectual activity. There is no human activity from which every form of intellectual participation can be excluded" (9). We agree.

v.

"shouldering more identity than we can bear"... seeking allies in academe

fifty-one

Nurturance

Kay Picart

fifty-two

Aliens and Others in Search of the Tribe in Academe

tatiana de la tierra

Our effectiveness depends on our capacity to be audacious and astute,
clear and appealing. I would hope that we can create a language more
fearless and beautiful than that used by conformist writers to greet the
twilight.

—*Eduardo Galeano*

I am a fat, slightly bearded lesbian. A white Latina of Colombian extraction. A pagan lacking in Catholic guilt. A hedonist who knows shame. I have been diagnosed with lupus. Drive a pink and purple pickup. Collect rocks. Been poor most of my life. Knew gold-plated Gucci wealth for a few memorable years. I am a writer. I speak and dream in Spanish, inglés, y Spanglish. I am a feminist, an activist, una gitana. I have a master's of fine arts in creative writing and a master's in library science. I am a teacher and a librarian. I am, with all my identifying quirks and contradictions, a part of the academy.

Yet I am the eternal outsider. From within the university system I carry a prognosis—regardless of how many years I reside here, an integral part of me will always be distant from the mainstream. I will never belong. I am, and always have been, Other. I am one of those smelly mismatched misfits, squawking weirdos, invisible meek clods, strange birds, stupid beings, or even worse, brainy ones. We are the marginalized, the outsiders, the queer ones, the immigrants. The aliens. We have no land to call our own, no comfort zone. We are dust and desert souls.

They told me, they told us: You don't belong here.

How many of us are "the weary travelers, the dislocated, those of us who left because we didn't fit any more, those of us who still haven't arrived because we don't know where to arrive at, or because we can't go back any more?" (Gómez-Peña, 38). How many of us in academe are eternally in search of our tribe?

"Others" are those who are not part of the dominant power structure. We are the ones who are not white, wealthy, or heterosexual. We are socially and economically disadvantaged. We are those who speak another language. Some of us—the immigrants, the poor, the gays, and those of us who are "of color"—are directly affected by homophobic, imperialist, anti-immigrant, anti–affirmative action, anti-poor, and anti-other legislation. Some of us are in solidarity with each other. All of us are gendered, racialized, sexualized, ethno-cized and class-ified beings. We exist on the outside of society while being a significant part of it. We do not belong, yet here we are.

We are all we have and so we become obsessed with who we are, with our history and identity. We must feel the vibration of the resonance of our identities. In "Documented/Undocumented," Mexican writer and performance artist Guillermo Gómez-Peña writes about this longing that so many of us Others have for ourselves:

> The recapitulation of my personal and collective topography has become my cultural obsession since I arrived in the United States. I look for the traces of my generation, whose distance stretches not only from México City to California, but also from the past to the future, from pre-Columbian America to high technology and from Spanish to English, passing through "Spanglish." As a result of this process I have become a cultural topographer, border-crosser, and hunter of myths. And it doesn't matter where I find myself, in Califas or México City, in Barcelona or West Berlin; I always have the sensation that I belong to the same species: the migrant tribe of fiery pupils. (37)

They told me, they told us: Go back where you came from.

I did not conceptualize my own otherness for many years; I just lived it. I was seven years old when my feet touched Miami asphalt. I did not speak English. I did not understand many aspects of U.S. culture, including the intense racial divide. This came much later. But I did know that I was Other, that I was inferior, that I was not meant to succeed.

They told me, they told us: English Only.

One day, as an adult, upon hearing the words for the first time, I instinctively identified with being a "woman of color," even though I am racially white. My alliances were not with white culture or politics; my experience as an immigrant in this country Othered and de-whited me. In her analysis of Cuban lesbian performance artist Alina Troyano, "Too Spik or Too Dyke: Carmelita Tropicana," Lillian Manzor-Coats conceptualizes the de-pigmentation of "color." "The racial imaginary of the United States seems to be a product of a binary structure where the only categories are the polar opposites white/nonwhite. Within this racial imaginary, Latinas/os automatically occupy the non-white position, regardless of their racial configuration" (39). As a light-skinned person I have white privilege. Also, I do not have a Spanish accent when I speak in English now, while my mother does and my father doesn't even speak English. Within the context of a society that bulldozes over otherness, though, I embodied the hatred that was bottled and distributed just for me and mi gente. We were belittled, stereotyped, tokenized, dehumanized, impotent.

How can anyone overcome a self-hatred that was born of a white, patriarchal social construction? Honestly, I don't know that I have quite accomplished this.

They told me, they told us: Cockroaches for dinner.

It could be said that everyone has equal opportunity to be an Other. Not all of those who are a part of the "mainstream" feel a sense of belonging or agree with this group's racist, sexist, and classist tenets. The "white trash" phenomenon is representative of the complexities of race and power. White does not always equal might. Being "white" or "brown" is no one's doing; it is what we are. Yet what we are does dictate, to a great extent, what we can hope to accomplish. Racism is a constant factor that affects all of us, all the time. African-American author, activist, and librarian E. J. Josey, who has been a librarian since 1953, defines racism as "a system of advantages that benefits all whites, whether or not they seek it. In America, whites are not simply in the majority. They hold most of the positions of power, they own most of the wealth and set most of the nation's policies, and they are for all these reasons the norm" ("To Be Black," 82). Institutionalized racism (and classism and sexism) in the academy translates into privileged white men making decisions that affect everyone within the system. And, often, this means that, in the classroom, the materials and pedagogy are of such white male heterosexual origin. We all learn our place within the system; we take our positions and occupy the space allotted to us, nothing more. To transgress is to endanger the little that is ours.

They told me, they told us: Too brown, too loud.

Like all people of color, Latinos exist outside the norm of pop culture in this country. Despite demographic predictions that Latinos are the fastest-growing minority, I am concerned about the glaring invisibility of Latinos in places that represent mass culture. Where are Latinos in Hollywood? (We are violent criminals, servants, and whores.) In literature? (Think fast—Julia Alvarez, Sandra Cisneros, Junot Díaz—there cannot be too many of us, as the room fills up quickly.) In Washington, D.C.? (Tending tables and washing dishes.) On the radio? (The select few who "make it" to mainstream airwaves are Anglicized for mass consumption.) In academe? (Scrubbing toilets or not there at all, though some of us are trying, against odds, to Be Somebody, Get Somewhere, Graduate.) After the glitter settles on the supposed Latin Boom, I want to know—Will Latinos ever be perceived as anything more than spicy and ridiculous "yo quiero Taco Bell" hot tamales? Will key issues that affect our survival in this country—bilingual education, immigrant rights, environmental racism, representation in the White House, equitable access to higher education and technology—ever be worked out in our favor?

They told me, they told us: Ghetto, ghetto, ghetto.

For many years now, the ethnic look has been saturating mass culture. White teenagers sport tribal tattoos and dreadlocks while their parents swing on Brazilian hammocks in the comfort of their living rooms. You could even be fooled into thinking that this is the Age of the Other. Queer is hip, salsa is happening, rap is here to stay. But are we anything beyond the flavor of the month?

We are still a quantifiable minority in every stratum of society, except that which corresponds to low wages and poor education. In comparison to non-Latino whites, for instance, as of March 1999, Latinos are three times as likely to be living in poverty (25.6 percent, compared with 8.2 percent for non-Latino whites); significantly less likely to graduate from high school (56.1 percent, compared with 87.7 percent); and less likely to graduate from college with a bachelor's degree or more (10.9 percent, compared to 27.7 percent) (U.S. Census Bureau). "Color-blind" theorists and anti–affirmative action politicians and racists are waving the flag of equality when, in fact, all is not equal.

They told me, they told us: Ignorance becomes you.

Legal challenges and state initiatives designed to eliminate affirmative action in educational institutions (and elsewhere) spell impending doom for people of color in academe. Affirmative action has had a positive impact on the presence of Others in higher education. A 1995 report from the White House stated that "Only in the wake of affirmative action measures in the late 1960s and early 1970s did the percentage of black college students begin to climb steadily" ("American Council on Education," 8). The same is true for other minority groups.

Ironically, Others are multiplying in meteoric rates in the United States as affirmative action programs are being challenged and eliminated. According to the U.S. Department of Commerce, 90 percent of the total U.S. population growth from 1995 to 2050 will be attributed to racial and ethnic minorities. Also, the non-minority youth population is expected to decline, while the minority youth population will more than double. All demographic statistics and trends in higher education point to a decrease in white student enrollment and an *increase* for students of color (DeEtta Jones). In the future, we can expect a more diverse student population on college campuses.

They told me, they told us: Proposition 209, Initiative 200.

Personally, I did not initially envision education beyond Miami-Dade Community College, where I obtained my associate's degree in arts in the early 1980s. I did not have high academic expectations for myself. My mother did not graduate from high school; she cleaned houses for twenty-one years. My father, who had a college education and spoke English at the time, had tried his hand at the "American dream" and failed. By the time I graduated from high school, my father was an entrepreneur living, mostly, in Colombia, with erratic success.

Even though I had been in honors programs in junior high and high school, I believed that my own road to "opportunity" was inherently limited. Thanks to federal financial aid and economic support from relatives in Colombia, though, I completed my bachelor's at the University of Florida. Twelve years later, after much traveling, activism, writing, publishing, and barely making a living, I went to graduate school, the result of a defining moment in my life. While at a writing retreat in the Northwest, I ended up in the hospital with a lupus "flare-up" in the form of pneumonia, pleurisy, and other painful manifestations. Since I was unemployed and uninsured, I went to Colombia to heal, where a relative paid for my therapies. For months, in the mountains on the outskirts of Santa Fé de Bogotá, I submitted myself to every treatment in my path that resonated with me—from intravenous oxygen and rebirthing to flower essences, intravenous chemotherapy, and walking barefoot in the mountains.

I did a lot of reading and thinking while the IV delivered molecular concoctions into my bloodstream. I entertained myself with far-out fantasies during the grueling solo three-hour walks: I would create a New Age adventure tour company in Colombia; I would have a baby and travel the world with her; I would go to Valledupar with a group of women and start a lesbian vallenato band; I would be what I've always wanted to be, a songwriter; I would stay on my mom's farm in the outskirts of Palmira and write the Great Colombian-American novel; I would go to graduate school and Do Something That Equaled Survival.

They told me, they told us: You get what you deserve.

I tried the farm idea first. I loaded up with a month's worth of supplies—groceries, writing tools, novels, rolls of black-and-white film—and relaxed into a writing mode. Two days later, after nightfall, a group of masked men came for me with their guns cocked. Supposed guerrillas of some sort, they had orders to interrogate and kidnap me. After playing their game for several hours, they left me intact and walked off with the worldly possessions that defined me at that time in my life: Nikon camera and lenses, Gucci watch and gold jewelry, Sony camcorder, professional recording equipment, Tarot cards, camping gear, music. At the crack of dawn I said goodbye to my mom's gardens and cows, and to the green mountains, the brightly painted farmhouses, and the forever fields of sugarcane that form the landscape on the winding path to town.

They told me, they told us: Go back where you came from.

Three months later, I was in graduate school in a bilingual MFA creative writing program on the border of the United States and Mexico, at

the University of Texas at El Paso (UTEP). The program was disappointing—the fact that we were on the border did not translate into having
courses or professors that reflected the immediate surroundings. British
literature and white heterosexual instructors and graduate students dominated the English department. Every once in a while, a Chicano or
African-American literature course was offered. The Spanish department
was parochial and male-defined. With the exception of one Colombian
instructor who included a significant amount of female writers in her literature courses, most of the required readings were by male authors.
There was not any palpable queer presence in the contents of the courses
in either of the departments, or any cutting-edge anything, for that matter.

I was not a happy graduate student, though I did eventually invent
ways to make my own work meaningful and I identified allies in the
process. I remember feeling, as a student, ripped off. There was no inherent support for me as a creative person or as a Latina or a dyke, no courses
that reflected my bicultural, bilingual reality, no critical feedback to my
writings that offered a basic understanding of who I was. (I remember
having to explain the concept of a lesbian femme in a writing workshop.
That was just the beginning.) I, along with the other Others, were
strangely alienated in a place that promised just the opposite. I developed
an Us-against-Them mentality and bonded with select Others in the program—the three Chicanas from Los Angeles and myself became the
"WCC" (women of color corner). We performed our work at a local art
gallery at a reading entitled "This Frontera Called My Lengua: A Reading
by Linguistic Terrorists." That was our way of surviving.

While being a student was disempowering, being a teacher was just
the opposite. I was a teaching assistant, which meant that I taught two
sections of English composition each semester. Immediately, I recognized
the potency of each of the components of teaching—creating a syllabus,
making lesson plans, selecting course materials, lecturing, and grading.

Because of our relative invisibility in academia, those of us who are
Others in the classroom inherently have particularly powerful personas
that we take with us. I occupied space in the classroom fully aware of who
I was and who my students were. At UTEP, 70 percent of the undergraduates are of Mexican-American descent; most are the first ever in their
family to attend college, and many never graduate. I wanted to teach in a
way that was respectful of my students and myself and that was also fun.
My approach to teaching English composition, which I experimented
with and developed along the way, entailed having a multicultural reader,
doing creative writing exercises as well as traditional lesson plans, coming
out in the classroom, and creating an environment that invited students to
play with words, including Spanglish and Caló.

My students were conscious of my Otherness—I was a stranger in *their* land, as well as an outsider to the university that we all attended. Instructors who identify themselves or are identified as Other wear a neon sign in academic settings. I was a queer role model for my gay students. They would visit during and after office hours and come out to me; one of them even came out in the classroom. Likewise, even though I am not Chicana, my students knew that I understood their culture, familia, economic situation, and their language. All of this had a tremendous impact in the dynamics of required English composition courses (de la tierra, "Coming Out").

By being one of the few recognizable faces in a sea of white academics, we, whether we want to or not, represent our raza. This is not necessarily a good thing. We are just who we are—individuals. We are not representatives of countries, gender, ethnicity, or sexuality. Yet, because there are so few of us, we often end up shouldering more identity than we can bear. Although it's unfair and unrealistic, it is part of our path. Likewise, it is part of our power. If we are conscious of this connection, and if we care, we can make our time in the classroom purposeful and more potent than it naturally is.

I remember Mrs. Garcia, a Cuban math teacher at Homestead Junior High. Unlike most of the "American" teachers, she wore makeup and clicked down the hall in high heels. She was brassy; she spoke loud and fast and in Spanish with her Latin students. She wasn't my teacher, but even so, I memorized her image and identified her as a person of power. She was an idol in the corner of my eye, and yet she was nothing more than a math teacher. She represented the possibility that even if I was poor and Colombian I could still, someday, be someone. It was that simple.

They told me, they told us: Matensen, matensen.

Many of us Others are in tune with the power of our identity. We expect more from ourselves and we know that more is expected of us. Our writings are historical documents, and our achievements, or lack of, represent the grace or doom of our culture. We forge our paths swinging our sharpened hand-held machetes. We often feel that our writing and our presence make our gente visible and maybe even powerful. During a speech at the National Council of Teachers in English Annual Convention in 1995 in San Diego, Chicana writer Sandra Cisneros expressed the hope that her stories "give name to communities that have been silent or distant, give voice to people who don't have a voice" ("Cisneros"). Going a step further, Alicia Gaspar de Alba explains the role of Chicana writers in "Literary Wetback":

> The Chicana writer, like the curandera (medicine woman) or the bruja (witch), is the keeper of the culture, keeper of the memories, rituals, the stories, the

superstitions, the language, the imagery of her Mexican heritage. She is also the one who changes the culture, the one who breeds a new language and a new lifestyle, new values, new images and rhythms, new dreams and conflicts into that heritage making all of this brouhaha and cultural schizophrenia a new legacy for those who have still to squeeze into legitimacy as human beings and American citizens. (245)

Why does a Chicana writer shoulder the entire history, imagery, and future of her people? With such a small handful of visible Chicana writers, each one's social and cultural responsibility is magnified. Cherríe Moraga cites one of the drawbacks. "There are so few latina lesbians who are getting national readership or national recognition that there's always a lot of weight attached to anything we produce. It's like wanting every latina lesbian novel to be the definitive when we have like two or three to choose from. I think the pressure is a little much" (de la tierra, "Cherríe Moraga," 6).

I agree. We are under intense pressure to represent and produce and succeed when we are only idiosyncratic beings. For five years, I was one of the editors of the Latina lesbian magazines, *esto no tiene nombre* and *conmoción*. I was convinced that if it weren't for these magazines, Latina lesbians would not be published or otherwise visible. And this is not far from the truth. Rarely are Latina lesbian writers, artists, performers, and activists featured within contemporary literature. Even though Latina lesbian visibility increased within our community as a result of the magazines that I edited from 1991 to 1996, our cultura continues to be apart from. Other.

They told me, they told us: Alien, alien, alien.

I think back to my own otherness—leaving my magical, mountainous country at seven years of age to be indoctrinated into North American culture; learning a foreign language as if it were a weapon for my survival; being a fat, savage teenager; being a member of the first Latin family in the neighborhood and listening to my mom explain plátanos asados to the rednecks; being so poor that we had to clean the carpet with our fingers; spending summers in Colombia and no longer being one of "them"; living as a "Resident Alien"; being branded with a diagnosis of lupus, incurable; loving women forever. And I know that regardless of ethnic and queer buzzwords, I will always be Other. It is the only place that I can call my own.

In her rock song "Alienation," Naomi Morena sings a Latina lesbian anthem: "Tell me where do I belong, my hair is short and my skin is brown. Won't take a man and I got no plans for the future." I remember jamming to this song, recorded in 1984, as a baby dyke in Miami and, eventually, meeting the author in Portland during my travels.

Part of my own path in the land of Otherness is to meet other Others.

We are, scattered throughout the world, sisters, familia. For many years, I was a gitana in search of Us—I drove, flew, walked, rode horseback, and swam anywhere that we were. I went to conferences, music festivals, teepees, communes, bedrooms, bars, bookstores, cafés. I have been an audience to so many of our awesome performers, a publisher of some of our talented writers and artistas, a consumer of the products that we stamp with our own seal of Otherness.

I have found that our deep-seated anger, a response to being belittled and virtually erased, is the fuel that ignites our work. Juanita Ramos, editor of the Latina lesbian anthology *Compañeras*, dedicates the book, "For Latina lesbians everywhere. With much love and the conviction that one day we will be able to live our lives to our fullest potential without anyone to oppress us." Achy Obejas, Cuban lesbian writer, cites incidents of "barbaric" racist remarks spewed at her during childhood and concludes that, in her role as a creative writing instructor, "There is nothing that gives me greater pleasure than correcting an American in English. It's the ultimate fuck you" (de la tierra, "Achy Obejas," 38).

Perhaps "fuck you" is at the heart of our identity. It's definitely a part of who I am. In my "coming to America" story, entitled "Wings," I wrote:

> I dreaded those public moments that highlighted the fact that I was a foreigner. Sometimes I sat at my desk, plotting my revenge. I would master the English language. I would infiltrate the gringo culture without letting on that I was a traitor. I would battle in their tongue and make them stumble. I would cut out their souls and leave them on the shore to be pecked on by vultures. Winged words would be my weapon.

They told me, they told us: Jodensen, jodensen.

Yet I realize that we have to evolve beyond our eternal rage. We have to survive, be functional, stay out of prison, dream, dance, live in peace, know beauty.

Today, I am everything that I ever was, and more, but my stomping ground is academe. After completing my MFA, I moved across the country again, this time to the Northeast, where I was the recipient of the Library Internship/Residency Program for underrepresented academic librarians at the University at Buffalo (UB). Once again, I was one of very few people of color in graduate school. One of my professors was African American; the rest were white. According to the 1998 *Library and Information Science Education Statistical Report*, 15.7 percent of full-time faculty in ALA-accredited programs were people of color; only 2.4 percent were Latin (Association, 20). I studied alongside a handful of African-American and Asian graduate students; there were no other Latinos that I knew of during the time that I was in the program. In

1996–97, 94 master's degrees, out of a total of 5,068, were awarded to Latinos who attended ALA-accredited library schools (114). In Buffalo, only one Latino received a master's during this time, along with 1 Asian or Pacific Islander and 4 African Americans (117). Considering that many of the students who attend UB are from the area, and that Buffalo has a significant Black and Puerto Rican population, these numbers are disproportionately low.

During library school, I saw things through the eyes of an Other. While library science revolves around keyword searching, databases, cataloging, reference sources, bibliographic retrieval, and the Internet, all of these topics also have political ramifications that are not usually explored in the classroom. The only exception at UB was the African American professor, who routinely included race, politics, and an international perspective in all of her courses. As a graduate student, I occupied myself with researching and writing about the Other side of library science—the digital divide; resources for Spanish-speaking patrons; the cataloging of Latina lesbian literature; Cuban libraries; the effect that Amazon.com and Barnes & Noble superstores have on publishing queers and authors of color; and the lack of people of color in library school and, correspondingly, in libraries and universities.

I was fortunate while in graduate school at UB because, as a result of the internship/residency, I had a built-in support system. Along with my own office, I had a mentor and a cadre of librarians whom I could count on to help me with my studies. Not coincidentally, most of the librarians who were there for me were also people of color. Along with academic support, though, I also associated myself with a creative lesbian group in the community and a Latino social and academic organization on campus. All of these different support systems, combined, provided me with the nourishment that allowed me to grow and graduate.

Being one of the few Others in academe can be a difficult and alienating experience. Racism, classism, and homophobia are present every step of the way. It takes grit to endure the isolation. It takes strength of character to proceed even when you are treated as a trespasser. It takes shape-shifting ability and wizardry to be able to walk and run with a nail in your shoe.

Being in solidarity with each Other is key to being successful in academe. We are each Other's strongest allies. We need to look into each Other's eyes, acknowledge our mutual presence, and, if possible, appropriate, and heartfelt, offer and seek support. We need to know that we also have white allies and that, many times, actively seeking what we need yields positive results. We need to know that sometimes it takes more courage *not* to fight.

We need to remember that our presence exists within an institutional system that is not designed in our favor, and that our part in the system is prescribed. Still, we are not powerless. As students, we are learning a discipline and a code of behavior, a language that puts us at another level, one that we can explore and inhabit, if we choose. As professors, we are in positions to create change, student by student, to be mentors, to select materials and teaching methods, to actively participate in and affect the discourse of academe. As students and as professors we can be subversive within the system; the fact that we are even a part of it is significant.

We have to remember that we have a right to be here. We have to consider that, today, we are few, but tomorrow, there will be many more of us. Our presence is more meaningful than we may realize. We are etching our names on the academic walls. *I was here.* We are writing about *us.* "One may write as if to say: 'We are here, we were here; we are thus, we were thus'" (Galeano, 125).

A key part of our evolution lies in our holistic identity, in honoring everything that we are, all of the time. We are always individuals, and at the same time we are a piece of the land or the body or the goddess that birthed us. We are our own independent republics, our own minorities. All of us who bring ourselves with us into the classroom are walking, talking, breathing replicas of many others like us. Wherever we are, we have a scent, we speak in a certain tone, we express ourselves with our personal décor. We can't get away from ourselves, or from our Otherness, even if we try.

> *They told me, they told us*
> *So many goddamn things*
> *That some of us even believe them.*
> *They told me, they told us*
> *So many goddamn things*
> *That some of us know better.*
> *They told me, they told us*
> *So many goddamn things*
> *That I invented alchemy all by myself.*
>
> *All the pain becomes a refrain*
> *The disempowerment a parade*
> *The fucked-up feeling, un festival*
> *The fuck-you-too, un carnaval*
> *The you-don't-belong-here, un madrigal.*

Originally written in 1996, el paso, tejas.
Revised 12 de marzo de 2000, buffalo, nueva york.

fifty-three

The Fire in My Heart[1]

Sunu P. Chandy

In 1992, approximately the midpoint between the date Bridge *was first published (1981) and now (2000), I wrote a letter to one of my professors voicing my disappointment after the peace studies committee at my college rejected students' recommendation to add* This Bridge Called My Back *to the program's required reading list. What follows here is a rough re-creation of the sentiments expressed in that letter.*

Dear ————,

I am writing to you in response to our conversation earlier this afternoon when you informed me that *This Bridge Called My Back* would not be included on the required reading list for the peace studies program. I was shocked when you told me that the committee found this book to be a "lightweight"—especially since, as you told me, no one on the committee had read the book before arriving at this conclusion. I looked up the definition of *lightweight*: "A person [or book in this case] of little ability, intelligence, influence, or importance." Now that I have confirmed that this word is just as disrespectful as it sounds, I must tell you that I am offended and outraged that the committee labeled such a groundbreaking book of writings by women of color as a lightweight.

I am so disappointed that this ignorance came from a group of professors concerned with the task of running a peace studies program. There are no women-of-color authors currently on the required reading list. Yet there are so many women-of-color writers who have smart and helpful commentaries on the state of our world and who would make important contributions to our curriculum. We need to think more about representation in our program. Who do you consider "heavyweight" philosophers? What do they look like?

A senior woman of color loaned *This Bridge* to me during my first semester at college. Having read *Bridge*, I will tell you that this book is both tremendously moving and life-changing. *Bridge* is the first book that I and so many women of color on this campus have found that gives voice to our experiences. *Bridge*'s authors validated our years of unwritten and often unspoken realities. To see these realities on paper for the first time is so affirming and sustaining for us. Perhaps for those of you who find your lives and voices in countless textbooks, novels, TV shows, and movies on a daily basis, it may be difficult to understand.

As you know, the writings in this book inspired us to start the first women-of-color group on our campus. Reading *This Bridge* has helped us to know that we are not alone in our multiple struggles. Reading *This Bridge* has enabled us to acknowledge areas where some of us have much privilege as well. *This Bridge* has given us a way to put women of color, our understandings, and our experiences of the world at the center. For us, it is very refreshing to be able to read about our own experiences, but *Bridge* also needs to be read by others who are concerned with social justice. Only then can our peace studies program begin to be inclusive of various critical viewpoints that are currently missing.

Did it occur to anyone on the committee to attend when Gloria Anzaldúa, one of *Bridge*'s editors, came here to speak? Had you attended, you would have witnessed a packed room enjoying her wisdom and insight. You would have seen her draw islands on the chalkboard and describe how women of color lay our bodies down as the bridges between such different groups of people. You would have enjoyed her humor and seen the caring she showed toward the women of color on our campus.

This Bridge also helped me to contextualize and validate what happens to women of color, wherever we go in the world. For example, when a group of students went on a program to study conflict resolution, it is true that we went to the Middle East with the purpose of studying the Palestinian/Israeli conflict. However, a larger conflict in our group became women's encounters with sexism and racism. The Mexican woman on the program did not feel safe, as she was continually harassed by those who mistook her to be Palestinian. Some of the women were constantly harassed because they were seen only as sex objects by some of the local men. As for me, I became tired of being called "brown sugar" as I walked through the market. These too were conflicts. These issues also needed resolution. These too were concerns of a global proportion. As many of the authors in *Bridge* recognize and demand, our experiences as women of color deserve attention.

This Bridge is also important because I am still called "nigger" when I walk down the streets of this town. There is a reason I carried *Bridge* as a refuge during my summer in D.C., my program in Jerusalem, and my trip to India. *This Bridge* reminds me that so many women of color before me have analyzed and acknowledged their oppression in this world and yet made the decision to continue their activism, again and again.

As for me, it is true that I came to this college to be a peace studies major, but I can leave peace studies. I can turn completely to women's studies, where *Bridge* is now one of the critical and defining texts. However, before I decide to leave completely, I want to help this program to change. We can not maintain an honest peace studies program without some analysis of race, gender, class, sexuality, and an understanding of the power differences these create.

I am only a student and you are a well-respected professor. In so many ways, I value your wisdom and humor and generosity. However, I cannot allow my fear to silence me, and let this incident pass without taking a stand. The committee was disrespectful in its dismissive decision not to include *This Bridge* on the required reading list for peace studies and in labeling this book as a lightweight. Furthermore, I find this incident symbolic of the larger lack of diversity and representation in our program.

I am writing this letter both to voice my disappointment and to express hope for change. As *Bridge* co-editor Gloria Anzaldúa wrote, "I am trying to make peace between what has happened to me, what the world is, and what it should be" ("La Prieta," 208). I know that ultimately this is also our work, individually and collectively as a program.

Sincerely,
Sunu P. Chandy

Following this letter, of course, one of my professors replied immediately, stating that he did not mean to offend. Before I graduated in 1994 with my degree in peace studies *and* women's studies, *Bridge* was placed on the "optional" reading list for peace studies majors. Our activism made other changes as well, like a new requirement that peace studies majors must take at least one women's studies and one African-American studies course. It did feel like tokenism and it did feel like the smallest of steps, but it was what we managed to achieve during this time.

Note

1. I borrowed this title from Cherríe Moraga's line in her preface to *This Bridge*: "the fire we feel in our hearts when we are insulted" (xviii).

fifty-four

Notes from a Welfare Queen in the Ivory Tower

Laura A. Harris

ghetto supastar/that is what you are/coming from afar/reaching for the stars/run away with me/to another place/we can rely on each other, uh-huh.
—Mya

I am of the vanquished, I am of the defeated. The past is a fixed point, the future is open-ended; for me the future must remain capable of casting a light on the past such that in my defeat lies the seed of my great victory, in my defeat lies the beginning of my great revenge. My impulse is to the good, my good is to serve myself. I am not a people. I am not a nation. I only wish from time to time to make my actions be the actions of a people, to make my actions be the actions of a nation.
—Jamaica Kincaid

In the past twenty years the academy opened its doors to the barbarians loudly clanging at the gates—people of color, feminists, and queers, as well as their theories and activisms, are now visible on many university campuses. Departments have been formed, educational requirements redesigned, and hiring practices politicized. These political movements aimed to create, from inside the ivory tower, theories that reflect real conditions outside the academy. Academic activists hoped that strong links between theories and activisms would thus be forged so that the academy's relationship to practice could be productively changed. However, this visibility—namely people, books, and theories—or so-called multiculturalism remains structured by a rigid class hierarchy. The academy, now the locus of much critical work purporting to report on and effect real change in the lives of the marginalized, from an office of my own with a view, is one of the most prominent long-standing cultural bastions of class elitism.[1] The structural power and class relations outside but also inside the academy obscure the possibilities for critique, let alone any dismantling, of the ways in which class disperses the barbarians at the gate and silences those within its walls.

This is my rant. I am part of the last generation of welfare moms who managed to make the system work right and who managed to work the system right to crash the gates of the academy. For thirteen or more years, ten of which I was a student, I received AFDC, Food Stamps, Medi-Cal, Section 8, deferred student loans, a bunch of credit cards, and often I worked under the table. To pay for my education, I amassed over eighty thousand dollars in debt (principal alone). No matter which way I look at it, this debt was the price of the ticket. But to whose event? Now, my biggest disappointment in assuming a new position as a tenure-track assistant professor in English, world literature, and Black studies at a small private liberal arts college has been the lack of experiencing a new economic situation parallel to my new middle-class professional standing. Did the system *work me*?

My identity as a welfare queen is consistently rendered illegible in the academy. I find myself unable to articulate my class difference as I wonder how it would affect those admissions ads and national ratings to advertise that, like bats in the belfry or madwomen in the attic, this college has a welfare queen ranting in its ivory tower. While the academy identifies me as a lesbian woman of color and is often eager to do so, it remains a troubled identifying coupled with my lived experience as a welfare recipient that frequently impacts my subjectivity in the academy's halls.

When I was still a student, every welfare mother in school followed the specter of welfare reform with a deepening sense of urgency and fear. There was a group of women in college who were welfare moms, smart and goal-oriented. We knew each other in small groups, ran into each other in the social service and university offices. We spoke among ourselves about being on welfare, but never once did we speak out in all those politically-charged theory classes. I can write about being a welfare mother, from a family of generations of welfare mothers, because I am not on welfare anymore. I now teach in those classes I used to attend, trying to illuminate somehow the recurrent and heated debates about the intellectual's role in the revolutionary consciousness of the duped underclass, working class, and masses. Which am I?

In July 1996 President Bill Clinton, in supporting the house and senate welfare bills, kept his election-year promise to "end welfare as we know it." Today, welfare has been replaced by workfare, the twenty-first century's rendition of indentured servitude. This legislation stripped women, children, legal immigrants, the elderly, minor drug and criminal offenders, poor communities of color, and poor white or white ethnic communities of access to public assistance, housing, medical care, education, food stamps, substance abuse treatment, and rehabilitation services. In reforming the welfare status of such a diverse cross section of the population, this federal legislation works in conjunction with draconian state ballot initiatives and legislation including but not limited to three strikes laws, Proposition 21, and anti-queer hate crime and anti-immigrant legislation to police these communities.[2] It is increasingly apparent that in a parallel manner poor people, women, immigrants, and queers are often under attack and scapegoated. This scapegoating suggests their interconnected centrality to any formulation of feminist, women-of-color, class politics, or queer theory and practice today.

In her foreword to the 1983 republication of *This Bridge Called My Back*, Cherríe Moraga argued that "the impetus to forge links with women of color from every region grows more and more urgent as the number of recently-immigrated people of color in the U.S. grows in enormous proportions, as we begin to see ourselves all as refugees of a world on fire" (n.p.). Decades later Moraga's statement remains urgent to an ever-growing impoverished class of peoples and nations in the face of recently enacted policies such as NAFTA, welfare reform, European unionization, and the MAI.[3] As *This Bridge* suggested initially, the poverty class most affected by these global economic changes is comprised of an ever-growing number of women of all racial, ethnic, and socio-cultural backgrounds. This call to action, advanced in *This Bridge* over twenty years ago, continues to be relevant though it has been largely ignored in the academy and elsewhere. Academic knowledges that confine women's issues and queer issues to a specific political, economic, racial, or sexual space, or that too narrowly limit discussions of power to cultural politics, are not equipped to address forms of resistance to overdetermining conditions of power and dominance.

While the current economic disappointment I experience is certainly not dire in the face of these other ongoing global atrocities, I point to my conditions only to expose a caste system in which poor women of all colors are systematically maintained at the lowest rungs of the economic ladder. These ever-increasing systematic erasures affect the workfare mom grossing less than minimum wage for her labor and the immigrant queer working in low-level jobs alike—both are now unable to obtain an education. Using a two-year cut-off limit, welfare reform denies access to higher education and student federal financial aid is no longer available to immigrants. One of the crises of class in this country used to be that some of us had to pay a very high ransom for our "equality" of educational opportunity. The crisis of class post–welfare reform is that many of us and our children will not be left that chance anymore.

Well-known jewish queer writer and activist Joan Nestle, recently teaching a group of students in a southern college, and speaking directly to this issue, asked of them what they believed constituted a contemporary gay political agenda. The students responded, "Marriage. . . . Gays in the military." Nestle allowed them to continue in this vein for a short period of time. She then inquired in a low tone, "What about a national minimum wage? What about healthcare? Aren't they gay issues?" (Steel). As we approach the new millennium we need to ask of various ethnic, feminist, queer, and other radical theories, What are people of color's issues, women's issues, and queer issues today? In addition to concerns pertaining obviously to the realms of race, gender, and sexuality, the answers to these questions need to include free and available economic stipends, housing, health care, and education.

How can feminist, queer, radical academic work speak with, rather than only about, disenfranchised communities in order to begin articulating these increasingly complicated political commitments? In this body of work, how can the voice of the welfare queen, the immigrant laborer, the sick elder, the queer adolescent be heard too? The critical thrust of *This Bridge* illuminated the limitations of white middle-class feminisms and the academic institutions out of which much of this ideology arose. More, however, than just a critique of whiteness, the academy, and feminism, *This Bridge* sought to further a conversation women of color had been having for some time: How do we address class, race, gender, *and* sexual politics? How do we produce self-critical knowledges enabling us to ask new and different questions? How do these urgent concerns work together; how do we work together to address these urgent concerns?

While these considerations may have been elided, for the most part, in the academy, as evidenced by the writings included in the original *Bridge*, feminists of color have acknowledged the necessary interdependence of oppressions and the imperative need for building unlikely coalitions for some time.[4] As early as 1980, Barbara Smith proclaimed, ultimately, any kind of separatism is a dead end. . . . [T]he strongest politics are coalition politics that cover a broad base of issues. . . . What *I* really feel is radical is trying to make coalitions with people who are different from you. I feel it is radical to be dealing with race and sex and class and sexual identity all at one time" (Smith and Smith, 126; her italics). Women of color continue to find themselves asking these same questions. In "Punks, Bulldaggers, and Welfare Queens: The Radical Potential of Queer Politics?" Cathy J. Cohen argues that "a truly radical or transformative politics has not resulted from queer activism." In a call reminiscent of Smith's entreaty for feminist coalitions with other marginal groups, Cohen maps out her own version of unlikely coalition-building: "I envision a politics where one's relation to power, and not some homogenized identity, is privileged in determining one's political comrades. I'm talking about a politics where the *nonnormative* and *marginal* position of punks, bulldaggers, and welfare queens, for example, is the basis for progressive transformative coalition work"(438).

A complicated identity politics is a basis for coalition politics, especially class-based coalition work. The historical movements, lesbian feminism, and queer politics referred to by Smith and Cohen emerged as semi-grassroots activism and then later attained an academic thrust. However, the academic institutionalizing of grassroots movements has failed at coalition-building of the sort they articulate. Coalition-building is thus absent in much politicized intellectual grappling with the complexities of identity. Indeed, it is precisely the academy's refusal to witness its own identity politics—middle-class privileged, male-dominated, predominately white, neo-liberal, ivy league struck, euro-ethnic—that renders it inept at translating or understanding a connection to other identities. Necessarily in such an atmosphere, identity politics becomes separatist, narrow, combative, exploitive, individual, and token where it might have functioned as guerilla warfare in the liberatory project of building coalitions.

The academy's failure to radically incorporate the emergent diverse presence within its walls manifests itself in various equal opportunity programs. Unfortunately, this form of integrating multiculturalism reveals the academy's alienation from its own racism, as well its less remarked upon class bias. Across the board, where efforts are made to diversify departments, curricula, and other academic structures, it is not the systematic foundation of the particular department, curriculum, or academic structure that itself is altered. Instead, existing conditions are augmented by adding token diversity, be it a highly recruited student or faculty member from an underrepresented group or a course examining a facet of the lives of the marginalized. Tokenism functions only to validate large-scale exclusion by providing a misleading veneer of diversity and transformation. The goal of these diversifying measures is never first to inquire what about western and european academic knowledges of histories, literatures, and sciences is inextricably linked to a legacy of unacknowledged dependence and exploitation. It's quietly assumed that new arrivals to the academy need not disrupt the serious (and of course unrelated) academic work constituting the academy's master narrative. Required courses remain status quo, a new ethnic studies course, often optional, is inserted into the curriculum, and faculties for the most part remain male, pale, and privileged. Even where faculty diversity is assertively sought, it is only valued if it re-inscribes the sameness of the academy's master narrative, especially that of class privilege.

At the most obvious level, these diversifying measures are racist. They are measures predicated upon the assumption that there is not anything biased about academic knowledge as it stands. The academy's racism results in a hierarchical ghettoization of ethnic studies departments, faculty, students, and coursework by their consistent relegation to the peripheries. Further, in universities in which faculty from underrepresented groups are brought in as joint appointments, a uniquely exploitive form of academic work requiring them to teach, advise, and serve in both status quo and ethnic or women's studies departments is forged. The work overload alone is staggering to their careers. Liberal academic multiculturalism is unable to counter white supremacy and bourgeois values, "knowledge," and modes of education.

On yet another level, the "multicultural" strategy operates to reinforce deeply entrenched class hegemony. For years, universities have identified racial diversity as a problem; committees have been formed, meetings called to order, programs outlined, and task forces set into place to solve the mysterious problem of race in the academy. But class, too, is a problem in the academy. It is a problem that institutions of higher education for the most part ignore.

One exception is a large public midwestern university that released via a community and governmental relations liaison a media alert addressing the ways in which higher education can break welfare cycles.[5] As the model case in their discussion, the study celebrates Nan, a welfare mother of two who—against all odds, including a massive heart attack—completed her bachelor's degree. The fact that Nan had to return to school almost immediately after coronary failure (thus risking her life) or risk losing her welfare benefits and therefore be unable to finish her degree is celebrated as an unprecedented success story. What it means for a welfare recipient and student to endanger her life in order to maintain her welfare benefits and pursue her education is glaringly absent from this university's task force's "analysis" of how higher education breaks a welfare cycle. This story indicates the academy's cruel indifference or blatant ignorance to the reality that much is lost, potentially everything, as we pull ourselves up by our bootstraps.

I am not suggesting merely that universities should develop affirmative action programs to combat class discrimination. In fact, my aim in part is to demonstrate the limited avenues of possibility affirmative action policy creates, namely because it fails to confront the problematic specificity of narrow academic self-definitions. I am arguing that questions of class in the academy have the potential to radically exert pressure, not only upon the particular socio-economic function fulfilled by liberal education, but on its racist and sexist narratives of exclusion as well. Importantly, the welfare queen promises a paradigm shift for knowledge about the world *and* the structure of academic institutions.

Since the economic privileges of being in a middle-class profession will indefinitely remain unavailable to me (go ahead, garnish my social security check), I thought the rewards of passing into an intellectual realm would suffice insofar as this passing potentially allows me to agitate for crucial transformation. Unfortunately, while all that the academy promises remains at times seductive and alluring, passing is never as pleasurable or empowering as imagined. I am never as good at it as I like to think or as others like to accuse. Instead, more than a few times in the first months of my job I have thought and perhaps too loudly complained: "Fuck this intellectual and behavioral middle-class sphere—*show me the money!*" Making it into the middle class cost a lot more money than I anticipated. Even where I do find satisfaction in the intellectual sphere, the middle-class behavioral expectations are unappealing and tiresome to have knowledge of, understand the implications of, and therefore ever perform, even subversively. Now, as I refuse to adopt the social niceties of collegial behavior, I have come to understand that the subject position of the welfare queen qua middle-class professional offers yet another avenue for resistance.

On my way to work one morning I saw a young coyote running in and out of the parked cars on the side of the street. Others saw him too as pedestrians were stopping and cars slowing. He probably came down from the Griffith Park canyons in the early hours of the morning and now found himself in the midst of Los Feliz, an upscale radically-chic urban neighborhood. I imagined the pup experiencing ecstacy and terror. This creature ran into the middle of the street, circled obsessively thirteen or fourteen times, then deposited a large steaming bowel movement right in the middle of the boulevard as everyone watched. A traffic jam ensued as people stopped, somewhat taken aback and silenced by the coyote's untenable action. I laughed aloud, always fond of small feral creatures, and also because at that moment the animal's reaction was a clever and apt expression of being caught out of place as an interloper from the tattered edges of civilization. I thought of how clearly the coyote's intestinal intuition represented my own ecstasy and fear in relation to the academy, my own daily urges in the face of a radically-chic academic milieu.

In *Race Rebels: Culture, Politics, and the Black Working Class*, Robin D. G. Kelley discusses the satisfaction of these urges as the revolutionary actions of daily life within African-American working-class communities. Kelley argues that such resistance constitutes a dialectical politics of moving out into space and public in a way that structurally alters both: "Politics is not separate from lived experience or the imaginary world of what is possible; to the contrary, politics is about these things. Politics comprises the many battles to roll back constraints and exercise some power over, or create some space within, the institutions and social relationships that dominate our lives"(9). He urges an understanding of everyday forms of revolution that not only resist but serve to shape struggles between workers and institutional powers, between "seemingly innocuous" individual acts and formal political structures (19).

Writing a cultural history of the working class from "way, way below," Kelley illuminates that theft and other forms of sabotage work through dialectic to incite the institutional formation of resistance movements. Theft, in his analysis, becomes transformative rather than deviant.

Individual acts make visible the political connectedness of the working and poverty class, so that they take agency in shaping the formal directions of political agitation. In other words, working people's resistance transforms space dialectically by explicitly drawing attention to contradictions between bourgeois expectations and poverty-class reality, paving the way for the organization of political dissent in unions and political action groups. I want my daily sabotage of the expectation that I could readily shed my identity as a welfare queen to embrace the behavioral and other middle-class codes of the academy to function to create space for formal re-considerations of class in the university by making visible pre-existing contradictions, thus introducing the possibility of transformation.

Let me offer a very basic example: I do not have cash to spend or credit cards on which to charge research funds. These funds consist of monies for which I *work* to apply and that go through college financial offices. Although once the funds are awarded the college expects grant recipients to later be reimbursed, I do not have the money and must agitate at the dean's office to have it allocated prior to producing the receipt. The notion that life is homogenously middle-class, that we have cash or credit to burn, that we all own homes, that we are coupled, that we are routinely stable and safe, and that this type of existence must be what we desire is embedded in the college's daily practices and intellectual structures. Perhaps, consistently, unpleasantly, and loudly exposing that gross untruth will cause the academy to implode, or, ultimately and ideally, the knowledges produced there will dismantle the assumptions of homogeneity. When Audre Lorde made her statement about the master's house, she did not mean do not get an education, do not speak forcefully, do not write critical essays, and do not live every day in the fray of the battle (you always are there). I believe she meant do not think the battle is ever done, do not think that because you made it everyone can, and do not buy into the prevailing myths.

I draw attention to the coyote's action in order to present by way of metaphor a form of resistance, analagous to the revolution of every day detailed by Kelley, one that is all too frequently overlooked or dismissed within the academy. Often, mainstream and academic efforts to reform institutions reinforce systems that do violence to marginalized subjectivities, rendering these potential revolutionaries complicit in silencing radical difference and subversion. At best traditional reform efforts provide a false and empty sense of betterment for individuals while failing to undermine master narratives of social control or spatial, economic, and ideological hierarchies. Transformation requires new strategic approaches. I advocate rejecting a politics of seeking incorporation or inclusion, and instead choosing a politics of everyday resistance. I argue for a politics of shredding the fabric of institutional regiment through refusal, sabotage, thievery, defecation. In doing so I acknowledge the necessary connectedness of subcultural resistance to other resistances, especially that of unlikely coalition-building.

As a student, forced to purchase exorbitantly priced textbooks from a university-owned bookstore, I chose to liberate texts, to change price tags, to damage texts so used prices could be had, and to otherwise circumvent paying the academy's prices. As a welfare-class-cum-middle-class professional I am liberating my Ph.D. degree from the fetters of a federal government that enacts harmful welfare reform policies and denies student financial aid to immigrants. In the academy, I refuse to be an American "success" story, to be another exotic animal in its multicultural petting zoo, or to walk quietly and self-contentedly down the halls to teach. I disdain the academy's class hegemony. I want to use the skills and knowledges of a welfare queen, equipped with the privileges I acquired along with my Ph.D., to rebuke the ivory tower's insidious hierarchies daily.

In the epigraph to this essay, Jamaica Kincaid expresses the needs fulfilled by a politics of everyday resistance. Kincaid articulates her desire that the future "remain capable of casting a light on the past such that in my defeat lies the seed of . . . victory." She enunciates how it might be possible for her to serve herself and in so doing to serve her people: "I only wish from time to time to make my actions be the actions of a people, to make my actions be the actions of a nation." Here, Kincaid acknowledges that the daily struggle to survive is also the struggle for transformation. Whether fusing political action with subjectivity or asserting the potential of a ghetto supastar identity, to survive we must foreground the aspects of our identities constructed as abject in the work that will produce transformation. Simply, the call to action for the new millennium is this: Radical women of color, while we build and work within coalitions, we must also individually and collectively put to use the myriad ways in which daily we can productively shit on the racist, elitist, anti-feminist, and queer-bashing regimes in each of our worlds.

Notes

I am ever indebted to Allegra McLeod for generous support and intelligent assistance, as well as to Phyllis Jackson, Maria Soldatenko, and Marina Harris for their insightful suggestions.

1. "Cultural bastions of class elitism" references institutional identities and practices, institutionally biased socio-economics, and academic stratification of "minority" members who function as a racialized class presence whose work can be ignored and exploited according to the logic of the academy's authority/knowledge, which is reflected in a parallel history of north american/western european class structures predicated upon the racialization of the "other" as a class of non-citizens whose labor can thus be appropriated.

2. Between California and Oregon alone—from California's propositions 21, 184, 187, 209,

226, and 227 to Oregon's measure 9—poor women, queers, immigrants, and children are aggressively under attack.

3. The Multilateral Agreement on Investment nullifies national sanctions, in particular enviornmental or labor sanctions, in favor of international economies.

4. At the fall 1998 Scripps Humanities Institute Conference, Angela Davis pointed to her early coining of the term "unlikely coalitions."

5. See www.nasulgc.nche.edu//WelfareStudentSuccess.

fifty-five

Being the Bridge: A Solitary Black Woman's Position in the Women's Studies Classroom as a Feminist Student and Professor

Kimberly Springer

Gloria Anzaldúa's autograph in my copy of *This Bridge Called My Back* reads, *"Para Kim, que te vaya bien con tus estudios. contigo, Gloria E. Anzaldúa 10.2.91."* I doubt she knew the significant role her words and *This Bridge* would play in my development as an activist, a student of women's studies, and a professor. *Bridge* not only introduced me to the feminism of Asian-American, Latina, and Native American women, but on a basic level this text showed me the possibility of even *being* a Black feminist.[1] However, this particular bridge could only take me so far and from that point on I began to create, if you will, an expansion. The bridge I envision is like one in movies featuring rainforests and uncharted jungles: rickety ol' planks strung together with rope that looks like it's seen many hardships. But the bridge *exists*; someone took the time to build it and it awaits use, as well as reinforcement for those who will follow. Through awareness, activism, and scholarship, I hope to reinforce the bridge by replacing a few well-worn planks with constructive criticism of Black feminism's past, as well as self-critique of my own Black feminist praxis.

In this essay, I recall demands from white peers in the classroom that I *be* the bridge over which they cross from being racist to interrogating their own privilege and my refusal to do so. I also gingerly step onto the bridge I now provide as a scholar-activist in my academic work. Through these experiences I reflect upon *Bridge*'s impact on my life, my relationship to Black feminism, and my understanding of coalition-building. Feelings of wonderment, rage, isolation, and transformation within *Bridge* were guideposts for the socialization I underwent from an assimilated, working-class girl into a Black feminist woman. Call them stages of Black feminist development.

Feminism, as theorized in *Bridge*, was a guide mapping many potential directions for my analysis of the complexity of Black feminism. With this personal narrative I demonstrate the continuing existence of Black feminist activism from Black women active in the 1970s (Kate Rushin, Beverly Smith, Barbara Smith, Beverly Guy-Sheftall, Audre Lorde), many still active today. I oppose a media-generated image of a second-wave/third-wave fracture and speculate on the possibilities for an intergenerational Black feminist theory. Rather than competing with the Black feminists who came before me, as much predominately white third-wave feminist literature attests, I see myself as the bridge between my foremothers and future Black feminists. Feminists must do coalition work on many levels simultaneously: connect with those outside the groups we choose to call home and examine our internal politics to determine what keeps us separated and reinventing the wheel.

Black Girlhood and Incipient Feminism

There are perils to growing up Black and female in the United States, but there are also unimaginable joys and triumphs. Watching my young second-cousin, Skylar, grow up, I'm simultaneously filled with pride and trepidation. Her mother reminds me of my own mother: the best mother possible, trying to raise a healthy, whole African-American girl in a society that devalues her based on her race and gender. I try to assist, reminding Skylar how smart, beautiful, and truly bold she is through creative feminist gifts and encouraging words. However, there is only so much I can do to protect her from the racist, sexist, heterosexist attitudes that will eventually try to shape her into someone other than who she was meant to be. I often compose letters and practice conversations I'd like to have when she is old enough to comprehend my meaning.

Dear Skylar Jade,

What's up, Skydee-dy-dee? Are you keeping Mama busy with your activities and questions and just all-around brilliance? I remember the time we tried to go see a holiday light festival. You were in the backseat all strapped in, asking me why we couldn't, after all, go. I'd left my wallet at home and explained the situation. You asked for the 3rd or 4th time and I lost my patience and, with a heavy sigh, said, "BECAUSE, Sky, I don't have any money on me." From the backseat I heard this pre-teen (though you were only 5) sucking of teeth and an exasperated "I was just ASK-ING." That, my dear, was what Alice Walker and other women in our family would call acting "womanish," but I had to laugh because you were so SASSY. I hope you remain secure in who you are—a complex almost-young-woman who'll keep questioning until satisfied with the answers.

Enclosed is a copy of Toni Morrison's The Bluest Eye. *Call me when you've read it. Kisses. Love, Cousin Kim*

Part of the message I received growing up was "Each one, teach one." I try to apply this edict as I reach back to younger Black girls who have yet to figure you that feminism is not a "white girls' thing" or a "bad word"; to help young girls and women see that female empowerment is not a crotch-grabbing "video-ho" and that we can, in fact, say, "Sister, that is fucked-up behavior." As my dear friend, another Kimberly, says, we need to bring our whole selves to the table, not just the newly sexually-empowered parts. I want to offer my Black feminist experiences as just one of many options to get them through the times when the news media, popular culture, and even some of their peers try to tell them that they're not intelligent and beautiful because they don't fit the dominant norms of beauty or that they are not keeping it real unless they are singing about some man paying the bills.

Preparing to graduate in the spring of 1992, I sat trying to decide what protest message to write on my mortar board. Among the sea of Greek letters and accolades for years spent partying, I wanted my cap to reflect my growing Black feminist consciousness. Not that I hadn't gotten my apolitical groove on to Public Enemy a number of times, but my years at the University of Michigan were my own flashpoint. Onto the television came another round of bulletins about the L.A. rebellion. A reporter asked a teenaged African-American girl a typically inane mainstream question: "What does the verdict in the Rodney King trial say to you?" I could feel my young sister's anguish as she choked out between tears, "It makes me feel like they think we don't matter at all." I knew then what to write on my mortarboard ("Burn, Hollywood, Burn"), but it was hard to see through my own tears as I felt similar feelings of worthlessness and defiance all at once. I think of that girl when I contemplate the shock of waking up from a deep assimilated sleep and into the cold reality of social injustice. How could I help her and others cross the icy waters of degradation threatening to overtake us all every time a bullet rips through the flesh of another sister or brother?

Identity Politics/Identifying Politically

What does it mean that a white man, a gay white man, introduced me to feminism? Is my feminism any less legitimate than that of my classmate who came to feminism following years of sexual abuse at her father's hands? Is it any less legitimate than that of my friend whose lesbian mother raised her with feminist principles, as if *Free to Be You and Me* were the sugar on every child's morning cereal?

My resident advisor, Jim, taught me many things that year. He taught me what it meant to think critically about power and privilege. He taught me what it meant to have my first real bona fide crush on a gay man and opt instead for being a dear friend. He also suggested that I take Introduction to Women's Studies during my first year. He led this horse to water, but he didn't have to make me drink. I partook of every reading, required and suggested, that I could get my hands on. Finally, there was something, or rather many "someones," who could explain just what the hell it was I felt as I learned about Black women's history for the first time, who all the powerful Black figures were in Boogie Down Productions' song "You Must Learn," why someone would want to spell *woman* "womyn," and the import of my senior high/junior college paper on *Bowers v. Hardwick*.

For me this mixing of cultures and political allegiances meant that, early on, I had an abiding belief in building coalitions across identities. It sounds clichéd, but I really could not see how one could harbor prejudices toward entire groups of people if one had experienced discrimination and also entered into intimate relationships with people different from one's self. I'm sure the label "sell-out" was tossed at my back, but I was too busy, thrilled by the activism and camaraderie, to notice. As an activist in anti-racist work, defending suburban Detroit clinics with reproductive rights organizations, studying social movements, I encountered people with differing political priorities. While it was never easy to negotiate all the demands and a few friendships fell by the wayside, I never regret trying to bridge the externally-imposed divides between my political interests. In those interests for women's, lesbian/gay, and people of color's rights, I had my own hands-on practicum in how power and privilege circulate to positively and negatively impact movement outcomes.

Just when I was discovering what each aspect of my identity had to do with the others, postmodern theorists (mostly white, European men) tried to suck *all* the damn air out of the room and tell me there was no "I." I was also discovering how my powerlessness and privilege lived side-by-side, making for a very confused, angry, but oddly exhilarated young woman. In my Intro to Women's Studies course, one of the *Bridge* essays I elected to read was the dialogue between Beverly and Barbara Smith. Not having a sister myself, I could only read in awe: two Black feminists in the same family? They captured precisely the conflict I felt while taking advantage of my educational privilege for eight months of the year, then going "home" to my family and Black community during holidays:

> There are ways we act when Black people are together that white women will
> never see in a largely white context. Now, I don't think this is about acting
> white in a white context. It's about one, a lack of inspiration. Because the way

you act with Black people is because they inspire the behavior. And I do mean
inspire. And the other thing is that when you are in a white context, you think
"Well, why bother? Why waste your time?" If what you're trying to do is get
things across and communicate and what-have-you, you talk in your second
language. (119, my emphasis)

Barely passing French my first year, I became bilingual in my Blackness
and my feminist inclinations. What I had yet to learn was how to defend
myself in this new language, this new land where different parts of me
fought to lay claim to my time and energy. The Black Student Union protest
or drive to a Clinic Defense in suburban Detroit? The United Coalition
Against Racism meeting or the Take Back the Night March? Like the 1970s
Black feminists I would later study, I was torn between two lovers and,
surely, feeling like a fool. I straddled the fence of my identity and burned out
quickly trying to bring an anti-sexist analysis to my "race work" and an anti-
racist sensibility to my "gender work." Not surprisingly, these two branches
never met. It was like trying to keep two lovers from finding out about one
another, but secretly wanting them to meet, fall in love, and forget all about
me. Bringing an anti-heterosexist perspective to either aspect of my activism
was, needless to say, an even rougher battle as I tried to be pro-lesbian/gay/bi
rights and *still* get a date with one of the SNAGs (Sensitive New Age Guys)
on campus. Was I being naive in thinking that, unlike Rushin in her "Bridge
Poem," I would somehow be exempt from translating for everyone who
selected which parts of me they wanted to encounter?

Inside the classroom a different battle was only just beginning. I tried
to defend myself in my women's studies classes where I was "The Only
One." The only Black woman, the only one who knew the importance of
talking about hair and its racial and gender implications for Black women.
The only one who thought, "You must be kidding" when professors at one
of the most prestigious universities in the country spoke of being ghettoized. Tell it to the folks in Cabrini Green. The only one who cringed and
slouched over self-consciously when a white professor declared, "Black
women don't have body image issues. There's just a different aesthetic in
the Black Community." Did you hear that, hips? You're just a different
aesthetic. Yeah. Right. Donna Kate Rushin's poem rang in my ears: "Sick
of being the sole Black friend to 34 individual white people." Sick of being
the sole person in the room unimpressed when professors tokenized bell
hooks on their otherwise all-white feminist theory syllabi.

The struggles with white feminists were not only with professors, but
with teaching assistants of the next generation of feminist activism too.
The TA for a required course interrogated me, "Well, 100–level students
will want to know. *Are* you a feminist?" It made me angry that all the

replies I could think of were not mine. Not the historically logical answer: "*Hell*, no, I'm not a feminist! Do I look like Sojourner Truth, waiting for some Northern suffragist to turn her back on me? I ain't no fool." That would be too "angry Black woman" and I might not pass the interview to facilitate the 100–level women's studies class, which I needed to fulfill my major. I opted for "Throw Her off the Scent Answer #2": "No, I'm not a feminist. I'm a *womanist*." While appeasing my Birkenstock-wearing, cultural-feminist TA, it did nothing for me but give me a reprieve from committing myself to feminism or to non-Black status in the eyes of some of my friends and relatives. Still, I felt so good and authentic that I went out and bought my *own* pair of Birkenstocks—militantly **black** ones.

I kept those broke-down sandals as a memento of what I saw as a simpler time in my feminist trajectory. It was easier in undergraduate school for me to parrot the lines of my real and imagined mentors on the need for socialist revolution, Black liberation, and patriarchy's downfall. It wasn't that I didn't believe those things but just that I didn't think about them much. It was much easier to take these principles as my own, rather than wrestle with my inner-life contradictions: my middle-class aspirations, my vast amount of book-learning, a decreasing belief in god, the ability to get instantly weepy at a strong rendition of the gospel hymn "Goin' up' a Yonder," the desire for a throw-down revolution Che Guevara–style, and a penchant for a Black Panther in a black leather coat.

In the Belly of the Feminist Beast

In the face of all that confusion I went to graduate school. Thinking I'd find out who I was and what I wanted to be, or at least buy myself a little more time, I applied to and was accepted into a doctoral program in women's studies. It seemed like a logical next step, building on my undergraduate major in women's studies and sociology. I could continue finding ways to remain politically active because I would still be a student—or so I thought.

The program I chose was, at the time, one of two offering a Ph.D. in women's studies. I assumed that it was a feminist program—after all, what else would a women's studies program be? Not until I began studying social movements and organizations did I understand it in the context of the institutionalization and professionalization of an area founded by activists. I entered a women's studies program in which most faculty and students *studied* women, but not necessarily tried to investigate or apply feminism.[2] This was, in fact, a double-sided realization: slight dismay that I could no longer assume that women's studies equaled feminist studies, but a determination to focus on feminist theory in my own work.

After another Black woman left the program for one more suited to her interests and sanity, I was once again the only Black woman in the program.[3] In addition to my status as the only Black woman, I also encountered many students who hadn't majored in or taken women's studies courses as undergraduates. This lack of training had significant consequences on my intellectual and activist outlook. It baffled me that a few women's studies graduate students in my classes professed to do women's studies, but flushed at the thought of having to enter a classroom and talk about feminist perspectives on film, religion, science, politics, or any number of other topics. Soon I learned that many of the women opting for a certificate in women's studies, wasting valuable class time in my feminist theory course with asinine debates about standard vacuum cleaners versus Dustbusters, merely added the certificate to their resume in the hopes of landing a scarce teaching position in their respective fields. That's when I decided that there's meeting women where they are and there's leaving their asses by the side of the road (or at a very nice rest stop) if you've got places to go.

It's a Love/Hate Thang

Recently three constellations saved me from chewing through the rope I was holding. My academic research, a few students, and a posse of Black, Asian-American, Latina, and white feminist friends were, and still are, my bridge between women's studies and feminism, between academic professionalization and activism. That's what the hyphen in scholar-activist means to me: I can still think critically, write, and teach about ideas of social justice, democracy, and equality, while encouraging students and myself to participate in direct action that makes those ideas practical tools for living.

Part of my struggle as a scholar-activist is my research on 1970s Black feminist organizations. I read about several organizations, searched them out to join up, but found that they'd all disbanded around the time I was saving my allowance for candy and *Archie* comic books. So I decided to discover what happened to these organizations and, more important, how they did it in the first place. How did they get a group of Black women together in the same room for something besides planning Women's Day at church or getting their hair done, which for a long time was my limited experience of women's organizing activities? Over the course of twelve years, several hundred, if not thousands, of Black feminists laid the groundwork for Black feminist activism and the expansion of what we call feminist issues (including, but not limited to, the right to *have* children and informed consent about sterilization as valid reproductive rights). Black feminists in at least five organizations in Boston, New York, Chicago, and San Francisco participated in consciousness-raising groups with white women and in groups of only Black women where they started to believe that they were not crazy for being Black *and* feminist.

Though these groups ceased meeting by the early 1980s, they left a legacy inspiring me to document their existence. Kitchen Table Press pinned a button stating, "Black Feminism *LIVES!*" to every copy of the reprinted Combahee River Collective Statement! This feminism lives in me as I read and re-read feminist-of-color writings and as I try to relay to my students the excitement and danger of a time in women's movement history that I wasn't around for either.

As an instructor on social movements, I struggle to teach about identity politics. Some postmodernists view identity politics as essentialist, reinforcing ideas of how marginalized people "naturally" are. Well, in some ways essentialism is *essential*. As the Smith sisters and the Combahee River Collective note, there once was, and still is, value in *identifying politically* with people who look like you. Yet as Bernice Johnson Reagon points out, this does not mean we don't ever open the door to the place we call home. In fact, it often behooves us to collectively tear the roof off our ideas of home and invite others in to see what we can make of the future.

As much as I complain about students' lack of historical context or wish I could just uncritically enjoy my *Entertainment Weekly*, I wouldn't trade in my feminism for anything in the world. Every time I experience a student having that °click° of how to think critically about discrimination and social change, I have that same spark of recognition all over again. We are still working on a bridge to somewhere exciting, dangerous, and new.

Incredibly enough, I've seen a few frat boys experience that click while some young sisters try to get over on me, Sister/Teacher, because, after all, "You know what it's like to be the only Black woman in a classroom of white folks *and* not have done the classwork because of last night's Kappa step show." At that moment Black feminist organizations' lessons come back to haunt me: do not assume that because someone looks like you, they share your political and personal objectives; I return to the idea of identity politics and remind myself there is much intragroup coalition work to be done. Moreover, I must be aware of how my own internal identity politics can impede internal critique and connections with the Black woman I hope to be and with other Black women.

One way I sought to make the exchange between activism and scholarship was to help organize a Black Feminist Salon while living in Atlanta. Unfortunately for me, I was moving away soon after the group formed, but it filled me with hope and pride that we could get several sisters to sit in a room and share what it means to be Black and feminist, lesbian, straight, and bisexual. Living about a thousand miles away from the Salon is disappointing, but just getting it together lets me know I can build community wherever I go. Whether that community is with other Black women or with feminist women and men in my predominately white mountain town, the bridges I've learned to build are internal and transport well.

There is so much work to be done around gender that I will not be left to my leisure even if I live miles away from a critical mass of Black sisters and brothers. The work heterosexual Black feminists need to do in conjunction with our Black lesbian and gay counterparts around homophobia in Black communities is unending. The dialogues that Black women of all sexual orientations need to open up with one another about sexuality and competition and "diva-dissing" could fill hours of conversation and anthologies yet to be conceived. Continuing to push for a redefined Black masculinity that does not replicate patriarchy's worst tendencies is a project just beginning in academia and the street.

Feminism, specifically third-world feminism, has been a bridge, a lifeline, and even an extension of my being. Yet sometimes I wonder how much longer I can continue being a bridge between cultures, races, and theories. As a member of the Black Feminist Salon in Atlanta said, "I consider it my activism whenever I leave the house." This is a lifetime of work. Social change is a process. I will often be afraid inside and outside spaces I call home. Perhaps I can persuade myself to look forward to the challenges and growth that will come as I continue crossing the bridge built by *This Bridge Called My Back* twenty years ago.

What Donna Kate Rushin calls for is not throwing in the towel because we're sick of white folks and everyone else who looks to Black women to be political Mammys. Instead, she affirms the work we need to do internally as well as externally to continue waging battles that have yet to be fought. Rushin's determined words warrant repeating: "The bridge I must be / Is the bridge to my own power / I must translate / My own fears / Mediate / My own weaknesses // I must be the bridge to nowhere / But my true self / And then I will be useful." Amen, sistah Kate, amen!

Notes

The author thanks AnaLouise Keating and Kimberly Wallace-Sanders for their extensive sisterly comments.

1. Equally critical in my personal-political Black feminist development was *Home Girls*, another Kitchen Table publication.

2. By the time I graduated from the program in 1999, I perceived students' greater dedication to critically engaging feminism.

3. The next year, sister Francis Wood came to the program, bringing heat and light.

fifty-six

This World Is My Place

Bernadette García

Concerning Alice Walker's poetry

He said it   he did   *It has its place*   *but I'd be very disappointed if you wrote like that*   wrote like what exactly? Like a Black Woman?   wake up little man

Where is this place and Who belongs there?

this Woman
    this wise beautiful woman   who weaves tapestries of words that touch people worldwide   are adored by   —Black   White   Poor Rich   Oppressed   Indigenous   Woman   Homosexual High School Drop Out   Man   Buddhist   Mormon   Ph.D....

or You
Understood   comprehended   appreciated   by pedantic   feather fluffing academic residents of the ivory tower   and their privileged wannabes

You can take your western eyes   off of my creations   saying   *it's ok but*   if my words are not mimicking   those slithering from your lips   if I choose to speak   to write   a language   other than patriarchy   paint through non-European eyes   compose music which comes from the rhythm of the earth   referring to my works as charming   ok   BUT   to be kept in their own place   not in your   serious consideration   publications   books   museums   anthologies   schools

THIS WORLD IS MY PLACE

this exclusive space   you've constructed around yourself   and a select few   is   rapidly   diminishing in size   confined to the barriers of your ignorance   and transparent tolerance   of me   we others   our creations   when will you discover that there is room for all of us   equally fifty-seven

Missing Ellen and Finding the Inner Life: Reflections of a Latina Lesbian Feminist on the Politics of the Academic Closet

Mirtha N. Quintanales

On April 30, 1997, an estimated 42 million people tuned in to watch *Ellen* on network television. In a historic moment, Ellen Morgan, the lead character of this sitcom, came out of the closet, declaring, "I'm gay! You hear that? I'm gay. And it sounds darn good." A couple of weeks earlier, Ellen De Generes, the actress/comedian who played Ellen Morgan, had made the cover of *Time* magazine. In an exclusive interview she had come out herself. Her words, "Yep, I'm gay," accompanied the cover photo.

It was the fourth month of my sabbatical leave and I was home. I don't watch much television, but I do buy *TV Guide*, regularly read through it, and choose programs I think might be worth watching. As an anthropologist who specializes in social movements and social change and ordinarily keeps a close media watch (certainly print media) on contemporary issues, I regularly buy and read *Time, Newsweek*, other weekly trade publications, and of course the *New York Times*. Nevertheless, I missed both Ellen Morgan's and Ellen De Generes's great moments, as well as the entire media blitz surrounding them. I was simply unaware of what was going on. A little over two years later, as I watched *Ellen* re-runs, caught up with this bit of network television history, and read up on the lives of those who had made it, I had to ask myself how I could have missed all this, and why.

Contemplating this particular omission, it occurred to me that it was symbolic of something that had changed in my life almost without notice. Unlike my decision to pass over the Miss America beauty peagant, the Olympics, O. J. Simpson's trial, or the Clinton-Lewinsky affair, there had been no conscious choice here. Ellen had slipped through the cracks of my consciousness as imperceptibly as I had slipped into the closet, and that closet had come to set the boundaries and color my perceptions of the world. Allowing myself to fully acknowledge and experience the great discomfort of my narrow confinement, I now felt motivated to open the closet door and take my first step out of it. Stepping out began with a review of the outer structures that had kept me in the closet for over a decade.

Flashback #1. It is 1980 and I am teaching a class entitled Lesbian Lives and Thought at an urban university in California. I have been invited to teach in the women's studies program as an adjunct while I begin to do research for my Ph.D. dissertation, approved by my graduate committee, on Latina lesbian feminists (it later changes). The class is fully enrolled. The students are all young women, the majority of them self-proclaimed "out" lesbians, as am I. So are other faculty members who teach in women's studies—full-time and adjunct, tenured and not. Several of us consider ourselves Latina lesbian feminists. I have been active in the women's movement for a long time, have been out since the moment I realized I was a lesbian, and can't even conceive of being closeted. In the following years I continue to be politically active (as an organizer, writer, public speaker) and to teach and work in affiliation with women's studies programs and conferences—always as an out lesbian.

Flashback #2. It is 1988. Within a year of completing my Ph.D. with a dissertation dealing with Cuban Americans, not my original Latina lesbian feminist project, I have my first tenure-track position at another urban university, this time on the East Coast. I have been hired to coordinate and teach in a Latin American, Caribbean, and Latino studies program, where I remain to this day. One of the first things I do when I arrive is to look for the visible, active feminist presence on campus to which I have become accustomed over the years, but meet only three women: the two women's studies faculty members and the director of the women's center. They are friendly and welcoming and soon to become my allies in what turns out to be a very challenging academic environment for me. None of them is a lesbian.

I know only one gay person on campus, a man with whom I share common friends outside the university. Unfortunately, within weeks of my arrival, I hear a high-level administrator crack gay jokes and ridicule this very same faculty member. Shortly after this incident, while having a conversation with a Latina on the administrative staff, I casually make a comment about my life or my partner. I watch her literally shriek and recoil in horror at the word *lesbian*, which has casually slipped out of my mouth. Wrongly concluding that I was making a pass at her, she quickly lets me know that she is not interested and is surprised and insulted when I tell her that neither am I. Pretty classic.

After a number of other similarly uncomfortable encounters, I begin to understand that I have to be careful, that perhaps it isn't wise to be open about my life. But I don't want to ignore gay and lesbian issues in the classroom, so I regularly integrate gay and lesbian feminist writings into my courses. Some students are very offended and feel free to openly voice their hatred. Others don't seem particularly to mind but present another kind of problem. A twenty-three-year-old student asks to watch a film with gay content at the university to complete a homework assignment because his parents will not allow him to watch it at home. Another student lets me know that she cannot read certain things because it's against her religion and her family values; her parents check her books and assignments for suitability. I hear students in their twenties refer to themselves and to each other as "kids" and sometimes get calls from their parents to report absences and inquire about their "children's" grades. If the homophobia, ignorance, or insensitivity I find among some of my colleagues, and the absence of a visible gay and lesbian community on campus do not sufficiently signal the need to be completely closeted, the situation with students now certainly does.

I begin to think of myself as a middle school or high school teacher who could possibly be accused of perverting the young and thus lose my job. I am particularly weary of the Latino students, 25 percent of our student population. I am aware of the importance of close family ties and religion in their lives. As one of only a handful of Latino faculty members on campus, I also realize that I am a role model for them. This is the case even as I have to tell them from time to time that "assistant professor" does not mean that I am simply an aid to some absent "real" professor. I have a Ph.D. in a legitimate academic discipline, and Latin American studies is a bona fide academic field, our courses as challenging as any other. I never stop bringing up gay and lesbian issues in the classroom but begin, on a regular basis, to try passing as straight. I call forth heterosexual credentials such as high school dating or a former marriage—in order to talk about gay and lesbian themes without drawing attention to my own identity and lifestyle. I hate myself for doing this but I feel I have no other choice.

It doesn't happen suddenly, but I gradually become solitary, withdrawn, taciturn, perpetually tired, indifferent, overweight, unproductive—my natural creativity and enthusiasm all but gone. Thankfully, through years of meditating regularly and doing other spiritual practices, I have learned to gain some distance from these negative states and circumstances and to simply be aware of them. I manage not to despair or feel totally trapped. During summer and winter vacations I participate in spiritual retreats and immerse myself in meditation, chanting, hatha yoga, the study of scripture, and other spiritual practices. These are periods of deep inner work, revelations, and transformation when I feel renewed and uplifted. I experience them as oases in the desert.

Yet the desert remains and I continue to reflect on what it means but still cannot understand it. I realize that to walk a genuine spiritual path is not easy, so I accept this difficult situation in my life as part of a process of inner purification. I tell myself that I am strong and willing to meet its challenges. The spiritual quest is indeed central to my life, but I mistakenly begin to think of it as separate from other aspects of who I am or what I do. Whenever the issue of my sexual orientation (among others) comes up, I brush it aside, telling others and convincing myself that a lesbian identity and lifestyle are no longer very relevant to my life, to my goals or to who I am as a person. As a spiritual seeker, I insist, I am beyond "all that." I do not yet grasp the homophobia and the lack of understanding of what it means to be "spiritual" that lie at the root of these deeply ingrained and misguided notions.

After some years and thanks to the efforts of one young "out" faculty member, and with the support of the women's studies program and a campus administrator, gay and lesbian studies begins to have a presence at the university. As the new millennium approaches, university administration invites the faculty to celebrate it with a Millennium Semester, an opportunity to develop and showcase new courses. Unexpectedly I am involved in planning a course on the lesbian and gay experience in global context with the colleague responsible for developing and teaching the first gay and lesbian courses on campus. We'd like to co-teach it and discuss it with the coordinator of the women's studies program and with the vice-president of academic affairs. The course proposal is written up and accepted, but before the master course list goes to press, I back down and decide not to be involved with it. I just don't feel "ready." My colleague agrees to teach the course alone but when the semester is about to begin has a schedule conflict and cannot teach it, so I have to do it. I am terrified at the prospect, but I am unable to refuse it this time.

I feel pressured by the little time I have to prepare for the course. I am also dismayed by the realization that I need to catch up with a decade of many changes, not only in the field of gay and lesbian studies but in the larger gay and lesbian world. It becomes evident to me that while I *had* always included materials on gays and lesbians in the classroom, in fact I had barely "kept track" of current gay and lesbian issues beyond reading the occasional article here and there. I had clearly maintained myself apart from the gay and lesbian community, both intellectually and in my daily life. How to bridge this gap on such a short notice?

Significantly, I am soon facing a class not of young, politicized "out" lesbians, but men and women whose lives and preferences and politics are a great unknown. I am still in the closet and after anonymously canvassing the students (I ask them to write in notecards about their identities and reasons for taking the course), I feel extremely vulnerable. The majority are heterosexual, wanting to learn more about gays and lesbians for a variety of reasons. I consider coming out to bring the wealth of my personal experience to the classroom, but this is only one of five courses I am teaching; the others are in Latin American studies. Once the word spreads, would my credibility elsewhere be questioned? I decide not to say a word. After a challenging semester of voluminous reading and preparation and of much personal reflection and discomfort, I begin to feel a longing for connection that goes beyond the academic.

I quickly learn where I might be able to find it. I am surprised by the sheer volume of gay and lesbian "cyberspace stations," so to speak, not to mention the numerous organizations, festivals, bars, and bookstores (small ones and large chains) filled with shelves of gay and lesbian and queer books and journals for mass consumption, to name only a few of the venues. I tell myself that I don't want to bother gay and lesbian friends I haven't seen for a while, friends who are surely too busy or too married to possibly understand what I am going through. I am too timid (and, I am afraid, too old and too proud—after all, I've been a lesbian for how many decades?) to set foot in a center or chat with cyber strangers. So instead, I buy armfuls of trade books, magazines, and newspapers every time I go out, rent every good gay and lesbian film I haven't watched—old and new—in over a decade, and finally discover Ellen Morgan in daily reruns on Lifetime: Television for Women.

I watch every episode with enthusiasm. And, like a devoted fan, I set out to find "everything Ellen." Now a habit, I also contemplate my experiences and observe my own responses, this time, to the magical world of sitcom. I have a feeling of community and comfort even as I notice that other than being a lesbian, I have, in fact, little in common with Ellen Morgan or any of the other characters on the screen. Suddenly it occurs to me that in real life I am quite alone in my living room, contentedly sipping seltzer with lemon as I sit in front of my television set late afternoons before dinner. It doesn't take me long to realize that I am the only one with whom I am truly keeping company and that the comfort I feel is my own and has been there all along waiting for me to just "tap into it."

I begin to understand that I really hadn't been missing Ellen and all she stood for, that instead I had been missing and denying parts of myself—the way I am in this body, in this lifetime, in this world. I feel very fortunate, at this point, to understand that neither "Ellen" nor any other character, real or fictional, nor any activity or set of circumstances—at work or anywhere else—is ultimately responsible for or capable of changing my predicament, my internal desert, the thoughts and feelings that led me to and kept me in the closet. It becomes evident that for the inner problem, so often reflected in the "outer" world around me, there could only be an inner solution, a solution completely in my hands. Even if I am unable to change outer circumstances–a cloudy day or institutional heterosexism—I *can* change my attitude, the way I think about myself and others and the manner in which I approach whatever I encounter on my path. In other words, I can take responsibility for the way I live my life.

I have long been aware of and sometimes have experienced deep contentment or joy as an inner state that "just is"–independent of any external factors. I know that I don't have to look for it anywhere "out there," that I can actually access it rather easily through meditation and other spiritual practices. This is no philosophy to me, this is something I have lived. However, like the majority of mortals, I have the tendency to forget and I had forgotten. But now I am able to remember, to experience this inner contentment, this joy, once again.

In a way I had been asleep, like Sleeping Beauty of the fairy tales. Yet Ellen Morgan is not the Prince who wakes me up. Neither are my new gay or gay-friendly colleagues and friends or the countless products of our modern culture, scholarly or otherwise, responsible for rousing Sleeping Beauty. Although they all play a role, it is the inner power of transformation that unfolds through spiritual practice *itself* that is ultimately the cause of the re-awakening. It brings the issue of "the closet" (academic and every other kind) to a head, engaging me in contemplation about myself, my life, my spiritual growth. It exposes and dismantles misconceptions and makes room for the inner light to shine forth and the eyes to open.

This *is* a process of spiritual purification, but as I realize now, it does not demand nor is it its goal that I lead a life of self-denial. On the contrary, the awakened spiritual energy seems to use absolutely everything in my life (including misguided notions or what I think are my "shortcomings" or "mistakes") to bring attention to the inner work and the inner goodness. It takes me step by step to total self-acceptance and the highest experience of joy, of love, which is always *there*. I find this truly amazing. It literally dawns on me that to be "spiritual" is to live always, no matter what I *think* or *believe* "is going on," with the awareness, the remembrance, of this ever-present divine state.

I am still a Latina, a lesbian, a feminist, and to large extent still closeted at work because I have found no good reason to be "out" any more than I am. But in truth, academic politics (or any kind of power discourse or praxis, in fact) is not my main concern at this point in my life. I want to know all of who or what I am, to become established in the highest state a human being can experience, and to serve humanity in whatever way I can. I try to be kind to and respectful of others and to do "what is right" on a moment-to-moment basis.

Sometimes this means speaking out or doing whatever is necessary on behalf of people who are suffering—near and far. Sometimes it means listening with complete attention to a student or simply eating well and caring for my body. Often it means correcting what I may have done half-heartedly or with anger, with a sense of self-importance or with a little too much attachment to results. Most challenging and most rewarding, "doing what is right" is being open to, acknowledging, and fully welcoming the many blessings—in any form they may appear—that are always showering upon my life; being aware of and allowing myself to experience the immeasurable greatness of my inner world: what I already have, what I already *am*.

fifty-eight

The Cry-Smile Mask: A Korean-American Woman's System of Resistance

Jid Lee

"I wish they were all like him," Susan whispered, looking at the back of the black man who had just turned around after asking her for a dance. "He's so nice. No bitterness or anger. If all black people were like him, we'd be living in heaven." A friend and former student, Susan stung me with her rudeness; I had to bite my tongue, struggling to smile. What I'd emphasized for the whole semester had evaporated somewhere in the space between us. She was praising a black man with a cheerful Uncle Tom smile, wishing all black people to be rid of the righteous pain and anger we'd discussed in class. I felt awkward. I couldn't correct her because she was no longer my student. I couldn't frown at her, either, because she was an exceedingly loving and compassionate person, who brought me chicken soup when I was sick and lifted me up with encouraging words when I was down. Facing this forty-year-old lady—so mature and loving yet filled with hackneyed racist clichés— I had to think.

Fortunately, I didn't have to go far. I already possessed a coping mechanism: the mask I'd been wearing since I came to the United States in 1980. When I smiled, it puckered into the face of an ancient Korean painter, Cry-Smile, carved by a mask maker a millennium and a half ago. Cry-Smile swore to the gods that until he finished painting the Buddhist utopia he had repeatedly seen in his dreams, he would not engage in any worldly activities. A life deprived of painting would await him if he allowed impure thoughts and acts to enter his life. He obeyed the gods, secluded himself, and worked. Sadly, however, he violated his oath when a neighbor woman visited him one day. When he raised his face from the painting, she gave a shy smile and he found himself returning an equally shy smile. His painted utopia paled in the vernal glances between the youths. For the rest of his life, Cry-Smile wore a face manifesting his name. Forever disabled from painting, but enabled to mingle with human beings instead, he smiled and cried at once, his face fleeting into pain and joy alternately.

In Susan's presence, I strengthened this Cry-Smile mask, pushing it into my face, feeling it stick with the adhesive force of a viscous panel. Only one third of an inch thick, my face—my mask—was strong enough to beat off Susan's rudeness. This burden of smiling always fell upon me, not on Susan or countless others who echoed such tired clichés. I was exhausted, struggling to weave a smile into the cry. Ulcer and headache were my daily companions, insomnia and wakefulness my nightly friends.

The Cry-Smile mask was effective, but its use came with collective as well as personal harm; it condoned my audiences' self-righteousness.

But the mask alleviated my students' resentment, opening a door; I could walk into their mind-set and modify it from within. I could "seduce" them into listening to my words, looking at the cry behind my smile. I couldn't persuade them to free themselves entirely from their preference for Uncle Tom's cheerful smile, but I could help them recognize the fallacy in this preference, acknowledge the legitimate anger, and participate in the fights to eliminate the root reasons for this anger. They could learn how to *perceive* and *love*, realizing that love alone may not change the world. Their love came with a smug, self-righteous ignorance about racism's power. Expecting everybody—regardless of race and gender—to be free of pain and anger, they could love only those just as cheerful and blissfully ignorant as they were. They loved without perceiving, happily oblivious to the mental violence experienced by those whom they shunned. I wanted to encourage them to perceive this violence, to extend their love for those shaped by this violence. I wanted to help them to love and perceive at once.

As a doctoral student at a midwestern university, I first realized that most students expected me to reinforce their stereotypes: as an Asian woman, I was to tell them how grateful Asian immigrants were for the opportunity to live in a free country far superior to our own oppressive native lands. Because I didn't accommodate this expectation, I became unpopular until I adopted my Cry-Smile mask. But when I moved to a southern regional university as a tenure-track assistant professor, I needed a much thicker mask, capable of withstanding the omnipresent, violent statements of racism and prejudice.

Two experiences during a 1995 course on autobiography illustrate this refashioning process. The first occurred during discussion of Benjamin Franklin's *Autobiography*. After praising Franklin's contributions, I described his overt contempt for Native Americans. One student, Richard, suddenly raised his hand and yelled at me, "You're being unfair, imposing today's liberalism on people who lived in the eighteenth century!" Although I explained that I simply wanted students to stop deifying Franklin and view him as a human being with merits and faults, Richard rejected my explanation, abruptly left class, and stormed into my department chair's office, where he accused me of suppressing his opinion. Because he needed my course to graduate, he refused to drop it. He remained through the end of the semester, constantly disturbing the class by verbally bashing my "radicalism." He did not again stand up in the middle of the class, but his persistent heckling served as a strong demoralizing force.

Although my mask was strong enough to withstand this first encounter, my interactions later that semester with Carla compelled me to measure the thickness of my mask and reinforce it. This new layer, I meditated, would be much more concealing and suggestive, softer in appearance but harder in reality. Carla's racism, emotionally and verbally violent, was even worse than Richard's open assault. Her attack occurred during class discussion of Anne Moody's *Coming of Age in Mississippi*, a book about the secret conspiracy between the local police in a rural southern town and the FBI agents who condoned and even protected the police's cooperation with the local Ku Klux Klan. Carla felt I was criticizing her country, became angry, and blocked me out by reading *Farewell to Manzanar*, Jeanne Wakatsuki Houston's autobiography about the Japanese-American internment. A book without an indictment of southern racism, *Farewell* was safe because it promoted an assimilationist image, without the anger of a Civil Rights activist. For Carla, *Farewell* was about a harmless Asian-American woman, a member of the model minority who did not threaten the hegemony of the majority. Carla's rejection of Moody's text in favor of Houston's reflects a position shared by many whites: "We don't like blacks, but we like Asians." When I asked Carla to put *Farewell* away she resisted, stating, "If you were teaching, I would." Her accusation annihilated my authority as a professor and exposed her belief that I had no right to discuss African-American experiences. She knew the history of U.S. slavery but was convinced that Asian Americans were treated exceptionally well. According to her, I owed compliments to this country.

Richard and Carla would not have reacted in this accusatory fashion had I been black or white. Had I been black, they would have expected and been prepared for the same materials and perspectives I introduced to them. They knew that if they assaulted a black faculty in the same crass manner, they would be instantly branded as racists. Had I been white and endowed with the privilege of being "radical," I would have been much less "guilty" of the fanaticism they and other students read into me.

As Frank Chin observes, white Americans' positive attitude toward Asian Americans is thinly disguised racism stemming from preference for a group that seems to follow whites' norms and accept their racism cheerfully (xxv). They do not realize that the model minority role is a survival tactic. Keenly aware of the brutal fact that minorities succeed only when they work twice as hard as the majority culture, Asian Americans swallow their anger and struggle to excel, exercising the only available alternative: wearing the cheerful mask of a subservient, diligent Asian who doesn't complain about discrimination. Whites' praise of Asian Americans, therefore, is "racist love," not "racist hate."[1] By showing racist love toward Asian Americans and racist hate toward other minorities, they shift racism's burden from the majority-centered system onto the minority groups themselves; and by emphasizing Asian Americans' relatively higher success rates (especially in business and education) against other minorities' lower success rates, they smugly promote the fallacious idea that the United States is full of opportunities even for minorities. To whites, Asian Americans are buffers justifying their racism.

Had it not been for *This Bridge Called My Back*, the loneliness that assaulted me after my interactions with these students would have lasted much longer. Rereading *Bridge* reaffirmed my belief that Asian-American and African-American women must establish a community. Praised as a happy, diligent model minority with no anger, Asian-American women have smothered their cries under a manufactured smile. United with the cries of African-American women, our cries could be heard more fully and we could find more support. As Toni Cade Bambara asserts, our wrath must be united ("Foreword"). Rereading *Bridge* reinforced my desire to move beyond the simplistic identity categories dividing us from each other. If I surrendered to the illusion that I, as an Asian-American woman, was shielded from the racism facing African-American women, I would be surrendering to the racist system's "divide and conquer" technique. I could not let this happen.

This sense of unity has been influenced by my deep commitment to African-American literature. Although black women's literature has been at the center of my work, I found myself dedicated to the whole African-American experience because I could identify with African Americans as a whole race, because I could feel what they felt, and because I had to wear a mask—much like their own—to survive. I was zealous for their literature not only intellectually but also emotionally. Paul Lawrence Dunbar was singing about my mask as he described his own: "We wear the mask that grins and lies, / It hides our cheeks and shades our eyes,— / This debt we pay to human guile; / With torn and bleeding hearts we smile, / And mouth with myriad subtleties." W. E. B. Du Bois was writing about my "double face"—my mask and my true face—when writing about his "double consciousness." Du Bois wore the mask of a mild, affectionate gentleman expressing his pain and grief in a non-threatening manner, the mask that put his white audiences at ease and moved them to appreciate his cries. His "double consciousness" was a smile that portrayed pain. It was a Cry-Smile mask.

Because I could identify with African-American writers emotionally, they became the core of my professional life in the United States. As traditional American literature came to me when I was growing up in Korea, African-American literature came to me when I was maturing in the United States. In Korea, learning about the United States and its culture and literature was one of the most important parts of education. Since Korean children begin learning English at the age of twelve, most Koreans are as familiar with English as they are with Korean. By the time I graduated from high school, I read Hemingway and Faulkner just as habitually as I read Korean authors. Going to a U.S. university for a Ph.D. in English and teaching English at an American university was a natural progression. I wished to continue learning American literature. This love of my major, so simple and so strong, sustained me against all the subtle and overt prejudices I suffered from my students. My commitment to people like myself—not only African Americans but all men and women of color—supported me during the violent backlash I faced in my classes.

With this sense of union, I continue my journey toward the making of a utopia, thickening my Cry-Smile mask whenever necessary. Each semester, I am faced with a new group of students repeating the same stereotypes: "I didn't know there was racism against Asians. Most Americans envy Asians because they perceive them as rich and well-educated. The internment of Japanese Americans during World War II shocks me." "Frankly, it's a little hard for me to believe what you say about Asians being discriminated against. They're white." "Those concentration camp days are over. We don't want to bring them up again." "Immigrants like you work so hard. They rise so fast. Look at how Asians make it in twenty, thirty years and how blacks who've been here for hundreds of years still live in the same old rot."

I can't count the times I have declared to my students, "The name of a model minority is bogus. Asians have suffered as much." "If we are white, why are we called a model *minority*? If we are white, why aren't we treated as whites?" "Those concentration camp days aren't over. When we entered a war with Iraq, the FBI agents made phone calls to innocent Arab Americans to find out if they had connections with Sadam Hussein or if they could in any way aid Iraq's war efforts. Our government was suspicious of an entire group of people, the Japanese Americans of 1991."[2] "Immigrants from Asia are a carefully screened group. Since World War II, this country did not accept Asians who weren't well-educated and financially capable. It's unrealistic to compare a carefully selected immigrant group to the masses of black people whose drive has been affected by violence and deprivation. We don't even ask middle-class whites to be exceptional. Why do we ask all blacks to be? Do we recognize our double standard in such a request?"

Yet in an age of educated ignorance, I maintain a mask thickened by similar double standards. If I lost control even for a short time, the class could be contaminated by students ready to express their clichés and erroneous preconceptions. Although I could not entirely eliminate students' resistance, I could at least keep them from disrupting the class. My southern mask became much more methodical and sophisticated than that worn in the Midwest. Crudely speaking, this mask had to be trickier and more mendacious, concealing my true thoughts while acknowledging a student's fallacious position. Only then could I assist them in unlearning their prejudiced views.

I no longer talk to my colleagues about my frustration and difficulties.

Those without my experiences would simply assume I was making excuses. As the only Asian faculty in my department, I had to establish a precedent not only for myself but also for other Asian female faculty who may find themselves at southern regional universities. I had to deal with people's preconceptions about Asian women and wear a smiling mask to avoid threatening them, but I had to stand my ground to keep myself against all odds. "What is a woman if she loses herself?" I asked myself every morning.

Repeatedly, I reminded myself that my Cry-Smile mask had nothing to do with the stereotypes of the nice, soft Asian female. I was myself: neither a submissive, giving Asian woman nor an aggressive, westernized woman manufactured as a rebellion against the stereotype. Certainly, I was aware of the "damned if you do and damned if you don't" situation. If I fit into the stereotype, some students and peers would take advantage of me; I would also be invisible, viewed as a second-class citizen. If I didn't fit into the stereotype, they would get mad at me because I broke the mold and I would get mad at them, too.

But still I smile. By smiling, I invite my students to enter a world foreign to them; I encourage them to change their attitudes. Changes are possible—and even powerful—when we aim for a long-term impact, when we give up the temptation to wish for an immediate outcome. With the smile in my Cry-Smile mask, I can give myself the patience to wait, to help my students change gradually from within themselves.

Recently, I witnessed the power of this patient waiting. I was teaching a class in autobiography again, four years since being challenged by Richard and Carla. "Seduced" by the abundant smile exuding from my mask, my students gently engaged themselves in the discussion of Franklin's hatred of Native Americans. Because I spoke with a smile enabling me to mingle with their self-righteous ethnocentrism, they could acknowledge the pains of Native Americans. They were prepared for Russell Means's *Where White Men Fear to Tread,* a Native-American political activist's autobiography about his war with the federal government. This book would have been called "fanatically radical" by students like Richard and Carla, but because I taught it with a thicker, more supple mask, it didn't invite violent verbal opposition. It was accepted, at least without overt resistance, as a record of a legitimate American experience. In four years, I had accomplished a major task for myself and my students: I had earned the ability to plant seeds for changes. I saw the smile of my Cry-Smile mask at work, envisioning the seeds blooming five years from now. I could see them taking the words from our class into their environment.

Notes

1. *Racist love* and *racist hate* are Chin's terms.
2. See Raskin.

fifty-nine

Andrea's Third Shift: The Invisible Work of African-American Women in Higher Education

Toni C. King, Lenora Barnes-Wright, Nancy E. Gibson, Lakesia D. Johnson, Valerie Lee, Betty M. Lovelace, Sonya Turner, and Durene I. Wheeler

I had to write so that somebody would realize what my life is like.

—*Ntozake Shange*[1]

We are African-American Women in Higher Education who hold a range of faculty, administrative, and clinical counseling positions.[2] We have gathered to tell our story, to speak from the particulars of our experiences. In coming together we engage in a collective process of "transforming silence(s) into action" (Lorde, *Sister,* 40). One common quality we bring to our view of work in the academy is our willingness to create humanizing change and the additional level of service this often entails. This commitment is integral to our work, yet it complicates both our lives and our professional experiences within the academy (Rains). It is this story we choose to tell.

A Metaphor to Begin the Story

As black women we came together to talk about what we do in our respective roles in academe. As we talked about the level of service infusing our work, we began to view the accompanying responsibilities as a kind of "third shift." Here we build on the main premise of Arlie Hochschild's *Second Shift*: after fulfilling job responsibilities in the paid labor force, working women return home to fulfill a majority of the household duties and family responsibilities. Society's support of this traditional division of labor renders women's "double shift" invisible. Our metaphor of the third shift builds upon Hochschild's idea, but articulates yet another level of unseen work and invisible contribution we make within the "white academy." We want you to witness our experiences, so we will describe the work that constitutes this "shift" within predominately white academic institutions. Our story, however, is primarily a story of the change processes we create to deepen the institution's humanist capacities. We share this process of change and transformation with you so that you can compare, draw from, alter, and use it in your own revolutionary work.

The metaphor of third shift is tied to the working-class labor of employees who work the third organizational shift. Third shifts generally occur from 11:00 P.M to 7:00 A.M, and have been referred to variously as the third shift, the swing shift, and the graveyard shift. We assert that the third shift pulls together the work done by earlier shifts throughout the day, and also prepares operations for the next day. Hence, this shift often carries the responsibility for both "breaking down" prior activities and production modes and "setting up" the subsequent work activities for the day shift. The third shift can also be the most taxing, for it requires that workers adjust their circadian rhythms to the demands of the job. In our case, we see a parallel between the rigors of third-shift workers and the physiological and psychological challenges we face as black women by taking on an additional level of responsibility in the white academy.

We also draw a connection between the metaphor of third shift and the euphemism of "Third World." Hegemony and patriarchy both devalue and make invisible women's labor worldwide, particularly in the case of women relegated to Third World status. At the same time that we acknowledge a common connection, we realize that the specifics of class, culture, ethnicity, sexuality, age, abilities, and religion differentiate our experiences. We do not mean to essentialize. Audre Lorde warns us as women not to diminish the real differences among us. And bell hooks challenges us not to create false harmony as it will be a shallow substitute for authentic solidarity. While we acknowledge and remain open to our differences as women, we simultaneously affirm and celebrate the enormity of contribution made by women's labor on a global scale.[3]

Using the metaphor of third shift, we position our invisible work as critical to the work of the academy. This metaphor is our first act of resistance. It is an act of reinventing ourselves. Through naming and telling our individual stories, we create a collective voice. With this voice we transcend the organizational arrangements that would isolate us from one another. Our first act of resistance is culturally resonant with the concept of divine Nommo, the belief that the spoken word has power to create reality.[4] Molefi Asante, one of the foremost scholars of African-centered themes in the Americas, the West Indies, and the African continent, speaks of Nommo as a fundamental belief in the generative and productive power of the spoken word.

Through our words, first spoken and now written, we deepen and expand the connections between us. This is the generative power of the spoken word. Maya Angelou tells of "deep talk," a phrase used in West Africa. Deep talk is the ever deepening spiral of revelation, truth telling, truth seeking, meaning making, and planning. There may never be an answer, at least not one answer. But the process is generative and leads to the discovery of new possibilities of identity, voice, community, and action. As black women in the academy, we know what it means to engage in this kind of "deep talk" with each other (Ferguson and King). Our deep talk generated this essay. As you read it our deep talk has the potential to spiral even deeper.

The kitchen table as a site of restoration and revolution also resonates in our theory of our role as change agents within the academy. Traditionally the kitchen table has held a distinctive place in black women's lives. Beyond its central role in family life, the kitchen has been a site for nurturing the woman-to-woman relationships that nourish community.[5] It is a dynamic site of action where black women hold multi-purpose community councils. In turning the tables on the kitchen as a site of gender role oppression, black women have skillfully used kitchen table consultations to resolve the problems of life. That is why kitchen table conclaves figure so prominently in black girl-to-woman rites of passage where earning a place at the table signals acceptance into womanhood. Like women before us, we sit around the kitchen table, talking deep—planning, strategizing, and healing each other's wounds.

In "Across the Kitchen Table: A Sister-to-Sister Dialogue" Barbara Smith and Beverly Smith model the kitchen table forum and its requisite deep talking. They create an ever deepening spiral of communal expression by courageously articulating their thoughts and experiences as black feminists in the Women's Movement. The resulting conversation is not staged or choreographed from some canonized text. Rather it is generated in the moment, between the biological sisters' relationship of mutual respect and trust. This context allows them to risk self-revelation, articulating the unarticulated, breaking the taboos, and thereby voicing the silences that denied and "white-washed" black feminists' experiences in the Women's Movement (117). The silences of class oppression, lesbian separatism, and homophobia in the black community are some of the dynamics they transform across the kitchen table. They initiate a process of change by making it possible to discuss what we had been afraid, unable, or unwilling to name.

Now, two decades later, we continue this kitchen table tradition. In essence, we bring the kitchen table into the academy. Our kitchen table is any site where we come together for the process of deep talking and with the purpose of creating change in the academy. Women have created kitchen table forums in multiple locations, kitchen tables notwithstanding. Kitchen tables are women's space, the place to which people gravitate to prepare and strengthen, cleanse and release, feel safe and become empowered. Generally speaking, kitchens are service-oriented spaces controlled by women. To humanize organizational space within the academy, it is essential that we create and re-create kitchen table forums. Making the opportunity for these sites of transformation is a part of the work of the third shift.

A "Griot" to Pass on the Story

The characteristics we discuss for this shift work apply to each of us gathered to tell her story. Yet we experience these characteristics differently depending upon our positioning within the academy and our respective institutional spaces. The stories we share reflect our experiences and herstories across the various institutions, spanning continuums of size (for example, large state universities versus small liberal arts colleges), variations in student populations (by age, socio-economic class, race, and ethnicity), emphases and orientations toward research and teaching, and other major dimensions. Our stories are composite scenarios that incorporate real experiences while masking the specific events any one of us has encountered within a particular institution. We make this choice to protect our own anonymity and confidentiality as well as the privacy of our students, colleagues, and the institutions for which we have worked. At the same time, our composite scenarios reflect patterns, commonalities of experience, dilemmas, and issues familiar to each of us and connected to the growing body of literature on women in general, and particularly women of color within the academy. For this reason, we create a fictional character[6] to share our stories with you. She is the bridge between our individual voices and our collective memory, the expression of our multi-tongues. She will speak to you in first person in the spirit of passing on knowledge through oral tradition, and as such serves as the griot for our individual and collective voices. She is Andrea.[7]

Who of you know how to carry your burden in the heat of the day?
—Mary Church Terrell[8]

Story One: Third Shifting in a Third Space

I am Andrea. Late one Thursday evening, I saw two colleagues in the hallway of my building. They looked exhausted and I greeted them warmly, curious about their obvious fatigue. Wearily seating themselves on a bench, they explained that they had been pulling up registration records throughout the day to review schedules of students at risk. They examined what particular combinations of courses might lead to in terms of student grade point averages, or student successes in completing their courses. "We know," one colleague said, "that taking too many science courses together is not generally a good idea for most students, even the strongest. But some advisors sign students up for classes that are sure to lead to poor grades, dropped courses, and frustration. Students who drop a course sometimes jeopardize their financial aid. Many wait so late to drop that they encounter complications—perhaps a snowballing effect in terms of doing badly in other courses, not to mention the emotional effects. So we're identifying scheduling problems and then calling the students in to help them revise their schedules and to recommend that they meet again with their advisors." "Is that a part of your job?" I naively asked. And now we're all beginning to laugh. "Well, yes and no," each of my colleagues answered. "Our jobs as administrators include a variety of functions and services for student support. While this particular task is not specified, while no one has asked us to do it, in order for us to provide effective academic services, we know this must be done."

This first scenario tells us much about the work of the third shift and reveals the surrounding cosmology. We assert three things. First, African-American women who engage in third-shift work are making a clear choice to humanize organizational space. Second, African-American women who engage in third-shift work are bearing added physical and emotional strain and fatigue in order to implement a culturally-motivated organizational vision (Ella L. Bell).[9] This vision mandates integrating organizational goals with humanist purposes to promote the well-being of both individuals and community. Finally, we assert that as African-American women who engage in third-shift work, we are contributing to the institution's mission and goals by identifying spaces where those goals are not being fulfilled.

Intentionally humanizing organizational space is historically aligned with the calling to racial uplift. Black women activists fought against racism, and fought to uplift the race through gaining civil rights and liberties (White). The values underlying this human rights activism can be purposefully applied in any organizational context or setting. Moreover, this humanist purpose transcends focusing solely on one's own race. It is a consciousness that reflects Alice Walker's womanist ideas of being "in charge and serious" ("Definition"). We see our identities as transcending the formal organizational positions assigned to us. Position is useful as long as it accomplishes the desired goal—individual and collective uplift. In fact, a distinctive characteristic of the third shift is its emphasis on achieving such outcomes.

The impetus for reshaping organizational space to make it more responsive to human needs and experiences is part of our womanist system of valuing. Yet the ability to identify what is in need of reshaping derives from what Linda James Myers describes as third space. Rather than emphasizing dichotomous thinking that values one side of a dichotomy above the other, Myers speaks of movement beyond dualism to a third, more creative and generative space (7). Working to explore this third space allows us to create new alternatives.

We apply a logic that womanist thinkers have referred to as a both/and epistemology—a form of creative problem solving that requires working through contradictions (Henry; Olguin; Collins). In the previous story, the women who pulled the files identified a contradiction in the institution's goal for student success: students were allowed to register for courses in ways that would make success unlikely. Taking up the burden included not only the labor of the third shift (that is, pulling the files during the late evening hours); it also included defining a way to counter the organizational inadequacy that put students in a position of imminent failure. This is one of the ways we take up our burden, in the heat of the day or, as in this case, the heat of the night.[10]

The theme of third space is also evident in the next story. Its greater length is to illustrate the cyclical nature of our third-shift work.

Story Two: Forming and Re-forming Coalitions

It's me again, An'drea. I'm a tenure-track faculty member. One of my first-year advisees was an African-American woman who was quite capable academically and well prepared to handle the rigors of this setting. Yet it was obvious to those of us who had worked with her that she entered the university with some emotional and interpersonal problems. In spite of this, you can imagine my surprise to hear from my colleagues that she had violated community standards.

I too am Andre'a. I'm an administrator in judicial affairs and also have an MBA. I informed my colleague, the student's advisor, that I had already begun to implement an action plan on this student's behalf and would work closely with another colleague in multicultural affairs to ensure that the student received the appropriate counseling, academic support, and (if necessary) legal advice.

I am also Andreah. I'm an administrator in multicultural affairs with a Ph.D. in political science. My colleague in judicial affairs and I quickly gathered comprehensive information so that full knowledge would inform the situation at hand. We then worked with the student, coaching and encouraging her through the process. Interestingly, each time my superior talked to me about her, the response was focused solely on protecting the institution from liability. Concern for the student's well-being appeared secondary, if not inconsequential. My colleague and I, however, continued to advocate for the student. Given her race and gender as well as our assessment of the sensitive nature of her counseling needs, we strongly recommended that she see the African-American woman psychologist on staff. As with many students, we employed a kind of shepherding process.

I am Andryah as well. I'm a psychologist at the student counseling center. The secretary who received the call referring the student to me was not told nor did she comprehend the urgency of the request that the stu-

dent be assigned to me. Nor did the other counseling personnel realize that this young African-American woman's crisis of identity and communal place could be more readily addressed by a counselor of the same race and gender. Ultimately, she was assigned to a white male counselor.

Alas, I too am N'dreia. *I'm dean of Academic Services and have a Ph.D. in public policy. I am in a meeting with other administrators whose concern about the student's situation prompts them to propose discussing it with the university ombudsperson. I am aware that an African-American woman with a law degree was hired to provide conflict resolution and mediation. I say: Why not bring Ondreyah in on this? They do not seem to hear me. So I push further by pointing out that Ondreyah's legal expertise would be beneficial here. No one objects, but I sense only mild support. I do not take the time to be baffled. However, I do offer to follow through myself to make certain that the student connects with Ondreyah. I feel satisfied that I have helped to re-form the current coalition to address this stage of the student's concerns. Including Ondreyah makes it more possible for the student's race, class, and gender identity to be sensitively addressed. The university will also have the benefit of additional legal expertise. Finally, I have intervened in a dynamic of invisibility in which it appeared that Ondreyah as well as all of her much-needed expertise would have been overlooked.*

This story never ends. But we will pause here to explore the meanings we derive from it. Primarily, we see this story illustrating the ways that we shepherd students through the process necessary to their well-being in the system. Our work on the third shift does not relate only to students or only to issues of race but to the university community as a whole. Yet we do acknowledge and own our unique awarenesses of race, class, gender, identity politics, and power relations. We are particularly attuned to these issues because they profoundly affect the potential for a just community.

Our internalized mandate to serve creates an open agenda. We may be involved with individual students, but we also find ourselves responding to personnel issues—such as an unfairly evaluated or harassed faculty or staff member. We may respond to campus politics. At other times, we find ourselves in the midst of conflicts between students and administration or we may be the contact person when desperately litigious parents threaten the university. At other times we may facilitate student-to-student conflicts and crises. We find ourselves third shifting through many such stories simultaneously.

In each of these scenarios we form and re-form coalitions. We identify the skills needed for the third shift (who we need to work with, and *how* we need to be engaged during each phase of the process). As our story indicates, our coalitions may include each other. But more often than not, we are continually forming coalitions that cut across boundaries. More significant, we make boundaries where they are needed, and undo boundaries where they are not needed. This process also requires us to determine how public or private each third-shift activity must be. We determine what is needed next and who can help, and in doing so we form or re-form a coalition, passing the baton to a trusted member of the team. The team member is one of us who is well-positioned in the organizational space (or shall we say in the "race") to help us achieve our goals.

Forming and re-forming coalitions also entails building the communal ethos necessary for responding to the situation at hand. We identify those individuals with a vested interest in some aspect of the situation, or we cultivate a vested interest in those who we feel would be receptive and could play a critical role in our collective response. This task requires a multiple consciousness such as that characterized by Mary McLeod Bethune's[11] leadership. According to Audre Thomas McCluskey, Bethune demonstrated specific qualities and adaptations that allowed her to embrace the conventions of white middle-class femininity while simultaneously working to subvert the effects of sexism and white racism (71). Using a highly adaptive leadership style, Bethune engaged in successful outreach for the purpose of "uplifting the black home and community" (72). Like Bethune, we work to create the forms of coalition that "bring forth community."[12]

"Mama, I'm walking to Canada, and I'm taking you and a bunch of other slaves with me."

—Alice Walker[13]

Historically, we see the ultimate level of skill at forming and re-forming coalitions in the person of Harriet Tubman. Her work to liberate enslaved African Americans by guiding them to freedom required extreme secrecy and risk, and yet could not be accomplished without diverse strategies of coalition forming and re-forming as each situation dictated (Hine and Thompson). We do not mean to equate our work at the turn of the twenty-first century with that of Tubman's nineteenth-century work. However, we acknowledge her as one of many (both known and unknown) black women historical figures who provide a prototype for our third-shift work. We carry this imprinting. We call it up as we engage in breaking down the previous shift and setting up for the next.

Our third shift requires us to be aware of how invisible we are. Though we are routinely asked to deal with matters of race, rarely are we consulted for our expertise in addressing broader institutional issues. In particular our white colleagues call upon us to deal with issues they perceive as involving anger, gender differences, cultural differences, or other emotionally-charged areas. We are often asked to facilitate, work through, or speak for issues that are out of bounds in terms of the institution's norms and, indeed, for the culture as a whole. This dynamic places us within what Chandra Mohanty refers to as "oppositional space within institutional space" ("Under Western Eyes").[14]

Sweet Grass Baskets and Third-Space Technologies

The third shift resembles the art of weaving sweet grass baskets.[15] The age-old patterns of basket design represent a sacred trust handed down by our African-American ancestors. They have entrusted us with an ethic of communal care[16] transformative in nature. Like the sweet grass baskets, our third-shift work requires weaving of knowledge and skills to produce communities where individuals and collectives can develop and thrive. We continue centuries-old patterns and designs, and also create new designs as needed by adding some new feature or adaptation to the cultural/communal prototype. The basic structure of the baskets, what one might call functional integrity, is preserved. Yet the new features are customized for contemporary use, equipped to handle the subtleties of modern-day racism, sexism, classism, and heterosexism.

In the case of the third shift, we apply third-space technologies. *Third space* refers to the new alternatives and possibilities that defy and transcend the oppositions and polarities that organizational cultures create. "Third-space technologies" is our response to bell hooks's call for the development of emotional technologies of recovery and resistance (*Teaching*). We use the word *technologies* to imply intricate details, steps, and procedures that can be taught and replicated. Two salient aspects of our method include kitchen table/collaboration and deep talk/articulation. Together, these aspects transform a particular context from restrictive to empowering organizational space.

The process of calling together a forum of sisters and the process of talking deep are intertwined. We do not have a step-by-step instructional manual, but rather an elaboration that honors the wholeness and complexity of our collaboration for change. We begin by creating opportunities to gather as a group of black women. It is important, within the white academy, to come together as black women so that we don't have to translate our experiences across race but can first become centered in our own experience and voice. We come together in a spiritual connection that counters the white academy's promotion of a color-blind value stance. Color- blind values diminish opportunities for the communal affirmation needed by those sharing a common social and/or cultural identity. Like Barbara Smith and Beverly Smith (113), we come together to speak our truths and create shared vision(s). Their collective voices became a tool for change in the Women's Movement just as our voices become tools for change within our academic locations.

Technologies of articulation and talking deep vary and respond to the persons and issues at hand. We tend to each other's concerns and needs at many levels: personal, social, spiritual, institutional. Because this process is emergent rather than proscriptive, our description here can not be exhaustive. Yet we are conscious of some common patterns. We give careful attention to each other and the issues, and raise consciousness by sharing how the issues affect us all. In this way we transform our individual experiences of isolation viv-à-vis the issues and their psycho-social repercussions for us in our respective roles. We push and challenge each other and ourselves to move vague discussions toward greater clarity, so that everyone understands the issues and how they can participate in resolution. We brainstorm, analyze, and critique various approaches, ideas, and solutions as well as possible reactions, consequences, and outcomes. One might say that we practice and rehearse, in the empowering space, what must be carried out in more restrictive space.

Within this kitchen table forum and its accompanying deep talk we develop Third-Space Technologies—the strategies for change that we will ultimately implement in our academic setting. It is our method for occupying oppositional space within the institutional space of the white academy. Third-Space Technologies are the product of Nommo. We act, we become, we live—the generative and productive power of the spoken word.

In pushing ourselves to become clear, we sharpen our methodology. In addition to kitchen table/collaboration and deep talk/articulation, it includes our movement from internal kitchen table space to more external spaces throughout the organization. In the organizational spaces beyond our kitchen table, we apply what we have dreamed and envisioned. These competencies include generating new alternatives to address issues or fulfill goals. This generative vision reframes dichotomies, resolves contradictions for the organization, and expands the organization's reach to achieve its mission fairly and equitably. It is a vision informed by our respective standpoints that reveal to us how organizations reproduce the dominant ideologies of exclusion and marginality.

We must learn to decode the activities, language, and strategies particular to the white academy. We must anticipate the ways racism, sexism, and classism are taking place. We have to translate what has cultural capital in the academy and how this reward system operates to exclude. Just as Ida B. Wells decoded and translated the white supremacist ideologies supporting mob violence against blacks during the postreconstruction era (McMurry), we too engage in decoding the academy's activities. Oppositionality in action is the way we apply these skills. It is a day-to-day application of the ethic of care as black women academics might interpret it.

Belenky, Bond, and Weinstock's research on the expression of this caring leadership mode among women of color led them to Barbara Omolade's[17] view that it is "a tradition that has no name." We name the tradition for ourselves as the third shift. In so doing, we transgress a social perception that devalues service and caring.[18] We invoke a new reality that moves us beyond the stereotypical mammy who "suckles and raises other people's chirren's."[19] This essay explains our contemporary tradition of lifting as we climb and its application in academe. The competencies and perspectives we apply help to create the kinds of "public home places" Belenky's research attributes to developmentally oriented leaders (15). These places allow both the individual and the community to thrive. They are places where all of us can transform our silences into action.

We end by talking deeper still. Our process of change supports and protects the individual's vision, and ultimately the consensual vision—the very mission and purpose of academic institutions. We see the individual's deepest vision connected to that which is most vitally alive in all of us, the level of dreaming (Lorde, *Sister*)–a theme that figures prominently in the cultural mythologies of diasporic African peoples (Asante). In the African-American cultural matrix, Martin Luther King publicly immortalized the power of dreaming in his "I Have a Dream" speech. Similarly, history documents that Harriet Tubman's underground railroad activities were often guided by prophetic dreams and that Madame C. J. Walker was propelled to millionaire status based on a formula for hair care preparations revealed in a dream (Hine and Thompson). Black writers in all genres reveal even more artifacts of dream symbolism.[20]

As African-American women in higher education we too find meaning in this symbolism. Our oppositional space within the white academy seeks to clearly discern the dreams that individuals wish to align with the organization's purpose. We seek to hold the community accountable to its stated purpose and mission for all of its members. We seek to help the organization interpret its mission in ways that support individual and collective growth and development within and across cultural and social differences. Our commitment is to the whole community. Yet we invest heavily in tending the dreamscapes of the marginalized. We come together as black women across kitchen tables of our own design in white academe. We realize that there is not one way, nor is there only one answer. So we generate new possibilities to support our students, our colleagues, our co-workers, and ourselves in actualizing dreams of wholeness in contexts of justice. Sweet grass baskets woven with our voices hold a collection of third-space ideas. We go to work. *We are Andrea.* At the day's end we remain Third World women living in a third space working a third shift. But we have learned that working the third shift has one irrevocable advantage: *we are awake while others sleep, and in that wakefulness,* we safeguard dreams.

Notes

1. Quoted in Wallace, 132.

2. We've held professional positions at a number of colleges and universities spanning the areas of academic support, admissions, clinical psychology and counseling, EEO compliance and affirmative action, human resource management, judicial affairs, minority and multicultural affairs, and a host of faculty appointments, both tenured and untenured.

3. Robin Morgan's extensive research compilation, *Sisterhood Is Global*, reports that women contribute two-thirds of all working hours. She writes that women are the world's proletariat: "While women represent half the global population and one-third of the labor force they receive only one-tenth of the world income and own less than one percent of world property" (1).

4. The belief that humans have the power to speak reality into being is a cultural artifact of African experience throughout the diaspora that underlies the oral tradition (Asante).

5. Kitchen table discourse is used by a number of black women writers, who position the kitchen as a site of communal action and construct the kitchen table as a transformative and revolutionary space (Marshall, "Making").

6. Derrick Bell's texts were instrumental in modeling the scholarly use of fictional characters to voice social issues and dynamics.

7. We selected the name *Andrea* to represent our collective identity and give voice to our story. However, in the spirit of African-American naming traditions, each of the "Andreas" would pronounce or write her name differently to reflect her own individuality. The following spellings and pronunciations include some of these variations in personal style as well as generational, regional, or other distinctions among us: An'drea, Andre'a, Andreah, Andryah, N'dreia, Ondreyah.

8. From a 1916 speech by Mary Church Terrell, a preeminent educator and the first president of the National Association of Colored Women, to the black women of Charleston, South Carolina (White, 23).

9. Historical models of women who made such sacrifices abound in the work of African-American women as they engaged in social change such as supporting the underground railroad, campaigning against lynching, and advocating for civil rights (Hine and Thompson).

10. Third-shift work does not take place solely in the private, backstage spheres of organizational life, but throughout all spheres. A third-shift goal is to create institutional politics and social arrangements that generate public discussion of issues relevant to the community.

11. Bethune founded the Daytona Educational and Industrial Training Institute for Negro Girls in 1904. She later engineered the school's merger with Cookman Institute, creating the coeducational Bethune-Cookman College, and became one of the nation's first women college presidents (McCluskey).

12. Beverly Wildung Harrison, womanist theologian, speaks of "bringing forth community" by responding with the fullness of one's humanity to another. By so doing, we "act-each-other-into-well-being" (217).

13. Walker's definition of a womanist includes the following dialogue: "'Mama, I'm walking to Canada and I'm taking you and a bunch of other slaves with me.' Reply: 'It wouldn't be the first time.'"

14. For Mohanty, this phrase indicates carrying out an agenda that opposes or resists institutional norms and practices.

15. Sweet grass baskets are coiled baskets made of long-leaf pine needles or dried grasses. The Gullah people, known for their artistry in creating them, are African-American descendants of enslaved Africans brought to the coastal islands of South Carolina. These multipurpose baskets' design can be traced back to Nigeria, Togo, Benin, and Ghana (Nichols).

16. Carol Gilligan's research found that women's system of morality is guided by the desire to determine and apply principles of justice in the context of caring relationships and communities. She refers to this morality system as an ethic of care ("Visions," 397).

17. Barbara Omolade, an African-American educator, activist, and writer, identifies a form of leadership among black women throughout the African diaspora that is rooted in egalitarian governing processes modeled on African tribal societies. Promoting the development of people and communities is central to this leadership tradition.

18. Gilligan discusses the devaluation of caring in our society and describes a dichotomy that reserves relational expertise for women and limits agency to the domain of men.

19. Many scholars note the mammy stereotype's pervasiveness and its insidious relationship to black women's construction as other in the white imagination (Bogle; Carby; Wallace). For an extensive discussion see Bogle.

20. See Langston Hughes's poem "Dream Deferred" and Lorraine Hansberry's gripping drama *A Raisin in the Sun* and its exploration of a black family pursuing the dream for a better life. A more recent example of dream symbolism is found in Gloria Ladson-Billings's book naming educators of African-American children as "The DreamKeepers."

sixty

Recollecting *This Bridge* in an Anti–Affirmative Action Era: Literary Anthologies, Academic Memoir, and Institutional Autobiography

Cynthia Franklin

Toward the end of the 1997–98 school year, our department was in the final rounds of a three-year struggle over the revision of the undergraduate English major. After a particularly tense department meeting—one during which many assistant professors called the present curriculum colonialist, outdated, and irrelevant to Hawai'i students—a senior colleague (white, male) e-mailed a "campaign document" to the department's sixty full-time faculty members. In it, he announced his interest in being elected to the hiring committee.[1] He promised, if elected, to screen for and oppose any job candidate whose application materials included terms such as "of color" or "colonial," or who otherwise evidenced signs that she (this hypothetical applicant was always a "she") or her work was politically motivated. A barrage of department-wide e-mails followed— one expression of support; several admonishments to the writer for his disrespect to junior colleagues; an incisive analysis of the "campaign document's" racism and sexism by one of the faculty's four women of color; memos calling the whole set of exchanges "silly"; and a few unapologetic assertions from the campaigning colleague stating that his target was "jargon" and "cultural studies imperialism," not people.

This bit of departmental history interests me not because it is important in and of itself, but because I suspect that others in academe have similar stories to tell. Furthermore, I believe that these stories are, taken together, significant. They speak to how affirmative action is being rolled back in universities in informal as well as official ways. More specifically, they point to a crisis in the relationship between the personal and the political.

In the 1980s, women of color, working from the insight that "the personal is political," gave expression to collective forms of identity politics, often in the form of multi-genre anthologies. Among the first and the most influential was *This Bridge Called My Back*. *This Bridge* helped create a paradigm shift in the academy, one that enabled progressive reforms and wide-ranging critiques of the academy's discrimination against disempowered groups. The late 1990s, however, was a time of backlash. And as my colleague's e-mails suggest, individually-aimed expressions of racism and sexism are often cloaked as intellectual arguments against theoretical language ("jargon") and the politicization of the academy ("cultural studies imperialism"). Furthermore, racist and sexist attacks often articulate with reactionary institutional practices that are supposedly politically neutral. At the same time, explicitly political positions—especially those premised on identity politics—are regularly dismissed on the grounds that they are either *merely* personal or only represent the interests of a "narrow" group. Such dismissals depend upon seeing identity politics as a strictly personal rather than political formation, one interchangeable with any assertions of identity. Thus, the meaning of "the personal is political" has become complex, various, and confused. Furthermore, as I explain in this chapter, my campaigning colleague's e-mails indicate how the language of marginalization can be co-opted. Indeed, personal narratives based on identity politics deployed in anthologies like *This Bridge* are even being used to perpetuate the individual acts of racism and the discriminatory institutional practices that these anthologies so powerfully oppose.

In one of his later missives, my colleague quoted a passage from Gloria Anzaldúa that he found in a Norton anthology. In this passage, Anzaldúa describes the rituals that she undergoes to begin writing. These include "wash[ing] the dishes or my underthings, tak[ing] a bath, or mop[ping] the kitchen floor." My colleague used this passage—initially published in *Borderlands*—to denounce the proposed curriculum's cultural studies component and to justify his "campaign document."[2] Noting that D. H. Lawrence, whom he described as "the whitest of the white and the malest of the male," expressed in his letters an affinity for jam making and floor mopping, this colleague expressed disappointment that Anzaldúa showed no sign of having read Lawrence's letters.

The Norton's inclusion of Anzaldúa removes her work from its specifically Chicana and activist contexts and recontextualizes it as a part of the literary canon. My colleague, reading this work in its new context, tries to further contain—and, indeed, discredit—Anzaldúa's aesthetic innovations, and the identity politics and insistence on the importance of material conditions integral to these innovations. The relevant antecedents for this passage become not Anzaldúa's lived experiences as a working-class Chicana writer, but literary, and canonically so. This substitution itself depends upon ignoring Lawrence's class position and the significance that he discloses his domestic proclivities not in his literary writings, but in his private letters. Thus Anzaldúa's writing becomes the unwitting emulation of the "minor" work of a dead white man of letters, rather than a materialist and political intervention into the elitist and ethnocentric realm of western literature. Moreover, as this analysis makes Anzaldúa into a second-rate rather than a revolutionary writer, it further undermines the literary and political claims of her writing by leveling the material and experiential differences between her and "the whitest of the white, the malest of the male"—if white guys as well as women of color can (and do) mop floors, it is, apparently, only white guys who can really write.

In his efforts not simply to invalidate Anzaldúa's politics, but to depoliticize her work altogether, my colleague bespeaks his desire for a clear separation between literature and identity politics. He also registers the threat that Anzaldúa's work poses to this split. His use of Lawrence signals his desire for white men's continued control over the domain of literature and his covert or unconscious investments in a hegemonic form of identity politics. Moreover, as he tries to delegitimate Anzaldúa's work in efforts to impede change at the levels of curriculum and hiring, he indicates that a relationship exists between Anzaldúa's writing and curricular reform and between this writing and hiring practices.

Rather than dignify his "campaign documents" with a direct response, some junior faculty members instead forwarded them to the university's sex equity specialist and to the civil rights counselor. The decision not to enter directly into department debate changed, however, when our campaigning colleague received fourteen of forty-four votes cast and made the final rounds of the hiring committee election. At this point, some women, myself included, sent a letter to the department. We explained that we were writing not to attack this colleague, but to express our dismay regarding our colleagues' support for his position: "Let's be clear about what such a vote means. First, it registers support for an ongoing climate in which junior faculty and their specializations will be the object of serious disrespect and derision. Second, this vote suggests that we support a policy of active discrimination against people on the basis of their race, gender, or politics. We remind people before they cast their votes that implementing such a policy is in fact illegal." Four of us signed this memo—three of us untenured; two, women of color.

Many colleagues responded to our memo with disapproval, even outrage. We received angry and sadly chastising responses to our "lack of collegiality" and "unjustified accusations of racism." Even those who agreed with our position expressed discomfort with our "harsh tactics," our references to the law, or our use of "threats" and "intimidation." Others flourished our letter as evidence that we opposed free elections and democracy. Our still-campaigning colleague sent a memo to the department likening us to the Polish Communist Party in place under Jaruzelski. In the next round of elections, our colleague received eighteen of fifty-five votes cast—enough to require yet another round of voting, although he ultimately was not elected. The following school year, those of us responsible for the offending letter were relieved of our heavy committee loads and advised to lay low.

I was stunned by the anger and disruption that our letter occasioned; our points seemed to me to be obvious and irrefutably true. I am still thinking about this moment in departmental history, especially the attack on Anzaldúa.

I believe that even as Anzaldúa's writing—particularly in its communal contexts and commitments—continues to inspire change in the academy, academic institutions have limited the oppositional force and revolutionary energy that this writing can continue to engender. The Norton anthology is at the center of literary canon making and is emblematic of the bourgeois individualism and elitism that Anzaldúa challenges in *Borderlands* and in *This Bridge,* with co-editor Cherríe Moraga and the other contributors. The Norton's incorporation of Anzaldúa's work—and their decision to excerpt a chapter from her individually-authored book rather than from *This Bridge* or *Haciendo Caras*—suggests how academic institutions work to co-opt, neutralize, and individualize oppositional forms of writing. Indeed, it is unsurprising that the Norton includes Anzaldúa's *Borderlands* essay "Tlilli, Tlapalli: The Path of the Red and Black Ink" rather than, for example, "Speaking In Tongues: A Letter To 3rd World Women Writers," a *Bridge* piece that takes up similar issues about writing from a more collective and explicitly activist perspective. The Norton's selection obscures *Borderlands's* grounding in and connection to *This Bridge,* and instead situates it as part of the literary canon. The movement of this writing into the mainstream of academe and my colleague's anxiety regarding Anzaldúa's inclusion and his subsequent efforts to contain her writing's transformative possibilities signal to me not that the war waged by Anzaldúa and other *Bridge* con-

tributors has been won, but rather the need to adopt new forms of oppositional writing.

In saying this, I in no way mean to discount the importance that *This Bridge*, *Borderlands*, and their successors continue to have for students, particularly as models for politicization and self-empowerment of women of color. *Bridge,* in particular, has played a crucial role in challenging the biases of what constitutes literature and theory. This anthology has been profoundly influential and is of continuing relevance in its critiques of individualism and its collective format; in its stress on community coupled with its insistence that feminism and women's community must be founded upon difference; and in its attention to how structures of racism, sexism, classism, and homophobia inform the everyday lives of women of color. Especially in the classroom, I continue to be moved by *This Bridge*'s revolutionary fervor, and to witness the passionate and politically power-ful student writings that it elicits. Nor do I wish to cast the Norton's inclu-sion of Anzaldúa in a purely negative light, since this makes possible widespread awareness of her work.

And yet, *Borderlands*—and Anzaldúa's and other women's writings in *This Bridge*—does not necessarily cause the disruptions that it once did in an academy still sorely in need of anti-racist and feminist transforma-tion. For teachers of ethnic and/or women's literature, this writing by now constitutes a familiar genre. And it has become commonplace in compo-sition classes to ask students to explore their ethnic and gender identities. Therefore, students can read, write, and circulate *Bridge-* or *Borderlands*-inspired narratives and poems in ways that are not threaten-ing to the academy. Whereas some professors can take the edge off this writing by viewing it in its Norton contexts, others such as myself can teach *Borderlands* alongside anthologies including *This Bridge,* and feel progressive for helping create a space within the academy for this litera-ture. Teaching this work can bring those in positions of authority a degree of comfort and satisfaction—a sense that as teachers we are part of the solution rather than the problem, and at very little risk, since Anzaldúa's work has been Norton-approved. In short, its acceptance blunts the chal-lenges it poses at present to those in dominant positions in the academy.

For students today, however new, crucial, and relevant the writings in *Bridge* and its successors remain, this writing appears as a part of (liter-ary) history, especially if students are introduced to it by a professor or a Norton headnote. Most students reading *This Bridge*—especially those born after it was published—do not encounter contributors as contempo-raries, but rather as figures in history. And as inevitably happens with all literature, some of its most powerful innovations and insights have become naturalized over time. Although of continuing influence and

inspiration, then, *This Bridge* often speaks to new readers with less direct-
ness and immediacy than it does to those who first read it during the
1980s. Given its place within literary history, it can inspire—but perhaps
no longer provide a direct model for—writing that will engender community and transform the academy.

Viewing Anzaldúa's work in its different contexts serves as a reminder
that its transformative power was not only bound to the genres it utilizes
but also to its moment of production. As the Norton recontextualizes
Anzaldúa's work, it illuminates the extent to which transgression is tem-
porally bound. Without discounting the connections between the politicization of students and the transformation of academic institutions, I
would nonetheless argue that today *This Bridge* and its successors are less
directly transformative for academic institutions than they are for individual students. The need, then, exists for new forms of writings that can
issue challenges to the academy.

In considering what these new forms might be, I have been thinking
about the extreme reactions to our letter regarding our department's hiring committee elections and what they reveal about the relationship
between the personal and the political. I am struck by how explosive our
memo was and by how personally our colleagues took it. In some ways,
differences between our missive and our campaigning colleague's were
leveled—both were widely perceived as troublemaking and mean-spirited. However, our colleague's attacks were attributed to his idiosyncrasies
and dismissed. In contrast, our letter, placing department members in
relation to larger institutional regulations and breaking with the myth of
department as family, proved more incendiary and less forgivable.
Paradoxically, it was precisely the impersonal nature of this letter that
made it so threatening to our colleagues on a personal level.

Responses to our letter demonstrated to me the power and importance of institutional structures and the strength of faculty desires to view
departmental relations and decisions apart from them. Our department,
in particular, prides itself on its collegiality and makes decisions based
upon people's feelings. One exasperated colleague has dubbed this "the
politics of hurt feelings." The perception that untenured or newly tenured
professors are not only invulnerable to insult, but also that we are "threatening" and "intimidating" to senior colleagues, revealed to me how willfully and conveniently blind our department is to factors of institutional
power and also the extent to which language about marginalization has
been co-opted and cut free of material groundings. In our department—
and in English departments more generally—the language of oppression
has been appropriated to describe anything from the neglect of medieval
poetics to the condition of full professors who oppose literary theory. In

short, dissonance exists between faculty members' personal feelings of marginalization and their institutional power. The vocabulary of oppression is regularly used to suture the divide between personal feelings and institutional privilege, and between those in the academy with differing amounts of institutional power. At the present moment, then, one in which the language of *This Bridge* is being used so inappropriately, legitimate claims to marginalization are often too easily dismissed or emptied of meaning as they coexist alongside trivial or unjustified ones.

Given this state of affairs, language that is most impersonal, even legalistic, can hit hardest on a personal as well as political level, in part because it refuses those in institutionally privileged positions the right to feelings of being marginalized or oppressed, and instead highlights the responsibilities, privileges, and power of institutional location. At this particular moment, when people with institutional authority are using language of disenfranchisement to enforce discriminatory politics, fighting this discrimination requires changes in strategy. Rather than employing language of marginalization or a personal framework, it can be effective, especially at the local level and for those with any degree of institutional privilege, to lay claim to institutional authority—or "the Master's tools"—in order to defend the civil rights laws that still exist and to work to make the laws and structures governing the academy more just. For students or for those without institutional privilege, however, personal narratives based on a politics of identity can retain their oppositional edge; I return to this point later.

To account for the transformations in the academy of the relationship between the personal and the political, first I examine a form of personal writing that is a successor to *This Bridge* and other multi-genre identity-based publications—the academic memoir. Academic memoirs—like my colleague's e-mails—demonstrate an important way that identity politics is being taken up and neutralized by those in positions of privilege. These memoirs, which constitute another, very different, response to *This Bridge,* can nevertheless also work—however inadvertently—to contain its revolutionary impulses. I find it no coincidence that in the paragraph that precedes his critique of Anzaldúa, my campaigning colleague quotes approvingly from Frank Lentricchia's "Last Confessions of a Literary Critic." This *Lingua Franca* article dramatically renounces the political approach to literature upon which the formerly Marxist critic made his reputation. Lentricchia's memoir, *The Edge of Night,* is written in the same vein. In both, Lentricchia attacks identity politics even as his portrayals of himself as an Italian American with working-class roots are energized and made possible by identity politics. Although Lentricchia's "Last Confessions" and his memoir share the "campaign document's" repudiation of "P.C." agendas and their role in literary studies, many academic memoirs are politically progressive in intent—indeed, many are premised on a naive or unreflective version of "the personal is political." Nonetheless, as these memoirs often collapse the personal and political, they demonstrate how doing so can have the same conservative effects as trying to prise them apart, as do my colleague and Lentricchia. Furthermore, the canonical literary form of memoir and its basis in bourgeois individualism—particularly when used by tenured faculty members—often is at odds with—and subsumes—politically progressive agendas found in *This Bridge* and the other identity-based anthologies upon which academic memoirs depend in significant ways.

From Anthology to Academic Memoir

Over the past decade, memoirs by well-established professors have been pouring from publishing houses at the same rate as identity-based anthologies were in the 1980s and early 1990s. This literary movement is both indebted to and departs significantly from the one initiated by *This Bridge*. So prevalent have memoirs by English professors become that, as David Simpson caustically remarks, "the award of tenure now seems to bring with it a contract for one's autobiography" (24).

Although much remarked upon in academic and popular venues, academic memoirs have been under-analyzed, particularly in terms of race and identity politics. Most critics have given them only cursory readings before dismissing them as a reaction against postmodernism, a fatigue with theory, unfortunate by-products of the academic star system, or the self-indulgent products of middle-aged academics undergoing identity crises.[3] In contrast, some feminist critics have championed the memoirs as the success of a democratic form of writing, or as the realization of the ideals embodied in the slogan "the personal is political," without interrogating the privilege that attends writing—and publishing—a memoir. Such celebrations also neglect how memoir as an individualist, bourgeois genre can depoliticize the personal. Furthermore, both popular and academic considerations have ignored the important linkage between the proliferation of these memoirs and contemporary crises in the academy—and in the wider public sphere—that concern issues of race and identity politics.

Memoirs provide academics with vehicles to struggle with and embody—and sometimes evade—the challenges, limitations, impasses, and inadequacies of theories of race and formulations of feminism. And as individual endeavors premised upon forms of feminist community and institutional privilege, these memoirs present the opportunity to think about how well-established academic feminists might use their institutional power in progressive and collectively-minded ways, and about the genre's possibilities and limitations in helping to mobilize a politics in keeping with *Bridge's* revolutionary agenda.

In an earlier project, *Writing Women's Communities: The Politics and Poetics of Contemporary Multi-Genre Anthologies,* I argue that *This Bridge* and anthologies inspired by it—for example, *Nice Jewish Girls, Gathering Ground, Making Waves, Calling Home, Haciendo Caras,* and *The Very Inside*—theorize and enact identity-based models of women's communities. These anthologies constitute an important part of a literary and social movement aimed at reaching non-academic audiences *and* clearing a space in universities for women of color and genres of writing usually excluded from the realm of the literary.

I view the current "memoir craze" as a turn away from the identity politics that characterizes these anthologies and toward poststructuralist analyses that highlight the constructedness, multiplicity, hybridity, and performative nature of all identities. The memoir is in a privileged position to play out the construction and complexity of identities that ethnic or racial labels can simplify, erase, or essentialize. Accompanying their poststructuralist play with identity and often camouflaged by it, many academic memoirs reinstate liberal humanist understandings of the centrality and uniqueness of individual consciousness. These memoirs, with their centering of the individual (however split or fragmented), often seem to forgo the collective and activist vision that fuels *This Bridge* and its successors' practices of identity politics, even as they retain a focus on identity.

Therefore, the movement over the course of the 1990s from multi-genre anthologies to more conventionally literary memoirs by tenured academics indicates to me that the "memoir movement" might be not only a way for academics to enter the wider public sphere; it also might signal a retreat from—or a giving up on—a form of identity politics that is collective, activist, and oppositional. A question that animates my interest in academic memoir, then, is: Can the genre sustain a politics that is not exclusively focused on the individual self? Must a focus on the individual happen at the expense of larger social and political identities and concerns? To explore this question, I consider the important role that memoir plays in white studies, an academic arena that intersects in significant ways with the memoir movement.

White Studies and Academic Memoirs

Jenny Bourne remarked over a decade ago that "identity politics is all the rage" (1). Today the same can be said for white studies. The centrality "white studies" has come to assume in literary and cultural studies is evidenced by the special journal issues (for example, the *Minnesota Review's* "The White Issue"), the many recent books with titles such as *A White*

Studies Reader, Off White, White, Whiteness, White Trash, Displacing Whiteness, or *The Social Construction of Whiteness,* and the renewed scholarly attention to Jewish Americans, Italian Americans, and other white ethnic groups.[4] As white studies scholars seek to understand the constructedness of whiteness, they often work to expose and undermine white supremacy, and/or to challenge the perception that whiteness automatically entails privilege or an absence of ethnicity.

On the one hand, such attention is crucial. Discourses racializing whiteness that expose its ideological force and function are precisely what some scholars committed to fighting racism have been calling for (see bell hooks and Hazel Carby). Furthermore, attention to the ethnic identities of white people can disrupt the hegemonic force of whiteness, productively challenge its naturalness, open possibilities for cross-racial alliances, and allow for an understanding of how some ethnic groups have achieved "whiteness" at the expense of others.[5]

At the same time, we are seeing a proliferation of studies that focus on white ethnic groups without attention to structures of race and racism. Such studies are licensed by and often merge with white studies, even as they may contribute to the privileging of whiteness that white studies was founded to challenge. All this attention to whiteness—especially given the slippage between white studies and white ethnic studies—can result in a recentering of it that is all the more disturbing given the present historical moment. If recent MLA calls for papers or the *PMLA* special issue on "ethnicity" are indicative of the current state of affairs in literature departments, explorations of "whiteness" too often can accompany a diminishing amount of attention to the decreasing numbers of racial minorities in universities, not to mention their worsening conditions in an era characterized by anti–affirmative action, anti-immigration legislation, and an exponential growth in what Angela Davis calls the prison industrial complex, which criminalizes the poor and people of color.[6] When a focus on the complexity of whiteness and white ethnic groups seems to be replacing attention to racial minorities and their cultural production, or when such studies place white ethnic texts in relation to those by racial minorities without engaging questions of institutional racism and unequal power relations, then I think that despite the excellence and integrity of much white studies scholarship, white studies as a movement can work to reinscribe rather than undermine the hegemony of whiteness.[7]

This is particularly apt to happen in memoirs that, through a focus on white ethnicity, participate in white studies. Although they have not been read as such, memoirs of the 1990s including Cathy Davidson's *36 Views of Mount Fuji,* Alice Kaplan's *French Lessons,* Jane Lazarre's *Beyond the Whiteness of Whiteness,* Frank Lentricchia's *The Edge of Night,* and

Marianna Torgovnick's *Crossing Ocean Parkway* importantly contribute to, at the same time as they are underwritten by, white studies. Furthermore, both white studies and academic memoirs are indebted to, even as they sometimes subvert the aims of, anthologies such as *This Bridge*. *This Bridge* provided a model for marginalized groups of women to assert their individual identities *and* to forge a positive collective identity. Today, we see academics in positions of privilege drawing upon the discourse developed in these anthologies in order to write memoirs in which they explore their uniqueness or render visible their feelings of marginality or (ethnic) difference. These memoirs demonstrate the problems with working to complicate a dominant racial identity using a traditional literary form. To varying degrees, these memoirs, with their focus on how *individuals* experience their dominant racial identities in complex and contradictory ways, suggest that even the most nuanced and sensitive memoirs can, especially in combination with white studies, displace and elide the need for work focusing on institutional forms of racism in the United States.

Affirmative Action in Beyond the Whiteness of Whiteness

These memoirs, however, need not (re)center humanism in a new "white studies" packaging. As Jane Lazarre's 1996 *Beyond the Whiteness of Whiteness: Memoir of a White Mother of Black Sons* demonstrates, memoir and white studies can come together in ways that are resolutely anti-racist and sensitive to how structures of race inform our intimate relationships and everyday experiences. At the same time, it raises questions about the work memoir can do in institutional contexts, and about potential limitations of an anti-racist politics premised upon intimacy and identification.

In contrast to many of her contemporaries, Lazarre uses memoir not as a (covert) return to individualism, but rather as the vehicle for transcending the self in order to "speak out against even the smallest injustice" (134). Indeed, her commitment to social justice results from and fuels her interest in writing and teaching memoir.

Lazarre's interrogation of whiteness also predates academic fashion. And whereas many white academics write memoirs in order to claim unmarked ethnic identities or experiences of marginalization, Lazarre's focus is on moving beyond "the whiteness of whiteness" that "is the blindness of willful innocence" (49). For Lazarre, whose husband and two sons are black, whiteness cannot be understood independently of blackness, and awareness of race is ever-present, and informs every decision she makes about her sons' lives (47).

Lazarre consistently refuses a perspective unmediated by historical analysis, and her memoir foregrounds U.S. history as important but not all-determining of personal relationships. In the first chapter, Lazarre tells of viewing a slavery exhibit, where she realizes that "without understanding slavery, we cannot understand the United States of America. And from that perspective it was clear to me that I would have to revisit the story of my life in a Black family " (20). The story Lazarre tells insists upon the ongoing significance of race and racism in the United States, even as she posits racism not as inevitable but as something to resist and overcome.

Lazarre's struggle against racism and her identity as a writer are based on her model of mothering. She explains that motherhood is "a story within which I could trace this human dilemma of the boundaries and pathways between self and others throughout the development of my children's lives" (118). For Lazarre, mothering means empathizing and identifying with her sons, and using her white privilege only when it can help them. Learning to see through her sons' eyes is "not only an aspect of narrative and aesthetic technique, but has an important ethical dimension as well" (71). Identification with them leads to what Lazarre calls "passing over" into blackness, to moments during which "I became my sons, Black Americans" (5).

As Lazarre chronicles the process of "passing over," she maintains the tension between having white skin and rejecting whiteness as a social identity. Nevertheless, the memoir increasingly focuses on how Lazarre comes to view her identity as "hidden" by her white skin (49). By the memoir's conclusion, Lazarre presents her journey beyond whiteness as nearly complete; she explains that among strangers, "I am always comforted by this thought: I am no longer white. However I may appear to others, I am a person of color now" (135). Although she distinguishes between her perceptions and material conditions, as I discuss later, this claim is problematic.

The memoir's structure enables Lazarre's dis-identification with whiteness through shifts in settings that become increasingly intimate. Whereas the first chapter is set at a slavery exhibit and the next two detail a mix of institutional and domestic contexts, chapter four, "Reunions, Retellings, Refrains," concerns Lazarre's experiences at her husband's family reunions, where she is surrounded by black people who love and accept her fully. Thus, Lazarre's full identification with a black vantage point seems enabled by the chapter's domestic settings.

In Lazarre's memoir, the political becomes increasingly personal. Successfully utilizing the genre of memoir, Lazarre sets forth what is in many ways a radical politics, one based on overcoming racism through empathy, love, and identification. And yet, the memoir's focus on familial relationships and its increasingly domestic settings often gloss over the limitations of such a model when the setting is institutional. One moment in the memoir gestures toward these limitations. When Lazarre relays her experience serving on a faculty hiring committee, she suggests how her model can fail her personally and politically. Lazarre's account stands out because it is the memoir's least processed and most vexed one; indeed, Lazarre describes the experience as one "accompanied by a confusion so powerful I know it is a signal of depth" (90). Because the details Lazarre provides are so telling, a lengthy summary precedes my analysis.

The section in question follows an account of Lazarre's discovery of her son's vulnerability as a black male when a white hospital staff mistakes his fear for violence. Lazarre next describes being on an almost all-white hiring committee conducting a search for a scholar in African-American history. When "Suzanne," a black, middle-aged finalist comes for a campus visit, Lazarre describes her as follows: "She has an impressive resume, including a privileged education, world travel, honors, and degrees. Yet, she seems held back professionally, somehow trapped" (91). During the interview, Lazarre notes the frayed T-shirt beneath her silk jacket, and observes that "She pauses for long moments before she answers questions, speaks low, and if someone disagrees with her she neither presses her point nor changes her mind; she remains silent. The only Black person on our committee, G., tells us he believes she is scared" (91–92). Describing her own response to Suzanne, Lazarre confesses to "a confusing ambivalence toward her which has nothing to do with her academic work or credentials. . . . I feel intimidated, yet I can see she is doing nothing intimidating" (92). Observing this candidate's performance with the student committee, Lazarre notes that "she is warmly engaged with them, sounding confident in her own purposes and attitudes about teaching" (92). That evening, when the committee takes Suzanne to a poetry reading, Lazarre is overcome by a desire to go home: *Something about her vulnerability—the clothes, the braids, the fear*" (92). . . . "She makes me think about my fear of rejection" (92). Lazarre presses the candidate, whom she is supposed to escort to a cab, to leave; Suzanne responds with cold dignity and Lazarre says, "in this passing moment of her anger, I sense her strength and feel relief" (93). When the committee reconvenes, Lazarre explains that, "In terms of objective standards, the key members of the committee decide, we cannot hire her. We need leaders on this faculty. If she were stronger, more brave . . ." (93).

Several nights later, Lazarre has a dream:

> I am walking after an elegant tall woman who is turning around every so often to talk to me over her shoulder. As she does so, I feel small, tolerated, and

> exposed, like a young child on one of those leashes people attach to toddlers as
> if they were dogs. The tall woman is self-confident, secure; *she has her nerve.*
> She wears her clothes well. . . . She is looking down on me and I am not meas-
> uring up. I wake up thinking about Suzanne's braids, the frayed neckline of her
> T-shirt beneath the silk jacket. (93)

As she again identifies with Suzanne's vulnerability, musing on ways "we
show up for interviews with old T-shirts visible beneath our new jackets,"
Lazarre recalls her relief in "finding armor that . . . enabled me to move
around" (94). Her thoughts return to Suzanne, and she wonders, "If most of
us had been Black, would she have seemed different, stronger, more free?"
(94). These thoughts remind her of a blues lyric, which in turn reminds her
of a moment of "musical intimacy" (94) during an Odetta concert, when the
audience joined together to sing "Amazing Grace." Singing reawakens in
Lazarre a sense of the awesome responsibility of mothering black sons.

Lazarre sandwiches her experience on the hiring committee between
discussions of her sons' vulnerability as black males. Thus she implicitly
posits the experience as part of a more general awakening about the vulnerability of being African American, a discovery crucial to the process of
"passing over" that the chapter chronicles. Only whereas Lazarre, in her
role as mother at the hospital, is able to see her son's "violence" as fear
and to comfort him, and whereas at a concert, she can merge her voice
with African Americans' in an expression of community, the job search
allows no such experience of "passing over." Lazarre neither knows what
Suzanne is thinking, nor does Suzanne tell her—as a white professor with
power over Suzanne's fate, Lazarre invites distrust, not identification or
personal disclosures. Suzanne's aloofness intimidates Lazarre, and, combined with her age, strips Lazarre of her maternal role. Instead, Suzanne's
response assigns to Lazarre the role of white oppressor, even as Lazarre's
perception of Suzanne's vulnerability and her identification with this feeling overwhelms her.

Suzanne catches Lazarre in the contradiction of occupying a white
social identity while desiring and identifying with a black one. Lazarre's
dream captures this contradiction. As the "I" who does not measure up,
Lazarre registers her empathy with Suzanne's vulnerability and her inability to mother Suzanne (lacking maternal authority, she feels like a young
child). The dream also conveys her sense that it is she who is being
judged—even infantilized—and found inadequate by Suzanne (that the
tall woman is racially unmarked—an anomalous ambiguity for Lazarre—
enables this interpretation). Moreover, by occupying the position of the
powerless woman, Lazarre arguably expresses her wish to dissociate herself from her position of institutional authority.

Lazarre does a better job exposing her feelings of personal discomfort and failure than she does analyzing the failures of her politics. Although she asserts that "objective standards" dictate the decision not to hire Suzanne, the reasons for rejecting her seem questionable. In addition to her impressive resume, Lazarre has noted that "Her intelligence and passion for her work are unmistakable" (92). It is Suzanne's "restraint" that seems to be her downfall for "key members of the committee" (92). Lazarre, however, does not address whether "restraint" should be so defining, particularly when Suzanne's response to students—and to Lazarre at the poetry reading—suggest that it is situational. Nor does Lazarre consider how restraint seems to be less the problem than the discomfort it arouses, the reminder it serves Lazarre of her institutional power and whiteness.

Lazarre's account leaves the fairness of the job search unaddressed. Her identification with Suzanne's vulnerability not only becomes unproductive in a situation in which this identification cannot be recognized, but, in fact, becomes counter-productive and unjust, since Suzanne's "failure" to see past committee members' institutional positions takes precedence over her qualifications. The professional arena remains intensely personal for Lazarre, and her politics are based upon a maternal model that too exclusively depends upon her feelings and her desire for recognition and intimacy.

The inadequacies of Lazarre's response suggest the limits for white people of countering racism in the academy through a maternal, or familial, model based on intimacy, love, and identification. This analysis also suggests the limits of doing anti-racist work in the academy through the genre of memoir. However sensitive to larger social and historical conditions, the focus in memoir remains on individual consciousness. Although crucial, this is not sufficient, particularly for academics who are all too adept at analyzing themselves in resistance to, rather than as part of, institutions.

Crossing Back, Moving Forward

This moment in Lazarre's memoir returns this essay to its starting point, and contributes to an understanding of how contemporary understandings of the personal as political can articulate with reactionary practices in universities. Although my colleague's political commitments—and his understanding of how the personal is political—could not be more opposed to Lazarre's, both of their stories indicate the need to rethink this relationship between the personal and the political. Their stories also suggest the importance of developing forms of writing that foreground institutional practices and policies without ignoring the significance of the personal. Twenty years after *This Bridge,* what might such forms look like? And how might *This Bridge* inspire or provide the basis for such writing?

In my teaching a graduate course in spring 1999 on contemporary academic memoirs, students' writing provided some possible answers to these questions. Their projects suggested how personal narratives influenced by *This Bridge* continue to issue important institutional critiques. Allison Yap, for example, wrote "An Absence Ever Present," a beautifully lyrical autobiographical narrative that is influenced by and implicitly engages work by Moraga, Anzaldúa, and Hélène Cixous. As she traces her family history, Yap effectively critiques dominant cultural discourses about motherhood, adoption, and racial identity. Another class member, Donna Tanigawa, has published a body of work that both reflects the influence of *This Bridge* writers and makes groundbreaking contributions to articulating issues of identity that are distinctive to Hawai'i. For her final class project, Tanigawa wrote of trying to get pregnant as a local Japanese lesbian with limited economic resources. In "Premature" (included in this volume), Tanigawa issues a scathing critique of the medical establishment, even as she preserves a sense of her and her lover's strength and agency and a formulation of sexuality and reproductive powers that resist definition by this institution. Both Tanigawa and Yap demonstrate how narratives premised on identity politics can serve counter-hegemonic purposes for those who address state agencies and institutions in which they are not authorized or privileged.

Class members also addressed the importance—and indeed, for those in the academy who are not well-established, the necessity—of finding alternatives to traditional and small press publishers. As the book publishing industry has become increasingly constricted, technologies developed since *Bridge*'s publication have made possible other means for reaching disparate audiences. Class members discussed how desktop publishing and the Internet can combat the elitism attached to book publishing and enable experimentation, collaboration, and freedom from academic conventions and marketplace pressures. Toward these ends, for his class project, Carlo Arreglo started the zine *Alibata*. The inaugural issue features memoir by Arreglo, his father's recipes for *mechado,* movie and CD reviews, a mock interview, and writings by friends. As he continues with this zine, Arreglo plans to use the Internet to reach various Filipino/a communities.[8] In the spirit of *Bridge,* his emphasis is on claiming his Filipino identity as part of a collectivity, and on building community to help counter the racism against and exclusion of Filipinos in the academy.

Yet another piece by Tanigawa—the first she wrote for the class—has been on my mind since I set out to write this essay because it so richly illuminates interrelations between different formulations of the personal as political and so directly speaks to ways to build upon *Bridge*'s interventions into the academy. Tanigawa begins this essay with personal narrative in a style reminiscent of *This Bridge*. Significantly, this narrative addresses—and evidences the overcoming of—writer's block. Tanigawa details the personal costs of having published writing that breaks cultural and family silences, and explores how graduate school has curtailed her creativity. Next, the essay details a series of events in which women faculty (white and of color) acted insensitively to local graduate students. This account includes excerpts from collectively authored e-mail in which Tanigawa and other graduate students called these faculty on misuse of their institutional power. In contrast to the essay's wry and intimate first section, the e-mail excerpts and accompanying commentary were at once impersonal and animated by anger.

Both sections of the essay involved, for Tanigawa, different kinds of risks and breakthroughs, and a willingness to work from and through positions of discomfort. Tanigawa's shift from a focus on personal feelings to one on institutional location—and her willingness to confront academic feminists with power over her—felt particularly risky and productive to me.[9] Indeed, Tanigawa's essay served as the impetus for this essay's account of departmental e-mail exchanges. Her essay impressed upon me the possibilities of circulating collectively written, local, ephemeral pieces of writing in a more formal and enduring format, one that allows for a wider audience and a different though related set of academic interventions.

Tanigawa's essay not only prompted me to address my colleagues' denial of their institutional privilege and location, but also to reflect upon my own institutional identity. I found this reflection uncomfortable. As Tanigawa's narrative makes clear, my discomfort is not idiosyncratic. Although Tanigawa's e-mail was directed to only a few faculty, Tanigawa tells of how they forwarded it to other women faculty, who responded as if they were being personally criticized for upholding institutional structures that are oppressive to local graduate students. I attribute their—and my own—discomfort and defensiveness to a sense that although left-leaning academics have become accustomed to thinking through identities of race, gender, class, and sexuality, an identity politics that foregrounds institutional location feels much more threatening. Not only are questions of institutional identity less theorized, they are more commonly disavowed or ignored. For academics whose work is premised upon oppositional alliances and/or marginalized forms of identity, attention to our institutional identities can be a source of anxiety because—unlike other dominant identities—they are chosen ones that, in various and complex ways, position us as part of rather than poise us against a hegemonic institution. Tanigawa's piece is powerful in its demand that faculty members acknowledge and reflect on how responsibly we are using our institutional power, and on how our institutional identities relate to our political commitments, personal feelings, and experiences of and/or claims to marginalization.

Tanigawa's essay also suggests an important linkage between personal writings and those that are institutionally directed: in her essay, the institutional account follows the more personal one, even as the collective, institutionally aimed writings she describes enabled a return to the personal. I am not, then, positing a developmental narrative: both modes are important, and each serves different purposes. Moreover, in their combination, something new happens to each. The two parts of Tanigawa's essay exist in a dynamic relationship, one that reinvigorates and reopens questions of how the personal is political, and the political, personal.

Looking to writing by graduate students who have received inspiration from *This Bridge* affords ways of seeing how its work can be continued. This new generation of writers remembers without memorializing, and rethinks without forgoing, *Bridge*'s conceptualization of community-based forms of activist writing and its formulation of the personal as political.

Notes

Thanks to Carlo Arreglo, Andrea Feeser, Candace Fujikane, AnaLouise Keating, Jacqueline Shea Murphy, Juliana Spahr, Donna Tanigawa, Pam Thoma, Beth Tobin, Allison Yap, and especially Laura Lyons, for generous and rigorous responses to drafts of this essay and for the many discussions that informed its arguments.

1. In this section, I withhold names and identifying tags, and rely predominantly on paraphrase rather than direct quotation for a few reasons: (1) to avoid a lawsuit, given murky copyright practices in regard to e-mail; and (2) denunciation of particular individuals is not the point here, but rather the larger issues that their actions speak to.

2. This passage comes from "*Tlilli, Tlapalli*," which I have located in two Norton anthologies—*Postmodern American Fiction* and *Literature by Women*.

3. See Simpson's *The Academic Postmodern* and Begley's "The I's Have It."

4. Whereas in the U.S. studies of ethnicity used to focus on white ethnic groups, since the inception of ethnic studies programs in the late 1960s until quite recently racial minorities have been the focus. The oscillation reflects an ambiguity inherent in the word's root: *ethnos* means both "all people" and "other people." Thus, who is considered to be "ethnic" has much to do with the academy's current political climate.

5. Important studies with an anti-racist focus include, for example, Ignatiev and Roediger.

6. The January 1998 *PMLA*, a well-advertised special issue on "ethnicity" coordinated by Sander Gilman, includes six articles, three of which concern Jewish identity. Although I found these essays exemplary in their scholarship and don't want to dismiss the importance of studying dominant or marginalized white ethnic groups, as a collective statement about the academy's position toward "ethnicity" I find the issue disturbing for its inattention to present-day racial inequities.

7. For considerations of such problems, see Hill or Chvany.

8. For information about *Alibata*, contact Carlo Arreglo at shoyu@aloha.net.

9. Because this e-mail addresses not only white feminists' racism, but also divides among women of color, Tanigawa's work reflects a shift since *This Bridge*. For analysis of this shift, see

Anzaldúa's introduction to *Haciendo Caras*. Also relevant here is the complex set of identity politics in Hawai'i that often include divisions among people of color who identify as "local" and those not from Hawai'i.

sixty-one

Healing Sueños for Academia

Irene Lara

I dream, and in my dreams I heal myself

> *Light streams through the windows, casting afternoon shadows on the audience. I sit surrounded by rows of older white people wearing pastel designer outfits. A white man stands in front, donning a navy-blue suit and a cardinal-red tie, flashing straight pearly whites and shiny black shoes. I am very aware of my differences as a twenty-something Chicana. Am I sitting up straight enough? I nervously wonder. Yet I am uncertain anyone sees me, making me feel both relieved and sad. This dream man moves his mouth, but I hear no sound. Clutching his chest, he suddenly falls to the floor. Still, no sound. His eyes are pierced with fear. His twisted mouth is wide open. Streaming out of it is a silence that resonates with such deep suffering that everyone freezes. Except me. With a confidence that surprises me yet feels familiar, I walk over and place my glowing brown hands above this white man's heart. With my eyes I tell him that his salvation depends on his faith in my ability to heal.*

This dream man is the internalized white man in me. He is the epitome of privilege I encountered at Stanford University. The one who yelled a chilling "Wetbacks go home!" at a showing of a United Farm Workers documentary. The one who humiliated me for asking about the role of colonialism in American history. The one who organized against Self-Defense Issues for Women, a course about the politics of violence. At times, I have swallowed his racist, sexist, homophobic, classist, and capitalist values and definitions of success. At times, I have also regurgitated them—mostly against myself. Why can't I speak in class? Why can't I write as easily as everyone else can? Why can't I feel this place belongs to me, too? What is the cost of these internalizations? A body, mind, and spirit desirous of soul retrieval (Avila, 169–219).

This white man is also who he is. And I *am* his healer. Western man needs me—a brown mestiza woman—whether he likes it or not. He also needs my ways of knowing. Cherríe Moraga taught me that when U.S. dominant society appropriates and commodifies "Other" spiritualities it marks a need for the wisdom of these ancient yet dynamic beliefs and practices. Our Earth faces ecological disaster. People continue suffering from social injustices. Alienation from self and communities persists. In this era of capitalist globalization, there is a great necessity for relief from physical, spiritual, and social afflictions. So, many of us (re)turn to indigenous and mestiza spiritual knowledges for empowerment[1]—knowledge powerful enough to survive despite patriarchal and colonial efforts at destruction.

This white man is also my great-great grandfather, the Californiano Luis Arellanes, who married my Chumash great-great grandmother on my mother's side, Gumercinda Lara. On my father's side, this white man is also my great-great grandfather, the Mexican hacienda-owner Refugio Aguilar, who never recognized his "illegitimate" daughter with my great-great grandmother, Ramona Torres. Whether I am comfortable with it or not, their genealogies live in my bones as well. Like other people of mixed race before me, I work to make peace with them. Because not to acknowledge and love all who I am is to be defeated, again. As Alice Walker writes, "To cut anyone out of the psyche is to maim the personality; to suppress any part of the personality is to maim the soul" (*Living*, 85). And my soul wants to fly!

My dream, a gift from spirit, reminds me that I am indeed engaged in "curandera work," healing work.[2] My tools are my words. The tools of neither the oppressed nor the oppressor "locked in mortal combat," but simultaneously of and beyond both in the creation of a third transformative space. Standing in rigid opposition is a strategy for survival, but this strategy has also killed us and will continue to sever our souls and assail our hearts. Western binary oppositions wound us in many ways.[3]

At school, I was taught to rely on my reason and deny my body's intuitive knowledge. Throughout my childhood, adolescence, and young adulthood, the oppressive messages were clear: "If you want to 'succeed': develop your reason, conceal your emotions, fragment your mind from your body."[4] A very eager student, I was initially rewarded for internalizing the binary lessons that regulated my behavior. Ignoring my achy body and staying up all night. Pretending I felt fine when I often felt exhausted, incompetent, or hurt. But by the end of my first year at Stanford, I experienced a costly effect of sustained mind/body fragmentation—an excruciating headache that lasted several months. After I was subjected to numerous medical exams, all the doctors could do was give me a vague diagnosis: stress. My eighteen-year-old body was telling me something was not right. But I did not have the support, tools, or language to understand.

With constant pain pulsating across my temples, spreading up through my crown and down to my eyes and nose, I felt that my body was betraying my will to be a "good" student. I could no longer study all of the time. My internalized white man also led me secretly to fear that my headache was caused by an innate inability to handle all of the rational thinking expected from me—brain overload. At the same time, I ambivalently felt a sense of relief for finally having what I perceived as a valid justification to slow down and rest. My head hurt so much for so long that I was compelled to reevaluate my schooling's emphasis on the mind. I was experiencing the impact of always thinking and not allowing myself to feel enough. I slowly began to heal my fragmented self and move toward wholeness and balance. I think and feel at once. Unlearning the western mind/body split and learning to listen to the wisdom of my whole self, my bodymindspirit, is a perpetual process.

Eight years later, a month before my Ph.D. oral qualifying exam, I excitedly drive past Stanford on my way to a conference in Cupertino where I am a main speaker. It is hard to believe that I once uncomfortably sat behind seminar tables. Now, a few miles south of my alma mater, I stand center stage and lecture to a predominantly white middle-class audience. As words—including my dream narrative—powerfully flow out of my mouth I feel that I am healing and forgiving my white man. *You need me whether you like it or not. I need you whether I am comfortable with it or not.* Elated, I head home on Interstate 280. As I drive through Ohlone land, I retrieve the pieces of my soul lost at Stanford. Those invisible to most western doctors' eyes. My fears, embarrassments, self-doubts. My innocence, enthusiasm, desires. My silences, loneliness, sleepless nights. *¡Irene! ¡Iiiiirene! ¡Ireeeneee! ¡Irenita! Irene, come back to me, I need you! ALL of you!* Two nights later, still reeling from the joy of the success of my speech and soul retrieval, I dream another white man.

I dream, and in my dreams I am a warrior

> *Lampposts spaced far apart create a dense pattern of dark shadows. It is late and I am afraid as a friend and I briskly walk toward my car. I stride ahead, fearing that a slow pace will make us likelier targets for violence. Sensing a man approaching, I instinctively move to the edge of the sidewalk. I quickly survey my surroundings. I don't want to be scared. Inhaling, I gather the courage to look up and make eye contact. In a flash, a white man socks me, spilling blood from my nose. Stunned, I begin to fall. He wears a scowl on his face. Still falling. His long nails are bruised, jagged. Still falling. He has bushy eyebrows and lashless brown eyes. I never hit the pavement. Instead, at the crossroads of faith and fear—knowing my friend is near—I pray for help.*

This white man is my "shadow-beast."[5] He reminds me that curanderas must be vigilant warriors, aware of those threatened by her power to heal as well as the ways our internalized oppressions sabotage our affirming work. Being engaged in healing work also means being engaged in a battle. Ours is a perpetual struggle against the "shadow-beasts" who attempt to subvert our transformative work by instigating anxiety, shame, or another stifling violence. This "thug" within and without is a live presence impacting our ability to fly.

As Laura Pérez reminded me, many relate the nose to the human faculty of instinct and intuition. The nose as a metonym for *gnosis*, "intuitive knowledge in spiritual matters" (*Webster's New World Dictionary*), however, is delegitimized in western modern thought. This dominant paradigm, especially since the Enlightenment's focus on science and the mind/body split in the seventeenth century,[6] privileges the rational mind as the sole origin of knowledge. The blow to my nose forcefully reminds me of those invested in maintaining the split. I am aware of the warning against scholarship and pedagogy that reintegrate the bodymindspirit as a legitimate and empowering source of knowledge. Yet like so many other women of color before me, I proceed with faith and courage "in the service of my vision" (Lorde). Redefining the meaning of warrior, I do not perpetuate the violence by punching back. Instead, I invoke the presence of all bodies, spirits, and consciousnesses engaged in similar healing battles. Collectively we will create a space from which to shape and embody "otro modo de ser human[a] y libre."[7]

After all, we need each other to fly.

Learning to Fly

Yet the question remains: How do we sustain the courage to bridge the sacred and the profane in our work, the spiritual and political in our lives, and our mind with our body? Perhaps, first of all, by remembering that these are constructed western binary ways of thinking. Feeding the interests of the dominant, these false splits keep us from ourselves, each other, and our visible and invisible world. With the aim of building a third space, I am learning how to use prayer to suture the ruptures that impede the collective hard work of personal, social, and cosmic transformation.

Early in 1999, I participated in a spiritual reading with Belen Cenizeros, a Yaqui medicine woman who spoke at the University of California, Berkeley. Looking at me, she emphatically stated, "You must pray a lot." This statement left me puzzled because I did not pray, or at least not in what is considered any traditional sense. But perhaps she is right. Many prayers, after all, are questions. And I have a lot of them. What if my scholarship has been a prayer all along? A prayer for understanding how my aching head signals a desire for change. A prayer for re-membering and re-imagining the sacred sexual feminine in our everyday lives. A prayer for relishing in the wetness of my own panocha. A prayer for making present the absences—however much suppressed—in the official histories of las Américas. Belen's words are gifts that continue resonating in my consciousness. *I must pray, I must pray.* I have reappropriated prayer back into my life.

I wrote this prayer as a beginning to my Ph.D. qualifying exam position papers because I desired integrity in my life. Throughout the arduous process of organizing, researching, writing, revising, and studying, I was also concerned with transforming the fragmenting processes of academia by drawing from all of my faculties. By consciously nurturing my reasoning abilities, spiritual strengths, and the wisdom of my body, I worked toward bringing my whole powerful self to the committee table. In conceptualizing my writing as a prayer, I attempt to embody what I am theorizing, the need for transformation. How might writing as a spiritual and political practice help us articulate ideas and feelings that in the effort to be "academic" enough might otherwise be lost to the cosmos? How might prayer open up other possibilities for speaking and acting transformationally and transrationally[8] within academia?

In the spirit of the Mayan philosophy "In Lak Ech"[9]—yo soy tu otro yo, I am your other I—I offer these words as a prayer for connection across differences and with the darkness, whiteness, and other "shadow-beasts" within.[10] For those of you in the midst of doctoral exams, tenure review, or another academic initiation process. For those of you writing your first research paper or healing from your undergraduate experience. For those of you who contemplate applying to college or leaving academia forever. For those of you made to believe you were not smart enough to go to school. For those of you tired of battling without healing. For those of you who desire to integrate your bodymindspirit, these sueños and prayers are my offering.

> May these words heal the de-spiritualization of the academy
> May these words heal the de-politicization of the spiritual
> May these words heal the de-eroticization of the body, mind, and spirit
> May these words heal our separation from ourselves, each other, and the visible and invisible world
> May these words "transfix us with love,"[11] so together we will soar
>
> In Lak Ech

Notes

The lives and words of many continue to touch and inspire me. Ana Castillo, Cherríe Moraga, Gloria Anzaldúa, Audre Lorde, Yvonne Yarbro-Bejarano, Laura Pérez, Norma Alarcón, Elena Avila, Laura Jiménez, Rosalía González, Yolanda Santiago Venegas, Macarena Hernández,

Christina Grijalva, Karina Céspedes, Luz Álvarez Martínez, Susana Renaud, N'tua N'tua Domayla, Elena Gutierrez, Luz Herrera, Rosa Hernández, Raúl Trejo, and the rest of mi familia, gracias.

1. While indigenous spiritualities largely draw from the beliefs and practices of indigenous people, mestiza spiritualities are more culturally hybrid. Both are subject to the legacy of colonialism in the Americas. They may draw from but are not limited to the multiple worldviews of North American, Meso-American, and South American indigenous peoples; Yoruba, Congo, and other African peoples; and Catholics, Protestants, Sephardic Jews, Muslims, and Buddhists. Writings on this topic include: Avila; Anzaldúa's *Borderlands/La Frontera*; Castillo; Delgadillo; Hernández-Ávila; Medina; Moraga's *The Last Generation*; Laura Pérez.

2. Laura Pérez, building on Ana Castillo and others, describes the work of Chicana artists as "curandera work" ("Spirit Glyphs," 41). Similarly, Morales associates the work of historians with the symbol of the curandera in "The Historian as Curandera."

3. Anzaldúa, *Borderlands/La Frontera*, 78. Throughout her innovative book, Anzaldúa elaborates the limits of oppositional tactics, develops the "borderlands" as a site of transformation, and explores the impact of various binary oppositions on our consciousness. I join many in gratitude for her healing role in my conscientización. I am also informed by the visionary work of Audre Lorde, who taught me about the limits of the "master's tools" in bringing about "genuine change."

4. Western oppositions establish fixed divisions, negate multiplicity, and have unequal social value. (For example: you're a thinker *or* a feeler; rational thinking is good, intuition is bad.) Furthermore, binary frameworks are racialized and gendered (thinkers are white and/or men [good]; feelers are people of color and/or women [bad]), thus occluding the role of power and hindering complex understandings of our multiple identities.

5. I draw from Anzaldúa's concept of the "Shadow-Beast" as the feared, distorted, suppressed aspects of our psyches. Especially see chapters 2 and 4 in *Borderlands/La Frontera*.

6. Descartes's philosophy plays an especially prominent role.

7. "Another way to be human and free" (my translation). Castellanos, *Meditación*, 73.

8. Arguing for the need to (re)integrate spirit and reason, Wilber distinguishes "transrational spirituality" from "what has historically served as prerational, ethnocentric, fundamentalist dogma."

9. Claudia Mercado, a member of the Los Angeles–based Latina performance group In Lakech.

10. In recognition of ancient understandings of prayers and dreams as sources of healing, I draw from a wide range of sources linking spiritual practices to material effects, including Gandhi's; Moraga's *Last Generation*; Matthews; Hernández's "Cascada de estrellas"; Metzger; and Castillos's "I Ask."

11. Harjo, "Creation Story."

vi.

"yo soy tu otro yo—i am your other i" . . .
forging common ground

sixty-two

my tears are wings

Chrystos

sixty-three

The Colors Beneath Our Skin

Carmen Morones

Hell breathed on us in Potash, California, on the edge of Death Valley and it was a battle to stay on the good side of God. I had a terrible thirst that nothing would quench but the lemons from Mrs. McBride's tree. That was the summer that I became a lemon thief.

Mrs. McBride, a retired schoolteacher in our neighborhood, paid me $3 a week to do her chores. There was her lemon tree to water, dishes to wash, laundry to hang, and, most boring of all, giving the old lady a manicure. We sat at her dining room table near the droning swamp cooler where the breeze fluttered my bangs and ponytail, providing an island of chill. It was here beneath the framed pictures of President Kennedy, Pope John XXIII, and the long dead Mr. McBride that the old lady stopped complaining about her aching joints and became kind as a fairy godmother. For the second week of my job, she had again placed before us two frosty goblets of iced tea and a fancy dish of speckled pink and white Mother's cookies. I was dying to grab a handful of the delicious-looking animal shapes and wash them down with that cool drink, but I couldn't. It wouldn't be polite unless she offered them.

While waiting for the viejita as she cleaned her cat eyeglasses with slow pained movements, I stared at her gallery of photos. President Kennedy had been assassinated by a communist. Pope John XXIII was poisoned by greedy bishops for wanting to help the poor, my mama said. Mr. McBride, I wasn't sure how he'd died, but he might have been a spy, with that black beret and camera-sharp eyes. If I had a wall of my own, a place to hang pictures in that dinky room I shared with my kid brothers, I sure wouldn't put up photos of dead people. I'd put up Glinda, the good witch from *The Wizard of Oz*, and George Harrison, the absolute fab, the cutest of the Beatles.

Mrs. McBride put her glasses back on, magnifying her blue eyes, bright and liquid as the Yucca Park pool. She checked to see if all the manicure supplies were on the mirrored tray, including nail file, tiny scissors, nail polish remover, and an elegant little bottle of "Rose Petal." Satisfied, she lifted her goblet to mine with great effort, her gnarly hands shaking. "Salud," she said in Spanish so good, she sounded like us Mexicans.

I would have preferred lemonade to the cold perfume and sugar taste of her Jasmine tea, but I was so thirsty I guzzled it down until there was nothing left in the glass but a pile of ice. Please ma'am, I'll have some more, I wanted to say and a handful of those cookies too, if you don't mind. But I was too embarrassed, I didn't want to seem como una muerta de hambre.

The old lady laid her wrinkled hands on the table, signaling it was time to start. I lifted her small hands and began inspecting her cuticles. How soft her palms were compared to my mama's. This viejita, still in her house robe, had probably never picked mangos for a patrón as my mama had back in Mexico when I was little. I didn't understand why she wanted her fingernails so pretty anyway, her knuckles were knobby and her hands were as spotty as a toad's. It was plain to see her cuticles hadn't grown even as high as a weed in an ant's garden. "Mrs. McBride, we don't need to trim your nails today, ok?"

"Oh really?" She sounded disappointed, and though it took her some pain, she immediately traced the skin around her nails. "My word, you're doing an excellent job, Odilia. As good as a professional." She winked at me. "But my nails—" she tapped her crooked fingers on the table. "They absolutely need filing and of course, a new coat of polish."

Though her nails were only slivers, I did my best to be gentle, filing them into little crescent moons. When I'd finished, Mrs. McBride smiled her approval. I uncapped the bottle of nail polish remover and winced at the fumes. They reminded me of last night, my papa's hot breath in my face, telling me I was a muchacha mala, no good, bad, a sinner. I felt like throwing up. The old lady didn't notice my disgust, as she had her eyes closed like she was falling asleep. I turned my head away from the fumes and gazed at the lemon tree outside her window.

For a moment the little tree's beauty captured me, its golden fruit shimmering in the noonday sun as if ready to catch fire. It was a miracle that the leaves weren't brown and shriveled up, that the lemons weren't stunted or rotting, that the tree could grow at all in this desert inferno. In Mariposa, where I was from, trees grew easily, especially lemon trees. The tree in our chicken yard was as tall as my papa, with limbs as thick as his wrists, while Mrs. McBride's tree was scrawny and only reached to the middle of her window. In Mexico, our lemons had been like fruit from heaven, little yellow suns that hung above my cousin Lola and me. We plucked them freely, tearing the rind with our fingernails, sucking the juice like a refresco, sighing at the out-of-this-world goodness. How I craved the taste of one now! "Odilia—"

She startled me. I dabbed the cotton in the solution and hurried to remove the chipped pink from her fingernails. "Odilia, are you having fun this summer?" Suddenly wide awake, she peered above her glasses at me.

I laughed nervously as I debated telling her the truth. Fibbing was a sin but she'd probably fire me if she knew how I resented helping my mama and her when I'd rather be dipping my gangly legs in the Yucca pool and watching the boys.

Mrs. McBride sipped her tea through a straw. "Are your folks taking you on any trips?"

"I think we're going to L.A." I tried to sound excited so she would believe me, but my words sank like a deflated inner tube. Most days, my papa came home from shoveling potash looking like he'd been fried and refried, and my mama was a zombie from the heat, the housework, and keeping up with the new twins.

"Disneyland?"

"Disneyland is for little kids," I said, rubbing the polish off her nail. If the truth be told, I liked Mickey Mouse cartoons but Disneyland was like another planet to me, a place for brats and overgrown babies. I'd never been and I never wanted to go.

"How *old* are you dear?"

"Twelve."

She peered over her glasses at me, her eyes roaming from my string bean arms to my goose neck and down again to my tits showing through my T-shirt like little mounds of masa. The heat rushed to my face and I hunched forward. "My goodness . . . you are becoming a woman." She said as though it was something to celebrate. "Are you prepared for that, Odilia?"

"Excuse me?"

She lowered her voice, "You know, womanly things?" I felt embarrassed as I thought of having to wear a bra and starting my period. "Does your mother talk with you about such things?"

I wanted to yell at her, hell no, there's no time for little talks. The only words my mama had for me were orders. "Ayuda con el casear o cuida los niños!" Housework or babysitting. The only things she had time to teach me were how to make the beans last longer or get the washing machine to work right. I shrugged. "I didn't think so." She patted my hand. "Well, if you have any questions, feel free to ask."

Who did she think she was that I would tell her anything private? Just because I was stuck here with her didn't mean I was going to blab my problems. I nodded anyway, just so she would shut up. I finished removing the chipped polish from her last finger. The cotton ball smeared with pink made me imagine a Kotex and things to come. There was one thing I would have liked to ask, that I wanted to know more than anything—could you predict when you were going to start? I would just die if I got a stain on the back of my skirt the way Tina Marshall did last year in sixth grade. But I was too embarrassed to ask. I opened the diamond-shaped cap, dipped the little brush in, and pulled out a thick pink pearl of polish.

"Uh—Odilia—" She pointed to the cotton balls. "Remember?" She splayed her fingers on the table.

"I'm sorry." I returned the brush to the bottle and began placing cotton between each stiff, knobby finger. How many more things could I do wrong today? I'd already accidentally broken a plate and dropped a basket of laundry. I feared the old lady would get fed up and fire me. If that happened, I'd make my mama wrong for standing up to my papa and insisting I take this job to buy clothes for school when he'd demanded I stay home to help her. "I'm sorry, ma'am."

"You're doing great, Odilia." I sighed with relief. She peered at me again and it struck me that she was studying me, using some mysterious sixth sense that could see more clearly than her bad eyesight. "Is everything okay at home?"

The viejita sounded sympathetic. She tugged at the thread that held me stitched together, like she was trying to rip open the skin that held the real me. She wanted to see the swirls of colors underneath, when I could only show her a brown blur. "Everything's okay, ma'am."

"Are you sure?"

"Yes, ma'am."

"No troubles?"

"No, ma'am."

"It's just that you seem . . . nervous today, like something is upsetting you." I let her words pass over me. All I wanted at that moment was to finish the manicure. I opened the bottle of polish and as I pulled out the brush, my hand shook. Afraid of dripping pink on her white plastic tablecloth, I stuffed the brush back in the bottle and twisted the cap on tightly.

"Are you sure you're alright, dear? You can tell me if anything is wrong." I wanted to say, Shut up, you nosey old lady. Shut the hell up and leave me alone! "No, ma'am," I said, gritting my teeth.

"Well alright, dear, if you say so." She sipped her tea.

Silence fell upon the room like an uninvited ghost standing between us. I wished I could have trusted her enough to tell her about my hidden hurts, but I could no more tell her the truth about my life than she could probably tell me about hers. Counting numbers inside my head, I steadied myself and began painting her fingernails.

She hummed a tune that sounded like a lullaby. "It's called 'Beautiful Dreamer,' ever heard of it, Odilia?"

"No, ma'am."

"It's an old song, one of Billy's and my favorites." She sipped her tea. "What are your dreams, Odilia?"

"Excuse me?"

"What are your dreams for yourself? You know, what do you want to be when you grow up?" No one had ever asked me that before. I knew what I didn't want: to be married and end up una esclava—a housewife and slave to a husband and a bunch of kids like my mama. And I didn't want to live in this hellhole for the rest of my life. But what was the key? How did one escape?

"Come on, dear, you can tell me. Just say the first thing that comes to mind."

As I brushed the glistening pink over her fingernail, I imagined how wonderful it would be if I could make anything happen like in a fairy tale. I might be a bird. Or a butterfly. A monarch butterfly, like the ones that migrate to Mariposa every winter. Beautiful, with bold orange and black wings. A butterfly flitting from tree to tree, gliding in the sunshine, soaring toward the sun without fear of burning. Of course, I couldn't share any of this with her.

She blew on her nails. "Oh, I see those bright eyes of yours staring off, getting lost in some secret place." She sighed. "You know, you remind me of myself when I was your age. I too was rather quiet, but Lord I was bursting with dreams." This viejita was different from any grown-ups I'd ever met in Potash. She poured herself into a room instead of being all locked up and proper like the others.

"Do you have a boyfriend, Odilia?"

Why the heck was she asking me that? I wished. I wished that one day Chris White would shine his emerald eyes on me. I wished he could see me as beautiful as Cinderella at the ball, my faded skirt changed into a bright mod dress, my cinnamon skin as lovely as an Arabian princess's, my goose neck as graceful as a swan's. Every night I imagined what it would feel like to run my fingers through his Beach Boy bangs and kiss his princely lips. But he was a doctor's son and I knew I was invisible to him. Having his love was an impossible dream, just like wanting to be a butterfly. "No, ma'am, I don't."

She laughed, fanning her polished hand. "Oh you will, you will soon enough."

"No way."

"That's what you say now. I know, I was like that at your age. Boys were the furthest thing from my mind. Growing up in upstate New York, all I wanted to do was read books and ride horses." She was very still like she was catching her memories in a net. "Oh, I wanted to be a writer like Miss Louisa May Alcott, but I was an only child with no siblings to write about. Then, I wanted to be a dancer like Isadora Duncan, a scientist like Marie Curie . . . and so on."

As I listened to her story I calmed down. She giggled just like a girl my age. "Well, when I finally grew up I settled on journalism. Newspaper reporting. Went to Columbia. That's where I met Billy." She looked up at his picture and sighed. "Goodness, that man would smile at me and I'd drop the pen right out of my hand."

I nodded as I shook the bottle of "Rose Petal." I still had one more hand to polish. Mrs. McBride played with her wedding ring, a gold band with a tiny diamond, which she turned round and round with such smoothness, it seemed the pain had disappeared from her hands. "After we got married, we joined the People's Press and went to Spain on assignment to cover the civil war. That was the best time of my life, Odilia." Her face radiated so much happiness and life, she seemed like a young woman hidden behind a wrinkled sagging mask. "We had love and we had a cause. Socialists," she said with pride. "Do you know what I'm talking about?"

I shook my head. "Socialism means equality. It means sharing the wealth of the land with working men and women. No bosses, Odilia. The workers run everything. No bosses. Can you imagine?" The truth is I couldn't. I didn't understand how it could ever happen that I would never have to work for anyone, that I could be my own boss, but I liked the idea, so I nodded.

Mrs. McBride looked pleased and didn't seem to mind that I wasn't working on her nails, but just sitting there listening to her. "It was a revolution, Odilia, and we were there, a voice for the people. Until my Billy got caught in the crossfire—" She had a faraway look in her eyes, like she was somehow back in that time and place where she last saw her Billy. Her lips quivered. She cleared her throat and returned to sipping her tea.

"Afterwards, I returned to the States. Came out to Potash in '39 to cover the strike against the chemical company." She stared at her goblet and turned it round and round as though she were looking into a crystal ball that showed her the past. "When I went to visit the strikers' homes— well, they were actually shacks—there were all these skinny Oakie children asking me for food and vying for my attention. They just melted my heart. You know, my Billy was an Oakie."

She stared at Mr. McBride's photo with admiration. "Billy always said, 'You can't plant a garden just by talking about it.' So I decided to stay. They were desperate to keep teachers here in those days." The viejita took off her glasses, and with shaking hands, wiped them with a white handkerchief that had her husband's initials. "Billy would have liked that, but that wasn't the only reason I stayed. I planned to write a book . . . about the war . . . about Billy and me. Out here there would be no distractions. But I never had the time. There was always so much to do . . . planning lessons, making home visits, trying to unionize the workers, setting up a free clinic . . . " She sighed. "Always so much work to do." She shook her head and laughed like someone had played a joke on her. "And that was before I got arthritis." Mrs. McBride put her glasses back on and stared at me with saucer eyes full of hope, full of expectations. "Now it's *your* turn, Odilia."

What was she talking about?! I didn't want to be a teacher, I hated grammar, and I sure as heck would not choose to stay in Potash. What happened to all her talk about dreams? She made me believe there *was a door I could open*, and now she'd shut it in my face. She was just like all the other grown-ups I'd ever known who made me believe something good was going to happen and then delivered the opposite thing. I wanted to fling the polish against the wall. "I have to go to the bathroom," I said, hurrying away in the direction of the bathroom but instead going out the back door.

Outside the heat flared in my face and the afternoon light blinded me like a giant flashbulb. I couldn't breathe, I was hyperventilating. I ran down the dirt pathway of the old lady's garden, past the row of prickly pears with spine-laced ears, beyond the blanket of fuchsia ice plant and the life-size statue of St. Francis. Help me, I prayed as I ran by. Stepping over the rock circle that surrounded the lemon tree, I threw myself at it, wrapping my arms around the small twisted branches, closing my eyes and burying my face in its leaves. Lola, I cried inside. My cousin Lola, the only person who had never lied to me but I had left behind in Mexico when I was seven. Little Lola with the curly black angel hair, the elfish smile, the twinkling fairy eyes, the small soft hands soothing the belt welts on my thighs, whispering funny things in my ear, making me laugh when I had been crying. Lola and me under the lemon tree, plucking the fruit and sucking the juice as if drinking a refresco. My Lola whom I waved adios to en Mexico for the last time. My little Lola who drowned in a well when she was five. Mi Lolita. My breath came back to me in gasps.

I plucked a lemon from the tree, lifted it to my mouth, inhaled the sweet citrus and bit through the thick rind. The sour juice jolted me and I threw it to the ground. I plucked another and another. Lemon after lemon, I plucked, bit, sucked, searching for the sweet juice of Mexico. I tasted every fruit until the tree was bare. But it had not quenched my thirst. I felt emptier, with a bigger hole in my heart, lonelier than the day I'd left Lolita. I stomped the fruit pile at my feet, squishing the pulp, squirting the juice, flattening the rind, destroying it. I kicked the trunk, yanked the leaves, tried to break the thorny branches. My hands were scratched and pricked, stinging and trickling with blood. My insides were a whirl. I wanted to throw up.

"Odilia," Mrs. McBride called from her back door, startling me.

Coming back to my senses, I saw the naked tree, robbed of its fruit, destroyed. I was ashamed of what I had done and couldn't face the old lady. Feeling like a cornered animal, I didn't know which way to turn: if I stayed the old lady would surely yell at me; if I went home my mama would break out crying for making her look bad by losing my job, my papa would beat me for humiliating la familia and having to spend money to replace the viejita's tree. I looked at the craggy hill casting a shadow upon the desert and ran toward it.

"Odilia!" Mrs. McBride called again.

I ran as fast as I could, trampling over the dirt in my flip-flops, moving against the pounding heat. Up the slope I climbed, passing between creosote, careful of sidewinders and tarantulas that might lurk beneath. My body stung from the cuts and scratches, but this pain was nothing compared to the ache in my soul. Up the hill I climbed, the sun drinking my sweat, turning the blood on my face and hands into trickles of dried red paint. As I climbed closer to the fiery mouth of the sun, I had no fear for I was offering myself to it.

At the top of the hill, the world was quiet. I looked below to Mrs. McBride's white stucco, the size of a doll house. I stared at the small patch of green garden and the lemon tree that looked like a twig. Even from this distance, you could tell by its nakedness that it was ruined. I felt sorry for the little tree and wished I hadn't hurt it, but something furious had come over me and I'd lashed out. Now there would be hell to pay. My eyes roamed the glittering gravel rooftops of our neighborhood until I recognized the lone brown patchwork roof of our house on Patton Street. I imagined my mama inside the kitchen making tortillas at the hot stove, the twins crying in their crib, my kid brothers making a ruckus. Would she think of me if I was gone, would she miss me?

In the distance, on the outskirts of town, clouds spewed like dragon's breath from the smokestacks of the chemical company where my papa worked. I could just see his hang-dog face igniting with anger when he heard what I'd done to Mrs. McBride's tree. No doubt, he'd beat the hell out of me. Who could I turn to in this lonely, colorless town, this desert valley as desolate as the moon? I scanned Potash from the looming white cross of St. Mary's church, to the school, the hospital, round and round the tracts of cookie-cutter houses and miles beyond to the Panamint Mountains, yet there was no one out there who could help me. I would leave Potash as unwelcome as I had arrived.

Mrs. McBride was now outside. The viejita looked as tiny as a stooped doll in her sun hat and pink robe as she shuffled across her garden. She saw the wreck I'd made of her tree. "Odilia!"

I heard her faraway voice and I knew I was really in for it. "Odilia," she called again.

Pretty soon everyone in the neighborhood would know my business. It was bad enough that I was already called a beaner and a spic by some of the white kids; would they now also call me a lemon thief? There was no hope, no way out. I laid down on a coffin-shaped rock, screaming inside as my bare thighs touched the burning stone and my dangling legs pressed the blistering earth. How could this be any worse than my papa beating me to death? I could take this. At least it was quiet up here except for the old lady's distant calls. I closed my eyes and the sun burned through my lids a fiery orange. Was this a preview of Hell, where I'd burn forever for my sins? It scared me but there was no turning back. I imagined myself becoming as hard as the rock on which I lay, but my thirst flared and my head throbbed from the heat. I called for my mama.

She didn't answer. The only sound was the sizzle of the afternoon heat. I was alone. Abandoned. I thought of Lolita and a huge sadness weighed upon me, for I realized that I would never be reunited with her again; we would be on the opposite ends of God's spectrum. "Perdóname, Lolita," I said, as though she could somehow hear me.

I surrendered myself to the merciless sun and waited for death. The heat was sucking the life out of me when a sudden breeze passed over my body. It blew from my head to my feet and up again, becoming as fierce as the wind on a cold winter night. It thrust open a door inside me and I felt myself regaining life. Clouds swirled within me and it began to rain. Water seeped throughout my body, mind and spirit, cleansing me, releasing all my pain. Just when I feared drowning in my grief, a winged shadow fluttered above me, parting the waters and filling me with a pink soothing light, a tender balm like the rose-petal touch of my beloved cousin. I heard her familiar lion cub's laugh and when I opened my teary eyes to look for her, I caught a glimpse of a wing flying toward the sun.

Was this real or was I imagining things?

I sat up and stared at the blue emptiness above, wondering if Lolita was an angel somewhere up there, if she could see me though I couldn't see her. What did it all mean? Something gleamed in the sky and fell downward. I watched the gold speck drift toward the earth, floating along a spiraling path above me until I could see that it was a feather. A beautiful golden feather landing in my wounded palm. As I stroked the heavenly softness, I knew that I was not alone. I now had the courage to step through the door that had been unlocked by the viejita.

"Odilia!" Mrs. McBride called, her voice closer than it had been before. I looked below. To my amazement, she was shuffling across the desert, following my footprints toward the hill.

"I'm coming!" I said, waving the golden feather in my hand.

sixty-four

Connection: The Bridge Finds Its Voice

Maria Proitsaki

The Greek woman's many attempts to "connect" with Third World lesbians and "Women of Color" . . . have been met with outright rejection. Unfortunately, being loud, aggressive and very Greek-identified, she has found a great deal of rejection in white, mainstream lesbian/feminist circles as well. Clearly she does not fit there either.

—Mirtha Quintanales, This Bridge Called My Back

There was hardly a river

I brought the food
I brought the water

Ah! I could sit there and watch
them whistling while working
layer upon layer of
freshly cut stone,
from the heart of Pindos

But the bridge would not stand still.

So they lured me in
to find the ring

How he rushed then!
How the boys grew nervous
and the whistling ceased . . .

Stone by stone they piled their frustration
on my shiny black hair

Vocal chords arranged in numbness

This arch is not of glory
You parade on my back

Sewn by night
in filthy quarters
are wings

Yet, I am not an angel

Shamelessly
My father's lash
Balances
Against the sun
before it leaps

It echoes in his lady's room,
where the china heart
of the arched ballerina
on the dresser skirts

—my back, my soul—

she misses a step
and I am voiceless

Could you ever translate
my suffering?

Note

The Bridge of Arta is the oldest and largest stone bridge in Greece, built over a river in Epirus, and named after the nearby town. A legend has it that its foundation, unsuccessful for years as the construction would collapse by night after each day's work, had finally required the sacrifice of the first builder's wife. In the legend's most widely anthologized version, the trapped woman calls down a curse upon the bridge, but when reminded of her brother (who might cross it and would therefore be at risk), she changes her words and blesses it instead. This revision of the curse, however, occurs in less than a quarter of the 333 documented Greek versions of the legend, the majority of which share an open-ended quality, concluding on a dynamic and far more intriguing note: the woman curses the bridge, thus undoing its construction and the meaning of her sacrifice.

sixty-five

The Body Politic—Meditations on Identity

Elana Dykewomon

First a testimonial: writing changes our lives. *This Bridge Called My Back* was among the collections of voices I was eager and desperate to hear as a young lesbian. I was listening for the whole voices of women whose lives were unlike mine. In love, anger, accent, intent along with content, *This Bridge* presented that range as well as words on a page can. Reading about other women's lives gives us two things: an understanding of difference, and a way into sameness. Almost every time we stop to listen to another woman's story, we hear something in it that resonates, and that resonance—of text with body—changes us. Yet we are not always "sisters under the skin." What we wear on our skins—race, ethnicity, money, country of origin, physical ability, appearance, religion, age—creates troubling barriers. *This Bridge* and books like it were my teachers—from them I learned how complex it is to make common cause, how absolutely necessary it is to find ways to bridge the divisions that institutions use to keep us powerless.

But our skins remain our first point of contact.[1] In the last twenty years, activists often find they are asked questions that these writings have already addressed—irritating questions because they mean starting again at step one. Often we want to go back and say—"Read. Here's a reading list, come back when you've finished it." (I imagine many women have wanted to say that to me as well.) But our reading doesn't always make us sensitive to the same issues in new situations; it doesn't always prepare us for our own defensiveness. It's easier to see how others operate from their privileges than how you or I, the readers, do. We have to work with how reading (and re-reading) translates into practice, in the moments when we're face to face.

This physical translation of thought preoccupies me lately. I am thinking about bodies in one way or another all the time—how it is that our bodies are the sites of so many competing stories. Sometimes it's almost impossible to get our own attention, let alone listen to someone else. It's more or less easy to say racism, capitalism, imperialism, patriarchy are the enemies, smash the state! But when we get down to the business of working with each other, when we look at each other, how do we understand these abstractions as they play out in relationships? In the dynamics of our organizations?

Bodies—my body, the bodies of lesbians I work with—are still the hardest things to get hold of. Why is that? I've been trying for months to write about what it means, one to one, when we take in each other's bodies. Say you're in a room of strangers and acquaintances who have come together for a cause—to plan a march, a conference, a picket line, a magazine, a web strategy, a support/action group. You look around. You listen. And everyone's body matters. What color, age, weight, what obvious disability, what gender presentation, which distinguishing marks, what tone of voice, what speaking pattern.

Our mothers and teachers told us never to judge books by their covers, that making assumptions because of appearance is superficial. But in fact we constantly judge by appearance—and there's nothing superficial about it. It's become part of our political commitment to count how many of us are women of color, how many disabled, old, young, working-class. How many like us/not like us. It has always been (from elementary school to action groups) part (if not most) of how we choose to be in a group. The judgments we make on appearance touch our best and worst motives, touch unconscious prejudices and desires, murky stuff. It's not shallow—it's the terrifically complicated thing we do. As we claim our identities, we make family/alliances as well as knuckle under to the available categories an oppressively hierarchical culture has created for us.

Books have been written about this—what the viewer's gaze does to the one being viewed/how we construct and project our personas. But I keep wanting to get at it what it means in daily life for those of us who struggle together in lesbian and other progressive communities—sometimes with wonderful and often with painful results. I want to work in groups where I know women won't harm, judge, or mock me because of what I look like. I want to be safe for the others I work with. And at the same time I want it to be possible to acknowledge that appearance influences our perceptions without falling into endless cycles of processing (in which the person who's asked to explain herself ends up taking care of those who've hurt her through their ignorance).[2]

Somewhere in this problem—how it is we reach out of ourselves and work with anyone—identity politics, separatism, nationalism, familial pride, internalized prejudice, gender theory, social roles, and our vision of working toward a just world get completely tangled up. Everything in U.S. culture tells us we have to look out for ourselves, watch our backs, trust only family. But it's easy to see that unless you're an able-bodied middle/upper-class white man (sometimes woman), going it alone will likely result in failure. And many of us find our birth families (however much affection we may have for them) confining for any number of reasons. We look around and injustice is everywhere. Our responses vary, of course, depending on our social positions and personal visions. But at some point we all decide we don't want injustice done to us. Out of that self-interest,[3] we realize we need to make common cause with others. But with whom? How do we get to we/us/them?

If I understand the arguments against "identity politics" correctly, basing our activism entirely on one identity inadvertently reaffirms the power of culturally constructed roles; this may lead to ranking oppressions (and therefore fighting about what's most important), and drawing boundaries that exclude making allies. We tend to resist being one thing only—the common cry of "don't put your labels on me" comes not so much from identifying with all humanity as feeling slighted in our individual complexity, invisible behind our labels. But isn't it important to lay claim to ourselves, to take on all the names for what we are or hope to become? I am, for instance, a dyke, a butch, a Jew, a writer, an ex–mental hospital inmate, a teacher, a former printer, middle-class, fat, disabled, middle-aged, an anarcho-separatist with an analysis of power relations. This is not the end of me; it's the starting point. Nor do I insist on all these words in every context: sometimes all that matters about me is that I'm middle class, or that I've been locked up, or that I'm fat.

Most folks, for instance, aren't used to looking at fat people—and of course it's impolite to stare, so they don't look—missing the contours of our bodies, the shape of our breasts or our complexions. I've been a fat activist for about twenty years, yet I notice how often I'm reluctant in new situations to insist on it as a legitimate part of my political resume. It's obvious why people "reject labels" that are culturally negative: it's usually positive to be called a writer, but most people don't mean to compliment you when they say you're fat. Fat activism hasn't been able to change much, not even the attitude that it isn't very important.[4]

What does it mean to be a fat activist? Like many other activisms, it contains two fronts: a civil rights component and a radical analysis of power relations. The civil rights component proposes that fat people have the same rights to employment and use of public facilities, the freedom to walk around the world without being ridiculed, and the right to be taken seriously. If you think this is obvious, you've never had to complain about the seats being too small in meeting rooms, classrooms, buses, airplanes, movies—never had to suffer the choice between public humiliation and "choosing" to stay home, isolated.

In her 1970s story "Advancing Luna—and Ida B. Wells," Alice Walker writes of Luna: "She was attractive, but just barely and with effort. Had she been the slightest bit overweight, for instance, she would have gone completely unnoticed, and would have faded into the background where, even in a revolution, fat people seem destined to go." Reading these lines in the late '70s, a minor observation in a story about the politics of rape between black men and white women, was a kick in the gut, and I determined I would not fade into the background.[5] Not much has changed since the 1970s—you don't see many four-hundred-pound women giving papers at national conferences or being advanced as role models. Believe me: there are plenty of brilliant, incisive, radical very fat women; they've just never been missed. Culturally they have been "identified out of existence"—they are "only" one thing, and they serve only one purpose—cautionary.

The analysis of power relations around body size tells us we live in a misogynistic culture that creates hierarchies among women, pitting us against each other and forcing us to compete for male approval. Many mechanisms of class mobility are played out through fear of fat. Women forcing their daughters to diet at the age of six (or sixteen) are no different from women who have complied with rituals of clitoridectomy or foot-binding. Women in almost every[6] society offer their daughters up to the prevailing cultural standards of beauty and usefulness for women. Men as a group control access to power and economic security—if women don't prepare their daughters to meet institutionalized male demands, they know their daughters will suffer in life.

You knew that, right? But you still find yourself complicit. While I don't mean to focus all your attention on the nature of fat oppression, it is definitely one major way we judge when we look at/can't see each other, and something that gets glossed over in organizations, even those committed to accessibility. Body grief touches women of all races, ethnicities, abilities, ages, classes. And that suffering is a deep psychic wound, requiring a constant internal balancing act. Very few fat women achieve the equanimity to go ahead and do whatever the hell they are inspired to do—and keep doing it, whether or not they get recognition or respect.

Part of this is the result of consumerism. We are led to believe that if we do not like some part of our bodies/physical identities, it is possible to change that part.[7] So if you don't change something generally perceived to be within your power to change, you're a failed consumer. It's worth considering how intense the disinformation campaign is that convinces most people that body size can be changed: even scientists and doctors now reluctantly will agree, when pressed, that "dieting" has a 95 to 98% failure rate.[8] If you suffer because of something that people believe can be changed, the suffering is your fault. Fat people, mostly women, are scapegoats for a myriad of cultural sins—fat means taking more than your share, a lack of intelligence, the moral failure to embrace "discipline" and "will power," laziness, indolence, sloth, greed. Fat women carry these sins on our skins so that thin and average-size people can feel good about themselves, feel as if they are in control of their lives.[9]

Fatness, although perceived to be a changeable characteristic, is an identity most fat people carry through life. Many other physical traits, of course, are perceived to be immutable. Both categories, the supposedly mutable and supposedly immutable, serve power structures. For instance, the category of "young black male" has acquired so many negative cultural meanings that even the mutable part—youth—has become fixed: we know how many young black men never get old. We are so used to these "slots" that we barely have to do more than glance around to orient ourselves. We see those who are from different physical groups than our own by the most generalized characteristics—not noticing variations of hair, hue, eyebrows, hands—or even statement. We don't look carefully at each other (I know exceptions exist). We're too nice and too competitive and too insecure all rolled up together in our separate ticking bundles. So we lump people together in groups and that makes it easier to imagine what they'll say, how they'll act. This may be a couple steps beyond stereotyping, but it stems from much the same desire: to anticipate social interactions, and make them safe.

So? How do we distinguish between claiming the identities that make it possible to make common cause and clinging to identities (both for ourselves and others) that reinforce hierarchical power structures? Are we just little-brained creatures who wind up with these limiting stories of reality because we can't look and are afraid to listen? Really, what changes the world is the power of a compelling story. But we seem to carefully limit the stories that reach us to those stories that won't push us to change.

What stories are we listening to, anyway? I was walking through the Boston Public Library last summer, and I happened on turn-of-the-nineteenth-century murals, John Singer Sargent's *The Triumph of Religion,* in the old building. Everyone in them (can I be remembering right?) looked white. The goddess Astarte was there, and Mary, but the natural evolution was toward men, the "king of kings." I was struck again by how reality belongs to the one who tells the story. If your story gets the foreground—the murals in public buildings, the majority of public school reading lists—it overpowers other stories that could be told. That the Boston Public

Library features these murals presenting a white, male, Christian religion as the "triumph" of civilization is directly connected to the derision heaped upon those who want an Afrocentric curriculum. Those murals, presented as truth, make the public believe that everyone who works in the library, and by extension, who works for the public, supports that "reality." Even if the head of the library, or the housing commissioner, should be a woman of color, she would be expected to uphold "civic values"—the story the mural tells—and act in the way that's appropriate to the slot. So our identities—our stories—are not only what we look like, but where we are.

"Occupying the slot" is a big part of how we function and what we expect from others. We may not "look the part," but if we have the part others will allow us to be the exception. When I stand in front of my English classes on the first day of school, that I have the slot of "teacher" works against what my students see: a fifty-year-old, short, fat, white butch who says her name is Dykewomon. I am sure some leave because of the dissonance between their images of teachers and fat queers. At San Francisco State, usually the biggest challenge to my students' conceptual framework is that fat women can be smart, rigorous, and industrious.[10]

But it's a struggle to change the slots we occupy—judge, professor, senator, author, electrician—that have been traditionally reserved for white men. We are expected, even when we manage to acquire one of those slots, to exhibit characteristics culturally defined for us: working-class women are tough; fat women are self-indulgent; middle-class women are politely controlling; women of color are righteous. We carry these expectations with us—both of ourselves and those we interact with. That's why it's so important to not allow a context to take you over.

Earlier in this essay I wrote: "sometimes all that matters about me is that I'm middle-class, or that I've been locked up, or that I'm fat." The more I think about this, the more I realize it's not true. I am never only a single way that I may be oppressed, nor am I only a single way that I may be oppressive. This is a shift in language: the physical/cultural character-istics translate as implicitly part of a social dynamic (I am fat/I will experience oppression; I am middle-class/I will participate in classist actions). If we don't take the power to identify ourselves with as many labels as we can, if we don't insist on knowing the people we work with in at least some depth, we run the danger of affirming categorization. By identifying our-selves—not as one thing, but as many—we can take a step toward recog-nizing each other.

But let's go back to the problems with "identity politics." On the one hand, saying out loud who we are, insisting on being in control of those definitions, is crucial to our ability to work with others. Yet if we cannot cope with simultaneity—the discomfort of having to allow that identity is both fixed and fluid, both singular and multiple—we are easily led into making common cause only with people as like ourselves as we can find; that is, drawing strict boundaries can lead to the same nationalism that has so recently devastated Europe and Africa, and on the local level makes it so difficult to work in coalition, to trust each other.

In the '70s and '80s, many lesbian groups splintered around narrower and narrower criteria—we used our differences to push each other away instead of as ways to negotiate boundaries and establish when we could trust each other, and when not. This splintering caused a great deal of pain (and certainly lesbians didn't invent the "splinter group"). Often it was attributed to separatism[11] and identity politics. But at this distance, I think it is more honest to attribute it to late adolescent zealotry and broader cultural influences. I used to watch those movies in which the government gets bent out of shape because a couple of aliens landed. And it occurs to me that we live in the shadow of a national paranoia. Everyone is always taking up arms to prepare themselves against an external(ized) threat. Even us. How could we not? The world is at war, and you want me to sit down in a multicultural, multiracial, multiclass group and make a magazine, plan a rally, start a lesbian institute?

But how is it possible to have worked for thirty years in the anti-war, anti-racist, women's and lesbian movements and still not be able to see the women next to me? Do the people I blur together threaten me? When women look at me, do they still see only one or two things, and expect me to behave a certain way because of that? Somewhere our analysis—or our practice— has failed us. I need my identity as a Jew, as a radical, as a writer, as a fat womon, as dyke, as white-skinned, as middle-class—sitting here writing, I think: it's too much to ask to have space for this list at every meeting. But why do I think that? It takes only a minute or three to say. And I want to have that information about the woman sitting beside me.

I don't want to imply that our inability to acknowledge/perceive each other is the constant—otherwise we would have no hope, and without hope we can't even begin to make movements for social change. It's because we find points of contact among our differences (that woman is as insecure, that one grew up with the same kind of music, this woman has an analysis of the interlocking systems of power that's close to mine, close enough) that we keep struggling to make a better world. We talk, read, watch documentaries, learn. But we have to know how our own systems of judgment work. We have to make space and time in our communities, in our political organizations, to keep talking about difference, to not allow good hearts and minds to be relegated to that "background" Walker described.

That's the hard part—often that conversation hasn't gone so well.

We'll have a clear goal, but when we stop to talk about how to get there and the differences in cultural expectations, class, style, ability, and trust come up, we hurt each other again. Once hurt, we feel sidetracked, curse identity politics, or look for a group to work with in which everyone is more like us. But suppose we were less fearful, more patient? What would that look like? I don't want someone coming up to me and saying, "You're the first fat woman I've known; tell me how it is for you"— that's not fun for me (and I've done it already). Maybe we should have naked pool parties where everyone coming in is told to check their body attitudes at the door—no competition for most beautiful, strongest, smoothest, lightest— and is invited to look at each other. This may not be as trivial as it sounds. Imagine Mideast peace talks going on in a place where negotiators had to first confront their bodies.[12] To deal first with our bodies—that's what we keep denying we're doing. And what we seem to need to do.

It turns out that life is long, for many of us. While I still want women to read—to read all the old books, and this new one you have in your hands—I want us to be able to take the reading and move into action. After reading comes talking. To be a part of lesbian activists' long conversation is the delight and heartache of my life. What I am listening and asking for now are new ways to work together with respect. Claim all your identities wherever you go. Ask others who they are, and what they think about who they are—don't rely on appearance and social slots. Harder to do than say, but not impossible—not for us.

Notes

My thanks to Dolphin Waletzky and SusanJill Kahn for feedback and suggestions.

1. While the Internet may change that, many of us participate on the web the way we do in the physical world: looking for discussion groups of lesbians of color, fat women, radical eco-athletes.

2. You know what I mean—somebody wants to know if you wouldn't be more physically able if you dieted or did acupuncture at $60 a pop—and then needs you to reassure her that she's really a good person after you point out how offensive her intrusion was.

3. I acknowledge that this is a big reduction of the philosophical debate on altruism's existence. My experience leads me to believe that, whether or not humans are capable of pure selflessness, being able to identify that our self-interests are better served in groups is what makes social change (and cohesion) possible.

4. This discussion of fat identity was originally one example in this paper—I expanded it here at the urging of the editors, which made me realize how rarely this subject is analyzed among progressive/radical political people.

5. This is another aspect of reading: the part we internalize as setting limits on our possibilities, rather than inspiring us. No writer can be responsible for the way every possible reader might take their words, but it's worth considering how little attention we pay to the exclusionary role writing can play.

6. I'd be surprised if there was a patriarchal society in which this didn't happen, but I'm trying to be careful about absolute statements.

7. Here's the hinge: physical realities exist but categories of identity are created. But this analysis—that our perceptions of bodies are socially constructed—seems to have played into consumerist demands for bodies exhibiting the markers of whatever kind of privilege/social access the

consumer wants. Another example: the current popularity of transsexual medical procedures in urban areas might be due in large part to twisting this concept of social construction in a way that ends up reinforcing it (you too can become a "real" woman or man). If you want male privilege, it's ultimately easier to become one than to fight the institutions. Capitalism has a big stake in making it more and more convenient to change yourself rather than change the world.

8. The truth about changing body size by dieting seems to be the opposite of what we all are hesitant to give up believing: dieting causes the majority of dieters to gain weight (the body thinks it's starving, metabolism becomes more efficient, so smaller and smaller portions of food cause weight gain) as well as having other extremely negative side effects, including heart disease and death.

9. This discussion of dieting and fatness has been going on for years among fat activists. If this is new information for you—read (she wrote, laughing). Still the best overview of both theoretical and personal perspectives is Schoenfielder and Wieserm's 1983 anthology.

10. But I've had students who've told me that the shock was having a lesbian teacher—in their countries of origin, homosexuals are considered immoral and unclean at best.

11. Although discussing separatism at length is another essay, I do want to say that I think separatism became the scapegoat for many kinds of disillusionment. Separatism is an essential, and continuing, part of organizing for social change, and those who put their primary energy into separatist organizations/positions make it possible for a spectrum to exist. I notice that coalition work is easier in places that have separate groups for Latina, African-American, Arab, Jewish, Native, Asian, disabled, fat, and old lesbians. We all need places to establish, confirm, and relax in our various identities. Those places make it easier to work in coalitions, knowing the coalition will support us even if it doesn't mirror us. It's also easier to assert our right to be taken seriously when others know we have both organizations and political analysis behind us.

12. Best experience at a conference: The 1982 Jewish Feminist Conference in San Francisco opened with in-your-face papers read by working-class, fat, dyke, Sephardic, and disabled Jews— papers that said: we're here, look at us, listen to us. Throughout that conference, and even at its dance, I was more comfortable in my own body and ideas, and more relaxed with everyone else's, than at any other conference I've ever been to.

sixty-six

Speaking of Privilege

Diana Courvant

I want to speak today about privilege. I have a need today to speak about privilege. Because I have a computer to record my words, because I know that I have been given the opportunity to speak to many people at many times, because I am sure that I will be given that opportunity again, I have a privilege. Today I will use that privilege to refuse to be silent, to speak up, even to raise my voice.

I need to speak about privilege because today I will ride a bus. I know from experience that the bus driver will not ask to see my bus pass. And I know from experience that while I am on that bus others will be asked. I cannot know the thoughts of every driver by whom I have the privilege of being transported, but I do know that regardless of the skin color of my driver, my skin is white, and the skin colors of those whose tickets are scrutinized make up a rainbow. I don't need to know the thoughts of any driver. I know I cannot leave my house without my privilege.

I need to speak today because I am privileged to own many books of words written by generous women of color. In the language of those books I am reminded of my life. I am reminded of la lucha. I am reminded that when I am filled with emotion demanding I struggle with my sisters, it is privilege that allows me to say, "Su lucha es mi lucha." When I am filled with the power of those words yet torn by my own oppression, it is privilege that allows me to take those words that generations have formed into a cry against racism and racist patriarchy and pretend that I can use them to describe my struggle against trans oppression. It is privilege that allows me to pretend my struggle can be invested with power equal to that of la lucha without generations of trans people cultivating, nurturing, growing our own language.

It is privilege that allows me to pretend that being a white woman confronting racism is hard. In dangerous moments I allow myself to think that it would have been nice to have been born of color, that I might have absorbed along my life's way the reality of racism instead of having to focus, to study, to force into visibility and to look at the racism entwining me that I have so often failed to see. In dangerous moments, allowing myself to take care of my disabled body becomes an excuse for not doing the work of confronting oppressions that privilege me. In dangerous moments, I do not notice that I have begun a thought with "I shouldn't have done that, but . . ."

It is not dangerous but terrible, when in the privilege of my ignorance I wound a sibling soul. It is terrible and it is privilege if I then go on to think that it makes a difference that I, *I*, **I** did not intend any harm. Very often in my life that sibling soul has given me the grace of forgiveness. In the midst of a hostile, oppressive world, that soul has trusted me enough to forgive me. It is privilege to believe that I earned that trust. It is privilege to believe that I somehow did something to cause that trust. It is a privilege to believe that anyone other than that forgiving soul is responsible for creating and nurturing the trust that has so benefited me.

It is privilege, too, when I speak into a microphone whether my voice is halting or fluid, whispered or strong. It is the privilege of a child who, no matter how other children sensed and punished difference, received extra encouragement from adults to break from silence by virtue of a white skin, a body appearing whole, a penis between two legs, and a mind whose intelligence was of the type most desired by the schools of the child's homeland. It is the privilege of a teen who, even when nearly an entire society conspired to silence the child's experience, was given a space by the schools to pretend in public, pretend for an audience, to practice what it would be like to no longer be silent, practice what it would be like to be oneself. It is the privilege of an adult who received an apprenticeship at activism, an apprenticeship that the adult's age and white skin allowed it to accept, even though the journeywomen activists had yet to seriously challenge their own adultism and racism. It is the privilege of being a resident of a society that speaks the language that resident began learning before birth.

The recognition that brings you to my words is also a result of privilege. It is the privilege of a transsexual person walking a path from male to female whose society permitted images of people walking the same path, but not paths in other directions. It is the privilege of a person whose body is sufficiently male or female to describe that person's own journey to a society that chooses to pretend that male and female are the only human sexes. It is the privilege of an activist who has lived long enough for others to notice that activist's work. It is the privilege of an unwrinkled skin that encourages others to assume that the words and ideas singing forth from that skin are not obsolete.

All of these privileges and many more demand that I speak today.

But many, *many* of the privileges that make that demand are not privileges that I enjoy. I cannot trust that if I need a public restroom, I will be able to find one that I can use without being harassed. I cannot trust that I will not be resented for the time it takes me to enter or leave a bus. I cannot trust that I will be able to find clothes that fit in materials I find ethical to buy and wear. I cannot trust that my body will be able to walk as well in an hour as it does now. I cannot trust that if I accept an invitation I will be welcomed when I arrive. I cannot trust that the queers with whom I mourned Matthew Shepard would ever, *ever* mourn a crime that took my life. I cannot trust that I will be allowed to do feminism in feminist institutions. I cannot trust that I will be considered the authority on my own life.

In one university classroom, a trans woman taking a class on queer issues was forced to sit through *Sally Jesse Raphael*. Sally's show was being used as the only source of the class's information about trans lives. Agencies concerned about institutional homophobia have begun to include trans issues in anti-oppression training but using non-trans trainers and requiring trans staff to attend. The instructors' privileges, both as supervisors/teachers and as non-trans people, have allowed them to assume that trans people's silent acquiescence is the same as endorsement . . . approval . . . congratulations.

Even when trans people do speak, they are not assumed to be the authorities on their own experiences. After being invited to a women's gathering in 1998, I said no. When asked repeatedly, and finally offered a scholarship so that I did not have to choose between paying for my health care or for my weekend's lodging, I said yes. The group of women responsible for creating the event moved to rescind that invitation in the most humiliating way possible: declaring that no penises would be allowed and challenging me, without ever meeting me, to describe my genitals so that it could be determined whether or not I was *welcome*. In response, I offered to have a conversation with any and all women who wished to step off the land long enough to have one. It was privilege that allowed the event's creators to ignore my offer. It was privilege again when rumors were spread for the next year that I had attempted to invade, regardless of the fact that I had said no, that I had been asked repeatedly, that because the event's policy was made clear I did not even desire, much less attempt, to set foot on the land. It was privilege that allowed the people who heard those rumors to let those statements stand, to never ask my story even when they had reasons to distrust the rumors. It was privilege that allowed both those who spread and those who heard the rumors to assume those words would never come back to me, that those who spoke would never have to take any responsibility for wounding me with patent untruths. It was privilege when on the anniversary of my humiliation, an ally of the event creators wrote a newspaper story about how the creators had been treated poorly for doing nothing wrong. It was a privilege of the writer that she could write the story without ever once contacting me, without having to consider my story, my feelings, my self.

In Washington, D.C., live two white women, one who had shared her home with me for a conference weekend, one who had shared with me a week of working against domestic violence. While I lived my life and did my work three thousand miles away, the two shared a conversation about me. They spoke about my male privilege, the privilege that they assumed allowed me to do the anti–domestic violence organizing that is my life's work. They spoke about how there were essential truths, that it is undeniable that men are men and that women are women, and that I was privileged if I didn't see that. They spoke about how my actions denying these truths were wounding to them. They spoke about how my own work, my own voice, my own visibility, my own self are proofs that transsexual and transgendered people are inherently privileged, privileged through and because of their trans experience. They spoke about how my actions were in truth all about hurting them, hurting feminism, setting back their own lives' work.

My father believes that the steps I have taken to connect my body and my society to my soul are in fact all about hurting him. It is a privilege for him to not have to adjust his perceptions of me, a privilege apparently worth the loss of a child. What a greater privilege it must have been for two women in Washington, D.C., to believe that someone who did not even know them at the time of decision turned her own life upside down, subjected herself to ridicule, harassment, vitriol, and risk of murder—all to maybe, someday, affect their work. What incredible privilege to see their own work, their own *selves* as so important. And yet, these two women did not speak of any privilege that they might share as non-trans people. Isn't it interesting that they could speak of my transsexuality in relation to my privileges—real, imagined, both—without ever once discussing their shared non-trans experience in relation to their own privileges? Perhaps if they had considered their privilege they might have asked themselves any number of interesting questions at that lunch:

Isn't it privilege to assume that our conversation will never be repeated to the object of it by the other feminists at our table? Isn't it privilege to assume that no matter how we stereotype, demonize, or deny the reality of trans people, our conversation will never reflect badly on us? Is it privilege that we assume that coming out as transgender or transsexual has more to do with us than with the trans person's own self? Is it privilege that we assume that in deciding to come out a trans person should weigh the preservation of our theories of gender more heavily than the preservation of the trans person's own integrity, sanity, life, or self? Is it privilege that allows us to ignore the inherent contradiction in assuming that even though we have done work against domestic violence, a trans person's anti–domestic violence work indicates a privilege we don't have? Isn't it privilege to assume a selfish, anti-woman motive, while ignoring the fact that the trans person who is now doing work to aid all survivors of domestic violence was twice told not to try to volunteer within our institutions, three times told that she would be called when training was to start, only to be forgotten, and once completed weeks of training only to be asked to resign? Isn't it privilege that we assume we don't need to verify stories targeting trans people as oppressive that appear in a press with a historic hostility to trans people? Isn't it privilege that we can freely claim that there should not be different treatment of people with different genders or sexes, when it serves us, and also claim that there are inherent differences between men and women that demand different treatment, when claiming that serves us? Isn't it privilege to claim that the personal is political, that life should inform theory, but that our theories don't have to be informed by some lives? Isn't it privilege that we refuse even to acknowledge the existence of intersex bodies, experiences, people, mutilations, when doing so would force revision of a theory that has served us? Isn't it privilege to assume that we see truth where trans people cannot? Isn't it privilege to feel wounded and attacked when someone speaks a personal truth that implicates us in oppression? Isn't it privilege to assume that a person should leave a truth unspoken if it makes us uncomfortable? Isn't it privilege when we assume that the ten or twenty visible trans people in the dis/united states are representative of all trans people? Isn't it privilege to assume that all trans people are visible . . . loud . . . white . . . MTF . . . and femme, because only they are seen and heard? Isn't it privilege that we need never acknowledge the possibility that there are many more trans people in the dis/united states who are silent because they have been silenced by the burden of pervasive oppression? Isn't it privilege to assume we will never have to endure anger or loud voices, or any other backlash when we deny the reality of trans people to the point that murder and suicide take almost half of those who manage to be noticed? Isn't it privilege that leads us to assume that our silencing of trans voices has nothing to do with ten or twenty visible people raising theirs up and shouting us down?

Isn't that privilege? To two white women in Washington, D.C., I say yes. *Yes, I agree with you.* To all of you receiving my words, I say yes. Privilege has absolutely everything to do with why I am not silent. Privilege has everything to do with why I speak up. Privilege has everything to do with why I am raising my voice. Privilege has everything to do with my refusal to let stand the theories and statements that demonize or erase *me*.

sixty-seven

The Latin American and Caribbean Feminist/Lesbian Encuentros: Crossing the Bridge of Our Diverse Identities

Migdalia Reyes

Introduction: A Personal Testimony

Many historical opportunities surfaced in the past twenty years for women of color in general, and for Latinas in particular. In spite of the tremendous effort that breaking ground took, Latina authors like Gloria Anzaldúa, Cherríe Moraga, Alma Gómez, and Mariana Romo contributed tremendously to giving voice to those of us who had been silenced. Feminist/lesbian writings like *This Bridge Called My Back* were twenty years ago the seed that gave birth to the momentum that many of us, as Latinas living in the United States, awaited. In my own experience, as someone who hung from the margin of the white women's feminist social movement, I found in the work of my Latina sister writers the awaited bridge that took me to my own identity, and revived the spirit of my soul.

And, because I grew up in rural Puerto Rico during the '50s and was well aware that gender oppression was a cruel reality, my search for a sense of identity led me to the Latin American and Caribbean Encuentros. My experience at the Encuentros served as a source of empowerment as well as a source of pain due to what I perceived as internalized oppressive values and attitudes and ignorance regarding sexual-emotional orientation, ethnicity, nationality, and class differences. While this last element has created a rift among women participants, bridging it provides an opportunity for us to come together to address our source of conflict. In my judgment, given clearly defined efforts for creating alliances, the rift may be focal to opening dialogue from a place of mindfulness regarding differences and similarities, and for acknowledging the merit of building strength through the formation of international coalitions.

Historical Background of the Encuentros

Latin American nations have historically held political and economic Third World vulnerability, leading women to share a common legacy of oppression. The Latin American feminist movement has proposed that while economic dependency, poverty, and colonial relationships with western advanced nations are key to understanding the conditions in which Latin American women live, patriarchal ideologies—such as traditional norms and values about women's social status and economic role, little access to formal political structures and educational resources, unequal division of labor and the exploitative nature of women's work, racism directed primarily at women of color (that is, of Native and African descent, and Mestizas), and the historical heritage of machismo and Marianismo—characterize women's lives. Despite these conditions, women have always organized. For example, organizing in the early 1980s biannual, region-wide Latin American and Caribbean feminist Encuentros offered women a vehicle for coming together and becoming politicized, and for developing strategies to fight against prevailing sexism, racism, economic disparity, neo/colonialism, and political repression. While the organizing efforts focused on heterosexual women's issues, in 1987 lesbian feminist women sponsored the First Latin American and Caribbean Lesbian Feminist Encuentro with the goal of building a lesbian social movement.

I attended the Second Latin American and Caribbean Feminist Encuentro, held in Peru, in 1983, and was beyond myself with excitement. My excitement grew as I thought about securing support and developing ties of solidarity with other Latina lesbians. However, I was disappointed that lesbianism was absent from the Encuentro's program, and felt pain that there was so much lesbophobia. It is not like this was a great surprise for me. Before attending the Encuentro, I was aware of the oppressive and repressive conditions that sexual minorities live under. In Puerto Rico and other Latin American countries many view lesbianism as a shameful illness or as something to maintain secret and invisible. The times it is publicly recognized are mainly when humiliating or making fun of a lesbian or gay person. Of course I knew that coming out is not an option for many lesbians because of existing forms of repression, persecution, torture, and in some countries death.

In spite of the hostile attitudes of most participants, many lesbians, most of whom were from the United States, chose to come out. Our decision was based on the need to be visible, to fight against lesbophobic values, attitudes, and behavior, and to support women unable to come out. Our visibility was received with a wave of fear, rejection, and mistrust. Some heterosexual women broke into tears and threatened to leave, while others refused housing with us. Our solution was to have a workshop on lesbianism with an open discussion about people's reactions. Approximately two hundred women attended the workshop; it served as a groundbreaking experience and a bridge that brought Latina lesbians together, prompting a very beginning effort at inclusion and solidarity.

The Third Feminist Encuentro was held in 1985, in Brazil. The organizers officially included a series of all-day workshops on lesbianism. These were not conflict-free; however, they were well attended and offered a space for dialogue between the heterosexual and lesbian women. One major accomplishment was the formation of a discussion group, led by women of various lesbian organizations from Mexico, to organize the First Latin American and Caribbean Lesbian Feminist Encuentro in Cuernavaca, Mexico, which took place in 1987, a week before the Fourth Latin American and Caribbean Feminist Encuentro, in Taxco, Mexico.

Once again I felt great enthusiasm about being part of a social movement that unified us as Latina lesbians. Furthermore, the idea of forming and being a member of a Latin American Latina lesbian network (La Red)—which the organizers proposed—meant an important process of political and social empowerment for me. However, conflict between the women of Latin America and the Latinas of the United States surfaced, as our differences became the target of debate. Because this time the women were all lesbians, for many women this division felt more painful and affected Chicanas the most. To make matters worse, the Mexican women held a closed meeting about how to keep the U.S. Latinas from participating in La Red. The result was four days of conflict and the need to employ a conflict resolution expert to guide the discussions. By the end of the Encuentro, and in spite of the conflict, different workshops took place, some women formed new alliances, and many embraced the conflict as a learning process. This process grew and at the Fourth Feminist

Encuentro, in Taxco, some lesbian women worked together to create and facilitate a workshop on lesbianism.

They planned the next lesbian Encuentro for 1990 in Peru. However, their early momentum did not last. Many of the Peruvian organizers received death threats from both ultra-right and ultra-left political groups, and they were forced to move the Encuentro to Costa Rica because of potential violence against the participants. The assumption made by some organizers was that Costa Rica, with its history of democracy, liberalism, and no army, was a perfect choice. The city of San José had a large and active lesbian organization, Las Entendidas, and a lively gay community. However, a week before the Encuentro, local newspapers published a series of sensationalist stories and editorials, with leads such as: "An invasion of 150 foreign lesbians, along with a group of Costa Rican lesbians is expected. They will corrupt and pervert the minds of innocent young women," and "Lesbians coming to Costa Rica to have a satanic orgy." Initially, some women who arrived in Costa Rica denied the possibility that such a level of homophobia could exist. After all, Costa Rica was incidentally celebrating one hundred years of democracy.

The uproar and anti-lesbian hysteria created by the press and the church pressured the government to attempt to stop the conference. Since the government officials did not know who the organizers were or where they would hold the conference, they enacted a law prohibiting entrance into the country to anyone considered undesirable—which meant not only controlling who entered the country, but deporting those suspected of being lesbians. Despite the danger, organizers decided to hold the conference but to do so in a secret location. The repression forced us to go underground, pledge secrecy, and agree to remain on the premises until the Encuentro ended.

The possibility of danger led us to develop strong solidarity ties and a protective attitude toward each other. As a result, the Encuentro offered a range of workshops and social activities held in a climate of harmony. Support and nurturance were displayed between the women from Latin America and the United States. However, this harmony was severed when on the last night of the conference a group of men surrounded the location in trucks and began shouting obscenities at the women and threatening to attack. The fear continued until the next day when the women could leave. This was due, in large part, to the help of the rural town police.

In spite of the lesbian-baiting, the Encuentro ended with a strong sense of solidarity among the women. Because of the vulnerability that coming out in public posed for the Latin American women, a group of foreign women called a press conference. They denounced those individuals and policies that had created the situation of fear and violence. The press conference was a great opportunity to organize for the civil rights of gay, lesbian, and transgender men and women. Moreover, the print media and TV news responded well, presenting a less distorted portrayal of lesbianism after some women filed a formal complaint with the United Nations Human Rights Commission.

La Grieta: The Rift

In 1992, Puerto Rico sponsored the Third Latin American and Caribbean Lesbian Feminist Encuentro. It was well organized with a series of structured workshops and events. However, the conflict between U.S. and Latin American lesbians once again surfaced and found its way into various workshops. For instance, one of the U.S. lesbians challenged the Latin American lesbians to take more risks in coming out publicly because, according to her, it was the only way to combat homophobia. A suggestion was made that the lesbians wear a brown bag over their heads to not be recognized while participating in a TV talk show addressing lesbianism and lesbophobia. Others went on to discuss how many struggles had been won in the United States by the gay and lesbian communities due to their bravery. Of course, women from Latin America reacted to such suggestions with pain and anger. Many felt that those who made such recommendations had no idea of the danger that being out posed for them. For example, a woman from Ecuador shared with me that she was once at a private birthday party when she turned her head—while kissing her lover—to find a machine gun put to her head. The military police had quietly entered the party to harass and arrest everyone.

The "they" and "we" rift—la grieta—resulted from the conflict generated between the two groups at the Encuentro. It created an emotional whirlpool for all of the participants. La grieta was particularly painful for me and the other women of Puerto Rico; we felt torn between both sides because of the U.S. colonial status of a self-identified Latin American island. Because of la grieta, the conference schedule was changed to include two separate workshops, one for the Latin American women and another for the U.S. Latinas, to address the painful and terrifying energy that surfaced. Two women from Los Angeles, a woman from Washington, one from Miami, and I facilitated the U.S. Latinas' workshop. We opened a space to discuss and process feelings, and to negotiate the political and emotional dispute that had surfaced. Most women's reactions were similar to those I experienced during the Encuentros in Peru and Mexico. They felt rejected and hurt by some of the Latin American women's accusations about their privilege as lesbians from the United States. While many of the feelings surfaced in what seemed like a never-ending cycle of hostility, a subsequent workshop brought both groups together to discuss sources of conflict and differences. Versions differ as to the outcome of this interchange. However, I observed that by the end of the Encuentro many women appeared to bridge some of their ethnic, class, political, and ideological differences, and seemed more willing to intermingle.

At the following Encuentro, held in Argentina in 1995, few Latinas from the United States attended. Providing a precise explanation for this is difficult, but assumptions may be drawn. Traveling to Argentina from the United States is very expensive and the registration cost for U.S. Latinas was much higher than that of Latin American participants. While the organizers of the Puerto Rico Encuentro promptly provided the Argentinean organizers a mailing list, many women from the United States did not receive the information until too late. Also, it would be safe to assume that the rift between Latin American and United States women had a disempowering impact.

Bridging the Rift: Creating Solidarity and Coalitions

To understand and deal with the rift that has surfaced numerous times during the Encuentros, it has been important for me to recognize the existence of significant differences between the experiences of Latina women from Latin America and those from the United States. Varied cultural and racial heritages, mixed social, economic, and political realities and ideologies, as well as regional differences contribute to the widely diverse identities of Latin Americans and of Latinos/as in the United States. Latina women, both from Latin America and the U.S., reflect this heterogenous reality. In addition, Latina women who have im/migrated to the United States or are U.S.-born present differences due to social group membership and levels of ideological awareness and political exposure to issues of ethnocentrism, racism, sexism, classism, and heterosexism. The Encuentros reflect such differences.

I have observed that the Encuentros' interactive, peer-led open debate format draws two common types of reactions that may lead to conflict. One reaction relates to ignorance, intolerance, and the belief in hierarchies of oppression (for example, a Latina lesbian from the Midwest in the United States who believes that she is more oppressed than a lesbian from El Salvador). The other reaction relates to denying—in the spirit of solidarity—that differences exist and insisting that conflict should be avoided by all means (for example, we are all sisters and class privilege is not an issue).

It is important to recognize that conflict over differences often grows out of ignorance and created assumptions. In my observation there is often a lack of knowledge, and stereotypical assumptions are often made about the history and the life conditions of different social group memberships, both from Latin America and from the United States. For example, ignorance about social movements presents a problem in cases where lesbian women from Latin America assume that gay and lesbian Latinos/as hold a position of power in U.S. gay and lesbian movements, when in fact this is far from true. Ignorance is often projected when Latina lesbians from the United States display an image of being as oppressed as lesbians from Latin America. Although often indirectly, U.S. Latina lesbians have access and exposure to information about, and resources on, institutionalized hetero-sexism, racism, and classism when compared to their Latin American counterparts. While written material on Latina lesbians is frequently unavailable, if not hard to publish, many Latinas from the United States have more access to literature on lesbianism (for example, via the Internet). Supportive services such as self-help groups and culturally competent psychotherapy often exist in the United States. Moreover, identifiable sexual-diversity communities promoting a gay-friendly environment are often a reality in some regions of this country. Unfortunately, during the Encuentros I have often observed some U.S. Latinas using these privileges to measure and judge the experiences of Latin American women. I have also observed competitiveness, arrogance, and attitudes of superiority exhibited when describing resources or information about social movements, organizations, and communities in the United States.

While developing a knowledge base and awareness, we must recognize that gay men, lesbian women, and transgender people—particularly those who live or come from societies with a history of violation of human rights and of hate crimes—face manifestations of oppression more severe than those encountered by people with access to more validating types of environments. For many lesbians in Latin America, coming out is extremely dangerous, if not impossible. Many gays and lesbians from Latin America continue to witness the horrors of repression. In some regions gay and lesbian bars are still raided—despite giving police officers financial compensation to stay away. Gays, lesbians, and transgender people have also reported violence and gang rape by police and the military. Deaths have also been reported.

Conflict: A Bridge to Dialogue

While giving life to conflict around differences is often accompanied by painful feelings, it is often necessary and can be extremely helpful when conducted within a context of open dialogue. It is critical that respect and sensitivity are used when addressing conflict, and that structured dialogue groups—conocimientos—are considered. The conocimientos could help participants get to the heart of their values and attitudes, unlearn oppressive ways of seeing differences, and understand the realities of others, without having to constantly compare and contrast their oppression and struggles with others'. The goal is to move beyond reactive resistance to a place of celebrating differences, where we can become and allow others to become politicized—crear consciencia—and empowered.

Creating consciencia offers a place where different participants share personal life experiences in order to enhance open communication and decrease intolerance and stereotyped assumptions about who they are. This method may enable U.S. Latinas to learn what Latin American women may perceive to be their power or privilege. Also, Latin American women, both heterosexual and lesbians, may listen to U.S. women regarding their marginalized status in the United States without comparing oppressions. Conflict resolution skills and clear ground rules may also be helpful tools during the conocimientos by bringing issues of differences out in the open and managing disagreements and confrontations if they arise. A framework grounded in the concepts of empowerment and conscientización is also a useful mechanism for creating respect and confianza.

While the Encuentros have often made me feel frustrated, I also recognize the opportunity that they have offered me to understand our struggles and how we have often been pitted against each other due to our own realities with internalized oppression. In my judgment, we as Latina lesbians from the United States must learn more about the social realities and conditions of sexual minorities from Latin America, especially those representing populations at risk. Furthermore, Latin American women, both heterosexual and lesbians, must understand that they are not the only victims of oppression and that hierarchies of oppression create antagonism and prevent our joining in a united front, and they must create coalitions.

In coming to bridge our differences, we must all form alliances and learn ways to share nuestras vivencias. Only in this spirit will feminist lesbians of the Americas discover a safe space for sharing with each other in empowerment, and welcome conflict simply because it may be a stimulating opportunity for further growth.

sixty-eight

Sitting in the Waiting Room of Adult and Family Services at SE 122nd in Portland, Oregon, with My Sister and My Mother Two Hours Before I Return to School (April 1995)

Ednie Kaeh Garrison

The irony strikes me two weeks later.

In the space of one day I have crossed two worlds. My shame in each of them pulls against the other. I want to exist in the seven hours between

Portland and Pullman. Moving. Traveling. Away from both. Toward some figuration of Annandale, perhaps, like a highly fictive moment I call home.

The memories that solidify that morning: the nervous anxiety generated by impatience for the two boys running so confidently among the waiting chairs, yelling and whooping their lack of concern; two girl-women in the corner braiding bright blocks of yarn into each other's hair; a man behind the nearest window speaking in Hindi or Farzi to a very tired woman and her sweating male companion; and my sister's belly eight months big. Her hands rubbing her aching hips. Her breasts swollen like our mother's for most of my childhood.

Mama spent hours of my childhood locked in the molded plastic chairs of Adult and Family Services. She would come home worn out, hot, and irritable as if this were a necessary and frequent part of the shame of Food Stamps. Just like the intrusive inspections of women in the grocery store who judged and condemned us for buying the wrong kinds of food with their tax dollars. Like the old lady who told me one day that she did not appreciate me being so fat on handouts from the government. Or the woman at the checkout stand who had to tell me it was a shame I was having kids at such a young age. My two-year-old brother was with me in line holding on to the colored coupons after I'd counted them. I was fourteen and not yet bleeding.

And today my sister-becoming-a-mother sits in a welfare clinic with our mother, who knows the inside of this desperate room with a smell that simultaneously recalls the slackness of her shoulders and the bitter cavities of resentment that have hovered about her for years.

I, the queer sister/daughter, shocked into the thought that this is the first time I have sat here in this triad of relations. Not merely in this particular room on the farthest side of town—the white side—where we lived for only a short time, years ago. But this is the first time I have sat waiting to hear how much will be allotted or whether the application for Medicare will be accepted/rejected. I harbor no shame for my sister or mother waiting here.

But shame is what I think of as I sit with them.

This is a room mothers sit in. My only comfort is as the child of a mother, while my sister is a mother, like ours. For me, this is another alienation, yet another distance that has stretched its walls around me.

I do not sit here like them. I am not the kind of woman my mother wanted us all to be. And yet Sarah, who is here and who is that kind of girl, is the one sister who is least scared of me. The sister who is making me an aunt. The sister who thinks loving women is good, sitting next to the mother who cannot love women because they remind her too much of herself, with me, who love women exactly because they do remind me of me. Only we three share these overlapping triangles. My other three sisters form other geometric relations.

I sit here in Adult and Family Services acutely aware of where I have been and of where I am at, but with no clear sense of where I will be. The only privilege I can count on is whiteness, but even that is no guarantee. The poverty of my youth, and the continued poverty of my family, reminds me that whiteness doesn't have to signify security. So I rely on knowledge.

Here in Pullman I can sit at my computer and play these thoughts around and around. It is a privilege I want to protect against the weight of my parents' disappointment, offset for years by the world in the television. A world that sometimes felt more real for the very reason that it wasn't ours. Those characters who had lives, while we just kept on.

And yet, the supposed insulation of this institution acts more like a cancer. It eats at my heart and my integrity, filling up the remaining emptiness with printed words and occasional affirmations. Even the ideas and the politics I cling to can't battle against the mold graduate school pours me into. Every crack and puncture and seam of my incomplete fit is cause for concern. Perhaps my dedication and discipline are not adequate.

I want to suture the incongruities. I want my presence in this environment to need my past like a backbone. I will not have it erased. Just as this place follows me into welfare clinics and my sisters' or parents' houses, welfare clinics and my sisters and my parents follow me here. The fabric of my diplomas are like the fabric of Food Stamps. Their colors refer to one another. Both of them have fed me.

I make no apologies. I will locate myself in all these worlds.

sixty-nine

Tenuous Alliance

Arlene (Ari) Istar Lev

I believe that each of us stands at a unique place, with our own particular view of this world, and that each of us tells the story of what we see with the only language we have. I keep growing, so my own perspective keeps shifting and the words I speak to tell my story continue to evolve. I have no doubt that the narrative I now tell you will continue to shift and transform as I continue my journey. I cannot wait, however, for the finished product—the perfect place or language or perspective—but must jump into the fray with all that I am at each moment and tell my story with all the truths I can contain.

I am a white-skinned Euro-American Ashkenazi Jewish lesbian. Ashkenazi means that during the two-thousand-year exile and dispersion of the Jewish people, my ancestors settled in Europe. After surviving numerous expulsions and pogroms they made their way from Eastern Europe to the United States three generations ago and settled in Brooklyn, the shtetl[1] of the New World. Most of my people who did not make that journey died in the camps and ovens of Nazi Germany. Being Jewish was not always an important part of my identity. My Jewish identity—insulated in the Jewish neighborhoods of Brooklyn—was something I tried to avoid, not knowing of course that this was the oppressors' hope, to whitewash my culture and history so that I could melt into the American dream, the Great White Hope.

Long before I realized that anti-Semitism existed—as a child of the sixties and an early student activist—I was engaged in anti-racism work. Racism was tangible and clear. I grew up amid the struggles of integration and busing; joined school groups committed to ending what we then called prejudice; hung out in mixed-race social groups, and to the horror of my family dated men, and later women, who were not only *not* Jewish, but weren't even white. In college I studied sociology and political science, minoring in women's and "minority" history. As a radical lesbian-feminist in my early twenties I studied in the great "think tanks" of the women's and gay liberation movements and took workshops called "Being a White Ally," and "Confronting Racism."

I do not say any of this to win points and be perceived as a "good ally"—or to lose points with those of you finding these attempts at white accountability puerile. I say this simply to identify where I stand on these issues. I am a woman who has taken the challenges of the last few decades to heart. I examine my language, my social groups, the neighborhood I live in, and the content of the classes I teach; I push myself, my friends, my students, and my clients to recognize our privileges and to not turn away from the ugliness of blatant racism, or the ubiquitous quality of its more subtle forms. My awareness of my white skin privilege is both a blessing and a curse, in the way that all awareness brings great responsibility. I take this responsibility seriously, and act with conscious intention against racism as often as I can. I am also painfully aware of my limitations, all that I do not do, cannot change, and all the ways that I walk with, and take advantage of, privileges others do not have.

As racial and ethnic awareness has grown in this country, it has challenged many white-skinned people to become aware of our own ethnicities, cultures, and histories. How can white people witness the rich language, music, food of non-white cultures and not wonder "where is the richness of my own culture?" In Yiddish there is a word, *tam*, which means taste or flavor; it refers not only to food, but to the essence, the fullness, the vibration of a thing. I needed to know more about the tam of my own community, the flavor of yiddishkeit.[2]

My journey back toward the words and rituals, food, and language of my own people has indeed been a fertile one. I have learned much about myself, my sense of humor, my love of learning and books, my ethical visions and political commitments. So much that I once thought uniquely mine is part of the customs and cultural ways of my people for centuries. I have also come to understand more thoroughly anti-Semitism and the centuries of expulsions and violence. I learned that we had been evicted from many countries long before Hitler decided on the Final Solution, and that European Jews—who were not considered citizens of the countries where they lived—were forbidden to enter many professions. Often the only livelihood allowed was money-lending and of course Jews were then labeled money-greedy people. I came to understand that contemporary anti-Semitic rhetoric had its roots in centuries of oppression. I learned that my embarassment about my "pushiness" and "smartness" was my own internalized oppression, and that being smart and pushy were some of my strong Jewish survival skills.

I have spent hours contemplating this tribe of people without a land, who have lived among the people of all other lands. I have learned that although I am a white-skinned Ashkenazi Jew, Jews are not white; they're dark-skinned people from the Middle East, and Sephardic Jews of Spain and the Iberian Peninsula. After the dispersion of the Jews from Palestine, thousands of years ago, Jews have settled in Africa, India, South America, and Asia, as well as in Europe, and because of intermarriage, conversion, and sexual exploitation now look identical to the native people of these lands.

Jews have been defined as a nation, a religion, and a race; however, Jewish identity overlaps national, religious, and racial categorizations. Jews live within the borders of many nation-states, practice different religious rituals or none at all, and are members of all the world's peoples. I am most comfortable seeing Jewish people as part of a diverse international tribe with similar religious, historical, and national identities. Seeing the Jewish people as simply a nation, *or* a religion *or* a race ignores the complexity of this tribe, with its roots deep in antiquity, who, though having lived among all the world's peoples have always been treated as "outsiders."

Though the Hebrew people once belonged to a strong nation, the dispersion of the Jewish people has meant that Jews, until recently, were without a national land for much of our history. When the Tibetan people became refugees, the Dali Lama, in his wisdom, summoned Jewish leaders to ask, "How have your people survived for so long without your land; what can you teach me to help my people survive?" For the past fifty years, due to great shifts in international power and loyalties, the Jewish people once again have a land to call their own. But "ownership" to a land that others too call home raises huge questions about the role of political and economic power in establishing legitimacy for a people's right to a "landed" existence, and—most poignantly—how easily an oppressed people can become oppressors.

Although Jews are a "nation" both historically and currently, most Jews do not live within the national border of Israel, and many do not feel connected to this ancestral home. Jews are also a religious entity, though the differences among us regarding religious beliefs, values, and practices are so enormous that the similarities are at times barely recognizable. So are Jews, therefore, a "race"? In Roget's thesaurus *race* indicates a "family, tribe, clan, genealogy, descent, caste, breed, sisterhood, mankind, and human species," and certainly Jews fit into those general guidelines. The word *race*, however, assumes that races are distinct and that people are genetically different from one another in scientifically provable ways—a concept that is questionable both biologically and politically.

European and Euro-American men originally developed the racial classification system outlining the three racial categories—Caucasoid, Negroid, and Mongoloid—to establish a pseudo-scientific pecking order. This system of racial classification is clearly flawed, creating a human hierarchy that serves not only to divide us into arbitrary groups and keep us separated from one another, but to reinforce an oppressive social system as if it is organically derived.

This standard racial classification system also renders entire groups of people invisible. Simply put, not everyone *fits* into this classification system. For instance, Caucasians are technically people whose ancestors come from the Caucasus Mountains in Russia; white people are, of course, the descendants of numerous European cultures with diverse tribal and national affiliations, not just descendants from the Caucasus Mountains. The tribal groups and nation-states of Europe have been warring with one another for centuries, have oppressed one another, and, until very recently in world history, saw each other as different racial groups. Our word *slave* comes from the Slavic people, who were once the slaves of many other European people. The word *Anglo*, often used for all white people, refers to white, English-speaking people from a particular geographical area of Europe. How did these diverse peoples become unified into one overarching category?

If all whites have been lumped together under this label "Caucasian," should all dark-skinned people be called "Negroes"? In this tripartite classification system where do American Indians or Puerto Ricans *fit*? Are all native peoples from North and South America the same racial group, and should they be subsumed under the category of "white" *or* "black"? Both Jews and Asians have been classified as "blacks" in various census forms over the past 150 years. Some groups of people, like Southeast Asians and Puerto Ricans, as well as many American blacks, have members that represent a diverse spectrum of colors. Should they be classified differently from other family members based on their skin color though they are technically of the same tribe or group, and, if not, which group should they be assigned to? What of "mixed-race" people; where do they *fit*?

These divisions are arbitrary. Jews are simply one of the most obvious examples of a tribe of people transcending the edges of national, color, and cultural parameters. In the United States, Jews have now been assimilated under the banner of "whiteness," a category that they do not easily fit into, as any member of the Aryan Nation will attest. Amoja Three Rivers[3] reminds us that "whiteness" is a political alliance, a way of creating an "us" (white people) and a "them" (dark-skinned people). There is a special word for Jewish racism; it is called anti-Semitism. But we must not forget that anti-Semitism is just another word for racism, a particularly virulent form of racism that transcends color. Without denying the privileges associated with having white skin, Jews can choose to reject any association with this white political alliance.

The truth is simply that we are all members of the human race. We, all of us, all humans, are a diverse people who come in many different colors, with differently textured hair; we speak different languages, worship different gods, wear different kinds of clothing, practice different spiritual and lifecycle rituals, have different habits and beliefs, but ultimately we are all one people. The cultural, language, color, and theological differences have been used to create power differences between us and are then used to discriminate, oppress, and even annihilate groups of people. It is the work of the *racists* to try to classify races as definably different from one another in a hierarchical way.

This does not mean that we should (or could) deny or dilute the value of our differences. Each group has unique qualities and distinctive attributes that should be honored and that collectively contribute to the mosaic of the human family. We each crave to be with our own people—to be around others who talk, think, move, and look like us—and feel a sense of "home" conveyed in the American black expressions "homeboy" and "homegirl." Smelling the foods of our grandmothers' kitchens, and seeing the familiar faces of those who look like us, is a universal feeling of homecoming. Each of us knows the sweet *tam* of our people, as well as the particular bitterness we have each endured. It is possible to denounce the discourse of "race" as a concept invented by the racists that encourages, justifies, and solidifies racism, and yet still celebrate our own unique cultures and tribal histories.

It is difficult to balance these two divergent truths: that, on the one hand, there is no such thing as race, and, on the other hand, ubiquitous racism exists and must be challenged. We are all impacted by racism, wherever we fall on the privilege/color/class continuum. Standing up against racism, without falling into the simplistic categorical divisions set up by the oppressors, is a difficult task. Knowing who we can trust as allies and who are our "enemies" can be a quickly shifting territory, while we balance within our own lives the realities of our own privileges, as well as our own oppressions.

As a Jew and lesbian I walk in this world with oppressions that are rarely visible. If I withhold my breath/spirit,[4] nobody needs to know that I am a Jew or a lesbian. The mainstream community will just assume by default that I am gentile and straight . . . isn't that what everyone is? It is a strange merger that exists within this lesbian body: to be a privileged white-skinned woman in a country where whiteness rules, and yet to be a Jew who knows that the history of racial bigotry is part of my people's history, that racism has followed my people like a rabid dog, from country to country, and from century to century.

The realities of color and culture in this world are that even if one wanted to renounce their inclusion in certain oppressed groups, no matter how much you try to assimilate, the power and history of oppression will not let you hide. There have always been light-skinned blacks and Latinos who have tried to pass, as there are Jews who try to pass, as there are Queers who try to pass, but, in truth, there is nowhere to hide from the oppressor's wrath.

A number of years ago I was part of a group of lesbian women working together to examine the relationships of racism, anti-Semitism, and classism. A white-skinned Latina from a well-to-do family questioned what made her a "woman of color" eligible for inclusion in women-of-color–only spaces when other white-skinned women were not included. In answer, another woman, the daughter of a white Jewish father and Puerto Rican mother, talked about going to Hebrew school in New York City, while her mother was the school's "cleaning lady." She said, "You are an 'other,' and if you do not see yourself that way, trust me, whites do." Our inclusion and identity within certain cultural groups make us vulnerable to social and economic realities that can never be whitewashed. Like Jews, Latinos, particularly those with light skin, share a similar experience, belonging to a people who live in many countries, cross all color lines, but share a clearly discernible and identifiable culture.

I believe it is important not to rank oppressions. Yet I also know that as painful as my invisible oppressions are they do not provoke street violence and racial slurs, and have not stopped me from attending the university or limited my job opportunities. I know that my white-skin privilege *is* a privilege that allows me to walk in this world with an illusion of safety that darker-skinned people cannot afford. As with all privileges there is the tendency to "forget" where you come from, to try to blend in and fit where you have not been allowed. Those who cannot hide are still the targets, and those who can hide often minimize the ugly truths about racial hatred. They often turn away from those who are targeted, as if it is too hard to acknowledge the privilege they have, how much they can lose, and the real dangers that others live with. Racism for most white people is something "out there" that they witness from the comfort of their living room, watching the violence on the evening news. They click their tongues and shake their hands and switch the station to something less stressful. They view themselves as non-racist and do not see themselves as participants in racist behavior but as somehow above or outside it. This of course veils their own racism and absolves them of any daily responsibility in the perpetuation of the racist system.

My students in the university "find it hard to believe" that U.S. blacks have been lynched in this country, this century, this decade. One black woman said she felt angry that I was reminding her how awful it still was. Other students have trouble "remembering" that within many of our lifetimes the Japanese were placed in concentration camps on American soil, while the United States fought the Nazis to release prisoners from German concentration camps. They often do not understand that repressing the Spanish language in our school systems today is an act designed not to encourage young Latinos to succeed in an English-speaking country, but to separate them from the very soul of their people—and *that* can never be considered success.

Most Jews know that hiding and passing do not work, which might explain the large presence of Jews in social justice movements. Even though one cannot see my otherness simply by looking, I have never been one to hide who I am, or be less than I am, even if who I am provokes fear or confusion in others. I have always chosen to be fully out as a raised working-class Jew and a femme lesbian. White-skinned Jews may pass for white on the streets; however, few have "forgotten" the real possibility of a knock at the door at midnight and the permanent disappearance of family members. In a world of power and privilege, haves and have-nots, the tides can turn quickly, and I know few Jews, whatever their wealth or apparent social privilege, who do not believe that it can happen again. I know that to the white supremacy groups that continue to grow in numbers, as an out Jewish lesbian, I am, and will always be, just one more "colored" person.

Most whites have turned their faces from the bitterness of blatant racism, but the dilemma for American Jews is that both whites and people of color alike have turned away from the daily realities of anti-Semitism, and refused to see the historical as well as modern similarities between the treatment of people of color and the treatment of Jews. Sharing the same enemy is not always the foundation for a strong friendship. To people of color, who live with the reality of racist violence each time they walk out of their home, I will always first be seen as a privileged, educated woman, and not necessarily someone trustworthy or safe.

The work of challenging racism, of undoing, unlearning, and fighting racism, is lifelong work. Inevitably white people are uncomfortable around you, and feel challenged. Inevitably you will disappoint people of color mostly because you will make mistakes, but also because there is so much to do and whatever you do can never be enough. For me, as a Jewish lesbian, it has also meant confronting anti-Semitism and homophobia within communities of color. This raises the stakes for forging ally-building strategies, and sadly makes my anti-racism work questionable, instead of more honorable.

I do know one thing: I became a more effective ally for people of color after I did my own homework. The more comfortable I became with my own legacy as a Jew, the more I could let into my heart the pride, and pain, that people of color experience. It became easier to look people of color in the eye, and realize that we are all much more than the lines that divide us. In our efforts to build coalitions across our differences, we cannot buy into the simplistic and racist categories, but must face the challenge of embracing the intricacies, depth, and complexities of the racial, cultural, and ethnic legacies we all bring to the table.

In twenty-five years of anti-racism activism, I thought that I had recognized and owned my privilege, but I did not realize how much white privilege I had until it was revoked, revoked when I first held my child in my arms, and took on the yoke of all it means in this culture to be a mother. Adopting a child of color meant that I was no longer fully a member of the white privileged elite; I was marked as a "nigger-lover," as my mother had warned me I would be, and indeed in the most powerful of ways, I am.

My oldest son is African American, the birth child of an unknown father and a mother who could not raise him. He now has an extended family, which includes his lesbian parents and three grandmothers—my mother, my partner's mother, and his birth grandmother—as well as aunts and cousins, both biological and adopted. Our family picture hangs on the wall of his grandmother's dining room, the only white faces on the wall (though not the only lesbian ones). He is being raised in a very queer family, of Jews and gentiles, blacks and whites, where his uniqueness is treasured.

The challenges of parenting (lesbian parenting) a child of "another" race in a racist world are enormous. I am raising a black son in a war zone, and I'm reminded of this each time I watch the evening news, realizing in terror that in this world my son's life isn't worth squat. I was warned by more than one African-American mom: they are only cute till six or seven, then they're in trouble. I worry that his childish antics will be seen as violence, that his teenage horseplay will be seen as dangerous; I worry that his mere presence will bring the white man's law down on his back, that someone will mistake his wallet for a gun. As one friend said, "The Black man is held to different standards." I fear that he will feel the loss of that certain *tam*, that flavor of living in African-American culture. Even though my own social circles and neighborhood are racially integrated and we try to give him all that we can of his own cultural heritage, there will be a loss for him to grieve. As Jana Wolff has taught, white parents are always "tour guides" within black culture, and it is a very real fear that the vibrancy of African-American culture "will be reduced to its souvenirs."

Although most Jews are of color and most Jewish people accept him as a Jew, my son will undoubtedly face rejection within the Jewish community in this country. Some people of color will pity him for growing up with white people. Many people, of all cultures, will think it is terrible that lesbians—and rather gender-bent lesbians for that matter—are raising him.

Being the white mom of an African-American child has not made me more conscious of racism. Nor has it made me a better anti-racism activist. It has made me more vulnerable. Wearing "practice anti-racism" buttons in public did not provoke the hostility that a small black child yelling "Momma" while running toward a white woman can.

Although I have lived my whole life "out," never hiding in any closets, I did not consciously realize that some of my survival skills have been skills of stealth, and that being out has always been a choice. I have learned to sound more educated, to use my hands less when I speak, to not reveal my sexual identity when it's dangerous to do so. Many of my skills are skills of privilege, and with my white skin I have been able to move freely in the world. These skills will not help my son, a tall black male, survive. My son must develop skills that I'm poorly equipped to teach him. I am challenged to raise my son to survive in a world I will always have limited access to. Although I have lost my membership in the white world, I have not necessarily gained admission to the black community. My family may be a threat to white supremacy and white racists have now targeted us as their enemy, but that does not make us any more welcomed into communities of color.

The simple divisions of human beings into categories of "us" and "them" simply do not fit in my life; my family spills outside of the boxes we've been assigned to. When I voice my opinions about the treatment of young black boys in the public school system it is viewed as a liberal white concern, not the voice of an angry mom. When the administrators realize that I *am* the mother of a black son is my privileged voice heard more clearly than black mothers' voices? If I use my voice to speak out, is this a positive way to use my privilege or am I disempowering black mothers by taking up so much space as a pushy Jew? Are my expectations that my son be treated with the same respect and dignity as white boys just the foolishness of white privilege, or is it good anti-racism practices?

There are no simple answers here. We are a complex people, us humans, with a complicated legacy, coming from rich and vibrant cultures, and we have been wounded deeply by one another. I have learned to not fall prey to the simplicity of the oppressors' definitions or to the simplistic divisions that divide us. The only hope for our children—all of our children—is healing the wounds that divide us, and ultimately that we are each other's healers.

My four-year-old son was swirling round and round in the kitchen, the way children can, with reckless abandon and nary a fear in the world. He stopped suddenly and looked at me, and asked, "Momma, are we still slaves?" He had just finished studying Martin Luther King Jr. in his Montessori pre-school and had been singing "We Shall Overcome" all week; we were beginning to prepare for Pesach (Passover). I wasn't sure which slavery he was referring to, but at the Passover table every year we are admonished to never forget that the Hebrew people were slaves in Egypt. I looked at him and said, "No, *we* are not slaves anymore, but we must never forget that we once were."

When my partner and I adopted another son at birth I became a mother for the second time. He was considered a "hard-to-place" child because he is bi-racial with a white Irish birth mother and an unknown black father; another potentially adoptive family withdrew from adopting him when they met his brown siblings. He is five months old, lighter skinned than his olive-complected momma, with big blue eyes. The reality of raising a bi-racial child with very light skin has been yet another layer of awareness for our family. Everyone of course wants to know "what" he is as they admire his blue eyes. I imagine they are thinking that *this* child will have it easier than his older brother, and sadly they are probably right.

Although he will experience less overt racism he will also develop his racial identity and pride from the example of his older brother, who is proud that he is of African descent (and assures me that he knows more about Africa than I ever will). When my oldest son overhears the news of a war overseas he knows enough to ask if someone is trying to hurt Africans. When speaking to himself in the mirror I hear him say, "I think my lips are the nicest part of my face."

At first I worried that my oldest son would feel still feel "alone" as the darkest person in our family, but although he asks many questions about skin color, he absolutely perceives his baby brother as African just like him. When my older son's biological grandmother called she never asked "what" he was—but only inquired, "How are my boys?"—warmly welcoming this light-skinned mixed-race child into *her* extended family.

As a Jewish mother, I bring one skill to my parenting that will serve this family just fine. It is a legacy of my oppression as a Jew, a tool honed sharp by generations of women who carried their babies from country to country wrapped in blankets at their breasts while their older children huddled around their skirts. I've been told that this skill may or may not serve my sons. I have been told that it just might break my heart. It has been suggested that my expectations for black men in racist America are too high—I've been told this by well-meaning blacks, and by not-so-well-meaning whites. I've been told that I cannot protect my sons.

I am a pushy Jewish mother and I bring the only skill I have—I expect my boys to survive.

Notes

1. Shtetl: the small village ghettos of European Jewry. Jews were confined to these townships because of their outward differences in clothes and lifestyles; their freedom of movement varied from country to country and during different eras but by and large Jews lived their lives within the parameters of the shtetl life.

2. Yiddishkeit: the culture of Eastern European Jewry, exemplified in the Yiddish language—the mother tongue of Eastern European Jewry. Language is so embedded in cultural identity

that my grandmother, who spoke fluent Yiddish, never called the language Yiddish; she called it Jewish, as in, "Do you speak Jewish?"

3. Amoja Three Rivers is the author of a wonderful book called *Cultural Etiquette*, which outlines respectful relationships between people of different cultures, and examines racist assumptions. She includes examples from the experience of people of color, as well as Jewish people.

4. In Hebrew, like Sanskrit and Latin, the root words for *spirit* and *breath* are the same word. When we hold our breath, we hold in our spirits.

seventy

Chamizal

Alicia Gaspar de Alba

(for Deena)

Tonight Sangre de Toro
slips smooth and cool
as prophecy
down my throat
or your tongue
tasting the deepest parts
of my hidden name

In your mouth I am
Teyali

daughter clinging to a chain-link fence
watching the bad woman whose name
shamed me, Mamá
driving off in a strange man's car
At Christmas and birthdays
she gave me Barbies
that I impregnated with cotton wads
and left in a drawer
to wait for the moment that never came
never too thrilled about playing with dolls
until now
contigo, muñeca,
mujer who loves the one
I've hidden

In your mouth I am
Teyali

handsome woman of your dreams, me dices,
whose hands draw out of you
your own secret self
the absolute gentleness
of your gaze bathed
like your house in blue light
A November afternoon
sitting across from you at dinner
plates of arroz con pollo
the pungent oregano
of our desire
poetry haunting my tongue

In your mouth I am
Teyali

four years old
and two women talking custody
my mother and my father's mother
going to court

I dream a chain-link fence
between Teyali and the ocean
in the distance the Guadalupe mountains
curve out of the earth
like solid breasts
I shovel the sand under the fence
but cannot tunnel back
to that body
of water whose name
was carved out of my tongue
the same name as mine

there are two of me and I
have always lived between two women
bridge, river, desert
claimed like el Chamizal
first by one country
then the other

broken treaties in my wake

In your mouth I am
Teyali

blindfolded woman
holding two swords
across my heart
The tarot positions you
in the place of fate
high priestess
you open me so gently
fold the pages back
and my history rises
like braille
under your fingers

Me preguntas, where have I been?
how did you find me?
I am the one with the shovel
the one digging for restitution

In you, in the deep gate of your body,
in the wet welcome of your mouth
I meet Teyali

Note

In 1963–64, by virtue of the Chamizal Treaty that stabilized the course of the Rio Grande, the United States isolated 823 acres of land along the Juárez/El Paso border, 437 of which were returned to Mexico, the remainder of which is in joint use by both countries. El Chamizal is now national park on both sides. It is the only piece of the Mexican north, lost to the United States in 1848, ever returned to Mexico.

seventy-one

Linkages: A Personal-Political Journey with Feminist-of-Color Politics

Indigo Violet

This Bridge Called My Back awakened deep truths for a generation, inspiring and influencing a plethora of writings and other works by U.S. women of color and Third World feminists. A generation of feminists of color offered vision and pathways for a revitalized, radical, and transformative social movement. A new generation of people are taking these lessons to heart—sharing stories with each other, deciphering our multiple ways of living and struggling in the world, and recognizing the entwined nature of our histories and our existence in America.[1] We are articulating the depth and meaning of interconnection. We are learning each other's languages, forging new identities. We're making movements.

We are radical women of color, pro-feminist men, and whites. We have been fundamentally transformed by the work of feminists of color who insist that we must contend with the intersections of race, class, gender, sexuality, and nation, teaching us that the personal is inherently political, and that our politics must be holistic—rooted in the erotic, in a sense of the divine. Women-of-color feminism offers models for building radical solidarity, working vigorously with difference to create coalitional identities of resistance. U.S. Third World feminism has proposed that we find wholeness in our contradictions and connection where there is seemingly disconnection. We've been inspired to mobilize an intuitive, practical, and intellectual knowledge that our togetherness can transport us to new worlds. With this knowledge we are rejecting a white western consciousness that has encouraged separation in order to enact pillage and build empire. In this sense, womanism has offered a praxis of decolonization by suggesting affinity across difference, and by encouraging the formation of identities and movements that resist the status quo.

Within the violent formation of America, upon our backs is the task of living within the chaos and creativity of multiple worlds and various ways of knowing in order to understand how to act and align ourselves. Women-of-color feminism "coax[es] us into the habit of listening to each other and learning each other's ways of seeing and being" (Bambara, "Foreword," vii). As Gloria Anzaldúa suggests, it is through recognizing how "our multiple-surfaced, colored, racially gendered bodies intersect and interconnect" ("haciendo caras," xvi) that women of color of diverse backgrounds begin to espouse a common politics and to affirm solidarity with each other.

At the turn of the century, we desperately need affinity and intercon-nection, coalitional spaces, shared political commitments. We need mul-ticultural and multi-class communities to which we are accountable and within which we collectively struggle. We need to better recognize the intersections of the personal and the political. We need healing and trans-formation.

A new generation has been coaxed into this process, inspired by the work of women of color who have come before us and who live among us. We have been enticed into doing this strenuous work with each other, to end segregation and to craft new worlds. We attempt, through engaging in collective work, to form those intellectual/political/interpersonal com-munities interested in justice. "Gloria urges us to cross, 'atravesar.' Cross the borders—the established ones, the chosen ones, the forced ones, the good ones. Recognize and accept—no, embrace—each part of our wholes. Through such recognition we become empowered, dignified human beings with the courage, strength, and confidence to act offen-sively" (Gutierrez, 4).

I have been involved in women-of-color spaces, both in intentionally formed groups and in spaces that responded to specific social, political, or institutional conditions. In a "women-of-colors" peer support group that I helped to found, Asian, Asian-American, Caribbean, Caribbean-American, African, African-American, Chicana, Puerto Rican, biracial, lesbian, straight, bisexual, middle-class, poor, and working women sat with each other weekly to discuss the dilemmas and strengths of being women of color in America. There we struggled over the identity "women of color," over class and educational differences, sexuality, racism, our diverse experiences with and understandings of sexism. We brought our personal and cultural histories to the room and shared them with each other. People joined and left the group, interpersonal tensions erupted, political differences emerged.

This group was my first concerted effort to bring women of color together to unearth a process of solidarity-making and alliance-building. As an engaged participant in the group, and through coming to know the struggles of women of color different from myself I learned to travel to different worlds, to incorporate people's histories—to know myself while simultaneously moving beyond myself. I recognized that the hard work of building a women-of-color identity involved coming to know ourselves better, to interrogate the self rigorously in dialogue with the world around us and the people within it, and to commit to this process, no matter how paradoxical, contradictory, and difficult it is.

This "personal" work was immensely political. We enabled new modes of being by attempting to be in relation. Our cultural space was politicized. We analyzed our experiences in relation to the social forces that we moved through and that shaped us. Our meeting helped to generate a new kind of power, a power useful in combating domination. That power was the force of relation, of border crossings, of subverting established ways of being, of ending a legacy of segregation. The power created in our "women-of-colors" room was the power of knowledge, that if we women wanted to come together we could. If we insisted on our linked experiences, then our linkages could be theorized. If we could meet in a room every week and theorize our own experiences and insist upon solidarity, we could make a movement. We attempted to be about inclusion, a commitment to acknowledge, understand, and struggle with difference, and a type of identity politics that moved beyond nationalist narratives. We attempted to speak each other's languages.

Identities in Relation

The work of building solidarity across difference involves facing history and the consequences of our diverse and varied locations in society. Many of us have embarked upon a search for wholeness in light of our experiences in America—histories of uprooting and migration, internal colonizations, and alienation from land and culture. In our attempts to grapple with the past, this search for and honoring of our cultural roots is part of a dynamic process through which identities of resistance are consciously constructed.

In Anzaldúa's words, we are often "haunted by voices and images that violated us, bearing the pains of the past, we are slowly acquiring the tools to change the disabling images and memories, to replace them with self-affirming ones, to recreate our pasts and alter them—for the past can be as malleable as the present" ("haciendo caras," xxvii). Haunted by voices and images, we are able to imagine a past and conjoined histories. We bring pieces of our identities of origin together into a wholeness that can be understood.

Doing work to understand the histories of our peoples and to simultaneously mark the parallels and intersecting histories of all who have been colonized and oppressed in America allows differently positioned people to begin making links with each other. Rather than attempting to re-member a past in search of a sovereign identity limited solely to our communities of origin, we can begin to re-member the past in order to grapple with the interconnectivity of our *mutual* living in America. Putting our identities in relation allows for new possibilities and new radical subjectivities. Choosing to empathically align ourselves with people who are different from us, and incorporating this kind of diverse knowledge into who we become and how we move in the world, is the work that informs radical feminist-of-color solidarity in America.

Feminists of color have been theorizing this work of bridging gaps, crossing borders, and traveling to new worlds in order to build and enact the unique consciousness that seeks decolonization on all levels. The holistic consciousness that women-of-color feminism has inspired insists on empathy, on building linkages, on recognizing that our movements through history and through the present must simultaneously take account of the personal, political, and spiritual. Radical women of color attempt this work among themselves, and they have inspired other justice-seeking people—pro-feminist men and anti-racist whites—to engage in this work as well.

Through theorizing the process of building empathy and connection, U.S. Third World feminism has offered an understanding of the intersectional nature of oppression, and a personal-political accountability to difference as well as to solidarity. This notion of being accountable to history, to the present, and to our allies as we build new selves capable of resisting separation resonates with one of feminism's central tenets: the personal as political. While we seek to end oppression, we must simultaneously interrogate how we may also be implicated in structures of domination. Accounting for the personal as political while doing concerted work together entails building dialogue and democratic spaces between feminists of color privileged/disprivileged in myriad ways. Exploring how individuals—including women of color—are implicated in perpetuating structures of inequality is some of the most challenging work of transforming our personal-individual interests into collective interest in combating domination. This new work fuels some progressive movements in the United States—making the personal political and demanding transformation that is simultaneously material, psychic, intellectual, and cultural.

Gloria makes it clear that "[W]e have not one movement but many. . . . Ours are individual and small group *movidas*, unpublicized *movimientos*—movements . . . of small groups or single *mujeres*" ("haciendo caras" xxviii). Our theories and movements provide a blueprint for how justice seekers of the twenty-first century can begin to enact radical politics in a time when mass movements have waned and where "white supremacist capitalist patriarchy"[2] remains entrenched. These new politics are fueled by people willing to work in various locations, shifting consciousness and culture through the acts of moving within and among communities, and making the links between class, race, and gender oppression. Feminists of color have built foundations for revolutionary transformation in America, and women of color's theories and perspectives are fueling these emerging, unpublicized movements.

The New University in Exile: Mobilization in the Academy

Where are those "interstitial spaces beyond the hegemonic where feminism and popular mobilization can reside"?
— *M. Jacqui Alexander and Chandra T. Mohanty*

April 1997, New York City. The lobby at 65 Fifth Avenue at the New School for Social Research is taken over. We have created a New University in Exile, to protest exclusion and discrimination in this world-famous "progressive" institution. A movement is in progress.

The New School's Graduate Faculty for Political and Social Science, founded as the University in Exile in 1933, had been a haven for scholars fleeing European fascism. In 1997, it was an embattled place where students and faculty intended to make the links between different yet parallel legacies of exile. At the end of the twentieth century, people of color, queer people, working people—our knowledges and histories ignored and erased—were in exile here. In 1997 New School faculty, students, and staff were facing, within the institution, a culture of Eurocentricism masquerading as progressivism—its racism insidious, its sexism covered up, its exclusionary practices unchallenged en masse. Unchallenged until this moment.

An opening ceremony inaugurates the New University in Exile. Two young feminists of color—a Chicana from California and an African-American woman from Maryland—together cut the ribbon. Cheryl Boyce Taylor shares powerful poetry that speaks of erasure in another part of New York City—the African burial ground. Drummers bring in the call. The walls are decorated with maps, posters, lessons. A chalkboard with recommended readings has been brought in: writings by people of color, contemporary radical thinkers, and others not deemed fit for the Eurocentric academism of this ivory tower. In this lobby classes will be held, teach-ins and demonstrations will occur, freedom songs will be sung, and for the first time in a long time, liberatory knowledges will be shared openly.

The space is inhabited by colorful people. It is a multiracial space, a radical feminist space, a queer space. The New University in Exile.

There are still people who insist on education as the practice of liberation. And many of us ended up at the New School during 1996–98, when the Mobilization for Real Diversity, Democracy, and Economic Justice began to expose the racism, sexism, and economic exploitation practiced by this institution known in the larger world to be "progressive" and "leftist."

We wanted anti-colonial knowledges. We wanted a multicultural curriculum that decentered Europe and looked transnationally at social, political, and artistic phenomena. We wanted faculty of color teaching us and working among us. We wanted to study and work in an institution that valued its workers, paying them livable wages and ample benefits. We wanted a thriving, equitable environment where radical intellectualism and human dignity would be the daily reality. We wanted gender studies that were vigorously concerned with the intersections of race, class, sexuality, and gender, that recognized Third World and U.S. feminism of color's central space in feminist theory. We wanted Professor M. Jacqui Alexander to be retained with a permanent faculty position. We wanted decision-making power at all levels, a participatory democracy where a diverse body of students and faculty would be involved in the shaping of university policy and curricula. We wanted a new consciousness to shape life in this university. We demanded that the New School live up to its promise of progressivism and diversity.

This Mobilization at the New School put women-of-color feminism into practice. We insisted on analyzing the interrelatedness of oppression and conditions of domination. Activists recognized ourselves—women, men, queer, straight, black, Latina, Asian, white—as a collective interested in liberatory knowledge production, equity, and justice. Our insistence upon linkages provided the force for our mobilizing.

We made a movement that challenged "how the institution functioned and how it relied on different kinds of exclusions and exploitations at different levels" (Alexander, quoted by Poitras). We stressed that these exclusions and exploitations had to do with race, class, gender, sexuality, and nation. We noted the linkages between the various forms of marginalization that we identified, and struggled alongside each other in a movement that sought diversity (in curriculum, hiring, and recruitment of students), democracy (participatory decision making to include students, staff, and marginalized faculty), and economic justice (an end to the exploitation of the security guards, administrative staff, and part-time faculty) at the New School.

Un Mundo Zurdo/A Left-Handed World

The New School's anti-racist, multiracial, pro-feminist, queer-friendly Mobilization for Real Diversity, Democracy, and Economic Justice enabled spaces of critique, dissent, and direct action to expose the university's unfulfilled promise of progressivism and diversity. We held public meetings, we organized demonstrations, we crafted demands, we attempted to negotiate, and, after being met by recalcitrant administrators and faculty members, some students and faculty went on a hunger strike.

Not coincidentally, diverse women of color—black, Latina, Middle Eastern, and Asian women—took leading roles in creating the spaces that enabled this kind of mobilizing. Women-of-color feminist theory and perspectives were fully present in the New School's mobilization, helping to provide analyses that enabled activists to link the fragments (events happening in classrooms and meetings), to the local (the New School's widespread institutional discrepancies), to the global (a world of oppression, domination, and exploitation). We were committed to a holistic and pervasive justice that relied on recognizing intersections and making linkages with each other and with our allies. The Mobilization sought to remedy myriad injustices that were perpetrated by the New School, yet which had implications far beyond the university.[3]

As events unfolded, and as we increasingly vocalized our experiences in the world and in the New School, many women of color came to know each other within this movement, to identify with each other, and to commit to concerted collective and political work with each other. We made the links between our personal discontent at the New School, our familial and individual identities, our histories and prior experiences. We began to put all of those things in relation, and eventually to articulate a politics of affinity—in which we differently and multiply constituted women of color began to see that we had common interests, common goals, and that we shared a familiar psychic terrain. We realized that the institutional practices of the New School were part of a larger historical force that was killing us—erasing our knowledges, removing our bodies, separating us from each other. We also recognized a larger context of national backlash against the small gains made to increase opportunities for people of color, and we grew in our outrage that a supposed "progressive" institution would be implicated in the racist/heteropatriarchal attitudes and practices that oppressed our communities.

Along with women of color, whites and men together began to craft coalitional identities of resistance within this movement. The process of putting our identities into relation and conversation and linking them with our political and ethical choices created a radical, multi-racial, sexually diverse, pro-feminist space. This space of camaraderie was engendered by the personal-political work that many of the mobilization's actors were willing to engage in. The personal-political work in this space included both confronting the exclusionary practices of the New School and interrogating ourselves as we related to the segregationist culture of the world around us. Ours was a movement that sought to transform the New School, and it simultaneously created liberated zones within the institution and within ourselves where the intellectual, the political and the personal, the erotic and the spiritual, coexisted.

We did not win. We did not get permanent positions for feminists of color who taught in gender studies. We did not get a new, enlivened curriculum. Workers still battle for their rights to dignity, good working conditions, and good pay. Eurocentrism still reigns supreme in prominent sectors of the New School.

However, we created radical and multiple spaces where feminism and popular mobilization could reside. We created networks that extend beyond the New School, beyond the academy. We saw how powerful intersectional politics and women-of-color theories are, mobilizing white people and men as well as women of color. We learned the difficulties of organizing around multiple issues and making the links between them, of making authentic multicultural alliances, and of invigorating feminism. We enacted some radical, anti-racist, pro-feminist, queer, unruly politics —with the New University in Exile we created what Anzaldúa calls "un mundo zurdo." We created an activist space that contained a "mixture of bloods and affinities . . ." where "Third World women, lesbians, feminists, and feminist-oriented men of all colors . . . band[ed] and bond[ed] together" ("La Prieta," 209). Through our activism, our strenuous personal-political work, we transformed *ourselves*.

Feminists of color have offered models for facing difference, for building radical multicultural solidarity, and for making ethical commitments that are counterhegemonic, subversive, and in the interest of justice and decolonization. This kind of movement—one that struggles through the personal as political, that pulls together fragments to make a holistic consciousness, that insists on the intersecting and interlocking nature of oppression and liberation—has given us new understandings of identity and politics in a "postmodern" world where material existence has necessitated new modes of analysis, theorizing, and organizing, new ways to imagine solidarity and struggle, and new social movements.

These new social movements that simultaneously account for the multiplicity of oppression as well as the multiplicity of identities-in-relation, like the Mobilization at the New School, are made possible only with the participation of feminists of color. In our mobilizing, our theories of intersectionality, difference, plurality, justice, and equity emerge and constitute the praxis upon which radical politics *must* be built. For it is women of color's feminist theories that are carving out a radicalism for the twenty-first century that works to dismantle the interlocking forms of domination in society. Women-of-color feminists and their allies, inspired by writings such as *This Bridge Called My Back*, have created models for radical movements that are multi-dimensional in scope and vision— demanding nothing short of a radical feminist revolution. The transformative work is as immensely personal as it is political, enabling what

Alexander and Mohanty call "a different order of relationships among people . . . understanding socioeconomic, ideological, cultural, and psychic hierarchies of rule . . . their interconnectedness, and their effects on disenfranchised peoples within the context of transformative collective or organizational practice" (xxviii).

We are changing culture, crafting a new order of relationships. In learning each other's languages, in meeting each other in diverse spaces, we can multiply ourselves. Women-of-color feminism has ignited a generation to *struggle where they are*, to make social change a revolt that is simultaneously psychic, material, erotic, and personal. Affinity and camaraderie across difference are the seeds sown by radical women with a vision. Through our rigorous attention to the vast interconnections we will realize multiple possibilities, new worlds, new ways of relating on our way to creating something that could turn out to be a decolonized and just future. A bridge has been made to a new generation who will carry the torch, honoring our ancestors.

Notes

I have to give thanks and praises to my people: to my teachers Jacqui Alexander, Ella Shohat, Meena Alexander, Nova Gutierrez, Aleyamma Mathew, Matthew King, Amit Rai, Amala Levine, Dina Siddiqi, Gary Lemons, Mustafa K. Emirbayer, Chéla Sandoval, Gloria Anzaldúa, Cherríe Moraga, Audre Lorde (presente), Papusa Molina, and María Lugones for their inspiration; to my compañeras/os in the Mobilization at the New School; and to all the radical women of color who organize, teach, and write, giving us language, clarity, and breath.

1. The "United States of America" has no name of its own. America actually includes two continents, an isthmus, and a plethora of islands. "America," when used to refer solely to the conglomerate of fifty states, is in effect an appropriation, an erasure of the heterogeneity and immense geographic and cultural expanse of the Americas.

2. bell hooks's eloquent description of "white supremacist capitalist patriarchy" offers an immensely useful summary of the forces we are up against.

3. We drew analogies and felt affinities with movements responding to the dismantling of affirmative action in California state universities, the student movement at the University of Massachusetts challenging the administration's capitulation to anti–affirmative action backlash, and the work of Derrick Bell in exposing the racism and sexism at Harvard Law School, and currently we are watching the struggle to retain ethnic studies at the University of California, Berkeley, and the student movement at the University of Texas-Austin demanding an Asian-American studies program.

vii.

"i am the pivot for transformation" . . .
enacting the vision

seventy-two

Girl and Snake

Liliana Wilson Grez

seventy-three

Thawing Hearts, Opening a Path in the Woods, Founding a New Lineage

Helene Shulman Lorenz

When I first became aware of *This Bridge Called My Back,* I understood it in the tradition of Latin American testimonios, the story of a whole group of oppressed people focused through the personal account of one. In testimonios, the idea is not necessarily to express individual subjectivity, uniqueness, or creativity but to give voice to what has been marginalized in the mainstream press. Often testimonios are co-authored and sometimes incorporate several people's narratives. Such stories are "prophetic" because they articulate the concerns of a whole population, their truth about economic, political, and cultural conditions.

Usually emerging where there has been a long historical silencing of certain ways of experiencing the world and an insistence on other stories that cover over suffering and support the status quo, testimonios can have tremendous power. The slaves' narratives and those of masters might as well have described different universes. One presented the plantation as hellish prison, the other as relaxed, pastoral heaven. In this discursive gap, energies build up as in the space between stored positive and negative electricity. When the gap is suddenly arced, it can cause a flash, an explosion, a lightning bolt. In this moment, a public recognition and articulation of alternative visions can be a stunning experience for both masters and slaves.

In 1980, during *Bridge's* creation, I had left the academic world where I taught philosophy and was active in the Latin American solidarity movement, working at a cultural center in Berkeley, California. Though I'd been involved in the women's movement since the 1970s and in the Civil Rights Movement before that, my idea of political work was limited by a frame of reference focusing on the dominant culture's economic and ideological dynamics. In my view then, the solution we sought was in political organization and oppositional movements. The goal was to replace one organizational hierarchy representing privilege with another representing those marginalized by privilege. I saw *This Bridge Called My Back* as an organizing effort.

Twenty years later, though *Bridge* has proven its enormous political potential in mobilizing oppositional voices, it has also made an equally profound theoretical contribution. It's said that you cannot really appreciate an answer until you have a question to accompany it. I now see levels of sophistication in this book that it has taken me years to grow into. I now believe that *This Bridge Called My Back* embedded, performed, and began to articulate what I call a "theory of reframing and restoration" emerging in multiple social locations and disciplines all over the world. Just as a spotlight illuminates and frames lead actors on a stage by deepening the shadows on the surrounding set, every discourse frames some ways of thinking and pushes others to the margin. A theory of reframing asks how margins are created, enforced, justified, denied, challenged, and recentered. It looks for what has been made to appear "natural" or "normal" in every social location; how this naturalization is enacted to create a frame or border pushing out difference; and how difference survives with a life of its own, and can then become a resource either to help strengthen the frame or else to question or rupture it.

A theory of reframing and restoration also looks for traces of older narratives, multiple ways to resituate our life-stories. In fragments of oral history, in received spiritual traditions, in symbols surviving from other eras, a practice of autoethnography begins to sift through sediments, recreating in discourse the kind of lived ecological diversity that surrounds us in our communities. This is not the creation of a master narrative or a return to an authentic "Golden Age." It is the re-creation of a kind of performance style practiced in many oral traditions where multiple voices and tellings of the past build up a many-sided and ongoing dialogue about provisional truth-in-perspective-for-the-moment. On a good day, sitting at a kitchen table, cooking together for family or community, telling stories near a fire, dancing to well-loved music—or alone at a computer with many fragments and dialogues trying to find a voiced conversation—a miracle is always possible. When spirit enters these rituals of restoration, a kind of cultural alchemy can temporarily cook what's raw, unite what's divided, give meaning to what's chaotic, and thereby enchant, refresh, and reanimate all participants. It is this experience of negotiated cohesion through dialogue leading to a shared feeling of grace that is sought in a theory of restoration. Knowing how to create such rituals is the special expertise of healers, curanderas, griots. In this sense, *Bridge* itself is a ritual of restoration, and it is perfectly consistent with the theory of the curanderas who created it that we go on talking together about it.

My new understanding of theory came out of the experience of shared personal and political defeats. In the decade after *Bridge* was published, many organizing efforts from which it had emerged ran into a wall. The Latin American revolutionary and solidarity movements I was involved in essentially collapsed. I don't want to rehearse the ongoing dialogue about why this collapse occurred, but it was clear that institutional change and finding sustainable common ground across differences in human experience was much more difficult than any of us, in our perhaps naive optimism, had anticipated.

During the late 1980s, a kind of "midlife crisis" sent me back to the drawing board to figure out a new way of understanding my social and political environment. I experienced a storyline meltdown: I suddenly could see, both in my own life and in the community around me, that the silences and absences in our stories were sometimes more potent and alive than the known and habitual. I was raised in a small and isolated Orthodox Jewish community, in the Adirondack Mountains, reeling from trauma of the Holocaust yet almost unable to speak about it. We all colluded to keep silent and unspoken borders in place as part of the conspiracy to fit in with and be safe among our majoritarian-culture neighbors. I knew and cooperated with the rule that I was never allowed to feel or name the unspoken because it was too dangerous. Only a circling of the wagons, a repression of difference, a united front in the face of an unpredictable world, would make possible our survival. We were Americans now.

Yet layers of other fragments are sedimented in my memory: my mother singing Yiddish songs with her brothers; my grandmother dancing at weddings to Eastern European music; stories about "No dogs or Jews" signs recently removed from nearby tourist resorts; pictures of my great-grandmother's grave in the Polish shtetl where every man, woman, and child was murdered; the constant layer of rebellion in me against "what girls could do" and were forbidden to do; and the knowledge that my father's depression and my mother's "migraines," tears, furies, and evolving medical symptoms were silent protest against the collapsed possibilities for education and creativity in their lives. Despite this multiplicity of unspoken yearnings, I also learned how to create and live in community, which I have done all my life. As a child, I experienced being embedded in an oral culture with a rich repertory of ritual, and a practice of self-in-community or self-in-participation with other people, the world, and what one could call the "unknown sacred" flowing through us.

My midlife reflections taught me that for a long time I'd been participating in a process where, at the margins of what is officially named, symbols loaded with shared meaning were hidden in plain view, elaborated, and passed hand to hand in poetry, music, dialogue, and performance. In my last year in the solidarity movement, 1989, I was the coordinator of the Guatemala News and Information Bureau and worked with the International Indian Treaty Council to arrange Rigoberta Menchu's tour. She was under death threat, so a group of us stayed with her all the time sharing stories, visits to the supermarket, and impromptu meals long into every night.

For years people in California's sanctuary movement had been quietly driving Guatemalans and Salvadorans, escaping the U.S.-assisted genocides in their countries, from the Mexican border to Oakland, where housing and work had been arranged for them. We put out the word through their networks that on a certain night Rigoberta would meet anyone who wanted to see her in the basement of a local sanctuary church. Of course, all indigenous Guatemalans knew that to walk the streets of California they had to relinquish their traje (traditional dress) and assimilate to local customs so that La Migra could not pick them out and deport them. Yet that night, over a hundred people in traje waited in a sea of color and traditional music, surrounded by the smell of flowers and village food cooking in the church kitchen. As Rigoberta entered the room, there was a hushed moment as everyone took in the symbolic significance of the scene. In full bloom here, against all odds, was a symbolic tree that had been hacked to bits in a genocide in its home place, now suddenly transplanted and alive with meaning. Then everyone in the room began to cry. The traje must have been carried across borders, in paper bags, hidden in suitcases, for thousands of miles at huge risk. The evening was one of the most inspiring I have ever spent, the whole roomful of people—indigenous and Ladino/a, gringo/a and Latino/a—in dialogue about what can survive and what can change, what is worth fighting for and what will be lost, all the while sharing food, music, song, and dance from two continents in what was surely a ritual of transubstantiation and renewal.

Though my own hometown was thousands of miles away and different in every particular, I recognized the story of having come here from a faraway place with its own life, story, music, food, language, costume, and values (or being different in any way from a dominant majority), and living in the margins of another culture where safety and survival—with dignity and values intact—was the issue. I was also familiar with the fact that in the room were many contradictory points of view and interests and a need sometimes to create something new and not-yet-spoken, alongside the traditions and symbols brought over from the past.

During this time, I began to dream of a new kind of social change movement in which instead of a fixed platform or party line, we could accept the necessity for community rituals of dialogue, evolution, and restoration. The starting point would not be obedience to a master narrative describing a single hierarchical and linear process, which always leads to scapegoating those with different and creative impulses. Rather, we might start with the recognition that every formulation was provisional and open to reframing; we would always need the ritual of community dialogue and storytelling to periodically restore energy to our projects.

These fragments and new thoughts came flooding into me as I spontaneously suffered processes of disintegration, reframing, and restoration in my personal life. I began to understand how everyone colludes to create a habitual, predictable worldview that defends the boundaries of the already-known. I began questioning how to host, in both personal and community life, a multiplicity of viewpoints and sedimented fragments of experience in such a way that the grace of restoration brought not only division and suffering but also compassion, dialogue, healing, and celebration.

During these years I studied at an interdisciplinary psychoanalytic institute and began leading community groups in transformative dialogues. I also returned to the university to teach psychology and philosophy. There, I rediscovered *This Bridge* and much of the literature that succeeded it, in an encounter of revelation and relief. By that time, *Bridge* had traveled from California to the margins of women's studies and other interdisciplinary programs in academia, where a shocking war of cultural values was tearing apart traditional disciplines. I was in a new place and began seeing *Bridge* with new eyes.

Unfortunately, academic departments can be extreme in building fortresses to guard the treasures of the past from the encroachment of newcomers. Many departments are frozen in the frame of a modernist mythology of fixed individualist egos in existential alienation from a mechanical and meaningless world. In my experience, women's studies departments could be particularly disappointing. At the last university where I taught, the chair of women's studies decided that a course on Cuban women's literature and a philosophy course in which *Bridge* was read could not be cross-listed with her offerings. Though several women of color on campus taught courses on literature by women, she made no attempt to dialogue with them. She had no time in two semesters to meet with any of us suggesting such inclusion because she was too busy. That year, she received an award for faculty excellence and was promoted to the position of dean.

From an established disciplinary perspective, there is still a profound suspicion of theories of reframing and restoration. Like all "wounded healers" (Hillman, 116–18) who come into the world under the myth of an orphaned divine child, there is a story of rejection of *Bridge* and its ways of thinking in many academic locations: "No room at the inn." Because it broke down older classification systems or symbolically inverted their meaning, many people did not know how to classify this work. Is it fiction? Philosophy? Literature? Sociology? Ethnic studies? Women's Studies? Psychology? In what department should it be read? The theory of reframing in *Bridge* is a problem for all frames, a challenge to conservative ways of thinking that find the present U.S. landscape the best of all possible worlds. Such people may claim that they do not understand these ideas, that they are not theoretical enough to be considered, or that they were already raised and dismissed by canonical thinkers. To imagine that the older frames of race, gender, sexuality, self, and other cut across the whole field of knowledge over an entire historical era, that they are connected with colonial impulses, that they serve and reflect power, privilege, and hierarchy, and that they are filled with arbitrary exclusions and absences which need to be renegotiated, would indeed be a revolutionary rupture in many disciplinary conversations.

Consequently, my daily life in the academic world is always a kind of agony. It seems that I am often sitting in a room where I-in-community-in-multiple-perspective seems to have disappeared, along with everyone I know well and everything I care about. (I cannot forget the moment when a Jamaican colleague asked an economist in a seminar we attended what the effects of his economic policy would be on women in the Caribbean. "Oh," he said without emotion, "they would be assigned to the permanent underclass of the late capitalist economy.")

It's been a terrible struggle for me to find the words and spaces to address the state of shock in which I frequently find myself within academic discourse. No other environment enforces in me this tendency to silence with the sheer weight of its inherited exclusionary practices. *This Bridge,* and the literature that has grown up around it and as a result of it, has been a tremendous source of strength and solace in my work. I know what it cost to wrench those stories out of self-silencing collusion, and bring them into communities that would rather not hear them.

Today, in what feels like another aeon, I teach about the cultural and imaginal construction of self and other in an interdisciplinary graduate program in psychology. I can see, from this vantage point, that when discourse becomes frozen in harsh oppositional stances—a dynamic that was locked both in my inner and in my outer worlds in the 1980s—the only point of exit is "below." Here I am imagining a bamboo plant that attempts to grow past a barrier like a cement sidewalk or a building blocking its growth. When it cannot, it will deepen its root system, sending out new growth below the surface, emerging across the street or in a neighbor's yard. The work of *Bridge* is like that for me now, a decisive moment when oppositional thinking went into new and deeper territory, and began to theorize around the existent dualities.

Bridge began at the border between several communities, selves, and discourses in the evolution of a symbolic frontier in-between and around the edges of living individuals and their current frames of reference. The "no-man's-land" border area has been created through the silencing of certain types of expression. *Bridge* named this space—a liminal threshold where new conversations could develop—as valuable, important, even central. Here, when distinctions between self and other, individual and community, are radically challenged because frames have been cracked by the shock of difference, unexpected ruptures can create the dialogues, performances, and rituals that stretch identity and identifications.

If we have no way to create liminal spaces, energies toward creative development are thwarted. Folk medicines and indigenous psychologies, including western psychiatric diagnoses, have many names for conditions of somatic distress in which the body performs a cultural practice, a symptom, which is really disguised resistance: neurasthenia, depression, hysteria, panic disorder, nervios, susto, crise de nervos, fraquaza. Marginalization can also be expressed by yearning, desire, fantasy, and dream—felt primarily as an uncomfortable accumulation of energy long before anything is expressed. Though these symptoms can be painful, they may evolve into dangerous resources. They are a kind of rupture of normalization expressed through the body, a scream of shock and noncompliance, the beginning of a new conversation. The energy could begin to emerge in word, song, or art and be carried from place to place. Anyone silencing messages contributes to the buildup of resistant potentials. In this state of being one can act as a border guard to collude in repressing what needs to be spoken; but energy also begins to accumulate outside our control in our bodies and souls. This energy can be tapped in rituals of restoration.

Transgressive culture can breach the policed silences of normalized hegemonic discourse and permanently break its capacities to frame the situation. In Latin America, the movements of liberation theology aimed at producing communities in permanent, ongoing dialogue about their own histories. Repeated rituals of shared reflection gave the most oppressed people a space to imagine alternative realities. Once they owned these rituals or were consciente, they could no longer be dominated. This critical practice of giving voice to suffering in local environments was called concientizaçao, as it first developed in the poorest Christian base communities in Brazil (Freire, "Adult"). We could imagine a whole spectrum of environments where, at one end, discourse and performance are highly controlled and frames are rigid and policed; at the other end, creativity, innovation, and spontaneous expression are celebrated and frames are permeable and provisional. What are the costs and benefits of living in such landscapes? Who pays? We need to understand how communities and individuals move across the spectrum to know how resources emerge for resistance and healing.

The "no-man's-land" *Bridge* named can be a territory for dialogical and intercultural encounters, where particular individuals in all their historical and cultural embeddedness may find Others about whom they care enough to reach across unimaginable gulfs of difference. Here, in the creation of a "Third Space" (Bhabha), the invisible edges, frames, or frontiers established by normalized discourse could become suddenly visible and negotiable. The territory appears through the expression of very particular and local experiences because the preceding scientific and national era focused on framing European local experience as "universal," repeatable, replicable, statistical, non-contextual, and ahistorical.

In the alternative paradigm, subjectivity is not primarily prophetic in the sense of representing a whole class or caste, nor is it personal and isolated in the sense of expressing the private interiority and reflection of an already universally constituted self-monad. Rather subjectivity is acknowledged to have potentials of reflexivity. Reflexive subjectivity, understood in most oral cultures as self-in-dialogue-and-community, makes possible a transgressive rupture of its own construction of self. Borders and defenses are noticed, owned, named, dialogued with, befriended. This interpretation of subjectivity attempts to create a dialogue among unacknowledged parts of our own personalities as well as our communities. It is an encounter between conservative border guards enforcing the current version of the socially constructed self and immigrant and exile experiences, symptoms, visions, and dreams longing to cross borders.

This Bridge Called My Back (along with later texts in cultural studies and postcolonial studies) attempted to break a hole in academia's fortress wall, an effort so far only partly successful, to let new symbolic energies enter the story. In doing so, *Bridge* de-centered every "inside" by asking us to consider our disciplines' and communities' patrolled borders or frames. By allowing us to think of ourselves and our worlds with one foot in older discourses and another at a growing, opening edge, the not-yet-voiced could begin to create new myths—new containers for new wine—beyond the limited already-known. This required a huge act of courage: to speak what the dominant culture has forbidden for centuries, to find the words for marginalized experiences that many have contrived to silence, to explore out loud the regimes that have been policed to deny love, hunger, pain, and exclusion. It's no accident that writers experiencing multiple marginalizations through dominant narratives on sexuality, race, nation, and/or gender were often the first to think about reframing. This body of work has surely challenged any simple identification with what it means to be "man" or "woman," me or you.

Once this theater of the margin has been successfully performed, it must have radical implications. From here on in, we might all have to think of ourselves as always with a social and personal frame that pushes aside a level of collective or personal unconscious we've collaborated in not hearing, one step beyond our current margin of understanding.

Nothing we say can be once-and-for-all. We might have to be endlessly open to revision within and without, while owning the history and density of the multiple descriptions that have made us what we are.

People with a theory of reframing play by different rules. They distrust statements of absolute idealization and identification, or clear and abstract binary opposites. They're interested in traditions but more interested in edges, frames, or frontiers. Their border guards become more curious, friendly, and experimental. They look for oppositions, dualisms, and conflicts in themselves and others as sites of brittle identifications, hoping to melt what's been frozen. Resembling the tricksters of folklore and fairy tale, conflating outside and inside, hated others with hated selves, they dare to walk to the edge of town and explore. Gloria Anzaldúa saw this clearly in her preface to the second edition:

> With *This Bridge* . . . hemos comenzado a salir de las sombras; hemos comenzado a acarrear con orgullo la tarea de deshelar corazones y cambiar conciencias (*we have begun to come out of the shadows; we have begun to break with routines and oppressive customs and to discard taboos; we have commenced to carry with pride the task of thawing hearts and changing consciousness*).
> Mujeres, a no dejar que el peligro del viaje y la immensidad del territorio nos asuste—a mirar hacia adelante y abrir paso en el monte (*Women, let's not let the danger of the journey and the vastness of the territory scare us—let's look forward and open paths in these woods*). (n.p., her emphasis)

In performing a theory of reframing and restoration, *This Bridge Called My Back* inevitably dug deep in the compost of traditional mythologies set aside through conquest in order to find what nourishes while separating out what poisons. In this project of cultural archeology, we can explore our own colonization and collusion with silencing agendas; but we also encounter older mysteries of renewal and healing. In sediments of inherited ritual, the alchemy of the creative act may imagine a transpersonal ground embedded in the personal and social frame: that in us and our communities which imagines "more" in dream, image, symptom, inspiration, or desire, even before we fully understand what we're reaching for, perhaps more understanding, more creativity, more community, much more than life offers in the current globalized economy.

The realm of the transpersonal "more," a sense of the sacred unknown ground of life, announces the presence of the numinous and uncanny, where we might realize that what we have already understood in life is only a small part of our potential. An exploration of the territory of spiritual renewal or symbolic healing can be expressed through traditional transpersonal myths of redemption and community. These myths are one way to imagine coming out of limited frameworks to build the open and sacred spaces in daily life where new healing energies will be welcomed. Such energies—named in narratives of various cultures as gods and goddesses, orishas, daimons, invisables, spirits—can give us the vision and strength to author new scripts for ourselves, our cities, and our surrounding environments.

In the images emerging from these rituals, we can begin to speak of the suffering and healing potentials that come through us from the world. Every night, dreams of nuclear disaster, lost children, border guards, and fleeing prisoners flood through the bodies of people everywhere. Every day we may become poets of lost or disarticulated voices in ourselves and our habitat, by spontaneously reaching for new words in the river of language and image that has shaped us and continues pouring through our experience. In this space of symbolic healing and restoration, the constructed walls of alienation between self and other, individual and community, inside and outside, past and future, may fall. In that instant we might glimpse the living ground of symbolic imagination, the mother of all creativity: our shared capacity for myth-making.

In making a space for symbolic healing rituals of a new kind, *This Bridge* could be viewed as a kind of original pilgrimage, a journey that founded a lineage, or Sangha in Buddhist terminology. A whole new generation of men and women come through undergraduate and graduate schools with *Bridge*, and more recent work by several original contributors, as founding texts returned to again and again. No longer content to accept the "received authority" of old frames, these students are creating a new culture where we search for absence as much as presence, dialogue more than contradiction, multiple perspectives rather than single narrative overview. This work has opened possibilities for many creative genres in writing and more complex ways of being present in an academic environment. Transdisciplinary by nature, it challenges the separations between subject matters as it reaches across borders to make needed connections between the personal and political. As in the tradition of liberation theology, it asks in a radical way: Who is served by the research, conferences, and writing we are involved in? The new lineage, in repeating the originary impulses, can be imagined as similar to the great annual pilgrimages to sacred landscapes that many cultural groups still perform. These rituals have the potential to create an environment for renewal in universities, though pilgrimages always require that we leave behind the security and comfort of our habitual worlds at least periodically.

For many of us in the academic world suffocating in the old paradigm, this work has created a small space to breathe in a landscape finally open enough for us to enter whole with all our doubts and suffering, silences and not-knowing, creativity and multiplicity, families and communities. In an educational culture that overvalues and overestimates the naturalized Eurocentric and patriarchal past, a ritual clearing for innovation has been built by theories of reframing and restoration.

Occasionally now, I experience a sublime joy while in dialogue with others at a critical and creative edge where we can see ourselves as both frame and rupture, fortress and challenger. Sometimes I'm a defender and sometimes I'm the one needing to break down walls. Little by little a new kind of clearing, a psychology of liberation, can emerge alongside the old frame of academic discourse. In that freeing space of crossroads, we can be as personal, consciente, theoretical, bodily, symptomatic, complicated, ethnic, queer, straight, conflicted, multiple, interpretive, wrong, provisional, daring, or creative as we need to be. This is healing myth for souls in protest against a conversation designed to marginalize and pathologize them. This lineage is one in which I take refuge.

seventy-four

Still Crazy After All These Tears

Luisah Teish

The wind blows leaves across the parking lot as women, children, and men enter the meeting room downstairs, the theater upstairs, or the lobby on the ground floor of the building anywhere we happen to be anytime.

They are smudged at the door, meet and greet each other, receive stones, candles, and flowers then seat themselves on pillows, chairs, and parental laps. The chitchat stops as the primal heartbeat of humanity, the African drum, calls the village together. We sing ourselves into community. Caressed by the undulating beat we sway and swoon in our seats until the drum fades and the house lights go out.

Kindred Spirits Call

Out of the warm dark silence comes the sound of the Shofar blown by a towering figure of a woman, a daughter of the Shekinah. Her horn announces "let the ritual begin."

A Black Muslim sister, wrapped in her choice of veils, recites a prayer for peace. We are transported to the Tower overlooking the rising sun. A manila-colored woman from the Philippines recites a prayer in Tagalog on behalf of the hungry, the homeless, and the disabled.

Lava flows and sizzles as Madame Pele dances across the floor to an ancient Hawaiian chant. The scent of her flowers, the flow of her hair and

her skirt leave us breathless on an imaginary beach basking in the noonday sun. Dressed in beads and feathers a black Native American elder
calls the Thunderbird, the Wolf, and the Salmon as our people did long
before Columbus came and the Buffalo went away. The ancestors are
called to the circle in perfect Yoruba by a priestess of Mayan descent.

Back to the Future

On these nights we call the deities and the ancestors, the animals and the
plants, the stars and the stones of every continent, culture, and era to
come be with us. In this room, in this sacred space, we are "kindred spirits," people who respect our earth, our cultures, our ancestors, and ourselves. We stand together, we pray, play, and struggle together. We trust
each other and are political *because* we are spiritual. Our spirituality
informs our political struggles, our years of high-risk living, loving, laughter, and tears. We have traveled over the mountains and through the
forests, around the globe to arrive at this common place . . . to inner and
outer sacred space.

For me the journey began with a childhood dream, a whispering on
the wind, a sense that I had come to earth to be someone with something
to do. That recognition developed in spite of the backdrop of late-1950s
racism in the segregated south, the pro-macho sexism of mid-1960s
counter-culture and the perpetual gynophobia of the Catholic Church. I
came to realize that these things stood in the way of my soul's purpose for
being here and I resolved to do something about it all.

So I began by questioning the nuns and the bible, by challenging segregation in the church, and by struggling to understand male-to-female
relationships. In a Consciousness-Raising '70s moment I realized that
"Eve Was Framed" and that my own future and that of generations to
come depended on changing the impact mythological images had on the
lives of real-life women, particularly women of color. Then I became
active in the women's spirituality movement.

That quest for understanding led to a great discovery . . . the sacred
myths of the African Goddesses Yemonja, the Great Mother of the Ocean,
Oya the Queen of the Winds of Change, and my personal Goddess
Oshun, the beautiful and generous Goddess of Love. These Goddesses
reflected the collective stories of generations of powerful women who
walked the earth as daughters of nature.

This information inspired me beyond reason, wrapped me in mystery
of the Divine Feminine, and made me crazy with faith, drunk on the possibility of paradise in this garden, this sacred place.

And far beyond my hopes and expectations was the discovery that
there were other crazy women who embraced the Goddesses with love

and reverence. These women were black, white, Latin, Asian, and Native American. They were midwives, artists, workers, and mothers. We were a beautiful bouquet of flowers. We worked together for many years performing rituals, staging demonstrations, writing articles addressing issues such as healings after rape, alternatives for battered women, defending women's sexual and reproductive rights, and combating violent pornography. The early '80s *felt* like progress.

The Future Shock

I made a commitment to Oshun that I would wrap my head in the cloth of power, honor my ancestors, and promote female power proudly in the world. To that end I have received initiations in Africa and the Caribbean, performed in Europe, and sat around firesides with indigenous clan mothers around the world.

In the midst of all this joy there came the shock and sorrow of the '90s. Big money and media mania engineered particular shifts in popular thought and culture. Many of those shifts encouraged institutional corruption and represented the loss of rights earned through blood and tears in the past.

A black Republican man led the parade against affirmative action in California, surprisingly. To this day I still can't comprehend just what a black republican is! The death of affirmative action was a crime and an insult to the memory of Dr. Martin Luther King, Fannie Lou Hamer, and the many people who died on the front lines fighting for our Civil Rights. The ancestors turned over in their graves.

Herrnstein and Murray's book, *The Bell Curve*, declared that black students were inherently inferior, a theory that had been disproved decades ago. Its publication and popularity announced that the same evil of educational racism as I had experienced in the segregated south would rise again.

My concern for the minds of our children went off the charts when I attended a Black History celebration at a midwestern college and found that *Sankofa* and *Malcolm X* had been replaced by *The Nutty Professor* as the feature film. And hard-core gangsta-rappers, *pre-dressed* in prison wear, scratched "black classical music" albums to create curse-ridden declarations of woman-hatred, the background music to drive-by shootings. I watched children that I'd delivered and taught graduate *into* the penitentiary instead of the university. Some died of crack overdoses and I buried them. This wiped the smile off my face.

Rastafarian dreadlocks, a specifically Afro-Caribbean spiritual hairstyle, became *the* measure of a black woman's blackness; yet they can (like the natural wig of the '60s) be purchased on silk strings at weaving salons, and some sisters refrained from performing spiritual head cleansings for fear of getting their hair wet. Soon even flaxen-haired white women began to wear them. At that point I no longer understood it; the symbolism was lost to me.

For sure, sweat popped out of my scalp when I experienced a complete break with reality in the person of a white Republican woman in a hot tub at my gym. She was fresh out of the military, and informed me emphatically that slavery happened because black people *needed* "a masochistic experience" and that "the Jewish holocaust *never really* happened!" I asked her "What happened to the belief that none of us is free until all of us are free?" She said *all that allness* was passé to a postmodern woman. I inhaled, smelled tar and feathers, and saw a modern KKKlan mother sitting in hot water with me. I thought she was crazy.

As we approached the end of somebody's millennium (not mine) the whole postmodern world seemed to be going crazy to me.

The Womanspirit Movement of the past decades had reclaimed a beautiful herstory and culture. But now I saw our contribution being usurped by exploitative and disrespectful cultural kleptocrats. Recovered Goddess images and indigenous body adornments such as Maori Moko, African nose rings, and Native American eagle feathers, usually awarded after a "rite of passage," became the purchased property of New Age dilettantes, so-called modern primitives, and gothic vampires.

And finally my heart was broken when pagan priestesses who had been my "sisters-in-struggle" in the Women's Spirituality movement referred to African spirituality in the negative and now chose the "Dark Goddess" as the scapegoat for their "sexual need" to sport whips, collars, and chains, the symbols of the slave-seller, the slavemaster, and the plantation overseer. I heard bloodhounds baying in the distance as the Promise Keepers, a conservative Christian men's international organization, promised to keep everyone in their "proper place."

Crazy with grief now, I ran off the road and took refuge in the forest, hoping to rest somewhere in an easy chair. But if I turned on the TV, read the paper, or opened e-mail I was again confronted with the encroaching foolishness of the " world outside."

I hid in the bushes and cried and I tried to forget that I had come here with a soul-purpose, with somewhere to go and something to do.

Kindred Lost and Found

In the midst of all these tears the drum sounded as ancestral figures rumbled in the bush. They rose up from under rocks; they came dancing from behind the trees. My kindred spirits. At first I did not recognize them in their multi-colored skins and spiritual traditions. But they dared to walk out of the wilderness with me, to accompany me on the road back to this place.

Now we take deep breaths as we enter this smoke-filled room. The herbs and flowers we smudge with come from equatorial rainforests where ancient trees, like us, have been burned by big business.

We hold our children on our laps, remembering those of *us* who stand in food stamp lines, duck bullets as we enter women's clinics, and run with our children from violent husbands and wives. We play the sacred drums and sing songs of freedom. Our voices ring louder than racial slurs, gender-class clichés, and politically correct half-truths.

We stand in a circle, hold hands, and call our ancestors from every direction, in every language. We dance for joy, for kinship, for peace. We dance for faith renewed. And we are happy to find each other, we who are still so crazy after all these tears.

seventy-five

"And Revolution Is Possible": Re-Membering the Vision of *This Bridge*

Randy P. L. Conner and David Hatfield Sparks

It is an unusually warm afternoon in Berkeley in October 2000. We've stopped to study in a café across the street from the main entrance to the university. We've been rereading *This Bridge Called My Back* and have been thinking about our memories of its emergence and our present reactions to it. We agree that to re-open *This Bridge* is for us reminiscent of Proust's indulging in madeleines.

To revisit *This Bridge* is to remember brisk wind, radiant light streaming into Victorian rooms, walls covered with posters, bookshelves overflowing with political and metaphysical texts, impassioned conversations with Gloria, Cherríe, and others living in a collective at 948 Noe Street in San Francisco, where *This Bridge* was compiled.

Revisiting *This Bridge* is to share once more Tex-Mex quesadillas and Indiana Shaker pie in our home on Noe Street, talking of our grandmothers—of Gloria's, a healer whose land had been stolen by whites; of David's, a suffragette who struggled against literary censorship and against the Indiana Ku Klux Klan; of Randy's, a midwife who defended her family and farm in Texas when the Klan arrived to "tar and feather" her socialist husband. At the Meatmarket Cafe and at Cafe Flore, we shared stories of the Vietnam period, of Gloria's brother badly injured; of

David's transformation from navy musician to anti-war activist, collective grocery worker, and gay father; of Randy's losing his job at the University of Texas after being grilled by the legislature for supporting gay rights and of his father's disowning him for being a conscientious objector, a "commie," and a "queer."

To revisit *This Bridge* is also to recall when we were asked to vacate our flat when lesbian separatists visited. While we recognized the need for women-only space, as we recognized the need for gay male space at events like Radical Faerie gatherings (roughly, gay men who frequently adhere to radical politics and "alternative" spiritual paths), we nevertheless resented being summarily dismissed, as men, from our own household, as if we were no different from William F. Buckley or John Wayne. We recall when Gloria's open friendship with us was challenged by separatists who refused to interact with men and when we were publicly shunned by a number of lesbians who privately befriended us. At times, this hypocrisy was difficult to bear.

Being shunned, as anyone who has endured this will know, is a very painful experience; it is hard to forget a sneer, eyes turned upward or downward so they will not meet yours, no response when you acknowledge the other's presence, a third party explaining that this person will not communicate with you because of your difference, or stepping silently into your friend's lodgings so that her separatist friends will not shun her as they have shunned you.

As *This Bridge* was being compiled, we were fighting for co-custody of Mariah after her new stepfather had told us we would never see her again. Many, including a woman lawyer, with little or no knowledge of Mariah's specific situation, insisted that she belonged with her mother. At a Gay Pride march to which we had brought Mariah, several Faeries with whom we were marching suddenly shouted "Breeders!" at us. Later, David was told by an older Faerie that he was not to be trusted because he had fathered a child; ironically, this individual had fathered children as well. Indeed, very few persons we knew other than Gloria and the Sisters of Perpetual Indulgence (an order of drag nuns) supported our struggle to share in the parenting of Mariah. (Who knew how fashionable queer parenthood would someday become!)

At the time of *This Bridge*'s publication, we still envisioned a revolution, one inspired by Marx and yet differing radically from prior revolutions. This revolution would bring about, hopefully without violence, a society no longer structured by economic class, gender, race/ethnicity, sexual orientation, physical ability, or religious affiliation; an America wherein individuality, diversity, and collectivity would be equally valued; in which indigenous and alternative spiritual traditions would nurture this pluralism while exposing the colonialist aspect of Christianity. We envisioned a society in which education would stress sharing over competition, enlightenment over career-building, community effort to improve the lives of others over academic isolationism. A culture in which the collective effort of communities would ensure an end to hunger, homelessness, lack of health care, political repression, and ecological disaster.[1]

We struggled with revolutionary concepts, attended meetings, marched in demonstrations. We read Marx and Malcolm X, Audre Lorde and Adrienne Rich, "Seth" and Carlos Castaneda. We explored spiritual paths, gravitating toward the pre-Christian European traditions of our own ancestors, the nagual shamanism and Basque spirituality of Gloria's ancestors, and—inspired by the women's spirituality movement—the reverence of goddesses of many cultures. We were certain of the multidimensionality of "reality," that "reality" embraces not only the material realm but also other realms of consciousness and spirit. We practiced divination, magic, and healing we learned from the Basque-American Tarot adept Angie Arrien, the Russian-American lesbian teacher Tamara Diaghilev, the Jewish-Wiccan priestess Starhawk, and others. We were especially inspired by the rich African-diasporic traditions Luisah Teish shared with us.

We assisted Gloria in organizing El Mundo Zurdo, a proto-multicultural reading series, at Small Press Traffic in San Francisco. This series nurtured the coming together of women, people of color, queer people, and others involved in the arts, including the poets Nellie Wong, Tede Matthews, and Maurice Kenny. Both El Mundo Zurdo and *This Bridge* challenged the radical movement as a whole to personalize its politics. They challenged us to examine and work through our prejudices. At a time when a majority of leftists insisted that atheism must accompany a radical political perspective, they challenged us to acknowledge and to celebrate the spiritual dimension of experience. For us, as gay males, *This Bridge* and El Mundo Zurdo encouraged us to acknowledge the key roles that women in general, and women of color in particular, had played in our own lives, as artistic and political comrades, kindred spirits, loving companions.

To revisit *This Bridge* is also to confront disillusionment.

In the years that followed *Bridge*'s publication, the dismantling and mainstreaming of the revolutionary movement(s)—due to governmental suppression, in-fighting, a desire to assimilate, and other factors—including the "McDonaldization" of the Soviet Union—left many of us feeling as if we had been betrayed by a lover or, as we might have phrased it two decades ago, been deserted by a comrade. Acknowledging the horrors of Stalinization, we had continued to hope that a democratic, visionary socialism might triumph over both Soviet-style totalitarianism and western capitalism. Now, in these days of "natural capitalism," this dream could not seem more remote.

Today's academics have largely exchanged Marx and community-building for Foucault and career-building. African-American statesman Colin Powell has endorsed presidential candidate George W. Bush, a Fundamentalist Christian and right-wing Republican. We are expected to vote for Al Gore as the "lesser of two evils." Actress and former radical activist Jane Fonda has allegedly been "born again." Mikhail Gorbachev performs in hamburger commercials and, like homophobic talk show host Dr. Laura Schlesinger, has been blessed by a Fundamentalist minister. Sinclair Lewis's and Margaret Atwood's dystopian visions in *It Can't Happen Here* and *The Handmaid's Tale* seem more plausible now than when they first appeared.

In such moments it seems that even the communities with which we once felt most intimately linked have abandoned many once-cherished values, chief among them being resistance to the status quo. Two decades ago, Pat Parker—with whom we shared brief, exhilarating conversations at Cafe La Boheme in San Francisco's Mission District—insisted—in one of the most potent essays in *This Bridge*, "Revolution: It's Not Neat or Pretty or Quick"—that we'd "had too many years of media madness" equating "'revolutionary eye make-up'" with revolution itself (240). We imagine how disheartened Pat might be to learn that fashion, youth, muscles, ideal weight, wealth, and sex toys now number among the most consuming passions of the queer and women's communities, when the "courage to be rich" has obscured the courage to resist. Pat also insisted on resistance to participation in the U.S. military. Today, many women, people of color, and queer people are devoting their energies toward overcoming the final barriers to full participation in the armed forces. While in recent years many voices have rallied against the homophobic "don't ask, don't tell" policy instituted by the Clinton administration, few have challenged the military per se as an institution entrenched in patriarchal, colonialist ideology.

Pat insisted as well upon the destruction of the nuclear family, as it remains "the basic unit of capitalism." "In order for us to move to revolution it has to be destroyed. And I mean destroyed" (242). While it might seem that many queer people are presently seeking to emulate the institution of the nuclear family, we feel strongly, after having thought about the issues for several years, that partnerships of two persons of the same sex or gender, or partnerships involving transgendered persons, together, in some cases, with the children they parent, represent a considerable challenge to traditional definitions of both marriage and the nuclear family. As partners and parents for more than two decades, we believe that queer and transgendered unions and families should be granted legal status. We also believe, however, that queer people and others must continue to develop visionary models of loving and parenting.

When we look toward our daughter and our extended family, our cynicism is somewhat lessened. Mariah, now in her late twenties, performs in plays, attends college, works at a grocery collective, and lives with her companion, Prado Gomez, a transgendered Apache/Chicano social activist, AIDS educator, and performer. Recently, our family has been involved in Gomez's recognition of his FTM identity, including his surgery and recovery. We are very thankful to have participated in this process; most important, we have witnessed Gomez's joy in being able to express himself more freely. Together, Gomez and Mariah are raising Jessica, who is now twelve. Mariah feels very fortunate to have experienced the presence of Gloria and other strong, political, spiritual, and artistic women in her life as she transited from childhood to adulthood, including having been instructed in drama—when she was a teenager and young adult—by Cherríe, who encouraged her to become an actor. While geographical distance and other concerns have resulted in her feeling somewhat abandoned by the strong women of her childhood, Mariah's creativity, compassion, and fierce independence owe much to the influence of Gloria and others.

With Mariah, we have written a book on queer spirituality, *Cassell's Encyclopedia of Queer Myth, Symbol, and Spirit*. Our book, for which Gloria has written the foreword, traces sacred beliefs and practices of same-sex love and gender diversity across many cultures and epochs. This book was conceived at 948 Noe, after Gloria placed a note under our door one night, as was her custom: "So . . . is there a gay/queer spirituality?"

Within our own extended family and within our community of friends, it seems—despite our moments of cynicism—that many people seem more at ease these days with inter-ethnic intimacy, same-sex relationships, and gender diversity. As Pat Parker insisted and as we continue to believe, only when persons of varying ethnicities, genders, and sexual identities—the inhabitants of Gloria's "borderlands," of El Mundo Zurdo—struggle together in alliance against oppression will revolution truly commence. Recently, in conversing with our close friend Susan Green, a musician, filmmaker, and environmental activist who works closely with the Hopi, it struck us that the coming-into-being of non-traditional families like our own bears a relationship to the current formation of alliances among diverse groups struggling for social justice and against the policies of the WTO and other organizations that threaten the well-being of workers, animals (as in the fur, meat, and pharmaceutical industries), and the environment.

Likewise, an earth-based spirituality movement that emerged at the time of *This Bridge*'s publication, illuminated by Teish, Tamara, Starhawk, Alice Walker (we recall Shug's sermon in *The Color Purple*), and others, continues to inspire us. This spirituality embraces indigenous, shamanistic, and goddess-revering traditions, nurtures collective effort to ameliorate life on the earth, and insists upon political opposition to forces of oppression. In *This Bridge*, Gloria speaks of the need to reclaim a "spirituality that has been hidden in the hearts of oppressed people under layers of centuries of traditional god-worship. It emerges from under the veils of La Virgen de Guadalupe and unrolls from Yemayá's ocean waves whenever we need to be uplifted from or need the courage to face the tribulations of a racist patriarchal world" (195).

In recent years, earth-based spirituality has been criticized on the grounds that it appropriates beliefs and practices from various cultures in a colonizing manner. Certainly, we must exercise extreme caution when adopting others' cultural traditions. While it is crucial to respect teachers who confine their sharing of wisdom to others of the same cultural background, we have been blessed to know spiritual teachers like Luisah Teish who are willing to share their wisdom with people of diverse heritage. Also in recent years, especially among academic feminists, reductionist attempts to denigrate and dismantle goddess reverence—and particularly to attack the work of archaeologist Marija Gimbutas—have become highly fashionable—while critiques of patriarchal religions have diminished profoundly. Perhaps the only spiritual traditions that today experience greater vilification than goddess reverence are African-based traditions such as Vodou, Santería, and the Yoruba religion, although this demonization most typically occurs in such horror films as *The Believers, Angel Heart*, and *The Serpent and the Rainbow* rather than in academic texts. In spite of such trends, however, traditions such as those we practice continue to grow stronger, as successive generations embark upon journeys of healing, creativity, and transformation.

In solitude and together with others, we honor the divine, the ancestors (biological and spiritual), animals, the earth, and our bodies. Each morning and evening, we carry out the simplest of rites with candles, incense, and water to honor the gods and spirits. In San Francisco, we have gathered with thousands of others to celebrate the Celtic holiday of Samhain by joining in a great spiral dance. In San Francisco, Los Angeles, San Antonio, and Austin, we've joined with Latinos and others to commemorate the dead during the ancient festival of the Día de los Muertos. In New Orleans, we've paid homage with Priestess Miriam Chamani to the lwas of Vodou, particularly to Ezili, goddess of love and the arts. This past summer, we celebrated the pre-Christian festival of the summer solstice with a myriad others in the streets of Paris.

We believe that the practice of an earth-based spirituality such as this, when linked to the forging of diverse intimacies and alliances, to community involvement, and to the creation and study of revolutionary works of art like *This Bridge*, may kindle in us a new vision of cultural transformation. In Gloria's words, "Change requires. . . . the alchemist and the welder, the magician and the laborer, the witch and the warrior"(*Bridge*, 196).

We will always treasure—as we cherish the inkwell, cup, quilt, button collection of our grandmothers —the experience of witnessing the birth of *This Bridge*. While we miss our nightly jaunts with Gloria, we look forward to carrying on our conversation with her at Cafe Pergolesi, or walking along the beach at Santa Cruz. We are grateful to have lived with her in a vortex of revolutionary fervor. We will always remember the women of *This Bridge* who did not shun us for being different, but who befriended us in the face of opposition, sharing Gloria's belief in the vision of El Mundo Zurdo, of honoring diversity in the borderlands. We pray that the hibernating bear may soon awaken, that the butterfly free itself from the cocoon, that the spirits of the tempest will vanquish apathy and cynicism and stir in us once more a passion for radical metamorphosis. "And revolution is possible," Pat Parker's spirit reminds us.

Note

1.This essay was written in October 2000, prior to the terrorist attack in the United States and the ensuing war in Afghanistan. We wish to make it clear that we do not look upon the destruction of innocent human beings—either by way of "guerilla" methods such as those used by the terrorists in New York or any bomb-girded martyrs, or by the use of imperialist/colonialist methods such as the destruction of Palestinian communities by Israelis or the killing of innocent civilians in Afghanistan by the U.S. military—as constituting acceptable revolutionary action.

seventy-six

Witch Museum

Alicia Gaspar de Alba

Long after Christianity had come, witchcraft survived in secret. On the Witch's Sabbath, the covens of thirteen would gather around their magic nine-foot circle, the fire would be lit beneath the cauldron, the scourge and pentacle and atham—the black-handled sacrificial knife—would appear and the ancient ritual invoking the evil one would begin.
　　　　　　　—Postcard of the Sabbat Circle at the Salem Witch Museum

I.
Fork up $2.75
and gather 'round
this scarlet Sabbat circle
inscribed with names all
witches worship, as you know.

　　　　Ashtaroth
Astarte　　　　　　Baphomet
Beelzebub　　　　　　　Asmodeus
　　　Lucifer Rex

If you're innocent
or just curious as a cat
with lives to spare
take your coat off,
have a seat (but don't
let foot or finger touch
the magic symbols if you know
what's good for you).
Twenty
minutes of the past
won't kill you.

Watch the story come back to life
in thirteen
Techno Sight and Sound
individually fired-up
scenes, latest concept
in witch museums.

II.
In France, a whirl of autumn
leaves makes girls
cry out "les sorcieres!"

In a northern province
of Argentina old women
step out of their houses
and talk to the wind:
"ya van cuatro tardes de viento,"
they say, and the wind
whistles their names
through the holes
of the cardos, petrified
sentinels of cactus
that line the crooked streets
of their solitude.

Where I come from
the wind is more alive
than the people's memory,
the border
between life and death
is called the Rio Bravo
and sand spinning
in the desert
a sure sign
of dust devils
come to drag you
out of your bed
at night,
come to feast
on the bones of the girls
in blue smocks,
three hundred head women
and counting.

No gift shops,
no souvenir Norwegian witches
or scarlet circles to manifest
the presence of those
who have never left.

Wind and leaf and sand are enough
if all we need is to be reminded.

seventy-seven

Forging El Mundo Zurdo: Changing Ourselves, Changing the World

AnaLouise Keating

The "no-man's-land" Bridge named can be a territory for dialogical and intercultural encounters, where particular individuals in all their historical and cultural embeddedness may find Others about whom they care enough to reach across unimaginable gulfs of difference. Here, in the creation of a "Third Space," . . . the invisible edges, frames, or frontiers established by normalized discourse could become suddenly visible and negotiable.

—Helene Shulman Lorenz

I am because we are. Without expecting sameness.

—Susan Guerra

When I first read *This Bridge*, over ten years ago, I was struck by contributors' repeated attempts to forge alliances and coalitions that do not ignore differences among women (and in many instances men) but instead use difference as a catalyst for personal and social transformation. Entering into the "unimaginable gulfs of difference" between self and other, they make visible the previously "invisible edges, frames, [and] frontiers" that divide us. Their willingness to actively engage in open conversations about differences enables them to insist on commonalities without assuming that their experiences, histories, ideas, or traits are *identical* with those of others. Instead, commonalities indicate complex points of connection that negotiate among sameness, similarity, and difference—a potent mixture brewed from all three.

This negotiation represents a radical departure from conventional practices. We've been trained to define differences oppositionally—as deviations from what Audre Lorde terms the *"mythical norm,* which . . . [i]n america . . . is usually defined as white, thin, male, young, heterosexual, christian, and financially secure" (*Sister,* 116, her emphasis)–and to regard these differences as shameful marks of inferiority. Driven by our fear of difference-as-deviation, we ignore, deny, and misname the differences among us. We hide our differences beneath a facade of sameness and erect rigid boundaries between self and other. But these differences don't go away just because we reject them. They grow stronger as we seek refuge behind stereotypes, monolithic labels, and false assumptions of sameness.

Risking great openness, *Bridge* authors expose the stereotypes, split open the labels, and challenge the false assumptions of sameness. They demonstrate that it's not differences that divide us but rather our refusal to openly discuss the differences among us. Thus, for example, in her letter to Barbara Smith, Mirtha Quintanales draws parallels between her experiences as an "essentially middle-class (and white-skinned woman)" immigrant from Cuba and the experiences of women identified as "black," "Third World," "white, poor, and working-class." While admitting that she "cannot presume to know what it is really like to be a Black woman in America, to be racially oppressed, . . . [or] to grow up American 'White Trash' and destitute" (152), she resists generalizations and stereotypes based on these labels and calls for new forms of unity that acknowledge the differences among us. Instead of denying these differences, she accepts and explores them: she opens herself to the lives of these others, allows herself imaginatively to feel their conflicts and pain, and uses this empathy and openness as pathways to explore possible points of connection.

This quest for commonalities culminates in Gloria E. Anzaldúa's concept of El Mundo Zurdo, the "Left-Handed World," a visionary place where people from diverse backgrounds with diverse needs and concerns co-exist and work together to bring about revolutionary change. As she asserts in "La Prieta": "We are the queer groups, the people that don't belong anywhere, not in the dominant world nor completely within our own respective cultures. Combined we cover so many oppressions. But the overwhelming oppression is the collective fact that we do not fit, and because we do not fit, *we are a threat*" (209, her emphasis). Anzaldúa replaces the oppositional definitions of difference I referred to above with a relational approach. She acknowledges that inhabitants of El Mundo Zurdo are not all alike; their specific oppressions, solutions, and beliefs are different, yet she insists that "these different affinities are not opposed to each other. In El Mundo Zurdo I with my own affinities and my people with theirs can live together and transform the planet" (209). Joined by their rejection of the status quo and their so-called deviation from the dominant culture, inhabitants of El Mundo Zurdo use their sense of difference to forge new alliances.

Anzaldúa's vision of El Mundo Zurdo grows from her radical "spiritual activism."[1] Unlike conventional religion, which relies on external standards and authorities, this spiritual activism has its source within the individual, an individual scarred by oppressive contacts with those s/he encounters. As Anzaldúa explains in her preface to "El Mundo Zurdo: The Vision," the final section of *This Bridge*, "We, the women here, take a trip back into the self, travel to the deep core of our roots to discover and reclaim our colored souls, our rituals, our religion. We reach a spirituality that has been hidden in the hearts of oppressed people under layers of traditional god-worship. . . . Our spirituality does not come from outside ourselves. It emerges when we listen to the 'small still voice' (Teish) within us which can empower us to create actual change in the world" (195).

Drawing on her indigenous beliefs, Anzaldúa develops what I have elsewhere described as a metaphysics of interconnectedness that posits a cosmic, constantly changing spirit or force that embodies itself in diverse material and nonmaterial forms. As she states in a 1982 interview with Christine Weiland, "[S]pirit exists in everything; therefore God, the divine, is in everything—in blacks as well as whites, rapists as well as victims; it's in the tree, the swamp, the sea. . . . Some people call it 'God'; some call it the 'creative force,' whatever. It's in everything" (*Interviews/Entrevistas,* 100).

I want to emphasize the pragmatic dimensions of the spirituality Anzaldúa describes. She enacts an alternate mode of perception, a holistic way of viewing ourselves and our world that breaks down self/other divisions and empowers individuals to work for psychic and material change on both personal and collective levels. On the personal level, her belief in an underlying constantly changing cosmic energy allowed her to develop a highly positive self-image that affirms her personal agency and enables her to resist the various forms of oppression she experienced both from the dominant culture and from her own culture. On the collective level, Anzaldúa's belief in a divine cosmic force infusing all that exists enables her to create a new identity category and a theoretical, ethical framework for social change. Positing a universal commonality, she can insist that—despite the many differences among us—we are all interconnected. As she explains in a 1991 interview, she believes that we are "almas afines," or "kindred spirits," and share an interconnectedness that could serve as "an unvoiced category of identity, a common factor in all life forms" (*Interviews/Entrevistas,* 164).

Replacing the "mythical norm" that defines "difference" as "deviation" with this unvoiced identity category, Anzaldúa creates a context for relational understandings of differences. Significantly, she does not deny the validity of each individual's experiences, beliefs, and desires. Instead, she views the individual as part of a larger whole and insists on a commonality shared by all things—no matter how different they appear to be, no matter how different they *are*. This faith in our underlying commonality infuses Anzaldúa's vision of El Mundo Zurdo. Viewed from this broader perspective, differences become less threatening. We don't need to break the world into rigid categories and hide behind masks of sameness which demand that we define ourselves in opposition to others. We can trust that, despite the many differences among us, we are all interconnected.[2] Sharing our differences through open-hearted listening, we can seek commonalities.

I am drawn to this vision of El Mundo Zurdo; it intoxicates me. But I don't live there, nor do I know anyone who does. And I wonder. . . . How do we enter into, how do we create, this visionary place where difference functions not to exclude but as a catalyst for community-building and change?

Changing Myself, Changing the World?

Near the end of "La Prieta" Anzaldúa makes the following confession: *"The pull between what is and what should be. I believe that by changing ourselves we change the world, that traveling El Mundo Zurdo path is the path of a two-way movement—a going deep into the self and an expanding out into the world, a simultaneous recreation of the self and a reconstruction of society. And yet, I am confused as to how to accomplish this"*(208). I, too, am confused about how to accomplish this task, how to materialize this visionary place. But like Anzaldúa, I believe that it entails a simultaneous two-way movement, that by changing ourselves (by changing myself), we/I can change the world.

And so, I begin with myself. I can't offer pronouncements on how we can transform the world, or even how you can transform yourself. But I can tell you about my own efforts to engage in this two-way movement. I am a mother, a writer, a teacher. These relational identities give me specific locations where I can begin working for change—today . . . in my home, in the written word, in the classroom. I've developed the following premises, which I attempt to embody throughout my life.

1. First, and most important, I've used this metaphysics of interconnectedness to design my own form of spiritual activism. Although I don't always see and feel it when I look at the world, I believe that we're all interconnected—materially and spiritually. As Inés Hernández-Ávila states (in this volume), "We are related to all that lives." This radical interrelatedness gives us—gives me—a responsibility to meet those I encounter with a sense of openness: my protective boundaries between self and other become permeable, begin breaking down. Exploring the differences between us, I seek commonalities between your experiences and mine. Empathy—the willingness to imaginatively enter your life through reading, through conversation, through storytelling—is crucial to this search. When "I" empathize with "you," I enact a relational form of thinking, a back-and-forth movement. Immersing myself in your stories, I listen without judging, I listen with open heart and open mind. I travel into your emotions, desires, and experiences, then return to my own. But in the return, I am changed by my encounter with you, and I begin recognizing the commonalities we share.

2. *Language has tremendous psychic and material power.* Like Anthony Appiah, I believe that "[S]ticks and stones may break our bones, but words—words that evoke structures of oppression, exploitation, and brute physical threat—can break souls" (43), and so I choose my words with great care. Language, belief, perception, and action are all intimately interrelated. The words we use shape what we perceive, which in turn shapes how we act. Language's creative power requires that I think carefully and thoroughly about the possible effects my words might have and the effects I desire. Since my goal is to awaken a sense of our radical interconnectedness, I try to use words that energize this perception. Whenever appropriate, I use inclusionary language and, as I'll demonstrate below, I do not identify people by categories unless the categories are relevant to the conversation.

3. *Categories and labels, although sometimes necessary, can prevent us from recognizing our interconnectedness with others.* As Andrea Canaan notes, "[T]he enemy is brownness and whiteness, maleness and femaleness. The enemy is our urgent need to stereotype and close off people, places, and events into isolated categories. . . . We close off avenues of communication and vision so that individual and communal trust, responsibility, loving, and knowing are impossible" (236). Whether we identify as "of color" or "white," we have *all* been trained to evaluate ourselves and each other according to existing identity categories. However, when we automatically label people by color or gender (or sexuality or religion or any other politically-charged characteristics and/or assumed differences, for that matter), we build walls and isolate ourselves from those we've labeled "different." These categories distort our perceptions, creating arbitrary divisions among us and an oppositional "us" against "them" mentality that prevents us from recognizing potential commonalities. Identity categories based on inflexible labels establish and police boundaries—boundaries that shut us in with those we've deemed "like" "us" and boundaries that shut us out from those whom we assume to be different.

4. *Out of all the categories we today employ, "race" is the most destructive.* "Race" is, for sure, one of the "master's tools," one of the most insidious tools of all. We've been trained to classify and evaluate ourselves and those we meet according to racialized appearances: we look at a per-

son's body, classify her, insert him into a category, make generalizations, and base our interactions on these racialized assumptions. These assumptions rely on and reinforce monolithic, divisive stereotypes that erase the incredible diversity within each individual and within each so-called "race." But racial categories are not—and never have been—benign; rather, they were developed by those in power (generally property-owning men of Northern European descent) to create a hierarchy that grants privilege and power to specific groups of people while simultaneously oppressing and excluding others. Racialized categories originated in histories of oppression, exclusion, land theft, body theft, soul theft, physical/psychic murder, and other crimes against specific groups of human beings. These categories were motivated by economics and politics, by insecurity and greed—not by innate biological or divinely-created differences. When we refer to "race" or to specific "races" we are drawing on and therefore reinforcing this violent history as well as the "white" supremacism buttressing the entire system.

5. *"Race" and racism are inextricably related.* We can't talk about one without also talking about the other. "Race" is built on and out of the oppressive history referred to above, and this fact must be acknowledged whenever I talk, write, or teach about "race."

These are my premises today, as I type these words. I'm sure they'll change in the coming years, but I work with what I know. Now I'll tell you about some of the ways I try to live out my beliefs.

My daughter, Jamitrice, was born in 1995 into a highly racialized world. Like the rest of us, she will encounter many messages designed to reinforce the oppressive belief in natural, god-given "races." While I can't prevent her from receiving these messages, I can invite her to question them and to recognize their tremendous limitations. At this point she's only five, not old enough to understand this racialized system. As Marguerite A. Wright explains, "Young children are developmentally inclined to treat people based on their character, as revealed by their actions, rather than on the color of their skin. As they grow older, this wonderful quality is lost to many of them as they learn some of the racial bigotry of previous generations" (261). Jamitrice still exists in this pre-racialized space, but I know the day will come when she'll leave it and enter—with her "new awareness (more accurately, acquired illusions)" (Wright, 196)—the "racial bigotry" we all inherit from our teachers, our classmates, the books we read, the TV shows we watch. In a few years, she'll ask me, "Mama, what am I?"—meaning "What's my 'race'?" Drawing on my belief in language's power to shape perception, I'll choose my words with great care and tell her our family stories—her grandparents and great-grandparents from Africa, China, England, Ireland, and

Spain. Because she needs to understand the systemic role racism plays in restricting our lives, as I tell her these stories I'll subtly point out the differences: our ancestors from Africa, China, and (to a lesser degree) Ireland experienced greater hardships because of their appearances and nationalities than those who immigrated from England and Spain. But I won't tell her "what" she is. I won't label her "Latina" or "black" or "white" (although I suppose any of these categories are accurate—since she has two grandparents from Panama, well more than one drop of African "blood," and extremely pale skin in the winter).

Even now, in our conversations or whenever she might be listening, I do not name people by "race." It's never "the 'white' woman" or "the Chicano" or the "Chinese-American boy" but rather "the lady in the red dress," "the man walking the dog," "the little boy in the green shirt." I offer my daughter a different way of perceiving herself and others, one deemphasizing "race." In this way, I challenge the conventional U.S. reading practice that encourages us to identify the bodies we encounter according to "race," defined simplistically by obvious physical differences. As I've just suggested, there *are* other ways to label people, when labels are necessary.

At a larger level, I attempt to instruct my daughter into what I'm calling a metaphysics of interconnectedness. She has not yet erected self-enclosed boundaries, and I try to nurture her intuitive sense of interrelatedness by demonstrating the many ways we're connected to others—not just to other humans (even those who don't look like us) but to everything around us, to animals, to the trees, to the water we drink. I use storytelling to encourage her to make imaginative leaps and draw parallels between her own emotions, experiences, desires and those of others.

As a writer, I try to shake—and sometimes even smash—the categories, demonstrating the limitations in the labels. I write about topics like this one, I challenge my readers (like I'm challenging you) to educate themselves about the history of racism and "race." I work on anthologies like the one you're reading right now. I put "race," "whiteness," and "white" (and sometimes also "black") in quotation marks to underscore their artificial nature. Simultaneously, I attempt to expose the "white" supremacy, as well as the economic causes and effects, behind and beneath racial labels. I emphasize the limitations in categorizing people by "race," and I interrogate recent developments in "whiteness" studies, especially the calls for positive "white" identities. Because "whiteness" and the concept of "white" people plays a crucial role in generating and maintaining a hierarchical, racist worldview, the construction of positive "white" identities inadvertently but inevitably supports this already-existing system. As Ian F. Haney López asserts, "Whiteness exists as the lynchpin for the systems of racial meaning in the United States. Whiteness is the norm around which other races are constructed; its existence depends upon the mythologies and material inequalities that sustain the current racial system. . . . Its continuation also requires the preservation of the social inequalities that every day testify to White superiority" (187).

As a teacher, I adopt a fluid both/and perspective that attempts to move beyond "race" while acknowledging the powerful roles it plays in our cultures and lives. Language, of course, is crucial and the trick is to talk about "race" in ways that do not trigger and thus reinforce the racial scripts my students have been trained to read. I continue using racialized categories but use them in new ways designed to wrench them from their previous usages and expose the arbitrary nature of racialized divisions. More specifically, I have developed for myself the following tactics.

1. I organize my teaching around this metaphysics of interconnectedness, and challenge self/other divisions based on "race" and other inflexible categories of difference. Whether teaching first-year composition, surveys of U.S. literature, women's studies, or graduate seminars, I introduce students to a variety of ethnic-, gender-, and class-inflected worldviews and emphasize that identities are shaped relationally—by personal, cultural, and historical issues. I structure assignments and discussions in ways that require students to grapple with these conflicting yet overlapping worldviews. I encourage them to draw connections between their own experiences and those of others, connections that do not overlook differences but rather use these differences to generate complex commonalities. By thus exposing them to a variety of perspectives and training them to examine multiple overlapping worldviews, I attempt to begin breaking down the divisions they've drawn between "self" and "other," between "us" and "them."

Reading plays a crucial role in this boundary-dissolving endeavor. When we read, we travel into the worlds of others. Even if these journeys are always partial, always incomplete, they can still be transformational. As they travel into the lives of their "others," students enact shifts in perception that expand their worldviews, enabling them to identify with those whom they had assumed were entirely different from themselves.

2. I delay racialization. I don't mention "race" first but rather begin with apparently general topics like "the American dream," "social protest," and "masculinity" then move into discussions about how "race" and other category differences influence these concerns. (Even when teaching courses that include "race"/ethnicity in the titles—like Latina/Chicana Authors or Native American Women Writers—I challenge students' stereotyped perceptions in ways I explain below.) For almost ten years I taught at an open-admissions medium-sized comprehensive university attended primarily by first-generation, working-class students who identify as "Hispanic" and "white." Because many believed that a college degree would enable them to advance economically, I found that organizing composition courses thematically, around issues related to the American dream, provided an effective entry into explorations of complex commonalities and differences. Generally, my students were firm believers in what Peggy McIntosh and others call the "myth of meritocracy." This belief—which maintains that the United States is a free democratic country where anything is possible and all doors will open to those who work hard—makes students callous and judgmental: they blame the individual for his or her failure to succeed. Focusing on the American dream enabled me to challenge this condescending belief. As students entered into the stories (the "American dreams") of individuals marked by "race" and other negatively-charged categories, they began recognizing how racism, sexism, and other forms of oppressive discrimination impede attempts to achieve success.

3. *I historicize and denaturalize "race."* When I (finally) mention "race," I do so in ways designed to challenge the belief in permanent monolithic "races." Like the larger U.S. culture in which they live, my students generally assume that "race" is an unchanging biological and divine fact, based on natural divisions among people. By historicizing "race," and by exposing the fluidity in racial designations, I demonstrate the limitations in this simplistic view. Take, for example, that notorious binary between the so-called "black" and "white" "races." Though we view them as permanent, transhistorical racial markers indicating distinct groups of people, they are not. In fact, the Puritans and other early European colonizers didn't consider themselves "white"; they identified as "Christian," "English," or "free," for at that time the word *white* did not represent a racial category. Racialization was economically and politically motivated. It was not until around 1680, with the racialization of slavery, that the term was used to describe a specific group of people. Significantly, then, the "white race" evolved in opposition to but simultaneously with the "black race." As peoples whose specific ethnic identities were Yoruban, Ashanti, Fon, and Dahomean were forcibly removed from their homes in Africa and taken to the North American colonies, the English adopted the terms *white* and *black*—with their already-existing implications of purity and evil—and developed the concept of a superior "white race" and an inferior "black race" to justify slavery.

Sometimes I use my own body and family history to expose and erode students' stereotyped binary perceptions. I draw on my African ancestry, the heinous one-drop rule the U.S. government and "white" people used to reinforce racial divisions and deny people of African descent basic rights, and identify myself as "black." I briefly inform students about my own family background—my grandmothers who tried to "pass" into "whiteness," the material benefits they accrued, the family losses they suffered. Since for much of the year I probably don't look "black," this self-naming also challenges my students to reflect on their assumptions about "race," and does so without reinforcing the existing stereotypes. Emphasizing that my family's history is not unique, I inform them that during the past three hundred years, many thousands of people have "passed" from "blackness" into "whiteness." I urge them to take this fact even further and recognize that our national history of passing means that many people now considered "white" are, in truth, actually of mixed descent. As Shirlee Taylor Haizlip notes, "Some geneticists have said that 95 percent of 'white' Americans have widely varying degrees of black heritage. . . . [and] 75 percent of all African-Americans have at least one white ancestor and 15 percent have predominantly white blood lines" (15).

My goal here is to reveal the limitations in the racial scripts students employ when they read—racial scripts presenting "race" as a permanent, monolithic component of each person's identity—and to pluralize "race" by emphasizing that all racialized identities take diverse forms. When students encounter information concerning the historical shifts and transformations in identity categories, they must reexamine their own preconceptions, as well as social representations of "race" and other categories.

4. *Whenever I talk about "race," I connect it with "whiteness" and racism, for these concepts are interlocking and interrelated.* As I've already stated, the history of "race" is a history of violent oppression on multiple levels. Generally, however, my students (of all colors) are unaware of this brutal history and the hierarchical dominant/subordinate worldview it relies on and reinforces. Nor do they realize the insidious role "whiteness" plays in buttressing this racist system. It's difficult to explore these issues in the classroom without inadvertently triggering solipsistic guilt in students who identify as "white" or complex mixtures of anger, shame, and pain in those who don't. These reactions aren't acceptable, for they reduce systemic racism to the personal, prevent "white"-identified students from acting, support already-existing stereotypes of "race," and replicate the hierarchical status quo. Moreover, these reactions ignore how "whiteness" serves as the unacknowledged framework, a framework affecting (poisoning) us all.

No matter how we identify—whether as "Hispanic," "Mexican," "Anglo," "American," "black," "white," and so forth—we all, to varying degrees, have learned to think, read, and act in "white" ways. We have internalized what Anzaldúa describes as a "white" "frame of reference" (*Interviews/Entrevistas*, 252). I want to assist students of all colors in developing an ethics of accountability that enables them more fully to comprehend how these oppressive racialized systems that began in the historical past continue misshaping contemporary conditions. Only then can they begin working for social change. But to do so, they first must recognize the constructed nature of "whiteness" and, more generally, of "race" as a whole.[3]

No two students, no two classes, are the same. Each class I teach is somewhat different, filled with students who have their own particular histories, beliefs, desires, and concerns. And so I modify and add to these tactics every semester, tailoring them to meet my students' specific experiences.

Taking Risks, Transforming Walls Into Thresholds

As I suggested in the introduction to this anthology, we're living in a place/time of nepantla: exiting from the old worldview, we have not yet entered or created new ones to replace it. We're questioning the barriers that divide us, and yet even as we acknowledge their limitations we cling to the labels and claim the power of self-naming in the face of erasure. In this essay I've shared my belief that a recognition of our radical interconnectedness offers one way to negotiate the divisions between "us" and "them," between "self" and "other."

Lest I be misunderstood, let me emphasize: this focus on spiritual activism, on a metaphysics of interconnectedness, must not be conflated with escapism. The spiritual components of life *cannot* be divorced from politics, sexuality, writing, or daily living. As Anzaldúa states in her introduction to "El Mundo Zurdo: The Vision," *Bridge*'s final section, "The vision of our spirituality provides us with no trap door solution, no escape hatch tempting us to 'transcend' our struggle. We must act in the everyday world. Words are not enough. We must perform visible and public acts that might make us more vulnerable to the very oppressions we are fighting against. But, our vulnerability *can* be the source of our power—**if we use it**" (195, her emphasis).

In part, this vulnerability requires that we let down our guard, relax some of the many defenses we've erected to shore up our fragile sense of self and protect ourselves from harm. We've been battered, in very different ways, by racism, sexism, classism, homophobia, and other forms of physical/psychic oppression and abuse. Identity politics has been extremely useful: we've invented and found specific names and labels that affirm us, give us self-confidence, agency, a sense of belonging, a place to call "home." But at some point—no matter how effective these labels seem to be—**they will fail us**. They will be walls rather than doorways.

Vulnerability—the willingness to occasionally let go of the labels—transforms these walls into thresholds. Differences don't go away . . . nor should they. But if we posit a shared factor of identity (call it "Spirit," call it "Soul," call it what you will), we can be open to the differences among us. Through conversation, through exchanging stories, through exploring our differences without defensiveness or shame, we can learn from each other, share each other's words. As we do so, we'll begin forging commonalities. Perhaps we'll even say, with Susan Guerra, "*I am because we are. Without expecting sameness.*"

Sure, we'll make mistakes. Hell, I'll bet I've made some in this essay. But to learn about each other, to grow closer, to create El Mundo Zurdo, we must take this risk.

Notes

Thanks to Gloria E. Anzaldúa for encouraging me to write this essay and for commenting insightfully on earlier drafts, to Caridad Souza for our conversations about this metaphysics of interconnectedness, and to Catherine Green, Lynda Hall, and Deborah Miranda for provocative comments on earlier drafts.

1. I discuss Anzaldúa's spiritual activism in the introduction to *Interviews/Entrevistas*.

2. This process of working with differences while exploring commonalities is incredibly complex, and merits a much longer discussion. In fact, it's my next project once this anthology is completed. For one example of this complex negotiation, see my "Back to the Mother? Feminist Mythmaking with a Difference."

3. For specific examples of how I assist students in recognizing the constructed nature of "whiteness" and "race," see my essay "Exposing 'Whiteness,' Unreading 'Race.'"

seventy-eight

In the Presence of Spirit(s): A Meditation on the Politics of Solidarity and Transformation

Inés Hernández-Ávila

I sit at my computer to write this essay, and I find myself constantly getting up to water the vegetable garden wash clothes hang them talk to my animalitos go for a bike ride, musing, musing, musing, wondering about my words, wanting spirit to speak through me, to take over.

She suddenly realizes she must shed her clothes, her masks, her layers, peel off the professor, mother, grandmother, cultural worker, woman, Nimipu (Nez Perce) woman from the north, India MexicanaTejana from the south, friend, lover, wife, human being, all of them, even though they are all her. As she peels, she weeps softly at the releasing, and she hears the drums beat, her heart beat, she hears a voice singing in the distance, calling her, and her tears well up the world. Tears of recognition, for her spirit, the spirit of all life, the spirit of love for the universe. The voice she hears singing is her own.

What does her spirit have to say?

Ancestors, the good ancestors from the beginning of time to the present, the ones who've gone ahead, the ones who were consumed in violence not of their making, in sickness often passed on through the generations, the children who passed on too early, the ones who had the chance to love and lead full lives, in the Spirit world, they are the light(ness) we need to see and feel. Theirs are the voices we need to hear with the ears of the heart. Theirs are the messages we should welcome with our intuition's blessing, and they are the ones who illuminate our work within and between our respective communities.

One of the elders I most respect, Maria Teresa Mejía Martinez, from the Conchero dance tradition of Mexico City, has counseled me, for times of crisis, or simply for when I'm doing my work, "Mija, entrégate a las ánimas. Entrégate, mija, y verás." My daughter, give yourself over to the spirits. Give yourself over, my daughter, and you will see. Las ánimas. Our loved ones who have crossed over into spirit, family, mentors, exemplary ones, those who understand how body/heart/mind/spirit can intimately connect, those who give inspiration for their courage, wisdom, dignity, honor, those who were activists on the front lines of justice struggles, and those who lived and gifted goodness, who gifted love.

They are the ones unrestrained by physical bodies, and so they see everything, beyond where our eyes could possibly take us, they have all the information we need to go forward alert and conscious. We hold them dear in our heart's memory, and they open paths of miracles for us. They are the ones we often visit in the land of dreams. They speak to us in signs, in songs that emerge suddenly during just-waking moments, in the swoop of a red-tailed hawk, the strut of a cat with attitude, the dancing smile of a stranger, the discovery of grace in our bodies, in the cherished calm of alone-time, in the precise second that we avert a completely planned action or proceed with an utterly unexpected one, every time we realize how precious and how short our embodied time is on this earth.

It's hard to be a human being and deeply painful to be conscious. The alternative? Death in life unconscious energy wasted dispersed como hoja al viento spent for nothing frustrated sickened. To care, to love with every part of our wondrous selves, with the memory of every palpable cell of our beings. To reach out embracing life, in honor of all that is good, beautiful, sensual, just, brave, wise, funny. Yes, funny, in honor of life-giving humor. Amoridolor, un difrasismo inventado hace muchos años por algunos de nosotros en Tejas. Love-and-pain entwined intimately as one loving truly loving knows.

The grandmothers make a decision. They call for a gathering. Women from all the directions make preparations for the journey. They make sure things are taken care of in the everyday world. They know the time has come. This is the message the grandmothers send.

I believe deeply that we do what we do because we love our people, our communities, we are linked through memory to loving family, to warrior sisters and brothers, mothers and fathers, grandmothers and grandfathers, women and men, to impeccable leaders, organizers, artists, healers, maestras y maestros, who gave their lives for the cause of universal peace and justice. We also give our lives, and the evidence is in each act we take to end the terror and degradation of genocide, repression, criminalization, starvation of body and spirit, violation of our human/civil/legal rights, woman-hating, people-hating, earth-hating that have been ours and our people's punishment for being so powerfully different. So that their/our suffering will not have been in vain, so that every ounce of energy they gave for liberation will count, so that our spirits will draw and give from such strength, we get up, we rise up, in beauty, in dignity, in conscious freedom.

We are related to all that lives.

Ann Daum writes of a female coyote inscribed in her memory. Kept in a makeshift cage on her family's South Dakota ranch, kept imprisoned so that her urine would scent the air, attracting other coyotes to the surrounding traps, "She didn't move," Daum says, "didn't look like the live coyotes I'd seen frozen in the headlights, or loping across the prairie pasture just after dawn. She looked dead, . . . except for her eyes, which were fixed on something, some hill or tree or bird outside the cage" (421). Coming from a background where it was ordinary to shoot coyotes, trap them, crush them into the earth with vehicles, rope them and drag them for miles, Daum says she dreams coyotes, dreams the end by fire of these wild animal relatives, and sometimes her dreams "wailed from inside rock and wire and wood, where there is, and always will be, a coyote living in a box" (422). This coyote is my sister; I will remember her and send her my wishes for her spirit to find peaceful freedom, just as another coyote who found earthly freedom through a girlhood gesture by Daum.

When she was twelve, Daum says she was shown "how easy" it is to break a mustang colt. The colt was hobbled from the start, and put through terror-filled moments until, in bleeding agony, he lay still in submission, "eyes wide and blank, breathing wretched, panicked whinnies through his open mouth" (422). . . . How easy. . . . Daum says that afterwards she tried to befriend the mustang, but "he wouldn't even see me. His eyes were dark and hard and faraway, and the part of him that had run on twelve thousand empty acres, I never saw again" (423). I feel for their broken spirits, and I know those eyes that go away, taking spirit far beyond the misery. The coyote, the young mustang are my relatives, as much as Daum herself, as much as anyone who reads this essay. I think of other life forms in much the same way I think of children. They are innocent of blame for what goes on in this world. And like children, these other life forms see and know more than we realize. There is no intellectual manipulation/justification to mask the hard, brutal, brazen face of cruelty.

It is not difficult to relate the coyote and colt to ourselves, to what we suffer(ed) through invasion, campaigns of genocide, the colonial projects that had as their unholy intent our erasure from the face of the earth, our complete dehumanization in the interests of outright theft and exploitation, targetting the women, the children, showing the men our fathers they could do nothing, crippling them all to rob them of their wholeness. We always had/have to be dominated, controlled, kept in rigid social cages until we are no good anymore, until our bodies/spirits/hearts/minds are so destroyed we can do nothing but die. We are throw-aways because we are the enemy. Particularly people of color, women of color (inexact as these terms are), of certain political persuasions, certain classes, certain levels of education, certain cultures and languages, certain sexualities, certain spiritualities. There are white allies, women and men, who are counted among us as well. In this scenario our lives and deaths are completely irrelevant, we are consumed and discarded. It is the role we were assigned in the original scripted narrative of colonizing nation(s). Now, the words have changed (only) slightly, global economy, "free" trade, child/woman/man labor repression, the (il)logic of capitalism and devastation of the earth. It is all we can do to face each day with clear consciousness and hearts strong. Some of us have more privilege than others, living in the belly of the beast. The greatest privilege? Knowing how to read and write, how to think things through and see it and name it all.

The women gather at the moment nestled between the night of full moon and the new morning. The colors of the embracing sky speak of the brilliance to come, and the soft wind whispers caresses. In the stillness there is the sense of birth, of rebirthing. The women care for a fire they have made. This fire is the bond between them all, the joining of Heart of the Earth with Heart of the Sky. They stand or sit in silence, sharing the fullness of consciousness with each other and with the cosmos, allowing their spirits to listen to each other's language of the heart, allowing themselves to travel to new places in a myriad of combinations with each other, the stars, the clouds, the night, with all of them as one, with the world of spirits accompanying each woman. There is no need for words. There have already been many, many words. Powerful words, outraged words, liberating words.

We know the story. We've lived it, named it, told it to each other, screamed it, worried over it, taken it upon our shoulders and into our wombs for such a long, long time, for centuries. It's a story that's been put upon us, slashed onto our bodies, branded into our hearts, nailed into our minds, causing us to despise our own spirits, viciously assaulting us so many times we've gone mad, or numb, and dumb, our spirits knocked out of our bodies and left for broken. The more rebellious we've been, the more mad we've been called, the more freakish, the more dirty, the more unacceptable, the more outcast. For many of us grief has become so familiar we've made a home for it in our lives, we tend to it, we serve it, we give ourselves over to it. For some of us the grief has turned into creative rage, to awesome deliberate coraje, for others grief has become a bitterness so deeply immobilizing it's hard to have faith in anything, much less ourselves.

But it is an old story, a shabby mean-spirited script, not the kind to keep, not the kind that nourishes, or ensures continuance. It is a lie. Not the violence, the violence is concretely manifest in us, in our communities, in the earth. It could not be more real. Those memories are etched each time more deeply, but we are much faster now in finding the sources of the pain, and by naming it, doctoring the wound(s). The old story that is a lie, the hechicería of the worst kind, is that we will never recover from the violence, or that we will recover only slowly, painfully. If our recovery is slow, it gives those in power more time to reap the benefits of their profane materialist consuming vampirish fortunes and privileges. But, here is the miracle. We have been recovering from the moment we began to question, know, and understand. From the instant we began to look for language to *name*. Otherwise our outrage would not be so powerful. The world would not have shaken, the earth would not have moved with us, through us, as she continues to do, because hers is the longest memory. She is the greatest witness.

Witness. We witness each other's sorrow, madness, rage, joy, abundant love. We must move up from the grief, the degradation, the violations. Anything is possible, nothing is impossible. Some say it takes a long time. Why? Once we learn to name it, once we gain command over it by releasing it through our tongues/hands/pens/creative forces/work, through our loving, why do we have to hold on to it? Whose game is this? Whose interests are being served by us holding on to disgraceful, horrifying memories in such a way that we replay over and over, going back to the place of defeat, going back and matching our energy to the actual experience again and again? What do the spirits say? They say, "Let go." Let go.

The joy the wonder the need for letting go not holding on not stifling not falling into patterns of destruction rejoicing at the nearness the sharing the telling the touching the laughter the good tears the loving. "Yo para querer no necesito mucha razón, me sobra mucho, pero mucho corazón."[1]

We are seers, we have seen the depths of degradation, and lived to tell of it, and in the telling we release la carga energética = the energetic charge of the violation, the retreat into ourselves, the near-autistic state where our faces are a wall and we are way behind, watching as other faces appear to search into our eyes for us, asking what's wrong. We live to tell of survival, and beyond.

To love, to laugh, to truly live, to have vision and promise, to believe in oneself and others, to life-work carefully, meticulously for something, alone and with others. We are the protagonists of these new stories. We are writing the scripts.

The women know when to form a circle around the fire. No one has to lead. They are paying such attention to each other that the moment is recognized and respected by everyone.

Autonomy, here is the connection. Self-autonomy, Gloria says in the first edition of *This Bridge*. Self-autonomy is the key to autonomy as peoples, as communities, and as communities in solidarity. How is a people, a community, free? When each individual realizes freedom from within, and thereby recognizes everyone else's right to it. In the old days we used to fight for the right to self-determination; at the same time we were rigidly prescribing party lines and agendas, allowing no deviation from ideology, theory, or platform. Those old days are still here, sad to say. The internal critique is still the hardest, but the most imperative. No matter what color, culture, race, ethnicity, gender, sexual orientation, class, nationality, religious/spiritual, economic, political persuasion (or not), we must talk more from the heart, with our own selves first, then with others. Mayan writer Martha Florinda Gonzalez Diéguez says for her people intelligence corresponds to the brain and wisdom to the heart. Ahí está el detalle. La sabiduria. Después de tanto luchar hay que reflejar en las enseñanzas del corazón. Qué es lo que hemos aprendido, digo, de sabiduría? In Cuba, I remember the saying "the revolution begins in the heart."

The quetzal's gentle tiny face shines with the true grace of freedom. Freedom is responsible. Freedom is accountable. Freedom is conscious. Freedom has conscience and understands consequence. Querer, poder, deber, it's that simple. An elder taught me this a long time ago. When the three coincide, then everything's in balance, it's a go. Do I want to do something? Do I have the power to do it? Should I do it? When there is a "no" to any one of these questions the issue becomes complicated; this is the test.

There are times when the path seems so solitary. Times when what we're going through we can't explain to our lovers, family, sisters, friends. And yet, we are not in a bubble that severs us from the universe. When my youngest son was a new teenager, an elder told him to take care with his steps because, he said, "The Creation is watching." This was not said to make him feel guilty at every move he made, but to help him be considerate, thoughtful, attentive, gentle in his ways, with himself, and with others. He learned he was not alone, and he was/is being protected.

Imagine the people who take other life forms for granted. Imagine the earth's heartbreak at being made insignificant, at being consumed carelessly, thoughtlessly, ignorantly. Imagine her mirroring eyes mirroring the desprecio. Remember the coyote's eyes, the colt's eyes, our own eyes in those moments when we face the mirror full of such deep heartache.

Imagine the earth waiting to be in solitude with us, wanting the embrace of our bodies as we drink in our solitary moments with her. Imagine the moonlit starry night bathing us with grace, cleansing us with quiet talk, nourishing us with breaths of wind as the trees tell us their stories with delicately swaying language. Imagine the reciprocal gratefulness for each other's existence, like those friends who are always there no matter the distance, the dearest trusted ones who do not know betrayal or deceit, who treasure us as we treasure them.

Standing together, the women communicate their wishes, longings, and affirmations to the fire, Heart of the Earth, Heart of the Sky. There is no First Speaker or Last Speaker. Standing with each other in a radiant circle of consiousness, at the same time, each woman offers her palabra, some with words, some silently, some with song, some with dance, each one following her heart's intuition, not thinking hard, but in effortless expression. Each woman respects the full circle and takes care not to call attention to herself, because many women's eyes are closed, as they softly sing, speak, or dance, or speak no words, but communicate with their bodies moving gently to and fro, some with arms outstretched, or with their faces turned upward reaching for the heavens. There are smiles of joy on the women's faces and in the rhythm of their bodies.

compassion forgiveness conscious illumination releasing letting go replenishing sensuous boldness humility energy wisdom renewing intelligence nurturing spirit body mind heart not taking time giving time to ourselves the struggles life's work replenishing our children, grandchildren, sisters brothers, friends, loved ones, the animals, plants, waters, birds, the earth, our universe sanctuary taking care loving healing creative anger power humor exuberance femalemale malefemale within each of us the land remembers listen remember the land the spirits care for the spirits will help take care of the rest respect respect respect each of us a center a center a center each of us trust earned respect constant conscious respect earning trust memory loving memory continuous continuance walk with the generations we are not alone radical transforming creative power radical trust

Many of the terms by which people identify us, by which we identify ourselves, can be somewhat useful for political expediencies, but fuzzy and even sometimes dangerous when used in a prescriptive manner. The only way to imagine communities of solidarity and transformation is by recognizing what Chandra Talpade Mohanty said some time ago, that difference is history (and herstory). For solidarity to exist there has to be consciousness, at least consciousness that it's hard to know everything about each other's herstories, personal and collective, and each person's or people's cultural responses to those herstories/histories. Among us women there are countless herstories, and herstories within herstories, centers within centers. Culling these herstories is part of the work many of us have been about for these thirty years plus.

We are only just beginning to know, through oral tradition, and oral herstory, through archival work, through language study—with indigenous languages we are beginning to see other ways of looking, of seeing that belong to us, other forms of creative expression and communication. We're not all alike and that's the beauty of it all. Yes, there are correspondences. When Hulleah Tsinhnahjinnie creates a piece called "Sovereignty Not Revolution" for her Aboriginal Savant Series, indigenous people anywhere can relate. In a similar manner, when Diné poet/scholar Laura Tohe writes an essay titled "There's No Word for Feminism," foregrounding the matrilineal society from which she comes, who of us would argue with her?

I've seen some recent writings that still focus on whose "feminism" is "first." I've also experienced on my campus a tension with a respected white feminist colleague over competing narratives having to do with our histories on the campus in a given moment. The issue is not about controlling the stories. It is about holding the stories, keeping them, caring for them, knowing that perspectives must/will shift when locations and experiences are distinct. White feminists are not at our center. For many of us, they never have been. White feminism, for me, has always been marginalized, on the periphery, where it should be. It's not about us, we're about us. I do recognize that there are white women who are good strong allies but we are also good strong allies. They are not leading us. We lead ourselves. And their narratives will never tell our stories the way we do. There are many, many centers.

In my graduate seminar last fall, one of the students, Sara Dutschke (who is Miwok), in critiquing a study of "indigenous aesthetics," posited a "Miwok aesthetics" in place of the more generic "indigenous aesthetics" the author was trying to establish. This is it. And even within the Miwok world there would be a negotiation of what "Miwok aesthetics" represents. There would not be an indigenous person who is non-Miwok attempting to tell Miwok people what their aesthetics, or by extension, their "feminisms," should be. Native nations respect each other's autonomy/sovereignty, just as they respect each other's Creation stories, belief systems, and ways of knowing; it is one of the major givens that make up the cultural protocols for getting along with each other, for working in unity and solidarity (if everything is at its best). If one Native nation does not respect another's sovereignty, there can be no understanding, no solidarity. There is nothing on which to build.

Still, at many women's conferences, in written works, in the media, Native people, Native women, are erased. Women's issues are often cast in black and white, and sometimes Latinas are included, sometimes other women's communities of color. This brings us full circle to spirit, to the spirit of the land. We are on Indian land. Throughout this entire hemisphere, wherever anyone lives, these are the original homelands of peoples indigenous to what is now known as the Americas. The spirits of the original peoples have been forgotten. One of the teachings from traditional people is to pay your respects to the spirits of the lands you are visiting or traveling over. Some do this with an offering of tobacco or with song. There is an understanding with the offering that you are asking permission to be on the land. In communities of women of color, the sisters who know this are the Santeras, Maori women, other indigenous women from other parts of the world. It is another given, another cultural protocol by which we recognize, show respect, and honor each other. I've heard the call for "new languages." The old languages are the new ones.

in thanksgiving for our people's prayers, ceremonies, good wishes, strong wills, courage, warrior spirits, commitment, for everything they have done for us to be here alive standing knowing ourselves respecting each other working together, in thanksgiving for the spirits of the earth and the universe, for their beautiful nuanced mystery and sacred intelligence, in thanksgiving for ourselves, for our triumphs, joys, wisdom, laughter, for walking this road in this life as women with compromiso

My mother's brother from Nespelem, my Uncle Frank, taught me a song that came to the Nez Perce from the Sioux a long time ago. A victory song for warriors returning from battle. I have been singing it often, offering it for the daily victories, large and small, anticipating, calling, creating the path for the victory of justice. I sing it to you now.

Notes

I want to thank Floyd Westerman for his beautiful song "Chante Waste Wi," which accompanied me in the writing of this essay.

1. Lyrics from the well-known Mexican love song "Mucho Corazón."

seventy-nine

continents

anne waters

out the window open. i hear voices of children screaming, playing, shouting names. antonio. yomi. natalija. physay. elizabeth. anna. leah. kwami. voices calling forth. children are playing together in the sunset before a new dawn.

a map lying on my desk locates my place in indigenous america. i do not know now who plays in china, africa, russia, mexico. in south america, australia, afghanistan, north america or central. i do not know whose voices i hear. what language or what gifts they bear.

but i hear the children of tomorrow. i hear their voices in australia, in the americas, in south africa, leading. i hear the voices of indigenous children. voices i could not hear i am now hearing.

the children are speaking and dreaming a new world. a world of love, community, passion, respect. no hunger. they are speaking and dreaming of a world of struggle.

they are speaking and dreaming our future. on all continents in all indigenous homes the children of today are talking our future.

eighty

now let us shift . . . the path of conocimiento . . . inner work, public acts[1]

Gloria E. Anzaldúa

an offering

As you walk across Lighthouse Field a glistening black ribbon undulates in the grass, crossing your path from right to left. You swallow air, your primal senses flare open. From the middle of your forehead, a reptilian eye blinks, surveys the terrain. This visual intuitive sense, like the intellect of heart and gut, reveals a discourse of signs, images, feelings, words that, once decoded, carry the power to startle you out of tunnel vision and habitual patterns of thought. The snake is a symbol of awakening consciousness—the potential of knowing within, an awareness and intelligence not grasped by logical thought. Often nature provokes un "aja," or "conocimiento,"[2] one that guides your feet along the path, gives you el ánimo to dedicate yourself to transforming perceptions of reality, and thus the conditions of life. Llevas la presencia de éste conocimiento contigo. You experience nature as ensouled, as sacred. Éste saber, this knowledge, urges you to cast una ofrenda of images and words across the page como granos de maíz, like kernels of corn. By redeeming your most painful experiences you transform them into something valuable, algo para compartir or share with others so they too may be empowered. You stop in the middle of the field and, under your breath, ask the spirits—animals, plants, y tus muertos—to help you string together a bridge of words. What follows is your attempt to give back to nature, los espíritus, and others a gift wrested from the events in your life, a bridge home to the self.

the journey: path of conocimiento

You struggle each day to know the world you live in, to come to grips with the problems of life. Motivated by the need to understand, you crave to be what and who you are. A spiritual hunger rumbles deep in your belly, the yearning to live up to your potential. You question the doctrines claiming to be the only right way to live. These ways no longer accommodate the person you are, or the life you're living. They no longer help you with your central task—to determine what your life means, to catch a glimpse of the cosmic order and your part in that cosmovisión, and to translate these into artistic forms. Tu camino de conocimiento requires that you encounter your shadow side and confront what you've programmed yourself (and have been programmed by your cultures) to avoid (desconocer), to confront the traits and habits distorting how you see reality and inhibiting the full use of your facultades.

At the crack of change between millennia, you and the rest of humanity are undergoing profound transformations and shifts in perception. All, including the planet and every species, are caught between cultures and bleed-throughs among different worlds—each with its own version of reality. We are experiencing a personal, global identity crisis in a disintegrating social order that possesses little heart and functions to oppress people by organizing them in hierarchies of commerce and power—a collusion of government, transnational industry, business, and the military all linked by a pragmatic technology and science voracious for money and control. This system and its hierarchies impact people's lives in concrete and devastating ways and justify a sliding scale of human worth used to keep humankind divided. It condones the mind theft, spirit murder, exploitation, and genocide de los otros. We are collectively conditioned not to know that every comfort of our lives is acquired with the blood of conquered, subjugated, enslaved, or exterminated people, an exploitation that continues today. We are completely dependent on consumerism, the culture of the dollar, and the colossal powers that sustain our lifestyles.

We stand at a major threshold in the extension of consciousness, caught in the remolinos (vortices) of systemic change across all fields of knowledge. The binaries of colored/white, female/male, mind/body are collapsing. Living in nepantla,[3] the overlapping space between different perceptions and belief systems, you are aware of the changeability of racial, gender, sexual, and other categories rendering the conventional labelings obsolete. Though these markings are outworn and inaccurate, those in power continue using them to single out and negate those who are "different" because of color, language, notions of reality, or other diversity. You know that the new paradigm must come from outside as well as within the system.

Many are witnessing a major cultural shift in their understanding of what knowledge consists of and how we come to know, a shift from the kinds of knowledge valued now to the kinds that will be desired in the twenty-first century, a shift away from knowledge contributing both to military and corporate technologies and the colonization of our lives by TV and the Internet, to the inner exploration of the meaning and purpose of life. You attribute this shift to the feminization of knowledge, one beyond the subject-object divide, a way of knowing and acting on ese saber you call *conocimiento*. Skeptical of reason and rationality, conocimiento questions conventional knowledge's current categories, classifications, and contents.

Those carrying conocimiento refuse to accept spirituality as a devalued form of knowledge, and instead elevate it to the same level occupied by science and rationality. A form of spiritual inquiry, conocimiento is reached via creative acts—writing, art-making, dancing, healing, teaching, meditation, and spiritual activism—both mental and somatic (the body, too, is a form as well as site of creativity). Through creative engagements, you embed your experiences in a larger frame of reference, connecting your personal struggles with those of other beings on the planet, with the struggles of the Earth itself. To understand the greater reality that lies behind your personal perceptions, you view these struggles as spiritual undertakings. Your identity is a filtering screen limiting your awareness to a fraction of your reality. What you or your cultures believe to be true is provisional and depends on a specific perspective. What your eyes, ears, and other physical senses perceive is not the whole picture but one determined by your core beliefs and prevailing societal assumptions. What you live through and the knowledge you infer from experience is subjective. Intuitive knowing, unmediated by mental constructs—what inner eye, heart, and gut tell you—is the closest you come to direct knowledge (gnosis) of the world, and this experience of reality is partial too.

Conocimiento comes from opening all your senses, consciously inhabiting your body and decoding its symptoms—that persistent scalp itch, not caused by lice or dry skin, may be a thought trying to snare your attention. Attention is multileveled and includes your surroundings, bodily sensations and responses, intuitive takes, emotional reactions to other people and theirs to you, and, most important, the images your imagination creates—images connecting all tiers of information and their data. Breaking out of your mental and emotional prison and deepening the range of perception enables you to link inner reflection and vision—the mental, emotional, instinctive, imaginal, spiritual, and subtle bodily awareness—with social, political action and lived experiences to generate subversive knowledges. These conocimientos challenge official and conventional ways of looking at the world, ways set up by those benefiting from such constructions.

Information your sense organs register and your rational mind organizes coupled with imaginal knowings derived from viewing life through the third eye, the reptilian eye looking inward and outward simultaneously, along with the perceptions of the shapeshifting naguala,[4] the perceiver of shifts, results in conocimiento. According to Christianity and other spiritual traditions, the evil that lies at the root of the human condition is the desire to know—which translates into aspiring to conocimiento (reflective consciousness). Your reflective mind's mirror throws back all your options, making you aware of your freedom to choose. You don't need to obey the reigning gods' laws (popular culture, commerce, science) and accept fate as decreed by church and culture. To further the self you choose to accept the guidance and information provided by symbology systems like the Tarot, I Ching, dowsing (pendulum), astrology, and numerology.

Throughout millennia those seeking alternative forms of knowledge have been demonized. In the pursuit of knowledge, including carnal knowledge (symbolized by the serpent), some female origin figures "disobeyed." Casting aside the status quo of edenic conditions and unconscious "being," they took a bite of awareness—the first human to take agency. Xochiquetzal, a Mexican indigenous diety,[5] ascends to the upperworld to seek knowledge from "el árbol sagrado," the tree of life, que florecía en Tamoanchan.[6] In another garden of Eden, Eve snatches the fruit (the treasure of forbidden knowledge) from the serpent's mouth and "invents" consciousness—the sense of self in the act of knowing.[7] Serpent Woman, known as Cihuacoatl, the goddess of origins, whom you think of as la Llorona[8] and sketch as a half-coiled snake with the head of a woman, represents, not the root of all evil, but instinctual knowledge and other alternative ways of knowing that fuel transformation.

These females are expelled from "paradise" for eating the fruit from the tree of knowledge of good and evil and for taking individual agency. Their "original sin" precipitates the myth of the fall of humankind, for which women have been blamed and punished. The passion to know, to deepen awareness, to perceive reality in a different way, to see and experience more of life—in short, the desire to expand consciousness—and the freedom to choose, drove Xochiquetzal, Eve, and Cihuacoatl to deepen awareness. You too are driven by the desire to understand, know, y saber how human and other beings know. Beneath your desire for knowledge writhes the hunger to understand and love yourself.

seven stages of conocimiento

You're strolling downtown. Suddenly the sidewalk buckles and rises before you. Bricks fly through the air. Your thigh muscles tense to run, but shock holds you in check. Dust rains down all around you, dimming your sight, clogging your nostrils, coating your throat. In front of you the second story of a building caves into the ground floor. Just as suddenly the earth stops trembling. People with pallid faces gather before the collapsed building. Near your feet a hand sticks out of the rubble. The body of the woman attached to that hand is pulled out from the debris. A bloody gash runs down one side of her face and one arm sticks out unnaturally. As they place her on the sidewalk, her skirt rides up to her waist, exposing a plump thigh. You fight the urge to pull her skirt down, protect her from all eyes.

The first aftershock hits. Fear ripples down your spine, frightening your soul out of your body. You pick your way through the rubble, dodging bricks, and reach your car; except for a few dents on the hood it's still in one piece. Coasting over the cracked bridge and pits in the pavement, you drive home at five miles an hour. One street over from your apartment, a fire spews smoke and flames into the sky. You unlock the door of your home to find it won't budge. Putting shoulder to wood you shove back books, plants, dirt, and broken pottery the earthquake has flung to the floor.

Every few minutes an aftershock rattles the windows, drying the spit in your mouth. Each time the walls sway, you run to a doorway, brace yourself under its frame, holding your breath and willing your house not to fall on top of you. The apartment manager comes to check and tells you, "No te puedes quedar aquí. You have to evacuate, the gas lines are not secure, there's no electricity, and the water's contaminated." You want to salvage your books, your computer, and three years' worth of writing. "I'm staying home," you reply as you watch your neighbors gather sleeping bags, blankets, food, and head for the sports field nearby. Soon most of the city and county keep vigil from makeshift tents.

You boil water, sweep up the broken cups and plates. Just when you think the ground beneath your feet is stable, the two plates again grind together along the San Andreas Fault. The seismic rupture moves the Monterey Peninsula three inches north. It shifts you into the crack between the worlds, shattering the mythology that grounds you. You strive for leverage in the fissures, but Tonan, la madre tierra, keeps stirring beneath you. In the midst of this physical crisis, an emotional bottom falls out from under you, forcing you to confront your fear of others breaching the emotional walls you've built around yourself. If you don't work through your fear, playing it safe could bury you.

Éste arrebato, the earthquake, jerks you from the familiar and safe terrain and catapults you into nepantla, the second stage. In this liminal, transitional space, suspended between shifts, you're two people, split between before and after. Nepantla, where the outer boundaries of the mind's inner life meet the outer world of reality, is a zone of possibility. You experience reality as fluid, expanding and contracting. In nepantla you are exposed, open to other perspectives, more readily able to access knowledge derived from inner feelings, imaginal states, and outer events, and to "see through"[9] them with a mindful, holistic awareness. Seeing through human acts both individual and collective allows you to examine the ways you construct knowledge, identity, and reality, and explore how some of your/others' constructions violate other people's ways of knowing and living.

When overwhelmed by the chaos caused by living between stories, you break down, descend into the third space, the Coatlicue depths of despair, self-loathing, and hopelessness. Dysfunctional for weeks, the refusal to move paralyzes you. In the fourth space a call to action pulls you out of your depression. You break free from your habitual coping strategies of escaping from realities you're reluctant to face, reconnect with spirit, and undergo a conversion.

In the fifth space your desire for order and meaning prompts you to track the ongoing circumstances of your life, to sift, sort, and symbolize your experiences and try to arrange them into a pattern and story that speak to your reality. You scan your inner landscape, books, movies, philosophies, mythologies, and the modern sciences for bits of lore you can patch together to create a new narrative articulating your personal reality. You scrutinize and question dominant and ethnic ideologies and the mind-sets their cultures induce in others. And, putting all the pieces together, you reenvision the map of the known world, creating a new description of reality and scripting a new story.

In the sixth space you take your story out into the world, testing it. When you or the world fail to live up to your ideals, your edifice collapses like a house of cards, casting you into conflict with self and others in a war between realities. Disappointed with self and others, angry and then terrified at the depth of your anger, you swallow your emotions, hold them in. Blocked from your own power, you're unable to activate the inner resources that could mobilize you. In the seventh, the critical turning point of transformation, you shift realities, develop an ethical, compassionate strategy with which to negotiate conflict and difference within self and between others, and find common ground by forming holistic alliances. You include these practices in your daily life, act on your vision—enacting spiritual activism.

The first stages of conocimiento illustrate the four directions (south, west, north, east), the next, below and above, and the seventh, the center. They symbolize los siete "ojos de luz" or seven chakras of the energetic, dreambody, spirit body (counterpart of the physical body), the seven planes of reality[10] the stages of alchemical process (negredo, albedo, and rebedo), and the four elements: air, fire, water, and earth. In all seven spaces you struggle with the shadow, the unwanted aspects of the self. Together, the seven stages open the senses and enlarge the breadth and depth of consciousness, causing internal shifts and external changes. All seven are present within each stage, and they occur concurrently, chronologically or not. Zigzagging from ignorance (desconocimiento) to awareness (conocimiento), in a day's time you may go through all seven stages, though you may dwell in one for months. You're never only in one space, but partially in one, partially in another, with nepantla occurring most often—as its own space and as the transition between each of the others. Together, these stations constitute a meditation on the rites of passage, the transitions of life from birth to death, and all the daily births and deaths in-between. Bits of your self die and are reborn in each step.

1. el arrebato . . . rupture, fragmentation . . . an ending, a beginning

The assailant's hands squeeze your throat. Gasping for breath, your scream eeks out as a mewling sound. You kick and scratch him as he drags you across the Waller Creek bridge. He shoves you against the rail. Heart in your throat, you peer at the wet rocks below lapped by the gurgling stream. If he throws you off the bridge bones will break, maybe your neck. He finally wrestles your bag from you and sprints away. Anger pulses through you. You snatch up a big rock and run after him. You survive este arrebato and witness his capture, but every night for months when safe in your bed, his snarl echoes in your head, "I'm going to get you, bitch." Footsteps behind you, people's sudden movements, stop your breath and your body responds as though he's attacking you again. Your relationship to the world is irrevocably changed: you're aware of your vulnerability, wary of men, and no longer trust the universe.[11]

This event pulled the linchpin that held your reality/story together and you cast your mind to find a symbol to represent this dislocation. In 1972 you first saw the huge round stone of the dismembered moon goddess Coyolxauhqui in Mexico City. She's lived in your imaginal life since then and this arrebato embeds her and her story deeper in your flesh. When Coyolxauhqui tried to kill her mother, Coatlicue, her brother Huitzílopochtlí, the war god, sprang out from the womb fully armed. He decapitated and flung her down the temple, scattering her body parts in all directions, making her the first sacrificial victim. Coyolxauhqui is your symbol for both the process of emotional psychical dismemberment, splitting body/mind/spirit/soul, and the creative work of putting all the pieces together in a new form, a partially unconscious work done in the night by the light of the moon, a labor of re-visioning and re-membering. Seven years after the attack, a psychic gives you a reading, telling you to find the scattered, missing parts of yourself and put them back together.

Every arrebato—a violent attack, rift with a loved one, illness, death in the family, betrayal, systematic racism and marginalization—rips you from your familiar "home," casting you out of your personal Eden, showing that something is lacking in your queendom. Cada arrebatada (snatching) turns your world upside down and cracks the walls of your reality, resulting in a great sense of loss, grief, and emptiness, leaving behind dreams, hopes, and goals. You are no longer who you used to be. As you move from past pre-suppositions and frames of reference, letting go of former positions, you feel like an orphan, abandoned by all that's familiar. Exposed, naked, disoriented, wounded, uncertain, confused, and conflicted, you're forced to live en la orilla—a razor-sharp edge that fragments you.

The upheaval jars you out of the cultural trance and the spell of the collective mind-set, what Don Miguel Ruiz calls the collective dream and Charles Tart calls consensus reality. When two or more opposing accounts, perspectives, or belief systems appear side by side or intertwined, a kind of double or multiple "seeing" results, forcing you into continuous dialectical encounters with these different stories, situations, and people. Trying to understand these convergences compels you to critique your own perspective and assumptions. It leads to re-interpreting the story you imagined yourself living, bringing it to a dramatic end and initiating one of turmoil, being swallowed by your fears, and passing through a threshold. Seeing through your culture separates you from the herd, exiles you from the tribe, wounds you psychologically and spiritually. Cada arrebatamiento is an awakening that causes you to question who you are, what the world is about. The urgency to know what you're experiencing awakens la facultad, the ability to shift attention and see through the surface of things and situations.

With each arrebatamiento you suffer un "susto," a shock that knocks one of your souls out of your body, causing estrangement.[12] With the loss of the familiar and the unknown ahead, you struggle to regain your balance, reintegrate yourself (put Coyolxahqui together), and repair the damage. You must, like the shaman, find a way to call your spirit home. Every paroxysm has the potential of initiating you to something new, giving you a chance to reconstruct yourself, forcing you to rework your description of self, world, and your place in it (reality). Every morning in ritual you turn on the gas stove, watch the flame, and, as you wait for the teapot to boil, ask Spirit for increased awareness. You honor what has ended, say goodbye to the old way of being, commit yourself to look for the "something new," and picture yourself embracing this new life. But before that can happen you plunge into the ambiguity of the transition phase, undergo another rite of passage, and negotiate another identity crisis.

2. nepantla . . . torn between ways

Pero, ay, como Sor Juana, como los transterrados españoles, como tantos mexicanos no repuestos aún de la conquista, yo vivía nepantla—un aislamiento espiritual.

—Rosario Castellanos, *Los narradores* (93)

*But, oh, like Sor Juana, like the land-crossing Spanish, like so many
Mexicans who have not recovered from the conquest, I lived nepantla—a
spiritual isolation. (Trans. GEA)*

There's only one other Chicana in your Ph.D. program at UT Austin,
Texas, a state heavily populated with Chicanos, and you're never in the
same class. The professors dislike the practice of putting yourself in the
texts, insisting your papers are too subjective. They frown on your
unorthodox perspectives and ways of thinking. They reject your dissertation thesis, claiming Chicana/o literature illegitimate and feminist theory
too radical.

Bereft of your former frame of reference, leaving home has cast you
adrift in the liminal space between home and school. In class you feel you're
on a rack, body prone across the equator between the diverse notions and
nations that comprise you. Remolinos (whirlwinds) sweep you off your feet,
pulling you here and there. While home, family, and ethnic culture tug you
back to the tribe, to the chicana indigena you were before, the anglo world
sucks you toward an assimilated, homogenized, whitewashed identity. Each
separate reality and its belief system vies with others to convert you to its
worldview. Each exhorts you to turn your back on other interpretations,
other tribes. You face divisions within your cultures—of class, gender, sexuality, nationality, and ethnicity. You face both entrenched institutions and
the oppositional movements of working-class women, people of color, and
queers. Pulled between opposing realities, you feel torn between "white"
ways and Mexican ways, between Chicano nationalists and conservative
Hispanics. Suspended between traditional values and feminist ideas, you
don't know whether to assimilate, separate, or isolate.

The vortices and their cacophonies continuously bombard you with
new ideas and perceptions of self and world. Vulnerable to spiritual anxiety and isolation, suspended on the bridge between rewind and fast-for-
ward, swinging between elation and despair, anger and forgiveness, you
think, feel, and react in extremes. Now you flounder in the chaos, now
feel cradled en la calma. In the transition space of nepantla you reflect
critically, and as you move from one symbol system to another, self-identity becomes your central concern. While the opposing forces struggle for
expression, an inner impasse blocks you. According to Jung, if you hold
opposites long enough without taking sides a new identity emerges. As
you make your way through life, nepantla itself becomes the place you
live in most of the time—home. Nepantla is the site of transformation, the
place where different perspectives come into conflict and where you
question the basic ideas, tenets, and identities inherited from your family,
your education, and your different cultures. Nepantla is the zone between

changes where you struggle to find equilibrium between the outer expression of change and your inner relationship to it.

Living between cultures results in "seeing" double, first from the perspective of one culture, then from the perspective of another. Seeing from two or more perspectives simultaneously renders those cultures transparent. Removed from that culture's center, you glimpse the sea in which you've been immersed but to which you were oblivious, no longer seeing the world the way you were enculturated to see it. From the in-between place of nepantla, you see through the fiction of the monoculture, the myth of the superiority of the white races. And eventually you begin seeing through your ethnic culture's myth of the inferiority of mujeres. As you struggle to form a new identity, a demythologization of race occurs. You begin to see race as an experience of reality from a particular perspective and a specific time and place (history), not as a fixed feature of personality or identity.

According to nagualismo, perceiving something from two different angles creates a split in awareness. This split engenders the ability to control perception. You will yourself to ground this doble saber (double knowing) in your body's ear and soul's eye, always alerta y vigilante of how you are aware. Staying despierta becomes a survival tool. In your journal you doodle an image of a double-headed, double-faced woman, una cara in profile and the other looking ahead. The twin-faced patlache of your indigenous queer heritage is also the symbol of la otra tú, the double or dreambody (energetic body). La naguala connects you to these others and to unconscious and invisible forces. In nepantla you sense more keenly the overlap between the material and spiritual worlds; you're in both places simultaneously—you glimpse el espíritu—see the body as inspirited. Nepantla is the point of contact where the "mundane" and the "numinous" converge, where you're in full awareness of the present moment.

You can't stand living according to the old terms—yesterday's mode of consciousness pinches like an outgrown shoe. Craving change, you yearn to open yourself and honor the space/time between transitions. Coyolxauhqui's light in the night ignites your longing to engage with the world beyond the horizon you've grown accustomed to. Fear keeps you exiled between repulsion and propulsion, mourning the loss, obsessed with retrieving a lost homeland that may never have existed. Even as you listen to the old consciousness's death rattle, you continue defending its mythology of who you were and what your world looked like. To and fro you go, and just when you're ready to move you find yourself resisting the changes. Though your head and heart decry the mind/body dichotomy, the conflict in your mind makes your body a battlefield where beliefs fight each other.

3. the Coatlicue state . . . desconocimiento and the cost of knowing

There is an underbelly of terror to all life. It is suffering, it is hurt.
—Ming-Dao

Three weeks after the doctor confirms your own diagnosis you cross the trestle bridge near the wharf, your shortcut to downtown Santa Cruz. As you listen to your footsteps echoing on the timber, the reality of having a disease that could cost you your feet . . . your eyes . . . your creativity . . . the life of the writer you've worked so hard to build . . . life itself . . . finally penetrates, arresting you in the middle del puente (bridge). You're furious with your body for limiting your artistic activities, for its slow crawl toward the grave. You're infuriated with yourself for not living up to your expectations, not living your life fully. You realize that you use the whip of your ideals to flagellate yourself, and the masochist in you gets pleasure from your suffering. Tormented by self-contempt, you reproach yourself constantly and despair. Guilt and bitterness gnaw your insides and, blocked by your own grand expectations, you're unable to function. You double over. Clinging to the rail, you look down. Con tus otros ojos you see the black hole of anger sucking you into the abode of the shadow. Qué desgracia.

Tú, la consentida, the special one, thought yourself exempt from living like ordinary people. Self-pity swamps you, que suerte maldita! Self-absorbed, you're unable to climb out of the pit that's yourself. Feeling helpless, you draft the script of victimization and retreat from the world, withdraw from your body, losing kinesthetic consciousness. You count the bars of your cage, refusing to name your demons. You repel intrusions, rout off friends and family by withholding attention. When stress is overwhelming, you shut down your feelings, plummet into depression and unremitting sorrow. Consciousness diminished, your body descends into itself, pulled by the weight, mass, and gravity of your desconocimientos. To escape emotional pain (most of it self-imposed) you indulge in addictions. These respites from reality allow you to feel at one with yourself and the world, gaining you brief sojourns in Tamoanchan (paradise). When you surface to the present your unrelenting consciousness shrieks, "Stop resisting the truth of what's really happening, face your reality." But salvation is elusive like the scent of a dim memory. De éste lugar de muerte viva the promise of sunlight is unreachable. Though you want deliverance you cling to your misery.

You look around, hoping some person or thing will alleviate the pain. Pero virgen santisima, you've purposely cut yourself off from those who could help—you've no desire to reconnect with community. Separated from all your tribes, estás en exilio en un destierro, forced to confront your own desconocimientos. Though you choose to face the beast depression alone you have no tools to deal with it. Overwhelmed, you shield yourself with ignorance, blanking out what you don't want to see. Yet you feel you're incubating some knowledge that could spring into life like a childhood monster if you paid it the slightest attention. The last thing you want is to meditate on your condition, bring awareness to the fore, but you've set it up so you must face reality. Still, you resist. You close your eyes to the ravening light waiting to burst through the cracks. Once again you embrace desconocimientos's comfort in willful unawareness. Behind your isolation is its opposite—a smouldering desire for love and connection. You pour ice water on that fire.

Last night cramps in your legs jerked you awake every few minutes. The lightest touch of the sheet burned your legs and feet. Finally you fell asleep, only to be roused out of your dreams by a hypo, a hypoglycemic incident—not enough sugar in the blood. Heart pounding, dripping sweat, confused, you couldn't remember what to do. Listing from side to side, you staggered to the kitchen and gulped down orange juice with two teaspoons of sugar. The thought of one night sleeping through a hypo and slipping into a coma te espanta.

Now you sag against the bridge rail and stare at the railroad tracks below. You swallow, tasting the fear of your own death. You can no longer deny your own mortality, no longer escape into your head—your body's illness has taken residence in all your thoughts, catapulting you into the Coatlicue state, the hellish third phase of your journey. You listen to the wind howling like la Llorona on a moonless night. Mourning the loss, you sink like a stone into a deep depression, brooding darkly in the lunar landscape of your inner world. In the night mind of the night world, abandoned to a maelstrom of chaos, you dream of your own darkness, a surrealist sueño of disintegration.

Beating your breast like a gothic heroine, you burst into the melodramatic histrionics of the victim. Cast adrift from all that's familiar, you huddle deep in the womb cave, a stone repelling light. In the void of your own nothingness, you lie in a fetal curl clutching the fragmented pieces and bits of yourself you've disowned. As you listen to the distant waves slapping the cliffs, your shadow-beast rises from its dark corner and mounts you, punishing you with isolation. Eres cuentista con manos amarradas, poeta sin saliva sin palabra sin pluma. Escondida en tu cueva no puedes levantar cabeza, estás cansada y decepcionada. Los días vuelan como hojas en el viento. Impaled bats infest your dreams and dark clouds move through your soul like shadows. You wallow in the ruins of your life—pobre de ti—until you can't stand the stench that's yourself.

On the edge of awareness, you seek comfort by blanking out reality and retreating into fantasies. You succumb to your addiction of choice—binge reading. During these gray foggy endless days and nights, you lose yourself in Lucha Corpi mysteries. Sucked into Laurell Hamilton's stories of Anita Blake killing and loving vampires and werewolves, you turn pagina after page to drown out la Llorona's voice, the voice of your musa bruja. Pero el viento keeps blowing and your black angelos (daemon) whispering, "Why aren't you writing?" But you have no energy to feed the writing. Getting out of bed is a Sisyphean task. Like the ghost woman you become a pale shade of your former self, a victim of the internalized ideals you've failed to live up to.

When first diagnosed with diabetes, your response was denial. This couldn't be happening, hadn't your body paid its dues? Why now, when you had the time and means to do good work? Digging in your heels you refused the reality—always your first line of defense to emotional pain. But the reality intruded: your body had betrayed you. You no longer had the agility to climb up to the roof to check the leak over the living room. Were you being punished for having been found wanting? No, it is you, not an external force, punishing yourself.

Back on the timber bridge, the wind shifts, whipping your hair away from your eyes. La Llorona's wail rises, urging you to pay heed. All seven ojos de luz blink "on." Your body trembles as a new knowing slithers up like a snake, stirring you out of your stupor. You raise your head and look around. Following the railroad tracks to the horizon, you note the stages of your life, the turning points, the rips in your life's fabric. Gradually the pain and grief force you to face your situation, the daily issues of living laid bare by the event that has split your world apart. You can't change the reality, but you can change your attitude toward it, your interpretation of it. If you can't get rid of your disease, you must learn to live with it. As your perception shifts, your emotions shift—you gain a new understanding of your negative feelings. By seeing your symptoms not as signs of sickness and disintegration but as signals of growth, you're able to rise from depression's slow suicide. By using these feelings as tools or grist for the mill, you move through fear, anxiety, anger, and blast into another reality. But transforming habitual feelings is the hardest thing you've ever attempted.

As you begin to know and accept the self uncovered by the trauma, you pull the blinders off, take in the new landscape in brief glances. Gradually you arouse the agent in this drama, begin to act, to dis-identify with the fear and the isolation. You sit quietly and meditate, trance into an altered state of consciousness, temporarily suspending your usual frames of reference and beliefs while your creative self seeks a solution to your problem by being receptive to new patterns of association. You observe how stimuli trigger responses from your body and how these reactions function. You urge yourself to cooperate with the body instead of sabotaging its self-healing. You draw a map of where you've been, how you've lived, where you're going. Sorting and resorting, you go through the trauma's images, feelings, sensations. While an internal transformation tries to keep pace with each rift, each reenactment shifts your ground again.

A paradox: the knowledge that exposes your fears can also remove them. Seeing through these cracks makes you uncomfortable because it reveals aspects of yourself (shadow-beasts) you don't want to own. Admitting your darker aspects allows you to break out of your self-imposed prison. But it will cost you. When you woo el oscuro, digging into it, sooner or later you pay the consequences—the pain of personal growth. Conocimiento will not let you forget the shadow self, greedy, gluttonous, and indifferent, will not let you lock the cold "bitch" in the basement anymore. Though modern therapies exhort you to act against your passions (compulsions), claiming health and integration lie in that direction, you've learned that delving more fully into your pain, anger, despair, depression will move you through them to the other side, where you can use their energy to heal. Depression is useful—it signals that you need to make changes in your life, it challenges your tendency to withdraw, it reminds you to take action. To reclaim body consciousness tienes que moverte—go for walks, salir a conocer mundo, engage with the world.

Periods of being lost in chaos occur when you're between "stories," before you shift from one set of perceptions and beliefs to another, from one mood to another. By realizing that it's negative thoughts (your reactions to events) that rouse the beast and not something "real" or unchangeable out there in the outer world, you avert being hijacked by past trauma and the demons of self-pity and doomsday ruminations. But you also know that grief and depression may originate in the outside world. You still grieve for this country's original trauma—the most massive act of genocide in the world's history, the mass murder of indigenous peoples. Before the European colonizers came to the "new world" there were five to seven-and-a-half million Indians in the territory between Mexico and Canada. By 1900 there were less than 250,000 left (Stiffarm). You descended from the world's oldest "races," thirty or forty thousand years old, and you cry out at the injustice, the waste. You mourn the devastation that the slave trade cost Africa and the United States. You lament the loss of connection to the Earth, a conscious being that keens through you for all the trees felled, air poisoned, water polluted, animals slaughtered into extinction.

Above, Coyolxauhqui's luz pulls you from the pit of your grief. Realizing that you always use the same tactics, repeat the same behaviors in each stage, breaks your paralysis. What you most desire is a way up, a way out. You know that you've fallen off a metaphorical bridge and into the depths. You look up toward la luna casting light in the darkness. Its bouncing light filters through the water. You want to heal; you want to be transformed. You begin the slow ascent, and as you rise feel as though you're passing through the birth canal, the threshold nepantla. Only when you emerge from the dead with soul intact can you honor the visions you dreamed in the depths. In the deep fecund cave of gestation lies not only the source of your woundedness and your passion, but also the promise of inner knowledge, healing, and spiritual rebirth (the hidden treasures), waiting for you to bear them to the surface.

During the Coatlicue phase you thought you'd wandered off the path of conocimiento, but this detour is part of the path. You bodymindsoul is the hermetic vessel where transformation takes place. The shift must be more than intellectual. Escaping the illusion of isolation, you prod yourself to get out of bed, clean your house, then yourself. You light la virgen de Guadalupe candle and copal, and, with a bundle of yierbitas (ruda y yerba buena), brush the smoke down your body, sweeping away the pain, grief, and fear of the past that's been stalking you, severing the cords binding you to it.

You realize you've severed mind from body and reversed the dichotomy—in the beginning you blamed the body for betraying you, now you blame your mind. Affirming they're not separate, you begin to own the bits of yourself you've disowned, take back the projections you've cast onto others, and relinquish your victim identity. Ésta limpia unclogs your ears, enabling you to hear the rustling of los espíritus; it loosens the constriction in your throat, allowing you to talk with them. Claiming the creative powers and processes of the unconscious (Coyolxauhqui), you thank your soul for the intense emotions y los desconocimientos that wrung consciousness from you. Though you try to thank the universe for your illness, emotional trauma, and habits that interfere with living fully, you still can't accept these, may never be fully present with the pain, never fully embrace the parts of self you ousted from consciousness, may never forgive the unconscious for turning hostile. Though you know change will happen when you stop resisting the dark side of your reality, still you resist. But despite the dread and spiritual emptying, the work you do in the world is not ready to release you.

4. the call . . . el compromiso . . . the crossing and conversion

At four in the morning, the pounding of your heart wakes you. It's banging so hard you're afraid it'll crack your ribs. You sit up gasping for air, fumble for the bed light, and pull the switch. Your arms are livid and swollen like sausages. Your face feels puffy and so hot it scorches your fingertips. Something slithers and swooshes against the inside walls. Bile rises, your stomach heaves. It feels like you've giving birth to a huge stone. Something pops out, you fall back onto the mattress in blessed relief. Is this what it feels like to die?

Cool and light as a feather, you float near the ceiling looking down at your body spread-eagle on the bed, a bed that's in the wrong place and reversed—the room is oddly elongated, the walls curved, the floor sloped. Though it's deep night and the light's off—but didn't you just turn it on?—you see everything like it was high noon in the desert. As you float overhead you bob into a white light—the lightbulb or the sun? You could glide out the window and never return. The instant you think this, you swoop back into the body. The re-entry feels like squeezing ten pounds of chorizo through a keyhole.

You get out of bed, stretch cramped limbs and stumble across the room like an arthritic patient. Soon energy zings up tu cuerpo (body) in an ecstacy so intense it can't be contained. You twirl around, hugging yourself, picking up speed and kicking the walls. Later you wonder if you made up an out-of-body story in an attempt to explain the inexplicable. It dawns on you that *you're not contained by your skin*—you exist outside your body, and outside your dreambody as well. If the body is energy, is spirit—it doesn't have boundaries. What if you experienced your body expanding to the size of the room, not your soul leaving your body? What if freedom from categories occurs by widening the psyche/body's borders, widening the consciousness that senses self (the body is the basis for the conscious sense of self, the representation of self in the mind)? It follows that if you're not contained by your race, class, gender, or sexual identity, the body must be more than the categories that mark you.

Leaving the body reinforces the mind/body, matter/spirit dichotomy you're trying to show does not exist in reality. The last thing you want to uphold is the Cartesian split, but thus far you haven't a clue how to unknot el nudo de cuerpo/mente/alma despite just having had an experience that intellectually unknots it. If el conocimiento that body is both spirit and matter intertwined is the solution, it's one difficult to live out, requiring that this knowledge be lived daily in embodied ways. Only then may the split be healed.[13]

What pulled you out of your body? Was the seven-seven you drank at the party still in your system when you took the Percodan? You know that mixing booze with drugs can end in death, so why did you do it? So that el jaguar, tu doble, que vigila por la noche could come from the south to stalk you, to pull you de tu cuerpo so you could experience . . . what, a different kind of knowledge? In the deepest part of night you followed the jaguar through the transparent wall between the worlds. Shapes shifted. Did you assume another pair of eyes, another pair of ears, another body, another dreambody? Maybe you took your physical body, and in this other place it metamorphosed into a jaguar.

Acts of self-abuse may lead to insight—or so you rationalize your experimenting with mind-expanding drugs. Insight originates from the light of the moon (Coyolxauhqui consciousness), enabling you to see through your identifications, through the walls that your ethnic cultural traditions and religious beliefs have erected. The lechuza eyes[14] of your naguala open, rousing you from the trance of hyper-rationality induced by higher education. An image flickers—nonverbal, brief, and subtle—signaling otro conocimiento: besides the mortal body you have a transtemporal, immortal one. This knowing prompts you to shift into a new perception of yourself and the world. Nothing is fixed. The pulse of existence, the heart of the universe is fluid. Identity, like a river, is always changing, always in transition, always in nepantla. Like the river downstream, you're not the same person you were upstream. You begin to define yourself in terms of who you are becoming, not who you have been.

These states of awareness, while vital, don't last. Yet they provide the faith that enables you to continue la lucha. When feeling low, the longing for your potential self is an ache deep within. Something within flutters its feathers, stretches toward the sky. You try to listen more closely, bringing all your faculties to bear on transforming your condition. Using these insights to alter your current thoughts and behavior, you reinterpret their meanings. As you learn from the different stages you pass through, your reactions to past events change. You re-member your experiences in a new arrangement. Your responses to the challenges of daily life also adjust. As you continually reinterpret your past, you reshape your present. Instead of walking your habitual routes you forge new ones. The changes affect your biology. The cells in your brain shift and, in turn, create new pathways, rewiring your brain.

On the path ahead you see otro puente, a footbridge with missing planks, broken rails. You walk toward it, step onto the threshold, and freeze, right hand clutching the past, left hand stretching toward the unknown. Behind, the world admonishes you to stick to the old-and-tried dominant paradigm, the secure relationships within it. Adelante, la Llorona whispers, "You have a task, a calling, only you can bring forth your potential." You yearn to know what that ever-present inner watcher is asking of you. Loosening your grip on the known and reaching for the future requires that you stretch beyond self- and culturally-imposed limits. By now you've found renmants of a community—people on a similar quest/path. To transform yourself, you need the help (the written or spoken words) of those who have crossed before you. You want them to describe las puertas, to hold your hand while crossing them. You want them to mentor your work within the Chicana, queer, artistic, feminist, spiritual, and other communities.

To learn what to transform into you ask, "How can I contribute?" You open yourself and listen to la naguala and the images, sensations, and dreams she presents. (La naguala's presence is so subtle and fleeting it barely registers unless tracked by your attention's radar.) Your inner voice reveals your core passion, which will point to your sense of purpose, urging you to seek a vision, devise a plan. Your passion motivates you to discover resources within yourself and in the world. It prompts you to take responsibility for consciously creating your life and becoming a fully functioning human being, a contributing member of all your communities, one worthy of self-respect and love. You want to pursue your mission with integrity, to honor yourself and to be honored. Holding these realizations in mind, you stand at the brink and reconsider the crossing.

Are you sure you're ready to face the shadow-beast guarding the threshold—that part of you holding your failures and inadequacies, the negativities you've internalized, and those aspects of gender and class you want to disown? Recognizing and coming to terms with the manipulative, vindictive, secretive shadow-beast within will take the heaviest toll. Maybe this bridge shouldn't be crossed. Once crossed, it can't be uncrossed. To pass over the bridge to something else, you'll have to give up partial organizations of self, erroneous bits of knowledge, outmoded beliefs of who you are, your comfortable identities (your story of self, tu autohistoria[15]). You'll have to leave parts of yourself behind.

The bridge (boundary between the world you've just left and the one ahead) is both a barrier and point of transformation. By crossing, you invite a turning point, initiate a change. And change is never comfortable, easy, or neat. It'll overturn all your relationships, leave behind lover, parent, friend, who, not wanting to disturb the status quo nor lose you, try to keep you from changing. Okay, so cambio is hard. Tough it out, you tell yourself. Doesn't life consist of crossing a series of thresholds? Conocimiento hurts, but not as much as desconocimiento. In the final reckoning it comes down to a matter of faith, trusting that your inner authority will carry across the critical threshold. You must make the leap alone and of your own will. Having only partial knowledge of the consequences of crossing, you offer la Llorona, who regulates the passage, a token. You pray, repeat affirmations, take a deep breath, and step through the gate. Immediately, a knowing cracks the facade of your former self and its entrenched beliefs: you are not alone; those of the invisible realm walk with you; there are ghosts on every bridge.

You stand on tierra sagrada—nature is alive and conscious; the world is ensouled. You lift your head to the sky, to the wingspread of pelicans, the stark green of trees, the wind sighing through their branches. You discern faces in the rocks and allow them to see you. You become reacquainted with a reality called spirit, a presence, force, power, and energy within and without. Spirit infuses all that exists—organic and inorganic—transcending the categories and concepts that govern your perception of material reality. Spirit speaks through your mouth, listens through your ears, sees through your eyes, touches with your hands. At times the sacred takes you unaware; the desire to change prompts it and then discipline allows it to happen.

With awe and wonder you look around, recognizing the preciousness of the earth, the sanctity of every human being on the planet, the ultimate unity and interdependence of all beings—somos todos un país. Love swells in your body and shoots out of your heart chakra, linking you to everyone/everything—the aboriginals in Australia, the crows in the forest, the vast Pacific Ocean. You share a category of identity wider than any social position or racial label. This conocimiento motivates you to work actively to see that no harm comes to people, animals, ocean—to take up spiritual activism and the work of healing. Te entregas a tu promesa to help your various cultures create new paradigms, new narratives.

Knowing that something in you, or of you, must die before something else can be born, you throw your old self into the ritual pyre, a passage by fire. In relinquishing your old self, you realize that some aspects of who you are—identities people have imposed on you as a woman of color and that you have internalized—are also made up. Identity becomes a cage you reinforce and double-lock yourself into. The life you thought inevitable, unalterable, and fixed in some foundational reality is smoke, a mental construction, fabrication. So, you reason, if it's all made up, you can compose it anew and differently.

5. putting Coyolxauhqui together . . . new personal and collective "stories"

Returning from the land of the dead, you wake up in the hospital bed minus your ovaries and uterus. Scattered around you en pedazos is the old story's corpse with its perceptions of who you used to be.[16] Como luciérnaga a light crosses your dark inner landscape awakening un saber (a knowing). You've passed a turning point—decided not to drag the dead self into the present and future just to preserve your history. Instead you've chosen to compose a new history and self—to rewrite your autohistoria. You want to be transformed again; you want a keener mind, a stronger spirit, a wiser soul. Your ailing body is no longer a hindrance but an asset, witnessing pain, speaking to you, demanding touch. Es tu cuerpo que busca conocimiento; along with dreams your body's the royal road to consciousness.

Before rewriting the disentegrating, often destructive "stories" of self contructed by psychology, sociology, anthropology, biology, and religion you must first recognize their faulty pronouncements, scrutinize the fruit they've borne, and then ritually disengage from them. Reflexive awareness and other aspects of conocimiento if practiced daily overule external instructions transmitted by your ethnic and dominant cultures, override the internal mandates of your genes and personal ego. Knowing the beliefs and directives your spiritual self generates empowers you to shift perceptions, te capacita a soñar otros modos of conducting your life, revise the scripts of your various identities, and use these new narratives to intervene in the cultures' existing dehumanizing stories.

After examining the old self's stance on life/death, misma/otra, individual/collective consciousness, you shift the axis/structure of reference by reversing the polarities, erasing the slash between them, then adding new aspects of yourself. To make meaning from your experiences you look through an archetypal psycho-mytho-spiritual lens, charting the various shifts of consciousness as they play out in your daily activities. You use your imagination in mediating between inner and outer experience. By writing about the always-in-progress, transformational processes and the constant, on-going reconstruction of the way you view your world, you name and ritualize the moments/processes of transition, inserting them into the collective fabric, bringing into play personal history and fashioning a story greater than yourself.

You shed your former bodymind and its outworn story like a snake its skin. Releasing traumas of the past frees up energy, allowing you to be receptive to the soul's voice and guidance. Taking a deep breath, you close your eyes and call back tu alma—from people, ideas, perceptions, and events you've surrendered it to. You sense parts of your soul return to your body. Another inhalation, more tendrils of spirit re-enter the places where it went missing. The lost pieces draw to you like filaments to a magnet. With a tender newly-formed sense of self you stand, wobbly. Sensing los espíritus all around, you face east, the direction of the visionary, offering a dream of the possible. Challenging the old self's orthodoxy is never enough; you must submit a sketch of an alternative self. As a modern-day Coyolxauhqui, you search for an account that encapsulates your life, and finding no ready-made story, you trust her light in the darkness to help you bring forth (from remnants of the old personal/collective autohistoria) a new personal myth.

After dismantling the body/self you re-compose it—the fifth stage of the journey, though reconstruction takes place in all stages. When creating a personal narrative you also co-create the group/cultural story. You examine the description handed to you of the world, picking holes in the paradigms currently constructing reality. You doubt that traditional western science is the best knowledge system, the only true, impartial arbiter of reality. You question its definition of progress, whose manifest destiny imperializes other peoples' energies and snuffs out their realities and hopes of a better life. You now see the western story as one of patriarchal, hierarchical control; fear and hatred of women; dominion over nature; science/technology's promise of expanding power; seduction of commerce, and, to be fair, a celebration of individual rights—freedom, creativity, and ingenuity. You turn the established narrative on its head, seeing through, resisting, and subverting its assumptions. Again, it's not enough to denounce the culture's old account—you must provide new narratives embodying alternative potentials. You're sure of one thing: the consciousness that's created our social ills (dualistic and misogynist) cannot solve them—we need a more expansive conocimiento. The new stories must partially come from outside the system of ruling powers.

You examine the contentions accompanying the old cultural narratives: your ethnic tribe wants you to isolate, insisting that you remain within race and class boundaries. The dominant culture prefers that you abandon your roots and assimilate, insisting that you leave your Indianness behind and seek shelter under the Hispanic or Latino umbrella. The temptation to succumb to these assimilationist tactics and escape the stigma of being Mexican stalls you on the bridge between isolation and assimilation. But both are debilitating. How can you step outside ethnic and other labels while cleaving to your root identity? Your identity has roots you share with all people and other beings—spirit, feeling, and body make up a greater identity category. The body is rooted in the earth, la tierra itself. You meet ensoulment in trees, in woods, in streams. The roots del árbol de la vida of all planetary beings are nature, soul, body.

Reframing the old story points to another option besides assimilation and separation—a "new tribalism."[17] An image of your tío's dying orange tree comes to mind, one still possessed of a strong root system and trunk. Tu tío grafted a sturdier variety of orange to it, creating a more vigorous tree. In similar fashion you "grow into" an identity of mestizaje you call the new tribalism by propagating other worldviews, spiritual traditions, and cultures to your árbol de la vida. You pick and choose views, cultures with transformational potential—a partially conscious selection, not a mestizaje imposed on you, but one whose process you can control. (You distinguish this mestizaje from acts of hybridization such as genetically engineering and modifying live organisms without their consent or consideration of their existence as integrated beings, or from acts resulting in cyborgian animal/machine hybrids.) A retribalizing mestizaje becomes your coping mechanism, your strategy of resistance to both acculturating and inculturating pressures.

Tussling con remolinos (whirlwinds) of different belief systems builds the muscles of mestiza consciousness, enabling it to stretch. Being Chicana (indigenous, Mexican, Basque, Spanish, Berber-Arab, Gypsy) is no longer enough, being female, woman of color, patlache (queer) no longer suffices. Your resistance to identity boxes leads you to a different tribe, a different story (of mestizaje) enabling you to rethink yourself in more global-spiritual terms instead of conventional categories of color, class, career. It calls you to retribalize your identity to a more inclusive one, redefining what it means to be una mexicana de este lado, an American in the U.S., a citizen of the world, classifications reflecting an emerging planetary culture. In this narrative national boundaries dividing us from the "others" (nos/otras) are porous and the cracks between worlds serve as gateways.

At first la nueva historia resembles Shelley's Frankenstein monster—mismatched parts pieced together artificially—but soon the new rendition fuels your drive to seek alternative and emerging knowledges. It motivates you to expose oppressive cultural beliefs, such as that all women are traicioneras (betrayers), queers are abnormal, whites are superior, and sparing the rod spoils the child, and replace these notions with new ones. It inspires you to engage both inner and outer resources to make changes on multiple fronts: inner/spiritual/personal, social/collective/material.

The new stories explore aspects of reality—consciousness, hope, intention, prayer—that traditional science has ignored, deeming these nonexistent as they cannot be tested in a lab. In the new stories, postmodern science shifts its orientation, no longer holding itself to what can be validated empirically by the five senses. It acknowledges non-physical reality, inner subjective experiences, and spirit. The world, from the depth of the sea to the highest mountain, is alive, intelligent, ensouled. In the fourth stage del camino de conocimiento you caught glimmers of this holistic story—a paradigm that's always served indigenous cultures. Beliefs and values from the wisdom of past spiritual traditions of diverse cultures coupled with current scientific knowledge is the basis of the new synthesis. The emerging narratives are multicultural. They not only insist on analyzing and combatting oppressive power systems, but advocate the need to collaborate and capacitar (empower) in realizing common goals.

The new accounts trace the process of shifting from old ways of viewing reality to new perceptions. They depict your struggles, recount your losses, re-ignite your hope for recovery, and celebrate the workings of the soul that nourish us with visions. They articulate unnamed, unvoiced, and repressed experiences and realities. The new versions of reality they offer demand that you employ alternative ways of knowing and re-wire your ways of seeing, thinking, feeling, and expressing. By using information derived from multiple channels and different systems of knowing you collectively create new societies. Together you attempt to reverse the Cartesian split that turned the world into an "other," distancing humans from it. Though your body is still la otra and though pensamientos dualisticos still keep you from embracing and uniting corporally con esa otra, you dream of the possibility of wholeness. Collectively, you rewrite the story of "the fall" and the story of western progress (Tarnas, 22)—two opposing versions of the evolution of human consciousness. Collectively you note the emergence of the new gatekeepers of the earth's wisdom.

Led by the light of the moon (Coyolxauhqui consciousness), you take the fifth step and see through the illusion of permanence—the fantasy that you can pull yourself together once and for all and live happily ever after. You again suffer otro espanto, and another dislocation. Surrendering the self, sacrificing a certain way of being, you go through the whole process again, repeating all seven stages of the cycle. Your inability to live with your old self is also a bodily function and not merely a mind thing—every seven years your body sheds its cells completely as it regenerates new cells. When the latest story/self/body ceases to be credible or is not developing the way you want, you reinterpret the story you imagine yourself to be living. Tu autohistoria is not carved in stone but drawn on sand and subject to shifting winds. Forced to rework your story, you invent new notions of yourself and reality—increasingly multidimensional versions where body, mind, and spirit interpenetrate in more complex ways.

In struggling with adversity and noting your reactions to it you observe how thoughts direct perceptions of reality. You realize that personal/collective reality is created (often unconsciously) and that you're the artist scripting the new story of this house/self/identity/essay under construction. You realize it's the process that's valuable and not the end product, not the new you, as that will change often throughout your life. Connecting the disparate parts of information from a new perspective, you re-member Coyolxauhqui in a new composition, temporarily restoring your balance and wounded psyche. Your story's one of la búsqueda de conocimiento, of seeking experiences that'll give you purpose, give your life meaning, give you a sense of belonging. It's a quest story of ordeal and distress, cyclic life-stages, and identity transformations. Like the heroine in a myth or fairy tale, after an arduous struggle in the dark woods, you return, bringing new knowledge to share with others in your communities.

Coyolxauhqui personifies the wish to repair and heal, as well as rewrite the stories of loss and recovery, exile and homecoming, disinheritance and recuperation, stories that lead out of passivity and into agency, out of devalued into valued lives. Coyolxauhqui represents the search for new metaphors to tell you what you need to know, how to connect and use the information gained, and, with intelligence, imagination, and grace, solve your problems and create intercultural communities.

6. the blow-up . . . a clash of realities

New knowledge occurs through tension, difficulties, mistakes and chaos.
                                                                —*Risa D'Angeles*

You fly in from another speaking gig on the East Coast, arriving at the feminist academic conference late. Hayas un desmadre. A racist incident has unleashed flames of anger held in check for decades. In postures of defiance, enraged women of color protest their exclusion from the woman's organization decision-making processes; "white" middle-class women stand, arms crossed, refusing to alter its policies. When they continue conducting business as usual las mujeres de color walk out.

The urgency compelling every woman to give testimony to her views is so thick you can almost taste it. Caras reflejan angustia and blanched looks of shock; eyes glint with hostility; feelings of disgust, bitterness, disillusionment, and betrayal clash, spatter, and scatter in all directions. These emotions flare through your body as you turn from one group to another like a weathervane. You lose yourself in the maelstrom, no longer able to find the calm place within as everything collapses into unresolvable conflict. You know that in the heart of the conflagration lies its solution, but your own anguish clouds true perception. Catching your co-presenter's eye, you both grimace in recognition. Though for years you've felt the tectonic bedrock of feminism shifting under your feet, you never imagined the seismic crack would be so devastating, the blow-out so scorching. El mar de coraje (anger) se te viene encima—you recoil from its heat. Trying to be objective, you distance yourself until you feel as though you're in an airplane observing safely from above.

Like most feminist conferences, this one begins as a bridge, a place of mutual access where thousands crisscross, network, share ideas, and struggle together to resolve women's issues. After fifteen years of struggle, of putting their trust on this common space, of waiting for the organization to deal with racism as it's promised, the women of color and some Jewish, working-class, and progressive white allies feel betrayed by their white middle-class sisters. Seething in frustration, they cancel their panels and workshops, quejandose que las feministas anglas do not allow their intellectual, emotional, and spiritual realities into this academic setting. They're tired of being treated as outsiders. They feel that whites still view issues of racism as the concern of women of color alone, anti-Semitism the concern only of Jewish women, homophobia the concern of lesbians, and class the concern of working-class and poor women. They accuse whites of reinscribing the imperialist tradition of dominance and call them on their white privilege.

White women accuse women of color and their allies of emotionalism—after all, this is the academy. Feeling unjustly attacked, they adamantly proclaim they're not racist but just following the organization's policies. Though their intentions—making "common ground"—are good, they don't realize that su base de acuerdo may be different or too narrow from el terreno comunal de otras mujeres and not really common at all. They ignore the input of mujeres de color in defining common ground.

You view most white women's racism as covert and always cloaked. An insidious desconocimiento, it refuses to allow emotional awareness and its threat into their consciousness. They deny their recognition of the situation, then forget having denied this recognition. This forgetting of having forgotten their denial (repression) is at the core of desconocimiento. Though most white feminists intellectually acknowledge racism, they distance themselves from personal responsibility, often acting as though their reality and ways of knowing are universal, not culturally determined. They assume that feminist racialized "others" share their same values and goals. Some view gender and race oppression as interchangeable. As members of a colonized gender, they believe they're experts on oppression and can define all its forms; thus they don't have to listen/learn from racial others. They herd women of color under the banner of their brand of feminism and impose their experiences and interpretations of reality, especially of academic life, on them—all racist acts.

The refusal to think about race (itself a form of racism) is a "white" privilege. The white women who do think about race rarely delve beyond the surface: they allude to the category, cite a few women-of-color texts, tack on a token book to their syllabi, and assume they've dealt with race. Though many understand the racism perpetrated by white individuals, most do not understand the racism inherent in their identities, in their cultures' stories. They can't see that racism harms them as well as people of color, itself a racially superior attitude. Those who see don't feel prepared to deal with race, though they do "feel bad" about it, suffering the monkey on their backs—survivor guilt, the guilt of privilege that, unac-knowledged, breeds greater guilt.

When their racism is exposed they claim they're the victims of attacks and are outraged at being "mauled" by these pit-bullish others. They use white privilege to coax women of color to toe the line. When that doesn't work they pull rank. They fail to meet the women of color halfway, don't bother negotiating the give-and-take between "majority" culture and "minority." Though they may pay lip service to diversity issues, most don't shift from positions of power. The privilege of whiteness allows them to evade questions of complicity with those in power; it gives leave to disre-spect other peoples' realities and types of knowledge—race and soul remain four-letter words. Their socialization does not allow women-of-color consciousness to transform their thinking. Afraid of losing material and psychological privilege, they drown others' voices with white noise.

Con nudo en la garganta, you look at your hermanas de color, chal-lenged warriors, who try to stop being victims only to fall into the trap of claiming moral higher ground, using skin color as license for judging a whole category of people. They're forced to belabor the point because most white women won't listen. Leading with their wounds focuses their energy on the role of victim: oh, poor me, I'm so oppressed. Though inad-vertently at times you too assume this attitude, you have little sympathy for it. Buying into victimhood forces you/them to compete for the coveted prize of the walking wounded. Many are driven to use the truth of their ill treatment as a stick to beat whites into waking up; they are the experts on oppression and thus don't have to listen/learn from whites. Some women of color—las meras meras—strut around with macha in-your-face aggressiveness. Hiding their vulnerabilities behind clenched fists and a "que se chinguen" attitude, they overlook the wounds bonding them to the other and instead focus on las heridas (wounds) that divide. As a writer one of your tasks is to expose the dualistic nature of the debate between whites and people of color, the false idealized pictures and other desconocimientos each group has but would rather ignore, and promote a more holistic perspective.

Seeing women from both camps throw words at each other like stones gives you stomach cramps. Apedradas (pelted with stones), each woman tries to regain her ground. Weaving her experience into a story-line where she's the one put-upon, she incites her allies to torch the bridge with inflammatory rhetoric. Pitting herself against the other (the enemy), she feeds las llamas her energy and repressed shadow parts, turn-ing the conference into a militarized zone where desconocimiento runs rampant. In full-frontal attack, each camp adopts an "us-versus-them" model that assumes a winner and loser, a wrong and right—the prevailing conflict resolution paradigm of our times, one we continue using despite the recognition that confrontational tactics rarely settle disputes for the long run.

You watch some women react to psychological violence in instinctive knee-jerk ways or in ways they've programmed themselves or have been programmed to respond. The usual tactics for dealing with conflict and threat are fighting, fleeing, freezing, or submitting. Those fighting or fleeing shut their ears and assume a hypervigilant guard mode to help them attack or escape. Those freezing separate their awareness from the reality of what's happening—they dissociate. Those submitting surrender their ground to more aggressive forces. All struggle to burrow back into their past histories, former skins, familiar racial and class enclaves even though these may be rife with discomfort and disillusionment and no longer feel like "home."

Caught in the middle of the power struggle, you're forced to take sides, forced to negotiate another identity crisis. Being coerced to turn your back on one group/person and favor the other feels like a knife to the heart. It reminds you of the seventies when other lesbians reprimanded you and urged you to abandon your friendships with men. Women of color will brand you disloyal if you don't walk out with them. Nationalistic fence-maintainers will label you malinchista; lesbians will think you not queer enough. You retreat from your feelings, take refuge in your head, priding yourself on equanimity, an objectivity detached from the biases of personal fear, anger, anxiety. As you observe others, pitying their misguided actions, you catch yourself feeling superior because you don't let your emotions take over. Not you, you've achieved spiritual and emotional equilibrium. You'd like to believe that detachment is always a strength, that remaining emotionally distant allows you to bring a sense of balance to conflicted situations. But instead of attaining spiritual non-attachment, you've withdrawn from painful feelings—a detachment that cuts you from your body and its feelings.

What takes a bashing is not so much you but the idea/picture of who you think you are, an illusion you're hell-bent on protecting and preserving at all costs. You overlook the fact that your self-image and history (autohistoria) are not carved in stone but drawn on sand and subject to the winds. A threat to your identifications and interpretations of reality enrages your shadow-beast, who views the new knowledge as an attack to your bodily integrity. And it is a death threat—to the belief that posits the self as local and limited to a physical body, a body perceived as a container separating the self from other people and other forms of knowledge. New conocimientos (insights) threaten your sense of what's "real" when it's up against what's "real" to the other. But it's precisely this threat that triggers transformation.

You think you've made progress, gained a new awareness, found a new version of reality, created a workable story, fulfilled an obligation, and followed your own conscience. But when you cast to the world what you've created and put your ideals into action, the contradictions explode in your face. Your story fails the reality test. But is the failure due to flaws in your story—based on the tenuous nature of relationship between you and the whole—or is it due to all-too-human and therefore imperfect members of the community?

The bridge buckles under the weight of these feminist factions, and as in the Russian "Tale of Two Goats on the Bridge" (MacDonald), the different groups butt each other off. With other in-betweeners (nepantleras) from both sides of the divide you navigate entre tres aguas trying to sustain some sort of dialogue among the groups. Pronto llegas a un crucero—you have to decide whether to walk off or remain on the bridge and try to facilitate passage. Though you've always been a bridge, not a separatist, es difícil decidir. From the eye of the storm you choose to hold fast to the bridge and witness for all camps. With only half the participants present at the roundtable, you use the forum to discuss the causes of the blow-up and possible strategies to resolve the conflict.

Often in the following days you and other nepantleras feel frustrated, tempted to walk out as the bridge undergoes more tremors. Negotiating cuesta trabajo. Las nepantleras must alter their mode of interaction—make it more inclusive, open. In a to-and-fro motion they shift from their customary position to the reality of first one group then the other. Though tempted to retreat behind racial lines and hide behind simplistic walls of identity, las nepantleras know their work lies in positioning themselves—exposed and raw—in the crack between these worlds, and in revealing current categories as unworkable. Saben que las heridas that separate and those that bond arise from the same source. Besides fighting, fleeing, freezing, or submitting las nepantleras usan otra media—they employ a fifth tactic.

Recognizing that the basic human hunger to be heard, understood, and accepted is not being met, las nepantleras listen to members of both camps. By attending to what the other is not saying, what she's not doing, what isn't happening, and by looking for the opposite, unacknowledged emotion—the opposite of anger is fear, of self-righteousness is guilt, of hate is love—las nepantleras attempt to see through the other's situation to her underlying unconscious desire. Accepting doubts and ambiguity, they reframe the conflict and shift the point of view. Sitting face-to-face with all parties, they identify common bonds, name reciprocities and connections, and finally draft a mutually agreeable contract.

When perpetual conflict erodes a sense of connectedness and wholeness la nepantlera calls on the "connectionist"[18] faculty to show the deep common ground and interwoven kinship among all things and people. This faculty, one of less-structured thoughts, less-rigid categorizations, and thinner boundaries, allows us to picture—via reverie, dreaming, and artistic creativity—similarities instead of solid divisions. In gatherings where people luxuriate in their power to prevent change instead of using it to cause transformation, where they spew verbal abuse in a war of words and do not leave space for others to save face, where feelings are easily bruised or too intense to be controlled by will alone—la nepantlera proposes individual and group rituals to contain volatile feelings and channel them into acts of conocimiento.

In gatherings where people feel powerless la nepantlera offers rituals to say good-bye to old ways of relating; prayers to thank life for making us face loss, anger, guilt, fear, and separation; rezos to acknowledge our individual wounds; and commitments to not give up on others just because they hurt us. In gatherings where we've forgotten that the aim of conflict is peace, la nepantlera proposes spiritual techniques (mindfulness, openess, receptivity) along with activist tactics. Where before we saw only separateness, differences, and polarities, our connectionist sense of spirit recognizes nurturance and reciprocity and encourages alliances among groups working to transform communities. In gatherings where we feel our dreams have been sucked out of us, la nepantlera leads us in celebrating la comunidad soñada, reminding us that spirit connects the irreconcilable warring parts para que todo el mundo se haga un país, so that the whole world may become un pueblo.

7. shifting realities . . . acting out the vision or spiritual activism

The bridge will hold me up.

—*Gabrielle in* Xena, Warrior Princess

You're three years old and standing by the kitchen table staring at the bright orange globe. You can almost taste its tart sweetness. You'll die if you don't have it. You reach for it but your arms are too short. Body quivering, you stretch again, willing yourself to reach the fruit. Your arms elongate until your small hands clasp the orange. You sense you're more than one body—each superimposed on the others like sheaths of corn. Years later after a few more experiences of bilocation, you describe it as a yoga of the body.[19] The ability to recognize and endow meaning to daily experience (spirituality) furthers the ability to shift and transform.

When and how does transformation happen? When a change occurs your consciousness (awareness of your sense of self and your response to self, others, and surroundings) becomes cognizant that it has a point of view and the ability to act from choice. This knowing/knower is always with you, but is displaced by the ego and its perspective. This knower has several functions. You call the function that arouses the awareness that beneath individual separateness lies a deeper interrelatedness "la naguala."

When you shift attention from your customary point of view (the ego) to that of la naguala, and from there move your awareness to an inner-held representation of an experience, person, thing, or world, la naguala and the object observed merge. When you include the complexity of feeling two or more ways about a person/issue, when you empathize and try to see her circumstances from her position, you accommodate the other's perspective, achieving un conocimiento that allows you to shift toward a less defensive, more inclusive identity. When you relate to others, not as parts, problems, or useful commodities, but from a connectionist view compassion triggers transformation. This shift occurs when you give up investment in your point of view[20] and recognize the real situation free of projections—not filtered through your habitual defensive preoccupations. Moving back and forth from the situation to la naguala's view, you glean a new description of the world (reality)—a Toltec interpretation. When you're in the place between worldviews (nepantla) you're able to slip between realities to a neutral perception. A decision made in the in-between place becomes a turning point initiating psychological and spiritual transformations, making other kinds of experiences possible.

Core beliefs command the focus of your senses. By changing some of these convictions you change the mental/emotional channel (the reality). In the Coatlicue state, an intensely negative channel, you're caged in a private hell; you feel angry, fearful, hopeless, and depressed, blaming yourself as inadequate. In the more optimistic space cultivated by las nepantleras, you feel love, peace, happiness, and the desire to grow. Forgiving yourself and others, you connect with more aspects of yourself and others.

Orienting yourself to the environment and your relationship to it enables you to read and garner insight from whatever situation you find yourself in. This conocimiento gives you the flexibility to swing from your intense feelings to those of the other without being hijacked by either. When confronted with the other's fear, you note her emotional arousal, allow her feelings/words to enter your body, then you shift to the neutral place of la naguala. You detach so those feelings won't inhabit your body for long. You listen with respect,[21] attend to the other as a whole being, not an object, even when she opposes you. To avoid miscommunication you frequently check your understanding of the other's meaning, responding with, "Yes, I hear you. Let me repeat your words to make sure

I'm reading you right." When an experience evokes similar feelings in both, you feel momentarily in sync. Like consciousness, conocimiento is about relatedness—to self, others, world.

When you're troubled, conocimiento prompts you to take a deep breath, shift your attention away from what's causing pain and fear, and call upon a power deeper and freer than that of your ego, such as la naguala y los espíritus, for guidance. Direction may also come from an inner impression, dream, meditation, I Ching, Tarot cards. You use these spiritual tools to deal with political and personal problems. Power comes from being in touch with your body, soul, and spirit, and letting their wisdom lead you.

By moving from a militarized zone to a roundtable, nepantleras acknowledge an unmapped common ground: the humanity of the other. We are the other, the other is us—a concept AnaLouise Keating calls "re(con)ceiving the other" (Women, 75–81). Honoring people's otherness, las nepantleras advocate a "nos/otras" position—an alliance between "us" and "others." In nos/otras, the "us" is divided in two, the slash in the middle representing the bridge—the best mutuality we can hope for at the moment. Las nepantleras envision a time when the bridge will no longer be needed—we'll have shifted to a seamless nosotras. This move requires a different way of thinking and relating to others; it requires that we act on our interconnectivity, a mode of connecting similar to hypertexts' multiple links—it includes diverse others and does not depend on traditional categories or sameness. It enacts a retribalization by recognizing that some members of a racial or ethnic group do not necessarily stay with the consciousness and conditioning of the group they're born into, but shift momentarily or permanently. For example, some whites embody a woman-of-color consciousness, and some people of color, a "white" consciousness.

Conocimiento of our interconnectivity encourages white women to examine and deconstruct racism and "whiteness." But perhaps, as Keating suggests, "white" women who are totally invested in this privileged identity can't be nepantleras: "I really think that 'whiteness' is a state of mind—dualistic, supremacist, separatist, hierarchical . . . all the things we're working to transform; I'm still not sure how this concept of 'whiteness' as an oppressive/oppressing mindset corresponds to lightskinned bodies, but I do believe the two are not synonymous."[22]

This move to a roundtable—generated by such concepts as nos/otras and retribalization—incites women of color to speak out and eventually refuse the role of victim. Though most identify with their mestizaje you wonder how much of a mestiza a person must become before racial categories dissolve and new ones develop, before committing to social concerns that move beyond personal group or nation, before an inclusive community forms. You wonder when others will, like las nepantleras, hand themselves to a larger vision, a less-defended identity.

This is your new vision, a story of how conocimiento manifests, but one with a flaw: it doesn't work with things that are insurmountable, or with all people at all times (we haven't evolved to that stage yet), and it doesn't always bring about immediate change. But it works with las nepantleras, boundary-crossers, thresholders who initiate others in rites of passage, activistas who, from a listening, receptive, spiritual stance, rise to their own visions and shift into acting them out, haciendo mundo nuevo (introducing change). Las nepantleras walk through fire on many bridges (not just the conference one) by turning the flames into a radiance of awareness that orients, guides, and supports those who cannot cross over on their own. Inhabiting the liminal spaces where change occurs, las nepantleras encourage others to ground themselves to their own bodies and connect to their own internal resources, thus empowering themselves. Empowerment is the bodily feeling of being able to connect with inner voices/resources (images, symbols, beliefs, memories) during periods of stillness, silence, and deep listening or with kindred others in collective actions. This alchemy of connection provides the knowledge, strength, and energy to persist and be resilient in pursuing goals. Éste modo de capacitar comes from accepting your own authority to direct rather than letting others run you.

Not long ago your mother gave you un milagro, a tiny silver hand with a heart in its palm, never knowing that for years this image has resonated with your concept of el mundo zurdo amplified here into the model of conocimiento; la mano zurda with a heart in its palm is for engaging with self, others, world. The hand represents acting out and daily implementing an idea or vision, as opposed to merely theorizing about it. The heart es un corazón con razon, with intelligence, passion, and purpose, a "mindfull" heart with ears for listening, eyes for seeing, a mouth with tongue narrowing to a pen tip for speaking/writing. The left hand is not a fist pero una mano abierta raised with others in struggle, celebration, and song. Conocimiento es otro mode de conectar across colors and other differences to allies also trying to negotiate racial contradictions, survive the stresses and traumas of daily life, and develop a spiritual-imaginal-political vision together. Conocimiento shares a sense of affinity with all things and advocates mobilizing, organizing, sharing information, knowledge, insights, and resources with other groups.

Although all your cultures reject the idea that you can know the other, you believe that besides love, pain might open this closed passage by reaching through the wound to connect. Wounds cause you to shift consciousness—they either open you to the greater reality normally blocked by your habitual point of view or else shut you down, pushing you out of your body and into desconocimiento. Like love, pain might trigger compassion—if you're tender with yourself, you can be tender to others. Using wounds as openings to become vulnerable and available (present) to others means staying in your body. Excessive dwelling on your wounds means leaving your body to live in your thoughts, where you re-enact your past hurts, a form of desconocimiento that gives energy to the past, where it's held ransom. As victim you don't have to take resposibility for making changes. But the cost of victimhood is that nothing in your life changes, especially not your attitudes, beliefs. Instead, why not use pain as a conduit to recognizing another's suffering, even that of the one who inflicted the pain? In all the great stories, says Jean Houston (105–6), wounding is the entrance to the sacred. Openings to the sacred can also be triggered by joyful experiences—for example meditation, epiphanies, communion with nature, sexual ecstasy, and desire—as in your childhood experience of reaching for the orange. Because most of you are wounded, negative emotions provide easier access to the sacred than do positive emotions.

You reflect on experiences that caused you, at critical points of transformation, to adopt spiritual activism. When you started traveling and doing speaking gigs, the harried, hectic, frenzied pace of the activist stressed you out, subjecting you to a pervasive form of modern violence that Thomas Merton attributes to the rush of continual doing. To deal with personal concerns while also confronting larger issues in the public arena, you began using spiritual tools to cope with racial and gender oppression and other modern maldades—not so much the seven deadly sins, but the small acts of desconocimientos: ignorance, frustrations, tendencies toward self-destructiveness, feelings of betrayal and powerlessness, and poverty of spirit and imagination. The spiritual practice of conocimiento: praying, breathing deeply, meditating, writing—dropping down into yourself, through the skin and muscles and tendons, down deep into the bones' marrow, where your soul is ballast—enabled you to defuse the negative energy of putdowns, complaints, excessive talk, verbal attacks, and other killers of the spirit. Spirituality became a port you moor to in all storms.

This work of spiritual activism and the contract of holistic alliances allows conflict to dissolve through reflective dialogue. It permits an expansive awareness that finds the best instead of the worst in the other, enabling you to think of la otra in a compassionate way. Accepting the other as an equal in a joint endeavor, you respect and are fully present for her. You form an intimate connection that fosters the empowerment of both (nos/otras) to transform conflict into an opportunity to resolve an issue, to change negativities into strengths, and to heal the traumas of racism and other systemic desconocimientos. You look beyond the illusion of separate interests to a shared interest—you're in this together, no one's an isolated unit. You dedicate yourself, not to surface solutions that benefit only one group, but to a more informed service to humanity.

Relating to others by recognizing commonalities does not always serve you. The person/group with conflicting desires may continuously attack you no matter how understanding you are. Can you assume that all of us, Ku Klux Klan and holistic alliance members, are in it together just because we're all human? If consciousness is as fundamental to the universe as matter and energy, if consciouness is not local, not contained in separate vessels/bodies, but is like air and water, energy and matter, then we *are* all in it together.[23] When one person steps into conocimiento, the whole of humanity witnesses that step and eventually steps into consciousness. It's like Rupert Sheldrake's concept of morphic resonance: when rats in a laboratory maze learn the way out, as time goes on rats in other mazes all over the world do it more and more quickly because of morphic resonance from previous members that have learned the hard way (311). Before holistic alliances can happen, many people must yearn for a solution to our shared problems.

But sometimes you need to block the other from your body, mind, and soul. You need to ignore certain voices in order to respect yourself—as when in an abusive relationship. It's impossible to be open and respectful to all views and voices. Though las nepantleras witness as impartially as they can in order to prevent being imprisoned by the other's point of view, they acknowledge the need for psychological armor (picture un nopal) to protect their open vulnerable selves from negative forces while engaging in the world. For attempting the best possible outcome not just for her own group, but for the other—the enemy—la nepantlera runs the risk of being stoned for this heresy—a case of killing the messenger. She realizes that to make changes in society and transform the system, she must make time for her needs—the activist must survive burn-out. When the self is part of the vision a strong sense of personal meaning helps in identity and culture construction. By developing and maintaining spiritual beliefs and values la nepantlera gives the group hope, purpose, identity.

You hear la Llorona/Cihuacóatl wailing. Your picture of her coiled serpent body with the head of a woman, shedding its skin, regenerating itself reminds you of the snake story in Genesis. A hunger to know and to build on your knowledge sweeps over you. You recommit to a regime of meditation, reflection, exercise. These everyday acts contain the sacred, lending meaning to your daily life.

Through the act of writing you call, like the ancient chamana, the scattered pieces of your soul back to your body. You commence the arduous task of rebuilding yourself, composing a story that more accurately expresses your new identity. You seek out allies and, together, begin building spiritual/political communities that struggle for personal growth and social justice. By compartiendo historias, ideas, las nepantleras forge bonds across race, gender, and other lines, thus creating a new tribalism. Éste quehacer—internal work coupled with commitment to struggle for social transformation—changes your relationship to your body, and, in turn, to other bodies and to the world. And when that happens, you change the world.

For you writing is an archetypal journey home to the self, un proceso de crear puentes (bridges) to the next phase, next place, next culture, next reality. The thrust toward spiritual realization, health, freedom, and justice propels you to help rebuild the bridge to the world when you return "home." You realize that "home" is that bridge, the in-between place of nepantla and constant transition, the most unsafe of all spaces. You remove the old bridge from your back, and though afraid, allow diverse groups to collectively rebuild it, to buttress it with new steel plates, girders, cable bracing, and trusses. You distend this more inclusive puente to unknown corners—you don't build bridges to safe and familiar territories, you have to risk making mundo nuevo, have to risk the uncertainty of change. And nepantla is the only space where change happens. Change requires more than words on a page—it takes perseverance, creative ingenuity, and acts of love. In gratitude and in the spirit of your Mamagrande Ramona y Mamagrande Locha, despachas éstas palabras y imágenes as giveaways to the cosmos.

ritual . . . prayer . . . blessing . . . for transformation

Every day you visit the sea, walk along Yemaya's glistening shores. You want her to know you, to sense your presence as you sense hers. You know deep down that she's not independent of humans, not indifferent, not set apart. At the lips del mar you begin your ritual/prayer: with the heel of your left foot you draw a circle in the sand, then walk its circumference, stand at the center, and voice your intention: to increase awareness of Spirit, recognize our interrelatedness, and work for transformation.

Then with feather, bone, incense, and water you attend the spirits' presence:
Spirit embodying yourself as rock, tree, bird, human, past, present, and future,
   you of many names, diosas antiguas, ancestors,
      we embrace you as we would a lover.

You face **east**, feel the wind comb your hair, stretch your hands toward
the rising sun and its orange filaments, breathe its rays into your body,
on the outbreath send your soul up to el sol,[24] say:
Aire, with each breath may we remember our interrelatedness
   see fibers of spirit extend out from our bodies
   creating us, creating sky, seaweed, serpent, y toda la gente.
   "El alma prende fuego,"[25] burns holes in the walls separating us
   renders them porous and passable, pierces through posturing and
      pretenses
   may we seek and attain wisdom.

Moving sunwise you turn to the **south**:
Fuego, inspire and energize us to do the necessary work, and to honor it
   as we walk through the flames of transformation.
      May we seize the arrogance to create outrageously
         soñar wildly—for the world becomes as we dream it.

Facing **west** you send your consciousness skimming over the waves
toward the horizon, seamless sea and sky. Slipping your hands into el ojo
   del agua
you speak to the spirit dwelling here en éste mar:
Agua, may we honor other people's feelings
   respect their anger, sadness, grief, joy as we do our own.
      Though we tremble before uncertain futures
         may we meet illness, death and adversity with strength
         may we dance in the face of our fears.

You pivot toward the **north**, squat, scoop sand into your hands:
Madre tierra, you who are our body, who bear us into life, swallow us in
   death
   forgive us for poisoning your lands, guide us to wiser ways of caring
      for you.
   May we possess the steadfastness of trees
   the quiet serenity of dawn
   the brilliance of a flashing star
   the fluidity of fish in our element
   Earth, you who dream us, te damos las gracias.

Completing the circle, retornas al **centro**, look down to the **underworld**:
May the roaring force of our collective creativity
   heal the wounds of hate, ignorance, indifference
   dissolve the divisions creating chasms between us

open our throats so we who fear speaking out raise our voices
 by our witnessing, find connections through our passions
 pay homage to those whose backs served as bridges.
 We remember our dead:
 Pat Parker, Audre Lorde, Toni Cade Bambara, Barbara
  Cameron, y tantas otras.

You raise your head to the **sky:**
May the words and the spirit of this book, our "giveaway" to the world,
 take root in our bodies, grow, sprout ears that listen
 may it harm no one, exclude none
  sabemos que podemos transformar este mundo
  filled with hunger, pain, and war
  into a sanctuary of beauty, redemption, and possibility
   may the fires of compassion ignite our hands
   sending energy out into the universe
   where it might best be of service
   may the love we share inspire others to act.

You walk back along the circle, erase the lines en la arena, leave a
 tortilla to symbolize
feeding the ancestors, feeding ourselves, and the nurturing shared in
 this book.
 Qué éste libro gather in our tribe—all our tribes—y alze nuestras
  voces en canto.
  Oh, Spirit—wind sun sea earth sky—inside us, all around us,
   enlivening all
  we honor tu presencia and celebrate the spirit of *this bridge*
  we call home.

We are ready for change.
Let us link hands and hearts
together find a path through the dark woods
 step through the doorways between worlds
 leaving huellas for others to follow,
 build bridges, cross them with grace, and claim these puentes our
  "home"
  si se puede, que asi sea, so be it, estamos listas, vámonos.

 Now let us shift.

        contigo,
        gloria

Notes

Quiero darle las gracias a mis "comadres in writing" por sus comentarios: a Carmen Morones, Randy Conner, Irene Reti, Liliana Wilson Grez, Kit Quan, and, most especially, AnaLouise Keating for her numerous, generous readings, right-on suggestions, and co-creation of this essay—les agradesco por animarme cuando me desanimaba. Thanks also to Bonnie Bentson and my graduate students in the Public Intellectuals Program at Florida Atlantic University.

A note on translations: I translate the first time a word or phrase appears and when the word or phrase appears much later and the reader may not remember what it means.

1. This essay is sister to "Putting Coylxauhqui Together."

2. *Conocimiento* derives from *cognoscera*, a Latin verb meaning "to know" and is the Spanish word for knowledge and skill. I call conocimiento that aspect of consciousness urging you to act on the knowledge gained.

3. *Nepantla* es una palabra indígena for an in-between space, el lugar entremedio, un lugar no-lugar. I have expanded this word to include certain workings of consciousness. See my "Border Arte." A slightly different version appeared in *NACLA Report* 27, no. 1 (July–August 1999).

4. *Naguala* is the feminine form of *nagual*, the capacity some people such as mexican indigenous shamans have of "shapeshifting"—becoming an animal, place, or thing by inhabiting that thing or by shifting into the perspective of their animal companion. I have extended the term to include an aspect of the self unknown to the conscious self. Nagualismo is a Mexican spiritual knowledge system where the practitioner searches for spirit signs. I call the maker of spirit signs "la naguala," a creative, dreamlike consciousness able to make broader associations and connections than waking consciousness.

5. Xochiquetzal is the Aztec goddess of love, del amor. Her name means Flor Preciosa, Precious Flower or, more literally, Pluma de Flor. Her cult descended from los toltecas.

6. Tomoanchan is one of the levels of heaven (paradise) according to Aztec mythology.

7. According to neurologist Antonio R. Damasio, consciousness is the sense of self in the act of knowing. The inner sense is based on images of feelings—without imaging you can't have feelings, you can't have consciousness (*Feeling*).

8. La Llorona is a ghost woman with long black hair and dressed in white who appears at night, sometimes near bodies of water, sometimes at crossroads, calling with loud and terrifying wails for her lost children. She has her origins in various prehispanic deities: Cihuacóatl, Xtabai, Xonaxi Queculla, and Autcanime. See my *Prietita and the Ghost Woman/Prietita y la Llorona*.

9. Toltec nagualism's idea of "seeing" beyond the apparent reality of the mundane world and into the spiritual was described to Carlos Castañeda by Don Juan.

10. The seven planes of reality are the physical, emotional, mental, Buddhic, atmic, monadic, and cosmic. Carolyn Myss, medical intuitive, makes a case for the seven chakras corresponding to the seven Christian sacraments and the sefirot of the Kabbala.

11. I wrote about this incident in one of the Prieta stories, "The Crack between the Worlds."

12. *Susto*, fright sickness, attributed to being frightened out of one's soul. Indigenous people in the Americas believe in the physicality of the soul. The Mesoamerican Mexica, called the Aztecs by the Spaniards, believed that a person had multiple souls which could be verified through the senses: these include the soul that animates the body and confers individual personality, aptitudes, abilities, and desires; the soul as breath; and the soul as an invisible shadowy double (Furst).

13. AnaLouise Keating, in one of her many generous readings of different drafts of this essay, made this comment to the mind/body split: "in various places throughout, you insist that you can't solve the cartesian mind/body split. yes & no. what you write *does* offer a solution—a solution that's difficult to live out in our lives, but the vision of spirit is the solution. it's finding pathways to manifest that vision in our lives (bodies) which is so damn tricky."

14. In south Texas, una lechuza is believed to be a naguala, usually una viejita (an old woman) who shapeshifts into an owl.

15. *Autohistoria* is a term I use to describe the genre of writing about one's personal and collective history using fictive elements, a sort of fictionalized autobiography or memoir; an autohistoria-teoria is a personal essay that theorizes.

16. "Canción de cascabel/Song of the Rattlesnake" is the title of the story.

17. I've borrowed the term from Rieff, who states that Americans should think a little less about race and a little more about class. Calling me "a professional Aztec," he takes me to task for my "romantic vision." I wish he'd attempted a more sensitive analysis of Chicano culture. Grace, you probably don't remember but I met you at UCLA on February 12, 1991—thanks for giving me this article.

18. I borrow this term from the "connectionist nets," the neural net consisting of billions of neurons in the human cortex. Connections are made in all states of consciousness, the most broad in artistic reverie and in dreaming, not in focused logical waking thought. The power of the imaginary must be utilized in conflict resolution.

19. *Interviews/Entrevistas*, 97. "'Yoga' means union of body with mind and spirit" (99).

20. Palmer; Keyes, especially her take on reframing.

21. The Latin term *respectus* comes from a verb meaning "to turn around to look back." It is the root of the word *respect*. You wonder if the word *perspective* comes from the same etymology.

22. According to AnaLouise in a comment she made while critiquing this essay.

23. Cognitive scientist and mathematician David Chalmer makes a similar point, claiming that consciousness is not confined to the individual brain and body or even to the present moment.

24. The charging of the sun is an ancient Mayan ritual.

25. Lhasa de Sela's (Mexican-American/Jewish) "El desierto."

Works Cited

Aanerud, Rebecca. "*This Bridge Called My Back* and Feminist Theory." Unpublished paper.

Abu-Jaber, Diana. *Arabian Jazz*. New York: Harcourt Brace, 1993.

Alameddine, Rabih. *Koolaids: The Art of War*. New York: Picador, 1998.

Alarcón, Norma. "Chicana Feminism: In the Tracks of 'The' Native Woman." In Trujillo, *Living Chicana Theory*, 371–82.

———. "The Theoretical Subject(s) of *This Bridge Called My Back* and Anglo-American Feminism." In Anzaldúa 356–69.

Alarcón, Norma, Ana Castillo, and Cherríe Moraga, eds. "Introduction." In *The Sexuality of Latinas*. Berkeley, CA: Third Woman, 1989, 8–10.

Alexander, Meena. *The Shock of Arrival: Reflections on Postcolonial Experience*. Boston: South End Press, 1996.

Alexander, M. Jacqui. "Not Just (Any) *Body* Can Be a Citizen: The Politics of Law, Sexuality, and Postcoloniality in Trinidad and Tobago and the Bahamas. *Feminist Review* 48 (1994): 5–23.

Alexander, M. Jacqui, and Chandra Talpade Mohanty, eds. *Feminist Genealogies, Colonial Legacies, Democratic Futures*. New York and London: Routledge, 1997.

———. "Introduction: Genealogies, Legacies, Movements." In Alexander and Mohanty, xiii–xlii.

Alexander, Susan M., and Megan Ryan. "Social Constructs of Feminism: A Study of Undergraduates at a Women's College." *College Student Journal* 31 (1997): 555–67.

Allen, Paula Gunn. *Off the Reservation: Reflections on Boundary-Busting, Border-Crossing Loose Canons*. Boston: Beacon Press, 1998.

Althusser, Louis. "Ideology and Ideological State Apparatuses." *Lenin and Philosophy and Other Essays*. New York: Monthly Review Press, 1971, 127–88.

American Council on Education. "Legal Developments Related to Affirmative Action in Higher Education: An Update for College and University Presidents, Trustees, and Administrators." June 1999.

Anderson, Benedict. *Imagined Communities*. London: Verso, 1991.

Andersen, Hans Christian. "The Ugly Duckling." *Fairy Tales*. Vol. 1, trans. R. P. Keigwin, ed. Svend Larsen, 1950. Odense, Denmark: Flensted, 1970.

Anzaldúa, Gloria E. "Border Arte: Nepantla, El Lugar de la Frontera." *La Frontera/The Border: Art about the Mexico/United States Border Experience*. Centro Cultural de la Raza and Museum of Contemporary Art, San Diego, CA, 1993.

———. *Borderlands/La Frontera: The New Mestiza*. San Francisco: Aunt Lute, 1987.

———. *Friends from the Other Side/Amigos del otro lado*. Ill. Consuelo Mendez. San Francisco: Children's Book Press/Libros para ninos, 1993.

———. "haciendo caras, una entrada." In Anzaldúa xv–xxviii.

———. *Interviews/Entrevistas*. Ed. AnaLouise Keating. New York: Routledge, 2000.

———. "La Prieta." In Moraga and Anzaldúa, 198–209.

———, ed. *Making Face, Making Soul/Haciendo Caras: Creative and Critical Perspectives by Feminists of Color*. San Francisco: Aunt Lute, 1990.

———. *Prietita and the Ghost Woman/Prietita y la Llorona*. San Francisco: Children's Book Press, 1995.

———. "Putting Coyolxauhqui Together, a Creative Process." In *How We Work*. Eds. Marla Morris, Mary Aswell Doll, William F. Pinar. Peter Lang, 1999.

———. "Speaking in Tongues: A Letter to 3rd World Women Writers." In Moraga and Anzaldúa, 165–73.

————, "*Tlilli, Tlapalli:* The Path of the Red and Black Ink." In *Norton Anthology of Postmodern American Fiction*. Ed. Paula Geyh et al. New York: W. W. Norton, 1997.

————. "*Tlilli, Tlapalli*." In *The Norton Anthology of Literature by Women*, 2nd ed. Ed. Sandra Gilbert and Susan Gubar. New York: W. W. Norton, 1996.

Aparicio, France R., and Susan Chávez-Silverman, eds. *Tropicalizations: Transcultural Representations of Latinidad*. Hanover, NH: University Press of New England, 1997.

Appiah, Kwame Anthony. "The Conservation of 'Race.'" *Black American Literature Forum* 23 (1989): 37–60.

Argüelles, José. *The Mayan Factor: Path Beyond Technology*. Santa Fe: Bear and Co., 1996.

Arreglo, Carlos. *Alibata* 1, no. 1 (1999).

Asante, Molefi Kete. *The Afrocentric Idea*. Philadelphia: Temple University Press, 1987.

Association for Library and Information Science Education. *Library and Information Science and Education Statistical Report*. Washington, D.C.: ALISE, 1998.

Avila, Elena. *Woman Who Glows in the Dark: A Curandera Reveals Traditional Aztec Secrets of Physical and Spiritual Health*. New York: Tarcher/Putnam, 1999.

Badran, Margot, and Miriam Cooke, eds. *Opening the Gates: A Century of Arab Feminist Writing*. Bloomington: Indiana University Press, 1990.

Baldwin, James. *The Price of the Ticket: Collected Nonfiction, 1948–1985*. New York: St. Martin's, 1985.

Bambara, Toni Cade. "Foreword." In Moraga and Anzaldúa, vi–viii.

————. *The Salt Eaters*. New York: Vintage, 1980.

Bannerji, Himani. *Thinking Through: Essays on Feminism, Marxism, and Anti-Racism*. Toronto: Women's Press, 1995.

Barker, Joanne. "Indian Made." Qualifying Essay. History of Consciousness. University of California, Santa Cruz, 1995.

"Indian™ U.S.A." *Wicazo Sa Review* 17 (Fall 2002).

Begley, Adam. "The I's Have It: Duke's 'Moi' Critics Expose Themselves." *Lingua Franca* (1994): 54–59.

Behar, Ruth. "Translated Woman." In *Translated Woman: Crossing the Border with Esperanza's Story*. Boston: Beacon, 1993, 275–359.

Belenky, Mary Field, Lynne A. Bond, and Jacqueline S. Weinstock. *A Tradition That Has No Name: Nurturing the Development of People, Families, and Communities*. New York: Basic Books, 1997.

Bell, Derrick. *Afrolantica Legacies*. Chicago: Third World Press, 1998.

————. *Faces at the Bottom of the Well: The Permanence of Racism*. New York: Basic Books, 1992.

Bell, Ella L."The Bicultural Life Experience of Career-oriented Black Women." *Journal of Organizational Behavior* 11 (1990): 459–78.

Berkhofer, Robert F. *The White Man's Indian: Images of the American Indian from Columbus to the Present*. New York: Vintage, 1979.

Berryman, John. *Stephen Crane*. New York: Sloan, 1950.

Bhabha, Homi. *The Location of Culture*. New York: Routledge, 1994.

————. "The Third Space." In Rutherford, 322–37.

Bhattacharjee, Anannya. "The Public/Private Mirage: Mapping Homes and Undomesticating Violence Work in the South Asian Immigrant Community." In Alexander and Mohanty, 308–29.

Birtha, Becky. "Is Feminist Criticism Really Feminist?" In *Lesbian Studies: Present and Future*. Ed. Margaret Cruickshank. New York: Feminist Press, 1982. Pp. 148–51.

Bivins, Larry. "Black Men in America: Prison Rates Rise." *Detroit News*, October 1996.

Bogle, Donald. *Toms, Coons, Mulattoes, Mammies, and Bucks: An Interpretive History of Blacks in American Films*. 1973. New York: Continuum, 1994.

Bordo, Susan. *Unbearable Weight: Feminism, Western Culture, and the Body*. Berkeley: University of California Press, 1993.

Bourne, Jenny. "Homelands of the Mind: Jewish Feminism and Identity Politics." *Race and Class* 29. (1987): 1–24.

Brah, Avtar. *Cartographies of Diaspora: Contesting Identities.* London and New York: Routledge, 1996.

———. "The Scent of Memory: Strangers, Our Own and Others." *Feminist Review* 61 (1999): 4–26.

Braidotti, Rosi. *Nomadic Subjects: Embodiment and Sexual Difference in Contemporary Feminist Theory.* New York: Columbia University Press, 1994.

Brand, Dionne. *No Language Is Neutral.* Toronto: Coach House Press, 1990.

Bright, Clare. "Teaching Feminist Pedagogy: An Undergraduate Course." *Women's Studies Quarterly* 3–4 (1993): 128–32.

Brown, Dee. *Bury My Heart at Wounded Knee: An Indian History of the American West.* New York: Henry Holt, 1991.

Bullough, Vern L., and Bonnie Bullough. *Cross Dressing, Sex, and Gender.* Philadelphia: University of Pennsylvania Press, 1993.

Butler, Judith. *Gender Trouble: Feminism and the Subversion of Identity.* New York: Routledge, 1990.

CAFRA News: Magazine of the Caribbean Association of Feminist Research and Action. Premier issue, 1986.

CaiRa. "Tse Tse TerroriSm #7—Welcome to the Transie Supermarket." *Willyboy* 7 (May 1999): 14–15.

Cameron, Barbara. "'Gee, You Don't Seem Like an Indian From the Reservation.'" In Moraga and Anzaldúa, 46–52.

Canaan, Andrea. "Brownness." In Moraga and Anzaldúa, 232–37.

Caraway, Nancie. *Segregated Sisterhood: Racism and the Politics of American Feminism.* Knoxville: University of Tennessee Press, 1991.

Carby, Hazel. *Reconstructing Womanhood: The Emergence of the Afro-American Woman Novelist.* New York: Oxford University Press, 1987.

Carrillo, Jo. "And When You Leave, Take Your Pictures With You." In Moraga and Anzaldúa, 63–64.

Castellanos, Rosario. *Meditación en el Umbral: Antología Poetica.* México: Fondo de Cultura Económica, 1985.

———. *Los narradores ante el público.* Vol. 1. México, D.F.: Joaquín Mortiz, 1966.

Castillo, Ana. "I Ask the Impossible: A World Meditation." University of California, Berkeley, Regent's Lecture, November 7, 1997.

———. "La Macha: Toward a Beautiful Whole Self." In Trujillo, *Chicana*, 24–48.

———. *Massacre of the Dreamers: Essays on Xicanimsa.* Albuquerque: University of New Mexico Press, 1994.

Cha, Theresa Hak Kyung. *Dictee.* 1982. Berkeley, CA: Third Woman, 1995.

Chalmer, David. "The Puzzles of Conscious Experience." *Scientific American,* December 1995.

Chin, Frank, Jeffrey Paul Chan, Lawson Fusao Inada, and Shawn Hsu Wong, eds. *Aiiieeeee: An Anthology of Asian-American Writers.* Washington D.C.: Howard University Press, 1974.

Chin Kee Onn. *Twilight of the Nyonyas.* Kuala Lumpur: Astra, 1984.

Christian, Barbara. "The Race for Theory." In Anzaldúa, 335–45.

Chrystos. "I Walk in the History of My People." In Moraga and Anzaldúa, 57.

———. "No Rock Scorns Me as Whore." In Moraga and Anzaldúa, 243–45.

Churchill, Ward, and Jim Vander Wall. *Agents of Repression: The FBI's Secret Wars Against the Black Panther Party and the American Indian Movement.* Boston: South End Press, 1988.

Chvany, Peter A. "What We Talk about When We Talk about Whiteness." *The Minnesota Review* 47 (1996): 49–55.

"Cisneros Shares Her 'Life Lessons' with Teachers at San Diego Convention." *English Journal,* February 1996, 97.

Clarke, Cheryl. "Lesbianism: An Act of Resistance." In Moraga and Anzaldúa, 128–37.

———. *Living as a Lesbian.* New York: Firebrand, 1986.

Clarke, Cheryl, Jewelle Gomez, Evelynn Hammonds, Bonnie Johnson, and Linda Powell. "Black Women on Black Women Writers: Conversations and Questions." *Conditions* 3 (1983): 88–137.

Cofer Ortiz, Judith. "The Story of My Body." In *The Latin Deli: Telling the Lives of Barrio Women*. New York: W. W. Norton, 1993.

Cohen, Cathy J. *The Boundaries of Blackness: AIDS and the Breakdown of Black Politics*. Chicago: University of Chicago Press, 1999.

———. "Punks, Bulldaggers, and Welfare Queens: The Radical Potential of Queer Politics?" *GLQ* (1997) 437–65.

Collins, Patricia Hill. *Black Feminist Thought: Knowledge, Consciousness, and the Politics of Empowerment*. New York: Routledge, 1992.

Combahee River Collective. "A Black Feminist Statement." In Moraga and Anzaldúa, 210–18.

Conner, Randy P., David Hatfield Sparks, and Mariya Sparks. *Cassell's Encyclopedia of Queer Myth, Symbol, and Spirit: Gay, Lesbian, Bisexual, and Transgender Love*. London: Cassell Academic, 1998.

Coombs, Mary. "Interrogating Identity." *Berkeley Women's Law Journal* 11 (1996): 222–49.

Crane, Stephen. *Maggie, A Girl of the Streets*. 1893. Ed. Thomas A. Gullason. New York: Norton, 1979.

Crenshaw, Kimberlé. "Whose Story Is It, Anyway? Feminist and Antiracist Appropriations of Anita Hill." In *Race-ing Justic, En-gendering Power: Essays on Anita Hill, Clarence Thomas, and the Construction of Social Reality*. Ed. Toni Morrison. New York: Pantheon, 1992, 402–40.

Damasio, Antonio. *Descartes' Error: Emotion, Reason, and the Human Brain*. New York: Avon, 1994.

———. *The Feeling of What Happens: Body and Emotion in the Making of Consciousness*. New York: Harcourt Brace, 1999.

D'Angeles, Risa. "Risa's Stars." *Good Times*, October 7, 1999.

Daum, Ann. "Coyote." In *Intimate Nature: The Bond between Women and Animals*. Ed. Linda Hogan, Deena Metzger, and Brenda Patterson. New York: Fawcett Columbine, 1998, 420–27.

davenport, doris. "The Pathology of Racism: A Conversation with Third World Wimmin." In Moraga and Anzaldúa, 85–90.

de Beauvoir, Simone. *The Ethics of Ambiguity*. Trans. B. Frenchman. New York: Philosophical Library, 1948.

de la tierra, tatiana. "Achy Obejas: She came all the way from cuba so she could write like this." *Deneuve* (April 1995): 38–39.

———. "Cherríe Moraga: Cultural Activist, Writer, and Mom." *conmoción* 1 (1995): 6–7.

———. "Coming Out and Creating Queer Awareness in the Classroom: An Approach from the US-Mexican Border." *Lesbian and Gay Studies and the Teaching of English Composition*. Ed. William Spurlin. Urbana, IL: National Council of Teachers of English, 2000.

de Lauretis, Teresa. *Technologies of Gender: Essays on Theory, Film, and Fiction*. Bloomington: Indiana University Press, 1987.

Delgadillo, Theresa. "Forms of Chicana Feminist Resistance: Hybrid Spirituality in Ana Castillo's *So Far from God*." *Modern Fiction Studies* 44 (1998): 888–916.

Deng Ming-Dao. *365 Tao Daily Meditations*. San Francisco: HarperCollins, 1992.

Devereux, George. "Institutionalized Homosexuality of the Mohave Indians." *Human Biology* 9 (1937): 498–527.

Diéguez, Martha Florinda Gonzalez (Maya Q'anjob'al from Guatemala). "Literatura Indígena: Mecanismo de Resistencia Cultural." Unpublished paper.

Dillon, Florence. "Tell Grandma I'm a Boy." In *Trans Forming Families: Real Stories about Transgendered Loved Ones*. Ed. Mary Boenke. Imperial Beach: Walter Trook, 1999, 3–8.

Doyle, Laura. *Bordering on the Body: The Racial Matrix of Modern Fiction and Culture*. New York: Oxford University Press, 1994.

Drake, Jennifer. "Third Wave Feminisms." *Feminist Studies* 23 (Spring 1997): 97–108.

Du Bois, W. E. B. *The Souls of Black Folk*. 1903. New York: New American Library, 1969.

DuBois, Ellen Carol, and Vicki L. Ruiz, eds. *Unequal Sisters: A Multicultural Reader in U.S. Women's History*. New York: Routledge, 1990.

duCille, Ann. "The Occult of True Black Womanhood: Critical Demeanor and Black Feminist Studies." *Signs* 19 (1994): 591–629.

Dunn, Kathleen. "Feminist Teaching: Who Are Your Students?" *Women's Studies Quarterly* 3–4 (1993): 39–45.

Dyer, Richard. "White." *Screen* 29, no. 4 (1988): 44–64.

Enloe, Cynthia. *Bananas, Beaches, and Bases: Making Feminist Sense of International Politics.* Berkeley: University of California Press, 1989.

Essed, Philomena. "Making and Breaking Ethnic Boundaries: Women's Studies, Diversity, and Racism." *Women's Studies Quarterly* 3–4 (1994): 232–49.

Fanon, Frantz. *Black Skins, White Masks.* New York: Grove, 1967.

Fausto-Sterling, Anne. *Sexing the Body: Gender Politics and the Construction of Sexuality.* New York: Basic Books, 2000.

Feinberg, Leslie. *Stone Butch Blues.* Ithaca, NY: Firebrand, 1993.

Ferguson, S. Alease, and Toni C. King. *Deep Woman Feelings: A Book of Contemplations.* Cleveland, OH: Blackberry Cobbler Press, 1997.

Fernea, Elizabeth Warnock, and Basima Qattan Bezirgan, eds. *Middle Eastern Muslim Women Speak.* Austin: University of Texas Press, 1977.

Fields, Gary. "Blacks Now a Majority in Prisons," *USA Today*, December 1995, 1A.

Findlen, Barbara, ed. *Listen Up: Voices from the Next Feminist Generation.* Seattle, WA: Seal, 1995.

Fonseca, Isabel. *Bury Me Standing: The Gypsies and Their Journey.* New York: Vintage, 1995.

Ford Smith, Honor. "Ring Ding in a Tight Corner: Sistren, Collective Democracy, and the Organization of Cultural Production." In Alexander and Mohanty, 213–58.

Foucault, Michel. *Herculine Barbin.* Trans. R. McDougall. New York: Pantheon, 1980.

———. *Language, Counter-Memory, Practice.* Trans. Donald F. Bouchard and Sherry Simon. Ithaca, NY: Cornell University Press, 1977.

Franklin, Cynthia G. *Writing Women's Communities: The Politics and Poetics of Contemporary Multi-Genre Anthologies.* Madison: University of Wisconsin Press, 1997.

Freire, Paolo. "The Adult Literary Process as Cultural Action for Freedom." *Harvard Educational Review* 40 (1970): 205–25.

———. *Pedagogy of the Oppressed.* 1970. New York: Continuum, 1994.

Furst, Jill Leslie McKeever. *The Natural History of the Soul in Ancient Mexico.* New Haven, CT: Yale University Press, 1995.

Galeano, Eduardo. "In Defense of the Word: Leaving Buenos Aires, June 1976." Trans. Bobbye S. Ortiz. In *Multi-Cultural Literacy*. Ed. Rick Simonson. St. Paul, MN: Graywolf, 1988, 113–25.

Gandhi, Mohandas K. *Book of Prayers.* Berkeley, CA: Berkeley Hills Books, 1999.

García, Alma. "The Development of Chicana Feminist Discourse, 1970–1980." In DuBois and Ruiz, 418–31.

Gaspar de Alba, Alicia. "Literary Wetback." *Massachusetts Review* (1988): 242–46.

Gest, Ted. "New War over Crack." *U.S. News and World Report*, November 6, 1995, 81–82.

Gibbon, Edward. *The Decline and Fall of the Roman Empire.* Vol. 1. New York: Heritage, 1946.

Gifford, E. W. "The Cocopa." *University of California Publications in American Archaeology and Ethnology* 31, no. 5 (1933): 257–333.

Gilligan, Carol. *In a Different Voice: Psychological Theory and Women's Development.* Cambridge, MA: Harvard University Press, 1982.

———. "Visions of Maturity." In Kourney et al. 384–97.

Gitlitz, David M. *Secrecy and Deceit: The Religion of the Crypto-Jews.* Philadelphia: Jewish Publication Society, 1996.

Gómez-Peña, Guillermo. *Warrior for Gringostroika.* Trans. Ruben Martínez. St. Paul, MN: Graywolf, 1993.

Gordon, Avery. *Ghostly Matters: Haunting and the Sociological Imagination.* Minneapolis: University of Minnesota Press, 1997.

Gramsci, Antonio. "The Intellectuals." In *The Prison Notebooks of Antonio Gramsci.* Ed. Quintin Hoare and Geoggrey Nowel Smith. New York: International Publishers, 1971.

Green, Rayna. "The Pocahontas Perplex: The Image of Indian Women in American Culture." In DuBois and Ruiz, 15–21.

———. "Rosebuds of the Plateau: Frank Matsura and the Fainting Couch Aesthetic." In *Partial*

Recall: With Essays on Photographs of Native North Americans. Ed. Lucy R. Lippard. New York: New Press, 1992, 47–53.

Grewal, Inderpal and Caren Kaplan, eds. *Scattered Hegemonies: Postmodernity and Transnational Feminist Practices*. Minneapolis: University of Minnesota Press, 1994.

Grewal, Shabnam, et al., eds. *Charting the Journey: Writings by Black and Third World Women*. London: Sheba Feminist Publishers, 1988.

Griggs, Richard. "The Meaning of 'Nation' and 'State' in the Fourth World." In *The Center for World Indigenous Studies Occasional Paper #18*, http://www.cwis.org/fwdp.html (accessed April 2000).

Guerilla Girls. http://www.guerrillagirls.com.

Gutierrez, Nova. "Borders and Crossroads: Gloria Anzaldúa's New Mestiza." Unpublished manuscript, 1992.

Haizlip, Shirlee Taylor. *The Sweeter the Juice: A Family Memoir in Black and White*. New York: Simon and Schuster, 1994.

Halberstam, Judith. "Transgender Butch—Butch/FTM Border Wars and the Masculine Continuum." *GLQ* 4 (1998): 287–310.

Hall, Stuart. "Cultural Identity and Diaspora." In Rutherford, 322–37.

———. "The Local and the Global: Globalization and Ethnicity." In *Culture, Globalization, and the World-System: Contemporary Conditions for the Representation of Identity*, 1991. Ed. Anthony D. King. Minneapolis: University of Minnesota Press, 1997.

Hammad, Suheir. *Drops of This Story*. New York: Harlem River Press, 1997.

Hammonds, Evelyn M. "Missing Persons: African American Women, AIDS, and the History of Disease." *Radical America* 20 (1986): 7–23.

———. "Race, Sex, AIDS: The Construction of the 'Other.'" In *Race, Class, and Gender: An Anthology*. Ed. M. L. Anderson and P. Hill Collins. Belmont, CA: Wadsworth, 1992, 329–40.

———. "Toward a Genealogy of Black Female Sexuality: The Problematic of Silence." In Alexander and Mohanty, 170–82.

Haney López, Ian F. *White by Law: The Legal Construction of Race*. New York: New York University Press, 1996.

Haraway, Donna. "Situated Knowledges: The Science Question in Feminism and the Privilege of Partial Perspective." In *Simians, Cyborgs, and Women: The Reinvention of Nature*. New York: Routledge, 1991, 83–203.

Harjo, Joy. "Anchorage." In *She Had Some Horses*. New York: Thunder's Mouth Press, 1983, 14–15.

———. "The Creation Story." In *Woman Who Fell from the Sky*. New York: W. W. Norton, 1994, 3.

———. *In Mad Love and War*. Hanover, NH: Wesleyan University Press, 1990.

Harjo, Joy, and Gloria Bird, eds. *Reinventing the Enemy's Language: Contemporary Native Women's Writing of North America*. New York: W. W. Norton, 1997.

Harrison, Beverly Wildung. "The Power of Anger in the Work of Love: Christian Ethics for Women and Other Strangers." In *Making Connections*. Ed. Carol S. Robb. Boston: Beacon Press, 1985.

Hartsock, Nancy. "Postmodernism and Political Change: Issues for Feminist Theory." In *Feminist Interpretations of Michel Foucault*. Ed. Susan Hekman. University Park: Pennsylvania State University Press, 1996, 39–55.

Henry, Annette. *Taking Back Control: African Canadian Women Teachers' Lives and Practice*. Albany: State University of New York Press, 1998.

Hernández, Inés. "Cascada de estrellas: La espiritualidad de la chicana/mexicana/indígena." In *Esta puente, mi espalda: Voces de mujeres tercermundistas en los Estados Unidos*. Eds. Cherríe Moraga and Ana Castillo. San Francisco: ism Press, 1988, 257–66.

Hernández-Ávila, Inés. "An Open Letter to Chicanas: On the Power and Politics of Origin." In Harjo and Bird, 235–46.

———. "Relocations upon Relocations: Home, Language, and Native American Women's Writings." *American Indian Quarterly* 19, no. 4 (Fall 1995): 491–508.

Herodian. *History of the Roman Empire*. Trans. and ed. Edward C. Echols. Vol. 5. Berkeley: University of California Press, 1959.

Herrnstein, Richard, and Charles Murray. *The Bell Curve: Intelligence and Class Structure in American Life*. New York: Free Press, 1996.

Hill, Mike. "Introduction." *The Minnesota Review* 47 (1996): 5–8.

Hillman, James. *Puer Papers*. Dallas: Spring Publishers, 1979.

Hine, Darlene Clark, and Kathleen Thompson. *A Shining Thread of Hope: The History of Black Women in America*. New York: Broadway Books, 1998.

Hochschild, Arlie, with Anne Machung. *The Second Shift*. New York: Avon, 1989.

hooks, bell. *All About Love: New Visions*. New York: William Morrow & Co, 1999.

———. *Black Looks: Race and Representation*. Toronto: Between the Lines, 1992.

———. *Feminist Theory from Margin to Center*. Boston: South End Press, 1984.

———. "Sisterhood: Political Solidarity between Women." In Kourney et al., 487–500.

———. *Teaching to Transgress: Education as the Practice of Freedom*. New York: Routledge, 1994.

———. *Yearning, Race, Gender, and Cultural Politics*. Boston: South End Press, 1990.

Houston, Jean. *The Search for the Beloved: Journeys in Sacred Psychology*. Los Angeles: Jeremy P. Tarcher, 1987.

Hrdy, Sara. *Mother Nature: A History of Mothers, Infants, and Natural Selection*. New York: Pantheon, 1999.

Hughes, Langston. *Montage of a Dream Deferred*. Henry Holt, 1951.

Hurtado, Aida. "Relating to Privilege: Seduction and Rejection in the Subordination of White Women and Women of Color." *Signs* 14 (4): 833–855.

———. "Sitios y Leguas: Chicanas Theorize Feminisms." *Hypatia* 13 (1998): 134–61.

Hwang, David Henry. *FOB and Other Plays*. New York: Penguin, 1990.

Ignatiev, Noel. *How the Irish Became White*. New York: Routledge, 1995.

Inayatullah, Sohail, and Ivana Milojevic. "Exclusion and Communication in the Information Era: From Silences to Global Conversations." In *women@internet: creating new cultures in cyberspace*. Ed. Wendy Harcourt. New York: Zed Books, 1999.

Jaimes Guerrero, Marie Anna. "Civil Rights versus Sovereignty: Native American Women in Life and Land Struggles." In Alexander and Mohanty, 101–21.

Jones, Christopher. "Women of the Future: Alternative Scenarios." *The Futurist* 30 (1996): 34–38.

Jones, DeEtta. "Leading Ideas: Demographic Shifts Call for Cross-Cultural Competence in Library Professionals." http://www.arl.org/diversity/leading/issue12/jones.html.

Jordan, June. *Affirmative Acts: Political Essays*. New York: Doubleday Anchor, 1998.

Kadi, Joanna, ed. *Food for Our Grandmothers: Writings by Arab-American and Arab-Canadian Feminists*. Boston: South End Press, 1994.

Kaplan, Caren, Norma Alarcón, and Minoo Moallem. *Between Woman and Nation: Nationalism, Transnational Feminisms, and the State*. Durham, NC: Duke University Press, 1999.

Kauanui, J. Kehaulani. "A Fraction of National Belonging: Anatomy of One 'Hybrid Hawaiian' in 1930s Racial Classificatory Schema." In *Beyond the Frame*. Ed. Angela Davis and Neferti Tadiar. Forthcoming.

Keating, AnaLouise. "Back to the Mother? Feminist Mythmaking with a Difference." In *Mary Daly*. Ed. Marilyn Frye and Sarah Lucia Hoagland. Albany: State University of New York Press, 2000, 294–331.

———. "Exposing 'Whiteness,' Unreading 'Race': (De)Racialized Reading Tactics in the Classroom." In *Reading Difference: Gender, Race, Class, Ethnicity, and Sexual Orientation*. Ed. Elizabeth Flynn and Patsy Schweickart. New York: Modern Langauges Association, forthcoming.

———. *Women Reading Women Writing: Self-Invention in Paula Gunn Allen, Gloria Anzaldúa, and Audre Lorde*. Philadelphia: Temple University Press, 1996.

Kelly, Joan. "The Doubled Vision of Feminist Theory: A Postscript to the 'Women and Power' Conference." *Feminist Studies* 5 (1979): 216–27.

Kelley, Robin D. G. *Race Rebels: Culture, Politics, and the Black Working Class*. New York: Free Press, 1994.

Keyes, Margaret Frings. *Emotions and the Enneagram: Working Through Your Shadow Life Script*. Muir Beach, CA: Molysdatur, 1992.

Khan, Ismith. *The Jumbie Bird*. Essex: Longman, 1961.

Kim, Elaine H. *Asian American Literature: An Introduction to the Writings and Their Social Context*. Philadelphia: Temple University Press, 1982.

Kingston, Maxine Hong. *The Woman Warrior: Memoirs of a Girlhood among Ghosts*. New York: Vintage, 1975.

Kirk, Robert. *The Secret Commonwealth of Elves, Fawns, & Fairies: A Study in Folk-Lore & Psychical Research*. 1691. London: David Nutt, 1893.

Kourney, Janet A., James P. Sterba, and Rosemarie Tong, eds. *Feminist Philosophies*. 2nd ed. Upper Saddle River, NJ: Prentice Hall, 1992.

Kulick, Don. *Travesti: Sex, Gender, and Culture among Brazilian Transgendered Prostitutes*. Chicago: University of Chicago Press, 1998.

Lacan, Jacques. *Ecrits: A Selection*. London: Tavistock, 1977.

Ladson-Billings, Gloria. *The Dreamkeepers: Successful Teachers of African American Children*. San Francisco: Jossey-Bass, 1994.

Lamming George. *In the Castle of My Skin*. Ann Arbor: University of Michigan Press, 1991.

Lang, Sabine. *Men as Women, Women as Men: Changing Gender in Native American Cultures*. Trans. John L. Vantine. Austin: University of Texas Press, 1998.

LaRocque, Emma. "Tides, Towns, and Trains." In Harjo and Bird, 361–72.

Latina Feminist Collective. *Telling to Live: Latina Feminist Testimonios*. Durham, NC: Duke University Press, 2001.

Lazarre, Jane. *Beyond the Whiteness of Whiteness: Memoir of a White Mother of Black Sons*. Durham, NC: Duke University Press, 1996.

lee, mary hope. "on not bein." In Moraga and Anzaldúa, 9–11.

Lentricchia, Frank. "Last Confessions of a Literary Critic." *Lingua Franca* (September/October 1996): 59–67.

Leuthold, Steven. *Indigenous Aesthetics: Native Art, Media, and Identity*. Austin: University of Texas Press, 1998.

Lewis, Gail. *Race, Gender, Social Welfare: Encounters in a Postcolonial Society*. Cambridge, UK: Polity Press, 2000.

Lhasa de Sela. "El desierto." *La Llorona*. Lyrics de Lela y Yves Desrosiers. Les Disques Audiogramme/Atlantic Records, 1998.

Lim, Shirley Geok-lin. *Among the White Moon Faces*. New York: Feminist Press, 1996.

———. *Crossing the Peninsula*. Kuala Lumpur: Heinemann, 1980.

———. "The Tradition of Chinese American Women's Life Stories: Thematics of Race and Gender in Jade Snow Wong's *Fifth Chinese Daughter* and Maxine Hong Kingston's *The Woman Warrior*." In *American Women's Autobiography*. Ed. Margo Culley. Madison: University of Wisconsin Press, 1992.

Lim, Shirley Geok-lin, and Mayumi Tsutakawa, eds. *The Forbidden Stitch: An Asian American Women's Anthology*. Corvallis, OR: Calyx, 1989.

Lorde, Audre. *A Burst of Light*. Ithaca, NY: Firebrand, 1988.

———. *Cancer Journals*. Trumansburg, NY: Crossing Press, 1979.

———. "The Master's Tools Will Never Dismantle the Master's House." In Moraga and Anzaldúa, 98–101.

———. "An Open Letter to Mary Daly." In Moraga and Anzaldúa 94–97.

———. *Sister Outsider: Essays and Speeches*. Trumansberg, NY: Crossing Press, 1984.

———. "Solstice." In *The Black Unicorn*. New York: W. W. Norton, 1978. 117–18.

———. "The Uses of Anger: Women Resonding to Racism." In *Sister Outsider: Essays and Speeches*. Trumansberg, NY: Crossing Press, 1984, 124–33.

———. *Zami: A New Spelling of My Name*. Trumansburg, NY: Crossing Press, 1982.

Lowe, Lisa. "Heterogeneity, Hybridity, Multiplicity: Marking Asian American Differences." *Diaspora* 1 (1991): 24–44.

———. *Immigrant Acts: On Asian American Cultural Politics*. Durham, NC: Duke University Press, 1996.

Lubiano, Waneemah. "Like Being Mugged by a Metaphor: Multiculturalism and State Narratives." In *Mapping Multiculturalism*. Ed. Avery F. Gordon and Christopher Newfield. Minneapolis: Univesity of Minnesota Press, 1996. 64–75.

Lugones, María. "Hablando cara a cara: An Exploration of Ethnocentric Racism." In Anzaldúa, 46–54.

———. "On Borderlands/La Frontera: An Interpretative Essay." *Hypatia* 7 (1992): 31–38.

———. "Playfulness, 'World'-Travelling, and Loving Perception." In Anzaldúa, 390–402.

Lugones, María, and Elizabeth Spellman. "We Got a Theory for You." *Women's Studies International Forum* 6 (1983): 573–81.

MacDonald, Margaret Read. "Tale of Two Goats on the Bridge." In *Peace Tales: World Folktales to Talk About*. North Haven, CT: Linnet Books, 1992.

Majaj, Lisa Suhair. "Arguments Against the Bombing." www.iraqaction.org.

———. "Boundaries: Arab/American." In Kadi, 65–86.

Manzor-Coats, Lillian. "Too Spik or Too Dyke: Carmelita Tropicana." *Ollantay* 2 (1994): 39–55.

Marshall, Paule. *The Chosen Place, the Timeless People*. New York: Vintage, 1969.

———. "The Making of a Writer: From the Poets in the Kitchen" In *Reena and Other Stories*. Old Westbury, NY: Feminist Press, 1983.

Massey, Doreen, B. *Space, Place, and Gender*. Minneapolis: University of Minnesota Press, 1994.

Matthews, Dale A. *The Faith Factor: Proof of the Healing Power of Prayer*. New York: Penguin, 1998.

Mattiessen, Peter. *In the Spirit of Crazy Horse*. New York: Viking, 1983.

McCluskey, Audre Thomas. "Multiple Consciousness in the Leadership of Mary McLeod Bethune." *NWSA Journal* 6 (1994): 69–81.

McCracken, Ellen. *New Latina Narrative: The Feminine Space of Postmodern Ethnicity*. Tucson: University of Arizona Press, 1999.

McDermott, Patrice. "The Meaning and Uses of Feminism in Introductory Women's Studies Textbooks." *Feminist Studies* 24 (1998): 403–27.

McDonnell, Janet A. *The Dispossession of the American Indian, 1887–1934*. Bloomington: Indiana University Press, 1991.

McMurry, Linda O. *To Keep the Waters Troubled: The Life of Ida B. Wells*. New York: Oxford University Press, 1998.

Medina, Lara. "Los Espíritus Siguen Hablano: Chicana Spiritualities." Trujillo, *Living Chicana Theory*, 189–23.

Metzger, Deena. *Writing for Your Life: Guide and Companion to the Inner Worlds*. San Francisco: Harper San Francisco, 1992.

Miller, Nancy. *Bequest and Betrayal: Mamoir of a Parent's Death*. New York: Oxford University Press, 1996.

Mohanty, Chandra Talpade. "Crafting Feminist Genealogies: On the Geography and Politics of Home, Nation and Community." In Alexander and Mohanty, 485–500.

———. "Introduction: Cartographies of Struggle: Third World Women and the Politics of Feminism." In Mohanty et al., 1–47.

———. "Under Western Eyes: Feminist Scholarship and Colonial Discourses." *Feminist Review* 30 (1988): 61–88.

Mohanty, Chandra Talpade, Ann Russo, and Lourdes Torres, eds. *Third World Women and the Politics of Feminism*. Bloomington: Indiana University Press, 1991.

Moraga, Cherríe. "For the Color of My Mother." In Moraga and Anzaldúa, 12–13.

———. "La Güera." In Moraga and Anzaldúa, 27–34.

———. *The Last Generation*. Boston: South End Press, 1993.

———. *Loving in the War Years: Lo que nunca pasó por sus labios*. Cambridge, MA: South End Press, 2000.

———. "Refugees of a World on Fire: Foreword to the Second Edition." In Moraga and Anzaldúa, n.p.

————. "A Tuna Bleeding in the Heat: A Chicana Codex of Changing Consciousness." CLAGS Lecture. December 2000.

————. "The Welder." In Moraga and Anzaldúa, 219–20.

Moraga, Cherríe, and Gloria Anzaldúa, eds. *This Bridge Called My Back: Writings by Radical Women of Color.* 1981. New York: Kitchen Table/Women of Color Press, 1983.

Morales, Aurora Levins. "And Even Fidel Can't Change That!" In Moraga and Anzaldúa, 53–56.

————. "The Historian as Curandera." In *Medicine Stories: History, Culture, and the Politics of Integrity.* Boston: South End Press, 1998, 23–38.

Morales, Rosario. "We're All in the Same Boat." In Moraga and Anzaldúa, 91–93.

Morena, Naomi. "Alienation." *conmoción* 3 (1996): 34.

Morgan, Robin, ed. *Sisterhood Is Global: The International Women's Movement Anthology.* New York: Anchor, 1984.

————. "Theory and Practice: Pornography and Rape." In *The Word of a Woman, Feminist Dispatches, 1968–1992.* New York: W. W. Norton, 1992.

Morris, Marla. *Curriculum and the Holocuast: Competing Sites of Memory and Representation.* Mahwah, NJ: Lawrence Erlbaum, 2001.

Morrison, Toni. *Beloved.* New York: Penguin, 1987.

————. *Paradise.* New York: Alfred A. Knopf, 1998.

————. *Playing in the Dark: Whiteness and the Literary Imagination.* New York: Vintage, 1992.

Moschkovich, Judit. "—But I Know You, American Woman." In Moraga and Anzaldúa, 79–84.

Moya, Paula M. L. "Postmodernism, "Realism," and the Politics of Identity: Cherríe Moraga and Chicana Feminism." In Alexander and Mohanty 125–50.

Mukherjee, Bharati. *Jasmine.* New York: Fawcett Crest, 1989.

Mullings, Leith. *On Our Own Terms: Race, Class, and Gender in the Lives of African-American Women.* New York: Routledge, 1997.

Mulvey, Laura. "Visual Pleasure and Narrative Cinema." *Screen* 16 (1975): 6–18.

Muñoz, José. *Disidentifications: Queers of Color and the Performance of Politics.* Minneapolis: University of Minnesota Press, 1999.

Myers, Linda James. *Understanding an Afrocentric World View: Introduction to an Optimal Psychology.* Dubuque, IA: Kendall/Hunt, 1988.

Narayan, Uma. *Dislocating Cultures: Identities, Traditions, and Third World Feminisms.* New York: Routledge, 1997.

National Institute of Drug Abuse (NIDA) Research Report—Cocaine Abuse and Addiction: NIH Publication No. 99–4342, printed May 1999.

Nhat Hanh, Thich. *Fragrant Palm Leaves: Journals, 1962–1966.* New York: Riverhead, 1999.

————. *Touching Peace.* Berkeley, CA: Parallax Press, 1992.

————. *Vietnam: Lotus in a Sea of Fire.* New York: Hill and Wang, 1967.

Nichols, Elaine. "Sea Island Celebration." *American Legacy* 5 (1999): 16–20.

Nielsen, Marianne O., and Robert A. Silverman, eds. *Native Americans, Crime, and Justice.* Boulder, CO: Westview Press, 1996.

Norton, Jody. "Transchildren and the Discipline of Children's Literature." *The Lion and the Unicorn* 23 (1999): 415–36.

O'Hartigan, Margaret Deirdre. "G.I.D. and the Greater Good." *Transsexual News Telegraph,* Summer 1997, 28–29.

Olguin, R. A. "Towards an Epistemology of Ethnic Studies: African American Studies and Chicano Studies Contributions." In *Ethnic Studies and Women's Studies.* Ed. Johnnella Butler and John C. Walter. Albany: State University of New York Press, 1991, 149–68.

Omi, Michael, and Howard Winant. *Racial Formation in the United States.* 2nd ed. New York: Routledge, 1994.

Omolade, Barbara. *The Rising Song of African American Women.* New York: Routledge, 1994.

Ong, Aihwa. *Flexible Citizenship: The Cultural Logics of Transnationality.* Durham, NC: Duke University Press, 1999.

Ordoñez, Juan Pablo. *No Human Being Is Disposable: Social Cleansing, Human Rights, and Sexual Orientation in Colombia.* San Francisco: International Gay and Lesbian Human Rights Commission, 1995.

Orr, Catherine M. "Charting the Currents of the Third Wave." *Hypatia* 12 (1999): 29–46.

Ortega, Eliana. "Poetic Discourse of the Puerto Rican Woman in the U.S.: New Voices of Anacaonian Liberation." In *Breaking Boundaries: Latina Writings and Critical Readings*. Ed. A. Horno-Delgado et. al. Amherst: University of Massachusetts Press, 1989, 122–35.

Ortiz, Simon, ed. *Speaking for the Generations: Native Writers on Writing*. Tucson: University of Arizona Press, 1998.

Owens, Louis. "*The Song Is Very Short*: Native American Literature and Literary Theory." In *Weber Studies: An Interdisciplinary Humanities Journal*. Vol. 12. Ogden, UT: Weber State University Press, 1995.

Oxford English Dictionary (OED). (The Compact Edition). Vol. 1. Oxford: Oxford University Press, 1971.

Palmer, Helen. *Enneagram: The Placement of Attention*. Credence Cassettes, 1994.

Paris Is Burning. Dir. Jennie Livingston. Academy-Maverick, 1991.

Pérez, Emma. "Sexuality and Discourse: Notes from a Chicana Survivor." In Trujillo, *Chicana Lesbians*, 159–84.

Pérez, Laura. *Altarities: Chicana Art, Politics, and Spirituality*. Forthcoming.

———. "Spirit Glyphs: Reimagining Art and Artist in the Work of Chicana *Tlamatinime*." *Modern Fiction Studies* 44 (1998): 41.

Pesquera, Beatriz, and Denise Segura. "There Is No Going Back: Chicanas and Feminism." In *Chicana Critical Issues*. Ed. Mujeres Activas en Letras y Cambio Social. Berkeley, CA: Third Woman, 1993, 94–115.

Pettiway, Leon E. *Honey, Honey, Miss Thang: Being Black, Gay, and on the Streets*. Philadelphia: Temple University Press, 1996.

Phillips, Caryl. *The Atlantic Sound*. New York: Alfred Knopf, 2000.

Pinar, William. F. "Introduction." In *Queer Theory in Education*. Ed. William F. Pinar. Mahwah, NJ: Lawrence Erlbaum, 1998, 1–47.

Piper, Adrian. "Passing for White, Passing for Black." In Shohat, 75–112.

Plaskow, Judith, and Carol Christ. "Introduction." In *Weaving the Visions: New Patterns in Feminist Spirituality*. San Francisco: Harper, 1989, 1–13.

Pocahontas. Walt Disney Pictures. Burbank, CA: Walt Disney Home Video, 1996.

Poitras, Laura. *Living the Legacy: Racism and Resistance in the Academy*. Documentary film with interview of M. Jacqui Alexander. New York, 1998.

Powell, Pat. *The Pagoda*. New York: Alfred Knopf, 1998.

Pratt, Minnie Bruce. *S/HE*. Ithaca, NY: Firebrand, 1995.

Quintanales, Mirtha. "I Paid Very Hard for My Immigrant Ignorance." In Moraga and Anzaldúa, 150–56.

Rains, Frances V. "Dancing on the Sharp Edge of the Sword: Women Faculty of Color in White Academe." *Everyday Knowledge and Uncommon Truths: Women of the Academy*. Boulder, CO: Westview Press, 1999, 147–74.

Ramos, Juanita. *Compañeras: Latina Lesbians*. 1987. New York: Routledge, 1994.

Raskin, Jamin B. "A Precedent for Arab-Americans?" *The Nation*, February 4, 1991, 117–18.

Reagon, Bernice Johnson. "Coalition Politics: Turning the Century." In Smith, 356–68.

Rhys, Jean. *Wide Sargasso Sea*. London: Andre Deutsch, 1966.

Rich, Adrienne. *Of Woman Born: Motherhood as Experience and Institution*. 1976. New York: Norton, 1987.

Rieff, David. "Professional Aztecs and Popular Culture." *New Perspectives Quarterly* 8 (1991). http://www.npq.org/issues/v81/p42.html.

Roediger, David R. *Towards the Abolition of Whiteness*. London: Verso, 1994.

Romany, Celina. "Ain't I a Feminist." *Yale Journal of Law and Feminism* (1991): 389–99.

Ruiz, Don Miguel. *The Four Agreements*. San Rafael, CA: Amber-Allen, 1997.

Rushin, Donna Kate. "The Bridge Poem." Moraga and Anzaldúa, xxi.

Rutherford, Jonathan, ed. *Identity: Community, Culture, Difference*. London: Lawrence and Wishart, 1990.

Sandoval, Chela. *Methodology of the Oppressed*. Minneapolis: University of Minnesota Press, 2000.

————. "U.S. Third World Feminism: The Theory and Method of Oppositional Consciousness in the Postmodern World." *Genders* 10 (1991): 1–24.

Santos, Richard G. *Silent Heritage: The Sephardim and the Colonization of the Spanish North American Frontier, 1492–1600*. San Antonio, TX: New Sepharad Press, 2000.

Sazama, Jenny. *Understanding and Supporting Young People*. Seattle, WA: Rational Island, 1999.

The Scarlet Letter. Dir. Roland Joffé. Burbank, CA: Walt Disney Home Video, 1995.

Schoenfielder, Lisa, and Barb Wieserm, eds. *Shadow on a Tightrope: Writings by Women on Fat Oppression*. San Francisco: Aunt Lute, 1983.

Segrest, Mab. "Reflections on Theory from Practice: Reality as Transformation." Paper delivered at the 9th Annual Duke University Women's Studies Graduate Conference, October 1998.

Sequoya-Magdaleno, Jana. "Telling the Differánce: Representations of Identity in the Discourse of Indianness." In *The Ethnic Canon*. Ed. David Palumbo-Lui. Minneapolis: University of Minnesota Press, 1995, 88–116.

Shakespeare, William. *A Midsummer Night's Dream*. Ed. Wolfgang Clemen. New York: Penguin-Signet, 1963.

Shakir, Evelyn. *Bint Arab: Arab and Arab-American Women in the United States*. Westport, CT: Praeger, 1997.

Shanley, Kathryn. "Thoughts on Indian Feminism." In *A Gathering of Spirit: A Collection by North American Indian Women*. Ed. Beth Brant. Ithaca, NY: Firebrand, 1984. 213–15.

Sharpley-Whiting, T. Denean, and Renee T. White. *Spoils of War: Women of Color, Culture, and Revolution*. New York: Rowman & Littlefield, 1998.

Sheldrake, Rupert. *Dogs That Know When Their Owners Are Coming Home and Other Unexplained Powers of Animals*. New York: Three Rivers Press, 1999.

Shohat, Ella. "Dislocated Identities: Reflections of an Arab Jew." *Movement Research: Performance Journal* 5 (1992): 8.

————, ed. *Talking Visions: Multicultural Feminism in a Transnational Age*. Cambridge, MA: MIT Press, 1999.

Short, Kayann. "Coming to the Table: The Differential Politics of *This Bridge Called My Back*." *Genders* 19 (1994): 3–44.

Silko, Leslie Marmon. *Ceremony*. New York: Penguin, 1977.

Simpson, David. *The Academic Postmodern and the Rule of Literature*. Chicago: Univerisity of Chicago Press, 1995.

Sinfield, Alan. *Cultural Politics—Queer Reading*. Philadelphia: University of Pennsylvania Press, 1994.

Sistren, with Honor Ford Smith. *Lionheart Gal: Life Stories of Jamaican Women*. Toronto: Sister Vision Press, 1989.

Smith, Barbara, ed. *Home Girls: A Black Feminist Anthology*. New York: Kitchen Table / Women of Color Pree, 1983.

————. "Toward a Black Feminist Criticism." *Conditions Two* (1977): 25–32.

Smith, Barbara, and Beverly Smith. "Across the Kitchen Table: A Sister-to-Sister Dialogue." In Moraga and Anzaldúa, 113–27.

Smith, Linda Tuhiwai. *Decolonizing Methodologies: Research and Indigenous Peoples*. London: Zed Books, 1999.

Spivak, Gayatri Chakravorty. "In a Word, Interview." *differences* (1989): 151–84.

————. *Outside in the Teaching Machine*. New York: Routledge, 1993.

Steel, Mel. "Joan Nestle: A Fragile Union." *Diva*, January 1999, 60–61.

Steinward, Jonathan. "The Future of Nostalgia in Friedrick Schlegel's Gender Theory: Casting German Aesthetics beyond Ancient Greece and Modern Europe." In *Narratives of Nostalgia, Gender, and Nationalism*. Ed. Jean Pickering and Suzanne Kehde. New York: New York University Press, 1997, 2–29.

Sterk, Claire E. *Fast Lives: Women Who Use Crack Cocaine*. Philadelphia: Temple University Press, 1999.

Stiffarm, Lenore A., with Phil Lane, Jr. "The Demography of Native North America: A Question of Indian Survival." In *The State of Native America: Genocide, Colonization, and Resistance*. Ed. M. Annette Jaimes. Boston: South End Press, 1992, 23–54.

Suleri, Sara. "Woman Skin Deep: Woman and the Postcolonial Condition." *Critical Inquiry* 18 (1992): 756–69.

Swartz, L. H. "Legal Implications of the New Ferment concerning Transsexualism." *International Journal of Transgenderism* 2, no. 4 (1998). http://www.symposion.com/ijt/ijtc0604.htm.

Takaki, Ronald. *A Larger Memory: A History of Our Diversity, with Voices*. New York: Little, Brown, 1998.

Tarnas, Richard. "The Great Initiation." *Noetic Sciences Review* 47 (1998): 24–33.

Tart, Charles. *Waking Up: Overcoming the Obstacles to Human Potential*. Boston: Shambhala, 1986.

Tate, Claudia. *Black Women Writers at Work*. New York: Continuum, 1983.

Thiong'o, Ngugi wa. *Decolonising the Mind*. London: James Curry, 1986.

"To Be Black and a Librarian: Talking with E. J. Josey." *American Libraries* (January 2000): 80–82.

Tobias, Sheila. *Faces of Feminism: An Activist's Reflections on the Women's Movement*. Boulder, CO: Westview Press, 1997.

Tohe, Laura. "There's No Word for Feminism in My Language." *wicazosa review: A Journal of Native American Studies* 15 (2000) 103–110.

Tompkins, Jane. *Sensational Designs: Cultural Work of American Fiction 1790–1860*. Oxford University Press, 1985.

The Transformation. Dir. Carlos Aparicio and Susana Aikin. Starfish Productions, 1997.

Trinh T. Minh-ha. *When the Moon Waxes Red: Representation, Gender, and Cultural Politics*. New York: Routledge, 1991.

———. *Woman Native Other: Writing Postcoloniality and Feminism*. Indianapolis: Indiana University Press, 1989.

Trujillo, Carla, ed. *Chicana Lesbians: The Girls Our Mothers Warned Us About*. Berkeley, CA: Third Woman Press, 1991.

———, ed. *Living Chicana Theory*. Berkeley, CA: Third Woman Press, 1998.

U.S. Census Bureau. "The Hispanic Population in the United States." March 1999.

Valerio, Anita. "It's In My Blood, My Face—My Mother's Voice, The Way I Sweat." In Moraga and Anzaldúa, 41–45.

Vizenor, Gerald. *Narrative Chance: Postmodern Discourse on Native American Indian Literatures*. Albuquerque: University of New Mexico Press, 1989.

Walker, Alice. "Advancing Luna—and Ida B. Wells." In *You Can't Keep a Good Woman Down*. San Diego, CA: Harvest Books, 1982, 85–104.

———. "Definition of Womanist." In Anzaldúa, 370.

———. *In Search of Our Mothers' Gardens*. New York: Harcourt Brace, 1974.

———. *Living by the Word: Selected Writings, 1973–1987*. San Diego, CA: Harcourt Brace Jovanovich, 1988.

Walker, Rebecca, ed. *To Be Real: Telling the Truth and Changing the Face of Feminism*. New York: Anchor, 1995.

Wallace, Michele. *Invisibility Blues: From Pop to Theory*. New York: Verso, 1990.

Walsch, Neale Donald. *Conversations with God*. New York: G. P. Putnam's Sons, 2000.

The Way Home. Dir. Shakti Butler. World Trust, 1998.

Web Grrls. http://www.webgrrls.com.

Weedon, Chris. *Feminist Practice and Poststructuralist Theory*. Oxford: Basil Blackwell, 1987.

West, Cornel. *The Cornel West Reader*. New York: Perseus Books, 1999.

White, Deborah Gray. *Too Heavy a Load: Black Women in Defense of Themselves, 1894–1994*. New York: W. W. Norton, 1999.

Wilber, Ken. "Liberalism and Religion—We Should Talk." *Shambhala Sun* (1999): 3.

Williams, Patricia. "Alchemical Notes: Reconstructing Ideals from Deconstructed Rights." *Harvard Civil Rights–Civil Liberties Law Review* (1987): 401–33.

———. *The Alchemy of Race and Rights: Diary of a Law Professor*. Cambridge, MA: Harvard University Press, 1991.

———. "Spirit-Murdering the Messenger: The Discourse of Fingerpointing as the Law's Response to Racism." In *Critical Race Feminism*. Ed. Adrien Katherine Wing. New York: New York University Press, 1997, 229–36.

Williams, Walter L. *The Spirit and the Flesh: Sexual Diversity in American Indian Culture.* Boston: Beacon, 1992.

Wilmer, Franke. *The Indigenous Voice in World Politics.* Newbury Park, CA: Sage, 1993.

Wolff, Jana. "Black unlike Me." *New York Times,* February 14, 1999.

Womack, Craig. *Red on Red: Native American Literary Separatism.* Minneapolis: University of Minneapolis Press, 1999.

Women of South Asian Descent Collective, ed. *Our Feet Walk the Sky: Women of the South Asian Diaspora.* San Francisco: aunt lute, 1993.

Wong, Nellie. "When I Was Growing Up." In Moraga and Anzaldúa, 7–8.

Woo, Merle. "Letter to Ma." In Moraga and Anzaldúa 140–47.

World Trust. http://www.world-trust.org. 1998.

Wright, Marguerite A. *I'm Chocolate, You're Vanilla: Raising Healthy Black and Biracial Children in a Race-Conscious World: A Guide for Parents and Teachers.* San Francisco: Jossey-Bass, 1998.

Yamada, Mitsuye. "Asian Pacific American Women and Feminism." In Moraga and Anzaldúa, 71–75.

———. "Invisibility is an Unnatural Disaster: Reflections of an Asian American Woman." In Moraga and Anzaldúa, 35–40.

———. "Mirror Mirror." *Camp Notes and Other Writings.* New Brunswick, NJ: Rutgers University Press, 1992, 56.

Yamamoto, Hisaye. "Seventeen Syllables." In *Seventeen Syllables and Other Stories.* Latham, NY: Kitchen Table/Women of Color Press, 1988, 8–19.

Yap, Allison. "An Absence Ever Present." In *Bearing Witness, Reading Lives: Imagination, Creativity, and Cultural Change.* Ed. Gloria E. Anzaldúa and AnaLouise Keating, forthcoming.

Yap, Arthur. "there is no future in nostalgia." In *The Poetry of Singapore.* Ed. Edwin Thumboo et al. Singapore: ASEAN Committee on Culture and Information, 1985.

Zack, Naomi, ed. *Women of Color and Philosophy.* New York: Blackwell, 2000.

Zavella, Patricia. "Reflections on Diversity among Chicanas." In *Challenging Fronteras: Restructuring Latina and Latino Lives in the U.S.* Ed. Mary Romero et al. New York: Routledge, 1997.

Zinn, Maxine Baca, and Bonnie Thornton Dill. "Difference and Domination." In *Women of Color in U.S. Society.* Ed. Zinn and Dill. Philadelphia: Temple University Press, 1994, 3–12.

Contributors' Biographies

Rebecca Aanerud earned her Ph.D. in English at the University of Washington in December 1998. She currently teaches in the English department and the women's studies program at the University of Washington. Her research focuses on U.S. constructions and representations of whiteness. She has essays published or forthcoming in *Displacing Whiteness*, *James Baldwin Now*, and *Working through Whiteness*.

A Palestinian living in Britain for over twenty years, **Reem Abdelhadi** has a B.S. in Business administration; a B.A. in human behavior and psychology; a postgraduate diploma in social psychology; an M.A. in mass communications; and is completing her Ph.D. thesis on Palestinian women's NGOs. A longtime activist, she is co-founder and member of various human rights, anti-racism, and women's organisations, and was the first elected Arab to the National Executive of the National Union of Students (UK).

Rabab Abdulhadi is an assistant professor of sociology at the American University in Cairo, Egypt.

Jeanette Aguilar is a twenty-seven-year-old Italian/Irish/Chicana who grew up in the San Jose area and currently lives in Oakland, California. She recently completed her undergraduate degree in community studies at University of California, Santa Cruz. Her work has appeared in *Las Girlfriends*, and she was editor of the journal *The Mirror Has Two Faces*, which focused on the creative works of mixed-race women. Currently studying film and video production, she's working on her next project, a short video about the daily experiences and adventures of a young queer woman of color.

M. Jacqui Alexander is a teacher, scholar, and activist writer who currently holds the Fuller-Maathai Chair in Gender and Women's Studies at Connecticut College. She has published numerous articles on the state and the legal production of heterosexuality, and edited, with Chandra Talpade Mohanty, *Feminist Genealogies, Colonial Legacies, Democratic Futures* (Routledge). Alexander has been active in struggles for lesbian and gay self-determination and curriculum transformation within the academy. She is a member of the Caribbean Association for Feminist Research and Action.

Evelyn Alsultany is a Ph.D. candidate in the program in modern thought and literature at Stanford University. Her work focuses on ethnic studies (theorizing multiethnic identity, Arab-American studies, and Latino studies) and gender studies.

Daughter of an Eritrean father and an Austrian mother, **Iobel Andemicael** was born and raised in New York City. After earning her degree in anthropology and intercultural studies from Haverford College, she was awarded a Thomas J. Watson Fellowship to do field research on cultural identity and social mobility in communities of African descent in Latin America. She is working on a collection of stories inspired by that fieldwork and completing a novel conceived during a year she spent in Egypt.

Anonymous: Raised in a predominantly white U.S. suburb by Indian immigrants and voted "shyest" in high school, she has made her ongoing personal project getting louder and sharing more of her thinking with the world, settling for nothing less than ending all oppression via building close relationships with many different people.

A Chicana from El Segundo Barrio of El Paso, Texas, **Berta Avila** is an independent, feral woman who alone raised a successful twenty-six-year-old daughter and is now raising a five-year-old. Her life is reflected with as much intensity in her poetry, her artwork, and her daughters' eyes. She considers herself a spiritual warrior who, like many others, has survived the harsh marginalization between the Mexican culture and the Anglo-Saxon community. She has found a spiritual yet passionate venue of expressing, through her poetry and artwork, the rage, despair, and oppression within her heart.

Mita Banerjee: I was born in Germany, the daughter of a (white) German mother and an Indian father. Growing up, I do not remember ever being conscious of the fact that I was non-white, not until I went to the U.S. through a university exchange program. Being an Americanist with a special emphasis on postcolonial literature has provided me with a framework, to a certain extent, within which to articulate my own existence as a hyphenated German woman in a country in which hyphenation still does not seem to be an issue.

Joanne Marie Barker: I'm a citizen of the Lenape nation of eastern Oklahoma. I am currently an assistant professor of Native American studies at University of California, Davis. I teach in the fields of Native jurisprudence, science and politics, and cultural studies. I care about indigenous struggles for sovereignty and self-determination, particularly as they intersect with women's rights and property rights.

Lenora Barnes-Wright has worked in higher education for the past thirteen years, most recently serving as associate dean of students and director of academic support at Denison University. Her areas of professional experience are post-secondary disability student services, multicultural affairs, academic support, and judicial affairs. Currently she has returned to graduate school full time to complete her doctoral work in cultural studies in education at Ohio State University. Her research interests include race, gender, class, and disability; student advocacy and mediation in higher education; and legal issues in higher education.

mary loving blanchard has published poetry and short fiction under the pseudonym *nia akimbo*. Currently she is working on a collection of poetry titled *making art, making love*. mary received her Ph.D. in the School of Arts and Humanities at the University of Texas at Dallas; she is an assistant professor of English at New Jersey City University, where she teaches literature and composition courses.

Renae Moore Bredin teaches in the women's studies program at California State University, Fullerton. She has published articles on Paula Gunn Allen, Leslie Marmon Silko, and Elsie Clews Parsons. She has also researched and published on issues of women and technology.

Hector Carbajal earned his B.A. in English at New Mexico State University and is currently studying history in the M.A. program in border studies at the University of Texas at El Paso. His creative writing has been featured in *The Thing Itself*, *El Ocotillo*, and *Frontera/Norte-Sur*. He is currently at work on a manuscript about growing up queer along the U.S./Mexico border.

Amy Sara Carroll: I spent my childhood in south Texas, but left the region to receive an A.B. from Princeton University, an M.A. from the University of Chicago, and an M.F.A. from Cornell University. Currently, I'm a Ph.D. candidate in Duke University's literature program, but live in Mexico City, where I'm doing dissertation research on performance art and poetry. My poetry and poem-prints have appeared in *Big Allis*, *Les Voz*, *Crayon*, *Mandorla*, *Bombay Gin*, *Seneca Review*, *Borderlands*, and *Faultline*. I've participated in the Latin America Writers Workshop and done residences at Saltonstall Arts Colony and Virginia Center for the Creative Arts.

Sarah Jane Cervenak is a graduate student in the Department of Performance Studies at New York University. She is interested in questions of materiality and spectrality in relation to contemporary black and Latina/o performance. She is a member and High Priestess of Spirit and Librian Dis/Harmony of the cult of the Shadow Beast and shares parenting of the Coatlicue twins with Karina Cespedes.

Karina Lissette Cespedes is a graduate student in comparative ethnic studies at the University of California, Berkeley. As a co-founder of the Cult of the Shadow Beast and Priestess of Chaos and Disorder, she is also a refugee from a world on fire—committed to questioning overt and phantasmic relations of power that keep us all "at the feet of madness, fate, and the State."

Sunu P. Chandy has been engaged in creative writing for the past ten years; her work explores the social and political insights sparked from the lived daily experiences of herself and those around her. In college, she organized the Audacious Sisters of Color women-of-color writing group and presentation; while living in India for ten months (1994–95) she organized writing workshops for young women at a community center in Kerala. Sunu completed her B.A. (Earlham College) in 1994, earned her law degree (Northeastern University School of Law) in 1998, and works as a civil rights attorney focusing on employment discrimination cases.

Chrystos is a Native American, born in 1946 and raised in San Francisco. A political activist and speaker, as well as an artist and writer, she is self-educated. Her tireless momentum is directed at better understanding how issues of colonialism, genocide, class, and gender affect the lives of women and Native people. For many years Chrystos has made Bainbridge Island in the Pacific Northwest her home.

Born in Washington, D.C., in 1947, **Cheryl Clarke** is a black lesbian-feminist poet and author of four books of poetry: *Narratives: Poems in the Tradition of Black Women*, *Living as a Lesbian*, *Humid Pitch*, and *Experimental Love* (nominated for a 1994 Lambda Award). Her poems, essays, and book reviews have been published in numerous feminist, lesbian/gay, and African-American publications. She was an editor of *Conditions*, a feminist magazine of writings by women with an emphasis on writing by lesbians, from 1981 to 1990. She's currently working on a new poetry manuscript, *Corridors of Nostalgia*. She lives and writes in Jersey City, New Jersey.

Randy P. L. Conner and **David H. Sparks**, queer activists since the '70s, are co-authors, with daughter Mariah, of *Cassell's Encyclopedia of Queer Myth, Symbol, and Spirit*. Conner is author of *Blossom of Bone: Reclaiming the Connections between Homoeroticism and the Sacred* and articles in *Queerly Phrased* and *Parabola*. Conner has taught humanities, literature, and religion, recently in the Public Intellectuals Program of Florida Atlantic University. Currently at work on a book on queer parenting, Sparks is an ethnomusicologist, composer, writer (*Afro-Hispanic Review* and other publications), and librarian who teaches humanities and information technology.

Diana Courvant is a writer, activist, volunteer, motivator, and educator dedicated to liberation. Co-founder, programs coordinator, and designated procrastinator of the Survivor Project—a Portland, Oregon, organization addressing the multiple issues and needs of trans or intersex domestic violence/sexual assault survivors—she has had her work published in a number of places. Bored by regular television, she adores her DVD player and enjoys munching on an enormous bowl of popcorn while marveling at her latest find from the used-disc bin, preferably something involving dykes, Muppets, or really cool special effects. She's still waiting for the one movie to have them all.

Joanne DiNova (Ojibway) is pursuing a Ph.D. in English at the University of Waterloo (Ontario), with an emphasis in discourse analysis and Native literature. She is a poet, an essayist, and the mother of a young daughter.

Elana Dykewomon has been a cultural worker and activist since the 1970s. Her books include *Riverfinger Women*, *Nothing Will Be as Sweet as the Taste—Selected Poems*, and the Jewish lesbian historical novel *Beyond the Pale*, which received the Lambda Literary and Gay and Lesbian Publishers Awards for best lesbian fiction in 1998. She brought the international lesbian feminist journal of arts and politics, *Sinister Wisdom*, to the San Francisco Bay Area in 1987, serving as an editor for nine years, and now lives in Oakland with her lover among friends, teaching and trying to stir up trouble whenever she can.

Nada Elia is scholar-in-residence in the Afro-American Studies Program at Brown University, as well as visiting scholar at the Pembroke Center for Teaching and Research on Women. Author of *Trances, Dances, and Vociferations: Agency and Resistance in Africana Women's Narratives*, she's currently working on a second manuscript, *Spell-Bound, Un-Bound: Conjuring as the Practice of Freedom*.

Chandra Ford is a doctoral student in the School of Public Health at the University of North Carolina. Her research examines the relationships between societal factors and health outcomes for "marginalized" groups. She is currently completing a book-length project about domestic violence among lesbians. And, like Sister Audre, she is a proud librarian.

Cynthia Franklin teaches contemporary U.S. literatures at the University of Hawai'i. Author of *Writing Women's Communities: The Politics and Poetics of Contemporary Multi-Genre Anthologies* (1997) and co-editor of *Navigating Islands and Continents: Conversations and Contestations in and around the Pacific* (2000), she's currently working on a book-length project on academic memoirs.

Bernadette García, queer Xicana Indigena mestiza, was born and raised in Colorado (El Paso, Boulder, Pueblo, y Huerfano counties). She earned her B.A. in music/piano at the University of Colorado, where her senior recital was a lecture/concert focusing on women composers, a performance that included piano solos, ensembles, y los Danzantas Aztecas de Grupo Tlaloc (Denver) in a celebration of women's creativity. Daughter, Auntie, Sister, Lover, Amiga, Prima, Student, Teacher, Musician, Poet . . .

Ednie Kaeh Garrison teaches women's studies at California State University, Fresno. She finished her Ph.D. in American studies from Washington State University in May 2000. Written early in her graduate career, her poem represents one effort to understand the fears and anxieties she experiences at "home" and at "school." As well, it attempts to articulate for her colleagues something of her struggle with loving ideas and learning while confined by a bourgeois institution; for her family it attempts to demonstrate (in a form they appreciate) just how much they've influenced the intellectual and political choices she makes.

A native of the El Paso/Juárez border and "the first Chicana fruit of her family," **Alicia Gaspar de Alba** is an associate professor of Chicana/Chicano studies at UCLA and holds a Ph.D. in American studies from the University of New Mexico (1994). Her publications include *Sor Juana's Second Dream* (1999); *Chicano Art Inside/Outside the Master's House* (1998); and poetry and fiction published in English, French, German, Spanish, and Mexican anthologies of Chicano/a literature. She teaches courses in Chicano/a art and popular culture, border consciousness, bilingual creative writing, and Chicana lesbian literature.

Nancy E. Gibson: I am an associate director of admissions and coordinator of student-of-color recruitment at Denison University. I received my bachelor's degree in public relations and have been working in admissions for eight years, coordinating multicultural recruitment efforts. I currently serve as a delegate to the National Association for College Admission Counseling, representing Ohio's private colleges and universities. I've given local and international presentations on diversity and multicultural. I am a native of Lincoln, Nebraska, a wife, and mother of two children.

Marisela Burns Gomez is a Creole woman, born and raised in Belize, Central America, until the age of thirteen, when she migrated to the United States. She's the youngest of three and the tía of three little kiddies. Currently working as a pediatrician and researcher in Baltimore, Maryland, she's also active in community organizing that focuses on adequate health care in communities of color. Existing to leave the world a more humane place, Marisela writes to maintain her sanity and to challenge the legacy of oppression.

Susan Morales Guerra: I'm a prodigal daughter of San Antonio, Texas, and San Antonio lives within me, but I reside in Oslo, Norway. A paradox of human traits, my two sons will tell you, but a loving one, they will also say. I work as a community organizer and as a writer, with degrees in social work and a major in comparative literature. In order to do both I believe there is always a story to listen to and there is always a story to tell.

Nova Gutierrez is a Chicana feminist educator, artist, activist, and writer from Robstown, Texas, living and working in New York City. Her paintings explore themes of fragmentation, loss, re-connection, and finding home. She has exhibited at the Clemente Soto Velez Cultural Center, Connecticut College ("Poets on Location"), the Tompkins Square Park Arts Festival, and the

Nuyorican Poets Café. Nova has an M.A. in gender studies and feminist theory from the New School for Social Research and is pursuing an Ed.D. in international educational development, with a concentration in gender studies at Teachers College Columbia University.

Nathalie Handal has lived in the United States, Europe, the Caribbean, and the Middle East. A researcher at the University of London and the director of Summer Literary Seminars (Dominican Republic), her work has appeared in numerous magazines/literary journals and anthologies worldwide. Her work includes a poetry book, *The NeverField* (1999), a CD of her poetry and improvisational music by Russian musicians Vladimir Miller and Alexander Alexandrov, *Traveling Rooms* (1999), and an edited collection, *The Poetry of Arab Women: A Contemporary Anthology* (2000).

Joy Harjo, a poet, musician, writer, and performer, has published several books, including *A Map to the Next World*; her first children's book, *The Good Luck Cat*; and a co-edited anthology of Native women's writing, *Reinventing the Enemy's Language*. She has released one CD, *Letter From the End of the Twentieth Century* (1997). A saxophone player, Harjo performs nationally and internationally solo and with her band Joy Harjo and Poetic Justice. A new CD, *Crossing the Border*, and a book of stories are forthcoming. She is of the Muscogee Nation and a member of the Tallahassee Wakokaye Grounds, and lives in Honolulu.

Inés Hernández-Ávila: I'm Nimipu (Nez Perce) and Chicana/Tejana/Mexican Indian. I'm a poet, cultural worker, associate professor and former chair of the Department of Native American Studies at University of California, Davis. My creative and scholarly work bridges the Native American and Chicana/Chicano communities. I continue to develop new ways of expression. I've begun working with relief printing, monoprint, and intaglio, although I am still a novice. My life is sustained by my spirituality, and by my love of dance and song. My beloved compañero, Juan Ávila Hernández, and I live in Woodland, California, with our precious familia de animalitos.

Leticia Hernández-Linares: I sing for my ancestors. I write because some can't. I learn through teaching. I go outdoors every day and give thanks for everything around me. I name my mothers Leticia del Carmen, Merceditas, Ana, Osún, and La Ciguanaba, for strength and inspiration; and my fathers Carlos, Abuelo, Serafín, Obatalá, for the words and the music. Constantly re-creating myself, soy tecpatl, artista, poet, vieja, los angelina, maestra, performer, salvadoreña, chicana, guide, gitana, guided, bruja, bard, tierra, water, música, fire, hopeful. (ciguanaba00@yahoo.com)

Simona J. Hill: I am an assistant professor of sociology at Susquehanna University in Selinsgrove, Pennsylvania, lecturer at the University of Pennsylvania, and a former director of the Pickett Community School in Philadelphia. I earned my B.A., M.A., and Ph.D. from the University of Pennsylvania. When I graduated with the doctorate in sociology in 1989 I was the first African-American woman since 1937 to do so. I am committed to higher education that enhances a person's abilities to think critically and act responsibly toward future generations. My academic mission is based on multiculturalism, community leadership, scholarship, and mutual empowerment.

Helen Johnson lectures at the University of Queensland–School of Social Science. Her visiting fellowships include the French University of the Pacific–New Caledonia, University of British Columbia and Dalhousie University in Canada, and University of Hawai'i–Manoa. Her articles have appeared in *Les Nouvelles-Calédoniennes, Australian Journal of Anthropology, Asian Journal of Women's Studies*, and *Feminista!* She has contributed to *A Reader's Guide to Women's Studies, A Reader's Guide to the Social Sciences, The Woman-Centred University: Interdisciplinary Perspectives, Encompassing Gender, Women's Studies: An Interdisciplinary Anthology*, and *Sexual Positions: An Australian Viewpoint*.

Lakesia D. Johnson: I am director of women's programs and affirmative action and an adjunct assistant professor of women's studies at Denison University. I received my law degree and master of arts in women's studies from the Ohio State University. My research areas include feminist legal theory, critical race theory, feminist critiques of mass culture, the history of African-American women in the United States, statutory civil rights, and employment discrimination.

Toni C. King: I hold a joint appointment as associate professor of black studies and women's studies at Denison University. I specialize in black women's studies, and use my multi-tongues as scholar, therapist, practitioner, storyteller, and poet to pass on stories of black women's recovery. In support of women's healing and growth, I have co-authored a book of meditations: *Deep Woman Feelings: A Book of Contemplations*, with S. Alease Ferguson, and developed personal growth workshops. My current research analyzes black women's bonds across the life span.

Donna Hightower Langston is chair of the ethnic studies department at Cal Poly. She is the author of four books. She was raised in southern California, the daughter of a teen mom who struggled with the welfare system and low-paying jobs. She is the mother of five and has a three-year-old granddaughter, Catalina. She is an enrolled member of the Cherokee nation, a quarter-blood, and primarliy identifies as racially mixed.

Irene Lara: Likes: sandia and scarlet red, sage, gardenias, and that my name means "peace." Loves: art, justice, and the erotic. As a University of California, Berkeley, Ph.D. student in ethnic studies, I co-founded the Chicana and Latina Studies Working Group and co-organized the "Oppositional Wetness: Mujeres Living Theory" conference. I am a facilitator and mentor for the National Latina Health Organization. I perform my poetry and have been published in *Voces: A Journal of Chicana/Latina Studies*. I plan to live in San Diego, with my compañero Raul, where I'll continue being an activist-scholar, teacher, and healer.

Jid Lee: When I was five years old, my grandmother told me about the genies who live in mountains. She said, "They come out of the mountains in the night and waylay travelers. If a traveler tells them a good story, they give them gold powder; if he tells them a poor story, they dump human feces on him." Whenever I write, I write with hunger for the genies' gold powder. I hope the story of Cry-Smile is one of the few stories for which the genies will give me a pinch of gold powder.

Valerie Lee: Professor, English and women's studies at Ohio State University. Womanist, folklorist, Americanist, theorist, I teach narratives about women who rebel and resist, and write books about women who conjure and console. My most recent book, *Granny Midwives and Black Women Writers: Double-Dutched Readings* (Routledge), is an interdisciplinary study that merges literature and folk medicine. My current research examines woman-authored modern/postmodern slave narratives.

Arlene (Ari) Istar Lev is a therapist, educator, and activist. She is a bridge-builder, and believes that complexity doesn't have to be complicated. She is Sundance's wife, and Shaiyah and Eliezer's momma. She can be reached at info@choicesconsulting.com (http://choicesconsulting.com).

Shirley Geok-lin Lim is chair professor of English at the University of Hong Kong and professor of English and women's studies at University of California, Santa Barbara. Her first book, *Crossing the Peninsula* (1980), received the Commonwealth Poetry Prize. She's published four volumes of poetry; three books of short stories; a memoir, *Among the White Moon Faces* (1996), which received the 1997 American Book Award; and a novel, *Joss and Gold* (2001). Lim's co-edited anthology, *The Forbidden Stitch* (1989), also received the American Book Award. *What the Fortune Teller Didn't Say* (1998) was featured in Bill Moyers's 1998 PBS special "Fooling with Words."

Helene Shulman Lorenz is a longtime community activist from the San Francisco Bay Area, currently teaching psychology and interdisciplinary studies at Pacifica Graduate Institute in Santa Barbara, California. Her book *Living at the Edge of Chaos: Complex Systems in Culture and Psyche* is an inter/cross-cultural exploration of ritual and healing. She is currently writing on Eurocentrism, racism, and decolonization in psychology. She has a Ph.D. in philosophy from Tulane University and a diploma in analytical psychology from the C. G. Jung Institute in Zurich, Switzerland.

Betty M. Lovelace, Ed.D., is director of multicultural affairs at Denison University, where she's responsible for the development and implementation of training and programming for students and staff. Previously she served as an executive administrator in a variety of educational, community, and business settings. She has also worked extensively within the areas of racial identity, multiculturalism, leadership development, work teams, and conflict resolution.

Renée M. Martínez is a parent, artist, and educator living in Los Angeles. In addition to completing a semi-autobiographical novel about a lesbian teen, she writes personal essays and political commentary. As a visual artist she works in various media, including acrylic and watercolor, wood and stone carving, ceramics, stained glass, and jewelry. Her father's people migrated to this country during the Mexican revolution; her mother's ancestors came from England, some as colonists. Her creativity is spiritually and politically inspired; it is part of her personal transformation from warrior into a Woman of Peace.

shefali milczarek-desai: my parents named me after a white flower that grows in india because i looked soft and delicate when i was born. i have rebelled against that meaning of my name and just about everything else. right now i'm finishing a joint-degree program i created between the law school and the women's studies department at the university of arizona. school is tiring, and i'm happiest hiking/biking/backpacking in the mountain ranges surrounding tucson. after i'm finished with this life of fighting/teaching/advocating, i will go live in the chiricahuas and write science-fiction novels.

Deborah A. Miranda is a mixedblood woman of European and Esselen, Ohlone, Costanoan and Chumash ancestry. She is a poet, scholar, and mother of two. Her first book, *Indian Cartography*, won the Diane Decorah Memorial Award from the Native Writer's Circle of the Americas and was published in 1999. Currently Deborah is assistant professor at Pacific Lutheran University, where she teaches writing poetry and autobiography, Native women's literatures, and women's studies.

Carmen Morones lives in Santa Cruz, California, with her husband, Andrew Baum. She has previously published poetry and short stories in *Revista Mujeres* and *Making Face, Making Soul/Haciendo Caras*.

Marla Morris is an assistant professor of curriculum studies at Georgia Southern University. She is the author of *Curriculum and the Holocaust: Competing Sites of Memory and Representation*.

Nadine Naber is a scholar-activist and co-founder of the Arab Women's Solidarity Association, North America. She is currently a professor of anthropology at the American University in Cairo and is expanding her dissertation into a book manuscript entitled: *Arab San Francisco: Beyond Arab Virgin/American(ized) Whore*. She received her M.A. in philosophy at San Francisco State University and her Ph.D. in socio-cultural anthropology from the University of California, Davis. She has written on migration, racialization, and gender among Arab Americans; radical Arab-American feminisms; Zionism—the forgotten "ism" within U.S. progressive politics; and the anti-globalization movement from a transnational feminist perspective.

Jody Norton was a lecturer in the Department of English Language and Literature and the women's studies program at Eastern Michigan University. S/he is the author of *Narcissus Sous Rature: Male Subjectivity in Contemporary American Poetry* (2000), and has published numerous articles on gender and transgender theory, aesthetics, radical pedagogy, and institutional theory, as well as U.S. literature and culture. S/he crossed over in May 2001.

Rosa Maria Pegueros is a professor of Latin American history and women's studies at the University of Rhode Island. She became an academic after earlier careers in law and community organizing. Currently, she is completing a translation of a book of interviews with survivors of La Matanza, the January 1932 workers' uprising in El Salvador. Her pieces have appeared in *Common Lives/Lesbian Lives*, *The Nation*, the *Providence Journal-Bulletin*, and other publications.

Minh-Ha T. Pham immigrated with her family of twelve to southern California from Viet Nam in 1975. Much of her writing explores the effects of immigration on the personal level—the people, politics, and stories that shape one's assimilation. She has been published in *A Community of Writers* (1999) and is coeditor of *Going There: Women of Color Writers on Creativity* (forthcoming). She is working on a novel and pursuing her Ph.D. in ethnic studies at the University of California, Berkeley.

Caroline (Kay) Picart is assistant professor of English and Humanities at Florida State University. Among her books are *Resentment and "the Feminine" in Nietzsche's Politico-Aesthetics* (1999); *Thomas Mann and Friedrich Nietzsche: Eroticism, Death, Music and Laughter* (1999); *The Cinematic Rebirths of Frankenstein* (2001); and *The Frankenstein Film Sourcebook* (2001) co-authored with Jayne Blodgett and Frank Smoot. She has also published scholarly articles on philosophy and popular articles in the United States, the Philippines, and South Korea. She has had solo exhibitions as an artist in South Korea and various parts of the United States.

Maria Proitsaki was born in Greece and received her B.A. from Aristotle University of Thessaloniki. She is currently a Ph.D. candidate at Göteborg University, Sweden, and is writing a thesis that examines the works of Nikki Giovanni and Rita Dove.

Mirtha N. Quintanales is a cultural anthropologist and former coordinator of the Latin American, Caribbean, and Latino Studies Program at New Jersey City University, where she has taught for the past thirteen years. She was a contributor to *This Bridge Called My Back* and feels very honored to be included in this anthology celebrating its twentieth anniversary.

Migdalia Reyes is a Boricua, born and raised in Puerto Rico. She has been an activist for thirty years, involved in social, economic, and political issues affecting marginalized populations. She has been a professor of graduate social work for twenty years at the University of Connecticut, and at San Jose State University in California. She has presented and published on U.S. Latina lesbians, Latin-American women studies programs, and organizing Puerto Ricans in the United States. Migdalia delivers services at a community mental health clinic to underserved populations, including people of color and sexual minorities.

Alicia P. Rodriguez was born in Cuba in 1962 and moved to the United States when she was four. As a college student she became involved in feminist, race, and multicultural politics. Professionally, she is a sociologist of education who explores issues of culture and identity. In raising her two young children, she's realizing the challenges of living one's convictions and passions. Since completing a postdoctoral fellowship at the University of California, Berkeley, Alicia has been focusing on being a mother and doing independent research while deciding her next career moves. She welcomes the career uncertainty and mothering certainty.

Kimberly Roppolo (Cherokee/Choctaw/Creek) is an instructor at McLennan Community College and a doctoral student specializing in Native literature at Baylor University, where she will take her Ph.D. in May 2002. Kimberly serves on the National Caucus of Wordcraft Circle of Native Writers and Storytellers. She is a member of the Association for the Study of American Indian Literatures. She has published in Robert Bensen's *Children of the Dragonfly*, *Paradoxa*, *Native Realities*, *News from Indian Country*, *Talking Stick Arts Newsletter*, and *Studies in American Indian Literatures*. She resides in Hewitt, Texas, with her husband and three children.

Chela Sandoval is associate professor of critical and cultural theory and Chicano studies at the University of California, Santa Barbara.

Caridad Souza is a co-founder with Karina Cespedes of the Cult of the Shadow Beast and Priestess of A Better Way. In her spare time she is a writer, educator, and research associate at the Centro de Estudios Puertorriquenos at Hunter College, City University of New York, working on racialized gender, culture, and sexuality. She is politically and psychically committed to the coming apocalypse.

Kimberly Springer is assistant professor of black studies at Portland State University. Editor of *Still Lifting, Still Climbing: Contemporary African American Women's Activism* (1999) and author of the forthcoming *Living for the Revolution: Black Feminist Organizations*, Kimberly holds a doctorate in women's studies and an abiding belief that public radio can change the world. She plans to do so through Colored Public Radio, an initiative designed to showcase the voices and perspectives of people of color in public and community radio.

Andrea M. Straub is a graduate student in education at Rutgers University. She is committed to continuing her research on the (un)consciousness of privilege in white women's racial identity formation. As the High Priestess of Mobius Strip Ideology, she is a devoted member of the Cult of the Shadow Beast and the Godmother of Sarah and Karina's the Coatlicue Child.

A native of San Antonio, Texas, **Jesse G. Swan**'s multicultural identity is informed by the disparateness of his family. With grandparents from south Texas, eastern Mexico, and the southern and midwestern United States, to say nothing of great-grandparents, Swan strongly feels the value of bridge-building and mestizo/a identity. Such multiple consciousnesses inform his scholarly pursuits as well, which include four areas: critical race studies, especially documenting the genesis of white supremacist discourse in English; Elizabeth Tanfield Cary, the first woman to write an original play and a modern history in English; John Milton; and the state of the academy.

Donna Tsuyuko Tanigawa, a yonsei lesbian of Japanese ancestry from Waipahu, Hawai'i, has published poetry and prose in numerous journals and anthologies. Although she labored for several years to write the piece in this collection, it is still "Premature." She teaches composition and women's studies at the community college level.

Writer, performer, and organizational ritualist, **Luisah Teish** is the author of *Jambalaya: The Natural Woman's Book of Personal Charms and Practical Rituals* and *Jump Up: Good Times throughout the Seasons with Celebrations from Around the World*. She is the founder of the School of Ancient Mysteries/Sacred Arts Center. (www.jambalayaspirit.org)

tatiana de la tierra is a generación ñ colombiana writer and librarian whose work focuses on South American memory and reality, immigration, identity, sexuality, subject headings, and publishing. Her creative writings have been published in anthologies and periodicals since 1987 and her plays have been produced since 1998. One of the founders and editors of the Latina lesbian magazine *esto no tiene nombre* and *conmoción* and the Latina lesbian writers' newsletter *el telarañazo*, currently she's a reference librarian at University at Buffalo. (td6@acsu.buffalo.edu)

Sonya Turner is a psychologist in the Health and Counseling Center at Denison University. She has a doctorate in clinical psychology. Her professional interests include stress management, multicultural issues, mood disorders, eating disorders, and psychological evaluation. She is a native of Cleveland, Ohio.

Max Wolf Valerio is a Latino/American Indian poet, writer, and performer who appeared in the first *Bridge* as Anita Valerio. He began his transition from female to male in 1989. He intends to find a new publisher for his memoir, *The Testosterone Files*; his poetry chapbook *Animal Magnetism* (1984) will be expanded and rereleased soon. He has appeared in numerous documentaries, including *Female Misbehavior* and *Gendernauts*, both directed by Monika Treut.

Susana L. Vasquez was born in Guayaquil, Ecuador, in 1970 and moved to Chicago when she was seven months old. Her Hungarian-American mother and Ecuadorian father divorced when she was two and she was raised by her mother. Susana attended the University of Illinois, receiving a B.A. in U.S./Latin American history (1992). She was active in the university YWCA and first encountered *This Bridge* in 1991. Since graduating, she has worked as a waitress, community organizer, and grant writer. She is currently the deputy director of The Resurrection Project, a Chicago nonprofit church-based community development organization.

An activist, teacher, and aspiring writer and performer, **Indigo Violet** is still reeling from the visionary power of women of color who are her sisters, mentors, and ancestors. She struggled and mobilzed through an M.A. in gender studies and feminist theory at the New School for Social Research, and she is currently a doctoral student in social justice education at the University of Massachusetts–Amherst. Indigo is identifying multiple places from which to work for revolutionary transformation. In community organizations, in schools, in neighborhoods and academia, she's trying to work it all out, trying to get free.

Anne Waters (Seminole) is editor of *American Indian Thought: A Philosophical Reader* (2001), coeditor of *Breaking Ground: An American Philosophy Anthology* (2001), and guest coeditor of *Hypatia*'s Special Issue on Intersections of American Indian Women and Feminism/Womanism.

President of the American Indian Philosophy Association, chair of the American Philosophical Association Committee on American Indians in Philosophy, independent scholar, certified mediator, educational curriculum development consultant, and editorial board member of *Ayaanwayaamizin: An International Indigenist Philosophy Journal* and *Radical Philosophy Review*, Anne has a Ph.D. in philosophy (Purdue University), a J.D. (University of New Mexico), and has received numerous awards.

Durene I. Wheeler: I am currently a doctoral student in cultural studies at Ohio State University. I have worked in the field of higher education and student affairs for the past ten years. My master's degree is in higher education and student affairs with a minor in counseling psychology. My areas of expertise are psychological development, self-esteem, and campus environment. I have utilized my race and gender as a foundation for reaching my students and colleagues on their various levels of development. I dream of becoming a faculty member after completing my doctoral work.

Judith K. Witherow: A mixed-blood Native American, Lesbian, differently-abled feminist, I was raised in an armpit of the northern Appalachians. Poverty and all that went with it will forever guide my pen. My partner, Sue, and I have been together for twenty-two years. During this time we raised my three sons and I was diagnosed with multiple sclerosis and systemic lupus. I've published in numerous anthologies, magazines, and alternative publications. In 1994 I won the Audre Lorde First Annual Award for Non-fiction. After two decades as an activist, I'm weary of standing on the bottom rung of the ladder below the glass ceiling, steadying it for women who have left others like me behind.

Editors' Biographies

Gloria E. Anzaldúa is a tejana patlache (queer) nepantlera spiritual activist. According to Numerology both her inner and outer self are number 7. Her most recent book is *Interviews/Entrevistas*, edited by AnaLouise Keating. Her book *Borderlands/La frontera: The New Mestiza* was chosen as one of the one hundred Best Books of the Century by both Hungry Mind Review and by Utne Reader. She's the author of two bilingual children's books, *Friends from the Other Side/Amigos del otro lado* and *Prietita and the Ghost Woman/Prietita y la Llorona*; editor of *Making Face, Making Soul/Haciendo caras: Creative and Critical Perspectives by Feminists-of-Color*; and co-editor of *This Bridge Called My Back: Writings by Radical Women of Color*. Gloria has played a pivotal role in redefining U.S. feminisms, culture studies, Chicano/a issues, U.S. American literature, ethnic studies, queer theory, and postcolonial theory. Her current book projects include *La Prieta*, a novel-in-stories; *Rewriting Reality*, a collection of autohistorias-teorías; and *Bearing Witness, Reading Lives: Imagination, Creativity, and Cultural Change*, an anthology she's co-editing with AnaLouise Keating.

AnaLouise Keating is a nepantlera, spiritual activist, and associate professor of women's studies at Texas Woman's University. According to the Tarot, her soul card is the High Priestess. Author of *Women Reading Women Writing: Self-Invention in Paula Gunn Allen, Gloria Anzaldúa, and Audre Lorde*, editor of Gloria E. Anzaldúa's *Interviews/Entrevistas*, and co-editor of *Perspectives: Gender Studies*, AnaLouise has published articles on critical "race" theory, queer theory, Latina writers, African-American women writers, and pedagogy. She's working on three projects: a multigenre anthology, *Entremundos: Creative and Critical Perspectives on Gloria E. Anzaldúa*; an anthology she's co-editing with Gloria Anzaldúa: *Bearing Witness, Reading Lives: Imagination, Creativity, and Cultural Change*; and a collection drawing on her personal experiences as a bisexual, light-skinned, mixed-"race" queer to explore pedagogy, transformation, "whiteness," and "race."

Index